Understanding Football Hooliganism

The research for this book was funded by the Amsterdam School for Social Science Research (ASSR) and the Netherlands Organisation for Scientific Research (NWO).

Cover design: René Staelenberg, Amsterdam
Cover illustration: Kees Spruijt

ISBN-10   90 5629 445 8
ISBN-13   978 90 5629 445 8
NUR 756

© Vossiuspers UvA – Amsterdam University Press, 2006

Understanding Football Hooliganism

A Comparison of Six Western European Football Clubs

Ramón Spaaij

For Ingmar

You who are in power have only the means that money produces,
we who are in expectation have those which devotion prompts.

Alexandre Dumas, *The Count of Monte Cristo*

Contents

Acknowledgements

The process of researching and writing this book has been long and winding. My prolonged stays in foreign countries and localities have helped me experience and appreciate the complex social, cultural and historical underpinnings of football fan cultures. It is clear to me that without the great variety of people contributing to the research project, each in their own ways, this book would never have been realized. Regretfully, not all can be personally acknowledged since many of those I have spoken to were guaranteed anonymity. I can therefore only mention some of the people who have offered me such good-natured support and assistance.

First and foremost, I thank Kees Schuyt for his encouraging advice and kindness. His enthusiasm has been a driving force from the beginning. Without his efforts this study would have amounted to only a fraction of what it has become. I am grateful to Ruud Stokvis for his helpful comments on drafts of this book and for our lengthy, stimulating discussions. His expertise in the field of sports sociology was an indispensable source of inspiration to my work. I thank the Amsterdam School for Social Science Research not only for generously funding my research, but also for providing such a pleasurable and intellectually stimulating environment. I have greatly enjoyed the friendship of Nienke Muurling, the kindness of the staff, and the customary football conversations with Hans Sonneveld and Teun Bijvoet. I also thank Gerd Baumann for inviting me to join the cultural anthropology programme in Vienna. I am grateful to Bert Schijf for his suggestions on earlier versions of this book.

In addition to my colleagues in Amsterdam, I also want to thank those who are based elsewhere but who have nevertheless contributed greatly to the realization of this book. Friend and former colleague Edward van der Torre continuously bombarded me with his neurotic passion for Sparta Rotterdam, provoking heated debates and humorous scenes on the terraces of his beloved stadium. Despite the physical distance that divides us, my professional relationship with Carles Viñas has been truly inspiring: *moltes gràcies per tot*. During my position at the University of Seville, Álvaro Rodríguez Díaz introduced me to the Sevillian way of life and amused me with his passionate monologues on sociology, football and politics. Thomas Herzog offered me a very different perspective, combining an admirable *Weltanschauung* with an unparalleled dedication to the promotion of anti-racism and a daily overdose of *cafelitos*. I thank Patrick Murphy, Eric Dunning, Mike Rowe, John Williams and Dominic Malcolm for making my visits to the University of Leicester both pleasing and intellectually challenging. I thank Ivan Waddington for arranging my stay at the Centre for Research into Sport and Society and for accompanying me to the Foxes. I also want to thank Heloisa Reis, Eladio Jareño, Edwin Winkels and Javier Durán González. I thank the staff at Amsterdam University Press for their help and advice, notably Marieke Soons. Much gratitude also to Adriënne Baars-Schuyt for her magnificent job in editing this lengthy volume.

This research would have amounted to only a fraction of what it has become without the efforts of a variety of individuals and organizations within the football community. I thank the board members, security officers, stewards and (former) players of the football clubs discussed in this book for sharing their stories and experiences. I thank Andy Brame and Bill Miller for hosting my customary visits to New Scotland Yard and for introducing me to the art of intelligence-led policing. I have thoroughly enjoyed the company of Martin Gooday at the Home Office and on match days. I am grateful to Kees Kerkhof, Henk Groenevelt, Graham Naughton, Nick Cross, Bryan Drew, Gordon Jaglall, Ramón Barba Sánchez and Ana Criado for providing me with useful data and, more importantly, great stories. I also thank the police officers who have contributed to the research project: Nigel, Andrew, Ian, Merv, Roger, Ramón, Pere, Henk, Miguel, Mark, Kevin and many more. Furthermore, I want to thank all the supporters who contributed to this book, even though not all can be personally acknowledged: Lloyd Richardson, Liam Tyrell, Kevin O'Callaghan, Quim, Aad Leeuwangh, Alex 'The Traveller' Ferguson, David Lloyd, Aitor Chacón, Nick, Bill Gardner, Ralf Bormans, Danny, Simon Zebregs, Pedro, Grunk, Tim Crane, Mook, Carles de Borja Ruiz, Carlo, Jordi, René Schouten, Daniel Crawford, Carol, Ton, Gary, Alberto, John Helliar, Olga, Steve, Lawrence Alexander, Joan, Rob Coxon, Cass, Alex, Rafa, Vicens, Geert Cuypers, Santi, Rob Allart, Joan Segura Palomares, Wim Cassa, Brian Belton, Dennis Turner,

Dave Gardner, Jose, Tom Greatrex, Stuart, Sergio, Eric Wilton, Andy Newbold, Renato, Florian, Paul, Francesc, and Michael, Rob and Bill and the lads.

And last but not least I thank my friends and family. I thank Jos for his patience in editing the cover illustration. I thank Martijn, Taco, Arnoud, Stefan and David for offering welcome distraction in times of crisis and uncertainty. I am also grateful to my parents for supporting me throughout the project. Their support has carried me through this long and intense period. I thank Alison for her love, patience and understanding over the past three years. Far more precious than any book, meeting her has been the ultimate reward of this research. I lovingly dedicate this book to her and to my brother. Ingmar has shaped my personal and professional development in countless ways and perhaps more than anyone.

Introduction

Football hooliganism periodically generates widespread political and public anxiety in a variety of European and non-European countries. In spite of the efforts made and resources invested over the past decades, football hooliganism is still perceived by politicians, policymakers, media and other actors as a disturbing social problem. Issues such as how to understand or explain hooligan behaviour continue to challenge social scientists, while at the same time instant answers and solutions are demanded from wider, non-academic audiences. Football hooliganism has long been viewed as an exclusively 'English disease', not only by journalists or the general public but also by academics. As recently as 1994, psychologist John Kerr (1994: x) claimed that manifestations of football hooliganism in other societies seem 'merely to imitate what has gone on in England over the past thirty years' and are 'a good deal less frequent and much less widespread.'

The common stereotype of football hooliganism as an exclusively 'English disease' no longer prevails. It has been replaced by a belief that, while in Britain football-related violence may be on the decline, hooliganism on the Continent is perhaps more serious and less effectively controlled. From this viewpoint, and in a rather sensationalist fashion, *The Guardian* journalist Richard Williams (2001) wrote that:

> [T]he catalogue of recent events suggests that football's social makeover may have been less than entirely successful. The new image may, in fact, be no closer to the truth than the old vision of uninterrupted mayhem which made it a pariah sport in the 80s. And if football has indeed been enjoying a period of relative calm, in which the increasing affluence of the players seemed to exist in a direct inverse ratio to the decreasing violence of the spectators, then it seems to be over now. From places as far apart as Hong Kong, Kurdistan, Leipzig, Brunei, Palo Alto, Shiraz and Nairobi, reports of violence suggest that the game has once again become a focus for people who want to fight and need an excuse.

1

Social scientific research supports the argument that football hooliganism is a transnational phenomenon with equivalents in countries as diverse as Germany (Ek, 1996), Argentina (Archetti and Romero, 1994), Italy (Dal Lago and De Biasi, 1994; Roversi, 2000), Peru (Panfichi and Thieroldt, 2002), Hungary (Pintér and Van Gestel, 2002), France (Mignon, 2001), Slovakia (Harsányi, 2005) and Greece (Astrinakis, 2002). But although there is some degree of academic consensus regarding the transnational nature of the phenomenon, the seriousness of football hooliganism and the need for more academic research is heavily disputed. Critics tend to give three major reasons why further research into football hooliganism is a more or less wasted effort.

First, football hooliganism has long been a, if not *the*, main field of interest in the study of football. The problem, then, is that research has focused disproportionately on a small minority of fans, largely neglecting other aspects of football culture that affect the vast majority of fans. King (2002: 3), for example, has argued that 'it may be the case that legitimate concerns about hooliganism have unreasonably biased research into football, so that issues such as the administration of the game and its political economy have been wrongly relegated to a secondary position.' Only as recently as the 1990s other important issues surrounding football have come to receive similar research attention, such as the globalization of football, the relationships between football clubs and their fans, football fan writing and racism (e.g. R. Taylor, 1992; Bromberger, 1993; Haynes, 1995; Merkel and Tokarski, 1996; Holland, 1997; Brown, 1998; Giulianotti, 1999; A. King, 2000; Brown and Walsh, 2000; Garland and Rowe, 2001; Sandvoss, 2003). But although it is true that other important aspects of football and football culture have long been under-researched, I see no reason why football hooliganism should not be studied as just one of the elements of football culture. In other words, sociological research into football should give hooliganism its proper position as only one of a number of important issues surrounding football (cf. Duke, 1991; Moorhouse, 1991).

Related to the issue of over-representation is a second common critique that football hooliganism is a very marginal social problem. Moorhouse (2000: 1464; see also 1991: 493) has argued that 'it is important to remember that football hooliganism is a quite unimportant part of all violent crime, let alone of social

2

nuisance.' I think the dilemma here is that although football hooliganism may realistically be a marginal element of all juvenile delinquency or violent crime, its public visibility and mediatization ensure its *perceived* image as a disturbing and recurrent social problem. This perception, in turn, has resulted in an ever-evolving range of constrictive policies affecting not only the small hooligan minority but also the match-day experiences of non-hooligan supporters, transforming the football ground into a Foucauldian Panopticon (Foucault, 1977).[1] In other words, while hooligan violence may not (or no longer), as some critics suggest, affect the experiences of the vast majority of football fans, policy measures targeting football hooliganism most certainly do (cf. Armstrong and Giulianotti, 1999a). I am reminded of this odd paradox every time I enter the gates of my local ground, (im)patiently joining a forty minute queue while fellow supporters routinely hold out their special club ID cards, have their names checked on a comprehensive list of banning orders, are rigorously searched and admitted into the ground one by one under close camera and police surveillance.

The public perception of the 'seriousness' of football hooliganism is also sustained, I would argue, by many prevailing stereotypes and popular fallacies surrounding the phenomenon. For example, incidents of racial abuse within football grounds are often erroneously attributed to the 'mindless thugs' of the hooligan subculture, even though research shows that many such incidents are not caused by football hooligans at all (Back et al., 1999; Garland and Rowe, 2001; Spaaij and Viñas, 2005a). Furthermore, hooligan behaviour is often explained in terms of comforting stereotypes far removed from the reality of the phenomenon. Consider, for example, the recent inquiry by two Spanish senior police researchers. Without providing any type of supporting evidence, they conclude that whereas 'some years ago the British hooligan was on the dole or an industrial worker, with a tattooed body', nowadays 'he belongs to the middle class, are [*sic*] racist and right-wing. They hate foreigners, blacks, Asians, Jews and immigrants' (Seara Ruiz and Sedano Jiménez, 2001: 135-136).[2] Interestingly, this inquiry was frequently cited in the Spanish media and the two researchers have been closely involved in the realization and evaluation of anti-hooligan policies.

A third major critique of research into football hooliganism is that the subject is now over-researched and 'overpopulated' (Marsh et al., 1996: 30; cf.

3

Moorhouse, 2000: 1464). I think there is some truth in this argument considering the enormous amount of books, articles and official inquiries on the nature and causes of football hooliganism. It is a topic that everyone seems to have an opinion on. But as the aforementioned examples demonstrate, the fact that football hooliganism is surrounded by a variety of, often fallacious, opinions and commonsense beliefs does not mean we are actually a lot closer to really understanding the phenomenon. In fact, one could argue that it is precisely because of the many contrasting opinions, both inside and outside academia, that more empirically grounded research is needed. The problem simply begins with the lack of a precise definition of the phenomenon. The label football hooliganism covers a variety of forms of behaviour which take place in more or less directly football-related contexts (Dunning, 2000: 142; Spaaij, 2005: 1; Frosdick and Marsh, 2005: 28).

There are, in my view, pressing reasons why football hooliganism remains an important subject for social science research. First and foremost, certain major issues have not been sufficiently explored and theorized. In Chapter Two, I will show that four theoretical themes are central to generating a deeper understanding of football hooliganism as a transnational phenomenon. These themes are: (i) the role of societal 'fault lines' in fuelling and contouring football hooliganism; (ii) the construction of hooligan identities and the attractions of the hooligan subculture; (iii) the social organization of football hooliganism; and (iv) the subtle yet vital interactions and negotiations between hooligans and significant others, and the (intended and unintended) effects of policies targeting football hooliganism. These aspects are temporally and spatially variable, and research into football hooliganism should therefore adopt a comparative approach.

There has been, up until today, little endeavour by academics to fully engage in the comparative study of football hooliganism. The numerous books, articles and conference papers on the subject have advanced our knowledge of the phenomenon, but they have failed to establish an integrative comparative framework for understanding football hooliganism as well as to identify the major cross-cultural commonalities and differences in football hooliganism (cf. Marsh et al., 1996: 57; 59). Systematic and detailed comparative research constitutes an important new departure in the study of hooligan subcultures, contributing to a deeper understanding of the phenomenon (cf. Giulianotti and Armstrong, 2002: 235;

4

Dunning, 1999: 153). Widening the base to include countries outside Britain can generate new knowledge on the cross-national and cross-local similarities and differences in football hooliganism as well as important new insight into the applicability of dominant theories on the subject. Comparative research into football hooliganism also has a more practical relevancy, since it can serve as a basis for more effective and more proportionate policies at international, national, regional and local levels. Research-based knowledge can provide practical help in, for example, assessing the intended and secondary effects of policy initiatives (cf. Giddens, 1997: 13). Although its main forms may have transformed to some degree, in most countries football hooliganism has not yielded to public efforts to contain or eradicate it (Dunning et al., 2002b: 218).

Considering the potential advantages of such research, I would argue that there is a need for systematic, in-depth comparative research into football hooliganism. Close empirical scrutiny enables us to generate a deeper understanding of football hooliganism and, eventually, to propose plausible explanations as to why the phenomenon occurs and persists. I therefore disagree with Armstrong's (1998: 21) statement that 'football hooliganism cannot really be 'explained'. It can only be described and evaluated.' This book seeks to develop a sociological understanding of football hooliganism as a transnational phenomenon by focusing on the extent and nature of football hooliganism in different national and local settings. I would argue that we should take into account not only variations in the extent and nature of football hooliganism *between* societies, but also dissimilarities and resemblances *within* countries and localities. Although manifestations of football hooliganism at different football clubs within one country may have much in common, football hooliganism is situated in the specific cultural and historical setting of individual football clubs and their wider communities. It is often overlooked that the extent of football hooliganism is not evenly or randomly distributed; not every country or football club is equally 'affected'. Comeron's claim (2002: 11) that football hooliganism is 'equally acute everywhere' is, in fact, incorrect. In this context, Van der Brug (1994: 194) has correctly argued that two major circumstances of football hooliganism remain unaccounted for. Why did traditions of football hooliganism develop particularly in some European countries but to a much lesser degree in other countries where professional football developed in similar ways? And why has football hooliganism emerged at some football clubs, but not at others? The central question addressed in this research can thus be formulated as follows:

How can we explain the extent and nature of football hooliganism at different football clubs and in different countries, and variations therein over time?

Football hooliganism is defined here as the competitive violence of socially organized fan groups in football, as we will see in Chapter One. For hooligan rivalries to develop and persist, the existence of at least one similar, oppositional fan group is a necessary condition.

The focus in this research on the manifestation of football hooliganism within different national and local settings has important theoretical implications for the study of football hooliganism. Recent comparative research has principally concentrated on general 'fault lines' as an explanatory factor for cross-cultural variations in football hooliganism (Dunning, 1999; 2000; Dunning et al., 2002; Frosdick and Marsh, 2005: 111-112). I would argue that although the concept of fault lines constitutes an important point of departure for comparative research into football hooliganism, to fully grasp the nature and sources of the phenomenon we should move beyond generality towards a more specific analysis of the ways in which football hooliganism is nested within particular fan communities. In other words, we need to analyze how general societal cleavages are interpreted and embodied in specific fan and hooligan identities and how they interact with more specific (local) social, historical and cultural factors. Such analysis enables us to identify the major patterns of cross-national and cross-local difference and similarity in the manifestation of football hooliganism. Moreover, we should not only develop an understanding of spatial, cross-case variations but also of within-case variations, that is, of changes over time, similar to what George and Bennett (2005) call process-tracing in within-case analysis. The extent and forms of football hooliganism are by no means fixed and unchanging. For example, research suggests that in the 1990s the dominant forms of English football hooliganism changed considerably due in part to transformations in English football (J. Williams, 2001; King, 2002; Spaaij, 2005).

In order to elicit contextual nuances, I will scrutinize the manifestation of football hooliganism at six professional football clubs from three major Western European cities – London (West Ham United FC and Fulham FC), Rotterdam (Feyenoord and Sparta Rotterdam) and Barcelona (RCD Espanyol and FC Barcelona) (see Chapter Two). I will demonstrate how important cross-national, cross-local and intra-city commonalities and differences can be identified in the extent and nature of football hooliganism. It must be emphasized here that the six local case studies included in the research are professional football clubs. The study will not focus on grassroots football, national teams or violence in other sports. This does not mean, of course, that spectator violence does not occur in these contexts. Research shows that spectator violence in sports has a long history and that football has been affected by fan violence at every level of the game (e.g. Bodin et al., 2005: 21-27; Frosdick and Marsh, 2005: 3-5; Murphy et al., 1990). An important difference seems to be that, to my knowledge, only professional football has been persistently affected by hooliganism, that is, competitive violence between socially organized fan groups. It is thus important to distinguish between different types of spectator violence and to carefully demarcate the subject of study, as I will show in Chapter One. We will also see how football hooliganism has much in common with other types of juvenile delinquency and male ritual violence in human society.

This book essentially consists of three parts. The first part introduces and conceptualizes the subject under consideration (Chapters One and Two), the second part deals with empirical case studies (Chapters Three to Nine) and the final part addresses the main findings and theoretical implications (Chapters Ten to Twelve). Chapter One discusses the concept of 'football hooliganism', the dominant theoretical perspectives on the subject and their main strengths and limitations in a comparative context. It is argued that the distinctive theoretical approaches to the study of football hooliganism have in common an almost exclusive focus on the nature and causes of English (and British) football hooliganism. Systematic, empirically grounded comparative research is needed to assess the strengths and weaknesses of these theories in a comparative context. In the final part of Chapter One I will examine key aspects of football hooliganism in a comparative context. It is suggested that despite significant cross-cultural variations, a number of key components in the construction of hooligan identities can be identified. In Chapter

Two I will outline four theoretical themes that emerge from the literature review in Chapter One. The chapter also discusses the case study sample and the research methodology.

In the second part of the book the focus is shifted to the six empirical case studies and their national contexts. Chapter Three explores the emergence and development of, and responses to, football hooliganism in England, the Netherlands and Spain as a context for the six local cases presented in Chapters Four to Nine. In these chapters the local manifestation of football hooliganism is examined within the culture and collective imaginary of each football club. I will describe the extent and nature of football hooliganism in these local settings as well as the development of football hooliganism over time. The third part explores the four theoretical themes outlined in Chapter Two through comparative analysis of the commonalities and variations in the extent and nature of football hooliganism in the different national and local settings. In Chapter Ten, I will examine the emergence and diffusion of football hooliganism, the role of fault lines in fuelling and contouring football hooliganism and the degree and forms of social organization. Chapter Eleven focuses on the development of formal and informal policies and their intended and unintended effects. In Chapter Twelve I analyze the construction of hooligan identities and the attractions of the hooligan subculture.

The analysis also draws upon my additional fieldwork since 2000 in various European and non-European countries. Interviews and observations at football grounds in places as diverse as Cádiz, Melbourne, Berlin and Antwerp have contributed to my experience and affinity with the subject. Regular visits to my local ground have also shaped my views on the subject. As a club with the typical 'no one likes us, we don't care' image, ADO Den Haag (The Hague FC) has been one of the epicentres of the persistent moral panic over football fan behaviour in the Netherlands.

1

Football Hooliganism: Concepts, Theories and Contexts

Introduction

A variety of academic research has sought to describe and explain spectator violence at football matches. Approaching the subject from a range of disciplines and theoretical perspectives, previous research contains a wealth of information on the meanings and causes of football-related violence worldwide. But as I will demonstrate in this chapter, certain key questions have remained insufficiently explored. The chapter is divided into four parts. The first section examines the concept and origins of football hooliganism and proposes a definition. I will show that football hooliganism can be perceived as a specific form of spectator violence at football matches and identify a number of key dilemmas that thwart the conceptualization of the phenomenon in a comparative context. In the second part of the chapter I will discuss the strengths and weaknesses of the dominant sociological approaches to the study of football hooliganism. I argue that a common weakness of these theories is their limited applicability in a comparative context. This issue is elaborated in the third section, which presents fan cultures as glocal phenomena and emphasizes the importance of local characteristics and social interactions in the development of football hooliganism. In the final part of the chapter I will shift my attention away from cross-national and cross-local specificities and towards key aspects of hooligan violence. It is argued that although their specific contents and outcomes tend to vary across localities, certain general processes and mechanisms can be identified in football hooliganism at a transnational level. I explore the moral and aesthetic values of violent confrontation as constructed and negotiated by football hooligans themselves.

What is football hooliganism?

Scholars from a range of academic disciplines have studied the relationship between sports and violence (Coakley, 1978; Atyeo, 1979; Goldstein, 1983; Smith, 1983; Guttmann, 1986; Elias and Dunning, 1986; Wann et al., 2001; Peiser and Minten, 2003; Kerr, 2005). In the social scientific debate, labels such as 'sports violence' and 'football-related violence' are often used as umbrella terms to refer to various types of violence in a sports context. These types are heterogeneous and require more precise conceptualization. With regard to the term 'football-related violence', an analytical distinction can be made between the violent conduct of players (on the pitch) and violence caused by spectators (off the pitch). The two types of football-related violence may require different explanations, even though they are intertwined at times (e.g. spectator violence triggered by violence on the pitch).

The distinction between player and spectator violence is only a first step towards the conceptualization of 'football-related violence'. Spectator violence is also a heterogeneous concept that groups together distinctive types of violent conduct among spectators. Elias (1971) has argued that spectator violence should be understood as an inherent feature of the game since modern football has, to varying extents, been associated with spectator violence ever since its early beginnings in nineteenth-century England. Throughout the development of football as a modern sport a certain level of spectator violence, although fluctuating over time, has always been present. But if we accept this general level of spectator violence at football matches, what about its specific forms? Can we identify differences in the forms of spectator violence throughout the history of the game, or have all types of spectator violence been evenly distributed in time and space? It is therefore necessary to analyze more accurately the different types of spectator violence at football matches. For present purposes, the concept of 'football hooliganism' needs to be delineated and defined more precisely.

There is no precise definition of 'football hooliganism'. It lacks legal definition, precise demarcation of membership and is used to cover a variety of actions which take place in more or less directly football-related contexts (Dunning, 2000: 142; J. Williams, 2001a: 1). For example, the *Report on Football Hooliganism in the Member States of the European Union* published by the Council of the

European Union (2002) groups together a variety of offences under the label 'football hooliganism', including violence against persons, damage to property, alcohol and drug offences, breach of the peace, theft and ticket touting. Contemporary scholars, such as Frosdick and Marsh (2005: 27-29), tend to acknowledge the problems in defining football hooliganism yet they avoid any attempt to propose a (working) definition of the subject in their own studies. The label 'football hooliganism' is thus a construct of the media and politicians rather than a social scientific concept. It is often used in a 'cover-all' sense, in which various forms of minor and more serious 'violence' are grouped together under the umbrella term 'football hooliganism' to refer to football fans who cause 'damage' to society. In this context, sociologists have studied the ways in which deviance and social problems are framed by powerful institutions and definers for purposes of public regulation (Becker, 1963; S. Cohen, 1972; cf. G. Pearson, 1998).

In search of a more precise conceptualization of football hooliganism, an ideal typical distinction can be drawn between spontaneous incidents of spectator violence and the behaviour of socially organized fan groups that engage in competitive violence, principally with fan groups of opposing football clubs (Spaaij, 2005b: 1; Giulianotti, 2001: 141; Stokvis, 1989: 148-152). The distinction between spontaneous violence and more socially organized or premeditated forms of spectator violence is historically observable in the shift from a pattern in which attacks on match officials and opposing players predominated over attacks on rival fans, to a pattern in which inter-fan fighting and confrontations between fans and the police became the predominant form of spectator violence (Dunning, 1994: 136). This shift has taken place in various European countries, but at different times.[1]

Football hooliganism is defined here as *the competitive violence of socially organized fan groups in football, principally directed against opposing fan groups.* For hooligan rivalries to develop and persist, the existence of at least one similar, oppositional group is necessary. The genesis of contemporary football hooliganism lies in (the media coverage of) the increasingly violent 'youth end' rivalries that emerged in the 1960s in England. Compared to the inter-group rivalries that developed from the 1960s onwards, the spectator violence that took place at football matches in the late nineteenth and early twentieth century was relatively unorganized, spontaneous and *ad hoc*. As Holt observes:

11

There are manifest continuities between the rites of violence in contemporary Britain and earlier periods. But the *specific forms* of hooliganism *are* new; football crowds were not segregated by age before the 1960s; youth did not congregate around parts of football clubs as their territory – they had a larger territory and community which they shared with their older relatives. When there were fights at football matches there was no dramatic media coverage (1990: 343). (emphasis in original)

Football hooliganism in its 'contemporary' sense thus refers to the social genesis of distinctive fan subcultures and their engagement in regular and collective violence, primarily with rival peers (Giulianotti, 1999: 49; Spaaij, 2005b: 1).

A universal phenomenon?

In the edited volume *Fighting Fans: Football Hooliganism as a World Phenomenon* (2002), Eric Dunning and his colleagues argue that football hooliganism should be viewed as a truly universal phenomenon (see also Hua, 2004: 88). Considering the definition proposed in the previous section, I find this argument problematic. Research into football-related violence suggests that some form of spectator violence at football matches is observable, to varying extents, in every part of the world where the game is played (cf. Young, 2000; Frosdick and Marsh, 2005; Bodin et al., 2005). However, the *specific* form of spectator violence which is the subject of this book (and, judging its title and contents, also the subject of Dunning et al.'s book) does not seem to be as worldwide as is suggested by the authors. Spectator violence at football matches *in general* may be perceived as a global phenomenon, but football *hooliganism* seems to me, first and foremost, a European and Latin American, and, to a far lesser extent, Australian phenomenon. Let me briefly explore this idea.[2]

Research suggests that several European countries have been affected by football hooliganism. Apart from persistent hooligan subcultures in Western European countries such as England (Dunning, 1999; Spaaij, 2005), Scotland (Giulianotti, 1999a), the Netherlands (Adang, 1998; Van der Torre and Spaaij,

2003), Belgium (Van Limbergen and Walgrave, 1988) and Germany (Ek, 1996; Dwertmann and Rigauer, 2002), hooligan formations are reported to exist, to varying degrees, in the following European nations: Italy (Roversi and Balestri, 2002; De Biasi, 1998), Austria (Horak, 1991), Poland (Piotrowski, 2004), Hungary (Pintér and Van Gestel, 2002), Romania (Beiu, 2005), the Czech Republic (Duke and Slepicka, 2002), Slovakia (Harsányi, 2005), Spain (Viñas, 2005; Spaaij and Viñas, 2005), France (Mignon, 2001; 2002; Hare, 2003), Greece (Astrinakis, 2002; Courakis, 1998), Cyprus (Murphy, 2000), Sweden (Andersson and Radmann, 1998), Denmark (Andersson and Radmann, 1998) and the former Yugoslavia (Colovic, 1999; 2002; Vrcan and Lalic, 1999).

Interestingly, in countries such as Portugal, Norway and Ireland there is a notable absence, or a relatively low level, of hooligan confrontations at football matches. With regard to the groups of young fans in Portuguese football, so-called *claques*, Marivoet (2002: 172-173) concluded that occasional incidents of violence are spontaneous and affective, and predominantly targeted at referees. Andersson and Radmann (1998: 151) have noted that at the level of club football, there are considerable differences between supporter cultures in Scandinavia. Hooligan subcultures are to be found, to varying degrees, in Sweden and Denmark, but not in Norway. Research by Bairner (2002) shows that football hooliganism in the Irish Republic and Northern Ireland has never assumed the significance which it has in several other Western European countries, although the rivalry between the two Belfast clubs, Linfield and Glentoran, 'can be more securely located in the realm of football hooliganism' (2002: 123).

In Latin America violent confrontations between opposing fan groups are relatively common, notably in Argentina (Archetti and Romero, 1994; Alabarces, 2002; Alabarces et al., 2005) and Brazil (Toledo, 1994; Pimenta, 2000; 2003; Reis, 2003). The emergence of militant fan groups in Argentinian football, *barras bravas* or *hinchadas*, can be dated back to the 1930s and 1940s and thus seems to have originated notably earlier than their European equivalents (Duke and Crolley, 1996: 276).[3] The scale and nature of Argentinian football hooliganism seems to have escalated from the 1960s onwards (Duke and Crolley, 2001: 108). Football-related murder became relatively frequent, on average about once in every three months (Romero, 1986: 7). The first *torcidas organizadas* in Brazilian football emerged in the late 1960s and early 1970s, in opposition to the more pacified, carnival-style *Charangas* that emerged as early as the 1940s. The competitive violence between rival *torcedores* escalated during the 1980s and the early 1990s as increasingly large numbers of youths were drawn to the fan groups (Pimenta, 2003: 43).

Traditions of football hooliganism in Latin America are not confined to Argentina and Brazil. Comparable fan groups can be found in countries such as Peru, Chile, Uruguay and Colombia. In Peru, a nation that experienced serious political violence, deepening economic recession and a breakdown of law and order in the 1980s and early 1990s, young members of the barras bravas tend to come from the most impoverished and marginalised sectors of the urban economy. They are, as Panfichi and Thieroldt (2002: 157) concluded, 'excluded from most educational and employment opportunities and other potential avenues of social mobility. Their main identities, therefore, lie precisely in their neighbourhoods or barrios, and in their football clubs.' From the 1980s onwards, and especially during the 1990s, football increasingly came to provide an opportunity for the expression of competitive violence by increasingly large numbers of youths.

Football hooliganism seems to be first and foremost a European and Latin American phenomenon. But although far less intense and widespread, comparable hooligan formations can be found in Australian 'soccer'. Crowd violence in Australian sports such as Australian Rules football, rugby and soccer is neither uncommon nor new (Warren, 1993; Vamplew, 1992; 1994a). Australian soccer has been popularly associated with hooliganism for decades, although Hughson (2002: 38) has argued that disorderly behaviour in soccer has been exaggerated and amplified by the mass media while, according to Mosely (1997: 168), 'incidents of violence in Australian Rules football and rugby league received far less attention and were painted in a different light.' The violence in and popular image of Australian soccer should be viewed within the context of the acculturation of immigrants through the involvement in sport, primarily associated with expressions of ethnic identity and nationalistic allegiance (Vamplew, 1994; Mosely, 1995; 1997; Hay, 2001). Spectator violence at soccer matches is almost invariably viewed to be attributed to ethnic tension because of the high level of ethnic community involvement evidenced in the sport throughout history and in contemporary times (Warren, 1995: 123). This ethnic tension is popularly perceived as problematic and

14

contrary to notions of assimilation and the 'Australianisation' of these social groups, hence the various attempts to 'de-ethnicise' the game (i.e. the banning of ethnic club names and symbols; cf. Hughson, 2002: 39; Mosely, 1997: 169-170). Matches featuring football clubs linked to communities from the former Yugoslavia have been a key source of conflict, but it is important to note that few injuries have been reported from crowd conflicts and few arrests are on record (Hughson, 2002: 38).

In the late 1980s and early 1990s youth fan groups emerged at Australian soccer clubs bearing some similarity to European and Latin American hooligan formations These fan groups emerged at a time when the international concern over English football hooliganism was at its height and a strong element of imitation appeared to exist in the creation of these groups (Hay, 2001: 88-89). Hughson (2002: 40) has argued that a key feature of Australian hooligan formations is the display of team colours, which usually reflect those of the homeland of the ethnic community with which it is affiliated. Violent confrontations between opposing hooligan formations occur occasionally but have been relatively infrequent (cf. Warren, 2003). Rather than being an integral feature of the Australian hooligan experience, fighting is 'an optional extra' (Hughson, 2002: 41).

In North America, spectator violence in soccer is rare and there is no equivalent of what I have termed hooliganism in this sport. More generally, while spectator violence in North American sports is neither uncommon nor new (Guttmann, 1986; Murphy et al., 1990; Dunning, 1999), it has not taken the form of competitive violence between rival fan groups characteristic of the European and South American soccer. Young (2002: 209) has argued that the majority of incidents of inter-fan violence occurring at North American sports matches involve individuals or small groups of supporters participating in activities such as common assault, drunken and disorderly behaviour and confrontations with the police. Less frequently episodes of fighting involving larger numbers of supporters have occurred.

In parts of Asia spectator violence at football matches has a long history, yet equivalents of self-declared hooligan formations engaging in violent confrontation do not seem to exist. Majumdar and Bandyopadhyay (2005) and Dimeo (2001) have shown that Indian football has witnessed a series of violent clashes, notably between rival fans of Mohun Bagan and East Bengal. One of the

15

worst tragedies in the history of Indian soccer occurred on 16 August 1980 during a league match between the two teams in Calcutta. Missile throwing and fights between opposing fans resulted in a stampede that caused the death of 16 fans (see Dimeo, 2001: 114-115; Gooptu, 2005: 698; Bandyopadhyay, 2005: 77). In the Middle East, deep-seated football rivalries occasionally spill over into violent confrontation between opposing fans. Football rivalries in Israel are closely related to ethnic and nationalist identities. Some sets of fans have a history of violent behaviour and high-profile matches are heavily policed in order to prevent confrontations between rival fans (Ben-Porat, 2001). However, the self-styled ultra groups that have emerged at several Israelian football clubs seem to be relatively pacified and when violence occurs, it is of a more spontaneous and unorganized nature than European and South American manifestations of football hooliganism. Similarly, with regard to spectator violence at football matches in Yemen, Stevenson and Alaug (2001: 181) have argued that when crowd disturbances occur 'they appear to be situational and opportunistic rather than planned or arising from long-standing animosities'.

In Japanese soccer unruly spectator behaviour does occur, principally in the shape of missile throwing and pitch invasions, but fighting between rival fans is extremely rare (Takahashi, 2002; cf. Shimizu, 2001). There are, to this date, no identifiable 'hooligan' groups in Japanese football. With regard to Chinese football culture, Hua (2004) argues that 'although football-related social disorder has occurred quite regularly, the mainstream media continue to deny its existence' (2004: 92). Incidents of spectator violence in Chinese football are often triggered by events on the pitch and are relatively spontaneous and unorganized when compared to European and Latin American hooligan encounters. Although Hua refers to spectator violence in Chinese football as 'football hooliganism', he concludes that 'rather than being well-organized and carefully planned acts of hooliganism [...] Chinese 'football hooligans' appear to be mostly young people affected by the atmosphere in the stadium.' Chinese football fans rarely set out to 'cause trouble' on purpose and violence tends to erupt as a result of spontaneous emotional outbursts (Hua, 2004: 90-91).

African soccer has a history of violence and disorder. Faulty organization and inadequate security measures at soccer grounds have played a large role in causing disorder, damage or deaths at soccer matches (Alegi, 2004: 244). On 9 July 2000, thirteen people died during a World Cup qualifying match between Zimbabwe and South Africa in Harare. Eight minutes from the final whistle, a South African goal scorer was hit on the head by a plastic bottle thrown from the stands, which halted the match. The police responded by using tear gas. In the ensuing stampede, thirteen people died and many were injured (Madzimbamuto, 2003). The following year Africa witnessed its worst sporting disasters. On May 9, 2001, 126 people died and dozens more were injured in a stampede at soccer match in Accra, Ghana. After the home team Hearts of Oak scored two late goals to beat Asante Kotoko, some of the visiting fans allegedly began destroying plastic seats and throwing them on to the running track surrounding the pitch. In response the police fired tear gas into the crowd, causing major panic and many to be suffocated and crushed to death. South Africa's most recent and worst-ever sport disaster occurred on 11 April 2001, when 43 people died and 158 were injured due to overcrowding at Ellis Park Stadium in Johannesburg (Alegi, 2004).

The occurrence of disorder and death at soccer matches in South Africa is not only related to inadequate infrastructures and security management. Violent confrontations between rival fan groups are relatively common, notably clashes between fans of the Kaizer Chiefs and Orlando Pirates. These confrontations resemble in some respects the violent encounters engaged in by hooligan formations, yet the inter-group rivalries in South African football are not related to a hooligan youth subculture and violent confrontations do not seem to be socially organized. In this context, Burnett (2002: 182-185) has argued that 'the South African 'soccer hooligans' are not an import of any kind, but are products of a society scarred by chronic poverty, in which some groups are marginalized in the social, political and economic spheres.'

In other parts of Africa spectator violence at football matches seems to be relatively spontaneous and unorganized and does not resemble the hooligan subcultures in Europe and Latin America. Spectator violence at football matches in Liberia, West Africa, has not been considered a social problem historically or today.[4] Armstrong (2002: 481) has noted that:

Fan disorder always seemed to involve the supporters of the big two teams [Invincible Eleven and Mighty Barolle], if not with each other then with fans of the smaller teams. But nobody I spoke with was ever aware of a 'hooligan' problem, and the fixtures were not occasions for chants and fights bound up in ethnic and socio-political antagonisms. Disorders tended to arise as a consequence of disputed refereeing decisions or cheating by players. In such instances, games have been abandoned after assaults on match officials.

In contrast, football-related violence in Mauritius has a long history. In the 1980s and 1990s there has been a catalogue of incidents, including assaults on rival fans, damage to stadia and buses, confrontations with the police, assaults on referees, players and officials, and pitch invasions (Edensor and Augustin, 2001: 95-98). Although these incidents seem to be relatively spontaneous and often related to events on the pitch, they are clearly embedded in wider ethnic and communal tensions throughout the island.

Towards a typology of football hooliganism

The brief overview of spectator violence and hooliganism at football matches worldwide suggests that football hooliganism is principally a European and Latin American and, to a far lesser extent, Australian phenomenon. My argument that football hooliganism can be viewed as a distinctive 'new' form of collective violence and juvenile subcultural identity in football should be qualified on two points. First, fights between rival gangs are by no means a new phenomenon (Pearson, 1983; Stokvis, 1991). In England, such fighting took place particularly in the streets in working-class areas, at cinemas, dance halls and at seaside resorts on public holidays. From the mid-1960s onwards, football grounds and their surroundings became one of its central and most persistent locations (Williams et al., 1986: 363). Football hooliganism should therefore perhaps not be understood as a sign of a rise in the level of social violence but rather as a relational shift and displacement in the level of violence of specific groups whose members are prepared for violence (Dwertmann and Rigauer, 2002: 80).

18

Second, in a limited number of cases, traditions of football hooliganism in Europe existed before the 1960s. For example, in Scotland, violent confrontations between rival fan groups of Celtic Glasgow and Glasgow Rangers have occurred since at least the 1920s (Murray, 1984). In the mid-1950s, Yugoslavian football witnessed a wave of spectator violence known as 'Zusism', consisting of armed confrontations between rival groups (Dunning et al., 1981: 342). In Catalonia, the deep-seated rivalry between fan groups of FC Barcelona and RCD Español (now RCD Espanyol) first turned radical in the 1920s. Español's fan club Peña Deportiva Ibérica was founded in 1923 within Barcelona's fascist circles to 'defend' the colours of Espanyol not only in football but also in regional political conflict. At stake was 'the affirmation of the principles of national unity in all areas of public life' (Culla Clarà, 1977: 50). In 1925, the fan group transformed from a sports grouping into a political body (Peña Ibérica) seeking to promote *Hispanidad* (Spanishness) among all sectors of Catalan society (Artells, 1972: 190). The group initially had a few hundred members, among them civil servants, students and army officials. Its main activity in the early years consisted of combating the 'anti-Spanish' and 'separatist' politics of FC Barcelona, both ideologically and physically. Peña Ibérica obtained a fearsome reputation for provoking (armed) confrontations at local derbies, which regularly resulted in injuries among spectators. At FC Barcelona, the Penya Ardèvol, led by the Olympic Greek-Roman wrestling champion Emili Ardèvol, regularly intimidated and assaulted fans of rival teams, most notably those of local rival Español (Sobrequés Callicó, 1998: 271-272). These early traditions of football hooliganism differ from their modern equivalents in that they were mostly local or regional and did not involve the regular attendance of large groups of young fans.

The proposed definition of football hooliganism as the competitive violence of socially organized fan groups in football corresponds in some respects with the framework for the comparative and historical analysis of spectator violence at football matches as proposed by Duke and Crolley (1996: 289-291). They use two criteria to categorize football-related violence in different societies and different historical periods: the degree of organization involved in acts of violence and the nature of violence. With regard to the degree of organization, Duke and Crolley draw an ideal typical distinction between spontaneous and organized forms of spectator violence. The second criterion, the nature of violence, contains three categories: attacks by fans on players and match officials, inter-fan fighting, and confrontations between football fans and the police.

My definition of football hooliganism can be located within the framework as principally involving socially organized (collective) violence between rival fan groups. However, inter-group fighting should not be viewed as an entirely separate category since hooligans also tend to be engaged in other types of violence to varying degrees. The framework proposed by Duke and Crolley therefore needs to be expanded to include a wider range of deviant behaviour. I also suggest that the authors' distinction between spontaneous and organized violence suffers two major flaws. First, I prefer to speak of *social* organization because most hooligan formations seem to be neither formally organized nor to generally exceed basic forms of synchronization and co-ordination (Van der Torre and Spaaij, 2003; Giulianotti and Armstrong, 2002; Adang, 2002). Second, the distinction is too dichotomous and requires an intermediate category that bridges the two extremes, since hooligan violence regularly erupts as a result of more spontaneous triggers, such as aggressive policing or on-field events. I would therefore propose the introduction of an intermediate category featuring spontaneous violence in socially organized fan groups, although I am well aware that the reality of football hooliganism is infinitely more complex and heterogeneous and cannot be fully captured in these analytical categories.

Table 1.1 shows the adapted framework for the comparative and historical analysis of spectator violence at football matches. The black cell relates to my definition of football hooliganism. The grey cells show related types of violence provoked by self-confessed hooligans. It is important to note that the distinctive types of violence often occur in combination, for example fighting and missile throwing. The extent of these types of violence varies in place as well as in time, as I will show in this book.

Table 1.1   Framework for the historical and comparative analysis of spectator violence at football matches.

Nature of violence		Degree of organization	
	Spontaneous	Spontaneous violence in socially organized groups	Socially organized
Violence against or fighting between rival fans			
Violence against players or match officials			
Violence against police officers or security staff			
Damage to property			
Missile throwing			
Intra-group violence			
Racial abuse or violence			

Source: Adapted from Duke and Crolley, 1996: 290.

The proposed framework is a useful instrument for analyzing the behaviour of socially organized fan groups in football. We should be aware, however, that it cannot fully account for the complex and heterogeneous nature of the phenomenon. At least five conceptual dilemmas can be identified. First, although football hooliganism primarily consists of competitive violence between rival fan groups, hooligans' violent behaviour is not restricted to inter-group fighting but may include missile throwing, vandalism, attacks on police or non-hooligan supporters, or racial abuse. At least in some countries, hooligan groups may consider the police a legitimate opponent, especially in the process of trying to separate warring parties (Galvani and Palma, 2005). Second, the violent behaviour of hooligan groups takes

21

place not only at or in the immediate vicinity of football grounds, but also in other contexts, for example city centres, pubs, nightclubs or railway stations (Dunning, 2000: 142). Third, football hooliganism involves a great deal of symbolic opposition and ritualized aggression which is easily confused with 'real' violence (Marsh, 1978). For many supporters identifying with football hooliganism, violence 'is not as central to their association as is sometimes assumed and rather the result of the "game" of confrontation and their willingness occasionally to turn symbolic opposition into physical encounter' (Armstrong and Harris, 1991: 434).

Fourth, even when self-declared hooligans are committed to the use of violence, their behaviour may be triggered by more spontaneous elements, such as aggressive policing or events on the pitch. The term 'organized' may in such cases be misleading. A common error, for instance within journalist and police circles, is to over-stress the degree of (formal) organization involved in football violence. This view portrays hooligan groups as paramilitary organizations in which 'ring leaders', 'generals' or 'lieutenants' initiate and co-ordinate riots. In reality, the degree of organization involved in football hooliganism appears to vary across cultures and localities. Even within British football the degree of organization involved in football hooliganism tends to vary significantly, as is suggested by the National Criminal Intelligence Service (NCIS):

> The amount and quality of this organization varies greatly between groups, from a highly disciplined, hierarchical criminal group that associates continuously throughout the week to a more casual grouping that comes together on the occasion of a football match with the intention of committing violent acts. (Private correspondence, December 2002)

Fifth, dissimilarities between countries complicate the conceptualization of football hooliganism. Self-declared hooligan groups have equivalent counterparts throughout Northern and Central Europe. Quite distinctive fan subcultures exist in more Southern parts of Europe and in Latin America. In countries such as Italy, Spain, Portugal and (parts of) France, so-called *ultras* are militant fan groups but their proclivities to violence vary substantially (Giulianotti, 2001: 142; Spaaij and Viñas, 2005: 80-81). Many ultra groups have certain characteristics of a formal organization, for example official membership, a board and recruitment campaigns (De Biasi, 1998: 216-218). Their basic function is to provide expressive and colourful support to the team and therefore they are not necessarily concerned with defeating or humiliating their peers through intimidation or violence (Giulianotti, 2001: 142; Mignon, 2001: 173). Although militant fan groups in Latin America (*barras bravas, hinchadas, torcidas*) resemble the European hooligan groups in some respects, there are also important differences. The barras bravas engage in political activity and, in addition, orchestrate violent confrontations with rival supporters (Duke and Crolley, 1996: 286-289). Configured like paramilitary task forces, the barras bravas 'carry out illegitimate tasks by means of violence and compulsion, and are used by sporting and political leaders for that purpose' (Alabarces, 2002: 34). Furthermore, it has been suggested that explanations centred on the diffusion of the modern variant of football hooliganism from England in the 1960s are not applicable to Latin America, since there has been a separate and distinctive evolution of the phenomenon on that Continent (Duke and Crolley, 1996: 289).

The aforementioned dilemmas illustrate the argument that football hooliganism is a complex and heterogeneous phenomenon. The level, forms and sources of football hooliganism seem to vary across countries and localities, presenting a case of great cross-national and cross-local variability. A fundamental question to sociologists in the field is how and to what degree existing theoretical frameworks can account for these variations. As we will see in the next section, there is reason to suggest that the dominant sociological approaches cannot fully account for the practical heterogeneity of the phenomenon.

Sociological approaches and their limitations

A key feature of the social scientific debate on football hooliganism is the long-standing dominance of British and, specifically, English theoretical approaches coupled with their almost exclusive focus on domestic forms of spectator violence at football matches. Within Britain, theoretical perspectives on football fan behaviour have come from a wide range of academic disciplines, including various strands in sociology, urban ethnography, anthropology, psychology, ethology, criminology, political science, public administration, communication science, and cultural studies. In contrast, the theoretical input of international scholars has been very limited, and there are no obvious international schools of theory (Young, 2000: 388).[5] Among sociological studies of football hooliganism, three quite clearly delineated theoretical approaches can be distinguished: (i) the Marxist approaches by Ian Taylor and John Clarke; (ii) the figurational approach of the 'Leicester School'; and (iii) the postmodernist approaches by Giulianotti and Redhead. These approaches will only be outlined briefly here, since they have been discussed at some length elsewhere (see Giulianotti, 1994a; Young, 2000; Frosdick and Marsh, 2005). While the different theorists have been highly critical of each other's works, it is important to note that, as we will see, their approaches are not necessarily mutually exclusive due to their distinctive focuses.

Marxist approaches

In his earlier contributions (1971; 1971a) sociologist Ian Taylor explained the emergence of football hooliganism in terms of the economic and social changes in society and football. Major changes in football itself, traditionally a male working-class sport, were believed to have alienated working-class fans from the game: commercialization, internationalization and professionalization. The sense of alienation experienced by working-class fans was further exacerbated by a more general alienation of parts of the working-class resulting from changes in the labour market and the decomposition of traditional working-class communities. Football hooliganism, Taylor argued, should be interpreted as a kind of working-class resistance movement, as 'the democratic response by the rump of a soccer subculture to the bourgeoisification of their game' (Taylor, 1971: 369).

A largely similar approach was developed by John Clarke (1973; 1978). He argued that hooliganism originated in the way in which the traditional forms of football watching encounter the professionalization and spectacularization of the game: 'it is one of the consequences of the changing relationship of its audience and the game' (1978: 50). Clarke stressed that specific subcultural styles enable young working-class males to resolve essential conflicts in their lives. Post-war youth subcultures were all examples of these symbolic attempts to resolve structural and

24

material problems. Football hooliganism, closely associated with the skinhead subculture in the 1960s and 1970s, is one such symbolic attempt.

The explanations of both Taylor and Clarke have been criticized as speculative theories lacking empirical confirmation. In his later work, Ian Taylor (1982; 1987; 1989; 1991) developed a different theoretical approach to football hooliganism. Reformulating his original thesis, he argued that the rise of a 'new' hooligan results from the culture of the upwardly-mobile, individualistic section of the (male) British working-class, which has done relatively well out of the restructuring of British industry and business in the 1970s and 1980s. The 'new' hooligan, in turn, has produced the jingoistic, racist and xenophobic behaviour of some English football fans abroad (cf. Williams, 1991: 173).

The figurational approach

Responding to early theories of football hooliganism, Eric Dunning and his colleagues at the University of Leicester developed an alternative explanation of the phenomenon. Their figurational sociological approach (Dunning et al., 1986; 1988) draws heavily upon Norbert Elias' theory of civilizing processes (1939). One of that theory's basic assumptions is that throughout recent history values of 'civilized' behaviour have penetrated the social classes in Europe; however, they have not yet fully penetrated the lower strata of the working class. The figurational approach explains football hooliganism in terms of the structure of the lower strata of society and the traditional relationship between members of these strata and football itself. According to Dunning and his colleagues, fighting is one of the few sources of excitement, meaning and status available to males from the lower working class. Their specific aggressive masculinity does not, however, simply derive from the manner in which lower-working-class communities are integrated into society at large. Lower-working-class communities also tend to generate norms or standards which, relative to those of groups higher up on the social scale, are conducive to and tolerant of a high level of aggression in social relations. The 'rougher' sections of lower-working-class communities appear to be characterized by feedback processes which encourage fall-backs on aggressive behaviour in many areas of social relations, especially on the part of males (Dunning et al., 1988: 208-209). In short,

25

although they emphasize that young men from the lower working class are not the *only* football hooligans, Dunning and his colleagues (1986: 240) stress that these youths 'seem to be the most central and persistent offenders in the more serious forms of football hooliganism.'

The work of the 'Leicester school' is by now the most widely known and consulted body of enquiry into the causes and nature of football hooliganism (Robson, 2000: 29). It has been an inspiration for many European scholars in the field for nearly two decades and has been praised on a theoretical as well as on a methodological level (e.g. King, 2002: 4; Young: 2000: 388). Nevertheless, the theoretical framework and methodology employed by Dunning and his colleagues have been criticized on various occasions (e.g. Armstrong, 1998; Armstrong and Harris, 1991; Giulianotti, 1999). It has been suggested that their theoretical approach operates on a high level of generality and has an aura of universalistic applicability and 'irrefutability' (Williams, 1991: 177). As King (2002: 4) puts it, 'in its less self-critical moments, Dunning's approach tends towards teleology.'

Postmodernist approaches

Steve Redhead's publications (1991; 1997; Redhead and McLaughlin, 1985) highlight the postmodernist influences in football culture. It is no longer possible, he argues, to explain football hooliganism through the classic prism of moral panics.[6] Redhead claims that, towards the end of the 1980s and into the 1990s, important changes occurred in masculine football culture. Football hooliganism gradually 'disappeared' into 'post-fandom', signalling a transition of football culture into popular fan and media culture. Redhead's work concentrates on the relation between supporter styles and pop music subcultures, within which he locates the 'style wars' of the football 'casuals' (seen as the new type of hooligans; see Chapter Three).

Richard Giulianotti (1991; 1994; 1995; 1999) has provided more ethnographically detailed descriptions of football fan behaviour. Like Redhead, he claims that football hooliganism 'in the modern sense' has evolved into a postmodern phenomenon. Giulianotti's work primarily concentrates on supporters of the Scottish national team and on Scottish hooligan formations. He argues that Scottish football fan behaviour derives from specific cultural and historical forces rather than from social structural factors. Scottish fans, especially those following the national team, are seen as seeking to distance themselves from the 'British hooligan' label and particularly from the unruly behaviour of English fans abroad. Their anti-Englishness has led them, in turn, to create a 'friendly' image for themselves. Giulianotti also uses the concept of 'post-fandom' to explain football hooliganism. Post-fans 'represent an epistemic break from older forms of football fandom in that they are cognizant of the constructed nature of fan reputations, and the vagaries of the media in exaggerating or inventing such identities' (1999: 148). Giulianotti asserts that the postmodern epoch of football hooliganism is signalled most obviously by changes in its political and media treatment.

It is not entirely clear in Giulianotti's analysis whether these postmodernist influences have come to replace more 'modern' forms of football hooliganism or co-exist with them in various constellations depending on the specific situations at different clubs and in different countries. Moreover, there appear to be important variations in the national trajectories of football culture and hooliganism, which thwart the division of spectator cultures into the categories 'traditional', 'modern' and 'postmodern'. Giulianotti (1999: 64) acknowledges these issues himself with regard to differences between the English and the Scottish experience. He points out that, in England, the attempt to construct a normalized, pacified, 'post-hooligan' identity sits uneasily with the continuing activities of football hooligans.

British theory and European evidence: a reappraisal of sociological approaches

It has been suggested that, despite obvious differences between rival sociological approaches to football hooliganism, they can be located within a common framework with regard to their predictions of the gender, race, age and class backgrounds of the typical football hooligan. In short, hooligans are male, white, working-class young adults (Frosdick and Marsh, 2005: 84-85). In my view, the reduction of these theories to such simplistic equations may have some merit as to identifying the core of the debate, but misjudges the diversity of Giulianotti's approaches. For present purposes, I would like to draw attention to another commonality of sociological explanations of football hooliganism. I argue that, due to their almost exclusive focus on domestic (British and particularly English) forms

27

of football hooliganism, the approaches converge in undervaluing and under-theorizing cross-national and cross-local variations in football hooliganism.

The range of international research published on the subject in the 1990s and early 2000s casts doubt over the universal applicability of the theories presented above. It seems unlikely that Giulianotti's notion of postmodern hooliganism or that of the 'new', post-class hooligan identified by Taylor is easily transferable to non-British contexts. The applicability of the work of the 'Leicester school' to European countries which lack the highly specific class structures found in England may also be limited, despite Dunning's claim that 'research on the social class of football hooligans [...] suggests that hooligans in other countries tend to come from social backgrounds similar to those of their English counterparts' (2000: 159). Dunning's interpretation of foreign research into football hooliganism seems to overlook significant contradictions. For example, Giulianotti (1999a: 32) has emphasized Scottish hooligans' social and economic incorporation within mainstream society, rather than their structural exclusion, while Harper (1990) has argued that hooligans 'come predominantly from lower levels of the social scale' while.

Similar contradictions can be observed in the work of Italian sociologists. In 1991, Roversi stressed that Italian ultras come predominantly from the working class. A decade later the same author suggested that: 'Even though the self-producing mechanism of the ultras groups closely resembles the principle of ordered segmentation proposed by Dunning, the social basis of the ultras does not consist predominantly of the lowest and roughest strata of society' (Roversi and Balestri, 2002: 142). Regretfully, Roversi's findings are flawed by his failure to distinguish between the 'genuine' ultra fan – engaging in the active and colourful support of the team – and the hooligan-type fan regularly seeking violent confrontation. His findings probably tell us more about the class backgrounds of young Italian football fans in general (the ultras) than about those of football hooligans. There are also important dissimilarities in the social composition of Italian ultra (and perhaps hooligan?) groups in different localities. Two studies carried out in Bologna and Pisa suggest that the social origins of the ultras vary according to the demographic context (Roversi, 1992; Francia, 1994). Especially ultras based in the richer North of Italy tend to come from more prosperous backgrounds (Podaliri and Balestri, 1998: 94).

Local and regional variations in the social backgrounds of ultras and hooligans also appear to exist in other Western European countries. Ek (1996: 73) has noted that West German hooligans come from all social classes and that, in the 1990s, there was an increasing dominance of young men from middle or upper-class milieus within hooligan groups. In contrast, football hooliganism in East Germany traditionally contained a strong element of social protest and provocation which can be located within the identity crisis of the East and its depressing social circumstances (Pilz, 1991: 117-119). In Spain, the ultra subculture has been appealing to young men and women from all social classes from its very beginnings, yet there are important regional and local variations. Historian Carles Viñas (2005: 190) has recently argued that 'the ultras form a complex variety in terms of their social situations, academic formation and family life'. Two recent sociological studies seem to confirm this idea. An ethnographic study of militant fan groups in Andalusia suggests that 77 per cent of the ultras are students, though comparatively many of them are engaged in vocational studies (no percentage is noted). Thirteen per cent work, and a further ten per cent are unemployed (Rodríguez Díaz, 2003: 118). A survey of 246 ultras of Frente Atlético (Atlético Madrid) concludes that almost half of the ultras are students, of which 24 per cent at a university level. Nine per cent of the ultras are unemployed (Adán Revilla, 2004: 91). Regretfully, both authors fail to draw a distinction between 'non-violent' ultras and those fans regularly engaging in competitive violence with rival supporters. Nor do they distinguish effectively between different types of work or education.

In a recent publication, Eric Dunning (2000: 161; see also Dunning, 1999: 158) acknowledges that 'it is unlikely that the phenomenon of football hooliganism will be found always and everywhere to stem from identical social roots.' He suggests that football hooliganism may be 'fuelled and contoured' by the major 'fault lines' of particular countries.

> In England, that means social class and regional inequalities; in Scotland and Northern Ireland, religious sectarianism; in Spain, linguistic sub-nationalisms of the Catalans, Castillians, Gallegos and Basques; in Italy, city particularism and perhaps the division between North and South as expressed in the formation of the 'Northern League'; and in Germany, the

relations between East and West and political groups of the left and right (2000: 161).

One of the differences that these variable patterns may make, Dunning argues, is that sectarianism and city particularism as bases for football hooliganism may draw in more people from higher up the social scale. A shared characteristic of all fault lines is that they involve variants of 'established-outsider figurations' (Elias and Scotson, 1965) in which intense ingroup bonds and correspondingly intense antagonisms towards outgroups are liable to develop (Dunning, 1999: 158).

The concept of societal fault lines provides an important new departure in the comparative study of football hooliganism and resembles in many respects the concept of cleavage structure coined by political scientists Lipset and Rokkan (1967). In the classical definition, a cleavage has three specific connotations. First, it involves a social division that separates people who can be distinguished from one another in terms of key social characteristics such as occupation, status, religion, or ethnicity. Second, the groups involved in the division must be conscious of their collective identity and be willing to act on this basis. Third, a cleavage must be expressed in organizational terms. This is typically achieved as a result of the activities of trade unions, a church, a political party, or some other organization that gives formal institutional expression to the interests of those on the one side of the division. The cleavage structure of a society is, of course, not immutable. Changes can occur as a result of changes in the social divisions that underpin cleavages, as a result of changes in the sense of collective identity that allows cleavages to be perceived by those involved, or as a result of changes in the organizational structure that gives political expression to cleavages (Gallagher et al., 1995: 209-215).

A major strength of the concept of fault lines is that it enhances our understanding of (variations in) the nature of ingroup and outgroup figurations in football and hooligan rivalries. I would argue, however, that due to the concept's high level of generality it seems to undervalue more specific aspects which co-shape the nature and development of football hooliganism. This includes (local or regional) historical and cultural specificity, football-related or hooligan-related local cleavages, interactions between hooligans and law enforcers, and formal and informal policies targeting football hooliganism. I will elaborate on this issue in the following section.

Fan cultures as glocal phenomena

Football hooliganism transgresses national boundaries and has undergone processes of globalization. Hooligan subcultures historically revolved around British terrace culture. On the Continent, football hooliganism underwent a process of cultural creolization as indigenous fan groups merged the adopted patterns with their own distinctive cultural forms (Dunning et al., 2002a: 223; Giulianotti, 2001: 143). Furthermore, the ultra subcultures dominant in countries such as Italy, Spain, and parts of France have come to influence supporter groups in Northern Europe, with similar fan groups being formed, to varying extents, in countries such as Germany, Austria, the Netherlands and parts of Scandinavia. In the 1990s British fan subcultures also started to experiment with aspects of the Southern European model, through the use of Latin chant patterns, musical bands and paraphernalia (Giulianotti, 1999: 64). For example, in 2004, an ultra-style fan group named Leeds Ultras emerged at Leeds United.

Recent changes in the football industry, for example the expansion of the Champions League, are believed to enhance the homogenization of football cultures. However, I would suggest that, as the aforementioned examples show, instead of leading to homogenization, the globalization of football cultures should be viewed as processes of hybridization or creolization (Giulianotti and Finn, 2000: 257; cf. Nederveen Pieterse, 1995; Hannerz, 1987). The intensity and rapidity of contemporary global cultural flows contribute to the misleading belief that the world is becoming a more singular place (Featherstone, 1990: 1-2). Many of the transnational cultural processes are incomplete and have not affected different countries to a similar extent (Hannerz, 1996: 6). Football is a social sphere in which the complex intertwinement of the global and the local can be observed *par excellence*. Football fan cultures can be viewed as 'glocal' phenomena (Robertson, 1992; 1995).[7] Although it is increasingly difficult to understand local or national experiences without reference to global flows (Maguire, 1999: 31; Sandvoss, 2003: 76), local cultural traditions and legacies continue to exert a strong influence over

31

patterns of behaviour. The fan cultures of particular football clubs 'share ritual elements, but at the same time each fan culture exhibits distinct forms of prescribed formal ritual behaviour and symbolism' (Back et al., 2001: 43). Although football culture appears to be changing with unprecedented speed, notions of post-fandom and post-hooliganism are not an evenly distributed and widely recognized phenomenon. In his detailed account of Millwall fandom, Garry Robson (2000: 6) correctly argues that:

> [T]hough growing numbers of individuals characterizable as […] post-fans do clearly exist, it is far from clear that the bases of participation for the majority have radically changed. This is likely to be most true, as is the case with Millwall, of small and medium-sized clubs with little or no appeal beyond their own historical and social-ecological limits.

Dissimilarities in the extent and forms of football hooliganism need to be understood in terms of the way hooligan subcultures are nested within the ritual and collective symbolism of each fan culture (cf. Back et al., 2001: 43). Besides important national variations in football hooliganism, there are also local and regional dissimilarities in the manifestation of hooligan violence. For example, academic research into English hooligan formations shows that not all hooligan groups in England are structured along identical lines in terms of their degree of organization and social composition (Dunning, 1999: 154; cf. Armstrong and Harris, 1991; Murphy et al., 1990). I would argue that although the fault lines of particular societies may in part explain cross-national dissimilarities in football hooliganism, they fail to account for more specific spatial and temporal variations (i.e. local fault lines). The latter type of variation should be addressed through close empirical scrutiny of the collective imaginaries of football fan cultures.

Within the context of national and local variability we should also examine the interactional dynamics of football hooliganism. Football hooliganism revolves around continuous interactions between the authorities, the local football club, its fan community, and hooligans. One way of approaching these inter-group dynamics is to focus on the effects of official attempts to curb football hooliganism. Murphy and his associates have argued that:

as the controls imposed by central government, the football authorities and the police have grown more all-embracing, tighter and sophisticated, so the football hooligans in their turn have tended to become more organized and to use more sophisticated strategies and plans in an attempt to evade the controls. At the same time, football hooligan fighting has tended to become displaced from an immediate football context and to take place at times and in situations where the controls are, or are perceived to be, weak or non-existent (1990: 89-90).

Approaches of this kind tend to highlight the large number of measures designed to curb football hooliganism: the segregation of home and away fans, fencing, closed-circuit television (CCTV), conversion to all-seater stadia, identity card schemes, intelligence-led policing, and so forth.

In recent years social psychologists have developed a more dynamic approach to studying the interactions between police officers and football fans. Whereas most scholars tend to concentrate on explaining football hooliganism in terms of the macro-social origins of conflictual norms, these authors emphasize more strongly the ways in which understandings and behaviours develop in context such that even those who initially and ordinarily eschew violence may come to act violently (Stott and Reicher, 1998; 1998a; Stott et al., 2001; Adang, 2002). I would argue that although cross-cultural differences in policing in Western Europe seem to have diminished (Della Porta and Reiter, 1998: 6), the contents and outcomes of supporter/police interactions may vary considerably across localities, depending, among other factors, on police professionalism and culture and on hooligans' and fans' perceptions of the police. We should remember that street-level interactions between law enforcers and the public produce more informal and unofficial sets of rules than the formal ones known publicly (O'Neill, 2005: 189; Van der Torre, 1999). In this context, Lipsky (1980: 82) has argued that 'to understand streetlevel bureaucracy one must study the routines of subjective responses streetlevel bureaucrats develop in order to cope with the difficulties and ambiguities of their jobs.'

Analysis of cross-national and cross-local overlaps and dissimilarities in football hooliganism should also include other forms of social interaction, notably the relations between hooligans and clubs, and anti-hooligan initiatives within fan communities. There are, for example, important dissimilarities with regard to the extent to which, and the forms in which, football clubs engage in the prevention of football hooliganism (Spaaij, 2005; 2005b). These diverse types of inter-group interaction add to the more obvious social interactions between opposing hooligan groups and intra-group negotiation, which are discussed below.

In this section I have argued that in order to enable a profound understanding of football hooliganism as a transnational phenomenon comparative research should focus not merely on general societal fault lines but principally on the manifestation of football hooliganism within individual fan cultures. The development of football hooliganism over time can only be fully understood if one also takes into account the diverse social interactions between football hooligans and 'significant others'. As we will see in the following section, these 'others' are crucial to the construction of hooligan identities.

Aspects of hooligan violence

If we accept that football hooliganism presents a case of great practical heterogeneity, where does this leave us? Can common aspects be identified, or should we merely describe and evaluate football hooliganism in individual, micro-level situations? The argument I seek to develop here is that although local contexts are crucial to understanding the precise nature and development of football hooliganism at different clubs and in different countries, certain universal aspects can be identified in the manifestation of football hooliganism. These aspects should be viewed as key components of football hooliganism as a transnational phenomenon.

Football hooliganism and social identity

A particular strength of the fault lines concept proposed by Dunning (1999; 2000) is its focus on established-outsider figurations in football rivalries. These figurations are of crucial importance to understanding the construction and maintenance of hooligan identities. In his detailed anthropological study of a Sheffield United hooligan group nicknamed 'the Blades', Gary Armstrong (1998: 3) stresses the significance of identity formation in football hooliganism:

> Essentially, what football hooliganism involves is the participants taking upon themselves various roles and identities. [...] [T]he very concept of identity is underplayed in most studies of hooligan causation, because crucial to Us is the construction and existence of Them or the Other. The problem, then, is how to interpret just how, in the hooligan debate, is the *'other'* constructed and maintained and given sufficient status to be worth confronting. (emphasis in original)

Hooligan formations construct their collective identities in terms of the perceived differences between self and the other. Social identity lies in differences, and differences are asserted against what is closest, which represents the greatest threat. Minimum objective distance in social space can thus coincide with maximum subjective distance (Bourdieu, 1990: 137).

Hooligan groups emphasize the differences between themselves and their opponents in two ways: first, in terms of (de)masculinization ('real' and 'hard' men versus 'boys' and 'poofs') and, second, in terms of club and/or city, neighbourhood, regional, ethnic, religious, nationalist or political allegiance (e.g. Feyenoord/Rotterdam versus Ajax/Amsterdam, or Athletic Bilbao/Basque/left-wing versus Real Madrid/Spanish/right-wing). With regard to the latter type, allegiances may also be shifted or suspended. This is illustrated by Harrison (1974: 604) in what he calls the 'Bedouin syndrome' in the football context, namely a tendency for *ad hoc* alliances to be built up according to the following principles: the enemy of your enemy is your friend, the friend of your friend is your friend, but your friend of one moment can become your enemy of the next. Thus, to use the previous example, Athletic Bilbao and Real Sociedad hooligans may temporarily suspend their local rivalry to form a temporal alliance based on their shared sympathy for Basque nationalism and jointly confront hooligans of 'centralist' Real Madrid.

35

There thus exists a common framework of interaction in which there is space for contact and co-operation as well as for distinction enacted by the use of violence (cf. Blok, 1997: 164). What is involved is not a deep-seated conflict of interest, since both parties share a commitment to engage in violent confrontation, but the emphasizing of minor, but nevertheless perceivedly fundamental differences between groups that tend to have much in common (e.g. in terms of age, gender, ethnicity, class, education, language, clothing and interests) and which share with each other a variable interest in particular leisure spaces, such as football grounds, pubs and nightclubs (cf. Giulianotti and Armstrong, 2002: 216). This is what Freud described as the 'narcissism of minor differences' in his 1917 paper *Das Tabu der Virginität*: how simply by displacement, by finding adversaries toward whom dislike can be directed, suspicion and dislike is set aside in the formation of groups (Freud, 1947). In other words, when people are alike in most respects, it is precisely the minor differences which will be made to serve as the basis and rationale for the aversion to otherness (cf. Ignatieff, 1998: 48).

> It is always possible to bind together a considerable number of people in love, so long as there are other people left over to receive the manifestations of their aggressiveness. I once discussed the phenomenon that it is precisely communities with adjoining territories, and related to each other in other ways as well, who are engaged in constant feuds and in ridiculing each other – like the Spaniards and Portuguese, for instance, the North Germans and South Germans, the English and Scotch, and so on (Freud, 1961: 61)

Importantly, the narcissism of minor differences does not automatically lead to violence (Blok, 1997: 178). In the football context, although the mocking and taunting of rival supporters is part of the 'game', the overwhelming majority of football fans do not engage in competitive violence. It is in their commitment to the use of violence in inter-group rivalries that hooligans distinguish themselves from non-hooligan supporters. In other words, for hooligans, 'violence constitutes the compelling form of social intercourse out of which their social group arises' (King, 2001: 571-572). Moreover, variations in the level and seriousness of hooligan violence may result from differences in broader social and political circumstances, among other factors. For example, the relative lethality of Argentinian football hooliganism should be viewed within the context of the comparatively high levels of social and state violence in Argentine society (Alabarces, 2002: 33-34).

In the first part of this chapter I emphasized that the label 'football hooliganism' is a social construct of media and politicians rather than a social scientific concept. How, then, do self-confessed hooligans themselves interpret their involvement in collective violence? Having stressed the specificities of football hooliganism in different local and national contexts, is there some sort of shared understanding among participants of the morality and aesthetic values of football hooliganism? I will address this question – to which the answer must be yes – by examining certain common aspects of football hooliganism in a transnational context.

Football hooliganism as meaningful action

Hooligan violence, like other types of interpersonal violence (Blok, 2000: 24), should not be seen as senseless and irrational, but as a changing form of interaction and communication, as a historically developed cultural form of meaningful action. More is at stake in hooligan fighting than an instrumental move towards a specific goal. If there are any goals involved, they can only be reached in a prescribed, expressive, ritualized way. As Blok (2000: 28) argues:

> Although violence may be primarily directed at the attainment of specific ends, such as wounding or killing an opponent, it is impossible to understand these violent operations in terms of these easily recognizable goals alone. There are often more effective ways to obtain these results.

Before examining what these specific goals might be, I will first discuss in more detail the moral economy and aesthetic values of football hooliganism to its (prospective) practitioners.

A basic assumption of sociological and anthropological studies of football hooliganism is that violence can be read, appreciated and decoded – that is,

37

understood – and that 'theories cast in terms of irrationality, mob psychology, individual pathology and simple instrumentality are to be rejected as incapable of explaining the social meanings of violence' (Downes, 1982: 29). Despite this common assumption, sociological and anthropological studies of football hooliganism diverge in both their theoretical and methodological approaches. In reaction to the speculative and distant theorizing of scholars such as Taylor (1971; 1971a), Marsh and his colleagues (1978) stressed the need for ethnographic fieldwork. This research method has become increasingly dominant among scholars of football hooliganism and has enhanced our understanding of the subcultural identity and motivations of football hooligans (see Armstrong, 1998; Armstrong and Harris, 1991; Hobbs and Robins, 1991; Van der Torre and Spaaij, 2003). What emerges from these studies is that football hooligans have a very intricate culture that has developed over many years. Strong emotional attachment to the collective is a central feature of their hooligan identity, which is produced and reproduced through processes of othering. The sense of 'being a hooligan' is a key part to that social identity; hooliganism is not something they do lightly or without passion (O'Neill, 2005: 26).

Football hooliganism can be perceived as a (youth) subculture with distinctive shapes, which revolves around particular activities, focal concerns and territorial spaces (cf. Clarke et al., 1976: 14). The principal territorial domain from which the subculture derives its visibility is the football stadium. Football hooligans are emotionally attached to 'their' ground, which is commonly perceived as home territory that needs to be defended. Over the years, however, violent encounters between opposing groups have increasingly been displaced to city streets, pubs, railway stations and so on, mainly as a consequence of the constrictive security measures in and around football grounds. The geographical meaning of the ground for football hooligans has altered accordingly, moving from being the 'front region' of hooligan confrontations to being a 'back region' in which interaction between competing hooligan formations is usually denied (Giulianotti and Armstrong, 2002: 224).[8] This process of displacement is not a singular development and should be understood as a variable product of ongoing interaction between opposing hooligan groups and law enforcers.

The use of the term 'subculture' requires some clarification in order to avoid ambiguities. Is this type of culture simply a segment of a larger culture, or is it something subordinate to a dominant culture? Is it something subterranean and rebellious, or is it substandard, qualitatively inferior (Hannerz, 1992: 69; cf. Thornton, 1997: 4)? The work of the celebrated Centre for Contemporary Cultural Studies at the University of Birmingham is of some interest here, perceiving subcultures as smaller, more localized and differentiated structures within one or other of the larger cultural networks (Hall and Jefferson, 1976). Subcultures are both identifiably different in important respects – their peculiar shapes and practices – from the culture from which they derive, but they also have things in common with their 'parent' culture (Clarke et al., 1976: 13). Hobbs and Robins (1991: 569) have argued that (English) hooligan groups do not conform to the idealized image of the teenage gang, somehow alienated from the parent culture. On the contrary, hooligans are viewed to celebrate their parent culture and stress apparent continuities with the past. In this context, hooligans' construction of social identity should be viewed as a dynamic and complex combination of distinction (e.g. being tougher and more masculine than the 'other') and compliance (e.g. embedded in, or celebrating 'mainstream' culture). The term 'subculture' emphasizes the differences between these youths and the rest of society, but we should remember that the youths who adopt a hooligan 'style' are socialized in a range of other sites, such as family, workplace and school.

From a postmodernist perspective, Giulianotti and Armstrong (2002: 218) take the issue of identity formation in football hooliganism a step further by arguing that hooligan identity may be regarded as a single constituent of a 'basket of selves which come to the surface at different social moments as appropriate' (Cohen, 1993: 11, paraphrasing Ralph H. Turner). They see this as having three consequences upon participation. First, time is critical in determining the exact degree of 'fit' between social context and identity. Second, the hooligan self must be combined with many other selves, perhaps simultaneously, as workmates, family, girlfriends/wives and non-football friends are encountered or accompanied within designated football spaces (pubs, the ground, railway stations). Third, within hooligan gatherings, there is a multiplicity of self identities available to participants, not only defined by the degree of involvement in fighting, but also by internal humour and self-parody

39

(Giulianotti and Armstrong, 2002: 218). A principal strength of the focus on the multiplicity of identities is that it views hooligan formations as loose associations with fluid instead of fixed boundaries and shapes. This enables us to understand, to some degree, how supporters who are not self-confessed hooligans come to participate in violent confrontations. As we have seen in an earlier section, this issue has been the subject of recent social psychological research into football hooliganism (Stott and Reicher, 1998; Stott et al., 2001; Adang, 2002).

In short, I would argue that the concept of subculture is applicable to football hooliganism only when it is qualified on two issues. First, I see the hooligan subculture as having fluid instead of fixed boundaries. Within hooligan formations there seem to be different levels of commitment to the group (i.e. core participants, followers, marginal participants, wannabes). I would argue that the core of the hooligan formation tends to be relatively permanent and cohesive, whereas the periphery of the group is constantly shifting, depending, among other factors, on processes of self-selection (Van der Torre and Spaaij, 2003). Second, and contrary to its traditional meaning, I use the concept of subculture in a less class-specific way (cf. Frith, 1987: 75-76). Recent research suggests that the social backgrounds of football hooligans vary across localities, depending on local and national circumstances (Alabarces, 2005; Spaaij, 2005a; Giulianotti, 1999; Viñas, 2005).

Earlier in this chapter I stressed that football hooliganism is a transnational phenomenon that transgresses the boundaries of individual societies. But does this mean that a notion of shared 'hooligan identity' among different hooligan groups exists, not only within one country but also across countries? Can we speak of football hooliganism as an 'imagined community' (Anderson, 1983), whose members will never know most of their fellow members, meet them, or even hear of them, yet in the minds of each lives the image of their communion? The answer to this question must be yes. In their detailed account of English and Scottish hooligan formations, Giulianotti and Armstrong (2002: 218) correctly argue that:

> The hooligan network is an informal and increasingly transnational phenomenon that has evolved gradually and rather haphazardly, particularly since the early 1980s. In most instances, it comprises individual hooligans from different formations who have met (usually fortuitously) and

exchanged personal details, with a view towards sharing subcultural information regarding fan violence or other common interests. In other circumstances, the network serves to tie some different hooligan groups through more formal friendships.

A shared cultural practice of football hooligans is their involvement, to varying degrees, in violent confrontation with opposing hooligans. It is their violence that distinguishes them from non-hooligan supporters, while at the same time their proclaimed loyalty to the club sets them apart from ordinary street gangs. Most hooligans are committed football supporters, with a broad knowledge of watching and playing the game (Giulianotti and Armstrong, 2002: 216), although in younger generations comparatively more hooligans appear to be principally attracted to football matches as a site for fighting (Van der Torre and Spaaij, 2003). Hooligans' club allegiance is demonstrated by their will to defend the honour of the team 'to the max', that is, including physical force. A similar logic applies to group solidarity; the group's reputation is defended and established through the use of violence.

Despite significant cross-cultural variations in the precise forms and social sources of football hooliganism and attendant terminologies, hooligan identities in these different parts of the world converge in their explicit concern with competitive violence against rival fan groups. This universally shared characteristic of hooligan identities can be found, for example, in the Argentinian term *aguante*. The term designates wider meanings than its strictly etymological reference (*aguantar* means 'to bear', 'to stand') and is linked to a rhetoric of the body and to a collective resistance against hardship and the 'other' (other fans, the police) (Alabarces, 2002: 36). In Argentinian fan discourse, *aguantar* means *poner el cuerpo* ('putting the body in'), that is, in physical violence. *Aguante* is essentially other-directed. It is through *aguante* that male football fans can distinguish themselves from the *no-machos*, who are disqualified as *hijos nuestros* (non-adults) and *putos* (homosexuals), and demonstrate to one another that they are 'real men', that they are 'macho'. Violence is thus not only a practice that is not rejected, instead it is deemed legitimate and more or less obliged (Alabarces, 2005: 1; Garriga Zucal, 2005: 39-48; Garriga Zucal, 2005a: 61).

41

The key aim of all hooligan formations is to successfully challenge their rivals through intimidation and violence. Hooligan encounters are essentially related to control over specific spaces, notably the defence of home 'turf' and the invasion of foreign territory (i.e. the ground and surrounding areas, neighbourhoods, cities). The (match-day) objective of the hooligan group is to secure or enhance its honour and status, by taking on opponents successfully, through 'standing' them in fights collectively, 'doing' or 'running' them (Giulianotti and Armstrong, 2002: 216).[9] The gravest humiliation in hooligan encounters is 'being done' or 'getting run', especially on home territory. Etymological equivalents of these actions can be found in several European and non-European countries, such as *rennen in je eigen stad* (getting run in your own city) in Dutch football hooliganism and *hacer correr* ('running') in Argentinian and Spanish hooligan confrontations.

Among hooligan formations there are broad definitions of how masculine honour can be won and lost, but these informal codes of legitimate action and their application to particular incidents are always negotiable, both within hooligan groups and between rival formations (King, 2001: 573; Giulianotti and Armstrong, 2002: 217). First, competitive violence is commonly perceived as a matter of hooligans only; hooligans should only fight each other (or the police) and not non-hooligan supporters (i.e. women, children or non-violent male fans). Honour can only be legitimately claimed through challenging, or responding to the challenge of, an equal (Bourdieu, 1977: 105). This informal code of action is occasionally broken and may cause fragmentation within hooligan formations or further escalation of inter-group relations. On a more regular basis, hooligans damage property (of non-hooligans) during encounters with opposing groups or missile throwing.

Second, although violent confrontation is a key aim, seriously injuring or killing the opponent is usually not. Serious injuries and deaths are relatively rare and often accidental, although there are significant cultural variations in the lethality of football hooliganism. While their rhetoric may suggest otherwise, most hooligans claim that they 'do not engage in confrontations with the aim of seriously harming their opponents, unless in their view there are "extenuating circumstances",' which are highly contestable (Giulianotti and Armstrong, 2002: 217). Related to this informal code of legitimate action is the idea that hooligans do not inflict more injury than necessary on a defeated rival (i.e. when lying helplessly on the ground).

There have been several cases in which this unwritten rule was broken, occasionally resulting in serious injury and even death.

Third, hooligan confrontations should ideally be a battle of physical contact (i.e. fist fighting). The use of weapons is generally considered a dishonourable practice since it implies distance between oneself and the opponent. As Alabarces (2005: 3) puts it with regard to Argentinian football hooliganism, 'the brick creates distances that need to be overcome, and the firearm is a thing of 'homosexuals'.' In reality this code of engagement is highly contestable and regularly ignored. Several hooligan groups hold a reputation for their use of offensive weapons (e.g. knives, bricks, bottles, sticks, belts). Some countries, cities and regions have a long cultural tradition of weapon-carrying (notably knives) by young people, while others do not (Giulianotti and Armstrong, 2002: 217). Fourth, group members are obliged to demonstrate complete loyalty to one another in violent confrontation. Those who do not enter the fight or abandon their mates in the middle of it will normally be 'expelled' and/or retaliated against. This code is crucial to the maintenance of group identity, yet it is often contested, especially among what can be termed 'opportunity hooligans' or marginal participants (i.e. self-declared hooligans in the periphery of the group) (Van der Torre and Spaaij, 2003: 44-45; Adang, 1997: 27).

In football hooliganism physical violence is a central means for asserting one's superiority over the opponent and demonstrating one's 'hard' masculinity, but it is not the only source of demasculinization of the 'other'. Symbolic demasculinization of opponents is not only enacted through physical force, but also through the use of a special vocabulary. Evidence of this verbal denigration is the frequent reference to rival fans and/or the team they support as 'wankers', which is usually accompanied by the mass gestured representation of the male masturbatory act (Dunning et al., 1986a: 172). Insults similarly denying the masculinity of opposing male fans focus on their assumedly deviant sexuality ('queers', 'sheepshaggers') or their alleged immaturity and lack of reputation ('who the fucking hell are you?', 'little boys'). Another recurrent theme is the ritual denigration of the community or assumed social circumstances of opposing fans ('You live in a caravan'; 'I can't read, I can't write, I can drive a tractor'). The rhetoric of football hooligans also incorporates, in a humorous and highly ironic way, certain media classifications ('we are the famous football hooligans', 'we are sweet'). These classifications serve as a prime means of communication within the football ground (Marsh, 1975: 7).

The fun of violence

In examining football hooliganism as social identity and meaningful action, I have already touched upon the role of violence in identity formation and the moral and aesthetic values of hooligan violence. Questions remain, however, as to what the specific goals of football hooliganism are and for whom this cultural practice is particularly attractive and rewarding. I will address these questions in the remainder of this chapter.

A central aspect of football hooliganism is the intense excitement associated with violent confrontation. Accounts of hooligans reveal how they experience an overpowering 'buzz' or adrenalin rush when confronting their opponents (Giulianotti, 1999: 52-53). Social scientists describe this experience in different terms depending on their academic discipline, such as Pilz's (1996) and Finn's (1994) use of the concept of 'flow', as developed by Csikszentmihalyi (1975), and Kerr's (1994; 2005) 'paratelic-negativistic metamotivational state'. The intense excitement hooligan violence arouses in its participants is inextricably related to the other side of the same coin: fear. The 'buzz' of football hooliganism is not only intimately connected to anticipation, but also to (overcoming) fear. Courage is not the absence of fear, but rather the sufficient discipline to perform when one is afraid (Collins, 1995: 189-190). The issue of fear is commonly addressed in the narratives of hooligans. As one Chelsea hooligan confesses, 'fear is a drug' and 'there is a very thin line between being hero and coward' (Foer, 2004: 102).

The pleasurable emotional arousal associated with violent confrontation is closely related to hooligans' anticipation and discussions of 'mayhem' and 'chaos'. They evaluate previous clashes and fantasize about upcoming events. Fighting is commonly described in erotic terms and compared to sex: 'It's better than sex. It lasts longer as well' (Foer, 2004: 102). In reality, it is the anticipation that precedes fighting that lasts for a relatively long period; the fights themselves are comparatively uncommon and brief. The majority of threats is never carried out and most pre-arranged fights never come into being, for instance because one group (or

44

both) fails to 'turn out' or because the police disrupt their plans. In other words, although it is the highpoint of the hooligan's existence, fighting itself constitutes a negligible length of time in the lives of these people (King, 2001: 570). Instead of focusing on how and why hooligans fight, one might therefore ask: if several young men so thoroughly enjoy fighting in the football context, why do hooligan encounters not occur more frequently? In contrast, *discussions* of fights are lengthy and ubiquitous.

In his analysis of collective memory and football hooliganism, Anthony King (2001: 570) correctly argues that 'it might be usefully asked how the violence in which these groups engage sustains group solidarity since the discussion of violence is the predominant social practice.' Using Weber's (1968) work on status groups and exclusive social intercourse, King provides a powerful analysis of the importance of collective memory to the maintenance and development of hooligan formations. Fights do not automatically promote group unity, since a fight is open to differing interpretations. Therefore:

> A common understanding of the meaning of a fight to the group has to be established as a collective memory for the hooligan firm to sustain itself. Without a common agreement on the meaning of a fight and its implications for the group as a whole, the group is simply a random sample of individuals who happened to have been in the same place at the same time [...]. Collective memory transforms the potentially random event like a fight into a powerful method of sustaining group solidarity because by agreeing upon a common version of events, individuals necessarily highlight communal interests and appropriate ways of acting in the future (2001: 572).

Collective memory is central to the apportioning of honour in hooligan confrontations. The collective memory of hooligan formations highlights the ways in which honour is won and 'individuals must protect this honour, even at the risk of personal injury, if they are to enjoy the benefits which come from membership of the group' (King, 2001: 574). As we have seen, there are broad definitions among hooligan groups on how honour can be won and lost. Importantly, honour and dishonour are not established by objective *a priori* rules but merely by intersubjective agreement, that is, 'by calls to order from the group' (Bourdieu, 1977: 15). The *post facto* meaning of a fight is highly negotiable and open to contestation. Even when a fight is won decisively, defeated groups appeal to various mitigating circumstances to redeem their honour (King, 2001: 573). 'In the course of this negotiation', King (2001: 580) argues, 'individuals of greater status are likely to have a greater influence over the decisions of this tribunal.' Nevertheless, apportioning honour between contestants is very rarely settled in full (Giulianotti and Armstrong, 2002: 218), as the following comment shows:

> If you talk to any member of the West Ham firm, they'll deny they were battered that day, or say that it wasn't their main mob, or that they were hit whilst they were waiting for the real faces to arrive and so on. But my pal Joe was travelling home by train later that evening and happened to share a carriage with some big West Ham faces. [...] Bags of finger-pointing, blaming and accusing each other of being too old (King and Knight, 1999: 110).

The excitement and anticipation associated with hooligan violence raises important questions regarding the specific ends of violent conduct. Most social scientific studies of violence focus on the causes or meanings of violence, that is, the question *why* violence occurs. According to Schinkel (2004: 16), the disproportionate focus on explanation ignores features of violence that only another kind of social science can uncover:

> The main problem with such differing perspectives as rational choice theory or theories of masculinity, for example, is that they reduce actions to means-end relations of some kind (either as rationally goals or as furthering an identity of masculinity). This is one way in which the researcher is totally blind for the action itself. The violence 'itself': that which remains when all causes are revealed, when external connections are uncovered, such as means-end relations, or meaning-facilitating constructions. What then remains is surely what one might consider as the most 'disturbing' of

46

all: a violence for the sake of itself, without morality, extrinsic meaning, but purely destructive. Evil, we might call it.

Schinkel argues that any instance of violence contains 'autotelic' aspects, a violence that is its own goal, in which means and end are melted together. Violent confrontation is thus not selected purely because it promotes a certain end, but also on the basis of an intrinsic attractiveness. This autotelic violence should be viewed as one aspect of (hooligan) violence and, arguably, a dominant one (2004: 20-21). The task for social science is thus to explain how and why some people seem to have a stronger will to violence than others.

Although accounts of hooligans highlighting the pleasurable emotional arousal derived from violence seem to confirm Schinkel's hypothesis, in specific social settings hooligan violence is perceived principally as a means to a clearly defined end. Certain hooligan and ultra groups view their violent behaviour as part of an existential political struggle which, in their own eyes, cannot be resolved by non-violent means. Left-wing groups such as Brigadas Amarillas at Cádiz CF, in Andalusia, claim to be involved in a *lucha* against fascism legitimating the use of violence against 'agents of fascism', that is, right-wing hooligan groups.[10] What remains to be explained is why some left-wing fan groups accept violence as a necessary strategy, while others pursuing the same cause do not. A similar dilemma can be observed in Australian 'soccer' hooliganism. The nature of fan and hooligan formations in Australian soccer should be understood within the context of the acculturation of immigrants through the involvement in sport, primarily associated with expressions of ethnic identity and nationalist allegiance (Hughson, 2002: 37). The authorities have labelled recent outbreaks of violence as 'ethnically based', yet at the same time senior police officers stressed that ethnic nationalism is merely used as a flag of convenience by young fans who wish to engage in collective violence. The latter view was shared by a journalist of *The Weekend Australian* (19 March 2005) in a background article on 'Rioting for kicks'.

These two examples raise crucial questions as to if, and to what extent, hooligan violence might be an end in itself, and why some people, and not others, do find violent conduct attractive and rewarding. Why do some fans resort to violence as part of 'ethnic' or 'political conflict', while the vast majority of supporters

47

equally identifying with ethnic or political nationalism do not? In other words, even when there is a perceived external goal, why do some people choose a violent means to realize this goal, while others do not (of course with the exception of autotelic violence, which is a goal in itself)? In addressing these questions, we must take into account aspects of male bonding and male adolescents' search for excitement and risk.

Football hooliganism, masculinities and adolescence

There is a fundamental tension between psychological and sociological explanations of the pleasurable emotional arousal derived from hooligan violence, although this tension is not always identified as such. Dunning (1999: 142), for example, claims that psychologist Kerr (1994) does 'little more than dress up in complex psychological jargon some relatively simple sociological ideas.' In my view, there are fundamental differences between the two approaches. Whereas Dunning analyzes football hooliganism within the specific class and community structures of British society, Kerr's (1994; 2005) reversal theory explanation conceptualizes the experience of arousal in violent behaviour as independent of social conditions. Thus, while Dunning argues that hooligan violence is appreciated principally in the lower strata of the working class, Kerr sees a paratelic-negativistic metamotivational combination as the source of hooligan fighting. Furthermore, Kerr's approach makes no reference to the key aspects of football hooliganism identified in this chapter, notably hooligans' construction of social identity, the specific norms of 'hard' masculinity, and the over-representation of young men in hooligan formations.

So which is the way forward? Each of these approaches has its particular strengths and weaknesses. Although the specific focus on 'ordered segmentation' in Dunning's approach seems to be of limited applicability in a comparative context, we must not undervalue the importance of the social mechanisms identified by Dunning, such as the established-outsider figurations in football and hooligan rivalries. Kerr's analytical description of thrill riots is of particular interest to the study of football hooliganism, but his approach insufficiently addresses the social processes and social conditions that structure the manifestation of football hooliganism. In other words, while we should not ignore psychological aspects of hooligan violence, we need to take into account the social mechanisms and social conditions that shape the hooligan experience. From this perspective, I will now address the question *for whom* participating in football hooliganism is particularly attractive and rewarding.

In his ethnographic account of Surma male stick-duelling, anthropologist Jon Abbink (1999: 227) reminds us that male ritual combat is a widespread cultural phenomenon which is often organized on the basis of territorial and/or age-group competition. Football hooliganism involves both types of competition. Hooligan encounters are essentially related to control over specific spaces and territories as well as 'male affairs' revolving around the construction of hard masculinity. The dominant English theories on football hooliganism converge in stressing that it is principally in working class areas that violent conduct by men is expected and endorsed. Aggressive masculinity is thus perceived as an epiphenomenon of social class. Dunning and his colleagues (1986; 1988), for example, have argued that the violent masculine style of football hooligans is generated by specific structural features of lower-working-class communities. Campbell and Dawson (2001: 69-70) have criticized this analysis for ignoring manifestations of macho masculinity in other forms and in other classes. Along similar lines, Giulianotti (1999: 156) has noted that contemporary masculine identities are complex and multi-faceted and cannot be pinned solely upon a singular class habitus. Football cultures, he argues, have always enabled the expression and appreciation of different forms of masculinity.

Scholars such as Van Stokkom (2000: 52-53) and Armstrong (1998: 302) contend that traditional masculine identity has devaluated in contemporary (Western) societies. The significance of work as an arena for male socialization into hard masculine identity has diminished as a result of the decline of many of the former 'macho' industries and occupations. Leisure – in particular football – replaces work as a site for the construction of hard masculinity. Football hooliganism is, in this view, not so much an issue of class but of disrupted masculinity (cf. Free and Hughson, 2003: 139). As Armstrong (1998: 156) argues:

> With the de-skilling of the workforce and the ending of exclusively male occupations the one surviving facet of masculine credibility that has come

down to the current group of young men is the ability to fight, and via that ability to hold a reputation. [...] [I]t is an asset that can attain male respect, and it is this that is available in [hooligan] gatherings and more than ever before unavailable in occupational cultures.

It is important, however, to emphasize that football cultures do not exist on their own as locations for the construction and contestation of hooligans' aggressive masculinity, but rather in complex interrelationships with other cultural sites, including the family, schools, labour markets, media representations and the legal system (see Mac an Ghaill, 1996: 394). Nor do hooligans develop just one form of masculinity: 'outside football, they adopt other masculine roles as partners, parents, children, workmates and social friends' (Giulianotti, 1999: 156). In this context, Free and Hughson (2003) have criticized what they call the 'new ethnographies' of football supporter subcultures for falsely dichotomizing the public and private domains. They argue that public and private domains and the gendered relations that characterize them are inextricable and should be studied as such. Elaborating on Armstrong's (1998) conclusion that hooligan activity rarely stretched beyond late twenties, they usefully ask: 'Should we not therefore see hooligan activity as part of a longer biography, its construction of "hard" masculinity a phase that a more "connected" form of masculinity thereafter complicates, if not fully replaces?' Masculinities can thus coexist, overlap and succeed one another within a single biography (Free and Hughson, 2003: 142).

The focus in this research on (national and local) variations in football hooliganism is reflected in 'doing' or 'performing' masculinities in hooligan formations. Connell (2000: 10) has noted that there is no singular pattern of masculinity to be found everywhere. Diversity is not just a matter of difference between cultures, periods in history or communities, but diversity also exists within a given setting. Masculinities are not homogeneous, simple states of being, but they are continually produced and reproduced. As we have seen, it is the interplay between a number of cultural sites that provides a filter through which masculinities are culturally produced and reproduced (Mac an Ghaill, 1996: 389). Hooligans' hard, hyperheterosexist masculine identity is 'constructed primarily in relation to difference, as something which is "not not-masculine" rather than as something

50

possessing an essence and substance of its own' (Frosh, 1994: 89; cf. Free and Hughson, 2003: 141). The 'other' (i.e. opposing hooligans) is systematically 'demasculinized' through ritual denigration of their physical and heterosexual prowess ('wankers', 'wimps', 'homosexuals'). Hegemonic masculinity is asserted through bodily performance, that is, physical violence:

> The bodily capacity to commit violence becomes, for many boys and young men, part of their sense of masculinity, and a willingness to put their bodies on the line in violence as a test of hegemonic masculinity (Connell, 2000: 218).

Research shows that the vast majority of football hooligans are boys and young men between 15 and 25 years old (Ferwerda and Gelissen, 2001; Adang, 2000; Armstrong, 1998). Football hooliganism is thus predominantly a male adolescent practice. This observation corresponds with studies of juvenile delinquency stressing the long-standing involvement of boys in riotous street cultures, subcultures and gangs, and violent crime (Carrabine et al., 2002: 38-39; G. Pearson, 1983; Giddens, 1997: 192-196). Male adolescents' involvement in various types of delinquency should be understood in terms of their specific life phase. In contemporary Western societies the stage of adolescence is almost a way of life between childhood and adulthood. Erikson (1968: 156) refers to this period as a psychosocial moratorium 'during which the young adult through free role experimentation may find a niche in some section of his society, a niche which is firmly defined and yet seems to be uniquely made for him.' While seeking some distance from parental controls, the social environment of youths expands and they increasingly gravitate towards friends for a sense of belonging and identity. Although not unique to the stage of adolescence, experimenting with certain forms of deviant or aggressive behaviour is characteristic of this life phase. Boys tend to seek prestige among peers by adopting a tough or masculine attitude. Participation in delinquency appears to be a normal part of (male) adolescents' lives and it is therefore unsurprising that most boys and young men commit some type of legal offence (Moffitt, 1993; Ferwerda et al., 1996; Junger-Tas, 1996; De Haan et al., 1999; Emler and Reicher, 1995).[11]

51

The plausible argument that participation in football hooliganism provides certain male adolescents with a sense of identity, belonging and status was elaborated by social psychologist Peter Marsh and his colleagues (Marsh et al., 1978; Marsh, 1978). Seeking recognition and excitement away from the routines of school and work, the football terraces enabled male adolescents to enter a process of 'character development' and 'graduation', an opportunity to achieve a sense of personal worth and identity through recognition from peers. Marsh concluded that social action on the terraces was guided and constrained by tacit social rules. These 'rules of disorder' enabled the display of masculine behaviour but, through ritualizing aggression, enabled the 'game' to be played in relative safety. Hence, much of what was labelled 'violent mayhem' was, in fact, highly ritualized behaviour which was far less physically injurious than it might seem (Frosdick and Marsh, 2005: 93). More recently, Marsh was obliged to revise some of his original conclusions in the light of the more lethal hooligan violence in the 1980s. He argues that football hooliganism 'shifted, in part, from a ritual to a more dangerous pattern of behaviour principally because of the inappropriate measures which were introduced to combat the problem and because of the extensive media distortion of true events at football matches' (Frosdick and Marsh, 2005: 94).

Following Marsh's thesis and studies of juvenile delinquency, football hooliganism can be viewed as principally adolescent-limited behaviour. Involvement in football violence is mostly temporary and diminishes as the young male enters adulthood, and can thus be seen as a rite of passage (Van Gennep, 1960) or, in similar terms, as *crime de passage* (Janssen, 1989). It would be erroneous, however, to view football hooliganism as exclusively adolescent-limited behaviour. In this context, we may draw upon Moffitt's (1993) distinction between adolescence-limited and life-course-persistent 'antisocial' behaviour.[12] Moffitt argues that the behaviour of adolescence-limited delinquents is mainly social mimicry of the 'antisocial style' of life-course-persistent delinquents. Life-course persistents serve as core members of revolving networks, by virtue of being role models for new recruits. Reflecting this analysis is perhaps the finding of some recent studies of football hooliganism that there are a growing number of older men involved in hooligan formations, often as 'semi-retired' hooligans but nevertheless with a great deal of status among peers (Van der Torre and Spaaij, 2003; cf. Giulianotti, 1999a;

Adang, 1997). Regretfully, research into football hooliganism provides little systematic analysis of individual or collective biographies of older hooligans. It seems that, besides seeking the rush of football violence, some older men may have economic interests in continuing their involvement in hooligan groups (e.g. drug trade, merchandising). I will discuss this issue in more detail in the final chapters of this book.

Conclusion

In this chapter I have sought to demonstrate the tendency of scholars of football hooliganism to avoid cross-cultural comparisons except in the most general of terms. The applicability of the dominant sociological approaches to football hooliganism in non-English contexts seems to be relatively limited. Recent attempts to rectify this imbalance have resulted in a growing awareness of cross-cultural variations in football hooliganism, but they have not generated a coherent analytical framework for the comparative study of football hooliganism. Furthermore, comparative research into football hooliganism tends to undervalue the importance of local characteristics and interactions in the development of football hooliganism, and variations therein across localities. In the following chapter I will outline four theoretical themes that emerge from the literature discussed in this chapter. These themes are seen as central to generating a deeper understanding of football hooliganism as a transnational phenomenon. I will also discuss the comparative case study and research methodology.

2

Research Outline and Methodology

Introduction

In the previous chapter I have discussed the main theoretical and methodological approaches to the study of football hooliganism. I have argued that there is a need for systematic, in-depth comparative research into football hooliganism which takes into consideration not only cross-national overlaps and differences but also variations at a local and an intra-city level. In this chapter I seek to develop this idea into a coherent research design. I will first outline four theoretical themes that emerge from the literature discussed in the previous chapter. These themes are seen as central to generating a deeper understanding of football hooliganism as a transnational phenomenon. I will then give an outline of the comparative case study. In the final part of the chapter the methodology of the research is presented.

Four theoretical themes

In the Introduction the following research question was formulated: how can we explain the extent and nature of football hooliganism at different football clubs and in different countries, and variations therein over time? The theoretical issues discussed in the previous chapter reveal four major themes that need to be addressed in order to answer this question. The first theme is *the role of societal fault lines in fuelling and contouring football hooliganism*. This theme is crucial to understanding cross-national commonalities and differences in football hooliganism and raises a number of important questions. What are the major fault lines of particular societies? What are the similarities and differences between the fault lines of individual societies? How do these fault lines shape the manifestation of football hooliganism? This first theme explores the concept of fault lines as proposed by Dunning (1999; 2000) in a comparative context. Applying this concept to the national contexts in which the six football clubs under study are embedded, we find significant variation

54

in the fault lines of these three countries (England, the Netherlands and Spain). The two fault lines in contemporary English society are social class and regional inequalities. The major cleavage in English society is class, based on accumulated social differences in, among others, type of occupation (factory-based manual work versus others), education, place and type of housing, income and the life experiences which stem from these (Budge, 1996: 19; cf. Gallagher et al., 1995: 216). This class cleavage overlaps with a territorial, centre-periphery cleavage, notably the socio-economic and cultural differences between the South-East of England and other parts of the country (e.g. the North) (Budge, 1996: 21). The class cleavage in English society is also evident in the country's traditional working-class football culture (Mason, 1980; Walvin, 1986), although in recent years the game has gradually attracted more fans from higher up the social scale (King, 2002; Giulianotti, 1999).

It has been suggested that 'Britain has perhaps the simplest cleavage structure in Western Europe' (Gallagher et al., 1995: 216). Indeed, with regard to football, Bale (1993: 60) has argued that elsewhere in Europe the sport is in many cases more socially heterogeneous than in Britain. In contemporary Dutch society no single dominant cleavage seems to exist. Class and religious cleavages were historically dominant, but 'secularization and a blurring of class boundaries have gradually eroded the strongly "pillarized" subcultures on which the traditional cleavage structure in the Netherlands rested' (Gallagher et al., 1995: 216; cf. Keman, 1996: 218-220). Although there are few if any remaining centre-periphery tensions in the Netherlands – perhaps socio-cultural differences between the West (the *Randstad*) and other parts of the country – local and regional identities prove remarkable strong.

The major fault lines in Spanish society are the centre-periphery cleavage and the class cleavage. The centre-periphery cleavage is crucial to understanding Spanish politics and culture. In fact, no other Western European country contains such a wide range of regionalist and (sub-) nationalist political and social movements as Spain (Gallagher et al., 1995: 216; cf. Giner, 2000: 162). The 1978 constitution saw the creation of a 'state of autonomies' with seventeen Autonomous Communities which have varying degrees of autonomy in legislation and administration. Four of these *Comunidades Autónomas* secured greater powers and

55

substantial autonomy from the very beginning – Catalonia, the Basque Country, Galicia and Andalusia – although others have obtained powers over similar areas, including education and health care (see Colomer, 1996: 200). The creation of these Autonomous Communities was followed by a rise in the expression of regional and national identity, which is reflected in every aspect of culture, including football (Duke and Crolley, 1996: 40). Spanish football has become inseparable from the expression of regional and (sub-)nationalist identities and cuts through all social classes (Ball, 2001: 16; Duke and Crolley, 1996: 5; Fernández Santander, 1990; Shaw, 1987; Colomé, 1999; Unzueta, 1999; Walton, 2001; Viñas, 2005). According to Crain (1997: 296), the cultural politics of 'the New Spain' has resulted in a blurring of class boundaries. She argues that the period of democratic transition:

> has been characterized by movements of regional autonomy in which regional elites and the middle and working classes have fashioned a self-conscious politics vis-à-vis the central state. Aiming to "decenter" the hegemony of diffusive national culture, these groups underscore internal differences and the plurinational composition of contemporary Spain.

The concept of fault lines constitutes an important new departure in the comparative study of football hooliganism since it enhances our understanding of cross-national variations in football hooliganism as well as of specific ingroup and outgroup figurations in football and hooligan rivalries. I would argue, however, that the concept does not provide a sufficient framework for the explanation of football hooliganism as a transnational phenomenon. The concept of fault lines operates on a high level of generality and therefore seems to undervalue more specific aspects which co-shape the nature and development of football hooliganism, as I have shown in Chapter One. We need to examine how general societal cleavages are reflected in specific fan and hooligan identities. Furthermore, the concept of fault lines attempts to explain variations in the *nature* of football hooliganism rather that variations in the *extent* of the phenomenon. It cannot adequately explain why some clubs and countries have more persistent hooligan traditions than others or why some young men, rather than others, find football hooliganism an attractive and rewarding activity. Importantly, although the fault lines of particular societies fuel and contour fan and hooligan identities, only a small minority of supporters engage in football hooliganism. Additional themes should therefore be addressed to generate a more profound understanding of the phenomenon.

The second theoretical theme is *the construction of hooligan identities and the attractions of the hooligan subculture*, which groups together a number of important questions. Who are most likely to become involved in football hooliganism? What are their motivations? How do they distinguish themselves socio-culturally? How are hooligan identities constructed and how do they develop over time? How did hooligan subcultures emerge in different national and local settings? Why do these subcultures persist? Most of these issues have examined to some extent in previous research, as discussed in the previous chapter, but they have not been systematically studied in a comparative context.

The third major theme addressed in this book is *the social organization of football hooliganism*. This theme features centrally in the academic and public debate on football hooliganism as well as in the definition proposed in Chapter One. Recent attempts by public prosecutors to convict hooligans as members of a criminal organization contrast starkly with academic studies portraying hooligan formations as loose associations with fluid instead of fixed boundaries and shapes (e.g. Giulianotti and Armstrong, 2002). The issue of social organization needs to be examined in a detailed and comparative manner in order to reveal cross-national and cross-local resemblances and variations. What are the degree and forms of social organization involved in football hooliganism? Does the social organization of football hooliganism vary across localities and over time? How can we explain similarities and differences in the degree and forms of social organization?

The fourth theoretical theme focuses on *the interactions and negotiations between hooligans and significant others and the effects of policies targeting football hooliganism*. In Chapter One I have shown how hooligans construct their collective identity in relation to the other (i.e. opposing hooligan groups, non-hooligan supporters). Interactions and negotiations between hooligans and significant others are also crucial to the development of football hooliganism over time, for example interactions with police or clubs. The development of football hooliganism is characterized by the evolving interplay between hooligan groups and efforts by the authorities to prevent or punish acts of hooliganism. The fourth theme raises a number of crucial questions: How do the interactions between hooligans and significant others influence the manifestation of football hooliganism? Do these interactions vary across localities and over time? What have been the intended and unintended effects of policies targeting football hooliganism? How have formal and informal policies shaped the development of hooligan subcultures?

The four theoretical themes are examined empirically in different national and local contexts. In Chapters Four to Nine I describe the extent and nature of football hooliganism at six individual football clubs. Each chapter has a similar structure. It first examines the 'club culture' in which fan and hooligan identities are nested, and which shapes fans' and hooligans' construction of self and the other. These issues correspond with two theoretical themes: the role of societal fault lines and the construction of hooligan identities. Each chapter then discusses the emergence and development of football hooliganism and anti-hooligan policies. Finally, each chapter analyzes the contemporary manifestation of football hooliganism, including the interactions and negotiations between hooligans and significant others and the social organization of football hooliganism.

In the remainder of this chapter I will discuss the ways in which the four theoretical themes are scrutinized empirically. I will successively outline the comparative case study and the research methodology.

Landscapes of fear: the good, the bad and the ugly in football stigmas

In this study I seek to show that not only overlaps, but also significant variations in football hooliganism can be found between geographically proximate cases. These variations cannot be fully explained in terms of differences in the development and popularity of the game or general societal fault lines, but require additional explanations as to how different trajectories in the manifestation of football hooliganism take shape. This study reflects a 'most similar systems design' in that it compares cases that are much alike in many respects, but differ with regard to the extent and nature of football hooliganism. I chose to focus on local manifestations of football hooliganism within three democratic societies in Western Europe – England, the Netherlands and Spain – because, despite significant variations, variables such as socio-economic structures and cultural traditions are comparatively similar in these countries (cf. Colomer, 1996: 5). In these countries football has also historically been the most popular spectator sport and the game has developed in broadly similar ways (cf. Giulianotti, 1999; Lanfranchi, 1997; Miermans, 1955).

I acknowledge that in countries such as Germany, Belgium and France equally interesting intra-city comparisons can be conducted, perhaps even more so since much of the academic research into football hooliganism has focused on the English situation. It must be emphasized, however, that very few studies have compared the manifestation of football hooliganism in two-club or multi-club cities, either in England or on the Continent. I would argue that English and European research has largely neglected intra-city variations in the extent and nature of football hooliganism. The importance of local and intra-city comparison is underlined by Giulianotti and Armstrong (2002: 228). They correctly argue that:

> In most instances of popular football fandom, greatest club-centred rivalries focus upon antagonisms with neighbouring clubs, particularly other city clubs. Intra-city rivalries give rise not only to the interminable rituals of argument and insult, in locations of work especially. They also germinate an ensemble of contrapuntal identities around each football institution so that the rival clubs symbolize opposing values and interpretations within the civic setting [...].

Focusing on the contrapuntal identities of intra-city rivals, I will now examine which clubs are suitable for intra-city comparison of football hooliganism in England, the Netherlands and Spain.

In *Sport, Space and the City* (1993), geographer John Bale deftly articulates the 'psychic cost' that football can generate. For many people, fans and non-fans, football can constitute a nuisance and sometimes generate real fear. Certain grounds present a strongly negative image and persistent stigma (Canter et al., 1989; Williams et al., 1989a). A survey by the Liverpool City council showed that 43 per cent of interviewed fans would not go to some grounds because they perceived a serious hooligan problem to exist (quoted in Bale, 1993: 95). Such stigmas, Bale argues, are often not based on fans' personal experiences but rather an aggregated public perception. Importantly, those who do not attend football matches tend to

59

have violence as a central theme in their accounts of the football ambience to a greater extent than those who are regular attenders. Non-attenders 'would have obtained their (amplified) images of the sport through secondary sources, obtaining a more violent image of the game than those who regularly attend' (Bale, 1993: 100).

The narratives of long-standing supporters also tend to pinpoint certain regions, cities and football grounds as 'hostile', 'nasty' or 'violent'. This type of labelling is essentially other-directed: none of the hundreds of supporters interviewed for this book qualified their own clubs as extremely hostile or violent, but rather as 'friendly', 'warm' and 'family oriented'. Stigmas affecting their own clubs were usually explained away as constructs of ignorant outsiders and the media. The tendency for most supporters to describe their team in a positive way was also found in recent fan surveys: three out of four fans consistently describe their club as 'friendly' (Sir Norman Chester Centre, 2002a: 30; 2002: 33). The social construction of landscapes of fear in football reduces the complex reality of football culture to a dichotomous logic of 'friendly' and 'nasty' clubs. In the three Western European countries under study, a number of spatially proximate football clubs tend to have diametrically opposed popular images. For present purposes, I will principally focus on the contrapuntal popular images of professional football clubs located in one city.

In England, a number of clubs are burdened by the violent reputation of a small minority of their fans. Among the main 'stadia of stigma' identified by Williams and his colleagues (1989) are clubs such as Liverpool, Chelsea, West Ham United, Everton, Leeds United and Millwall. These stigmas hardly correspond with recent official statistics on football-related arrests for 'violent disorder', which tend to be concentrated disproportionately in the lower leagues (see Table 2.2).[1]

Table 2.1 English football clubs with highest number of arrests for violent disorder in the 2003/04 season*

Club	Number of arrests for violent disorder
West Ham United	107
Portsmouth	70
Hull City	64
Plymouth Argyle	39
Tranmere Rovers	35

Source: Home Office, 2004.

Note: *Clubs with 35 or more of their fans arrested for violent disorder throughout the season.

At the other end of the continuum there are a number of football clubs with very 'friendly' public images. People often refer to these football grounds as places they are 'happy to take the kids to' (personal interview with Arsenal fan, September 2004) and where 'visiting hooligans do not even turn up because they know there will be no one to fight' (personal interview with British Transport Police officer, November 2003). These positive popular images are in part reflected in the comparatively low number of arrests at these clubs, as listed in Table 2.3.[2]

Table 2.2   English football clubs with smallest number of arrests in the 2003/04 season*

Club	Number of arrests for violent disorder	Total number of arrests
Crewe Alexandra	0	5
Charlton Athletic	0	7
Fulham	0	8
Watford	0	8
Gillingham	0	10

Source: Home Office, 2004.

Note: *Clubs with 10 or less of their fans arrested throughout the season.

Of particular interest in the context of this book are apparent variations in popular images and arrest figures at different football clubs in London. Personal contemplations of supporters living outside the English capital highlight the perceived differences between geographically proximate football clubs. As one Nottingham Forest fan asks:

How can four clubs, all located within five miles of each other geographically, be so socially distant from each other? Unassuming Charlton, Wombling Wimbledon, Suburban Crystal Palace and then savage, nasty, malicious Millwall. I'd read and seen all about the problems Millwall have with their fans but nah, I thought, hooliganism's on the wane isn't it? Perhaps it is, generally, but it's alive and well and truly kicking in Deptford and Peckham. (quoted in: Robson, 2000: 22)

The behaviour of Millwall and West Ham United fans is commonly perceived as being qualitatively different from spectator behaviour at clubs such as Fulham, Charlton Athletic and Crystal Palace. Though all may constitute interesting case studies, I chose compare West Ham United of East London, the club with the highest number of arrests for violent disorder in the 2003/04 season, with West London Fulham FC, with one of the lowest arrest records in the same season. Despite being located in one city, the two fan communities have very distinctive popular images; to put it bluntly, the former as 'violent' and the latter as 'friendly'. As I have said before, these stigmas do not adequately reflect the reality of football fandom at these clubs since they are (contestable) labels constructed by 'outsiders'.

My choice to include West Ham United and Fulham FC was in part based on pre-existing contacts with supporters of both clubs, which made my access to the two fan communities considerably easier. At a later stage of the research project I became aware of the 'added value' of Charlton Athletic, a football club located in the same area as West Ham United, but with a distinctive popular image and with very different hooligan traditions. This point was also suggested to me by John Williams, director of the Sir Norman Chester Centre for Football Research at the University of Leicester. Regretfully, at that stage no funds were available for additional long-term fieldwork in England.

In the Netherlands, four clubs have been particularly burdened by their supporters' reputation for violent behaviour: Feyenoord, Ajax, FC Utrecht and ADO Den Haag. These reputations correspond to a large extent with recent official statistics on football-related arrests shown in Table 2.4.[3]

Table 2.3 Dutch football clubs with highest number of arrests in the 2002/03 season*

Club	Number of arrests
Feyenoord	246
FC Utrecht	159
PSV	157
Ajax	147
ADO Den Haag	120

Source: CIV, 2003.

Note: *Football clubs with 120 or more of their fans arrested throughout the season.

In contrast with the persistent negative stigma suffered by some Dutch football clubs, other clubs are commonly praised for their 'friendly' atmosphere. This positive image is used by some football clubs as a powerful symbol of collective identity, portraying themselves as 'a community club for the Frisian country' (SC Heerenveen) or 'a gentlemen's club' (Sparta Rotterdam) in opposition to the perceived 'hard' nature of some urban working-class football clubs (e.g. Joustra and Kuiper, 2001; Sonneveld, 1986; Bol and Van Netburg, 1997). These images are reflected only in part by official arrest statistics, as listed in Table 2.5.

Table 2.4 Dutch football clubs with smallest number of arrests in the 2002/03 season*

Club	Number of arrests
Emmen	0
FC Volendam	0
Veendam	1
Sparta Rotterdam	3
RBC Roosendaal	4

Source: CIV, 2003.

Note: *Football clubs with 4 or less of their fans arrested throughout the season.[4]

Only two Dutch cities host two or more professional football clubs, Rotterdam (Feyenoord, Sparta and Excelsior) and Eindhoven (PSV and FC Eindhoven). Neither of the two Eindhoven clubs are burdened by persistent negative stigma, although PSV supporters have occasionally grabbed media headlines for incidents of violence, racism and nuisance. In Rotterdam, a stark contrast can be observed between the city's two largest clubs, Feyenoord and Sparta. Whereas Feyenoord hooligans are widely perceived as 'one of Europe's most violent football followings'

(Metropolitan Police officer, September 2003), Sparta's dominant public image is one of 'a club without hooligans' (ADO Den Haag supporter, August 2004). It seems logical, therefore, to include Feyenoord and Sparta as the Dutch case studies.

At first sight, the landscapes of fear in Spanish football are more difficult to identify since it is often viewed that spectator violence at football matches in Spain is comparatively rare. A Council of Europe report (1998: 39) concluded that 'Spanish football culture no longer contains large-scale hooliganism [as opposed to the early 1990s]. [...] Outbreaks of spectator violence are now rare.' The 'family-oriented' image of the Spanish game seems to correspond with official arrest statistics. In the 2002/03 season a total of 74 fans were arrested and a further 565 people were ejected from football grounds in Spain (Comisión Nacional Contra la Violencia en Espectáculos Deportivos, 2003). These figures are significantly lower, in absolute as well as in relative terms, than the number of arrests at English (3,982) and Dutch (1,647) football grounds during the same period, although they may be more an indication of differences in policing strategies and less of differences in the 'real' extent of spectator violence in the three countries. Unfortunately, Spanish arrest figures do not compare the number of arrests per club.

There are nevertheless some persistent negative stigma in Spanish football, which are closely related to political antagonisms. Clubs such as Real Madrid, Atlético Madrid, RCD Espanyol and Valencia CF are regularly associated with hooliganism and right-wing extremism, due to the occasional racist and violent behaviour of a small section of their fans (Spaaij and Viñas, 2005; Viñas, 2005).[5] The cities of Madrid, Barcelona, Seville and Valencia all constitute interesting cases in this sense, hosting two or more professional football clubs with contrasting popular images. The most striking example of contrapuntal fan identities within one city is, arguably, the case of FC Barcelona and Espanyol. FC Barcelona is popularly perceived within Barcelona and Catalonia (and, in fact, worldwide) as a community club with rich cultural heritage and symbolic meanings. Espanyol, on the other hand, is persistently burdened by its deep-seated negative popular image within Catalonia as a 'violent', 'fascist' club (Colomé, 1999; Duke and Crolley, 1996). I therefore chose to include these two clubs in the research.

The six cases included in the research can be differentiated along two dimensions, as shown in Table 2.6. The first dimension is geographical, that is, the city and country in which they are located (London/England, Rotterdam/the Netherlands and Barcelona/Spain). The second dimension involves the dominant popular image of the six football clubs, distinguishing clubs with a 'violent/hostile' image from those with a 'non-violent/friendly' image. The three 'non-violent/friendly' cases can be viewed as 'deviant cases' (Lijphart, 1971) that offer the potential for establishing new propositions and for expanding the nature and scope of existing theory on football hooliganism. Let me reiterate that the identified popular images may be nothing more than distorted stereotypes concealing the reality of spectator behaviour and fan identity at these clubs. Media images seem to play a central role in sustaining or altering the public images of particular fan cultures, 'providing more stable forms of meaning and interpretation in a globalising culture in which "seeing is believing", especially when those images are repeated time and time again' (Urry, 2000: 180). Public representations of the landscapes of fear in football do not exist separate from fans' self-definitions, but are inextricably intertwined. Many supporters are, in Giulianotti's (1999: 148) words, 'cognizant of the constructed nature of fan reputations, and the vagaries of the media in exaggerating or inventing such identities.' In the following chapters the extent and nature of football hooliganism in the three countries (Chapter Three) and at the six football clubs (Chapters Four to Nine) are examined in detail.

Table 2.5   Case study sample

City (Country)	Type of popular image	
	Violent/hostile	*Non-violent/friendly*
London (England)	West Ham United FC	Fulham FC
Rotterdam (Netherlands)	Feyenoord	Sparta Rotterdam
Barcelona (Spain)	RCD Espanyol	FC Barcelona

A methodological note

The method adopted in this research is the comparative case study.[6] The case study method enables close empirical scrutiny of football hooliganism in its real-life context. It allows detailed description and analysis of the emergence, development, nature and sources of the phenomenon. Previous detailed empirical research into football culture and football hooliganism demonstrates the strengths of the case study method (e.g. Marsh et al., 1978; Armstrong and Harris, 1991; Armstrong, 1998; Robson, 2000). A problem with these investigations is that their emphasis on empirical data in a specific geographical area may make the findings difficult to generalize to another time or place (Bailey, 1994: 58), although, as Flyvbjerg (2001) rightly argues, this is not necessarily the case.[7] I attempt to reduce the problem of (cross-national) generalizability by using multiple cases instead of focusing on a single case study. Although the manifestation of football hooliganism is examined separately within individual cases, these cases are also systematically compared. A major advantage of such comparison is its potential contribution to theory development. The principal purpose is not description, as with 'configurative-idiographic' case studies (Eckstein, 1975), but rather the comparative case study is 'heuristic' in that it is used to develop theory from particular instances. I would argue that the case study method used in this research is, in fact, a combination of the 'heuristic' and the 'disciplined-configurative' case study. Although it seeks to develop theory, the focus is also on understanding and interpreting the cases.

The research method used in this study is qualitative fieldwork. In order to establish a detailed picture of football hooliganism at the six football clubs, I have generated detailed, in-depth information on the basis of long-term qualitative research amongst football hooligans, fans, club officials, police officers and other actors. I have used similar data sources at each football club to establish a systematic and coherent comparative methodology. The eight main types of data were: interviews, participant observation, fanzines, official documents and databases, literature, newspaper reports, Internet websites and (official and private) video footage.

The semi-structured interview was a major method of data collection throughout the research. Interviews were conducted with a wide range of actors at each of the six clubs: hooligans, ultras, supporters, club officials, police officers, fanzine editors, club historians, journalists, and so on. Potential interviewees were selected through snowball sampling. Initial contacts within fan communities and institutions of football clubs were kind enough to help me expand my network of interviewees. Clubs were initially contacted through board members, general managers or safety officers. I subsequently approached other club representatives, such as security staff, board members, (former) players and managers. I also benefited greatly from pre-established contacts with national and regional police forces. These contacts had been established during research carried out between 2000 and 2003 (Spaaij, 2001; 2002; Van der Torre and Spaaij, 2003). In addition, I used contacts within the European police intelligence exchange network co-ordinated by the Centraal Informatiepunt Voetbalvandalisme (Dutch National Football Intelligence Unit; CIV).

My contacts within the local fan communities were established in broadly similar ways. Initial fan contacts were the basis for further contacts with supporters, supporters' organizations, fanzine editors, ultras and hooligans. Once introduced to some of 'main faces' within the local hooligan and ultra cores I was able to expand my network of interviewees. Interviews were usually conducted outside match days in pubs, at people's homes or, occasionally, at my own place. It must be stressed, however, that I only interviewed a small section of these formations (see Table 2.7). At Fulham FC it was considerably more difficult to recruit self-declared (former) hooligans for an interview due to the present-day absence of an identifiable hooligan group. In fact, of the four 'hooligan interviewees' at Fulham, only one claimed to engage in hooligan encounters at present, while the other three viewed themselves as 'retired' (all three of them were widely viewed as 'main faces' in football hooliganism at Fulham in the 1970s). Moreover, this one self-declared hooligan did not, according to his accounts and my own observations, claim any 'hooligan membership' at Fulham matches, but instead at his first team West Ham United. Since he was banned from that club, he attended Fulham's home matches along with friends who supported Fulham. He argued that when it comes to football hooliganism, 'Fulham ain't such a club'. I nevertheless decided to include him in the Fulham sample since he was particularly knowledgeable about the historical development of football hooliganism at Fulham.

The research was in all cases openly presented as 'for a book'. Scholars such as Corrigan (1979), Armstrong (1998) and Giulianotti (1993; 1994) successfully adopted this strategy in initiating their respective fieldwork. This research stance had a twofold effect. On the one hand, at each of the six clubs a number of fans and hooligans were particularly interested in my work. In the case of Sparta Rotterdam, for example, I was the first researcher to pay attention to their activities. Members of the hooligan group were highly co-operative and provided me with video footage, photos and newspaper cuttings. They also invited me to travel with the group on various occasions and allowed me to tape record group and individual interviews. On the other hand, some hooligans and ultras were most certainly alarmed by my 'for a book' approach. They suspected – unfoundedly – my allegiances to the police or club. In fact, on a number of occasions even my proposal to conduct an informal, non-recorded interview was turned down with great suspicion. This suspicion was partly fuelled by my lack of productivity: the compilation of the book took me nearly four years, which cast aspersions on my dedication or credentials (Giulianotti, 1995a: 7). Fortunately, several of my contacts within Dutch hooligan groups were already familiar with a previous book (Van der Torre and Spaaij, 2003), which they were eager to tell their friends and which seems to have increased my credibility.

Table 2.6   Interview categories

	West Ham	Fulham	Feyenoord	Sparta	Espanyol	Barcelona
Fans	16	31	18	15	15	15
(male)	(14)	(25)	(17)	(12)	(12)	(11)
(female)	(2)	(6)	(1)	(3)	(3)	(4)
(Former) hooligans/ultras*	15	4	13	16	26	22
(male)	(15)	(4)	(13)	(16)	(22)	(20)
(female)	(0)	(0)	(0)	(0)	(4)	(2)
(Former) board members, club managers and players	2	2	2	3	5	2
Ground safety and security, community schemes	7	6	6	9	4	6
Club historians and local writers	4	2	2	3	2	2
Official supporters' clubs	1	1	2	3	4	3
Independent supporters' initiatives	2	4	2	-	-	-
Fanzine editors and contributors	4	3	3	6	3	4
Local journalists	1	1	1	1	2	4
Politicians and government officials	3	3	5	3	5	5
Police officers**	13	10	17	6	5	5
Total	68	67	71	65	71	68

Note:

* Self-declared members, mostly key figures within the fan group. It is important to note that not every Spanish ultra identifies with the use of violence in inter-group rivalries. Furthermore, in the case of FC Barcelona, militant fans do not label themselves as 'ultras' but rather as 'radical supporters' or 'hooligans'. This deviant self-categorization should be understood in the context of the negative connotations of the term 'ultra' within Catalonia and, to a lesser extent, in Spanish society at large (see Chapter Three; see also Spaaij and Viñas, 2005; 2006).

** Including intelligence officers, spotters, match commanders and regular officers policing football matches.

Participant observation

A major part of the fieldwork consisted of participant observation at football grounds and related spaces, including public houses, nightclubs and railway stations. Participant observation did not concentrate exclusively on football fan behaviour, but also on clubs' security policies, police strategies and interactions between supporters and law enforcers. In the early stages of fieldwork at a new site observations were mostly made from a distance (in a specific section of the ground, in the streets, in a pub) without actually positioning myself among hooligans and ultras, even though from the start I socialized regularly with non-hooligan supporters and a number of hooligans and ultras. It was only after establishing direct rapport with my subjects that observations became more genuinely participant. In other words, the degree of participation shifed during the research from 'passive' to 'moderate' observation (Spradley, 1980: 59-60).[8] Observations were not merely a means for collecting specific data, but equally for obtaining a 'feeling', albeit a rather restrained one, for what it is like to be in a particular social situation. On the basis of such experience the researcher is more able adequately to make sense of what hooligans and non-hooligan supporters have to say and the ways in which they describe their social world (Marsh et al., 1978: 119).

Fanzines

Football fan writing, especially so-called 'fanzines', provide an insider's view to football culture. They represent an alternative network of ideas and lifestyles compared with the usual portrayal of fans in the popular press (Haynes, 1993: 21). The importance of football fanzines as both a subject and data source for academic research into football culture is often underestimated, but, more recently, it has received increasing academic attention (for example King, 2002; Giulianotti, 1997; Jary et al., 1991). Football fanzine writing can also be useful for research into football hooliganism because it offers a supporter's view to issues such as spectator violence, club policies and policing. Football hooliganism is a recurrent theme in several of the fanzines listed in Table 2.8. Some fanzines are written in part by and for hooligans and therefore contain much information on the matter, for example

Bulldog (FC Barcelona), *Ultras Español* (RCD Espanyol), *Lunatic News* (Feyenoord) and, to a lesser extent, the national Spanish fanzine *Super Hincha*. I have also analyzed a number of official club magazines that regularly discuss issues such as hooliganism and security policies.

Table 2.8	Types of fan writing analyzed as part of the study	
	Fanzines (F) / official (club) magazines (O)	National fanzines
West Ham	Over Land and Sea (OLAS) (F) On The Terraces (OTT) (F)	When Saturday Comes
Fulham	There's Only One F in Fulham (TOOFIF) (F)	When Saturday Comes
Feyenoord	Lunatic News (F) King of the Gasstation (F)*	Ultras Magazine
Sparta	In The Winning Mood (ITWM) (F) Kasteelnieuws (O) Het Sparta Supportersnieuws (O) Pro Sparta (O)	Ultras Magazine
Espanyol	Ultras Español (F) Gol Sur Ultrazine (F)* Fanatics (F) North Supporter (F)	Super Hincha El Jugador No. 12* Super Ultra* Revista Hinchas*
Barcelona	Bulldog (F)* Gent Culé (F)* Quicir (F)* Sang Culé (F)* Almogàvers (F)*	Super Hincha Hinchas y Supporters* Torcida Antifeixista* El Jugador No. 12* Super Ultra* Revista Hinchas*

Note: *Fanzine is no longer published.

Official documents and databases

Increased focus on intelligence-led policing has resulted in a more systematic recording of incidents of spectator violence at football matches (Spaaij, 2005; 2005a). This development has been particularly significant in countries such as England and the Netherlands, where annual disorder logs and evaluation reports list the main trends and incidents in a particular season. These official documents are an important data source because they provide insight, albeit biased, into the prevalence and nature of incidents of spectator violence and football hooliganism. I had access to reports from a range of institutions in each country, including, to varying degrees,

71

police units, football associations, football clubs, and national, regional and local governments. My fieldwork in the Netherlands benefited greatly from access granted by the Justice Department into police and judicial databases, including those of the Centraal Informatiepunt Voetbalvandalisme and the Politie Rotterdam-Rijnmond (Rotterdam-Rijnmond Police).

Fieldwork in England was conducted in co-operation with the Public Order Intelligence Unit CO11 (New Scotland Yard, Metropolitan Police Service), the Football Disorder Unit (Home Office), the Football Intelligence Section (British Transport Police) and local police units. I also received assistance, though to a far lesser extent, from the National Criminal Intelligence Service (NCIS) and the Football Banning Orders Authority. In Spain I obtained policy documents and annual reports from the Comisión Nacional contra la Violencia en Espectáculos Deportivos (National Commission against Violence at Sporting Events), the Consejo Superior de Deportes (Higher Sports Council), the Generalitat de Catalunya (Catalan Government) and, to a lesser extent, the Cuerpo Nacional de la Policía (National Police Force) and Mossos d'Esquadra (Catalan Police Force).

Literature

A useful source for the study of local fan and hooligan cultures was the available body of club-based literature, such as official and unofficial club histories and fan ethnographies. The titles of these publications can be found in the Bibliography. Some club historians were interviewed personally by the author in order to retrieve more specific pieces of information concerning the historical development of fan cultures and spectator violence. At two clubs I came across writings specifically dealing with the subject of football hooliganism. Pennant and Smith have published, individually and jointly, first-hand accounts of the emergence and development of football hooliganism at West Ham United (Pennant, 2000; 2002; Pennant and Smith, 2002; Smith, 2004). I also made use of journalistic accounts of football hooliganism at Feyenoord (Van Gageldonk, 1996; 1999). Certain academic studies were of particular relevance to my research, notably the work of Catalan historian Carles Viñas (2001; 2004; 2005) and Dutch sociologist Ralf Bormans (1996; 2002). These and other authors have also personally contributed to my research by allowing me to use their archives.

Newspaper and magazine reports

It is not within the scope of this research to give a complete historical overview of incidents of spectator violence and football hooliganism at the six football clubs under consideration. Analysis of newspaper and magazine reports can nevertheless provide important insight into public and media representations of fan cultures and football hooliganism. It should be noted that I have not analyzed the newspapers listed in Table 2.10 in their entirety, as some scholars have done (Maguire, 1986; Dunning et al., 1984; Lewis, 1996). Instead, I have examined only a selection of newspaper reports dealing with fan culture and football hooliganism at the six football clubs. These reports were obtained through several channels. Some hooligans and ultras were kind enough to let me use their personal scrapbooks containing hundreds of newspaper cuttings on the subject. Fellow researchers in the Netherlands and Spain allowed me to use their archives containing numerous folders of carefully systematized newspaper and magazine articles. Furthermore, club historians at the different clubs helped me locate relevant reports in club or personal archives. I also accessed a variety of national and local newspapers in printed form, on microfilm and online at libraries and city archives in London, Rotterdam and Barcelona.

Table 2.9   Newspaper sample (selections only)

	Local/regional newspapers	National newspapers
West Ham	Evening Standard Stratford and Newham Express* Newham Recorder East London Advertiser	The Times The Daily Telegraph The Sun The Daily Mail
Fulham	Evening Standard Fulham Chronicle* Hammersmith and Fulham Times	The Times The Daily Telegraph The Sun The Daily Mail
Feyenoord	Rotterdams Dagblad Rotterdams Nieuwsblad*	Algemeen Dagblad De Volkskrant NRC Handelsblad De Telegraaf

| *Table 2.9* | Newspaper sample (selections only) (continued) |

Sparta	Rotterdams Dagblad	Algemeen Dagblad
	Rotterdams Nieuwsblad*	De Volkskrant
		NRC Handelsblad
		De Telegraaf
Espanyol	El Periódico de Catalunya	El País
	La Vanguardia	El Mundo
	Avui	Diario As (Catalan Edition)
	Sport	Marca
	Mundo Deportivo	
Barcelona	El Periódico de Catalunya	El País
	La Vanguardia	El Mundo
	Avui	Diario As (Catalan Edition)
	Sport	Marca
	Mundo Deportivo	

Note: *Newspaper is no longer published.

Internet websites

Internet websites on the subject of football hooliganism provide an insider's view to the hooligan subculture. They contain press reports, real-time video clips and message boards where self-identifying hooligans exchange experiences and threats. I have studied websites associated with the specific hooligan formations under consideration as well as websites on hooligan and ultra subcultures in general (see Chapter Eleven). The data gathered from these websites have principally been used as background material in order to obtain a 'feeling' of the rhetoric, activities and motivations of self-identifying hooligans. It must be noted, however, that previous research has shown that relatively few experienced hooligans are involved in these websites and that many participants in message boards can be termed as 'wannabes' or 'cyber hooligans' (Van der Torre and Spaaij, 2003).

Official and private video footage

A final data source was video footage of football-related disorder involving fans of the clubs under study. Two types of video recordings can be distinguished. First, I used police footage of fighting and missile throwing inside and outside football grounds. Second, some hooligans and ultras provided me with private video footage of spectator violence and hooligan confrontations, usually the exploits of their own group recorded by members of the group. This video material was used merely as background information on the composition of hooligan formations and the dynamics of disorder.

Conclusion

In this chapter I have outlined four theoretical themes that are seen as central to generating a deeper understanding of football hooliganism as a transnational phenemenon. These themes are investigated empirically at six football clubs in three Western European cities (London, Rotterdam and Barcelona). I chose to include in the research football clubs with contrasting popular images, differentiating between clubs with persistent negative stigma (as 'violent' or 'hostile') and those with a more positive popular image (as 'non-violent' or 'friendly'). Through a comparative case study I seek to provide a detailed and systematic understanding of the phenomenon under study. In the following chapters attention is shifted to the empirical case studies. Chapter Three examines the emergence and development of football hooliganism and anti-hooligan policies in England, the Netherlands and Spain. In Chapters Four to Nine, I will analyze the extent and nature of football hooliganism at individual football clubs.

3

Setting the Stage:

On the Emergence and Development of Football
Hooliganism in England, the Netherlands and Spain

Introduction

The tragedy at the Heysel stadium in Brussels, on 29 May 1985, played a major role in the development of a concerted, European response to football hooliganism. Less than three months after the disaster that caused 39 deaths and over 500 injuries, the Council of Europe introduced the European Convention on Spectator Violence and Misbehaviour at Sports Events (Council of Europe, 1985). The agreement was designed primarily to enhance the prevention and control of spectator violence at football matches, promoting co-operation between the football authorities and the police and highlighting the importance of segregation of opposing fans, alcohol bans and the prohibition of potentially dangerous objects. By the mid-1980s, football hooliganism was a recurrent issue not only in England but in several Western European countries, although it was not perceived to be equally acute everywhere (Senado, 1990). Countries such as Italy, the Netherlands, Germany and Belgium were already faced with a pattern of disorder at football matches caused by domestic hooligan groups. In contrast, countries like Spain, France and Portugal had comparatively little experience with football hooliganism, except for the occasional misbehaviour of foreign supporters visiting their territory, the English in particular. Cross-national differences in the extent of football hooliganism at this early stage should be viewed within the context of the diverging national trajectories of the phenomenon in Western Europe and beyond. In other words, although football hooliganism is a transnational phenomenon, important national variations occur in the extent, nature and development of hooligan subcultures.

In this chapter, I will analyze the emergence and development of football hooliganism in England, the Netherlands and Spain. The chapter provides a detailed examination of the national contexts in which the local manifestations of football hooliganism in London, Rotterdam and Barcelona are embedded. It is argued that there are important overlaps and dissimilarities in the origins and evolution of the phenomenon as well as in the policies developed in the three countries.

Origins and development of the 'English disease'

Every form of spectator violence, including fighting between opposing fans, is observable, to varying extents, throughout the history of English football (Walvin, 1994; Dunning et al., 1984; Hutchinson, 1975; Holt, 1990). From the 1960s onwards, a gradual shift took place from a pattern in which attacks on match officials and opposing players predominated over attacks on rival fans, to a pattern in which inter-fan group fighting and confrontations between fans and the police became the predominant form of spectator violence (Dunning, 1994: 136). This shift was closely related to the emergence of so-called 'youth ends' at English football grounds. Groups of young working-class fans began to congregate in the cheaper sections of the grounds, usually directly behind one of the goals. At many English football stadia, first at those in the North of the country, certain areas of the ground became the exclusive territory of groups of young fans to the exclusion of the older football citizenry, representing a significant break with traditional ways of watching football (cf. Hobbs and Robins, 1991: 554).

This process of segregation by age had been occurring in an embryonic form as early as the interwar years, but was becoming more prominent in the 1960s. In particular, England's 1966 World Cup victory attracted large numbers of young fans to the stadia. The groups of young fans that congregated in the youth ends played an important part in the development of English terrace culture, replacing earlier chants and songs with a more complex and often obscene and symbolically violent repertoire. Regular television coverage of football seems to have accelerated this trend, producing a rapid diffusion of songs and chants among increasingly competitive rival fan groups (Williams et al., 1986: 365; cf. Dunning et al., 1988: 164-165). The increasing competition between youth groups of opposing football

77

clubs gave rise to an evolving network of inter-group rivalries. Opposing groups increasingly attempted to 'take' each other's home territories by intimidating, pushing or physically attacking their opponents.

Early youth end rivalries were mainly concentrated in the North of the country and, as early as the late 1950s, Liverpool and Everton fans obtained the title 'Merseyside Maniacs' for their train-wrecking exploits. From the mid-1960s onwards, increasing numbers of Northern football fans began testing their newly acquired reputations for 'toughness' on trips to the South, especially to London. Changes of this kind spurred on the embryonic London youth ends to develop greater levels of social cohesion (Williams et al., 1986: 366; Dunning et al., 1988: 166-167). During this period young Manchester United fans 'took' the home 'turf' of several Southern youth ends, including those at West Ham United and Arsenal. Such events were often widely reported in the British press and generated both apprehension and anticipation among local groups of young fans. For example, in the build-up to Manchester United's visit to Cardiff City, in September 1974, media and public expectations of crowd trouble seemed to overshadow the news status of the game itself (Jones and Rivers, 2002: 3; Dunning et al., 1988: 176).

Although evidence suggests that spectator violence at football matches in England was probably on the increase in the first half of the 1960s (Chester, 1968), it is certain that in this period the phenomenon also became an artefact of a moral panic over football fan behaviour.[1] Football hooliganism began to be perceived, especially from the mid-1960s onwards, as a national social problem. For the first time action was taken by the state and local governing bodies to tackle football-related violence, whereas before it tended to be regarded as a problem to be dealt with by the football authorities on their own (Dunning et al., 1982: 153). The growing official and public concern over football hooliganism should be understood within the context of the persistent moral panic over the behaviour of English working-class youth, notably youth subcultures such as the teddy boys, mods and rockers (see Cohen, 1972; Cross, 1998).

The preparations for the 1966 World Cup, hosted by England, acted as a catalyst for the materializing of football hooliganism as a cause for national concern. The staging of the World Cup meant that English fans were about to come under the close scrutiny of worldwide media. In the build-up to the event, the popular press in

England began to increasingly focus on 'football hooliganism' as a potential threat to the image of the English abroad (Williams et al., 1986: 362-363). Incidents of inter-fan fighting were now reported more frequently in national and local newspapers and were presented in a more dramatic relief, often using a military rhetoric (Hall, 1978). This upsurge in media reporting on spectator violence at football matches coincided with television becoming a prominent feature of English social life, increasing the public visibility of the phenomenon (Walvin, 1986: 67). By defining match days and football grounds as times and places in which fighting could be engaged in, the media, especially the popular press, appear to have played a role in the early development of English football hooliganism. The more-or-less sustained portrayal of football as a venue for inter-group fighting seems to have attracted growing numbers of male adolescents to the game (Murphy et al., 1990: 117; 122). Although this pattern of events was not limited to football, 'its regularity, its ubiquity and, later, its international nature gave football an added fame' (Walvin, 1986: 67).

In the late 1960s several youth ends in the South of England began to be dominated by a new youth subculture: the skinheads. Aggressively proletarian and chauvinist, the skinheads constructed their collective identity and style in sharp contrast to the image and dress style of the mods (Hebdige, 1979: 55; Clarke, 1973: 16). The skinhead subculture selectively reaffirmed certain core values of traditional working-class culture, in a uniform that can be viewed as a kind of caricature of the model worker (cropped hair, Doctor Martens boots, sta-prest trousers, Ben Sherman shirts, braces) (Cohen, 1972; Clarke, 1976: 99). The skinheads added to the youth ends a common style and uniform and an enhanced sense of collective identity celebrating aggressive masculinity and physical toughness. These features seem to have contributed to the intensification of collective territorial identifications and inter-group rivalries.

Dealing with football hooliganism: early security measures and their effects

The English authorities' initial responses to football hooliganism principally involved the expansion of the number of police officers at football matches and the segregation of opposing supporters within the ground. Segregation generally took two forms: the use of lines of policemen to separate the two sets of fans and the erection of dividing fences on terraces shared by home and away contingents (Dunning et al., 1988: 167). At this stage, segregation was still largely voluntary and therefore rarely totally enforceable; it depended on rival fans choosing to watch from separate locations in the company of their fellow supporters. Over the years, segregation strategies expanded rapidly both within and away from the ground. The entrances for home and away supporters were separated and perimeter fences were erected, many of which were high and crowned with spikes and barbed wire, producing an image of football fans as 'caged animals' (e.g. *The Observer*, 1 December 1974). Away supporters were escorted to their section of the ground by police officers and special trains and coaches carrying away fans became operative, being monitored en route by the police (Lord Justice Taylor, 1990: 7; Canter et al., 1989: 108).

Early segregation of rival fan groups inside the stadium failed to have a noticeable preventative effect. In turn, however, it had a number of unintended consequences. First, segregation seems to have enhanced the sense of solidarity and collective identity among members of the youth ends since it underlined their distinctive nature (Marsh et al., 1978: 59; Pratt and Salter, 1984: 213). Opposing parties were now physically separated by dividing fences and police officers, creating strong ingroup and outgroup feelings. Second, segregation within the ground resulted in the partial displacement of football hooliganism. Whereas fighting between opposing hooligan formations inside football stadia became increasingly rare, hooligan encounters began to take place more frequently on other locations, notably in the streets, in pubs and at railway stations (Giulianotti and Armstrong, 2002: 222-226; Dunning et al., 1986: 169). In general, instead of effectively reducing the problem early responses to football hooliganism seem to have inadvertently stimulated the social organization and planning involved in hooligan confrontations. In the late 1960s hooligan groups tended to be organized on a relatively loose and *ad hoc* basis. Small groups of young fans – united primarily by neighbourhood ties or through friendships formed at work or at school – would forge alliances in a match-day context for purposes of confronting rival fans (Murphy et al., 1990: 90). As official controls gradually came to have a more serious impact on the opportunities for fighting in and around football grounds, and as inter-group rivalries began to be displaced outside the grounds, the young fans who were most deeply committed to participating in football hooliganism began to plan their activities more consciously.

The evolvement of English hooligan formations can be characterized as a process of co-production. A major consequence of the imposition of controls and punishments was to displace the problem into areas where the controls were, or were perceived by hooligans as being, weak or non-existent (Dunning, 1999: 153; Spaaij, 2005: 7). For their part, the authorities responded to each innovation by the hooligans by producing harsher punishments and tighter and more comprehensive controls. This ongoing process involved a gradual widening of controls, first to the immediate vicinities of grounds and then to the major points of entry into the towns and cities where matches were played (Dunning, 1999: 152). It is within this process of co-production that the notorious 'super hooligan' groups came into existence, for example the Inter City Firm at West Ham United, Headhunters at Chelsea, Zulu Warriors at Birmingham City, Gooners at Arsenal, Soul Crew at Cardiff City and the Service Crew at Leeds United. The emergence of these groups marked a transformation in the nature of English football hooliganism, featuring a more distinct identity between those actively seeking violent confrontation and the rest of the youth end (Williams, 1991: 167). The groups developed an elite self-conception based on their perceived sense of superiority in terms of toughness, masculinity and style. As Thornton (2003: 49) argues, 'gone were the days of the mass exodus and scrapping on the terraces. Now the gangs were much tighter and better organized, finding strength in smaller, self-reliant groups.'

A key aim of these hooligan formations is to successfully challenge their opponents. They may use more complex strategies to escape police observation and 'infiltrate' the territory of their rivals. Hooligan groups tend to travel to away matches using regular railway services, private coaches, cars or transit vans rather than special football trains or coaches. They also eschew the forms of dress and the club emblems that are worn by many non-hooligan supporters, preferring instead a 'casual' style. The casual designer fashion began as a post-mod, post-skinhead subculture in the 1977/78 season, initially in the North of England and later in London (Thornton, 2003: 44-48; Redhead, 2004: 396-397). By the early 1980s the casual style had a strong hold on British terrace culture, triggering a widespread interest in, and competition in terms of, expensive (continental) designer labels and leisure wear such as Fila, Sergio Tacchini, Pringle, Lacoste and Ellesse (e.g. Jones and Rivers, 2002; Redhead and McLaughlin, 1985). The rise of the casual style can be seen to some degree as a strategy of hooligans to not stand out among regular supporters, enabling them to circumvent official controls. However, as Williams (1991: 174) has correctly argued, in cities such as Liverpool the casual designer fashion seems to have represented more a defiant masculine celebration of economic depression and unemployment in the face of an overwhelming pressure to consume.

The crisis of English football in the 1980s

The changing outlook and modus operandi of the hooligan groups contributed to an increase in the extent and seriousness of English football hooliganism in the late 1970s and the first half of the 1980s. Official and public concern over football fan behaviour culminated in 1985, a tragic year for both English and European football. The disturbances provoked by Millwall fans at Luton Town in April 1985 were perceived by journalists and politicians as evidence of the 'return' of large-scale hooliganism inside English football grounds. On 11 May 1985, 56 people were killed and more than 200 injured when fire broke out in a wooden stand at Bradford City. On the same afternoon, a 15-year-old boy was killed in Birmingham following the collapse of a wall during fighting between Birmingham City and Leeds United fans and the police. Only weeks later, on 29 May 1985, European football was shocked by the tragedy that unfolded shortly before the kick-off of the European Cup final between Liverpool and Juventus at the Heysel stadium in Brussels. With television channels around the world broadcasting live, a charge of Liverpool fans across one of the terraces led Juventus supporters to flee in panic, causing a crumbling wall to collapse and contributing to the deaths of 39 people, most of them Italians. The tragedy that unfolded that night 'was quickly considered to be the nadir of a history of football hooliganism that had preoccupied a generation of sports administrators, journalists, sociologists and politicians' (Chisari, 2004: 201). Responding to the immediate political and public outcry, the international football authorities took dramatic steps to restore the public's confidence in the game. The UEFA banned English clubs from European competitions for a period of five years, with Liverpool receiving an additional two-year ban. International guidelines for curbing spectator violence at football matches were set up in a European Convention on Spectator Violence and Misbehaviour at Sports Events.

The Heysel disaster had a severe impact on the international image of English football as well as on the authorities' responses to the behaviour of English supporters at home and abroad. An official inquiry by Lord Justice Popplewell in 1986 raised awareness of the issue of spectator safety at football grounds and, in particular, revived the controversial debate about the use of membership schemes. In the 1970s and early 1980s a number of clubs had already experimented with membership schemes in an attempt to prevent 'unwanted' fans from entering their grounds (R. Taylor, 1992). Leicester City, for example, launched its own partial membership scheme only five months prior to the Heysel tragedy. At Luton Town, following the incidents provoked by Millwall fans in April 1985, a home-fans-only membership scheme was introduced. This scheme constituted the first systematic attempt by any football club to exclude all away fans (Murphy et al., 1990: 218-219). The British government and, in particular, the Prime Minister at that time, Margaret Thatcher, determinedly supported the use of identity cards and membership schemes as the most effective way of enforcing exclusion orders at football grounds (Marsh et al., 1996: 118). The Football League and the government agreed on the introduction of so-called '50 per cent membership schemes' at all league grounds. The Football Spectators Act installed in 1989 proposed the creation of compulsory identity cards for spectators at all levels of professional football in England and Wales.

Official policies targeting football hooliganism in the second half of the 1980s relied almost exclusively on measures of punishment and control. Several specific devices were introduced during this period. Closed-circuit television (CCTV) systems were introduced at football grounds in an attempt to enhance the control and surveillance of football supporters. A new offence of 'disorderly conduct' was introduced in 1986 as part of a general review of British public order legislation (the Public Order Act). Although this new legal term was not, as Lord Justice Popplewell had initially recommended, designed specifically as a football-related offence, its practical implementation certainly demonstrated its relevance in that context (Williams et al., 1989: xxxvii). The policing of football matches increasingly concentrated on close surveillance and intelligence gathering, using instruments such as mobile surveillance 'hoolivans', hand-held video cameras and plain-clothes 'spotters' to identify hooligan 'ringleaders'. The function of the covert spotter rapidly developed into a more fixed office within police strategy. Throughout the country officers were deployed to 'infiltrate' hooligan groups, and to collect evidence against those most centrally involved (Armstrong and Hobbs, 1994: 122). On the basis of intelligence gathered during lengthy covert inquiries, dozens of alleged hooligans were prosecuted in the late 1980s. Five Chelsea fans were sentenced to up to ten year's imprisonment. However, subsequent trials collapsed due to irregularities in the way in which police evidence was prepared, notably the fabrication of evidence and procedural laxity of investigating officers (Williams et al., 1989: xxxvii; Reville, 1988: 12-14; Spaaij, 2005b: 6; Ward and Hickmott, 2000).

English football after Hillsborough

The spiral of increasing containment and surveillance in and around English football grounds came under severe criticism in the aftermath of the tragedy at Hillsborough, Sheffield, on 15 April 1989. During an FA Cup Semi Final match between Liverpool and Nottingham Forest, 96 Liverpool supporters were crushed to death on the terraces. Charges of 'hooliganism' left a lasting impression on the disaster and were reinforced and seemingly legitimated by journalists, politicians and academics (Scraton, 2004: 184). Despite these allegations, an official inquiry into the events concluded that the main causes of the disaster were overcrowding and a failure of police control (Lord Justice Taylor, 1990). It seems that the dominant law-and-order approach, notably the erection of high perimeter fences, was at the heart of the disaster:

> The determining cause, if this is the appropriate word, of the Hillsborough disaster was, indeed, the way in which the Leppings Lane terrace, like so many of the 'popular ends' at English soccer grounds, had been reconstructed over the years as a caged-in 'pen' from which there was no means of escape at a predictable moment of crisis of mass spectator excitement and anxiety (I. Taylor, 1989: 95).

Evidence suggests that this situation was not unique to the Hillsborough ground. In fact, Hillsborough was considered by the football authorities to be one of England's best grounds (Scraton, 2004: 185; Lord Justice Taylor, 1990: 4). The 1986 Popplewell inquiry speculated that if perimeter fences had been erected around the pitch at Bradford City, where a fire broke out in a wooden stand in 1985, the death toll would have been much higher. The importance of his recommendation of adequate exits in the fences was not widely noticed at the time amidst continuing concerns over hooliganism (Johnes, 2004: 143). Crowd management at English football grounds in the 1970s and 1980s almost exclusively concentrated on public order and the prevention of hooliganism. Repressive policing was coupled with engineering measures such as the perimeter fencing and penning, leading some theorists to describe football grounds in terms of a 'prison' metaphor (Bale, 1993).

The inquiry by Lord Justice Taylor into the Hillsborough disaster set off a new approach to crowd management at football grounds in Britain. His final report discussed a number of fundamental problems facing British football, notably the poor state of football grounds and the effects of hooliganism and segregation on the general experiences of football spectators. Taylor made a number of important recommendations, including: (i) the gradual replacement of terraces with seated areas at all venues by the end of the twentieth century (with all First and Second Division grounds being converted into all-seater stadia by the start of the 1994/95 season and all Third and Fourth Division grounds by 1999/2000); (ii) the instalment of CCTV systems at all football grounds; (iii) the formation of an Advisory Design Council to advise on ground safety and construction and to commission research into this area; (iv) the prohibition of perimeter fences of over 2.20 meters tall or with spikes on the top; and (v) the prohibition, by creating criminal offences, of three specific activities within the ground: missile throwing, chanting obscene or racialist abuse, and going on the pitch without reasonable excuse (Lord Justice Taylor, 1990: 76-82). Importantly, the Taylor Report also rejected the compulsory membership scheme. The clubs and the football authorities welcomed this conclusion since they objected to the detrimental effect of the membership scheme on their principal source of revenue: gate receipts (Murphy et al., 1990: 217; R. Taylor, 1992: 170). Much in line with the persistent political and public concern over football hooliganism, Taylor also advocated certain important disciplinary methods of control. Taylor acknowledged that seating and other controlling measures could not be guaranteed to minimize hooliganism, but they were, in his view, the best available option. He argued that apart from comfort and safety, seating had distinct advantages in achieving crowd control. With the assistance of CCTV, the immediate detection of troublemakers would be enhanced dramatically (Lord Justice Taylor, 1990: 12).

The impact of the Taylor Report was reinforced by the huge popularity of the 1990 World Cup hosted by Italy. The tournament 'demonstrated the inadequacy of English football grounds but also the potential market for football if it was properly organized' (King, 2002: 103). The modern Italian stadia confirmed Taylor's conclusions regarding the run-down state of football grounds in England. At the same time, the tournament showed that the transformation of the consumption of football was potentially hugely lucrative. It led to an interest in football among sections of society which had previously shown limited interest in the game, principally due to the success of the English team (ibid.: 104). The British government was, at this point, no longer content for football to govern its own affairs. The introduction of all-seater stadia was forced upon generally reluctant clubs by a government that saw football as an embarrassment and irritation (Johnes, 2004: 144). The Football Spectators Act (1989) regulated the creation of the Football Licensing Authority (FLA), which was given considerable powers to impose conditions on football clubs and to suspend or refuse licenses. In addition to the FLA, several government agencies and other bodies developed their own detailed guidance on managing aspects of public safety at sports grounds (Frosdick and Sidney, 1999: 210). The need for such guidance was underlined by the complacency and sheer neglect of spectators' interests found at many football clubs (Inglis, 2001: 89; cf. Elliott and Smith, 1999).

Post-Hillsborough initiatives to 'clean up' English football have steered attention towards the safety and comfort of all spectators. Improvements in spectator safety and comfort have not simply been the result of all-seater requirements, but rather of a capital change in attitude among those at the operating level. This transformation involved the recognition that safety and security are two separate issues that must be kept in perfect balance (Inglis, 2001: 90-91). Significant improvements in the attitudes of football clubs towards issues of spectator safety and comfort were realized by the late 1990s. This change is vividly described by Inglis:

> Had you sat down with the directors of a typical football club circa 1990 and asked them what was their policy towards 'customer care', you would have almost certainly have been met by a prolonged and embarrassed silence. Only 5 of the 92 League clubs even had a safety officer, and some of those were part-timers. Now, a decade later every club has one, not to mention a statement of intent, a stewards' training manual and maybe even a customers' charter and an annual survey of supporters' attitudes (2001: 89-90).

The transformation of English football in the 1990s has not been limited to the issue of spectator safety, but is closely related to the reinvention of the game itself. The stadium changes forced upon the football industry by the government 'compelled it to reassess its finances, its treatment of its consumers and, indeed, its whole image and future' (Johnes, 2004: 144). Most of the larger English football clubs have undergone profound changes. The political economy of the league has been completely restructured through the creation of the Premier League, in 1992, in order to assist the top clubs in their pursuit of increased television and admission revenues (King, 2002: 3). The shift towards all-seater stadia enabled both the attraction of wider audiences to the game and the reduction of potentially lethal crowd disturbances.[2] Attendances at football matches in Britain had been declining since the 1950s, except for a slight increase immediately after 1966, the year in which England won the World Cup. In the 1985/86 season, the first season after the Heysel disaster, British football attendances had fallen to 16.5 million compared to 41.3 million in the 1948/49 season (Football Trust, 1991: 9). The transformation of the game in the 1990s has resulted in a steady increase in crowd attendances. In the 2003/04 season attendances exceeded 27 million, for the first time in 34 years (Spaaij, 2005b: 7).

Along with the socio-spatial transformation of English football grounds, the experience of attending a Premier League match has changed significantly for most people. Football supporters are nowadays far less likely to experience large-scale hooligan confrontations in and around football grounds. Seven out of ten fans participating in Premier League surveys claim never to witness inter-fan fighting at football matches, although the experience of some travelling fans is different (J. Williams, 2001: 40-41; Sir Norman Chester Centre, 2002: 31-32). Scholars have attributed this perceived decline in football hooliganism to a variety of factors: shifts in youth culture (Redhead, 1997); the socio-spatial transformation of football stadia and a focus on crowd management and public safety (Inglis, 2001; Frosdick and Sidney, 1999; Garland and Rowe, 2000); new intelligence-led policing initiatives and harsher penalties for football-related offences (Garland and Rowe, 2000); the cultural transformation of the sport, informally via events such as the media presentation of the 1990 World Cup and commercially via the new pricing and marketing strategies of football (King, 2002); and the rise of a football fanzine culture (Haynes, 1995).

There is no consensus amongst academics on the extent and seriousness of contemporary football hooliganism in England. Some have suggested that the decline in football hooliganism is imagined rather than real, since English hooligan formations continue to be active in both domestic and international contexts. From this point of view, the British media may have been deliberately 'playing down' or 'covering up' recent incidents of hooliganism (Powley, 1999: 34-36; King and Knight, 1999: 217-218; *The Observer*, 4 October 1998). Dunning (1999) has argued that the 'myth of disappearance' is mainly the consequence of a de-politicization of football hooliganism by the authorities and the media. The occurrence of football hooliganism in England, according to Dunning (1999: 133), has become 'less "newsworthy" and hence less frequently reported, particularly by the national media.' Official statistics seem to confirm the idea that the 'disappearance' of English football hooliganism in the domestic context is perceived rather than real. The number of football-related arrests in England has generally been on the decline over the last decade (NCIS, private correspondence, 2002; Home Office, 2004), though this is not a clear-cut linear process, as is shown in Table 3.1.

Table 3.1 Football-related arrests in England, 2000/01 to 2003/04 seasons.*

Season	Number of arrests
2000/01	3,391
2001/02	3,214
2002/03	3,355
2003/04	3,010

Source: Home Office, 2002; 2003; 2004.

Note: *Includes league matches only, due to the incompatibility of arrest rates for other types of matches (see Home Office, 2004: 6 for an explanatory note). There are some inconsistencies with earlier Home Office reports (2002; 2003) which may distort comparison between seasons.

In contrast, the number of recorded incidents of football-related 'disorder' listed in Table 3.2 shows a steady increase in recent years: from 206 during the 2002/03 season to 317 in the 2003/04 season, an increase of 54 per cent. The British Transport Police has also recorded a significant increase in number of 'serious' incidents involving football fans travelling by public transport, notably on trains and at railway stations (British Transport Police, 2004; personal interviews, September 2004). Moreover, NCIS recently reported a 44 per cent increase in recorded incidents inside English football grounds whereas, intuitively, disorder in and around football grounds, at least in the Premier League, seems to have diminished. The main forms of spectator violence within football grounds are relatively minor, such as missile throwing and inter-fan skirmishes (NCIS, private correspondence, 2004). Certain recent incidents inside the stadium were widely reported in the British media, notably those during FA Cup matches at Millwall (26 October 2004), Chelsea (27 October 2004) and Everton (19 February 2005). These incidents temporarily 'revived' media attention for football 'hooliganism'. *The Guardian* (29 October 2004) wrote how 'Hooligans launch fightback' and a journalist of the *Evening Standard* (29 October 2004) asked: 'Is it coming back?'.

Table 3.2   Recorded incidents at professional football matches in England, 2000/01 to 2003/04 seasons.

Season	Number of incidents
2000/01	156
2001/02	189
2002/03	206
2003/04	317

Source: Data provided by NCIS.

Both media reports and statistics on football-related arrests and recorded incidents are flawed by the fact that they group together qualitatively distinctive types of offences in the football context. Table 3.3 provides a more detailed picture of the main types of football-related offences resulting in arrest. The three most common types of offences are public disorder (34%), alcohol offences (30%) and violent disorder (10%). Although Table 3.3 is substantially more detailed than the previous two tables, it shows the serious difficulties in analyzing the development of football hooliganism on the basis of official statistics. We are left clueless as to the precise backgrounds of the public order offences, that is, whether they were spontaneous or premeditated, directed at rival fans or at the police, individual or collective, and so forth.

Table 3.3   Main types of football-related offences in England, 2001/02 to 2003/04 seasons.

Type of offence	Number of arrests			
	2001/02	2002/03	2003/04	% of total
Public disorder	1,109	1,097	1,019	34%
Alcohol offences	986	979	889	30%
Violent disorder	248	342	408	10%
Pitch incursion	205	256	176	7%
Breach of peace	n.a.*	311	179	5%
Ticket touting	144	95	51	3%
Missile throwing	61	54	65	2%
Racist chanting	46	71	53	2%

Source: Adapted from Home Office, 2003; 2004.

Note: *Figure for 2001/02 is not available. This category is therefore under-represented in the percentage of total.

Tables 3.1 to 3.3 demonstrate that spectator violence at football matches in England has not disappeared. They do not, however, provide a reliable and more precise indication of the extent and development of football hooliganism. Official statistics on football-related violence have some serious limitations and need to be placed in context (Spaaij, 2005b: 4; Evans and Rowe, 2002: 37; Home Office, 2004: 2). First, definitions of what constitutes a ('serious') 'incident' may vary across localities and among individual police officers. Second, arrest statistics may reflect more trends in police strategies and productivity and less actual developments in spectator violence or hooliganism. Significant variations in police strategies occur between as well as within police forces. For example, in recent years the Metropolitan Police have made relatively few arrests at professional football matches in East London in comparison with matches played in West London. These variations do not reflect differences in the problems experienced in the areas, but rather the comparatively high degree of proactivity of policing football in West London (Metropolitan Police, 2003).

Third, the vast majority of hooligan confrontations nowadays takes place away from football grounds, notably at railway stations, in city centres or at pubs. The relative unpredictability of such locations may thwart the police's ability to arrest participants. Even when police officers anticipate violent confrontation, hooligans tend to disperse before the police arrive at the scene (so-called 'hit-and-run' tactics) (Spaaij, 2005b: 4). The relocation of hooligan encounters also seems to have influenced media reporting on the subject. Many hooligan incidents are never related to their football-related origins by the media or the public and are regularly described as ordinary pub fights (NCIS, private correspondence, 2002). The vast majority of confrontations between rival hooligans takes place on locations where no football journalists are normally present. This may prevent journalists from personally observing the incident and producing a story and photograph. Also, the casual fashion may obstruct identification of participants and the groups they represent.[3]

Rather than having 'disappeared', important transformations have occurred in the dominant forms of English football hooliganism. The overwhelming majority of hooligan confrontations take place away from the stadium. Elements of the 'super hooligan' formations of the 1980s still exist today, but most of these groups are significantly smaller than in the past. The decline in group membership is most visible at the larger Premier League clubs. Hooligan formations at these clubs remain active, but they tend to pick their clashes more carefully and occasionally with prior agreement of the opponent. Several hooligan formations at lower-league football clubs have been attracting new young recruits in recent years (King and Knight, 1999: 219). Both NCIS and New Scotland Yard argue that the involvement of new young practitioners in football hooliganism is currently increasing (personal interviews, September 2003 to November 2004). Crucially, these developments have not occurred to the same extent everywhere, just as football hooliganism has not been quelled at all football venues (J. Williams, 2001: 41). Also, it is important to note that although English football hooliganism has far from disappeared, much football-related violence appears to be relatively unorganized and *ad hoc* and not the product of competitive violence between rival hooligan formations (Garland and Rowe, 1999: 43-44). Whereas recent police strategies have been relatively successful in reducing hooligan confrontations in and around English football grounds, they seem to have more difficulty policing the unorganized violence that may involve fans who are not committed hooligans but come to be involved in disorder relatively spontaneously (Garland and Rowe, 2000: 144-145; personal interviews with senior police officers, May 2003 to January 2004).

In short, although English football hooliganism has far from disappeared, its extent and forms have changed considerably over time. In general, the phenomenon has become less visible and the number of regular participants has somewhat decreased. In the following section I examine the continuities and changes in Dutch football hooliganism.

Football hooliganism in the Netherlands: patterns of continuity and change

English football culture has had major influence on the development of football fandom in the Netherlands. Dutch fans introduced various elements of English terrace culture into their own practices, such as songs, chants and the display of scarves and flags. In the 1970s Dutch football experienced the emergence of so-called 'sides' or *zijden*, first at football clubs in the country's four main cities: Amsterdam (F-Side), Rotterdam (Vak S), The Hague (North Side) and Utrecht

(Bunnikzijde). These sides had much in common with the British youth ends and emerged as a result of a similar process of segregation by age. The sides predominantly consisted of young supporters in their teens and early twenties who congregated in specific areas of the ground, usually in the cheaper sections behind one of the goals. These areas were soon transformed into the exclusive territory of young fans to the exclusion of the older football citizenry.

The emergence of sides marked the beginning of an important discontinuity in the extent and nature of spectator violence in Dutch football. The frequency of spectator violence at professional football matches in the Netherlands appears to have been comparatively low until the 1970s and there are no indications of an early tradition of football hooliganism. Throughout the history of Dutch football some inter-fan fighting has occurred, but this fighting does not seem to have involved more than uncommon, spontaneous outbursts of spectator violence (Miermans, 1955). Early incidents of spectator violence usually took the form of missile throwing or assaults on players or the referee. Spectator disorderliness was only occasionally directed at rival supporters. Incidents were usually triggered by events on the pitch, such as a controversial refereeing decision or defeat (Van der Brug, 1994: 176). This pattern gradually changed in the mid-1970s as a consequence of the emergence of the sides and their increasingly violent repertoires and inter-group rivalries. Spectator violence at football matches became increasingly detached from the match itself (Van der Brug, 1986: 223). Some sides were already the subject of official and public concern in the early 1970s. FC Utrecht's Bunnikzijde obtained an early notoriety for its alleged violent behaviour. The occasional incidents provoked by members of the Bunnikzijde encouraged members of opposing sides to respond to these aggressions in a similar way, setting in motion the development of an early network of inter-group hostilities. These early incidents were relatively spontaneous and unorganized. Although the fan groups attended football matches without planning violent confrontation, they often did not refrain from the use of violence when challenged by their rivals. Anticipation of disorder was principally based on the early (mediated) reputations of rival sides.

The emergence of football hooliganism in the Netherlands can be understood as a continuation of fights between rival (youth) groups in other contexts (Stokvis, 1991). Such fighting initially took place between youths from different city districts and from different villages. From the mid-1970s, these inter-group rivalries were in part relocated to the football context as the different groups began to jointly occupy the terraces of their local football grounds (Custers and Hamersma, 2005: 23; Köster, 2005: 71; Vos, 2006). Traditional inter-group rivalries were temporarily suspended on match days and re-created in terms of club allegiance, reflecting in many respects the 'Bedouin syndrome' described by Harrison (1974: 604; see Chapter One).

The behaviour of English supporters on Dutch territory played an important role in the transformation of the pattern of spectator violence at football matches in the Netherlands. During the return match of the UEFA Cup final between Feyenoord and Tottenham Hotspur, on 29 May 1974 in Rotterdam, visiting supporters attacked home fans in adjacent sections of the ground. Over 200 people were injured during the incident that has been dubbed 'the day Dutch football lost its innocence' (*Rotterdams Dagblad*, 20 April 2002). While shocking the Dutch authorities and the wider public, the incident enhanced the interest of several young supporters in English terrace culture and hooliganism. Supporters of several Dutch clubs travelled to cities such as London, Manchester and Liverpool to directly experience the atmosphere of English football grounds. Visits of British clubs to the Netherlands were increasingly viewed with enthusiasm and anticipation by members of the Dutch sides. Affiliates of Ajax's F-Side attended the annual pre-season tournament in Amsterdam, which gave them the opportunity to observe the notorious hooligan groups of Manchester United and Leeds United (Pieloor et al., 2002: 22).

At this early stage of football hooliganism in the Netherlands, the four main sides were involved in the vast majority of hooligan confrontations. Early inter-group encounters set off a spiral of competitive violence which revolved around the groups' aim to successfully challenge their opponents by invading their territory and fighting them. Typically only a small proportion of all affiliates of the sides were actively involved in violent confrontation; many young fans joined the sides merely to 'have a good time' among peers and to experience pleasurable excitement. The main sides rapidly established a reputation for toughness and 'mindless' violence. The first televised domestic football riot, on 24 October 1976, pictured FC Utrecht supporters challenging and chasing Ajax fans with bicycle chains. These early reputations and the growing media coverage of hooligan incidents seem to have enhanced the national diffusion of the phenomenon. Young supporters throughout the country began to organize themselves in sides and imitated the behaviour and style of the pioneering sides. In several cases, this process of imitation became particularly visible after young home fans were attacked or intimidated by one of the established hooligan groups. The reputations of the established sides also had an impact on the development of certain Belgian and German fan groups, which, parallel to British influences, began to import certain elements of the Dutch hooligan scene into their own practices. Young fans of the Belgian Club Bruges, for example, created their East Side after interacting with Feyenoord hooligans during a friendly match between the two teams in 1980 (Verleyen and De Smet, 1997: 16).

It was also during this early period of football hooliganism in the Netherlands that the label *voetbalvandalisme* (football vandalism) began to be increasingly used to refer to a variety of behaviours that took place in more or less directly football-related contexts. The use of this term among politicians, journalists, academics and the general public has its origins in the official and media concern over train wrecking exploits of young football fans in the mid-1970s (e.g. Hartsuiker, 1977). Most academic studies of the time adopted a similar terminology, using 'vandalism' as an umbrella term for activities as diverse as missile throwing, fighting and verbal abuse (Siekmann, 1982; Van der Brug, 1986). From the mid-1990s, these types of behaviour have also been increasingly referred to by academics and journalists as 'football violence', 'football crime' and 'hooliganism' (Adang, 1997; Bol and Van Netburg, 1997; Ferwerda and Gelissen, 2001; Van Gageldonk, 1996). The Centraal Informatiepunt Voetbalvandalisme (CIV) and other governmental institutions continue to use the term *voetbalvandalisme*. These labels are, to varying degrees, all misleading since they group together distinctive types of offences caused by football supporters, including what I have defined as football hooliganism. I will return to this issue in the discussion of the current shapes of football hooliganism in the Netherlands.

The development and containment of Dutch football hooliganism

Football hooliganism became a prominent subject on the Dutch political agenda in the second half of the 1980s. The Heysel disaster heightened fears over the potential

95

lethality of football hooliganism and resulted in the introduction of a number of internationally agreed countermeasures. Domestically, the frequency and seriousness of hooligan confrontations increased considerably due to the continuing national diffusion of the hooligan subculture and the radicalization of several inter-group rivalries. Media coverage of spectator violence also became more extensive in this period. Live television broadcasting of an UEFA Cup match between Feyenoord and Tottenham Hotspur, on 2 November 1983, brought to people's homes serious fighting between opposing supporters on the terraces. More than 50 supporters were treated for minor injuries and three English fans were taken to hospital for treatment of stabbing wounds. The stabbing of one English supporter by a home fan was repeatedly broadcasted on national television. The Dutch broadcasting company NOS described the disorder as 'degrading scenes that have absolutely nothing to do with football' (*NOS Nieuws*, 2 November 1983).

Other widely reported incidents involved the throwing of home-made bombs and other missiles. An international fixture between Holland and Cyprus in October 1987 was suspended after a Dutch fan threw a bomb onto the pitch, injuring Cyprus's goalkeeper. On 27 September 1989, an Ajax fan was arrested after throwing an iron bar onto the playing field during a European Cup match between Ajax and Austria Wien. During a league match between Ajax and Feyenoord, on 22 October 1989, two Feyenoord hooligans threw home-made nail bombs into a home section of the ground injuring fourteen Ajax supporters. One home fan suffered an arterial haemorrhage. Riot police immediately cleared the entire away section and all 500 visiting fans were searched at the exit (*NOS Nieuws*, 22 October 1989). The incident was widely reported by national and international media. The BBC concluded that 'Holland was fast taking over as Europe's most troubled footballing nation' (*BBC News*, 22 October 1989). *The Times* (25 October 1989) published an article with the title 'Dutch bewildered by rising tide of hooliganism', stating that 'the Dutch reputation for football violence is rapidly overtaking that of the British as the worst in Europe.'

In response to the perceived threat of football hooliganism, the Dutch authorities introduced several security measures. Early containment strategies concentrated principally on the segregation of opposing supporters and the deployment of increasing numbers of police officers at 'high-risk' matches. Fences were erected inside the stadia to separate visiting supporters from the home crowd and to prevent pitch invasions. In addition, a number of working groups and commissions were established to study potential measures to contain hooligan violence, recommending, for example, better co-ordination between police forces and the instalment of security officers at all league clubs. In the second half of the 1980s the improvement of the co-ordination between different governing bodies and the establishing of a more integrated approach to tackling football hooliganism became the key objectives. This period witnessed the creation of the Centraal Informatiepunt Voetbalvandalisme, in 1986, which has the task of gathering, analyzing and disseminating football intelligence and co-ordinating national databases on football-related violence. Similar to the situation in England, intelligence-led policing gradually became a central tenet of Dutch anti-hooligan policies (Cachet and Muller, 1991: 100).

At the same time, several football clubs began to invest in the specialization of their security and safety regimes, spurred on by national and international regulations. Compliance with international requirements was enhanced by the renovation and relocation of various Dutch football grounds. FC Utrecht's Nieuw Galgenwaard, the first modern and multifunctional Dutch football stadium completed in 1982, served as an example both nationally and internationally (Tummers, 1993: 104). The stadium was considered the first to meet post-Hillsborough safety requirements and was included in the Taylor Report (1990) as a European best practice. In 1989 the Dutch football association, the Koninklijke Nederlandse Voetbalbond (KNVB), agreed with the clubs to convert all league grounds to all-seater stadia before the turn of the century. The clubs also gradually improved their ticket procedures and controls, installed CCTV systems and invested in their steward organization (see KNVB, 2003; Heijs and Mengerink, 1993).

The priority of football hooliganism on the Dutch political and media agenda was enhanced in the second half of the 1990s due to the country's co-hosting, with Belgium, of the European Championships in the year 2000. In the period leading up to the event, politicians and 'experts' voiced their concerns over how hooliganism could seriously damage the country's international reputation. These concerns were reflected in both national and international media reports. A newspaper survey suggested that 80 per cent of the population expected serious

97

disorder during Euro 2000 (*Algemeen Dagblad*, 23 October 1999). A British journalist wrote:

> Hooliganism has declined in Britain in recent years, but in the Netherlands it has got worse [...] After gun battles in Rotterdam, Dutch police fear Orange disorder will wreck the Euro 2000 tournament. (*The Guardian*, 2 May 1999)

Both organizing countries took a number of precautionary measures in a bid to prevent disorder during the tournament. Key fields of interest were international police co-operation and the management of intelligence, ticket management and entry controls. Most of this interest appears to have been relatively short-lived. The CIV stressed that although the Euro 2000 tournament proved that secure ticket management and tight entry controls could have a positive effect on spectator behaviour, the good practices were soon forgotten or shoved aside by most football clubs. It was also argued that clubs' security policies continued to lack the commitment and priority needed to effectively reduce football hooliganism (CIV, 2001; *Nederlands Dagblad*, 17 December 2001; *Zwolse Courant*, 14 December 2001).

The contemporary management of Dutch professional football features the recognition that security and safety are two separate issues and that customer services and fans' experiences are to be taken seriously (Tummers, 1993: 131-135; COT, 1998: 8). The shift towards a more customer-orientated approach sits uneasily with the continuing emphasis on the containment of football supporters, notably the compulsory membership scheme and travel regulations. The compulsory membership scheme, the so-called 'club card' program, has been a particularly contentious issue. A first experiment with the membership scheme was conducted in 1989 at five 'high-risk' clubs. Match tickets were sold only to supporters holding an identity card issued by their club. On the first day of the operation a large number of fans successfully circumvented the new scheme by attending the match without actually possessing a club card. Following the initial failure of the experiment, the membership scheme was temporarily abandoned. But after renewed official concern over football hooliganism and further attempts to commercialize the game, a comparable membership scheme was introduced at all Premier League clubs in the 1996/97 season. Officially, the club card principally functioned as a service card, that is, as a means for improving the club's service to its customers (Cotass, 1995). It was nevertheless viewed by many fans as merely another attempt by the authorities to crackdown on a violent minority at the expense of non-violent football fans (e.g. *Algemeen Dagblad*, 2 April 1998; *Algemeen Dagblad*, 27 April 1998).

The controversy surrounding the compulsory membership scheme entered a new phase with the proposed introduction of a club card with photo identification. From the start, fan organizations and several football clubs protested against the photo identification, claiming that clubs would lose a significant part of their income if fans were no longer allowed to purchase match tickets without an identity card (*Algemeen Dagblad*, 5 September 1998; *Algemeen Dagblad*, 14 September 1998). As a result of the continuing resistance by fan organizations and clubs, the identity card scheme was eventually given a non-compulsory status. Clubs were left to decide whether or not to issue club cards and, consequently, most clubs only utilize the card scheme to manage ticket sales at 'high-risk' fixtures. Five Dutch football clubs oblige their fans to submit personal data plus a photo, four of which only in the application procedure for an 'away card' required for attending away matches. By 2004, ADO Den Haag was the only club to request a photo card from its fans for both home and away matches (CIV, 2004: 5).

In addition to repressive and techno-preventative strategies for tackling football hooliganism, in the late 1980s several football clubs and local governments began to experiment with social preventative fan projects, similar to those launched in Germany (see Schneider, 1991; Homan et al., 1991; Hahn, 1987). These projects seek to reduce football hooliganism through improving the relations between football clubs and young fans as well as through enhancing the social skills and life chances of young 'risk' supporters (Van Dijk et al., 1991: 1-2; Ferwerda, 1999). Fan co-ordinators are key participants in the local projects, maintaining contacts with young supporters and hooligans, organizing social activities and providing additional services. Despite the local popularity of many of these fan projects, the social preventative approach to tackling football hooliganism has been overshadowed by the continuing dominance of repressive and techno-preventative strategies. The creation of the Landelijk Informatiepunt Supportersprojecten (LIS;

99

National Information Centre for Fan Projects) and recent media attention to the fan projects at Cambuur Leeuwarden and FC Groningen have only marginally rectified this imbalance. In the early 2000s a so-called 'perpetrator-orientated' approach to policing football hooliganism was introduced in order to crack down on known football hooligans. This approach focuses on the close monitoring of individual hooligans in the football context as well as in everyday life (see Ferwerda and Adang, 2005). Following the first positive results of the *Hooligans in Beeld* (Hooligans in View) project at Vitesse Arnhem, a similar approach was introduced in other police districts. In some cases the project has had the unintended effect of polarizing the relations between hooligans and the police. Police officers involved in the projects have occasionally been the subject of intimidation and violence (CIV, 2004: 4; personal interviews with senior police officers, October 2004).

The extent and nature of contemporary football hooliganism in the Netherlands

Football hooliganism in the Netherlands continues to be officially and publicly perceived as a disturbing social problem, despite public efforts to contain or eradicate the phenomenon. Habitually, political demand for more effective governmental action and additional legal provisions ensues widely reported incidents of 'hooliganism'. A closer look at Dutch football hooliganism reveals that the countermeasures taken over the years have fundamentally altered its main forms. Opportunities for fighting within football grounds have gradually diminished and hooligan encounters in and around the stadia are currently less common. At the same time, segregation and other security measures have led to a process of displacement. Hooligans have increasingly relocated their fighting away from football grounds to new locales, such as in city centres and at railway stations. Early containment strategies also failed to prevent train vandalism and the occasional looting of shops (Van der Brug, 1994: 177).

A number of serious incidents in the second half of the 1990s show that football hooliganism in the Netherlands has far from disappeared. On 16 May 1996, Feyenoord and PSV Eindhoven hooligans fought in Rotterdam forcing police officers to fire warning shots. After a match between FC Utrecht and Feyenoord, on 26 October 1996, rival hooligans pelted each other and the police with stones. Seven police officers were injured. On 17 May 1998 hooligans of Ajax, PSV and Feyenoord fought before and during the Cup Final between Ajax and PSV in Rotterdam. The celebration of Feyenoord's national championship, on 25 April 1999, escalated into a prolonged riot in which four fans were injured by police bullets. Moreover, during this period the rivalry between Ajax and Feyenoord hooligans escalated (see Chapter Six). On 16 February 1997 the two rival hooligan formations pre-arranged a fight near the A10 highway. The confrontation never fully materialized because the Ajax hooligans retreated after observing the larger, heavily armed group of Feyenoord hooligans. Renewed encounter between the rival formations took place five weeks later, on 23 March 1997, although on this occasion there had been no prior agreement between the two groups. During the fight a 35-year-old Ajax supporter died after being stabbed and beaten with various objects.

The statistics compiled by the CIV support the idea that Dutch football hooliganism has far from disappeared. Table 3.4 shows that the total amount of football-related arrests has not changed markedly during the three previous seasons, but is significantly higher than in the 2000/01 season (a 58% increase in the 2001/02 season). Considering the arrest rates in the 1998/99 and 1999/2000 seasons (1546 and 1550, respectively), it seems that the comparatively low level of arrests in the 2000/01 season is an exception rather than an indication of earlier arrest rates. In general, recent arrest rates are higher than those in the late 1980s, when the CIV first began to record the number of arrests at football matches (1021 arrests in the 1988/89 season and 950 in 1989/90), but comparable to those in the mid-1990s (with the exception of the 1994/95 season, with a total of 1933 arrests). It is extremely difficult to assess the precise meanings of these fluctuations in the number of football-related arrests, since they may be indicative of changes in police strategies and registration capacities rather than of changes in the extent of spectator violence at football matches. The CIV acknowledges this issue, 'it is impossible to draw conclusions with regard to the increase or decline of football hooliganism on the basis of the number of arrests' (2003: 23). Moreover, the arrest rates do not distinguish between different types of offences and therefore tell us little about the extent and development of specific forms of spectator disorderliness, notably football hooliganism.

Table 3.4   Football-related arrests in the Netherlands, 2000/01 to 2003/04 seasons.*

Season	Number of arrests
2000/01	1,193
2001/02	1,887
2002/03	1,647
2003/04	1,837

Source: CIV, 2001; 2002; 2003; 2004.

Note: *Includes arrests at league, cup, European Cup and friendly matches as well as international fixtures.

The statistics on football-related 'incidents' listed in Table 3.5 exhibit similar pitfalls. The CIV (2003: 11) defines an incident as 'an event requiring additional police deployment whereby the behaviour of a group of supporters aims at the following: (a) seeking a confrontation or; (b) causing damage or; (c) committing public violence or; (d) making discriminatory remarks or; (e) violent behaviour by supporters directed at the police and club security personnel (e.g. stewards).' This broad definition obstructs more specific analysis of the development of football hooliganism, since it includes both physical and verbal offences and does not distinguish between different types of violence (i.e. fighting, damage to property, missile throwing).

Table 3.5   Recorded incidents at professional football matches in the Netherlands, 2001/02 to 2003/04 seasons.*

Season	Number of incidents
2001/02	117
2002/03	96
2003/04	98

Source: data provided by CIV.

Note: *The CIV first began to record 'incidents' in the 2001/02 season. There are no figures available for the 2000/01 season.

Table 3.6 gives a more detailed overview of the main types of football-related offences in the Netherlands. The three most common types of offences are public disorder (41%), violation of General Municipal Bylaws (11%) and disregarding an order (7%). However, in an earlier section of this chapter I have argued that it is not possible to draw any conclusions regarding the development of football hooliganism on the basis of these statistics.

Table 3.6   Main types of football-related offences in the Netherlands, 2001/02 to 2003/04 seasons.

Type of offence	Number of arrests			
	2001/02	2002/03	2003/04	% of total
Public disorder	729	545	910	41%
Violation of General Municipal Bylaws	218	147	250	11%
Disregarding an order	148	134	79	7%
Insulting public official	78	121	83	5%
Rowdy behaviour	101	92	71	5%
Violation of ID Act	150	84	32	5%
Vandalism	39	78	25	3%

Source: Adapted from CIV, 2002; 2003 and 2004.

Recent academic studies have asserted that contemporary football hooliganism in the Netherlands is more complex and less surveyable and predictable than in the past (COT, 1999: 23; Spaaij, 2001: 31). Within this general development a number of major patterns can be distinguished. First, as we have seen, physical confrontations between rival fan groups inside football stadia have become relatively uncommon from the 1980s onwards, even though spectator violence in and around Dutch football grounds has far from disappeared. Hooligan confrontations occasionally take place within football grounds. Small-scale disorder inside football stadia is comparatively common, including damage to property and assaults on stewards. In this context, Adang (1998: 32) has made the important point that:

> Violence or the damage that results from it outside grounds is valued differently. Inside the ground violence is often less threatening and risky (apart from the use of bombs) than outside, because inside the stadium opposing supporters are always separated by fences. Moreover, they are searched before they enter the ground.

Instead of effectively reducing the extent and seriousness of football hooliganism, containment policies have had the unintended consequence of displacing hooligan confrontations to new locales. Hooligan formations may go to great lengths to escape police observation and to confront their rivals at unexpected times and locations. They occasionally seek to circumvent compulsory travel arrangements by arriving in the city where the match is played on the night before the match, or by turning up as a 'third party' at football matches which do not involve their own team. The CIV and some journalists have recently suggested that this type of circumvention is on the increase (CIV, 2004; *De Gelderlander*, 23 February 2005; *Eindhovens Dagblad*, 26 February 2005). One newspaper claimed that 'the risk of a second Beverwijk is growing rapidly' and that 'the relative quietness in and around football grounds is only an appearance' (*BN De Stem*, 1 March 2005). From the late 1990s onwards, hooligan groups also began to increasingly confront each other at pre-season or mid-season friendlies, occasionally involving temporary (transnational) inter-group alliances. For example, FC Twente supporters fought a joint combination of Club Bruges and ADO Den Haag hooligans in August 1999. In January 2002, NAC hooligans were attacked by a coalition of FC Groningen and the Belgian Germinal Beerschot supporters. Another site of contestation is the local nightlife and the major dance events organized throughout the country. Rival hooligans have occasionally confronted each other at such venues, for example at Dance Valley in 2004 (*De Volkskrant*, 23 August 2004; *Haagsche Courant*, 2 March 2005).

A more general feature underlying these specific developments is the growing level of planning and co-ordination involved in Dutch football hooliganism. In response to constrictive official controls, several hooligan formations have become more co-ordinated and calculating in confronting their opponents and escaping police observation. They manage instrumental communication with some rival groups, for example in negotiating the conditions of pre-arranged confrontation in terms of location, time and informal codes of legitimate action. These confrontations often take the form of 'hit-and-run' fights, that is, brief but serious disorder after which both groups disperse to avoid apprehension. This development closely resembles contemporary hooligan encounters in England, as I have shown earlier in this chapter.

Hooligan violence may also be directed at the police or security staff, ranging from individual assaults to collective confrontation. Some Dutch hooligan groups view the police as a legitimate opponent (Van der Torre and Spaaij, 2003b: 31; Ferwerda and Gelissen, 2001: 92-93). The CIV observed a polarization in the relations between police officers and hooligan formations from the early 1990s onwards. Police officers considered their influence on hooligans to be declining and, to avoid further endangerment, they were increasingly substituted by riot police on match days (CIV, 1991). In recent years, hooligans have occasionally attacked police officers and riot police en masse. The most widely reported incident of hooligan violence against the police took place after a match between Feyenoord and Ajax, on 17 April 2005. Hundreds of Feyenoord supporters attacked riot police officers and pelted them with stones and bottles, injuring 42 officers. In the aftermath of the incident the police displayed photographs of suspected Feyenoord fans on television and the Internet.

The features and developments described in this section indicate that the extent and forms of Dutch football hooliganism have altered considerably over time. The phenomenon was initially limited to a small number of fan groups, but through an ongoing process of national diffusion the hooligan subculture gradually spread across the country. Although football hooliganism has gradually become somewhat less visible and the number of regular participants has somewhat decreased, hooligan confrontations have also become more co-ordinated and planned as police and club controls tightened. I will now examine the origins and development of football hooliganism in Spain.

Ultras, hooligans and supporters: politics and violence in Spanish football

The emergence of youth ends in Spanish football occurred significantly later than in England and the Netherlands. This delay seems to be closely related to the specific political and cultural developments in twentieth-century Spain, most notably the military dictatorship from 1939 to 1975. The relative isolation, restricted media coverage and firm repression during the Franco regime appear to have delayed the diffusion of foreign youth subcultural styles. From the mid-1970s onwards, Spanish football culture increasingly opened up to foreign cultural influences. The growing access to these foreign influences was particularly visible in the styles and tastes of the newly emerging youth groups. Young fans had traditionally been only marginally represented in Spanish football stadia. The official fan clubs characteristic of Spanish football culture, so-called *peñas*, consisted principally of older supporters. In the second half of the 1970s, young supporters began to increasingly distance themselves from the more traditional forms of football fandom in Spain, claiming that most *peñas* benefited from the club without actively supporting it. Many young fans preferred to increase their visibility and create a more passionate atmosphere within the ground, using as reference models the Italian and British supporter styles. Their demand for a more prestigious fan model coincided with clubs' desperate attempts to attract more young supporters and to rejuvenate their crowds. Football attendances were declining due to the sport's Francoist image, and the average age of those attending football matches was increasing (Acosta and Rodríguez, 1989). Football clubs viewed the youths as an important new source of support and facilitated them free or reduced-price tickets, travel to away matches and (money for) material such as flags and drums.

Many of the newly emerging youth groups were initially embedded in traditional *peñas*. Some of these fan groups held a reputation for their visual and vocal support, including large banners and drums. As the number of young participants in these groups increased, differences in the behaviour and tastes of young fans and older group members became more manifest. At several football clubs groups of young fans, who were now in the majority, abandoned their *peñas*, while at some clubs they were expelled after accusations of aggressive or violent behaviour. The process of segregation by age resulted, in the early 1980s, in the emergence of the first self-identifying ultra groups with their exclusive territory within the ground to the exclusion of the older football citizenry. These groups were strongly influenced by their Italian and British peers whom they considered to be more prestigious than the traditional *peñas* (Spaaij and Viñas, 2005).

Crucial to the diffusion of the hooligan and ultra subcultures were the interactions between Spanish supporters and prestigious British and Italian fan groups. Young members of the Real Madrid fan club Las Banderas directly observed the behaviour of West Ham United fans during a European Cup Winners Cup tie in 1980, as was later recounted in the fanzine published by the ultra group Ultras Sur:

We had the opportunity to see one of the most violent fan groups in the world. [...] Can you imagine what the future ultras thought when observing these masses enter our stadium? There were no confrontations between both fan groups because the truth is we wouldn't have had the slightest chance. Once inside our stadium, the hooligans [...] destroyed everything they could. [...] The young Real Madrid fans decided to end the shame of being attacked in our own stadium. Never again! (*En el fondo hay sitio*, vol. 1, no. 5, 1991: 3)

In the following year, a group of young Real Madrid fans interacted with ultras of Inter Milan on the occasion of a European Cup match between the two clubs: 'We spent the night talking about football, hooliganism and the organization of ultra groups with these experienced Italian ultras, and we decided to denominate ourselves exactly that: ultras' (ibid.: 5). These contacts inspired the young fans to create the ultra group Ultras Sur after they were expelled from their *peña*, due to their alleged involvement in incidents of vandalism and physical violence.

In addition to inter-group interactions during European club competitions and friendly matches, two other factors had a decisive impact on the diffusion of Italian and British supporter styles. Growing television coverage of foreign football competitions led to an increased awareness among Spanish youths of the differences between indigenous and foreign styles of football fandom. Media coverage of foreign manifestations of football hooliganism had a similar effect. In the aftermath of the Heysel disaster the Spanish media began to report more frequently on incidents of football hooliganism in Western Europe. It has been argued that although the frequency of spectator violence at football matches in Spain started to increase around this period, the media treatment these incidents received was 'disproportionate' and 'much higher than its real extent' (Castro Moral, 1986: 38; Durán González, 1995: 308). At the same time, the Heysel disaster constituted a landmark for young Spanish fans identifying with the hooligan subculture. References to Heysel in the graffiti and chants of Spanish ultra groups were commonplace (e.g. Acosta and Rodríguez, 1989). A second factor that enhanced the emergence of militant fan groups in Spanish football was the 1982 World Cup in Spain. The event facilitated young supporters to directly experience the styles and behaviour of prestigious foreign fan groups, notably Italian, English and Scottish supporters (Spaaij and Viñas, 2005: 82). In the aftermath of the tournament, the number of ultra groups in Spanish football multiplied and the already established youth groups began to develop their activities more seriously.

A similar process of imitation was central to the subsequent diffusion of the hooligan and ultra subcultures across Spain (Durán González, 1995: 192). The pioneering militant fan groups Ultras Sur and Boixos Nois played a major role in the national diffusion of the new fan models. Both groups functioned as a yardstick by which the newly emerging fan groups measured their own activities. By the mid-1980s, almost every First and Second Division club fostered a radical fan group on its terraces (Spaaij and Viñas, 2005: 84-85). The songs, rituals and symbols of the most prestigious foreign and Spanish groups were copied by the new fan groups and were perceived as status symbols. The fanzine *Revista Ultras*, launched in 1985, facilitated contacts between Spanish ultras throughout the country and regularly published reports on developments in foreign football cultures, most notably those in Italy and Britain.

The Spanish ultra subculture emerged in a period of rapid political, social and cultural transformations. Spain's transition to democracy was characterized by processes of de-ideologization and de-politicization and an attendant diminishing of social mobilizations, while a prolonged economic crisis particularly affected working-class youths. The ultra subculture functioned as a site for cultural and political contestation, as a symbolic attempt by young fans to create a space and identity of their own in a changing society (Acosta and Rodríguez, 1989; Adán Revilla, 2004: 99-100). Characteristic of the early stage of the Spanish ultra subculture was the spontaneous and unorganized nature of the fan groups and the colourful atmosphere inside the stadia, including large banners and flags and pyrotechnical elements (smoke bombs, flares). Despite the elements of formal organization among certain militant fan groups, in terms of official membership and recruitment campaigns, the practical organization of the groups was very limited. The groups generally consisted of numerous small subgroups with heterogeneous attitudes towards the use of violence and politics. Most group members met only on match days in their specific section of the ground. Informal leadership was primarily based on *fama* and *notoriedad*, that is, on reputation for toughness.

From the start various political tendencies existed among the militant fan groups, closely reflecting the deep-seated regional and national identities in Spanish football and society at large (see Fernández Santander, 1990; Shaw, 1987; García Candau, 1996; Unzueta, 1999). Most Basque, Catalan and Galician fan groups identified with left-wing pro-independence, notably Boixos Nois and Herri Norte Taldea (Athletic Bilbao). Groups such as Madrid-based Ultras Sur and Frente Atlético (Atlético Madrid) associated with centralist and right-wing ideology. At this point often heterogeneous and flexible, these political tendencies would intensify and distort with the passing of time, transforming into a key feature of the hooligan and ultra subcultures in Spain (Spaaij and Viñas, 2005: 84). Political oppositions gradually came to dominate inter-group rivalries.

The emergence and development of Spanish football hooliganism

The emergence of socially organized groups of young fans with their own tastes and practices had a noticeable impact on the frequency of inter-fan fighting at football matches in Spain. In the early 1980s the reported incidence of inter-fan fighting was quantitatively low but on the increase, from 6 incidents between 1975 and 1981 to 23 incidents between 1982 and 1985 (Castro Moral, 1986). This increase was closely related to the emerging network of inter-group rivalry and violence (García Ferrando, 1990). From 1985 the frequency of fighting between rival fan groups increased more rapidly (Viñas, 2005: 249-253). During this period football hooliganism in Spain also came to be defined, for the first time, as a disturbing social problem. The growing official and public concern over football hooliganism was triggered by both international developments (e.g. the Heysel disaster) and incidents provoked by affiliates of domestic fan groups. Furthermore, the inter-group hostilities that were established in football were reproduced, albeit to a far lesser extent, in other sports (Spaaij and Viñas, 2005: 85). The attendance of members of Ultras Sur and Boixos Nois at their clubs' other sporting teams (i.e. basketball and handball) played a key role in the diffusion of inter-group rivalries. These rivalries were occasionally performed through violent confrontation. For example, during a basketball match between Real Madrid and local rival Estudiantes in the 1986/87 season, affiliates of Ultras Sur assaulted members of the opposing fan group Demencia.

The increase in the extent and seriousness of football hooliganism in the second half of the 1980s was closely related to the changing collective identity and territorial identifications of the ultras. As the notoriety of the fan groups extended, more and more young fans began to identify with them, either officially or as non-members. The ultras' sections of the ground (*grada* or *curva*) were increasingly viewed as contested territory and growing numbers of young supporters began to take pride in defending their home territory and 'running' their rivals. Many young fans sought to establish individual and collective reputations for toughness in the football context. Violence directed at opposing groups was increasingly perceived as legitimate. Many militant fan groups also viewed it as justifiable 'self defence' against allegedly disproportionate or aggressive police methods. Crucially, similar to the English youth ends and Dutch sides, only a minor part of the ultras regularly participate in violent confrontation. A survey by Adán Revilla (2004: 95) among members of Frente Atlético found that 33 per cent of the ultras had never been involved in inter-fan fighting, and a further 38 per cent had participated only once.

Early hooligan rivalries in Spanish football were mainly local and regional. Hostilities between opposing hooligan formations were particularly fierce in two-club or multi-club cities such as Seville, Barcelona and Madrid (for an overview, see Spaaij and Viñas, 2005; Viñas, 2005). These hostilities tended to reflect deep-seated local football rivalries and were enhanced by the relatively frequent contacts between members of opposing groups, in the football context as well as in everyday life. In this context, it is important to note that the frequency of encounters between hooligan formations located in different parts of the country has generally been comparatively low due to long travel distances and the amounts of time and money that need to be invested in attending away matches in remote areas, especially since most matches are played on Sunday afternoons or on weekdays. Apart from local and regional derbies and high-profile matches (e.g. a cup final or a European Cup match), the number of visiting supporters and hooligans is usually comparatively small. Recent figures show that the number of ultras travelling to away matches is gradually declining, with the exception of local and regional derbies and high-profile matches (Comisión Nacional contra la Violencia en Espectáculos Deportivos, 2004: 12; Viñas, 2005: 185-186).

In addition to changes in the collective identity and territorial identifications of the ultras, the escalation of Spanish football hooliganism was also closely related to two other developments: the emergence of the skinhead subculture and the politicization of the ultra subculture. The skinhead subculture became an influential youth style on the terraces of several Spanish football grounds from the mid-1980s onwards, co-existing with and gradually replacing subcultural styles such as the mods and heavies. The skinheads added to the fan groups a common style and uniform and an enhanced sense of collective identity celebrating aggressive masculinity and physical prowess, similar to the situation in England in the second half of the 1960s. The homogenization of the style and uniform of the ultras coincided with the expansion of radical political ideologies and symbology among the militant fan groups, which increasingly became major symbols of group identity. Many fan groups began to identify explicitly with either neo-fascism and National Socialism or with communism and left-wing pro-independence. In reaction to the rise of right-wing skinhead groups, the Skinheads Against Racial Prejudice (SHARP) movement sought to challenge the stigmatization of the skinheads as racists and fascists. SHARP was represented on the terraces of several Spanish football grounds, primarily those in the Basque Country, Galicia, Catalonia and parts of Andalusia.

The politicization of the ultras tends to take place by osmosis, through contacts with specific environments (football, music festivals), rather than as a result of ideological training or fixed and consistent political ideologies (Adán Revilla, 1998: 123; Casals, 1998: 72). As one ultra commented:

> Most ultras have no idea what left-wing or right-wing ideologies are really about. They simply want to be part of the ultra fashion, using political symbology as an excuse for engaging in racist and violent behaviour. I mean, very few ultras have actually read Marx, Stalin or Hitler. (Personal interview with a member of Brigadas Amarillas, November 2005)

The superficiality and changeability of these ideologies can be illustrated by the radical transformations that some militant fan groups have experienced, notably Boixos Nois (from left-wing to right-wing ideology) and Riazor Blues (Deportivo La Coruña) (from right-wing to left-wing ideology) (Spaaij and Viñas, 2005: 86-87). While punctual connections with the far right in Spain exist, the right-wing extremism of certain ultra groups is primarily located in the periphery of official politics and has been referred to as 'lumpenpolitics' (Casals, 1995: 269). Right-wing and left-wing symbologies have in common that they both function as a means for the construction of self and the other and for the provocation of 'outsiders'. For many ultras, they are constituent elements of their search for identity, adventure and prestige among peers.

The politicization of the ultra subculture resulted in an escalation of the conflict between politically opposed fan groups. In addition to violent confrontations between rival hooligan formations, other types of violence provoked by ultras also increased significantly from the late 1980s onwards, such as attacks on members of other youth subcultures (i.e. punks), ethnic minorities, homosexuals or transvestites (Pallarés et al., 2000: 104). A number of high-profile incidents in the early 1990s heightened official and public concern over the behaviour of the ultras and skinheads, condemning their violent behaviour as 'senseless' (*violencia gratuita*) (see Spaaij and Viñas, 2006: 147). The transformation of the ultra subculture also affected young fans' self-categorizations and, in particular, the meanings of the ultra label. At present, several militant fan groups reject the use of the term 'ultra': 'We are radical, we are violent, we are hooligans, but we are not ultras' (personal interview with a member of Boixos Nois, April 2004).

In the beginning the term 'ultra', borrowed from Italian fan groups, was perceived as prestigious and as a way to distinguish the most loyal and vociferous supporters from 'regular', older fans. From the late 1980s onwards, 'ultra' increasingly came to be popularly viewed as a synonym for *ultraderecha* (right-wing), even though many of the individuals and collectivities naming themselves as such did not share this ideology. During this period certain militant fan groups began to position themselves as 'anti-ultras' in order to distinguish themselves from 'those who merely use football as a platform for fascist organizations' (*Torcida Antifeixista*, vol. 5, no. 4, 1995: 12). Demographically, the anti-ultra movement is mainly supported by left-wing fan groups in the North of the country, most notably in the Basque Country, Galicia and Catalonia. The attitudes of the anti-ultras, and of anti-fascist fan groups in general, towards racial abuse are diametrically opposed to those of their right-wing counterparts, even though both may consider the use of violence in inter-group rivalry as legitimate.

The politicization of the ultra groups fundamentally altered the national network of inter-group rivalries and allegiances. Political antagonism was commonly expressed in dichotomous categories (separatism versus anti-separatism, communism versus neo-fascism or left-wing versus right-wing) generating new forms of inter-group conflict and aggravating traditional inter-group rivalries. At the same time, the process of politicization also stimulated identification and co-operation between like-minded fan groups. Shared identification with either left-wing or right-wing extremism enables punctual or more permanent contacts between members of different groups and the temporal suspension of inter-group conflict. In the Basque Country, Catalonia and Galicia, anti-fascist fan groups are united in the collectivities Euskal Hintxak, Escamots Catalans and Segadors, and Siareiros Galegos, respectively (Viñas, 2004: 119-120).

Tackling football hooliganism: the development and effects of governmental and club policies

Football hooliganism was long perceived by the Spanish authorities and media as principally a foreign problem. The 1985 Heysel disaster was interpreted by journalists as evidence of the seriousness of the 'English disease' in other Western European countries (Viñas 2005: 42), but also seems to have triggered growing media focus on the behaviour of domestic fan groups. Following Spain's ratification of the European Convention on Spectator Violence and Misbehaviour at Sports Events, in 1987, the government adopted a series of measures aimed at containing spectator violence in the realm of sport, and football in particular. This development was principally a response to the growing official and public concern over the behaviour of the ultras. In 1988 the Senate set up a special commission of inquiry to study the extent and nature of spectator violence in sports and to propose countermeasures, drawing on experiences in other Western European countries

113

(Senado, 1990). Several measures proposed by the European Convention and the commission of inquiry were included in 1990 Ley del Deporte (Sports Law). The Royal Decree 75/92 instated in 1992 regulated the creation of the Comisión Nacional contra la Violencia en Espectáculos Deportivos (National Commission against Violence at Sports Events). The commission's core activities include the analysis of incidents of spectator violence and the proposing of punishments. In addition, the Royal Decree 769/93 regulated the responsibilities of organizers of sports events and, specifically, the function of the security co-ordinator at football clubs. Spain also signed police co-operation agreements with various member states of the European Union in order to improve the monitoring and control of the movements of football fans between these countries (Council of Europe, 1998).

The expansion of security and safety regulations had a profound impact on the socio-spatial environment of Spanish football grounds: home and visiting supporters were segregated, high perimeter fences and netting were erected to prevent pitch invasions and missile throwing, control rooms and CCTV systems were installed within the ground, and the number of police officers and security staff at football matches increased considerably. Police surveillance was also operative outside the ground. Visiting fan groups were often escorted to and from the ground, and the police began to exchange pre-match intelligence on the potential security risks of particular matches and fan groups. In recent years, most grounds have witnessed the removal of high perimeter fences and a decrease in the average number of police officers inside the stadium, as the police were increasingly substituted by private security personnel contracted by the clubs. The police, security staff and stewards pay special attention to the interdiction of various objects, such as racist and neo-Nazi symbology (i.e. on flags, banners or clothing), weapons, alcoholic beverages and *bengalas* (flares). The official concern over, and prohibition of, flares was closely related to two tragic incidents. In 1985 a spectator died after being hit by a rocket flare during a match between Cádiz CF and Castellón. Seven years later, in 1992, a thirteen-year-old boy was mortally wounded by a maritime flare launched from the opposite stand during a match between Espanyol and Cádiz. Although on both occasions the perpetrators were not ultras but 'regular' supporters, the incidents enhanced the official and public concern over the behaviour of the ultras.

The prohibition of flares is viewed by many ultras as but one example of the stigmatization and criminalization of young football fans. They feel that the ever-expanding range of security measures has a profoundly negative influence on their match-day experience (although some degree of police presence is generally viewed as necessary; see Adán, 2004). The conversion of football grounds into all-seater stadia, in accordance with UEFA regulations, is seen as particularly disturbing because it seriously diminishes the opportunities for free movement on the terraces and the organization of large choreographed displays. The ultras have regularly used national fanzines such as *Super Hincha* and *El Jugador No. 12* as platforms for protest against alleged state repression and criminalization. They argue that the authorities indiscriminately equate the entire ultra subculture with football hooliganism, even though in reality only a small minority of ultras regularly participates in violent confrontations. As one ultra put it:

On the terraces there are all sorts of people, normal and abnormal people, but this reflects the society in which we live. There is violence, there is intolerance, but that doesn't mean that there doesn't exist passion and solidarity as well. The terraces are a mirror of society and to describe us as cages of violence is the most absurd thing one can do. [...] We are not the devils of society. We are like the rest of the youth (*El Jugador No. 12*, no. 24, May 2000: 20).

The ultras also tend to stress their important social, cultural and economic functions in Spanish football culture: 'Without ultras, the football grounds are like theatres or cinemas, where people go, applaud and return to their homes without sentiment. If it wasn't for the ultras, [football] wouldn't move millions of people' (*Super Hincha*, vol. 8, no. 85, December 2000: 10).

The alleged positive functions of ultra groups have traditionally been appreciated by football clubs. They welcomed the groups' vocal and colourful support and their potential for intimidating referees or players of the opposing team. Many clubs facilitated members of the militant fan groups free or reduced price tickets, an exclusive territory within the ground, travel to away matches, and office or storage space within the premises of the stadium. These facilities played a major role in the expansion of the ultra groups, enabling them to recruit new members and organize their activities and choreographed displays more extensively (Durán González, 1996: 93-102). Due to the escalation of football hooliganism at various Spanish clubs in the late 1980s and the attendant moral panic over the behaviour of the ultras, most clubs have gradually become less willing to be publicly associated with the militant fan groups. Some clubs attempted to decrease the power of the ultra groups by ceasing their support to the groups or by banning the most persistent offenders. But although club directors tend to publicly condemn incidents provoked by members of the ultra groups and commonly deny accusations of facilitation, at several clubs one or more types of facilitation have simply continued, for example at Real Madrid, Atlético Madrid and FC Barcelona (Viñas, 2005: 179-181). At the same time, the clubs have sought to contain hooligan violence inside the stadium by professionalizing their security regimes and crowd management. In the 1990s some clubs tried to strengthen their control over the ultra groups by legalizing them into official *peñas*. Thus, while the National Commission has repeatedly stressed the urgent necessity for clubs to give no direct or indirect support to groups which do not have a formal status (Council of Europe, 1998), many of the most violent fan groups are now official fan clubs. The involvement of some of their members in violent incidents has nevertheless continued.

The extent and nature of contemporary football hooliganism in Spain

Recent journalistic and police accounts of the violent proclivities of certain ultra groups suggest that football hooliganism in Spain has far from disappeared (Salas, 2003; Madrid, 2005; Ibarra, 2003; Seara Ruiz and Sedano Jiménez, 2001). These accounts contrast to a large extent with the findings of a Council of Europe report published in 1998. The report concluded that Spanish football culture no longer contains large-scale hooliganism, as opposed to the late 1980s and early 1990s. 'The preventative and the control measures applied in the past few years, while not eradicating the problem, have certainly brought it within manageable proportions. Outbreaks of spectator violence are now rare' (Council of Europe, 1998: 39). The data collected by the National Commission give a more ambiguous picture. Table 3.7 shows that the number of ejections at football matches has increased significantly in the early 2000s (from 264 in the 2000/01 season, to 521 in 2002/03; only in the 2003/04 season the number of ejections decreased slightly to 497). The number of arrests has remained relatively stable, with the exception of an eighteen per cent increase in the 2002/03 season and a comparable decline in the following season.

Table 3.7   Football-related arrests and ejections in Spain, 2000/01 to 2003/04 seasons.*

Season	Number of arrests	Number of ejections
2000/01	54	264
2001/02	55	373
2002/03	65	521
2003/04	53	497

Source: Data provided by the Comisión Nacional contra la Violencia en Espectáculos Deportivos.
Note: *Includes league, cup and European Cup matches. Excludes friendly matches and international fixtures.

To give a more detailed overview, Table 3.8 lists the main types of football-related offences leading to arrest or ejection. The three most common types of offences are public disorder (29%), abuse or assault of a police officer or security staff (17%), and the possession or use of fireworks (12%). The arrest statistics do not provide a clear and reliable picture of the frequency of spectator violence and, even less so, of the extent and development of football hooliganism. For example, the sudden increase in the number of arrests for drug offences seems to be principally related to growing police attention for this type of offence rather than to rapid changes in the frequency of drug consumption among supporters.

Recent studies of football hooliganism in Spain point to important transformations in the ultra subculture from mid-1990s onwards and an attendant decline in the frequency of hooligan confrontations (Spaaij and Viñas, 2005; Viñas, 2005; Adán Revilla, 2004). The combination of intense politicization, escalation of inter-group violence and growing police repression activated a process of fragmentation and polarization. This process contained a number of aspects. First, political antagonisms not only enhanced inter-group conflict but also conflict within militant fan groups and between fan groups of the same club. At several Spanish football clubs small cores of fans separated themselves from the main group and displaced their activities to different sections of the ground, as a way of conflict de-escalation.

Table 3.8   Main types of football-related offences in Spain, 2001/02 to 2003/04 seasons.

Type of offence	Number of arrests and ejections			
	2001/02	2002/03	2003/04	% of total
Public disorder	149	141	170	29%
Abuse or assault of police or security staff	81	116	75	17%
Possession or use of fireworks	70	61	52	12%
Missile throwing	26	75	40	9%
Alcohol offences	17	37	51	7%
Damage of property	26	34	14	5%
Drug offences	0	21	104	8%

Source: Data provided by the Comisión Nacional contra la Violencia en Espectáculos Deportivos.
Note: The figures for 2000/01 are based on the commission's annual report. For reasons unknown to the author, they do not correspond completely with those mentioned in later evaluations and reports.

Second, groups of young supporters began to contest the politicized nature of the ultra subculture. They argued that pseudo-ideologies destroyed the original ultra spirit and divided the groups internally, producing a destructive situation: 'If someone is interested in political causes it is fair to acknowledge those causes, but not in football stadia. What have Hitler or Stalin done for our clubs? Nothing' (*Super Hincha*, vol. 3, no. 19, March 1995: 8). The key aim of these groups is to return to the art of innovative choreographed displays, without the politics and violence that have come to dominate the ultra subculture. This fan model is particularly attractive to those young fans who previously looked upon the ultra groups as too radical and aggressive, and it has therefore played a major role in the attraction of new male and female fans to the game. Increased (feelings of) safety within most Spanish football grounds has also contributed to this development (Adán Revilla, 2004: 96; Spaaij and Viñas, 2005: 90).

Physical confrontations between opposing hooligan formations are currently less common than in the late 1980s and early 1990s. Constrictive controls and surveillance limit the opportunities for hooligan encounters in and around football grounds. Fighting is more likely to occur away from the ground, usually in the vicinity of the stadium, but growing police surveillance has gradually diminished the opportunities for large-scale confrontations near the stadium. Hooligan encounters occasionally result in serious injury and death. In the last decade two supporters died as a result of fighting between rival fan groups outside the ground. On 8 December 1998, Real Sociedad supporter Aitor Zabaleta was stabbed to death by a member of Frente Atlético's section Bastión after a UEFA Cup return match between Real Sociedad and Atlético Madrid. Five years later, on 7 October 2003, at the conclusion of a cup match between Compostela and Deportivo La Coruña, Manuel Ríos Suárez, a 31-year-old affiliate of Riazor Blues, died after receiving a ferocious kick from a former Riazor Blues member while he was trying to stop a fight between rival fans.

These recent fatalities have set off a public debate on the organized nature of the hooligan formations in Spanish football. During a recent high-profile court case eleven alleged members of Bastión were recently cleared from accusations of forming an illicit organization, although eight of them were sentenced to 20 months imprisonment for public disorder (*El Mundo*, 30 November 2005). It seems that the degree of co-ordination and planning involved in hooligan encounters is generally limited. The vast majority of Spanish hooligan groups have not developed advanced strategies for escaping police observation and successfully confronting their opponents, and pre-arranged encounters are rare. In this context, it is also important to mention that the casual style is relatively unpopular among Spanish hooligans when compared to English and Dutch hooligan formations. Only a handful of small subgroups identify themselves as casuals and adopt the casual fashion, principally as a means for escaping police observation and distinguishing themselves from the more traditional ultra style. A major reason for the relative unpopularity of the casual style among Spanish hooligans is the commitment of many militant fan groups to publicly expressing political and club symbols. I will discuss this issue in more detail in Chapter Ten.

In sum, the extent and nature of Spanish football hooliganism have changed considerably over time due to transformations in the ultra and hooligan subcultures and public efforts to contain or eradicate spectator violence. Within this general pattern, a wide variety of regional and local overlaps and dissimilarities can be identified regarding the precise nature and development of ultra and hooligan subcultures, as I will show in Chapters Eight and Nine.

Conclusion

In this chapter, I have described the development of football hooliganism and anti-hooligan policies in England, the Netherlands and Spain. Official responses to football hooliganism have much in common and have grown increasingly similar due to expanding international legislation and co-operation. International monitoring of the movement of football fans is currently on the increase as a result of growing co-operation and information exchange between European Union member states. National policies targeting football hooliganism have been predominantly reactive. Early security measures included the expansion of police presence at 'high-risk' matches, the segregation of home and away fans, and tougher penalties for offenders. The arsenal of security measures has expanded rapidly over the years, resulting in increasingly constrictive forms of containment and surveillance in and around football grounds. The growing focus on spectator safety and customer services in recent years can be seen as a counter-development producing a more 'spectator-friendly' environment (i.e. the conversion to all-seater stadia and the removal of high perimeter fences).[4]

Despite these recent changes, the dominant strategies for tackling football hooliganism in each of the three countries remain predominantly repressive and techno-preventative. These strategies have been increasingly influenced by technological developments, such as the use of CCTV systems and computer databases (cf. Frosdick and Marsh, 2005: 153). Important variations occur in the precise nature of these strategies. Constrictive membership schemes and travel regulations are part and parcel of the Dutch approach. In England, the Football Disorder Act introduced in 2000 enables the police to prevent suspected, not previously convicted supporters from travelling abroad, something which is not (yet) legal in the Netherlands and Spain. There are also variations in the extent and nature of intelligence-led policing. Investments in 'football intelligence' have been less systematic in Spain. Police officers at football matches in Spain tend to operate in a more *ad hoc* manner (on-the-spot de-escalation and dispersal of offenders), whereas in the Netherlands and England the policing of football matches is generally more related to making arrests and issuing banning orders. These different strategies are reflected in arrest statistics, which reveal the comparatively low level of arrests at football matches in Spain. I will show in the remainder of this book that significant local and intra-city variations in the policing of football also occur.

A final pattern of dissimilarity that should be mentioned here relates to the status of social prevention in policies targeting football hooliganism. Social prevention projects in Dutch football have been comparatively common since the late 1980s, but these programmes have never obtained the same political priority as knee-jerk law-and-order responses. The emergence of fan projects should be understood within the context of a wider tradition of youth prevention projects in the Netherlands. In Spain and England there are no fan projects specifically targeting football hooliganism. Most English football clubs have established community schemes aimed at strengthening the ties between clubs and their local communities and attracting local youths to the game. Although contemporary football community schemes in England do not tend to focus on the issue of hooliganism, several schemes were originally launched, in the 1970s, as a countermeasure to football hooliganism with the idea of involving young people in a variety of football-related activities. A number of English football clubs have also launched anti-racism campaigns as a means for promoting tolerance and multiculture in football, but these projects do not specifically target football hooliganism Social prevention schemes are comparatively uncommon in Spanish football. The first local fan project started in 2004 in Càdiz and primarily targets racism and xenophobia rather than hooliganism (see Spaaij and Viñas, 2006). A major reason for the relative lack of fan projects in Spain seems to be the authorities' historical reliance on repression, notably during the Franco regime. Although some changes were observed in some contexts, the transformation of Spanish police forces occurred at a relatively slow pace during the transition to democracy, retaining, for a while, most of its pre-democracy ethos (Jaime-Jiménez and Reinares, 1998: 184-186).

In this chapter, I have shown that in addition to cross-national overlaps and dissimilarities in policies targeting football hooliganism, important variations can be observed in the extent and nature of football hooliganism itself. These variations are discussed in more detail in Chapter Ten. In the following chapters I will examine the local manifestations of football hooliganism in London, Rotterdam and Barcelona.

4

'Them Were the Days': The Past and Present of Football Hooliganism at West Ham United

Introduction

The East End of London has a deep-seated image of deviance, deprivation and violence. Within this historical context, it is perhaps unsurprising that the contemporary hooligan formation at West Ham United holds such a widespread reputation for toughness and determination, both nationally and internationally. In a recent hooligan memoir, it was argued that 'West Ham must be the most televised mob in history. [...] They had it all. The numbers, the names, the bottle and the organization. Especially the organization' (King and Knight, 1999: 100). It is because of this reputation, and its complex yet strong relation to East End culture, that the case of West Ham United is of particular interest to this study. Considering the historical embeddedness of West Ham fan culture in local working-class culture, I argue that the manifestation of football hooliganism at West Ham United should be examined within the context of the core values and historical development of the East End. Although important demographic changes have taken place in the post-war era, local cultural traditions continue to exert a strong influence on the collective identities of West Ham fans and hooligans.

This chapter first analyzes the dominant features of East End culture and their relation to fans' and hooligans' construction of collective identity. Then I will describe the emergence and development of football hooliganism at West Ham United and of official responses to the perceived threat of hooligan violence. In the final part of the chapter, I examine the changes and continuities in football hooliganism at West Ham United from the late 1980s onwards. I seek to show that the extent and forms of football hooliganism at West Ham have changed substantially over time due in part to the ever-evolving interactions between hooligans and law enforcers.

Football in the community: the local rootedness of West Ham fan culture

The symbolic meaning of West Ham United are closely related to the club's historical ties with the local community. The club was founded in the docklands of East London in 1895 as Thames Ironworks Football Club. Its founding father was Arnold Hills, the owner of Thames Ironworks and Shipbuilding Company Limited. From the beginning of his career, Hills showed a strong interest in the living conditions of the company workforce. He wished to create a fellowship between all sorts and conditions of workers and to improve the co-operation between workers and the management. Hills set up a variety of corporate facilities, notably music and sports clubs, and Thames Ironworks FC was created as a football club for company workers. In 1900 the club divorced from the parent company and took on the name West Ham United Football Club. The club maintained its close ties with the local community and came to be publicly viewed as a community club for East London. At this early stage, directors and board members shared a similar background and status; they lived in the East End, most of them in the relatively affluent area of East Ham and in Essex (Korr, 1986: 31). Their socio-economic status was well above that of the players and the vast majority of fans. Most fans and players were working-class people who cherished the community spirit of the club. According to one supporter:

> The great thing about West Ham and the East End was the community spirit. You were looked after by your neighbours. Players didn't earn very much money. Players only earned 8, 9 or 10 pounds a week. So they were really very much the same as we were and our parents were. They lived there and used to get on the bus or train to go to the ground. A lot of the players were locals. (Personal interview, December 2003)

At the time when West Ham United was founded, East London was suffering severe economic depression. The docks – historically an important source of employment for East End men, as were the railways – experienced years of economic crisis and industrial unrest, culminating in some mass strikes. Working conditions in the docklands were unhealthy, wages were inadequate, and the spirit was demoralizing.

These conditions reflected to some degree everyday life in East London. In the second half of the nineteenth century the area had to endure various depriving circumstances, such as poverty, a constant housing crisis, unsanitary conditions and a cholera epidemic that killed almost 4,000 East Enders. A study conducted in the 1880s estimated that 35 per cent of the East Enders were living below the poverty line (Booth, 1902). The pressures of unprecedented population growth, deepening economic problems, growing unemployment and the additional burdens on an already inadequate housing stock saw an increasing unrest among East Londoners.

The East End's 'unparalleled image of filth and depravity' was constructed in relation to the increasingly affluent and prosperous City of London (Hobbs, 1988: 102). The more prosperous and 'civilized' City of London looked upon East London with disdain. The latter's working-class culture, cheap housing, foul-stinking prime and diverse opportunities for both legal and criminal work made the area a focus of various moral panics (O'Neill, 2002: xix). The East End was in many ways perceived as the 'embodiment of evil'. The Jack the Ripper murders in 1888 served to compound to the East End's deviant image: 'it confirmed the reputation of its occupants and reinforced the image of the area as a dangerous and parasitical "no-go" area, inhabited by individuals ill-equipped for productive enterprise within the normative order' (Hobbs, 1988: 108). At the same time, the East End was notorious for its organized protest and its close-knit nature. Outsiders, including police, were often treated with suspicion by the local working-class population. The area has been systematically portrayed as a power base for fascism and racism (White, 2002: 126-127). In similar ways, West Ham supporters have been repeatedly accused of collective racism, especially in the late 1970s and early 1980s (cf. Dunning et al., 1988: 182; Garland and Rowe, 2001). One journalist claimed that, by the late 1970s, Nazi emblems and copies of the National Front's fanzine *Bulldog* had 'become part of Hammers' machismo' (*Sunday Times Magazine*, 20 September 1981).

Life in the East End: continuity and change

The East End was a place with an entrenched social order and class solidarity, something which is often lost in the image of hardship and 'nastiness'. People's poverty was 'accompanied by a sense of family, community and class solidarity, by a generosity towards others like themselves, by a wide range of attachments, by pride in themselves, their community and their country and by an overflowing vitality' (Young and Willmott, 1992: xv). East London was characterized by a typical Cockney, a sense of humour and a vibrancy in the community which are still remembered with great fondness by those who lived there (O'Neill, 2000: 75).[1] At the same time, crime was crucial in the primary formation of East End culture and remains an enduring feature of life in the East End (Hobbs, 1988: 108). Balancing between legality and illegality, 'ducking and diving', is a common practice in East End life. The practice of 'ducking and diving' can be described as 'pursuing a form of resolutely autonomous, marginal entrepreneurialism in which the boundaries between legal and illegal, crime and speculative endeavour, are always ambiguously defined' (Robson, 2000: 64). This custom is more concealed and less violent than the business of the area's hardened criminals.

Some of East London's most notorious criminals seem to have possessed a sort of glamour and celebrity status, most notably the twin brothers Reginald and Ronald Kray in the 1960s. Both had been quite successful boxers and were involved in various episodes of street violence before they became 'professionals of violence'. The twins had a desperate desire to be noticed and acquired a widespread reputation for toughness. They fostered personal connections with all sections of society, from villains to show-business personalities and members of the aristocracy (Hobbs, 1988: 52). The element of glamour distinguished the Kray twins from their South London counterparts Charles and Edward Richardson: 'while the Krays were being fêted by West End celebrities and living like film stars, the Richardsons were getting on with business in their dark, mysterious, other London' (Robson, 2000: 56).

The 'business' enterprises of the Krays and Richardsons went for a long time unhindered by the police principally because they did not challenge social reality but reinforced it by conforming to behaviour traditional in entrenched urban working-class districts. Trouble, toughness, smartness, excitement, and autonomy featured prominently in the careers of both twins (Hobbs, 1988: 58; cf. Miller, 1958). More generally, it can be said that in East London there is a strong cultural connection between admired masculinity and violent response to threat. Violence is not merely glorified, it is also so closely tied to masculinity that 'aggression becomes central to the boy's notion of manhood' (Campbell, 1993: 31). Hard masculinity and autonomy (the capacity to 'look after oneself') are major virtues for many young men growing up in the East End. Within this historical context, it is perhaps unsurprising that the East End has produced both champion boxers and hardened criminals. Boxing offers determined boys the quickest way to fame and fortune; and for some, so does crime.

Apart from striking continuities in the core values of East End culture, the area has also experienced important changes in the post-war period. World War II had a profound impact on East End life. Its docks, railways and dense population made East London an attractive target for German bombers. In September 1940 German aircrafts bombed the area with daylight and nigh-time raids that left homes, docks, warehouses and factories burning. At a later stage of the war, in August 1944, West Ham's Upton Park ground was hit by a V1 flying bomb which landed on the pitch in front of the South Bank, destroying a large part of the cover at that end of the stadium (Northcutt and Shoesmith, 1997: 77-78). The post-war period was characterized by the redevelopment and modernization of the East End. With the bomb damage leaving less housing than ever available for rent, and crowded worn-out districts no longer being fit for modern living, an extensive redevelopment scheme was envisaged (White, 2002: 41). Much of the old housing was destroyed and replaced by municipal flats. By the 1950s there was an overall decline in the population of East London, with increasing numbers of families moving out of the war-ravaged East End to make their homes on the new, outlying suburban estates in the South East of England, notably in Essex (O'Neill, 2000: 273; Young and Willmott, 1992: xxiv).

The docks also underwent profound changes. In the 1960s the East and South London docks became engaged in a prolonged battle over the regeneration of the port of London. As a result of changing patterns of trade in British ports and improvements in handling techniques which reduced labour requirements, the number of registered dockworkers and associated personnel in East London declined dramatically (Hill, 1976: 1). By the end of 1981 the last remaining enclosed upstream docks ceased to be operational, and with their closure came the job devastation in port-related local trades and services (Palmer, 2000: 162-164; O'Neill, 2000: 312). The closure of the docks contributed to the erosion of the traditional way of life in the East End of London. Post-war changes in the structure and culture of East London were also closely related to the new waves of immigration into the area; at first predominantly East Pakistani (Bangladeshi from 1971) and later also people from the West Indies and the Caribbean.[2] At the start of the Twenty-first century, self-declared 'whites' were a minority in the East London boroughs of Newham and Hackney. These boroughs remain among the most deprived neighbourhoods in England (Mumford and Power, 2003: 9). At the same time, parts of East London are nowadays major sites for urban regeneration and they are gradually becoming more 'middle-class' by criteria of occupation, education and property-ownership (see Butler and Rustin, 1996).

As a result of the ongoing transformation of East London, traditional kinship networks and the strong feelings of community characteristic of East End life have become more dispersed. Defining the boundaries of the East End, where it begins and where it ends, has become an increasingly difficult task. Its Western boundary indisputably lies at the border of the City of London and its Southern boundary is the river Thames. The problem lies in defining its Eastern and Northern boundaries, neither of which can claim any distinctive physical barriers (Hobbs, 1988: 88). The East End nowadays seems to include suburban towns such as Romford, Barking and Dagenham as well as most of urbanized Essex. East London is essentially a disparate community bonded by a culture rather than by any single institution or governmental agency. Hobbs (1988: 87) has argued that this 'one-class society' locates its own boundaries in terms of subjective class definition: 'east of the City of London you are either an East Ender, a middle-class interloper, or you can afford to move sufficiently far east to join the middle classes of suburban Essex.'

How do these features of East London culture relate to the collective identity of West Ham United supporters? West Ham United is commonly viewed as a community club for East London.[3] For decades an omnipresent feature of the East End has been the attraction that football, and in particular West Ham United, has been holding for its residents (Korr, 1978: 213). For a long time the vast majority of fans lived relatively close to the ground, at walking distance or short bus distance. The post-war transformation of East London has had a significant impact on the geographical distribution of West Ham supporters. Many fans now live outside East

London, notably in the South East of England and particularly in Essex. In contrast, only a marginal part of the minority ethnic population of the East End seems to attend matches of West Ham United. A 1999 survey found that only 0.2 per cent of the season tickets holders at West Ham United defined themselves as British Asians, despite the large Asian population in East London (Sir Norman Chester Centre, 2000: 12-13). At the same time, like most major English football clubs West Ham attracts a growing proportion of middle-class fans. A 2001 survey suggested that 51 per cent of the season ticket holders at West Ham United were among the highest income categories, earning over 30,000 pounds a year (Sir Norman Chester Centre, 2002: 7).

Despite the important changes in the social composition of the club's fan base, West Ham United remains a key symbol of identity for many self-identifying East Enders. The club continues to represent an 'imagined community' (Anderson, 1983) that once was but has changed for good. This sentimental notion is well captured by one supporter:

> It's about identity. But not so much as it was because most people used to live within twenty minutes walk from the stadium. Now people are spread out right across South East England. It's identifying with something that is East End, that is rough, that is as a community. A fabled community because it doesn't exist anymore, if it ever did. Everyone worked together either in the docks, the railways or related industries. Everyone lived together. Everyone went to the match together. The part of being in a romantic part in the world which is associated with crime, poverty, but also solidarity. (Personal interview, November 2003).

In the remainder of this chapter I will relate the core values of East End culture to the manifestation of football hooliganism at West Ham United. I argue that the hooligan subculture should not be viewed as a counter-culture that is alienated from the conventional values in East End culture. Rather, West Ham hooligans seem to celebrate a heightened version of the core values of local culture. Toughness, ingroup solidarity, smartness, territoriality, excitement and autonomy all feature prominently in the collective identity and behaviour of the hooligans. In a way, the 'cool' violence of hardened criminals such as the Kray twins may have provided role models for male adolescents who moved around the fringes of the East London underworld, in that way helping in the formation of a partly older, 'street smart' backbone for the hooligan formation (Dunning et al., 1988: 169). Also, just as the Kray brothers in the 1960s, West Ham's hooligan formation possesses a sort of glamour and celebrity status. There is a variety of books, articles and films recounting the careers of the Krays and large amounts of money have been involved in this business (Pearson, 1995: 318-319). In a later section I will show that football hooliganism at West Ham United has become highly commodified.

'War on the terraces': the emergence of football hooliganism

East London has a long history of violent subcultures. Violent conduct has also been noticeable, in several forms and to varying degrees, in local football. As early as 1906, a bad tempered battle between local rivals West Ham United and Millwall FC, located in South East London (South of the Thames), spilled over into violence on and off the pitch, including fist fights between rival fans. The Football Association demanded that West Ham should post warning notices to prevent future brawls between spectators (*East Ham Echo*, 21 September 1906; Northcutt and Shoesmith, 1997: 15-16).[4] Both West Ham supporters and, to a larger extent, Millwall fans held an early reputation for intimidating match officials and opposing players and fans. In the 1920s and 1930s West Ham fans occasionally abused and attacked the referee (Pearson, 1983: 30). Visiting fans retained a healthy respect for the East and South London dockland areas where the reputation, especially of Millwall fans, had for a long time induced caution on the part of outsiders (Dunning et al., 1988: 166; cf. Robson, 2000: 27).

In the mid-1960s important changes took place in the pattern of spectator violence at West Ham United. The club's 'golden years' drew large crowds to home and away matches, including large numbers of local youths. The 1966 World Cup hosted and won by England boosted West Ham's national and international image since the England team fielded three of the club's key players: Bobby Moore, Geoff Hurst and Martin Peters. West Ham fans still refer to 1966 as 'the year West Ham won the World Cup'. Goals by Hurst (3) and Peters in the final against West

Germany inspired a local newspaper to the headlines: 'West Ham 4 West Germany 2' (*Stratford Express*, 1 July 1966). Two years earlier, the club had won its first FA Cup beating Preston North End at Wembley. In 1965, West Ham beat Munich 1860 to claim the European Cup Winners' Cup, again at Wembley. During this period groups of young West Ham fans increasingly began to congregate in the North Bank of the Upton Park stadium. This area of the ground gradually became the exclusive territory of young supporters to the exclusion of the older football citizenry, representing a significant break with traditional ways of watching football in East London.

Also during this period, large contingents of Northern football fans began to travel more regularly to London to support their teams and to test their newly acquired reputations for toughness (see Chapter Three). On 6 May 1967, Manchester United fans visited Upton Park in anticipation of their club's league title. Young Manchester United fans were rapidly gaining notoriety for their violent exploits throughout the country, and their trip to East London came to be perceived as one of the Northern fans' first successful challenges in the capital. The match was marred by various outbreaks of violence. Before kick-off one Manchester United fan invaded the pitch pursued by police officers, of which around 80 were on duty. During the match bottles were thrown and fights were plentiful. Over twenty people were taken to hospital. After the match, Manchester United fans allegedly robbed market stalls near the ground and fights erupted between rival fans in the streets (*News of the World*, 7 May 1967).

The interaction with Manchester United fans that day marked an important change in young West Ham fans' commitment to confronting opposing fan groups. It soon became particularly fashionable among local youths to 'take' the opposing fans' section of the ground (Pennant and Smith, 2002: 23). Their behaviour also began to receive growing media attention and Upton Park was increasingly portrayed as a place were local youths could fight. Of particular importance in this context was the renewed confrontation with Manchester United fans in September 1967. Days before the match journalists reported on the club's 'new war on hooligans' in order to preserve the good name of the club (*Stratford Express*, 1 September 1967). In an effort to 'stamp out violence', police chiefs ordered that 'anyone found causing a nuisance or starting trouble will be arrested and charged.'

Extra police would be deployed at high-profile matches at Upton Park and the club prohibited supporters to carry sticks and banners. During the match, police had great difficulty in keeping a gangway clear between a large number of home fans and about 500 Manchester United supporters. Abuse and threats were allegedly exchanged between the two opposing factions and beer cans and pennies were being thrown. About a dozen home fans were removed from the premises (*The Times*, 5 September 1967).

Football hooliganism rapidly transformed into an influential youth subculture in East London. Members of the Mile End gang gained notoriety around East London for their involvement in football violence. The group's reputation was based not only on its participation in football hooliganism, but also on its violent rivalries with other local youth groups, notably those from Barking and Dagenham. Inter-group conflict was often disputed on the North Bank during home matches: 'We used to have a lot of in-fighting between fans. Between different groups. Gangs that had no contact with each other during the week but only on match days' (personal interview with former member of the Mile End gang, September 2003). In the late 1960s, football hooliganism became intertwined with the skinhead subculture. The skinheads emerged against the backdrop of fundamental changes in East End life in the post-war period, including the redevelopment of the slum areas damaged by German bombs, changes in the labour market, the influx of new waves of immigrants and the relocation of many East End families to the new estates being developed around the outer suburbs. These changes were seen as eroding the traditional sense of community and many of the communal meeting places that played a vital role in East London life (O'Neill, 2000: 280; Palmer, 2000: 164). The skinheads, then, sought to reassert, in a heightened and stylized form, the values associated with the traditional working-class community, which were expressed in dress, style and appearance, and in activities. A central feature of the skinhead style was the collective identification of masculinity with physical toughness. The skinhead style was 'aggressive, communal, and non-magical, rooted firmly in confronting the day-to-day problems of the manual labourer in an increasingly hostile world; just like Dad' (Hobbs, 1988: 129).

As one of the remaining communal meeting places in the lives of many East End men, football became a major focus for local groups of skinheads. The skinhead subculture provided a common style and enhanced the territorial identifications of young West Ham fans. The stadium and the East End as a whole were increasingly perceived as places that had to be defended against outsiders (i.e. opposing hooligan groups). In addition, the young hooligans regularly set out to confront their rivals at away matches in order to enhance their status as the best 'firm' in the hierarchy of hooligan oppositions (cf. Armstrong, 1994: 299). As a former hooligan commented:

.

> I see it as very territorial. The East End has always had, I mean, was always seen as an area of London that is deprived. The people are very proud generally. And they don't like people coming in. And what we wanted to do as a group, we wanted to defend our territory in the East End of London, which was West Ham, but we also wanted to go out to other parts of London and up and down the country to say 'we are the hardest, we are the best and we can take on anybody if we want to'. (Personal interview, October 2003)

For many young West Ham fans, being involved in football hooliganism was an attractive lifestyle, part and parcel of being young. Football hooliganism was a sense of adventure, loyalty and enthusiasm, coupled with a passion in defending the team's honour against rival fans (Pennant and Smith, 2002: 15). At this early stage, the overwhelming majority of self-identifying football hooligans were in their teens and early twenties. As we will see in the remainder of this chapter, the age structure of the hooligan formation has changed considerably over time. Moreover, the degrees of planning and co-ordination involved in football hooliganism at West Ham increased significantly over the years, as did the national and international reputation of the hooligan group.

The myth and reality of the Inter City Firm

The hooligan subculture at West Ham United expanded rapidly in the first half of the 1970s, attracting local youths as well as male adolescents from other parts of South East England who wanted to be part of the action. Although by that time West

Ham hooligans already held a widespread reputation for toughness, it was from the mid-1970s onwards that the hooligan formation became notorious for its alleged elaborate organization and tactics. Members of the different subgroups inhabiting the youth end temporarily suspended their inter-group hostilities on match days in order to jointly confront the hooligan groups of opposing teams. In other words, ingroup and outgroup relations were temporarily redefined in terms of club allegiance. Together these different subgroups sought to secure their status as the best 'firm' in the country: 'We used to have a lot of friction and trouble among each other. We knew we had to get together 'cos otherwise we were never going to be nothing. So we got together. We wouldn't have any more in-fighting and that worked out pretty well' (personal interview with former member of Mile End group, September 2003).

As part of this process of temporal unification, West Ham hooligans increasingly began to refer to themselves as the Inter City Firm (ICF), a name that was picked up by the British media. *The Sun*, for example, referred to the group as 'the most feared gang of soccer hooligans in Britain' (17 June 1983). From the late 1970s to the mid-1980s, the ICF had approximately 150 core members, but for 'high-profile' matches the formation could call on the services of up to 400 young men (Dunning et al., 1988: 179). The activities of self-identifying ICF members demonstrated greater levels of planning, co-ordination and tactical sophistication than the earlier forms of football hooliganism at West Ham, principally as an attempt to escape official controls and to successfully challenge their rivals. The name of the group refers to the regular inter-city trains which the hooligans preferred over the special football trains and official supporters' club coaches. This mode of travel maximized their chances of escaping official control and enabled them to inject an element of surprise into their operations (ibid.: 179). The ICF also eschewed the forms of dress and club emblems worn by non-hooligan supporters or those worn by hooligans groups which ICF members considered as 'having no pride in their appearance'. Their adherence to the casual designer fashion seems to have had a twofold function: on the one hand, to avoid marks which would identify them as football fans to the police; and, on the other hand, to affirm their self-styled elite conception.

The ICF used relatively complex strategies to escape police observation and to infiltrate home territories on their visits to away grounds (ibid.: 180). Experienced ICF members made use of a group of younger fans nicknamed the 'Under Fives' in order to gather information on the numbers, locations and dispositions of opposing fans and the police. West Ham hooligans often roamed the streets and pubs near away grounds in search of local hooligan groups. Occasionally they would travel to other parts of London to launch surprise attacks on their opponents on their own territory. But despite the greater levels of planning and co-ordination involved in football hooliganism at West Ham United from the late 1970s onwards, the ICF's degree of organization is often exaggerated in media and police accounts. One journalist wrote how the ICF organized fighting in and around football grounds 'with military-style precision' (*The Times*, 3 February 1988). Other media reports claimed that the ICF 'hold regular meetings to plan their campaigns' (*The Times*, 6 August 1983) and that ICF members 'often meticulously plan the trouble and start it' (*The Sunday Express*, 17 August 1986). In reality, the degree of organization in football hooliganism at West Ham seems to have been generally limited. As a former ICF member put it:

> Again this is another myth that I believe is out of proportion to what really happened. Some core members did occasionally sit down to discuss what they were going to do. But then everybody just followed. It really was this herd instinct. Policing was quite ineffective so there was never much of a barrier to us doing what we wanted to do. Quite often, especially in London, you travelled to a tube station, waited until you were there in sufficient numbers and then just moved as a herd. No one really said, like, "meet at Mile End at seven". You just waited until you were in sufficient numbers and then off you went. (Personal interview, October 2003)

Apart from a small group of core members and certain relatively close-knit subgroups, the cohesion of the ICF appears to have been relatively limited. Crucially, group cohesiveness decreased as one moved from the centre of the group to the periphery. The ICF attracted a large number of followers in the periphery of the group who were in many cases 'friends of friends'. Thus, while several young men identified themselves as ICF members, many did not know each other personally: 'People picked up our name and said "this gang, they all know each other". But none of us knew everyone. When I was arrested with eleven people I didn't know three of them. Never met them before. And they were supposed ringleaders like me' (personal interview with former ICF member, September 2003).

Local and national media repeatedly expressed their concern over the escalating violence of West Ham hooligans. In a pre-season report, the *Stratford and Newham Express* (15 August 1975) warned its readers that 'there are potential killers on your terraces.' The report showed photographs of a range of weapons allegedly carried by West Ham hooligans, including knives, baseball bats, a mountaineer's ice pick, sets of Chinese fighting sticks and an air pistol. Journalists also highlighted the pervasive and costly police operations at West Ham. For example, a massive security operation was staged to prevent fighting between West Ham and Manchester United hooligans on 25 October 1975. Pubs and shops kept their premises closed as the sale of alcohol was prohibited. Three times the average number of police were assigned to the match (*Evening News London*, 25 October 1975). Despite these measures, serious fighting took place inside the stadium and hundreds of fans invaded the pitch to escape the fights. Over 100 people were injured and the police arrested 38 fans and ejected 132 supporters. The match was held up for over 15 minutes (*Evening News London*, 27 October 1975; *Stratford and Newham Express*, 31 October 1975; *The Sun*, 27 October 1975). Local journalists condemned the disorder and emphasized flaws in the security operation. The police announced that they would start collecting and disseminating photographs of 'London's worst soccer thugs' so special police squads could recognize troublemakers and either stop them going into the ground or remove them from the terraces before violence erupted (*Evening News London*, 27 October 1975).

In addition to their hatred towards Manchester United fans, West Ham hooligans established a deep-seated rivalry with their equivalents at Millwall. Before and after a testimonial match for legendary Millwall player Harry Cripps at The Den, in May 1972, opposing hooligans fought outside the ground. This incident set off the mutual hatred continuing today between the two hooligan formations (Pennant, 2002: 287). In September 1976, Millwall fan Ian Pratt died at New Cross station following a scuffle with West Ham fans that led to his fall from a train.

Within hooligan circles the rumour spread that Pratt had actually been pushed onto the train tracks, but no one was ever charged for his death. The incident was constructed by West Ham hooligans as a sign of their superiority, for example in chants such as 'West Ham boys, we've got brains, we throw Millwall under trains.' Millwall fans, on the other hand, pledged their revenge and awaited patiently a match between the two teams, which came in October 1978 after West Ham's relegation to Division Two (Dunning et al., 1988: 178). In the weeks prior to the match, Millwall fans distributed leaflets pledging revenge for the death of Ian Pratt (*Evening Standard*, 5 October 1978; *Stratford and Newham Express*, 7 October 1978). Police responded to the threat by tripling the usual number of officers and by introducing extensive searches and strict segregation.

The rivalry between West Ham and Millwall hooligans has not only been very intense at times, it is also somewhat distinctive in its nature. At first sight, the two hooligan formations seem to have much in common. They are located in a part of London that has a persistent image of deviance, deprivation and violence, and both hooligan groups adhere to similar cultural values: 'They're like two brothers, but only one of them can be king [...] They have the same kind of outlook and it all amounts to looking after yourself and being able to back it up' (*Evening Standard*, 26 September 2003). However, the mutual perceptions of West Ham and Millwall hooligans reveal certain subtle yet vital perceived differences. Both hooligan formations construct their own identities in terms of the perceived differences between self and the other. Social identity thus lies in differences, and differences are asserted against what is closest, which represents the greatest threat (Bourdieu, 1984). For Millwall fans, this contest is enacted entirely in terms of toughness, virility and cultural authenticity within 'Londonness'. Whereas West Ham fans are perceived as tough, volatile and 'plastic' Cockneys, Millwall fans perceive themselves as very tough, extremely volatile and 'authentic' Londoners (Robson, 2000: 175).

In contrast, West Ham hooligans commonly perceive Millwall fans as 'backward' and 'criminally insane' (e.g. Pennant, 2000: 36). The East End is viewed by West Ham hooligans as more 'friendly' and 'open' to outsiders, more adapted to mainstream society, whereas South East London is seen as sinister and backward. More specifically, West Ham hooligans claim only to attack rival hooligans and not non-hooligan supporters and accuse their South East London counterparts of not drawing this distinction:

> If you were on a train, and you had a West Ham shirt on, and they [Millwall hooligans] would get on, they would slap you. West Ham hooligans wouldn't do that. They might not approve, they might say something, but they would never harm you. We would never do that. They're just scum. I regard them as nothings. (Personal interview with ICF member, October 2003)

More generally, West Ham supporters emphasize that their club has been much more successful than Millwall and that this has created a deep sense of jealousy among Millwall fans: 'They hate us 'cos they can never be what we are' (personal interview with West Ham supporter, September 2003).

Overview of the emergence and early development of football hooliganism

In his early work on the subject, Ian Taylor (1971; 1971a) explained the emergence of football hooliganism within the context of the alienation of fractions of the working class resulting from changes in the labour market and the decomposition of traditional working-class communities. More specifically, he argued that football hooliganism was the response of lower-working-class supporters to the bourgeoisification of professional football. I would argue that the emergence of football hooliganism at West Ham United was less related to changes in the game itself, and more to both the continuities and changes in East End life. The studies by Clarke (1973; 1976) and Hobbs (1988) on youth subcultural styles are of particular interest here. The hooligans and the skinheads celebrated a heightened and stylized version of certain core features of traditional working-class culture at a time when the East End was undergoing rapid change, notably aggressive masculinity, excitement, autonomy and (ingroup) solidarity.

The emergence and early development of football hooliganism at West Ham United involved a number of processes. The crowd at Upton Park became increasingly segregated by age in the mid-1960s as groups of young fans began to create their exclusive territory on the North Bank. The violence provoked by Manchester United fans in 1967 and the rise of the skinhead subculture enhanced the commitment of these young fans to physically defending their territory and honour against opposing hooligan groups. Local youth gangs came to temporarily suspend their inter-group hostilities on match days in order to jointly confront the hooligan groups of opposing teams. West Ham hooligans established a number of violent inter-group rivalries. The early development of football hooliganism at West Ham United was characterized not only by the escalation of inter-group rivalries, but also by the ongoing interactions between hooligans and law enforcers. Early security measures failed to effectively reduce football hooliganism in and around the ground. Hooligan confrontations continued to take place despite the growing number of police officers, the segregation of home and away supporters and police surveillance at potential trouble spots. At this stage, the risk of apprehension and of serious punishment was relatively low for participants in hooliganism; most offenders were merely ejected from the ground. As opportunities for fighting inside the stadium gradually decreased, the hooligans began to relocate their activities to new locales and developed more complex strategies for escaping police observation and successfully challenging their rivals. In the following section I will examine this development in more detail.

'Birch these thugs': responses to football hooliganism

In the previous section, I have shown that early security measures failed to effectively reduce the frequency and seriousness of football hooliganism at West Ham United. Rather than containing or eradicating the problem, the segregation of opposing fans and the growing police presence inside the stadium resulted in the displacement of hooligan confrontations away from the stadium to new locales, such as underground and railway stations, and pubs. Security policies expanded steadily from the 1980s onwards as official and media concern over football hooliganism deepened, especially after the tragedies at Heysel and Hillsborough and a series of widely reported domestic hooligan incidents. West Ham United's efforts to contain spectator violence also increased significantly during this period due to persistent national and international pressures, for example in the aftermath of an incident involving West Ham fans in Spain. West Ham's European Cup Winners Cup tie against Castilla, on 17 September 1980 in Madrid, was overshadowed by visiting supporters' alleged 'disgraceful behaviour' (*Daily Telegraph*, 19 September 1980; *The Times*, 17 September 1980). During the match, played in Real Madrid's Santiago Bernabéu stadium, West Ham fans reportedly urinated and spat on home fans, pelted the pitch with beer cans and intimidated and attacked riot police officers and local supporters. English journalists condemned the behaviour of the West Ham fans, portraying them as 'scum' and 'animals' (*The Sun*, 18 September 1980). Spanish newspapers allegedly wrote that 'never in the history of the stadium has there been such uncivilized and bestial behaviour' (*Daily Telegraph*, 19 September 1980). West Ham fans, on the other hand, accused the police of brutal behaviour and regarded the fans' misbehaviour as a legitimate response to disproportionate police methods (*The Times*, 19 September 1980).

Notwithstanding its contested nature, the incident had serious consequences for the club. The UEFA punished West Ham by ordering the return match at Upton Park to be played behind closed doors. The game was played in a 'strange, eerie atmosphere' in front of officials and media totalling 262 (Northcutt and Shoesmith, 1997: 149-150). After the match, local supporters gathered in the streets of the East End to celebrate West Ham's 5-1 victory. The international and national pressures exerted on West Ham enhanced the club's sense of urgency in tackling football hooliganism. Up until then the club had not demonstrated a profound, long-term interest in containing or eradicating football hooliganism: 'It was only after the incident in Madrid that the club really began to take the issue seriously. Before that time, it was never really punished or anything, so there was no need to take full responsibility. It was always possible to point a finger at someone else, for instance the police' (personal interview with club director, September 2003). Ironically, only days before the match in Madrid the club had sought to positively influence the behaviour of its fans. Team captain Billy Bonds sent every club member a letter asking them to behave properly in Spain. Members of the official supporters club were required to submit photographs and passport numbers when applying for a ticket (*The Times*, 19 September 1980).

The club's growing commitment to reducing football hooliganism was reinforced by a number of widely reported incidents in the first half of the 1980s. On

1 May 1982, West Ham and Arsenal fans fought inside and outside Highbury stadium. West Ham hooligans let off a smoke bomb during the match to create confusion and they attacked rival hooligans while the match was suspended for twelve minutes. Hundreds of fans spilled over onto the pitch to escape the fighting (*Daily Telegraph*, 6 August 1983). At the underground station near the stadium, 24-year-old Arsenal fan John Dickinson was stabbed to death during an assault by West Ham hooligans. An FA Cup match at Birmingham City, on 18 February 1984, was suspended twice after West Ham hooligans invaded the pitch in an attempt to get the match abandoned (as West Ham were losing 3-0). National and local newspapers wrote how the incident had been premeditated and organized and condemned the disorder in headlines such as 'Birch these thugs', 'Damn West Ham!' and 'The yobs will never beat us' (e.g. *News of the World*, 19 February 1984; *The Times*, 20 February 1984; *The Sunday Express*, 19 February 1984). For ICF members, the public outcry was a source of excitement and fun. Anticipation of disorder had set in motion a process of self-selection, as subgroups and individuals eager to confront their Birmingham rivals joined the ranks of the ICF:

> [E]veryone kept all the cuttings about their exploits and laughed as we read that it had all been supposedly planned and organized. That was a load of bollocks, but when we hit the train station that morning and saw the West Ham turnout, we just knew that something would be on. The firm was so big that we had to follow in separate trains. Every firm and nutter from Tilbury to Canning Town and Mile End turned up. We were sure that Birmingham would also have their firm out for the day. That was the magic pulling power of the FA Cup (Pennant, 2002: 266-267).

During this period the reputation of the ICF came to take on mythical proportions. Cognizant of the constructed nature of fan reputations, ICF members consciously played up their notoriety. For example, they used their own 'calling cards' which they left on their victims, as did certain other hooligan formations. The cards read: 'congratulations, you have just met the ICF.' At the same time, investigators of the murder of John Dickinson condemned what they called the 'conspiracy of silence' surrounding the hooligan subculture at West Ham, as fans were extremely reluctant to give any information. This 'conspiracy of silence' closely reflects the values celebrated by West Ham hooligans and, more generally, the dominant values of East End culture, notably a strong ingroup solidarity and a profound distrust of representatives of society's master institutions (cf. Hobbs, 1988). As a self-declared West Ham hooligan put it: 'We pride ourselves in sticking together whatever happens. We look after one another' (*The Sunday Express*, 17 August 1986). East London police officers considered the close-knit nature of the ICF as having a deterrent effect on their intelligence gathering: 'It's very difficult to build up relations with prominents. They tolerate you, but they won't tell you things. That's part of the East End culture. You don't talk about your mates, that's the worst you can do' (personal interview with a football intelligence officer, September 2003).

In the mid-1980s a team of police officers began to closely monitor West Ham hooligans in order to unravel their activities and tactics. They accompanied West Ham fans to away matches and, in turn, other police districts monitored 'their' supporters on their way to Upton Park (*The Job*, 9 March 1984). The Metropolitan Police opened special investigations into alleged ICF 'ringleaders' (Operation White Horse and Operation Full Time). In January 1987, after months of presumed police 'infiltration' into the ranks of the ICF, twelve alleged hooligan leaders were arrested at their homes as part of what was dubbed 'Britain's biggest crackdown on football hooliganism' (*Stratford & Newham Express*, 24 January 1987). During the raids police found weapons such as knives and also a number of videos and newspaper cuttings on football violence. The court was told how plain-clothes police officers had 'posed as hooligans, taking notes of the ringleaders' activities' (*The Times*, 3 February 1988; *Newham Recorder*, 11 February 1988; *Daily Mirror*, 3 February 1988). The prosecution also showed fragments of the 1985 *Hooligan* documentary in which self-declared ICF members boasted about their desire for fighting. Eleven men were charged with conspiracy to cause affray, but they were cleared on all charges due to unreliable police evidence. The judge claimed that the logs kept by the officers 'were not safe'. Some of the accused received substantial financial compensation.

Parallel to these high-profile court cases, a special police investigation was carried out into the confrontation between West Ham and Manchester United supporters on a ferry boat from Harwich to Hook of Holland, the Netherlands, on 7

141

August 1986. Both sets of fans were on their way to pre-season friendly tournaments, in Groningen and Amsterdam respectively. Violence erupted after West Ham hooligans allegedly taunted the Manchester United supporters. The latter reportedly decided to take revenge for the stabbing of a 16-year-old Manchester United fan near Upton Park in 1985 (*The Times*, 9 August 1986; *Daily Mirror*, 9 August 1986). During the confrontation five people were injured, three of them needing urgent medical treatment for stab wounds. The ferry was forced to return to Harwich midway through its journey because of the fighting. After six months of police investigation, three West Ham fans were sentenced to six years imprisonment, while two others were acquitted (Pennant, 2002: 357-358).

The police investigations and the 'ferry riot' further enhanced the ICF's notoriety and fuelled the myth surrounding the hooligan formation. Journalists commonly portrayed the group as a 'heavily-armed gang' that organized hooligan confrontations with 'military-style' or 'commando-style' precision (e.g. *The Times*, 3 February 1988; *Daily Mirror*, 3 February 1988). At the same time, the ever-expanding range of security and safety measures in and around football grounds began to have a more profound impact on football hooliganism, both nationally and locally. After the Heysel disaster, calls were made for a partnership between the government and the football authorities, but the enthusiasm of clubs was generally limited as hooliganism was believed to lie largely outside their control (Houlihan, 1991: 184). Only after Hillsborough and the publication of the Taylor Report (1990) more rapid and profound changes started to occur (see Chapter Three).

The policing of football hooliganism at West Ham United was specialized and became increasingly intelligence-led. As a senior police officer commented:

> When I first came to police West Ham, in the 70s, you went to a huge briefing in the gym. And they said: "Well, we're playing such and such today. They wear these colours. The opposition will go in that end of the ground. The West Ham fans will go in that end. You're standing down here. Off you go." And I thought that was appalling, you know. What are they going to tell me about the prominent group that's coming from wherever. How are they going to get here? That's a lot better nowadays

with the focus on structural intelligence gathering and analysis. (Personal interview, October 2003)

Having faced painful defeat in the high-profile court case against alleged ICF leaders, the police sought to standardize and routinize their intelligence operations in the football context. Special intelligence officers and spotters were installed to gather intelligence on the activities and dispositions of hooligans. The police's investments in intelligence gathering and close surveillance created a belief among West Ham hooligans that whereas in the past they had usually remained anonymous to law enforcers, now 'the coppers know who you are and if you step out of line, they know which door to come and knock on' (personal interview with ICF member, October 2003).

The increased risk of apprehension and serious punishment seems to have put off several long-standing ICF members:

> The arrests pulled a lot of people off. At the time they were talking about doing ten years [in prison]. Some of the Chelsea boys did get ten years. That pulled a lot of lads off and they stopped going. That's when it started to die. When the punishment became more serious than what the crime was, it wasn't worth doing no more. (Personal interview with former ICF member, September 2003)

Although the high-profile court cases against alleged ICF 'ringleaders' in the late 1980s had collapsed, they nevertheless send out a clear message to experienced West Ham hooligans: the police began to take the issue very seriously. For some older hooligans, changes in their personal lives also played a major part in their decision to lessen their involvement in football hooliganism:

> I think people realized it wasn't going to last forever. 'We've had the crack, we've had the laugh but if we don't stop now we're gonna get ourselves in too deep.' It was a close shave in the trials, although they [the police] lied. If they had gone back a few years earlier and had the prove then we would have been in real trouble. The old warning signs came up and said 'that's

143

it'. For me, it changed the day my boy was born. Once he was born I decided that I didn't want to leave him without a dad. Simple as that. (Personal interview with former hooligan, October 2003)

Football hooliganism at West Ham United was also affected by the socio-spatial transformation of the ground: the terraces were replaced by numbered seats, a control room and CCTV system were installed and the club specialized its steward organization. These changes enabled the club and the police to more adequately monitor the movement of fans and to identify individual offenders, significantly reducing the anonymity of fans and hooligans in and around the ground. Ticket procedures and controls were automatized and tightened and ticket prices increased rapidly. But changes in football hooliganism at West Ham United were not only related to increasing external pressures. With the rise of the rave subculture, certain streetwise hooligans became heavily involved in the organization of lucrative 'warehouse' parties across London and Essex. Although occasionally such parties were a site for confrontation between opposing hooligan formations – as were punk gigs in the 1970s – they also diverted the attention of some ICF members from football hooliganism: 'There was lots of money involved in raves. Why would you run the risk of being arrested for violent disorder at a football match if you can earn thirty-odd thousand pounds in one weekend? And you have to say they were very good at that. The real East End entrepreneurial spirit, you know, always close to the edge of the law' (personal interview with senior police officer, September 2003).

As a result of the aforementioned developments in official security policies and the local hooligan scene, the forms of football hooliganism at West Ham United gradually became more controllable and predictable for the authorities. Opportunities for large-scale confrontations have diminished due to close police and camera surveillance, and the number of regular participants in hooligan confrontations has decreased. The ICF also picks its clashes more carefully than in the past. Whereas in the 1970s and early 1980s hooligan confrontations occurred almost on a weekly basis, the ICF now operates more occasionally, usually only three or four times per season. For 'needle' matches against deep-seated rivals, the ICF can still count upon the services of 200 to 300 affiliates. For low-profile fixtures hooligans' commitment to fighting their opponents is usually very limited. As one senior police officer put it:

> I would say it's not a week-in-week-out threat. It's big games only. It's almost like a sleeping giant. A couple of times per season they'll put out a very large group that needs looking after. And needs looking after well. The rest of the time they are fairly manageable [...] It depends on the opposition, on the histories between the two and even on what day it is. (Personal interview with football intelligence officer, September 2003)

In the following section I will examine the contemporary shapes of football hooliganism at West Ham United in more detail.

Overview of the development and effects of official policies targeting football hooliganism

The case of West Ham United demonstrates that the manifestation of football hooliganism is dynamic rather than fixed. Crucial to understanding within-case variations are the interactions between hooligans and law enforcers. As we have seen, international, national and local responses have all played a major role in the development of football hooliganism at West Ham United. A major consequence of the imposition of controls and punishments was to displace the problem into areas where the controls were, or were perceived by hooligans as being, weak or non-existent (cf. Dunning, 1999: 153). Hooligan confrontations also became increasingly planned and co-ordinated. But as controls and punishments grew more pervasive by the 1990s and police and club operations became more organized, opportunities for large-scale fighting diminished and many experienced hooligans lessened their involvement in hooligan confrontations. These developments, along with changes in youth culture and the ageing of core hooligans, resulted in a decline in football hooliganism at West Ham United. Football hooliganism also became more controllable and predictable for the authorities due to close surveillance and intelligence gathering, which enabled them to regularly prevent hooligan encounters and arrest offenders.

In the remainder of this chapter, I will show that although the extent and forms of football hooliganism at West Ham United have changed considerably over time, the hooligan subculture has far from disappeared. Skilled hooligan entrepreneurs also profit from the ongoing commodification of football hooliganism, thereby securing the notoriety of the ICF. Their successful involvement in the hooligan entertainment industry closely reflects the dominant core characteristic of East London's culture, which is entrepreneurial ability (see Hobbs, 1988: 140).

Terrace legends: nostalgia or revival?

The hooligan subculture has become increasingly commodified in recent years. West Ham hooligans' active involvement in 'hooligan entertainment' can be traced back to 1985, when self-declared ICF members starred in a documentary broadcasted on national television. The *Hooligan* documentary looked at the activities of the ICF and questioned its members about their motivations. The documentary enhanced the group's national and international reputation and revealed some of the ICF's characteristic arrogance: 'Such were our own successes, we were always grabbing the headline news and when we brought our style, pose and culture to people's living rooms via the *Hooligan* documentary, it was as if a romantic light had been shone on us' (Pennant, 2002: 393). A few years later, an ICF member worked as a consultant for producer Alan Clarke's television movie *The Firm*, which was released in 1989. Actor Gary Oldman played Bex Bissell, a respectable estate agent obsessed by football violence. He leads the fictional Inter-City Crew and plans to unite rival domestic hooligan 'firms' in order to confront foreign hooligan formations during the 1988 European Championships in Germany. By focusing on the obsessive, addictive violence of some well-off men, the movie teases then current sociological explanations of football hooliganism.

Self-declared (former) hooligans also discovered new ways of securing or enhancing their groups' reputations, for example through so-called 'hit and tell' fan memoirs (e.g. Allan, 1989; Ward, 1989; Francis and Walsh, 1997; Brimson and Brimson, 1996; 1997; King and Knight, 1999; Jones and Rivers, 2002; for an analysis of this type of literature, see Redhead, 2004). From the mid-1990s onwards the 'hit and tell' literature expanded rapidly as experienced hooligans became increasingly aware of the potential financial profit involved. Representatives of a variety of larger and smaller hooligan formations have published their accounts of hooligan confrontations and of developments in the British hooligan subculture. In 2003, London's leading sports bookshop Sportpages stocked 45 hooligan-related books (*Evening Standard*, 2 June 2003). Some former West Ham hooligans have been prominents in this book industry. In the early 2000s they published a number of books on the hooligan experience at West Ham United (Pennant, 2000; 2002; Pennant and Smith, 2002; Smith, 2004). One author also co-operated with a former Chelsea hooligan in a recent compilation (Pennant and King, 2003). Certain former ICF members also contribute regularly to the West Ham fanzine *Over Land and Sea*. Although not writing exclusively on the subject of hooliganism, they regularly comment on recent incidents of disorder and recount the heydays of football violence at West Ham. According to the editor, their stories boost the sale of the fanzine: 'The stuff they write, people want to read it. People like their stories and, to be honest, they are quite prominent figures among West Ham fans.' The entrepreneurial abilities of certain ICF members also show in their successful merchandising of hooligan paraphernalia. On match days the stalls outside Upton Park offer T-shirts, caps, hats and pins with the ICF logo. In November 2003, one stall was selling T-shirts showing a pub (frequented by Tottenham Hotspur hooligans) with smashed windows. The photo was taken just after the pub had been attacked by West Ham hooligans, on 29 October. The inscription read: 'London travel card: £ 4.50, ticket for the match: £ 30.00, smashed up bar by ICF: priceless!' (personal observations, November 2003).

The ongoing process of commodification – in print, film and paraphernalia, and on the Internet – reproduces the widely shared belief among (former) West Ham hooligans that the ICF has long been Britain's most notorious and hardest hooligan group. As one former ICF member argued: 'Although the team was poor standard, we were top of the league. And that's the way it always was. If it came to a row we would hold our own against any of them. And they knew that and all. They could never copy what we have done. None of them' (personal interview, September 2003). Central to this self-image is the idea that the heydays of football hooliganism are over, that is, a deep-seated nostalgia about the art of football violence in the

1960s, 1970s and the 1980s. Older (former) hooligans tend to argue that the current ICF generation will never be able to live up to the group's legacy:

> It's a joke compared to what we had [...] I cannot see them having much joy in it. They certainly won't have like we had [...] we had the element of surprise, we had the element of numbers, we had the element of organization. All the things that I don't think they've actually got. (Personal interview with former ICF member, October 2003)

But although the frequency of hooligan confrontations and the number of self-identifying hooligans have diminished considerably, certain serious incidents in the early 2000s suggest that football hooliganism at West Ham United remains a persistent phenomenon. Furthermore, following the club's relegation to the Championship (previously the First Division) in 2003, public fears over the behaviour of West Ham supporters resurfaced. The final match of the 2002/03 season, on 11 May 2003 at Birmingham City, was marred by spectator violence due to West Ham fans' frustrations over their team's relegation. After the match opposing fans engaged in a street fight for almost 30 minutes. Various fans were seriously injured by missiles. Relegation to the Championship meant that West Ham would be reunited with long-standing rivals both on and off the pitch. The Metropolitan Police expected that throughout the season the ICF would attempt to confront some of its old enemies. Media reports in the build-up to the 2003/04 season voiced these fears:

> Football is bracing itself for its most violent season in years as many of Britain's worst hooligans lay plans to attack rival gangs. Police fear there will be regular outbreaks of trouble at or around games in the First Division [...] the hostility between hardcore elements attached to clubs such as Cardiff City, Millwall, Stoke City, Nottingham Forest and West Ham United means clashes are inevitable [...] Football intelligence specialists in police forces across the country say the inclusion in the First Division this season of promoted Cardiff City and relegated West Ham will reopen some

bitter rivalries. Both have large travelling supports which contain known troublemakers (*The Observer*, 3 August 2003).

In the 2003/04 and 2004/05 seasons a number of confrontations took place between ICF members and long-standing opponents. A group of around 200 West Ham hooligans attended a Tuesday night Carling Cup match at Cardiff City, on 23 September 2003. They arrived by train early in the afternoon and were escorted to a local pub by the police. During the afternoon there were a couple of minor fights around the area where small groups of hooligans had dispersed. Inside the stadium West Ham hooligans were challenged by young Cardiff supporters singing 'Where's your famous ICF?'. In response, West Ham fans questioned the masculinity of the young fans in chants such as 'Little boys', 'You're supposed to be at home' and 'Sheepshaggers'. The ejection of a West Ham fan by the police during the match triggered conflict between young ICF members and police officers, who used batons to keep the group at bay. As the police tried to escort the away fans back to the railway station after the match, they were attacked with bottles by a group of Cardiff fans.[5] After a league match between the two teams at Upton Park later that season, on 28 February 2004, opposing fans fought outside the ground and West Ham fans attacked police officers. Cardiff fans assaulted a steward and ransacked an official club shop. Police claimed that both groups had been in contact with each other prior to the match via mobile phones.

On other occasions West Ham hooligans used more elaborate strategies for challenging rival hooligan formations. On 29 October 2003, a group of approximately 100 ICF members smashed up a pub frequented by Tottenham Hotspur hooligans five hours prior to a Carling Cup match at White Hart Lane. The police arrested 93 West Ham hooligans at the nearby Northumberland Park. In October 2004, a group of 50 young hooligans travelled to Bournemouth, where the local team played Cardiff City in a Carling Cup tie. The hooligans attacked Cardiff fans drinking in a pub before the match. Two Cardiff fans were hospitalized and four men were arrested. Incidents of this kind demonstrate that West Ham hooligans still occasionally plan and co-ordinate confrontations. They may arrive on foreign turf long before kick-off, or even at matches their team is not involved in, in order to inject an element of surprise. The hooligans' main modes of transport are train services, cars, transit vans and (private) coaches.

'We hate Millwall': local rivalry continued

West Ham's two-year spell in the Championship also meant renewed confrontation with local rival Millwall for the first time in ten years. In the build-up to the match, on 28 September 2003, journalists predicted a 'powder keg' derby with an extremely high potential for spectator violence. One newspaper argued that 'amid all the talk of rucks and riots it's easy to forget that there's a football match to be played ... though the result may not dominate the headlines' (*Evening Standard*, 26 September 2003). The Metropolitan Police classified the match as maximum risk (so-called category C+) and staged one of the largest security operations ever seen at a football match in London. Nearly 800 officers were deployed and the police utilized overt and covert surveillance cameras, spotters and a helicopter to deter and identify troublemakers (*Newham Recorder*, 24 September 2003; *The Guardian*, 27 September 2003). The match was moved from Saturday afternoon to Sunday noon for safety reasons and an alcohol ban was imposed at the ground in a bid to prevent drunken behaviour (*News of the World*, 28 September 2003).

Taunts and speculations among opposing supporters and hooligans were plentiful in the weeks before the match. Various rumours were spread via the Internet and newspapers: disorder had presumably been planned by Millwall hooligans, over 100 Millwall fans reportedly bought tickets for home areas, and Millwall fans threatened to vandalize the Bobby Moore statue outside Upton Park (*Evening Standard*, 26 September 2003; *The Guardian*, 27 September 2003; *News of the World*, 28 September 2003). To prevent the vandalizing of the Bobby Moore statue, it was covered with a protective sheet and a former ICF member guarded it the night before the game (personal observations, September 2003; *Evening Standard*, 2 October 2003). In reality, no serious disorder occurred before, during or after the match. Groups of West Ham hooligans sought to confront their opponents outside the ground, but high-profile policing prevented physical confrontation between the two sets of fans (personal observations, September 2003). After the game the Millwall fans were kept for 40 minutes to allow West Ham supporters to disperse. Due to pre-match intelligence indicating pre-planned disorder, the return match at The New Den, on 21 March 2004, was dubbed 'the biggest football policing operation ever undertaken by the Metropolitan Police', with 1,188 officers being on duty (*Evening Standard*, 19 March 2004). West Ham and Millwall hooligans were monitored by spotters and police officers throughout the day. During the match West Ham fans attempted to invade the pitch and damaged seats and the toilet areas. Opposing supporters also pelted each other with missiles. According to one journalist, the match proved that 'the heartbeat of football hooliganism remains strong' (*Daily Express*, 22 March 2004).

Although the rivalry between West Ham and Millwall hooligans remains intense, it has gradually become less physical and more ritualized due in part to pervasive police controls and surveillance preventing physical confrontation, and changes in the local hooligan scenes. Occasionally, however, the hooligans succeed in circumventing police observation, for example after a local derby on 21 November 2004. During the match at The New Den, West Ham supporters opened their usual repertoire of verbal abuse directed at Millwall players and fans. Millwall's player manager Dennis Wise was insulted throughout the match, as was goalkeeper Graham Stack because of his alleged involvement in a rape case. Both players were pelted with coins and a mobile phone. West Ham supporters also sought to denigrate their opponents by mocking the perceived slum character of South East London: 'You live in a caravan', 'Pikies, pikies, pikies', 'No one likes you 'cos you're scum' and 'Does the social know you're here' (personal observations, November 2004).

Hooligan reputations were negotiated throughout the match. Provocations by home fans were rebutted with chants such as 'Little boys, little boys, little boys.' One Millwall fan challenged the away supporters to come over to and fight. He was wearing a surgical mask, referring to Millwall's mythical hooligan subgroup The Treatment. West Ham fans were unimpressed and asked: 'Who's the wanker with the mask?' After the final whistle the atmosphere turned more aggressive as West Ham fans vandalized seats and threw them at the police and home supporters, but physical confrontation was prevented by the police. Later that night, after the extensive police operation was discontinued, a group of Millwall hooligans travelled to the East End and attacked a pub frequented by ICF members.

151

'Where's your famous ICF?': the current shapes of football hooliganism at West Ham United

The ICF still holds a widespread reputation for toughness, despite important changes in the extent and nature of football hooliganism at West Ham United. Although this reputation is creatively acted out by (former) hooligans, it has also come to occasionally burden non-hooligan supporters attending away matches. In an attempt to enhance their status as a good 'firm', local hooligan formations may confront regular West Ham supporters mistaking them for, or claiming them to be, ICF members. During the club's two-year spell in the Championship several incidents of this kind occurred due in part to the often less pervasive security regimes in this league. After a match between Wigan Athletic and West Ham, on 3 January 2004, a group of young Wigan hooligans attacked West Ham fans on their way to the railway station, as the away supporters were not escorted by the police. On the Internet self-identifying Wigan hooligans claimed victory over ICF members, but the latter dismissed these claims since attacking 'scarfers' (non-hooligan supporters) was considered illegitimate. Three weeks later, on 25 January, a West Ham supporter was stabbed outside a pub in Wolverhampton and another fan had multiple defensive wounds to his hands and arms after they were attacked by local hooligans. On other occasions, West Ham fans have similarly been burdened by the reputation of the ICF. As one fan argued:

> There is no doubt that smaller teams, especially from backwater towns and cities, see us as a target, a trophy if you like. Because of the ICF we are a valuable scalp I'm afraid. The fact that there are less cameras and general security than at the Premiership level is another factor [...] Stoke, Sheffield United and Burnley will all be dangerous. (Personal interview, January 2004)

The composition of the ICF has changed significantly over time. The overwhelming majority of the ICF members of the 1970s and early 1980s are no longer, or only sporadically, involved in hooligan confrontations. Although many former hooligans claim missing the 'buzz' of football violence, they argue that pervasive controls and punishments have deeply affected the hooligan experience: 'the odds are against us now. The 1970s and 1980s, them were the days' (interview with former ICF member, December 2003). Many former hooligans seem to have found a substitute for the buzz of football hooliganism in family, career, other forms of leisure, or hard drugs. At the same time, a small proportion of long-standing ICF members are still centrally involved in football hooliganism, seemingly 'addicted' to the hooligan experience and their status within the hooligan scene, despite the fact that some of them have successful businesses and steady families.

> For some who are really successful in a wide range of businesses, being involved in hooliganism is very riskful 'cos they have a lot to lose. Like the arrest the other day. They may be facing three years in prison. But it's the buzz... Some pulled out for a few years, but they just miss it too much. They need that buzz. They know people look up to them at West Ham and they want to secure that status. (Personal interview with ICF member, December 2003)

The age structure of West Ham's hooligan formation has therefore changed considerably. In the mid-1970s the majority of hooligans were in their late teens or early twenties. Today, the average age of ICF members is approximately 30 years old. Of the seven West Ham fans pleading guilty to affray in relation to the disorder at a match between West Ham and Cardiff City, four were between 35 and 38 years old. One well-known ICF member, with over 50 previous convictions, was 46 years old (*The Western Mail*, 6 January 2005; *Evening Standard*, 6 January 2005; *The Sun*, 6 January 2005).

In addition to this older section, in the early 2000s the hooligan formation has attracted a group of young men in their late teens and early twenties. This group has been involved in a number of recent hooligan confrontations. The group consists of around 30 core members, but for high-profile fixtures or when disorder is expected it can call on the services of up to 100 young men. The age structure of the hooligan formation as a whole currently ranges from 17 to 45 years old. Although this age structure seems to largely correspond with that of other long-standing hooligan formations in Britain (see Chapter Three; cf. Giulianotti, 1999: 52),

153

because of the relatively small number of younger hooligans at West Ham United the percentage of older hooligans is comparatively high. According to one football intelligence officer:

> They seem to be older here at West Ham compared to some other groups in London. The younger group are there but they're quite small. There's a good spectrum from the whole lot together. But the people that run with the group are quite old at West Ham. Say 30 upwards. There is a younger element, 17 to 20 years old, but that group is quite small. (Personal interview, October 2003)

Earlier in this chapter I have argued that football hooliganism at West Ham United is characterized by hooligans' strong territorial identifications, that is, their commitment to physically defending their club's and community's (and their own group's) honour. Due to the aforementioned demographic changes in the area, at present only a minority of West Ham hooligans actually live in the East End, although many were brought up there or have strong emotional ties to the area. Many ICF members live in East End diaspora in Essex, and some hooligans live even further afield, in places such as Surrey, Norwich, Cambridge or Milton Keynes. Notwithstanding these changes in the geographical distribution of West Ham hooligans, the core values of traditional East End culture still feature prominently in the collective identity and behaviour of the hooligans. These values – including the rules, strategies and codes of violence (cf. Hobbs, 1988: 124) – are passed on from generation to generation and structure hooligans' construction of self and the other. Thus, even though their social situations may have changed, West Ham hooligans' attachments to the aggressive aesthetics of working-class masculinity at football and elsewhere seem undiminished (J. Williams, 2001: 46).

This leads us to one of the main controversies surrounding football hooliganism at West Ham: the material circumstances of the hooligans. From the 1980s onwards, journalists have repeatedly stressed the relatively affluent nature of West Ham hooligans. According to one journalist, the majority of ICF members 'have well-paid jobs and take pride in their appearance. Many are married with children and are home owners' (*The Sunday Express*, 17 August 1986). Others wrote how a 50-year-old company director was centrally involved in the 'ferry riot' in 1986 (*Daily Mirror*, 10 November 1987; *Daily Telegraph*, 10 November 1987). Recently, newspapers reported that Tony Clarke, MP for Northampton and director of Northampton Town Football Club, had an ICF tattoo (a crossed hammers crest with the letters ICF) on his chest. Clarke denied to have ever been a member of the ICF, claiming that he 'did not know there was such a thing as membership' (*News of the World*, 12 September 2004; *The Sunday Times*, 12 September 2004; *The Express*, 15 September 2004). In a recent article titled 'Shame of middle class sons jailed as soccer thugs', one journalist wrote of 'fears of a new breed of middle class soccer thugs' as a judge's son and a London Underground manager were convicted for their involvement in football-related violence (*Evening Standard*, 6 January 2005).

It has been argued that the media accounts of the relatively affluent, middle-class hooligan – perhaps inspired by movies such as *The Firm*, which highlight the hooligans' 'flash' lifestyles – detract from the fact that the ICF and other English hooligan groups are rooted in traditional working-class culture (Williams, 1991: 175; Hobbs and Robins, 1991). The data presented by Dunning and his colleagues on the occupational and social class characteristics of 141 self-confessed ICF members suggest that: 'whilst the nucleus of the ICF contains a minority from higher up on the occupational scale, it is clear that the overwhelming majority [...] come from the lower levels of the working class' (1988: 190).[6] In the mid-1980s, several ICF members worked as builders, electricians, mechanics, market traders or army personnel. The data suggest that 32 ICF members were unemployed and 36 earned money from casual work or in the black economy as ticket touts, bouncers or musicians. Many ICF members were earning money through typical East End endeavours:

> You weren't dealing with hard-core criminals. It was mostly petty stuff. Like selling designer labels. Ducking and diving is what East End boys do anyway, you know. Anything to make a living or pull a scam. 'Here lady you can have one orange for 25 pence or four for a pound.' That sort of mentality. (Personal interview with former ICF member, September 2003)

The data presented by the authors raise the problem of class measurement and changes over time. Hobbs and Robins (1991: 557-558) take the career of one ICF member as an example. He worked as a bouncer and has since gone on to organize security arrangements at major sporting events, write a number of best-selling books, run his own mini-cab business, acted as a script consultant on various movie productions. They argue that: 'If this man is lower working class, we would suggest that many professional groups, if achievement, media profile and monetary reward are considered, should be classed as distinctly lumpen' (1991: 558). In fact, several older ICF members who were, or who still are, centrally involved in the hooligan subculture have progressed significantly in their professional careers. Nearly all ICF members are employed and some have been particularly successful in business. Certain group members were involved in organizing lucrative dance or rave parties in and around London. One well-known ICF member, who was formerly a market trader, is now a successful record company director. Some others hold jobs as office clerks or managers in the City of London.

In general, the nucleus of (former) ICF members appears to have experienced a degree of upward social mobility. As a former ICF member commented: 'Our group was nearly all in work, you know. Many run their own business. If you asked them now, like a bloke was a market trader, he used to work for somebody else and now he owns the store' (personal interview, September 2003). In this context, it has been argued that conventional class analysis finds it hard to classify the upwardly mobile and re-located home owning fans and hooligans, whose material circumstances suggest incorporation but whose attachments to working-class values seem undiminished (cf. J. Williams, 2001; Robson, 2000). Relatively few West Ham hooligans are obviously 'middle class'. Although several hooligans have 'got on', they are not beyond their cultural roots and male friendship networks (Williams, 1991: 177). Embodied class consciousness remains crucial to understanding the collective identity and behaviour of West Ham hooligans.

A final issue to be addressed here is the heterogeneous ethnic composition of the hooligan formation at West Ham United. Although the vast majority of hooligans are white males, some of the group's core members are black or minority ethnic, both historically and at present. Several black participants are endowed with a hypermasculinity to be feared, that is, they are commonly viewed as superior fighters and appear as daunting oppositional threats. Contrary to their image of overt racism in the late 1970s and early 1980s, only a small minority of West Ham hooligans seem to have publicly associated with the National Front during this period (Pennant, 2002: 376-377). In a 2002 BBC documentary a well-known ICF member was exposed as being 'at the front of trouble' during the European Championships in 2000 and as an active member of the right-wing organization Combat 18. There are, however, doubts about the susceptibility of West Ham hooligans to right-wing ideologies, as the following comments suggest: 'He [a fellow hooligan] tried to get a right-wing element started here, but very few people are into that. I don't take it very seriously, and most people think he's a bit of a tosser really'; 'Race has never been an issue with any of us. I don't judge a man by his skin. I judge him by what he's got here [points to his heart]' (personal interviews with West Ham hooligans, December 2003). Furthermore, racist ideologies are often inconsistent and more related to provocation (i.e. 'winding up' the opponent) and 'having a laugh'. On one occasion ICF members reportedly fought on behalf of the Socialist Workers' Party against the National Front (Dunning et al., 1988: 182). Some hooligans were, for a while, members of the anti-Nazi league and Communist Party, although 'none of us were really communists, it was a kind of fashion to have the badge' (personal interview with former West Ham hooligan, November 2003).

Conclusion

Crucial to understanding football hooliganism at West Ham United is the hooligans' celebration, in a heightened form, of the core values of traditional East End culture. The habitus of West Ham hooligans has not changed fundamentally over the last three decades, despite important changes in the material and social circumstances of several hooligans. Few hooligans actually live in East London due to major demographic changes in the area. Many hooligans live in Essex or even further afield, yet they closely adhere to the dominant values of the hooligan subculture and of East End culture in general, notably tough masculinity, excitement, autonomy, smartness and a strong sense of ingroup solidarity and intense antagonism towards outsiders.

In this context, we should also take into consideration a related feature of East End culture: entrepreneurial ability. Several hooligans have been engaging in market trading or petty crime from an early age, earning money to keep up with the latest fashion and to attend football matches. Some (former) hooligans have used their entrepreneurial skills to become centrally involved in the hooligan entertainment industry. This type of entrepreneurship resembles to some degree Giulianotti's notion (1999) of 'post-hooliganism'. Hooligans are particularly recognizant of the constructed nature of fan reputations and they have been successful in playing up their public image and making financial profit. However, this 'post-hooliganism' cannot be seen, as Giulianotti seems to suggest, as replacing physical violence. Rather, it sits uneasily with the continuing activities of West Ham hooligans, influencing the negotiation of the *post facto* meaning of a fight. The comments by a former ICF member on an incident provoked by West Ham hooligans in North London capture this tension well: '[The incident] could seriously harm the backing for the film deal signed on the ICF book. Reckless actions like this cannot be condoned' (*OLAS*, 321, November 2003: 16-17).

The development of football hooliganism at West Ham United should be understood not only in terms of the evolvement of inter-group and intra-group relations, but also by the interactions between hooligans and law enforcers. I have demonstrated that a major consequence of early security measures was to displace the problem into areas where the controls were, or were perceived by hooligans as being, weak or non-existent. Hooligan confrontations also became increasingly planned and co-ordinated. From the mid-1980s onwards, however, as controls and punishments grew more pervasive and police and club operations became more organized, opportunities for large-scale hooligan confrontations diminished and many experienced hooligans lessened their involvement in football hooliganism. One of the key moments in this process was the court case against alleged ICF ringleaders. Although the defendants were acquitted, a signal was sent to the hooligans that the police were beginning to take the issue very seriously and that the heydays of football violence were over. Football hooliganism gradually became more controllable and predictable for the authorities due to close surveillance and intelligence gathering, which enabled them to regularly prevent hooligan encounters and to arrest offenders.

Despite these changes, football hooliganism at West Ham United remains a persistent phenomenon. In recent years the hooligan formation has attracted new young recruits and a number of older hooligans is still centrally involved in confrontations with opposing groups. Although far less frequently and in smaller numbers than in the 1970s and early 1980s, the hooligan formation occasionally goes to great lengths to confront its rivals and to escape police observation. Group members and non-hooligan supporters are also regularly challenged by rival hooligan formations seeking to enhance or secure their status in the hierarchy of hooligan oppositions. In this hierarchy, the ICF continues to be viewed as one of Britain's most fearsome and organized hooligan groups and therefore as a valuable scalp, even though most older hooligans feel that 'them days are gone'.

5

Football Culture in SW6:
Fulham FC, the 'Friendly' Club

Introduction

Fulham Football Club holds a widespread reputation as a 'friendly' club. This image not only informs the collective identity of Fulham fans, but it also tends to structure the expectations and dispositions of opposing supporters and law enforcers. The case of Fulham provides a fresh look at theoretical explanations of football hooliganism. Theoretical approaches to the subject attempt to explain under which structural or cultural conditions hooligan behaviour is likely to develop, but they fail to fully account for the conditions that underlie the absence of such behaviour. The study of football clubs without a persistent hooligan subculture may provide an important new departure in the academic debate on football hooliganism. I argue that Fulham's 'non-hooligan' traditions should be understood in terms of the habitus and collective identity of its fans and the ways in which this identity is constructed in relation to significant others. Any attempt to understand and explain the club's 'friendly' image and the absence of a persistent hooligan subculture should therefore take into consideration the dominant values of Fulham fan culture and their relation to structural issues as well as to the construction of self and other in football rivalries. At the same time, I seek to show how the 'friendly' image downplays the existence of a hooligan subculture at the club in the 1960s and 1970s, which is generally viewed as a minor and temporary 'excess' compared to the persistent hooligan problems at other football clubs.

This chapter is divided into three parts. The first part analyzes the origins and development of Fulham fan culture and the ways in which fan culture shapes the collective identity and habitus of Fulham fans. It looks at the club's historical ties with the local community and the deep-seated local rivalry with Chelsea FC. Then I will examine the extent and nature of football hooliganism at Fulham and changes therein over time. In the final part of the chapter, I discuss recent developments in Fulham fan culture and hooliganism and their effects on fan identity and the interactions between supporters and law enforcers.

'Feeling Fulhamish': the sources of Fulham fan culture

The single biggest influence on the formation and early development of Fulham FC was the Church. In 1879 St Andrews Sunday School began to organize a football team which played at public sport places in the borough of Fulham. The key founding fathers were Reverend James Cardwell of St Andrews Church, churchwarden and leader of the Fulham Conservatives Dr Patrick Murdoch and Sunday school teacher Tom Norman, who were motivated by the Christian desire to provide local boys with some healthy recreation (Turner, 2004: 8).[1] Their wish to encourage sporting activity among young people was driven by the belief that football's robust game was an ideal way of combating urban degeneracy (Walvin, 1994: 59). It was not until the 1890s that the club – which changed its name from Fulham St Andrews to Fulham FC in 1888 – really began to take off. Football in South West London had become increasingly popular and together with local rival Stanley FC Fulham attracted the best amateur footballers in the borough. Having evolved into a more ambitious entity, in 1896 the club took over the destroyed Craven Cottage site located in London's SW6 district and turned it into a reasonably adequate sports ground. Fulham became a professional organization that gradually progressed from local to national competitions.

In an attempt to follow Fulham's example, in 1905 two local businessmen, the Mears brothers, established a rival club in Fulham: Chelsea FC. Chelsea moved into the Stamford Bridge ground, which was until then used almost exclusively by the London Athletic Club. Over the years Fulham and Chelsea developed distinctive profiles and personalities. Both teams were comparatively unsuccessful until the mid-1950s, when Chelsea's results improved periodically. Chelsea claimed the 1955 League Championship and, in the 1960s and early 1970s, the club experienced a comparatively successful period in the top division. In 1970 the club won the FA Cup and a year later it added the European Cup Winners' Cup to its honours. Meanwhile, Fulham failed to secure its place in the First Division.[2] The club obtained the image of an intimate family club, an image that was created in part by the three generations of the Dean family that were in control of the club for most of the twentieth century (Turner, 2004: 30).

The relatively intimate nature of Fulham FC came to be reflected more significantly in home attendances from the 1970s onwards. The club experienced its highest average attendances during two post-war spells in Division One. Between 1949 and 1952, and from 1959 to 1968, attendances at Craven Cottage regularly exceeded 30,000, contrasting starkly with the club's situation after 1968. Fulham constantly bobbed between the Second and Third Division and average home attendances fell steadily: from just over 10,000 in the 1974/75 season down to 4,200 by 1995/96. As home attendances fell below 10,000, Chairman Tommy Trinder publicly condemned the club's problematic situation:

> [The home attendances] are disastrous! Unless we get 10,000 at each home game, we lose money. That is just our break-even figure. Obviously, to make money available for new players we need many more supporters. Everyone at the club spent hours talking over this problem. And nobody knows the answer. We do all the right things. The team play attractive football. There are personalities like Bobby Moore and Alan Mullery [...] Our facilities are first class. Despite all this, our crowds are poor [...] I am hoping that if we stay in the promotion race, our support will grow. We have local competition from Chelsea, Queen's Park Rangers and Brentford. Even so, with our recent record we ought to have a bigger following (*Evening News London*, 25 October 1975).

By the mid-1990s Fulham's situation had hit rock bottom. Club historian Turner (2004: 128) wrote how 'supporters, tired of being short-changed by dodgy chairmen, incompetent managers, poor teams, second-rate players and inadequate facilities, drifted away.' In the opening weeks of 1996, being ranked second from bottom in the Division Three and 91st in the entire Football League, Fulham lost away at Torquay United, the team ranked 92nd and last in the entire Football League. This defeat still constitutes a key event in fan discourse as it exemplifies for many long-standing fans the hardships of supporting Fulham FC and the meanings of 'Fulhamish', as we will see in the following section.

A sense of place: the sources of collective fan identity at Fulham FC

Three inter-related themes are central to understanding contemporary fan culture at Fulham: the historical rivalry with Chelsea, the strong emotional attachment to the ground and the club's bizarre ups and downs throughout its history. The perceived differences between Fulham and Chelsea are seen to be reflected to some degree in the differences between the two localities. Despite being geographically close, the two areas have developed a distinctive character in the post-war era. Chelsea was one of the hearts of London's 'Swinging Sixties'. Local adolescents were drawn to the variety of fashionable music halls and bars in King's Road and Fulham Road (White, 2002: 341-351). The fashionable nature of the area mirrored, and still mirrors, the glamorous image of the club. For many local boys, Chelsea was (and is) the club to support. As one Fulham supporter claimed:

> Chelsea were the glamour team at the time. I was at primary school in Fulham and I was the only Fulham supporter in my class, of 30 kids. Everybody else who liked football supported Chelsea. A year later I went to secondary school and it was exactly the same. Me and another boy supported Fulham out of 70 boys (Personal interview, November 2003).

The distinctive personalities of the clubs are also ascribed to differences between the two football grounds. In 1970, local historian Whitting (1970: 217) wrote:

> The former [Craven Cottage] boasts a picturesque riverside setting, a lush green turf and a compactness which brings an exciting atmosphere even when the attendance only reaches 15,000; the latter [Stamford Bridge] well situated near an underground station, has three separate grandstands and excellent terraces which provide a good view, however crowded the ground.

Although many Fulham supporters claim that Craven Cottage is the most attractive football ground in Britain in the ornamental sense, central to Fulham fan culture is, above anything else, supporters' strong emotional attachment to the ground. The ground evokes memories and excites anticipation; its beauty 'is the special, environmental kind, appreciated only to people who relate the setting to their emotional attachment' (Hopcraft, 1988: 141). It possesses its own social-geographical character, emblematic of the fan community (Giulianotti, 1999: 70). For most supporters, the ground's unique location on the bank of the river Thames, adjacent to Bishop's Park and in the vicinity of a variety of animated pubs and restaurants, symbolizes the area's particular feel. The ground's overpowering yet intimate atmosphere is reinforced by the picturesque Cottage built in 1888. As the twentieth century progressed, 'what had been admired as a state-of-the-art facility became a much-loved anachronism, a throwback to a simpler age' (Turner, 2004: 13). Long-standing Fulham supporters feel as close to the ground as to the club itself. For all that has changed at a club level, the ground remains a major source of fans' pride and passion.

> Craven Cottage is like home to me. Because it's the only place that since the age of ten I've been going to regularly. Nowhere else have I gone that regularly. And funnily, I wouldn't always stand in one place or have a specific seat in one stand. I would always go to different places all around the ground 'cos I love the whole thing. It has its own special attractions, which other people can't understand. I mean they come here and say "it's a shit hole, it's desperate". No, it's beautiful! You've got the Thames, you've got the views, that lovely old stand and the little Cottage in the corner. For me it's home. (Personal interview with Fulham fan, October 2003)

Fulham's problematic situation from the second half of the 1970s onwards seems to have enhanced fans' emotional attachment to Craven Cottage as well as their ingroup solidarity. At a time when on-field performances were mostly disappointing and home attendances were steadily declining, Fulham supporters constructed a sense of self based on a combination of humour and irony, often referred to as 'Fulhamish'. Football itself remained a source of entertainment, but increasingly the team became the subject of supporters' mockery and disbelief: 'You used to take the piss out of yourselves at Fulham. To be honest, simply because there wasn't much else to do' (personal interview with Fulham fan, October 2003). Fulhamish is seen as being not only the ability to ridicule yourself and your team, but also the habit to fail the final hurdle, triggering a downward spiral into football obscurity: 'It's a unique word that is an integral part of the Fulham vernacular, epitomizing the hapless aura that has surrounded the club in the past – that unique and often baffling ability to throw away golden opportunities' (Mascall, 2001). Similarly, as we will see, it also applies to Fulham's bizarre upsurge in recent years as the club raced through the divisions and signed on multi-million pound players and high-profile managers. As one supporter put it:

> Even I say to my kids now 'enjoy this Premiership because if you're going to support Fulham for the rest of your lives, you're gonna see bad times.' Some of the stuff that kept us going through the 80s and 90s was some of the wise-cracking. The football was so bad, small crowds, and the jokes were just hilarious. (Personal interview, October 2003)

Supporters' strong emotional attachment to Craven Cottage should also be viewed within the context of the post-war gentrification of South West London. Chelsea had become an up-and-coming area for middle-class owner-occupiers and tenants since the 1920s, but after the Second World War this process accelerated and spread (White, 2002: 63). Several traditional working-class neighbourhoods in Fulham were converted into more affluent middle-class communities through the remodelling of the housing stock, that is, the extension of the system of private ownership of domestic property. Estate agents came to occupy a substantial proportion of commercial property in the area. This transformation was accompanied by the growth in cultural and leisure services. The upgrading of the area resulted in rising property values and the relocation of original working-class occupiers, who were no longer able to pay the increasing rents (Glass, 1963). The tightly-packed terraces which had housed working-class families employed in the heavy industry that dominated Fulham's riverside were rapidly replaced with young professionals who had a very different socio-economic outlook.[3]

165

The gentrification of the area has fundamentally altered the geographical distribution of Fulham supporters. Whereas historically many Fulham fans lived relatively close to the ground, at present only around twenty per cent live in the SW district, notably in the districts of Fulham (6,2%), Putney (3,7%), Wimbledon (1,7%) and Wandsworth (1,7%). Other areas with a substantial number of registered Fulham supporters are Kingston (13,3%), West London (7,6%), Twickenham (6%) and Sutton (4,2%) (data provided by Fulham FC, December 2003). A 2002 survey suggests that Fulham fans live on an average distance of 21 miles from Craven Cottage; it takes them an average 44 minutes to get to the ground on match days (Sir Norman Chester Centre, 2000: 12-13). Despite their physical distance from the ground, supporters' emotional ties with the local area remain strong. Three out of four Fulham fans were born locally (Sir Norman Chester Centre, 2000: 7), and for many of them Craven Cottage symbolizes the 'old Fulham' in which they were brought up: '[O]ur local club [...] is the final piece of old Fulham left in the area, representing a community that has been forced away due to high house prices' (*TOOFIF*, no. 71, September 2000: 12).

Craven Cottage is a key symbol of Fulham fan culture, but at the same time it has also been a major source of unrest and conflict. From the mid-1970s onwards, the ground became the source of bitter financial disputes which threatened the very existence of the club. As property values increased Craven Cottage became a prime location for property developers. At the same time, Fulham's prolonged financial malaise had been aggravated by the building of the Riverside Stand, in the early 1970s, and by the club's relegation to Division Three in 1980. 'Debts mounted as attendances fell, and the likelihood of Fulham ensuring a secure financial position from footballing activities steadily diminished' (Turner, 1994: 280). The disputes over Craven Cottage reached their first climax in the mid-1980s.[4] Chairman Ernie Clay sold the club and the ground to property company Marler Estates, which sought to merge Fulham and the West London club Queen's Park Rangers in order to leave Craven Cottage free to develop. The plan was scorned by opposition from the local council, the football authorities and the general public. Former Fulham player Jimmy Hill started a campaign to save the club and eventually gathered the resources to buy the club, but not the ground. A long-term solution to the ground issue was still not reached.

The disputes over Craven Cottage resurfaced in the early 2000s following Fulham's promotion to the Premier League. In the second half of the 1990s the club experienced a bizarre upsurge. In 1997 Fulham won promotion to Division Two, its first promotion in fifteen years, and only weeks later Harrods owner Mohamed Al Fayed announced to the public that he had purchased the freehold of Craven Cottage, along with a major shareholding in the club. His aim was to take Fulham to the Premiership within five years. The plan was realized in just four years, mainly owing to the injection of substantial sums of money into the team. Promotion to the Premiership, in 2001, brought an influx of new players to Craven Cottage and led to a significant increase in home attendances. Average home attendances increased from 4,200 in the 1995/96 season to almost 20,000 five seasons later. The club's new supporters include a variety of foreign nationals and tourists who seem to be principally attracted by the team's Premiership status and high-profile foreign players (e.g. French, Dutch, Japanese, and American) as well as by the fact that Fulham is one of the few Premiership clubs where one can obtain tickets fairly easily.[5] In recent years the club has also attracted, like most Premier League clubs, an increasing number of 'upper-middle-class' supporters, some of them local residents. A 2003 survey suggests that 54 per cent of Fulham FC season ticket holders fall within this category, compared to 45 per cent in 2000 (*Fultime*, September 2003: 47; Sir Norman Chester Centre, 2000: 6-7). Another survey, carried out for the club in 2002, indicates an even higher proportion of 'upper-middle-class' supporters (57%). The unemployment rate among Fulham fans is only 0.2 per cent, compared to a London general household average of 7.1 per cent (data provided by Fulham FC, December 2003).

Promotion to Division One and the Premiership also meant that Craven Cottage's inadequate infrastructure and facilities became a pressing problem. The ground needed extensive renovation and as a Division One and Premiership club an all-seater stadium was compulsory (within three years after promotion to Division One). From April 2002 to July 2004 Fulham shared the Queen's Park Rangers ground while Craven Cottage was being refurbished. Many Fulham fans feared that the club would never to return to its spiritual home as Al Fayed's ambitious plan to develop the ground into a state-of-the-art stadium, at an estimated cost of approximately £80 million, did not get beyond the drawing board. The alternative long-term solution was in some respects even more ambitious: to build a brand new stadium at another location near White City, West London, putting the considerable development value of Craven Cottage towards the new ground. Many long-standing Fulham supporters strongly opposed to this plan and yearned to return to the club's historic riverside home. In 1999 a group of dedicated fans created the Fulham United campaign, arguing that Fulham FC and Craven Cottage were the only remaining symbols of a community that had been eroded by post-war gentrification.

Moreover, during the first season of the ground share, a group of Fulham supporters began to grow more wary of the club's promise to return to Craven Cottage within two years and therefore founded the Fulham Supporters' Trust (FST), which sprang from the Back To The Cottage (BTTC) campaign. The FST researched the plans for a new Fulham stadium and worked with *The Guardian* to reveal new information on the ground issue (e.g. *TOOFIF*, no. 91, August 2004). Its original aim was 'to convince the club that the best thing is to remain at Craven Cottage and not to build a new stadium somewhere else' (personal interview with chairman of FST, September 2003). Over time, however, the FST has incorporated the more general aim of developing a fruitful dialogue with the club in order to enhance the influence of supporters on the decision making process. The FST has evolved into a well-informed discussion partner with over 2,000 members. It has increasingly taken over the role of the official supporters' club, which is viewed by many supporters as too uncritical of club policies.

The ground issue deeply divides the fan community. On the one hand, some long-standing fans argue that there is no rational motive for the club to stay in the SW6 district: 'I know there's a brand name which is associated with the borough, and of course the emotional side. But in terms of ease of access for supporters, there's no logical reason why it needs to be in SW6. That may have been true in the 1920s and the 1930s, but certainly not in the 80s and 90s' (personal interview with Fulham fan, December 2003). On the other hand, a section of Fulham supporters are so attached to Craven Cottage that they reject any proposal that suggests moving the club to another site. They claim that they would rather see Fulham play in the lowest regions of the Football League than to move away from Craven Cottage. These supporters feel that many new fans cannot quite understand the meaning of Craven Cottage, since they identify more with the brand name and with high-profile players.

Their discomfort is occasionally voiced in chants such as 'Where were you when we were shit?' Furthermore, they neither believe nor hope that their club will ever be 'the new Chelsea' or, in Al Fayed's vision, 'the Manchester United of the South'. As one fan commented:

> Everything is against Fulham ever being a big club. The problem we have now is that although we are in the Premiership we cannot make it pay with gates of 20,000. But then again, if we had a 40,000 capacity stadium we wouldn't fill it. Deep down I believe that Fulham is a First Division club with a maximum following of, say, 25,000. (Personal interview, September 2003)

Fulham supporters were temporarily united in the Summer of 2004 when Fulham returned to a refurbished, 22,000 capacity Craven Cottage. Rather than the state-of-the-art development originally proposed, the plans were scaled back and a temporary 'make do and mend' approach was adopted (Turner, 2004: 186). The Fulham Supporters' Trust publicly expressed its gratitude towards chairman Al Fayed. In an open letter and in the *TOOFIF* fanzine, the FST thanked him for acknowledging the fact that Craven Cottage 'is a unique setting for football, and it is the charm and history of the ground that makes Fulham so special'. However, as a long-term solution is still being worked out, the FST continues to campaign for a definitive return to the club's historic riverside home.

In the remainder of this chapter I will relate the three main themes addressed in this section – the historical rivalry with Chelsea, the strong emotional attachment to the ground and the club's bizarre ups and downs throughout its history – to the manifestation of football hooliganism at Fulham. These themes are crucial to understanding 'Fulhamish' fan culture and, specifically, the contemporary 'friendly' identity and image of Fulham supporters. I will show that the small core of supporters who stayed loyal to the club in times of hardship constructed a more light-hearted self-image based on humour and irony, in opposition to what they perceived as the 'glory hunters' and 'hooligans' at several other British clubs, notably local rival Chelsea. Within this context I examine the emergence and development of football hooliganism.

The emergence and development of football hooliganism at Fulham

The rivalry between Fulham and Chelsea has historically been fierce, but matches between the two teams have rarely been marred by spectator violence. The relatively low level of spectator violence at local derbies can in part be explained by the historical ties between the two sets of fans. The fixtures were originally arranged in such a way that Fulham and Chelsea played at home alternately. Many local fans watched both clubs, especially in the late 1940s and 1950s, even though they generally had a strong preference for one or the other (Whitting, 1970: 217). Only occasionally did (relatively minor) incidents of spectator violence take place during derbies. In October 1928, a Professional Charity Fund match at Craven Cottage reportedly caused some 'unsavoury incidents' on the terraces. After a Fulham player was sent off, a small group of home supporters 'made their disagreements with the referee's decision very apparent'. The football authorities ordered Fulham to post warning notices around the ground. The club was also required to insert in each issue of the official club programme for a period of four weeks a special warning that any interference by spectators with the officials of a match or further infringement of the official regulations may result in the ground being closed. The club objected to these conditions, which were seen as reacting unjustifiedly on Fulham's recognized reputation for fair play (Turner, 1994: 73).

By the 1960s the two clubs had developed distinctive profiles and personalities. Chelsea was the more glamorous and successful club, attracting large numbers of local youths to Stamford Bridge. Reflecting the developments at other major clubs in London (see Chapter Three), Chelsea's home crowd became increasingly segregated by age. Young fans created their own exclusive territory within the ground to the exclusion of the older football citizenry. The youth end, nicknamed 'the Shed', became known for its vibrant and intimidating atmosphere, but from the mid-1960s onwards it was also commonly associated with football hooliganism. The growing hooligan reputation of the Shed attracted local young males who saw involvement in football hooliganism as a source of excitement and adventure. The skinheads, with their emphasis on aggressive masculinity, also found a welcoming environment on the terraces of Stamford Bridge (Brimson and

Brimson, 1997: 40). In contrast, the youth end at Fulham never obtained a comparable reputation for toughness. The club's successive relegations in the late 1960s partly excluded its youth end from the emerging network of hooligan rivalries at the major London clubs. Chelsea hooligans saw young Fulham fans as 'friendly' neighbours rather than as respectable opponents. As a former Chelsea hooligan put it:

> There would be no trouble today. No way. Fulham don't have a mob, and if they did they would be indistinguishable from the Chelsea boys. Many of Chelsea's top and oldest faces lived in Fulham. You don't smash up your own back yard and fight with your old schoolmates. Although a couple of years on Chelsea did just that. Came out of Craven Cottage and demolished the Fulham Palace Road. That was when Chelsea was attracting every half-wit vandal residing in the south-east of England. A lot of the original Chelsea firm were very pissed off about that (King and Knight, 1999a: 60).

But despite the perception of Fulham as a club without a hooligan 'firm', the diffusion of inter-group rivalries also affected the youth end at Craven Cottage. Groups of young Fulham supporters congregated in the Hammersmith End, directly behind one of the goals. As 'taking' the opponent's territory became a popular terrace fashion, various hooligan groups attempted to invade the Hammersmith End, often with relative ease since the police undertook little action to prevent such invasion. The 'taking' of the home end was viewed by several young Fulham fans as a humiliation and they began to defend their territory more actively. This occasionally resulted in running battles between opposing fan groups, as groups of visiting supporters tended to congregate outside the home end and push their way in, often long before the start of the match. The young fans inhabiting the Hammersmith End were at the forefront of a brief terrace fashion, carrying black and white walking sticks which were regularly used as offensive weapons during fights with rival hooligans. Clubs soon prohibited the carrying of walking sticks (Watt, 1993: 121-122). Fulham hooligans celebrated their walking sticks in terrace chants such as 'Walking sticks where are you?' However, as the Hammersmith End was only sporadically sold out in the late 1960s, abundant space enabled the

171

opposing fan groups to inhabit different parts of the home end without physical confrontation. Visiting supporters habitually took over a corner part of the terrace, while Fulham supporters gathered around the green pole in the top centre of the stand (see Mascall, 2002: 77). This process often passed without serious fighting.

Although the defence of home territory and the invasion of foreign turf became a central concern for several young Fulham fans, only a limited number of young males regularly participated in violent confrontation with opposing hooligan formations. Some Fulham hooligans held a widespread reputation for toughness, which was celebrated in certain chants and songs.[6] These notorious fighters were usually treated with respect because of their fighting ability and bravery: 'He wasn't one of those people who would stand in the back and say "forward". He would be at the front and lead the charge across the Hammersmith End or down the Fulham Palace Road' (personal interview with former Fulham hooligan, October 2003). Apart from being renowned fighters, they were also seen by some as 'nutters' who 'steamed in' without thinking. The nutter, according to Marsh and his colleagues (1978: 70-71), is acceptable in that he demonstrates the limits of legitimate action, that is, he demonstrates to other fans what they should not do. As a former hooligan commented:

> He's just mad. He has a record as long as your arm. You would sometimes see him and maybe two or three others going into an end of the opposition on their own. At West Brom once, the whole ground opened up and there were four of them, him and three of his friends, and they just took on anyone that would come. That's crazy, really. (Personal interview, November 2003)

The core of Fulham's early hooligan formation consisted principally of young males from working-class council estates in Fulham and West Kensington. Especially the youth gangs from the large Clem Attlee Court held a reputation for aggressive and violent behaviour (*Fulham Chronicle*, 18 April 1975). A group of skinheads living in the Clem Attlee estate ran its own buses to away matches and regularly provoked fights with opposing fans. Although most young Fulham supporters kept their distance, many recall how this group was often useful as a kind of protective force at

172

away matches: 'If you were in a bit of a situation, being outnumbered, you were grateful to see them because it boosted your numbers. If you had a problem they would get involved' (personal interview with Fulham fan, October 2003).

Football hooliganism at Fulham was at its height in the late 1960s and early 1970s, but during this period the hooligan formation was still comparatively small and less notorious than the hooligan groups at clubs such as Chelsea, West Ham United, Millwall and Manchester United. Some Fulham hooligans themselves acknowledged the more violent reputations and the larger extent of certain other hooligan formations. As one former hooligan commented:

> I dreaded visits from clubs such as West Ham, Man United and Chelsea. The biggest fighting I've ever seen at Fulham was when we played Portsmouth in the FA Cup. They are like Millwall. They may have had at the time only 10,000 supporters, but 8,000 of them were men, big men, and nasty. The one place where you never went wearing colours. At Millwall and West Ham you would never do that either. (Personal interview, December 2003)

For young males living in South West London Chelsea was the team to follow (Ward, 1989: 106), especially after Fulham's successive relegations in 1968 and 1969. Chelsea was also the most attractive option for boys and young men identifying with football hooliganism due to the reputation of the Shed and the opportunities for confronting the hooligan groups of other major clubs. Once the exploits of Chelsea hooligans became part of youth folklore, this became a self-perpetuating process which still persists today.[7] At the same time, home attendances at Fulham dropped steadily in the early 1970s and football hooliganism gradually disappeared.

In the early 1970s, a group of Fulham supporters formed what is still referred to today as Fulham's 'hooligan firm'. The Thamesbank Travellers (TBT) first began to run their own coaches to away matches when the official supporters' club stopped facilitating travel arrangements. The TBT eschewed travel by train in order to avoid police controls and official restrictions. The group's main objective was to have a pleasurable day out, which usually included hefty drinking. For most

TBT members, confronting rival fans was not a major priority: 'We would have more trouble if the pub wasn't open at the time we arrived in a town. Not if there was a bunch of hooligans waiting for us' (personal interview with TBT member, January 2004). Usually, violence was only deemed legitimate as a form of self-defence. The group was regularly a target for opposing supporters who physically attacked them or damaged the coaches. In order to protect themselves and their coaches, TBT members did not allow opposing fans to 'take liberties', which occasionally forced them to confront their aggressors. As a former TBT member claimed: 'If I could avoid it, I would. Sometimes you get somebody up the north somewhere and the only way out is you gonna have to hit him. We never went out for it, you were going for a day out. However, people were not going to take liberties with us, that's for sure' (personal interview, October 2003).

Contrary to the myth surrounding the group, the accounts of TBT members reveal that the group should not be viewed as a typical hooligan formation. Group members' occasional involvement in violent confrontation was principally a response to intimidation and assaults by rival fans rather than an attempt to enhance the group's status in the hierarchy of hooligan oppositions. Compared to most English hooligan formations, the TBT also had a more positive public image. In 1974 Manchester United fans grabbed news headlines after allegedly 'brawling in city centres, smashing windows and damaging cars' at a match against AS Ostend in Belgium (Williams et al., 1984: 192). Shortly after the incident TBT members travelled through Belgium on their way to Fulham's friendly match against the Dutch club Helmond Sport. The English press described their behaviour as a credit to England:

At a time when the Minister of Sport, Mr Dennis Howell, has called for stricter measures against rampaging soccer fans, 22 Fulham supporters, in the shape of the Thamesbank Travellers, have been called a credit to England [...] So good was the supporters' behaviour that he [a Belgian police officer] described them as: 'A credit to England and such a nice change to have football supporters who know to behave themselves.' (quoted in Ferguson, 2003: 37)

The activities of the TBT diminished from the mid-1980s as many group members, now in their late thirties, were increasingly constrained by family and work responsibilities. By the early 1990s the group had virtually disappeared. Despite the TBT's gradual disappearance, the myth surrounding the group still persists. In recent discussions on Internet message boards some young Fulham supporters claimed that they wanted to 'get a firm back' at Fulham, similar to the TBT, in order to challenge their rivals at Chelsea. In response to these internet postings, a self-declared Fulham supporter wrote that the activities of the TBT 'are illegal and dangerous therefore they are all criminals [...] they must change there [*sic*] ways for their own good and the good of others especially for Fulham FC.'[8] Contemporary representations of this kind contrast starkly with the reality of the TBT.

Overview of the emergence and early development of football hooliganism

Despite its deep-seated image as a 'friendly' club, in the mid-1960s Fulham experienced the emergence of a hooligan formation. Football hooliganism at Fulham emerged as part of a national network of inter-group rivalries and was preceded by the segregation of the crowd by age, as young supporters began to create their own exclusive territory within the ground. Territorial identifications played a key role in the construction of ingroup and outgroup relations. Young supporters' commitment to physically defend their territory and to establish a reputation for toughness was enhanced by the attempts of opposing fan groups to 'take' the Hammersmith End. The hooligan group was nevertheless limited in both its extent and its reputation, and by the mid-1970s football hooliganism at Fulham had largely disappeared.

The relatively limited extent of football hooliganism at Fulham should principally be understood in terms of the club's declining situation in the late 1960s, its 'friendly' image and the popularity of local rival Chelsea. The overwhelming majority of local youths gravitated towards the more successful and glamorous club in the area, and male adolescents identifying with football hooliganism were increasingly attracted by the reputation of the hooligan formation at Chelsea. Furthermore, although a small group of Fulham supporters regularly engaged in football hooliganism, many hooligans acknowledged that their group was considerably smaller and less notorious than the hooligan formations at the major

175

clubs in London. In this sense, football hooliganism at Fulham contained elements of both resistance to and compliance with the club's dominant fan culture. In the following section, I will show that in recent years the 'friendly' fan identity has become a more dominant source of Fulham fan culture, increasingly defining football hooliganism as 'not for the likes of us'.

'Not for the likes of us': football violence as cultural trauma

The 'friendly' reputation of Fulham supporters has developed in relation to the sustained media attention for football hooliganism at Chelsea and at other clubs in London. Chelsea and the local authorities introduced a series of measures to prevent what a local newspaper called the 'disgusting behaviour by hooligans' in the aftermath of a number of violent incidents involving Chelsea fans (*Fulham Chronicle*, 19 February 1982). In the mid-1980s a police investigation was carried out into the activities of assumed 'ringleaders' of the hooligan formation Headhunters. In March 1986, after months of alleged police 'infiltration' into the ranks of the Headhunters, nine Chelsea fans were arrested for conspiracy to cause affray. Five of them were sentenced to five to ten years imprisonment, but they were later released due to unreliable police evidence. The court case generated widespread media attention, securing the status of the hooligan formation in the hierarchy of hooligan oppositions. National newspapers wrote how Chelsea hooligans gave Nazi salutes and how they planned confrontations with military-style precision (*Daily Mail*, 9 May 1986). The link between Chelsea hooligans and the far right was sustained in media reports in the 1990s and early 2000s. Members of the right-wing organization Combat 18 allegedly 'commanded' the Headhunters, assaulting rival supporters as well as 'defiant' Chelsea fans (*News of the World*, 12 February 1995). Club chairman Ken Bates repeatedly accused the national press of stigmatizing the club. In 1984 he banned the tabloid *News of the World* after publishing a sensationalist report on 'soccer's savages'. According to Bates:

> I don't deny there is a hooligan problem at Stamford Bridge [...] What differs is the press treatment of Chelsea in that they are the only club consistently criticized, consistently persecuted and consistently

176

emphasized. If Chelsea has the worst reputation in the country it is because of irresponsible reporting (*News of the World*, 30 September 1984).

Compared to the widespread reputation of Chelsea hooligans, football hooliganism at Fulham has been relatively unproblematic and insignificant, especially from the 1980s onwards. As part of Fulham supporters' construction of self, violence provoked by 'the other' has often been fiercely condemned. Perceived differences between self and the other are also sustained and reproduced by the perceptions of the authorities and the media. After Fulham supporters were attacked by local fans in Swansea, on 9 January 1993, a senior British Transport Police officer publicly acknowledged that 'Fulham's travelling supporters have an exemplary record of good behaviour' (*TOOFIF*, no. 25, March 1993: 36). Local and national newspapers have regularly reported how well-behaved Fulham supporters were assaulted by opposing fans. Neglecting previous incidents of spectator violence and hooliganism, one local newspaper reported that the 'first ever violence in the club's 114-year history', on 21 August 1993, was caused not by home fans but by visiting Cardiff City supporters (*Fulham Chronicle*, 26 August 1993). Around 50 Welsh fans climbed over fences into a home section of the ground and onto the pitch, assaulting home fans and forcing the players to leave the field for 22 minutes as stewards and police officers tried to stop the disturbances. The police claimed they were well prepared for the violence and that they had prevented a premeditated fight between Cardiff hooligans and an alliance of Chelsea and Queen's Park Rangers hooligans before the match. Fulham chairman Jimmy Hill condemned the behaviour of the away fans, claiming that although the trouble 'has been tried to be passed off onto a small minority, the 1,700 [Cardiff] supporters who were there did nothing to help the general situation but they responded to the violence... they did not discourage them' (*Fulham Chronicle*, 26 August 1993).

More recently, in 1999, opposing fans attacked Fulham supporters on two separate occasions. On 7 August 1999, during a First Division match at St Andrews, a group of twenty Birmingham City supporters attacked Fulham fans, knocking one of them unconscious. Three coaches carrying away fans were pelted with stones and bottles (NCIS, 2000; *Fulham & Hammersmith Chronicle*, 19 August 1999). On 18 September 1999 Fulham and Queen's Park Rangers played each other for the first time in sixteen years at Craven Cottage in what was termed 'the battle of West London' (*News of the World*, 19 September 1999). A group of away supporters attacked Fulham fans inside the stadium just before kick-off and spectators spilled onto the pitch in order to avoid the disturbances. During the first half the hostilities resurfaced as police officers and stewards attempted to separate the two sets of fans. Rival supporters confronted each other outside the ground after the final whistle (NCIS, 2000; *Fulham & Hammersmith Chronicle*, 23 September 1999).

Fulham's 'friendly' image was temporarily discredited in the aftermath of the most tragic event in the club's relatively meagre history of spectator violence. After a league match at Gillingham's Priestfield Stadium, on 28 March 1998, a small group of Fulham fans encountered a group of Gillingham supporters in a narrow alleyway outside the ground. There was a brief scuffle between the two groups during which punches were thrown. One Fulham supporter, 24-year-old Matthew Fox, died from head injuries after he was punched around the side of the head and fell, hitting his head on the side of the kerb. There had been no historical rivalry between the two sets of fans, but in November 1995, during an ill-tempered match between the two teams, a Gillingham player had his leg broken by Fulham's Martin Thomas, ending the player's career and enraging Gillingham fans. The renewed confrontation between both sides turned out to be one of 'bad blood'. Throughout the match opposing supporters allegedly attempted to confront each other and Fulham fans were pelted with missiles, such as bottles and coins. Stewards struggled to keep feuding supporters apart (*The Times*, 30 March 1998). When a bottle hit a young girl on the head and the local police allegedly failed to respond to the incident, the mood among the away fans changed: 'Normal people who you know wouldn't normally get upset were going potty. We pointed out the bloke who threw it to the police but they did nothing' (*Fulham & Hammersmith Chronicle*, 2 April 1998). After the final whistle both sets of fans filed out into the streets and various Fulham supporters were assaulted, some of whom needed hospital treatment.

Looking at it from the perspective of Fulham supporters and club officials, the violence at Gillingham can be seen as cultural disorientation, that is, a clash or ambivalence within the fan culture 'emerging suddenly, rapidly and unexpectedly, and embracing the core areas of cultural components, such as basic values, central beliefs, and common norms' (Sztompka, 2000: 453). The death of Matthew Fox produced cultural trauma in the sense that it disturbed the collective fan identity and the delimitation of the borders of the category 'we', as opposed to 'them'. It represented a fundamental threat to Fulham supporters' sense of who they are, where they came from and where they want to go, resulting in an identity crisis and a struggle to re-establish and reshape a collective identity through a searching re-remembering of the collective past (see Alexander, 2004). A week after the tragic incident the club organized a minute's silence before the home match against Preston North End in memory of the deceased. The club and its fans were desperately trying to come to terms with the events and their potential damage to Fulham's 'friendly' self-image. The editor of the Fulham fanzine *There's only one F in Fulham* (TOOFIF) wrote:

> It remains ironic that a Fulham fan should have been involved. We have gained a merited reputation for friendliness and our (good) behaviour has been commented upon many times in the past. This is a situation we must now strive to restore (*TOOFIF*, no. 58, April 1998: 5).

Supporters and stewards blamed crowd control failures, claiming that the match was seriously under-policed – with 60 officers policing a crowd of over 10,000 – and that police should have held back the two sets of fans from leaving the ground at the same time. These accusations were sustained by media reports on the long-running dispute between Gillingham FC and the Kent police over the costs of policing football matches (*Fulham & Hammersmith Chronicle*, 2 April 1998; *The Times*, 30 March 1998). At the same time, however, most Fulham supporters were aware of the fact that the incidents at the Priestfield Stadium could not merely be ascribed to crowd control failures or the misbehaviour of Gillingham fans. When Gillingham scored their second goal, a group of Fulham fans scaled the fence to confront rival supporters. They also hurled coins and bottles into the home end. Several long-standing supporters claimed that it was the worst hatred they had ever witnessed from a Fulham crowd (*TOOFIF*, no. 58, April 1998: 10-11).

One explanation offered by fans was that the attitudes of opposing supporters towards Fulham had changed since the arrival of Mohamed Al Fayed. From this viewpoint, whereas before many smaller clubs identified with Fulham because of their clubs' similar situations and Fulham's reputation as a 'friendly' club, now they resented Fulham's financial prosperity and claims to fame and fortune: 'We are no longer one of them' (*TOOFIF*, no. 58, April 1998: 14). A second explanation was that recent changes in Fulham's fan community had increased the potential for violence. Some Fulham supporters expressed their concern over what they perceived as the declining moral values of a section of the club's following. A small group of young fans in the Hammersmith End were seen to identify with football hooliganism. During the official inquiry into Fox's death, the police received a series of anonymous telephone calls claiming that Fox orchestrated hooligan confrontations at Fulham as well as at the English national team (personal interview with football intelligence officer, September 2003; *The Times*, 30 March 1998).

In fact, Fox was part of a small group of Fulham fans that became known to the police for its relatively boisterous behaviour in the mid-1990s. The core of the group consisted of around 30 young males in their early twenties from South West London. Some group members were students, while others were employed as decorators, postmen and civil servants, among others. For the local police, the group was much easier to control and monitor than the substantially larger and more violent hooligan formation at Chelsea. Although group members occasionally responded to provocations by opposing fans, they did not actively seek confrontation with rival hooligan formations nor did they identify themselves as a 'hooligan' group, and neither did the police. According to a local football intelligence officer:

> They wouldn't go out looking for violence. They wouldn't attack opposing fans, but they would stand up to anyone that attacked them. They weren't what you might call category C hooligans. We wouldn't categorize them as hooligans when compared to other clubs. They were never a real problem to us (Personal interview, September 2003).

Instead of enhancing the rivalry between Fulham and Gillingham supporters or the violent proclivities of the group, Fox's death seems to have led to the reshaping of group identity, as group members agreed that 'things had gone too far'. By intersubjective agreement the violence at Gillingham was framed as transgressing the group's core values and tacit social rules (cf. Marsh et al., 1978). Thus, although they did not identify with football hooliganism before the tragic incident, now their willingness to resort to violence became even more inhibited. Their collective identity was reshaped in accordance with the re-establishing of the dominant fan identity at Fulham.

This collective identity is important not only in limiting the hooliganism of Fulham fans, but also in producing a relatively sanguine and non-aggressive approach on the part of visitors to Fulham (cf. Williams et al., 1988: 41). Despite occasional (spontaneous) incidents, hooligan groups travelling to Craven Cottage normally do not anticipate violent confrontation because of the low-key profile of Fulham supporters. In other words, hooligan honour is not won at Fulham: 'At Fulham there is absolutely no point in coming to fight. There is no one to fight' (personal interview with West Ham hooligan, September 2003). Because of the negative sanctioning of hooligan behaviour and the relatively non-aggressive approach on the part of visitors to Fulham, young supporters interested in becoming involved in football hooliganism are likely to either follow one of the more notorious football clubs (e.g. Chelsea) or eschew their hooligan proclivities. Through this process the delimitation of the borders of the category 'we' (i.e. the 'friendly' Fulham fan), as opposed to 'them' (the violent other), is reproduced. Matches against Fulham may also serve as an opportunity for visiting hooligan formations to challenge other, more competitive fan groups in London. On several occasions the author has observed how Metropolitan Police officers sought to prevent hooligan formations attending their team's away match at Craven Cottage from confronting rival hooligan groups in the City of London. As a senior police officer argued: 'The main problem is that these groups travel around the city. Fulham matches are usually unproblematic, but when they play a big club and that mob tries to confront other major hooligan groups, then we have a lot of work on our hands' (personal interview, November 2003).

The collective identity of Fulham fans is thus reproduced in the interactions and negotiations between supporters and the police. Police officers highlight that Fulham supporters are 'right at the bottom of the hooligan league table' (personal interview with senior police officer, September 2003). Or, in the words of a football intelligence officer: 'If there was a league table for hooliganism, Fulham would be at the bottom of the Conference [a minor league].' This perception is reflected in official statistics on spectator violence; Fulham supporters were not involved in any of the registered incidents of football-related violence in the 2002/03 and 2003/04 seasons (British Transport Police, 2003; 2004).[9] Occasionally, however, the deep-seated hatred towards Chelsea boils over into spontaneous disorder. The West London derby at Craven Cottage on 19 March 2006 was marred by crowd disorder. After the final whistle Fulham supporters invaded the pitch to celebrate their team's momentous victory (1-0). Some of them ran to the away section and goaded the Chelsea fans. Minor fighting took place between opposing fans on the pitch. The club launched a major internal investigation into the incidents.

In accordance with the low-key profile of Fulham supporters, intelligence-led policing principally focuses on the intentions and behaviour of opposing fans. Matches at Craven Cottage are only very occasionally classified as 'high risk' ('category C'), mainly depending on the reputation and dispositions of the away contingent. Furthermore, local police intelligence officers invest most of their resources into spectator behaviour at Chelsea and Queen's Park Rangers. The number of police officers deployed at home matches of Fulham is systematically lower than at matches of one of these clubs (data provided by the West London police intelligence unit, January 2004). Only a small group of Fulham supporters, consisting of a dozen young males, is monitored more intensively by football intelligence officers. Although the group does not engage in hooligan confrontations, the police seek to prevent the group from developing into a hooligan formation by close surveillance and deterrence (albeit to a smaller extent than in their operations at Chelsea and Queen's Park Rangers). The police and the club also co-operate closely to identify and arrest offenders at home matches and to impose banning orders. Because of this 'proactive' approach the arrest rates at football matches in West London are relatively high compared to those at matches in other parts of the capital (Metropolitan Police, 2003). At the same time, police officers are well aware of the non-hooligan traditions of Fulham.

This non-hooligan image is celebrated by supporters and club officials alike. Club officials seek to maintain Fulham's non-aggressive, family atmosphere. Over the last three decades the club has had a relatively small (lower-league) fan base, stimulating close personal contacts (and informal social controls) between dedicated supporters and certain club officials and players. Fulham also implements a community scheme aimed at strengthening the club's ties with the local community, and local youths in particular, in order to attract new fans. One of Fulham's main assets, club officials argue, is precisely its 'friendly', feel-good atmosphere.

Conclusion

In this chapter I have sought to show how the collective identity of Fulham fans is shaped within the fan community and how it is generally sustained and reproduced, but also occasionally contested, by opposing supporters, the police and the media. This collective identity can be seen as a relation of difference, that is, it is constructed through the perceived differences between self and the other. The proximity of Chelsea and the historical rivalry between the two clubs is crucial to understanding Fulham fan culture and the relatively low level of football hooliganism at the club. Long-standing Fulham supporters tend to define themselves against what they perceive as the 'hooligans' and 'glory hunters' at Stamford Bridge and at certain other English football grounds. In short, they present a self-image of being more authentic and good-tempered than their (local) rivals.

This process closely reflects Giulianotti's (1995) analysis of the 'friendly' image of supporters of the Scottish national team. Giulianotti argues that the 'anti-Englishness' of the Scottish fans led them to create a 'friendly' image for themselves, in opposition to the English hooligan label. At the same time, there are also differences between the 'friendly' images of Scottish fans and Fulham supporters. The Scottish case seems to provide evidence for the mutability of hooligan behaviour over a relatively short period of time (cf. Frosdick and Marsh, 2005: 100). Prior to the 1980s Scottish fans were regarded as exemplars of the British heavy-drinking, macho style of hooligans. In the 1980s, according to Giulianotti, the Scottish fans began to create the distinctive 'friendly' image, radically transforming the meanings of violence and heavy drinking. The case of Fulham, on the other hand, is one of continuity rather than of change and involves a searching re-remembering of the collective past, that is, of the club's non-hooligan traditions.

This tradition of non-violence is in part an 'invented tradition', meaning 'a set of practices, normally governed by overtly or tacitly accepted rules and of a ritual or symbolic nature, which seek to inculcate certain values and norms of behaviour by repetition, which automatically implies continuity with the past' (Hobsbawm, 1983: 1). Although it is true that the club has a relatively meagre history of spectator violence, the contemporary 'friendly' fan identity tends to downplay the manifestation of football hooliganism in the 1960s and 1970s, which is generally viewed as a minor and temporary 'excess' compared to the persistent hooligan problems at other football clubs. The tradition of non-violence is reproduced in media and police accounts praising the exemplary behaviour of Fulham supporters and regularly condemning the behaviour of opposing fan groups. It must be stressed, however, that the extent of the hooligan subculture at Fulham has been relatively limited and impermanent. Football hooliganism gradually disappeared from the mid-1970s onwards due to two main factors: on the one hand, the rapid decline in home attendances as a result of club's problematic situation (e.g. two successive relegations in the late 1960s) and, on the other hand, a process of self-selection as the overwhelming majority of local young males identifying with football hooliganism gravitated towards Chelsea or towards one of the other notorious clubs in London. Importantly, the introduction of security measures – such as the segregation of opposing supporters and increasing police presence – does not seem to have played a significant role in the decline in football hooliganism at Fulham.

The impermanent and limited nature of football hooliganism at Fulham should also be related more directly to the social sources of Fulham fan culture. In their study of spectator behaviour at Watford FC, Williams and his colleagues (1988: 64) argued that 'the fundamental reason why football hooliganism is not a major problem in Watford is because of the generally affluent and cosmopolitan nature of the local community.' This argument is also valid, to some degree, for Fulham. Craven Cottage is located in a comparatively affluent part of London and the club attracts an increasing number of 'middle-class' supporters. At the same time, many working-class fans nowadays live outside the area due to post-war gentrification. They view Craven Cottage and Fulham FC as the only remaining symbols of the old (working-class) community. Middle-class and working-class supporters alike tend to celebrate the club's 'friendly' image and non-hooligan traditions, as opposed to the perceived hypercommodified and 'violent' nature of Chelsea fandom and at certain other English football clubs. This collective project of presenting hooliganism as 'not for the likes of us' is crucial to understanding why football hooliganism is not a major problem at Fulham.

6

'Rotterdam Hooligans!': The Origins and Evolution of Football Hooliganism at Feyenoord

Introduction

Feyenoord Rotterdam is a football club with deep-seated working-class traditions, historically representing the working-class community in the South of Rotterdam. The values celebrated in Feyenoord fan culture closely reflect the core characteristics of traditional local culture. These values are also adhered to, in a heightened or distorted form, by members of the hooligan formation at the club. The hooligan group holds a widespread reputation for violence and has regularly been portrayed by the media and the police as a 'criminal organization' that orchestrates hooligan confrontations with a military-style precision. Because of this persistent hooligan image, Feyenoord supporters are subjected to a wide range of pervasive controls and impositions seriously affecting their match-day experience. Despite important changes over time, the hooligan subculture at Feyenoord continues to attract local young men seeking risk, excitement and recognition from peers. Central to contemporary football hooliganism at Feyenoord are the diverse strategies developed by hooligans to circumvent, frustrate and manipulate security policies. I will argue that these diverse strategies and the continuous public efforts to contain or eradicate football hooliganism make the case of Feyenoord of particular interest to this research.

This chapter begins with an examination of the fan culture and collective identity of Feyenoord supporters. Then I will analyze the emergence and early development of football hooliganism at Feyenoord. More specifically, I will examine the escalation of inter-group rivalries and the sources and development of the antagonism between Feyenoord and Ajax hooligans. In the final part of the chapter I will discuss the recent developments in football hooliganism at Feyenoord and the subtle yet vital interactions and negotiations between hooligans, supporters, police officers and club officials.

Sterker door strijd: football and working-class culture in South Rotterdam

Feyenoord is one of the few Dutch football clubs that attracts a nationwide fan base. Historically, however, Feyenoord was essentially a community club for the working-class areas in the South of Rotterdam. The club, founded in 1908, functioned as a key source of excitement and local pride in the lives of many deprived families on the South bank of the river Meuse. The Feijenoord district experienced rapid growth from the 1850s onwards with the expansion of the docks, which became a cornerstone of the local economy. It is estimated that before World War I more than half of the local population worked in the docks (Van de Laar, 2000: 351). Large numbers of migrants from different parts of the country (notably Zuid-Holland, Noord-Brabant and Zeeland) moved to Rotterdam in hope of better employment opportunities. This migration was enhanced by the diminishing employment in agriculture and the displacement of industrial employment to the port city (Burgers, 2001: 13). The arrival of large numbers of migrants caused an urgent need for housing, particularly in the South of Rotterdam where the majority of newcomers settled down.

The predominantly unskilled manual workers benefited only marginally from the development of the port. Supply of work force usually exceeded demand, especially before World War I. Most workers did not have fixed contracts and were unable to earn a full wage. When there was no work available, for example in times of economic recession, the working-class families in South Rotterdam lived in sheer poverty (Bouman and Bouman, 1952). Poor working conditions and poverty gave rise to social problems such as public drunkenness, public disorder and prostitution, giving the area a bad reputation in the rest of the city (Van de Laar, 2000: 201). Although the local elites initially perceived the docks as an important source of economic growth and employment, they increasingly saw them as endangering the stability and social order of the city. The dockworkers and their occasional mass protests against poor working conditions were regarded with disdain. The moral panic over economic, social and cultural life in South Rotterdam revolved around the idea that a large uncivilized mob lived there that threatened social order. At the same time, this idea gave rise to an awareness of the social needs of the impoverished sections of society (Van de Laar, 2000: 228).

In an attempt to reduce some of the social problems in the area, the local authorities created alternative means for working-class recreation, such as cinemas and sports facilities. Admission to sports clubs was largely confined to the more privileged sections of society. The working classes merely participated in sporting activities within their own local communities and with limited means, for instance boxing, illegal swimming and playing football in the streets. The establishment of Feyenoord, in 1908, is generally viewed as the start of the diffusion of football to the working classes in Rotterdam, despite the fact that the more profound transformation of football into a 'people's game' occurred only after World War I (Miermans, 1955: 119). Feyenoord rapidly developed into an important social institution in South Rotterdam. Many young men growing up in the area considered the walk to the ground, in the company of their fathers, brothers or friends, as the highlight of the week (Van Wijnen, 1989: 157; Oudenaarden, 1994: 19). As a former club director recalled:

> My whole life took place in South Rotterdam: work, family, friends, football. You never crossed the river to go into the city. You stayed on the South bank, which was a town of its own with a distinctive character and culture. Feyenoord had a very important social function in the area. I derived a lot of pride and satisfaction from being involved in the club, especially during the hardships and poverty before the Second World War. (Personal interview, October 2004)

Having emerged as a typical working-class club, Feyenoord fan culture has always closely reflected the core characteristics of local working-class culture, shaping the team's image of 'hard workers' as expressed in the club's sentiment *Geen woorden maar daden* ('no words, but deeds'). In the aftermath of World War II, when the city was attempting to restore the extensive damage of German bombings, Feyenoord supporters reinterpreted this image as reflecting Rotterdam culture in general, corresponding with the city's post-war motto *sterker door strijd* ('stronger through struggle'). In other words, Feyenoord gradually came to represent the city of Rotterdam as a whole rather than exclusively the traditional working-class community on the South bank of the river Meuse.

The dominant image of Feyenoord as a working-class club still persists today, despite important changes in the relationship between the club and the local community. After World War II Feyenoord gradually transformed from a regional club into a high-profile club with a nationwide fan base. In the 1920s and 1930s the club had already come to attract growing numbers of supporters from surrounding areas, especially after its promotion to the Premier League in 1921 (Bormans, 2002: 17). This process accelerated from the 1960s onwards. In the 1960s Feyenoord won four national championships and in the 1970s the club experienced its most glorious moments, winning the European Cup (1970), the Intercontinental Cup (1970), the UEFA Cup (1974) and two national championships. These successes secured Feyenoord's status as a high-profile club and enhanced the heterogeneity of its fan base in terms of geographical and class distribution. The club attracts an increasing proportion of middle-class supporters and, by 2001, only 24 per cent of Feyenoord's 21,654 season ticket holders lived in Rotterdam and a further 16 per cent in the outer surroundings of the city (data provided by Feyenoord, 2002; Van der Torre and Spaaij, 2003: 13).

Another major development that has been central to the changing relationship between Feyenoord and the local community on the South bank of the river Meuse is the demographic transformation of the area. The arrival of non-Western immigrants in Rotterdam during the post-war period was characterized by its great ethnic diversity, including substantial numbers of newcomers from Turkey, Suriname, Morocco and Cape Verde Islands. In 2003 around 55 per cent of the population of the Feijenoord district consisted of non-Western immigrants. In certain areas of the district the percentage of inhabitants of non-Western origins exceeded 70 per cent (Gemeente Rotterdam, 2003: 79; COS, 2004). The influx of large numbers of non-Western immigrants has eroded the traditional social cohesion in South Rotterdam and has resulted in the homogenization of the socio-economic composition of the area, featuring comparatively low levels of education and relatively high levels of unemployment. This development was enhanced by the fact that many descendants of the first generation of Dutch migrants, who had arrived in South Rotterdam in the late nineteenth and early twentieth century, decided to leave the area. Their upward social mobility in terms of education and income was translated into geographical mobility as many families abandoned the area and moved to the more modern and spacious suburbs (Burgers, 2001: 17). South Rotterdam is among the city's most problematic areas in terms of socio-economic deprivation (Rood-Pijpers, 1995: 195; 212; COT, 2000; Gemeente Rotterdam, 2003). In the late 1960s and early 1970s manifest conflict emerged between the different ethnic populations in the area and between inhabitants and the police. From the mid-1970s inter-ethnic tensions no longer escalated into large-scale disorder and riots, but minor conflicts between neighbours, nuisance, juvenile delinquency and vandalism remain permanent social issues (cf. Rovers, 1995: 222-223; 262).

The construction of fan identity at Feyenoord

The collective identity of Feyenoord supporters is constructed in relation to the club's historical rivalries with Sparta and Ajax. Feyenoord supporters' strong feelings of hatred towards the latter have gradually come to overshadow the local rivalry with the former. The antagonism between Feyenoord and Sparta was at its height in the first half of the twentieth century and mirrored the distinct social realities on the South and the North bank of the river Meuse. Sparta's club officials regarded the emergence of working-class clubs such as Feyenoord with disdain, accusing them of a lack of discipline and civilization. Feyenoord was regularly portrayed by the local media as a team of villains that did not belong in the Premier League, notably in 1921 when Feyenoord gained promotion while Sparta was relegated (Oudenaarden, 1994: 59; Huijzer, 1998: 47). This negative image reflected to some degree the wider concern of the local elites over the social problems in the South of Rotterdam. The rivalry between Feyenoord and Sparta thus echoed (and to some degree still echoes) perceived differences in the tastes and customs of Rotterdam's higher and lower classes. From the 1960s the growing discrepancy between the two clubs in terms of size and successes and the rapid demographic changes in Rotterdam have led to a decline in the intensity of local rivalry from the perspective of Feyenoord supporters (see Chapter Seven).

Nowadays the collective identity of Feyenoord supporters is primarily constructed in relation to Ajax Amsterdam. The antagonism between the two teams goes back to the 1920s and to a number of close battles over the national championship in the early 1930s (Wolff, 1971: 109-113). For many Feyenoord supporters, confrontations between the two teams symbolize a 'clash of cultures' between the cosmopolitan and haughty nature of the capital (Amsterdam) and the worker spirit of the port (Rotterdam) (Bormans, 2002: 56). The relationship between Feyenoord and Ajax is commonly expressed in popular clichés that highlight the dominant images of both cities: Feyenoord's hard workers versus the sophisticated, technical game of Ajax; immovability and no-nonsense versus metropolitan elegance; assiduity and strong-mindedness versus virtuosity (Vermeer and Van Vrijaldenhoven, 1994: 4). These perceived differences are central to Feyenoord supporters' construction of self and the other. It has been suggested that since many supporters do not live in either of the two cities, supporting one club or the other means more than geographic commitment: 'it is a mentality, a feeling of being in tune with a club' (Huijzer, 1998: 49). The two contrasting play styles largely seem to be an 'invented tradition'. For example, during a match between the two teams in 1921, Feyenoord's sophisticated, technical game was allegedly frustrated by the rough play of their rivals. The Feyenoord team has, in fact, always contained players with exceptional technical skills (Bot, 1994: 54).

Feyenoord fan culture reflects in many respects the core characteristics of traditional working-class culture in South Rotterdam, notably its no-nonsense ethos, strong ingroup solidarity, territoriality and aggressive masculinity. But although these values shape the collective identity of Feyenoord supporters, they are interpreted by different types of supporters in different ways. As Bormans (2002: 10) argues:

> Different people from all places and from all classes visit De Kuip. Followers come to watch the game, supporters also like to experience some atmosphere, and for the hooligans the football party is only truly complete if they can also have a fight. All these different types of people together create the Feyenoord feeling that is the foundation of the club and that is passed on from generation to generation.

In the remainder of this chapter, I will examine the identity and behaviour of a specific section of Feyenoord supporters: the hooligans. I will show that the hooligans celebrate a heightened or distorted version of the core characteristics of Feyenoord fan culture, emphasizing their identification with the club and the city and their focus on physical prowess. Their violent rivalry with Ajax hooligans can be viewed as a radicalized version of the general antagonism between Feyenoord and Ajax supporters.

'Trouble on the terraces': the emergence and development of football hooliganism

The emergence of a youth end in Feyenoord's De Kuip stadium can be dated back to the late 1960s. In 1969 young supporters of Vak G and Vak S, located at opposite sides of the ground behind the goals, decided to transform Vak S into the central point of reference for the club's youth. The groups of young fans that gathered in that section of the ground sought to create a passionate atmosphere through chants and the display of flags and scarves. They copied various rituals and symbols of English terrace culture, such as the songs 'You'll Never Walk Alone' and 'We Shall Not Be Moved', which were perceived as more prestigious than domestic football chants. The group was characterized by its heterogeneous composition in terms of age, gender and social backgrounds, but the overwhelming majority of young supporters were white working-class youths from Rotterdam and its outer surroundings. Inter-fan fighting was, at this stage, relatively infrequent and small-scale. Certain young fans located in Vak G held a reputation for toughness because of their occasional involvement in missile throwing, vandalism and minor fighting (Van Gageldonk, 1996: 15-16). However, matches against Ajax usually passed without incident even though home and away supporters were not segregated. Fighting between opposing supporters occurred only occasionally, for example during a match between the two teams on 17 September 1972, when a small group of Ajax supporters steamed into Vak S and punched home supporters (Bot, 1994: 91).

The year 1974 marked the beginning of a hooligan subculture at Feyenoord. The UEFA Cup Final return leg between Feyenoord and Tottenham Hotspur, on 29 May 1974, was overshadowed by spectator violence and is commonly referred to as 'the day Dutch football lost its innocence' (*Rotterdams Dagblad*, 20 April 2002).

During half-time Tottenham supporters assaulted home supporters and pelted them with seats. Part of the home crowd responded to the aggressions, generating a full-blown riot in the stands in which over 200 people were injured. Several supporters were taken to hospital or were treated at the scene by medical staff (Van Vrijaldenhoven, 1996: 57). The incident shocked Feyenoord's fan community and the local authorities as such widespread violence had not been seen before on the terraces of De Kuip. As a former board member recalled:

> The Tottenham Hotspur incident was something we had never seen before. Large-scale fighting between rival supporters had, to my mind, not occurred before at Feyenoord. And I have been involved in the club since the Second World War. After 1974 fights between opposing fans became more common both inside and outside the stadium. (Personal interview, October 2004)

In the aftermath of the incident domestic inter-group rivalries became more and more characterized by physical confrontations. Vak S was increasingly perceived as the exclusive territory of young supporters seeking to establish a reputation for toughness, both collectively and individually, and many of those who felt intimidated by the atmosphere moved to different sections of the ground. At this early stage, confrontations between rival fan groups – principally those at Feyenoord, FC Utrecht, Ajax and FC Den Haag (see Chapter Three) – were relatively unorganized and spontaneous. Fans' anticipation of disorder was principally based on the early reputations of their opponents. According to a Feyenoord hooligan:

> In those days you wouldn't go out looking for trouble. Rather you would firm up for away travel because you knew about their reputation. I mean, I had seen dozens of Utrecht fans waving bicycle chains above their heads saying, like, you're going to get your heads kicked in. That was unheard of back then. It both frightened and fascinated me. (Personal interview, February 2005)

During the second half of the 1970s the extent and seriousness of football hooliganism increased. A group of young Feyenoord fans began to identify closely with football hooliganism, seeking to enhance its status in the hierarchy of hooligan oppositions. Vak S came to be viewed as territory that had to be defended against attacks by opposing formations, whereas the Feyenoord hooligans also sought to successfully challenge their opponents on their own turf. Violent confrontations between rival groups usually took place in or around football grounds, or en route to the ground. As we will see, early prevention strategies, such as the segregation of home and away fans, the erection of fences and the deployment of larger numbers of police officers resulted in the partial containment of football hooliganism inside the stadium. At the same time, however, they led to the gradual displacement of hooligan encounters to new locales.

In addition to domestic hooligan rivalries, matches against German and English clubs tend to be regarded by Feyenoord hooligans as particularly challenging. The hooligans have regularly sought to challenge the status of English hooligan groups, especially those with which a deep-seated rivalry has been established. Given the historical antagonism between the two sets of fans, the disorder during a UEFA Cup match against Tottenham Hotspur in Rotterdam, on 2 November 1983, should hardly have come as a surprise. More than 50 supporters needed medical treatment after groups of opposing fans fought each other in a home section of the ground. One police officer was in a serious condition after being hit on the head with an iron bar. The stabbing of an English supporter was broadcasted on Dutch national television. Television commentators described the disorder as 'degrading scenes that have absolutely nothing to do with football' (*NOS Nieuws*, 2 November 1983). More recently, on 5 November 1997, a Champions League match between Feyenoord and Manchester United was marred by spectator violence. Riot police officers prevented a clash between rival supporters in the city centre before the match. Near the stadium a group of 50 Feyenoord supporters pelted the coaches transporting English fans with stones and bottles (*Algemeen Dagblad*, 6 November 1997). The skirmishes continued inside the stadium. One of the gates at the bottom of the away section was left unlocked by accident, causing a confrontation between rival hooligans (private and police video footage; *Algemeen Dagblad*, 6 February 1998).

Matches against German opponents have traditionally been a major source of excitement and anticipation for Feyenoord hooligans. Their hatred towards German hooligans is based in part on analogies with the Second World War. During the war Rotterdam suffered major bomb damage and, during a raid in November 1944, De Kuip was used by the Nazis to gather local males. Against this background, visits to Germany are seen as particularly challenging:

> Germany is a different experience because the we-feeling is so much stronger. It has a different feel to it, more intense than your average game. It goes back to the war, we still have to avenge that. Everybody does something crazy there, whether you are a nutter or a decent boy. (Personal interview with Feyenoord hooligan, April 2002)

There is ample evidence of the relatively high potential for (hooligan) violence at encounters between Feyenoord and German clubs as well as of the draconian measures taken by the authorities to prevent trouble. For example, a European Cup match between Werder Bremen and Feyenoord on 3 November 1994 resulted in 500 arrests. Over 250 Feyenoord supporters were arrested before the match on their way to Bremen. They were accused of vandalizing a train, arson, missile throwing and the possession of drugs, and were sent back to the Netherlands. A further 150 Feyenoord supporters were arrested throughout the day. Almost 100 Werder Bremen supporters were arrested for throwing stones at the Feyenoord fans after the final whistle (*Volkskrant*, 4 November 1994; *Volkskrant*, 5 November 1994; *Rotterdams Dagblad*, 4 November 1994). Feyenoord hooligans have also fought German opponents at matches between the two national teams, occasionally forming temporary alliances with certain other Dutch hooligan groups to confront their common enemy. Before a match between the two countries on 24 April 1996 in Rotterdam, Feyenoord and Den Haag hooligans jointly confronted their German counterparts.

One of the most serious incidents took place before and after a friendly match against Bayer Leverkusen, on 30 January 1999. There were no compulsory ticket or travel arrangements for this friendly encounter, which enabled supporters to travel freely to Germany and to buy their tickets at the stadium. The Dutch and

German police were therefore unaware of the precise number of hooligans and supporters that would attend the match. Small groups of hooligans and supporters from different parts of the Netherlands travelled by train, car or transit van to Leverkusen. Several hooligans and supporters arrived in Cologne or Leverkusen on the night before the match, provoking a number of minor fights in pubs and nightclubs. After the match violence erupted when German police officers forced the Feyenoord supporters to remain in their section until the home fans had dispersed. A 22-year-old hooligan set fire to a ticket boot. The total damage was estimated at 270,000 euro (for a more extensive description of the incident see Spaaij, 2001: 64-65). In the aftermath of the incident 50 Feyenoord supporters were arrested on the basis of police video footage and photographs, many of whom were unknown to the police prior to the incident and unrelated to the hooligan formation. Many experienced hooligans were present in Leverkusen, but most of them remained on the background of the disorder spurring on young participants eager to prove themselves to their peers. A total of 65 Feyenoord fans were banned from all Dutch football grounds for a period of two to four years, and from all German football grounds for a period of five years, for their alleged participation in the disorder. The club also decided to ban all Feyenoord supporters from away matches in Europe for a period of eighteen months (*Algemeen Dagblad*, 1 February 1999; *Algemeen Dagblad*, 1 November 1999).

The escalation of the Feyenoord – Ajax rivalry

The competitive violence between Feyenoord and Ajax hooligans has played a central role in the development of football hooliganism in the Netherlands. The hostility between the opposing hooligan formations can be viewed as a heightened version of the general animosity between the two sets of fans. Official and public concern over this inter-group hostility is in part related to the anti-Semitic abuse during matches between the two teams from the 1970s onwards, focusing on the popular image of Ajax as a club with Jewish roots. Young supporters of clubs such as Feyenoord, FC Utrecht and FC Den Haag taunted their rivals from the capital with chants like 'Ajax is een jodenclub ('Ajax is a Jew's club') and, occasionally, by waving Israelian flags. The forms of anti-Semitic references changed in the 1980s.

Abusive chants such as 'Ajax Jews, the first football deaths', 'We go Jew hunting' and 'Ajax to the gas chamber' replaced the early, relatively innocent songs and symbols. These chants were occasionally accompanied by Nazi symbols and Palestinian flags. In reaction to these provocations members of the F-Side started to use the term 'Joden' ('Jews') as a badge of honour, naming themselves 'super Jews'. This pro-Semitism has come to constitute a key feature of contemporary Ajax fan culture, making the club extremely popular in Israel, more than any domestic club in that country (Kuper, 1999: 122).

Anti-Semitic references during matches between the two teams are not confined to the hooligan subculture. Most Ajax and Feyenoord supporters agree that pro-Semitic and anti-Semitic chants and symbols should be viewed as part of the football experience. As one Feyenoord supporter argued:

> We found it normal to sing that. It was part of Feyenoord versus Ajax, the battle between Amsterdam and Rotterdam, the thriller against the archenemy. You want to nag them, and Ajax fans do the same in return, calling us rednecks. Loving one club means hating the other. Feyenoord and Ajax supporters cannot live without each other, because a match against yourself is simply impossible (Bot, 1994: 90).

In the collective imaginary of Feyenoord and Ajax supporters, the term 'Jew' is detached from its original meaning and transforms into a more symbolic meaning that has more to do with Ajax and Amsterdam than with Judaism, Jewish culture or the state of Israel (Bormans, 2002: 124). Within this moral framework, anti-Semitism and pro-Semitism are two sides of the same coin. They both function as key themes in the construction of self and the other, in the delimitation of the borders of the category 'we', as opposed to 'them'.

> Ajax supporters walk around with Israelian flags and all that. They call themselves super Jews. I don't understand why we can't say: 'You are shit Jews'. I mean, politicians and journalists condemn us for doing so even though it is basically the same thing. Ajax fans themselves hardly worry about it anymore. (Personal interview with Feyenoord hooligan, November

197

The rivalry between Feyenoord and Ajax hooligans escalated in the 1980s. In addition to the regular, usually minor confrontations and missile throwing before, during and after matches between the two teams, the conflict between the opposing hooligan formations featured a number of high-profile incidents. During a League match between the teams at the Olympic Stadium in Amsterdam, on 22 October 1989, two Feyenoord hooligans threw homemade bombs into a home section of the ground. The bomb contained fireworks and small bullets injuring fourteen Ajax supporters, one of whom suffered an arterial haemorrhage. The riot police immediately cleared the entire away section and all 500 Feyenoord fans were searched extensively. Five supporters were arrested. The incident was widely reported in national and international media. The BBC argued that Holland was 'fast taking over as Europe's most troubled footballing nation' (*BBC News*, 22 October 1989). The reputation of Feyenoord hooligans was enhanced in 1991, when the country experienced its first hooligan-related death. A notorious Feyenoord hooligan stabbed FC Twente supporter Erik Lassche to death on the night before Feyenoord's away match in Enschede. He was convicted to five years in prison for manslaughter (data provided by Rotterdam-Rijnmond Police, 2003; *Rotterdams Dagblad*, 6 February 1998; Van Gageldonk, 1999: 89; 121).

Physical confrontations between Feyenoord and Ajax hooligans gradually became more planned and co-ordinated. Hooligan encounters increasingly took place away from the ground as controls and surveillance in and around football stadia grew more pervasive. The hooligan formations regularly sought to challenge each other at unexpected times and locations to escape police observation. For example, on 21 May 1995, a group of 60 Ajax hooligans attacked a television studio seconds before the start of the talk show *Lief & Leed* featuring Feyenoord and FC Utrecht hooligans. They smashed the windows of the studio's bar with stones. The Feyenoord hooligans chased their rivals down the studio and the streets, but these had retreated after the initial attack (Van Gageldonk, 1996: 94-97; *NOS Nieuws*, 21 May 1995). The determination of Feyenoord and Ajax hooligans in challenging each other culminated in 1997. On 16 February 1997, the rival hooligan formations arranged a fight near the A10 highway, but the pre-planned confrontation never fully materialized. The Ajax hooligans retreated after observing the larger, heavily armed group of Feyenoord hooligans. The police quickly arrived at the scene and forced the Feyenoord hooligans to return to their cars. Further down the A10, the police searched every car for offensive weapons. No arrests were made despite the large number of weapons found by the police, such as baseball bats, chains and knives.

Journalists attempted to interview the hooligans on the spot. One Feyenoord hooligan challenged his rivals on national television, arguing that the Ajax hooligans were 'real pussies' because they ran away (*NOS Nieuws*, 16 February 1997). Ajax hooligans responded to these accusations by appearing on the local television channel AT5, claiming that their rivals had violated the agreements by gathering 300 people instead of 50 people as agreed. The media appearances of Feyenoord hooligans in the aftermath of the incident illustrate the group's self-image as the most fearsome and toughest hooligan formation in the Netherlands. Experienced hooligans have occasionally co-operated with journalists and writers to present this image to the outside world. Journalist Paul van Gageldonk wrote two books on the hooligan group, two hooligans appeared in the television documentary *De Harde Kern* (1998) and a number of notorious hooligans featured in books by King and Pennant (2003) and by Vos (2006). The CIV (1998: 33) has strongly condemned the role of journalists in producing documentaries, books and magazine articles on football hooliganism, arguing that such programmes and writings tend to enhance hooligan rivalries and violence.

Serious confrontation between Feyenoord and Ajax hooligans occurred on 23 March 1997, although on this occasion the fight had not been pre-arranged. Feyenoord played an away match against AZ in Alkmaar, whereas Ajax played in Waalwijk against RKC. Although a revenge attack by Ajax hooligans was expected, none of the Feyenoord fans knew exactly where and when this attack would take place. On their way to Alkmaar, on the A9 highway, the Feyenoord hooligans spotted a group of 100 to 150 Ajax fans in a distant field. Hundreds of Feyenoord hooligans abandoned their cars rushing towards their rivals. The first confrontation lasted only twenty to thirty seconds before the Ajax hooligans retreated. A minute later they confronted their rivals once again, but they were forced back by a larger group of Feyenoord hooligans. Carlo Picornie, a 35-year-old Ajax hooligan, died after being beaten with several objects, including a hammer. Although the confrontation at Beverwijk was generally perceived within hooligan circles as a 'victory' for the Feyenoord hooligans, in hindsight most hooligans deeply regret the event. Football hooliganism, they argue, is not about killing people:

> I had a very bad feeling about what was going to happen. But basically we had no choice: we had to show up in order not to lose face. Looking back, I deeply regret the fight because someone died. It was never my intention to kill anyone, you know. You just want to fight and humiliate the opponent, that's all. (Personal interview with Feyenoord hooligan, November 2001)

Overview of the emergence of football hooliganism

The emergence of football hooliganism at Feyenoord was preceded by the segregation of the crowd by age. Groups of young fans began to congregate in specific sections of the ground, which were increasingly viewed as their exclusive territory. From the mid-1970s young Feyenoord fans came to establish violent rivalries with their counterparts at other football clubs in the Netherlands, seeking to enhance their status as a good 'firm' in the hierarchy of hooligan oppositions. Their identification with hooliganism marked the beginning of a fan subculture at Feyenoord that persists today. In this subculture the core values of local culture – notably hard masculinity, ingroup solidarity, territoriality and excitement – are reinterpreted in a more heightened version, containing elements of both resistance of and compliance with the parent culture.

The emergence of football hooliganism at Feyenoord should not be understood in terms of the changing relationship between the club and its fans, as was suggested by Ian Taylor (1971; 1971a). Rather, it can be viewed as a new youth subcultural style that was strongly influenced by developments in Britain and that is structured in accordance with local traditions and legacies as well as with certain key themes in Feyenoord fan culture, notably the deep-seated rivalry with Ajax and the fierce hatred towards German opponents. The 'turf wars' of Feyenoord hooligans not only involve the symbolic and physical defence of (specific sections of) the ground, but also of the club and Rotterdam as a whole. As one hooligan commented: 'We fight for our club and city, really. We are the most loyal supporters and we take on anybody who mocks our club or our city.' Even though several hooligans do not actually live in Rotterdam, identification with the city and with local culture is a key theme in their construction of self and the other.

Football hooliganism after 'Beverwijk': threat and response

The disorder at Beverwijk and the subsequent crackdown on hooliganism by the authorities had a profound impact on the short-term development of football hooliganism at Feyenoord. Experienced hooligans initially kept a low profile because of ongoing police and judicial investigations, resulting in a temporary decline in the number of arrests and reported incidents (CIV, 1998: 32). Forty-five Feyenoord hooligans and eight Ajax hooligans were imprisoned or banned for a period of up to four years for their role in the confrontation. 'Beverwijk' and subsequent controls and impositions also had a more long-term effect on the activities and composition of the hooligan formation. Several older hooligans have ceased to be centrally involved in the group, although many of them continue to participate as 'semi-retired' group members (i.e. they turn up when violent confrontation is expected). The frequency and seriousness of physical confrontations between Ajax and Feyenoord hooligans have also diminished in recent years. Matches between the two clubs are nevertheless regularly marred by spectator violence, notably missile throwing, vandalism and violence against police officers. On 15 April 2004, dozens of Ajax supporters invaded the pitch and assaulted several players of the Feyenoord Reserves team after a match in Amsterdam. Feyenoord hooligans swore to avenge the attack, claiming that the Ajax hooligans had violated the informal codes of legitimate action by physically attacking players: 'Players have nothing to do with hooliganism, they should be left alone. It should be a matter of hooligans only' (personal interview, November 2004; see also *Haagsche Courant*, 17 April 2004).

The core of the hooligan formation at Feyenoord currently consists of approximately 100 people between the ages of 15 and 45, but for high-profile matches the number of participants may increase to over 400. (As we will see, the group as a whole is nowadays less visible than in the past, especially during football matches.) Almost all hooligans are males, although some women occasionally

201

accompany their boyfriends or husbands. The hooligan formation is characterized by its heterogeneous ethnic composition. The vast majority of group members are white, but there are a significant number of group members from Surinamese, Cape Verdian, Moluccan and Indonesian descent. Several older black participants hold a widespread reputation for physical prowess, notably a small section of older hooligans nicknamed 'riot negroes'. Around three-quarters of the hooligans live in the Rotterdam region, significantly more than the percentage of season ticket holders at Feyenoord (40%) (Spaaij, 2001: 47; Van der Torre and Spaaij, 2003: 13). The hooligan formation should not be viewed as a homogeneous and fixed entity. Group cohesiveness decreases as one moves from the centre of the group to the periphery and there are different degrees of commitment to the group. The core of the group, which is comparatively small, is relatively permanent and cohesive. In addition, there are many people who are only occasionally or incidentally involved.

The core of the hooligan group includes two distinctive segments: an 'old' and a 'young' section. Despite important overlaps, they can be seen as heterogeneous groups with their own practices and tastes. The older section, Sport Club Feyenoord (SCF), consists of supporters who were already centrally involved in hooliganism before the disorder at Beverwijk. The SCF has become more fragmented in recent years due in part to pervasive police controls and serious punishments. The vast majority of group members are between 28 and 38 years old, but several hooligans in their forties are still involved in the group. Most SCF members have known each other for years and maintain close friendships with fellow group members, even though many of them do not see each other as regularly as in the past due to geographical distances and their demanding family lives (Spaaij, 2001: 49). The SCF essentially consists of several small, close-knit subgroups which often operate autonomously and which are seated in different parts of the stadium during home matches. Notorious subgroups include those from Dordrecht, Gouda and South Rotterdam. The latter group was at the forefront of the disorder during a dance event in Renesse in July 1996. A group of 100 Feyenoord hooligans provoked a fight and intimidated members of the Amsterdam-based band Party Animals because, during a performance in Amsterdam, band members had burned a Feyenoord flag on stage. There are also SCF subgroups from other parts of the country, notably from the East and the South.

The Rotterdam Jongeren Kern (RJK; 'Rotterdam Youth Core'), currently named the FIIIR (the third generation of Feyenoord hooligans), emerged in the aftermath of the confrontation at Beverwijk. The young hooligans were primarily attracted to football by the notoriety of the SCF and they were eager to establish a reputation for toughness, both collectively and individually. Many of them appear to have less affection for the club than their older counterparts. The core of the RJK consists of approximately 40 young males between the ages of 15 and 25. Although some group members are of Moluccan descent, the group predominantly consists of white males. Some individual members allegedly hold racist beliefs and the group has occasionally fought with Moroccan youth groups, but there is no evidence to suggest that 'whiteness' is perceived as a symbol of collective identity. In fact, RJK members attacked alleged neo-Nazis during a right-wing demonstration on 26 January 2002 in Rotterdam (private video footage; *Algemeen Dagblad*, 28 January 2002; *Searchlight*, April 2003). The majority of RJK members live in Rotterdam, notably in South Rotterdam and in the Crooswijk and Kralingen areas. A section of the group that lives in South Rotterdam was previously known as a local youth group regularly involved in incidents of vandalism, nuisance and intimidation.

Regular contacts exist between SCF members and their younger equivalents. Many young hooligans perceive their more experienced counterparts as role models, although they increasingly seek to exceed the reputation of the SCF. Certain older hooligans are closely involved in the activities of the young hooligans. The older hooligans tend to encourage the youths to 'keep up the good work'. Others, however, have less sympathy for the young hooligans, viewing them as regularly violating informal codes of legitimate action. FIIIR members hold a reputation for indiscriminate violence, that is, for assaulting non-hooligans: 'They often do stupid things. I mean, they even go after innocent people who have nothing to do with hooliganism' (personal interview with SCF member, September 2002). For example, eighteen young Feyenoord hooligans (including two females) were arrested after a 'queer bashing' incident in a park in Rotterdam, on 16 January 2000. The hooligans intimidated and assaulted a number of alleged homosexuals. The police found bricks and baseball bats in the hooligans' cars (data provided by the Rotterdam-Rijnmond Police in 2002). The youth core operates not only at Feyenoord, but occasionally also at home matches of Excelsior, the third professional football club in Rotterdam. Some RJK members live in the vicinity of the Excelsior ground in the Eastern part of the city. On several occasions young Feyenoord hooligans have provoked incidents at Excelsior. For example, on 7 December 1998 a group of young hooligans attacked Telstar supporters during a League match between Excelsior and Telstar. Feyenoord hooligans are also regularly involved in fights in local nightlife and at major dance events.

Certain general patterns can be identified in the social backgrounds of the hooligans. Very few hooligans are long-term unemployed and the vast majority earn a moderate income. Many older hooligans are skilled manual workers employed as builders, dockworkers, carpenters, bouncers, and so on. They perceive football hooliganism, and Feyenoord in general, as an important source of excitement and identity in their lives. Young hooligans either work or are still in school. Many of them have a relatively low level of education. They tend to dislike school and experience problems with teachers and fellow students. Their parents often do little to prevent their sons from engaging in delinquency and hooliganism. Parental neglect is in several cases related to the disruption of families or to drug or alcohol abuse. Several young hooligans grow up in a social environment (family, school, neighbourhood, football club, nightlife) in which aggression and the threat and use of violence are part of everyday life. Their reputation for physical prowess provides them prestige among peers and is used to intimidate other young men in everyday life. Within their friendship groups physical prowess, risk taking and the ability to 'look after yourself' are dominant values. 'Sissy' behaviour is viewed with disdain. The quest for risk and excitement features centrally in their activities: 'It's the excitement, the kick, you know. The idea that you're going to beat up your opponent. You're afraid, but you go anyway even though your rivals may have a much larger group waiting for you' (personal interview with Feyenoord hooligan, September 2002).

A recurrent theme in the contemporary public debate on football hooliganism at Feyenoord is the allegedly organized nature of the hooligan formation. Attempts to prosecute hooligans as members of a criminal organization have failed. The Dutch Supreme Court concluded that there was insufficient evidence to sustain that the disorder at Beverwijk was the result of a structured criminal organization rather than of initiatives of incidentally co-operating individuals or groups of people. At the same time, the judges sustained that the events had 'an organized character' (Hoge Raad, 10 July 2001). Notwithstanding the popular image of the hooligan group as a highly structured and organized entity, the social organization of football hooliganism at Feyenoord is generally limited to basic forms of co-ordination and synchronization. There is no formal leadership. Informal leadership is based on seniority, physical prowess or organizational skills. As a long-standing hooligan argued:

> There is no formal hierarchy or anything. Of course there are people who co-ordinate certain activities, who say 'we go there at this time'. There is always someone who first says that, but they are different people and not just one particular person. It's impossible to single out genuine group leaders. The only hierarchy is in terms of seniority. Older, long-standing hooligans usually have more status than younger ones. That's logical, isn't it? I mean, that's how it works in companies too. (Personal interview, October 2004)

The hooligan group consists of several small subgroups that merge in anticipation of violent confrontation. When violence is expected, supporters who identify with the group and with hooliganism are likely to be present, whereas others will prefer to stay away in order to avoid trouble (Van der Torre and Spaaij, 2003: 44). Importantly, the group as a whole is less visible today than it was in the past, especially during football matches. Only a section of the hooligan core regularly attends home matches, and those who do are not located collectively in a single section of the ground. Four factors limit the degree of organization of the hooligan group: (i) the physical dispersion of hooligans (in terms of residence, their location within the ground, meeting places); (ii) the internal masking of information on past, present and future events, in reaction to police and judicial investigations; (iii) the social distance between older and younger hooligans; (iv) the generally limited need for co-ordination at regular matches (when anticipating confrontation, the co-ordination and synchronization of group activities are temporarily increased) (Van der Torre and Spaaij, 2003: 26-27). Furthermore, few experienced hooligans are nowadays eager to be publicly perceived as group leaders due to the risk of apprehension and conviction as such.

Experienced Feyenoord hooligans are streetwise and have developed a practical understanding of the opportunity structures for football violence and of police strategies. They regularly spur on young recruits to participate in violence, while they themselves may remain on the background because of police presence or camera surveillance. This in part explains the relatively high number of first offenders among those arrested for football-related offences (approximately 80% on average; see Van der Torre and Spaaij, 2003: 60). Furthermore, certain 'regulators' within the group, mainly older hooligans, specifically engage in logistic tasks, such as obtaining tickets for specific sections of the ground or arranging travel to away matches. Their organizational skills are also used in other spheres, notably in the organization of lucrative dance parties and festivals, or in crime.

The management of football hooliganism: the development and effects of security policies

There is a long history of official attempts to contain football hooliganism at Feyenoord. Early security measures concentrated exclusively on repression and techno-prevention. The number of police officers deployed at matches in De Kuip gradually increased in reaction to the perceived threat of football hooliganism. From the late 1980s onwards police strategies began to focus more and more on the apprehension of offenders and on the issuing of banning orders. Special arrest units, video equipment and street-level police officers were used to identify troublemakers. The police and the Justice Department also invested in the faster and more effective prosecution of those arrested. Inside the stadium a number of techno-preventative measures were introduced. Segregation of home and away supporters was realized through the erection of dividing fences. The stadium was divided into four separate sectors in order to restrict the movement of opposing supporters within the premises of the ground. The pitch was fenced off from the stands in its entirety to prevent pitch invasions. After a high-profile incident during an international fixture between Holland and Cyprus in De Kuip in October 1987, when a bomb was thrown onto the pitch, high nets were erected behind the goals in a bid to prevent missile throwing. The renovation of De Kuip in the early 1990s paved the way for a more spectator-friendly approach to the management of football matches, which, at the same time, further reduced opportunities for collective violence in and around the ground. Numbered seats replaced the terraces, a ditch replaced the high perimeter fences, entrance controls were automated and a CCTV system was installed. The club also expanded its steward organization in an attempt to improve the social control within the ground and to reduce police presence. Furthermore, a tunnel was built to safely transport away supporters from the railway station to the away section of the ground.

The authorities also developed a social preventative approach to tackling football hooliganism at Feyenoord, albeit to a much lesser extent. In the second half of the 1980s the local government, the club and the police launched a social prevention project targeting football hooliganism through the improvement of the relationship between the club and young supporters. Two fan co-ordinators were assigned to run the project and at a later stage one youth worker was added to the project staff. They organized social activities such as football tournaments for supporters and local youths. Part of the project was the creation of a club house as a meeting place for young fans and the fan co-ordinators. The club house was closed down shortly after due to the aggressive atmosphere and the club's persistent financial problems. On one occasion, hooligans smashed the windows of the club house and assaulted police officers attempting to restore order. By the 1990s the social preventative approach to football hooliganism at Feyenoord had lost most of its original scope and priority, especially when compared to the wide range of repressive and techno-preventative measures introduced over the years. Recent attempts by the local government and the club to reinstate social prevention have yet to be evaluated. In the 2005/06 season a pilot project was started. This project is implemented by two 'fan coaches' and principally targets young supporters who are not yet integrated into the hooligan group in order to prevent them from becoming involved in football hooliganism.

Another central aspect of anti-hooligan policies at Feyenoord are the ticket and membership regulations set up by the Dutch football association (KNVB). The club participated in an experiment with a compulsory membership scheme in the 1989/90 season. Hundreds of Feyenoord fans protested against the scheme by showing up at their team's away match against FC Utrecht without a membership card. They were eventually allowed into the ground by the police in a bid to prevent conflict escalation. Once inside the stadium Feyenoord supporters mocked the authorities with chants such as 'Stick that card up your ass' (*NOS Nieuws*, 13 August 1989). The football authorities nevertheless introduced a membership scheme in the 1996/97 season. The club also uses a special membership scheme for away matches. This membership card is provided only to supporters who regularly attend away matches and who have never received a banning order. In 2001 only 1,500 Feyenoord supporters received a so-called *uitkaart* ('away card'). Responding to persistent pressures by international and national governing bodies to tackle football hooliganism, in the late 1990s the club threatened to ban all away supporters in case of serious disorder. This ban was first implemented in 1999 after the disorder in Leverkusen. Despite the risk of severe punishment, hundreds of Feyenoord supporters defied the ban and travelled to European Cup matches in Norway, Portugal and Germany (*Algemeen Dagblad*, 24 September 1999; *Algemeen Dagblad*, 6 October 1999; *Algemeen Dagblad*, 22 October 1999). A large banner displayed by defiant supporters summed up their frustrations: 'You can't ban a Feyenoord fan!'

Although ticket and membership regulations are perceived by hooligans as reducing opportunities for collective violence in and around football grounds, they have been creative in their attempts to circumvent these regulations. In the early 1990s the CIV expressed its concern over the forgery of tickets among Feyenoord fans and over their attempts to force their way into the ground through intimidation and violence, especially during Feyenoord's 1992/93 championship season (CIV, 1993: 27). Many hooligans possess multiple membership cards and have established facilitating networks for obtaining tickets for away matches, mainly due to Feyenoord's nationwide fan base and to their contacts with opposing hooligan groups. Despite the pervasive controls and impositions, most hooligans are positive about the opportunities for attending matches: 'If we want to go somewhere with 200 people, we do it. Nobody can stop that, not even ticket regulations. For certain away matches we get tickets from opposing hooligans. And when they visit us, we just return the favour' (personal interview with SCF member, September 2002). Police officers also detect flaws in the membership scheme. As a senior police officer commented:

The away membership is not flawless. Forty members of the youth core obtained away cards. There were 4,000 applicants and a random draw was applied. You would expect that only a couple of these boys would receive such a card, not the entire group. Moreover, officially you can only get an away card if you have been a season ticket holder for some years and have not been convicted or banned in the past. Most of these youths certainly don't qualify for that. (Personal interview, April 2002)

In addition to the ticket and membership regulations described above, a key element of the security regime at Feyenoord is the so-called *combiregeling*, which affects both hooligans and non-hooligan supporters. This policy measure, introduced nationally in 1984, obliges Feyenoord supporters to travel collectively to away matches by train, coach or car and under close police and steward surveillance. Tickets for the away section of the ground are sold only to supporters complying with the compulsory travel arrangements. Most supporters perceive this measure as negatively influencing their match-day experience since it obstructs free movement. For example, it forces Feyenoord supporters living in the East of the country who wish to attend their team's away match against, say, FC Twente to first travel to Rotterdam and then join the other away fans on a train all the way back to their original point of departure. The *combiregeling* is currently used less frequently by the authorities than in the past, especially at 'high-risk' matches (so-called 'Category C'), due in part to the continuous protests of fan organizations. Fan protests nevertheless continued in the early 2000s, occasionally taking on an organized, large-scale form. On 20 February 2000, supporters and hooligans of various Dutch clubs, including Feyenoord, jointly demonstrated against the *combiregeling* before Feyenoord's away match in Tilburg against Willem II. During the protest the police arrested 236 fans. Supported by the official fan club, several Feyenoord supporters and hooligans successfully appealed against their fines and banning orders, arguing that their arrest and punishment were unfair and disproportionate (Van der Torre and Spaaij, 2003: 99; *Rotterdams Dagblad*, 7 March 2000; *Rotterdams Dagblad*, 26 April 2000).

Parallel to formal, mainly repressive and techno-preventative, policy measures targeting football hooliganism club officials have adopted an informal style of co-optation and dialogue. As early as the late 1970s the club attempted to enhance the self-regulation among hooligans by employing notorious hooligans as an 'order service'. The hooligans received free match tickets and they regularly took advantage of their positions by engaging in vandalism and fighting without being arrested (Van Gageldonk, 1996: 19). Although club officials publicly condemned hooligan violence, there was always some sort of dialogue between the two parties and the club regularly facilitated hooligans free match tickets. The relationship between club officials and hooligans altered in the late 1990s as club officials increasingly sought to distance themselves from the hooligan group (Bormans, 2002: 154). Dozens of hooligans allegedly involved in the confrontation at Beverwijk were banned for a period of up to four years. According to an SCF member:

> In the past the board regularly approached us for a meeting and we were always available for dialogue, but when we wanted to discuss our banning orders after Beverwijk they refused. After the A10 incident [on 16 February 1997] we had a meeting with [the chairman] and we promised him that there would be no more pre-arranged confrontations with Ajax hooligans. But he seems to have forgotten that the fighting at Beverwijk was not organized. [...] He probably would have said 'the four-year banning order is non-negotiable,' but at least we would have had the chance to tell him our side of the story. Suddenly they did not want to talk to us anymore. (Personal interview, October 2004)

In recent years club officials seem to have reinstated to some degree their informal policy of co-optation. At the same time, the club's security officers actively co-operate with the police in a bid to reduce football hooliganism.

Interactions and negotiations between hooligans and police officers

In the mid-1980s senior police officers within the Rotterdam-Rijnmond Police force noticed that repressive, short-term police strategies failed to effectively reduce football hooliganism. The extent and seriousness of spectator violence at Feyenoord increased and hooligans regularly succeeded in circumventing controls and impositions. In reaction to the perceived threat of football hooliganism the Rotterdam-Rijnmond Police created a special unit of *supportersbegeleiders* ('fan attendants') with the task of establishing a relationship with hooligans and gathering intelligence on their activities and intentions. This task reflected the wider concept of community policing and was driven by the idea of enhancing social controls through *kennen en gekend worden* ('to know and to be known') (Spaaij, 2002: 29). The fan attendants initially worked at home matches only, but in 1989 they also started to attend Feyenoord's away matches. Their unit gradually expanded to three full-time and eight part-time employees in the early 1990s. Through their continuous interactions with hooligans, street-level police officers developed a more profound knowledge of the behaviour and backgrounds of the hooligans. Fan attendants observed that football hooliganism at Feyenoord was closely related to other forms of juvenile delinquency in Rotterdam. Rumour had it that several Feyenoord hooligans were centrally involved in the disorder in the city centre on the Queen's Birthday celebrations, on 30 April 1989. The fan attendants contacted investigating officers and were able to identify suspects. Their awareness of the intertwinement of football hooliganism and juvenile delinquency led them to extend the focus of their work. For this purpose, the football unit merged with local youth workers into a so-called 'youth team' (COT, 1999: 20).

Fan attendants attempt to reduce spectator violence through persuasion, exemplary behaviour and warnings. They have established a certain degree of mutual respect and trust with older hooligans, which is used at times to convince hooligans to refrain from violence or to obtain relevant information on hooligans' expectations and intentions. The relationship between fan attendants and hooligans is nevertheless fragile. A major difficulty in the activities of the fan attendants is to establish a balance between their police function and the need to maintain fruitful contacts with hooligans. Fan attendants are generally regarded with disdain and suspicion by the hooligans since they have regularly been involved in the identification and apprehension of supporters. Others do not tolerate their presence at all and may approach them in an overtly hostile manner. In order to not to disrupt their relationship with hooligans, fan attendants often tolerate infringements such as in-fighting and minor drug trade or drug use, but they generally act against serious vandalism or violence directed at opposing supporters or at the police. Fan attendants and the club's security officers have also realized a certain degree of respect among hooligans through their assistance in certain issues, for example by co-organizing the funeral of a deceased hooligan or by helping hooligans who wish to appeal against a banning order (Spaaij, 2002: 29). On the other hand, arrest or the submission of incriminating evidence against hooligans damage the police officers' relationship with their subjects. As a senior fan attendant commented: 'If I had the knowledge and a week after the riot at Beverwijk they [his superiors] had asked me to point out who might have thrown a punch ... I could tell them, but that would destroy a decade of hard work' (personal interview, April 2002).

The episodes of serious hooligan violence in the 1990s had a significant impact on police strategies. An awareness emerged of the urgent need for improving the co-operation between the different regional police forces and for expanding the method of intelligence-led policing. A special task force was set up within the Rotterdam-Rijnmond Police force to study the opportunities for improving the collection, analysis and dissemination of intelligence on football hooliganism. The task force concluded that the position of fan attendants was particularly vulnerable since their assignment was unclear and risky when confronted with criminal intelligence (Politie Rotterdam-Rijnmond, 1999: 29). Subsequent attempts to reduce these difficulties were only in part successful. The disorder during the celebration of Feyenoord's National Championship on 25 April 1999 highlighted the intertwinement of football hooliganism and other forms of juvenile delinquency. Supporters and local youths fought the police, the windows of 93 stores were smashed and 25 shops were ransacked. Police officers, threatened by supporters, opened gunfire injuring four people. The riot was widely reported in the international press. The *International Herald Tribune* described the incidents as 'a new dimension in soccer violence' (27 April 1999). The *New York Times* speculated that 'soccer fans may have returned police gunfire during rioting in Rotterdam' (27 April 1999).

Fan attendants' relationship with Feyenoord hooligans and their ability to positively influence fan behaviour have deteriorated in recent years. Senior police officers and fan attendants argue that their knowledge of the hooligan group has gradually diminished due to a number of factors.[1] Rapid change of staff, due in part to work-related stress, has been a major issue of concern. Information is often not fully documented and therefore the resignation of senior fan attendants leads to a (temporary) decline in institutional knowledge and expertise. In many cases new recruits have to establish a trust relationship with their subjects from scratch. The decline in police knowledge is also related to developments in football hooliganism at Feyenoord. Experienced hooligans tend to operate in a more secretive manner than in the past due to their fear of punishment. They may also spread disinformation in order to mislead the police. The emergence of the youth group has further complicated contacts between fan attendants and hooligans. Whereas certain older hooligans view such contacts as largely inevitable and instrumental (i.e. as a source of information and negotiation), most young hooligans consciously avoid any contact with police officers.

Feyenoord hooligans occasionally confront police officers in an aggressive and violent way due in part to recent conflicts with police officers and fan attendants. After a match between Feyenoord and Ajax, on 17 April 2005, hundreds of Feyenoord supporters attacked the riot police and pelted them with stones and bottles. Forty-two police officers were injured. In the aftermath of the incident the police displayed photographs of suspects on television and on the Internet. In April 2004 a number of fan attendants quit their jobs after four plain-clothes officers were forced to draw their guns when attacked by a group of hooligans (personal interviews with senior fan attendants, November 2004; *Rotterdams Dagblad*, 30 July 2004). In a bid to contain football hooliganism at Feyenoord, the Rotterdam-Rijnmond Police force has recently adopted a 'perpetrator-orientated' approach (see Chapter Three). The Regional Intelligence Service gathers and disseminates intelligence on notorious hooligans, who are being closely monitored at football matches as well as in everyday life. Police officers periodically visit hooligans at their homes. This approach has resulted in a further polarization between hooligans and the police. Police officers involved in the project have been intimidated or assaulted on occasion and hooligans have damaged the home of one fan attendant.

Feyenoord hooligans are aware of the fact that the opportunities for large-scale collective violence in and around football grounds are currently limited. They perceive the wide range of security and safety measures in and around De Kuip as inhibiting hooligan confrontations:

Inside the stadium the odds are basically against us now. I mean, you are quite likely to be arrested at some stage if you commit an offence inside the stadium. And the opportunities for confronting opposing fans have also decreased considerably. Missile throwing may still be common, but fighting is relatively rare, especially at home matches. (Personal interview with SCF member, October 2004)

At the same time, hooligans have developed strategies for circumventing controls and impositions. As we have seen, the vast majority of hooligan confrontations take place away from the ground on locations where police controls are, or are perceived by hooligans as being, relatively weak or non-existent. Confrontations with rival hooligan groups are occasionally pre-arranged. Hooligans also regularly seek to circumvent ticket and membership regulations in order to attend matches on their own terms. They use their contacts with police officers and fan attendants to negotiate banning orders, sometimes with success: 'The police try to maintain a good relationship with us. I am officially banned, but they allow me to attend matches as long as I behave myself. Hilarious, really. If we want something, we will double-cross them just as easily. It has always been like that' (personal interview with SCF member, August 2002).

Experienced hooligans also use certain substitutes for large-scale physical confrontation, which may generate similar excitement and fun at times (Van der Torre and Spaaij, 2003: 75-77). They regularly intimidate representatives of media and cultural institutions. In December 2000 hooligans threatened local cinemas to prevent the broadcasting of the Ajax documentary *Daar hoorden zij engelen zingen* and in March 2001 they disrupted the play *Hooligans*. Hooligans may also force the authorities to take exorbitant measures to prevent hooligan confrontations. Although these measures are normally a source of frustration since they reduce the opportunities for fighting, at times hooligans thoroughly enjoy the costs and efforts made by the authorities to prevent disorder, especially when in their view the potential for disorder is relatively low. They occasionally spread disinformation about their intentions and monitor how police officers respond to this information. Disinformation may also lead to sensationalist and incorrect news reports. For example, in 2000 the website of a Feyenoord hooligan led to a series of media reports on the alleged co-operation between Dutch hooligan formations during Euro 2000 dubbed the 'Orange hooligan army'.

Furthermore, experienced hooligans use their bureaucratic competences and networks to frustrate or to appeal against security policies. They appeal against what they perceive as disproportionate travel regulations, ticket prices for away matches, banning orders and police methods. Their protests are regularly supported by non-hooligan supporters as well as by the official fan club. The independent fanzine *Lunatic News* is also used as an instrument for criticizing the undesired consequences of official policies. These types of fan activism blur the distinction between hooligans and non-hooligan supporters. In 2002 Feyenoord supporters lodged a formal complaint against the Amsterdam riot police for their disproportionate use of violence and the injury of a number of fans during an away match against Ajax. The accusation was sustained by the Commission for Police Complaints (*Rotterdams Dagblad*, 11 November 2003). Hundreds of supporters claimed financial compensation for their unjust arrest after a home match against Ajax, on 23 April 2006. The police arrested 799 supporters in order to prevent conflict escalation, among whom many women and children. Supporters also lodged a complaint against the Mayor of Rotterdam, Ivo Opstelten.[2]

Conclusion

The wide range of security and safety measures introduced to contain or eradicate football hooliganism has significantly reduced the opportunities for hooligan confrontations in and around football grounds. Large-scale physical confrontations between opposing hooligan formations are nowadays relatively uncommon. The composition of the hooligan group has changed substantially over the last decade. The number of regular participants has somewhat declined and the age structure of the hooligan formation has broadened. In the 1970s and 1980s the majority of hooligans was in their teens and early twenties, but at present several group members are in their thirties and forties. Apart from these changes, there are striking continuities in the focal concerns of Feyenoord hooligans. The majority of hooligans come from working-class backgrounds and have relatively low levels of formal education. They celebrate in a heightened or distorted form the core values of local culture, which are reflected to some degree in Feyenoord fan culture, notably hard masculinity, ingroup solidarity, territoriality and autonomy. Although certain older hooligans have experienced a degree of upward social mobility, they are not beyond their cultural roots and male friendships networks (Williams, 1991: 177). Their involvement in football hooliganism as well as, for many hooligans, their involvement in the club constitutes a major source of excitement and identity in their lives. Young hooligans seek recognition and excitement away from the routines of school and work (cf. Marsh et al., 1978). Many of these male adolescents grow up in a social environment in which aggression and the (threatened) use of violence are part of social life.

The organization of the hooligan group is relatively limited. Leadership and hierarchy are informal and based on seniority, status or organizational skills. Over the years, however, the degrees of planning and co-ordination involved in football hooliganism have increased substantially in reaction to pervasive controls and impositions and as part of the escalation of inter-group rivalries. Streetwise hooligans have developed strategies for circumventing police controls and successfully challenging their rivals, displacing their activities to new locales and occasionally engaging in pre-arranged confrontations. At the same time, they regularly seek to frustrate or manipulate police strategies through negotiation, intimidation, disinformation or the collection of intelligence on potential flaws in police tactics. The interactions and negotiations between hooligans and law enforcers are a vital element of football hooliganism at Feyenoord and a source of excitement and fun for many hooligans. Hooligans also enjoy manipulating the media through disinformation and sensationalist accounts, and they have regularly intimidated journalists. On the other hand, experienced hooligans have also co-operated with journalists to present their image of physical prowess and sovereignty to the outside world. They are aware of the constructed nature of fan reputations and on occasion they deliberately manipulate these reputations, notably in the aftermath of high-profile incidents.

Characteristic of contemporary football hooliganism at Feyenoord are not so much, as Giulianotti (1999) has suggested, the changes in its political and media treatment, but rather hooligans' diverse strategies for experiencing the 'buzz' and for manipulating security policies and media representations. These strategies are an inherent part of the hooligan experience at Feyenoord and they substitute, in part, physical confrontations with opposing hooligan formations. In addition to their role as fan activists, however, experienced hooligans regularly seek violent confrontation with long-standing rivals. In recent years the hooligan formation has come to attract a significant number of young recruits eager to establish a reputation for toughness among peers. In spite of the efforts made and resources invested, the club's persistent hooligan image continues to attract young males identifying with football hooliganism.

7

'Decency and Tradition': Continuity and Change in Spectator Behaviour at Sparta Rotterdam

Introduction

Supporters of Sparta Rotterdam celebrate their club's widely recognized reputation as a 'gentlemen's' club with deep-seated non-hooligan traditions. This reputation is reflected in the historically low level of spectator violence as well as in the prolonged absence of a hooligan subculture at the club. The prolonged absence of football hooliganism should be understood within the context of the contrapuntal collective identities of Sparta and Feyenoord supporters and the distinctive social realities the two clubs symbolize. The case of Sparta provides a striking example of intra-city variations in the extent and forms of football hooliganism and changes therein over time. Sparta's 'friendly' image contrasts starkly with the persistent hooligan stigma of Feyenoord supporters. At the same time, a small number of young fans have started to identify with football hooliganism in recent years, a development which features elements of both resistance to and compliance with dominant fan culture. Recent episodes of hooligan violence contest the club's 'friendly' image and reveal the subtle yet vital interactions between the club and its supporters.

This chapter first examines the wider context of Sparta's image of a 'gentlemen's' club through an analysis of the sources of fan culture and the historical rivalry with Feyenoord. I will then describe the development of spectator behaviour at Sparta during the period of the escalation of inter-group rivalries in Dutch football and the ways in which this escalation was framed within Sparta's fan community. In the final part of the chapter I will analyze the recent emergence of a hooligan formation at Sparta and the challenges this development presents for the collective identity of supporters.

The making of a 'gentlemen's' club

Sparta Rotterdam is commonly portrayed as an elite club and a 'gentlemen's' club. This dominant image can be traced back to the early beginnings of the club. Founded in 1888, Sparta is one of the oldest football clubs in the Netherlands. The club played a pioneering role in the early development of Dutch football. At this early stage the game was played exclusively by young men from the upper classes. With the emergence of a number of working-class clubs in cities such as Amsterdam (Blauw Wit), Utrecht (DOS), Deventer (Go Ahead), Den Haag (ADO) and Rotterdam (Feyenoord), in the early twentieth century football gradually spread across all social classes. The old elite clubs, adhering closely to the tastes and behavioural codes of their class, regarded these newly emerging working-class clubs with disdain and feared that their roughness and lack of civilization would undermine the game (Miermans, 1955: 145; Cocheret, 1963: 12; Van Emmenes, 1972: 5). Many members of the upper classes sought to re-establish social distance by taking up more exclusive sports, including rugby and hockey (Stokvis, 1989: 28). Apart from being an elite club, Sparta was a driving force behind the innovation and professionalization of Dutch football. In 1893 the weekly newspaper *Nederlandsche Sport* wrote how 'Sparta has made football into something where people go to' (quoted in Tummers, 1993: 33). Sparta was the first Dutch football club to play against a foreign opponent, the English club Harwich and Parkeston FC, in 1893. The club also stimulated the creation of the Dutch Football Association (NVB) and the Dutch national team. Sparta became one of the most successful football clubs in the early history of Dutch football. The club won the national championship five times in seven years between 1909 and 1915.

Sparta's contemporary public image of *fatsoen en traditie* ('decency and tradition') in part derives from the club's move to the district of Spangen in the West of Rotterdam in 1916 and, more specifically, to the picturesque and charming stadium Het Kasteel (The Castle). The stadium and local area have been major themes in the development of Sparta's fan community and the construction of self and the other. Het Kasteel is the oldest football stadium in the Netherlands and has come to symbolize Sparta fan culture and the club's particular feel.

The building is more than a stadium, it is the symbol of the football club with the richest traditions in the Netherlands. [...] If there is one place in the Netherlands where football is culture, it is here. A castle is the appropriate home of such an institution (Tummers, 1993: 32).

Historically most fans lived at walking distance from the ground or in one of the adjacent neighbourhoods North of the river Meuse. The sense of close-knit community is remembered with great fondness by long-standing supporters and is passed on from generation to generation. Spangen and adjacent neighbourhoods in the West and North of the city were among the oldest working-class areas in Rotterdam. Because of Sparta's elite status, working-class men often had great difficulty in becoming club members. Applicants appeared before the club's admission's committee and only people from wealthier backgrounds or with good connections in club circles had a chance to be allowed into the club. This system of admission was abolished as late as the 1960s and contrasted starkly with the situation at Feyenoord, where there had never been such strict admission regulations. Unlike Feyenoord, Sparta never wanted to be a 'people's club'.

The rivalry between the two largest football clubs in Rotterdam historically reflects socio-economic and cultural differences between two parts of Rotterdam separated physically as well as symbolically by the river Meuse. Sparta was founded South of the river, but as early as 1889 the club moved to the North bank, evolving into a community club for the North-West of Rotterdam. Feyenoord, on the other hand, represented the working classes in the South of Rotterdam (see Chapter Six). The two clubs symbolized the distinctive social realities North and South of the river Meuse and the social distance between the upper and lower classes in Rotterdam (Sonneveld, 1986: 62; Huijzer, 1998: 11). The antagonism between the two clubs was at its height before the 1960s. For a long time local derbies were one of the few matches were large contingents of away supporters could be present due to the relatively short distance between the two grounds. Despite this geographical proximity, many Sparta supporters were reluctant to visit the South side of the city. They ritually refuse to cross the Meuse and many have done so only sporadically, for example on the occasion of Sparta's Cup Final against PSV in 1996, which was played in the Feyenoord stadium. The Southern part of Rotterdam is perceived by many Sparta fans as a somewhat remote and uncivilized place: 'We always considered them to be less intelligent, rednecks you know. It's not their fault, but they have always been a bit backward' (personal interview with Sparta supporter, October 2004). This view corresponds with the perceptions of Feyenoord supporters:

> If you lived in the South you never went beyond the bridge or the tunnel. You were from the South and you stayed there. And automatically that made you a Feyenoord supporter. We regarded those from the North as posh pricks and Sparta supporters saw us as rednecks (Bormans, 2002: 52).

The rivalry between Sparta and Feyenoord supporters gradually transformed from the 1960s onwards due to two parallel developments. The first development was the commercialization and professionalization of Dutch football. The introduction of professional football in 1954 meant that the richest football clubs often attracted the most talented players. Sparta experienced a decade of success under the management of Englishman Denis Neville. The club won the National Championship in 1959 for the first time since 1915, and in 1962 and 1996 Sparta won the national Cup. From the 1960s onwards Sparta's successes gradually declined and became overshadowed by those of the richest club in Rotterdam. Feyenoord's National Championship in 1961 marked the beginning of the club's 'golden era', which culminated in its victory in the European Champions Cup and the World Cup for club teams in 1970. During this period Feyenoord's fan base expanded rapidly, both regionally and nationally. Sparta, on the other hand, evolved into a more modest club in the Dutch Premier League with a comparatively small following. Between the 1970s and the 1990s average home attendances fell from 10,000 to approximately 5,000 (data provided by Sparta, April 2003). This development has transformed the antagonism between the two sets of supporters from a two-way rivalry to an unrequited rivalry: 'a Feyenoord supporter does not normally cheer if Sparta loses, but a Sparta fan celebrates Feyenoord's defeat like a victory' (Bormans, 2002: 55). Also, after Sparta's relegation to the First Division in 2002, East Rotterdam-based Excelsior came to be perceived as a minor rival. Due to

Excelsior's status as a sister club for Feyenoord, Sparta supporters commonly nickname their lower-league rivals as *Zuid 2* ('South Rotterdam 2').

The second development that influenced the historical rivalry between the two clubs was the profound demographic change in Sparta's local environment. The traditional working-class community was characterized by its pre-war housing and predominantly white working-class population, among which many dock workers, craftsmen, tradesmen and civil servants. Due to overcrowding and the deterioration of housing and living conditions, many people abandoned the area and moved to the modern, relatively spacious suburbs in the periphery of the city or even further out. Social mobility was translated into geographical mobility: those who could afford it left the area (Burgers and Engbersen, 2001: 252; Schadee, 2002). They were replaced by immigrants from non-Western countries such as Suriname, Turkey, Morocco and the Netherlands Antilles. The ethnic diversity of the area increased, but there was a homogenization of the socio-economic composition of the local population: comparatively low levels of education and income and high unemployment (Van der Torre, 1999: 42). The influx of newcomers was perceived by the traditional inhabitants as a sign of decay and reinforced their desire to move. Large-scale renovation in West Rotterdam failed to prevent those who were able to afford it from moving to 'better' neighbourhoods.

Demographic change and the decay of industrial employment in Rotterdam eroded the foundations and social cohesion of the traditional culture of the area, gradually transforming into a 'culture of unemployment' (Engbersen et al., 1993). Spangen is currently one of the most deprived urban areas in the Netherlands, despite the fact that the area shrugged off to some degree its reputation as an open drug scene and a 'no-go area'. In the 1990s the public visibility of drug abuse and drug trade in the area caused major protest and resentment among inhabitants versus the authorities that failed to produce a safe and comfortable living environment. There were also persistent inter-ethnic tensions in the area. In 2003 approximately 80 per cent of the total population of Spangen (just over 10,000) were 'non-Western immigrants', compared to an average of 62 per cent in the whole of West Rotterdam (Gemeente Rotterdam, 2003: 78; COS, 2003).

The demographic transformation of the area has radically altered the geographical distribution of Sparta supporters. Only a small minority of supporters still live in the area and most fans are based in other parts of the city or in one of the many adjacent suburbs, notably Alexanderpolder, Ommoord, Capelle aan den IJssel, Nieuwerkerk aan den IJssel, Vlaardingen, Schiedam, Krimpen aan den IJssel and Zevenkamp (data provided by Sparta, April 2003). Very few of the new residents of Spangen seem to have an interest in the club. The perceived discrepancy between the club and its local environment is reflected metaphorically in rumours about the club's motives for relocating the ground's main entrance. Rumour had it that club officials were so ashamed of the ethnic Spangen which cared so little about the club that they had deliberately built the stadium's main entrance at the undeveloped side of the area (Verkamman, 2002: 19).

The ground issue is a central theme in contemporary fan culture at Sparta. Conflicts on the relocation and development of Het Kasteel surfaced in the 1970s. The club systematically turned down proposals by the local government to relocate the stadium. After two decades of negotiation between club directors and the local authorities, the stadium was eventually renovated in its entirety. Many supporters argue that although they are emotionally attached to the ground, there is no logical reason for the club to remain in Spangen. They accuse club directors of decision making on the basis of the 'false sentiment' that the club must remain where its roots are and therefore having failed to anticipate the profound demographic changes in the area. To secure the club's future, many fans argue, Sparta should move to where its fan community is based, for instance in the East of the city or in adjacent suburbs. This argument in part derives from the fact that the club has failed to successfully strengthen its ties with the local community, that is, to attract a multi-ethnic crowd. Club officials have made several attempts to win the support of young second-generation or third-generation immigrants living in Spangen. In collaboration with the local government the club runs a school project which aims to attract local kids by facilitating free tickets and organizing meetings with players and managers. Some of the club's black and minority ethnic players are actively involved in the project because of their status and popularity within the ethnic communities. The project has not (yet) succeeded in attracting a substantial number of local citizens to the club (personal interview with board members, September 2004; cf. Van Dijk et al., 2000; Van Dijk, 2002).

The collective identity of Sparta supporters is constructed in relation to the local rival Feyenoord. Despite the declining intensity of the local rivalry and the profound demographic changes in the areas these clubs represent (see also Chapter Six), the contrasting collective imaginaries of the two fan communities persist today. Sparta supporters continue to define themselves in opposition to the alleged 'rough' and 'uncivilized' nature of Feyenoord fans. These representations of self and the other structure the boundaries of 'reasonable' behaviour and explain why football hooliganism is generally regarded within Sparta's fan community as 'not for the likes of us'.

'Not for the likes of us': the place of violence in Sparta fan culture

Spectator behaviour at Sparta is commonly perceived by the authorities and the media as 'friendly' and unproblematic. In the club's early years fan behaviour occasionally caused minor concern on the part of the football authorities, notably fans' alleged intimidation of referees. On three occasions, in 1896, 1911 and 1921, the football authorities demanded that Sparta should post warning notices to prevent future incidents. In 1896 Sparta's board posted a warning notice reading:

> With regard to the events during last Sunday's match between RAP from Amsterdam and Sparta – during which referee Trom suspended the match after being hissed continuously – the Board politely yet urgently requests that in the future all people involved co-operate better [...]. It should be prevented that people become overpowered by partiality from which all kinds of unpleasantness can emerge. The good game of the guests should be acknowledged as much as that of Sparta; one must obey the referee's decision and not inflict harm on him because of the implementation of his function (quoted in: Sonneveld, 1986: 76).

Club officials and supporters have regularly protested against punishments ordered by the football association. They argued that the incidents were always minor and that the club had an exemplary record of spectator behaviour. The punishments were seen as disproportionally severe for such a 'quiet' and 'civilized' club (Sonneveld,

1986: 76; Cocheret, 1963: 65). The behaviour of Sparta supporters has been perceived by club officials and fans as being much better than that of most sets of fans in the Netherlands.

Sparta's image as a 'friendly' club became a central theme in the construction of collective fan identity from the 1970s onwards. In the mid-1970s Dutch football experienced the emergence of violent rivalries between opposing groups of young fans, so-called 'sides' (see Chapter Three). Public anxiety over football hooliganism initially focused on four clubs: Feyenoord, Ajax, FC Utrecht and FC Den Haag (now ADO Den Haag). Journalists portrayed these clubs as having large numbers of violent supporters on their terraces. Sparta supporters were occasionally mentioned in media reports on spectator violence at football matches. Between 1970 and 1980 Sparta fans were mentioned in twenty reported incidents (Van der Brug, 1986: 281). Only in seven of the twenty reported incidents Sparta supporters were reported as being the aggressors. In five cases the incident involved missile throwing (e.g. fireworks, bottles or sausages). On one occasion, on 23 October 1974, Sparta supporters allegedly damaged a train carriage. Furthermore, at a home match against Twente on 13 May 1973, home fans 'had to be held back by the police' after a controversial refereeing decision (Van der Brug, 1986: 264). Compared to the number of serious incidents of spectator violence during this period, the incidents provoked by Sparta supporters were relatively minor. None of the reported incidents involved inter-fan fighting.

The incidents provoked by supporters of other Dutch football clubs had a significant impact on Sparta fan culture. They enhanced the self-image of Sparta supporters as being more 'civilized' and 'decent' than certain other football crowds in the Netherlands, notably those at Feyenoord, Ajax, FC Utrecht and FC Den Haag. In fanzines and official club magazines supporters and club officials have repeatedly criticized the behaviour of opposing supporters as well as the passive and ineffective responses of the authorities to football hooliganism. In 1984 the editor of *De Spartaan*, the magazine of Sparta's official fan club, wrote:

> In our club magazine we have protested for many years against the fights and vandalism in and around football grounds. The police have done almost nothing and neither has the [football association] and the Justice

225

Department. Only the UEFA was a bit stricter. Sparta, one of the most innocent clubs, was fined by the KNVB, but the riots at Ajax and Feyenoord have merely continued (*De Spartaan*, no. 792, October 1984: 3).

Both supporters and club officials argued that offenders were only marginally punished and that the club received insufficient financial compensation for incidents provoked by visiting fans, such as damage to fences or the ransacking of food stalls inside the stadium. Moreover, it was claimed that the football authorities were ducking the issue and punished 'decent' clubs which suffered from the misbehaviour of opposing supporters (e.g. *De Spartaan*, no. 752, November 1979: 3). They also blamed visiting teams for not taking full responsibility for the behaviour of their supporters. In the aftermath of the local derby on 15 November 1970, during which Feyenoord supporters threw smoke bombs at Sparta's goalkeeper and damaged a fence, the editor of *De Spartaan* wrote: 'The boards of these clubs [the more notorious clubs] fail to promote a sense of decency and respect for the opponent among the rough part of their support' (*De Spartaan*, no. 661, December 1970: 9). Similar accusations were made after supporters of Holland Sport (now ADO Den Haag) threatened and assaulted the referee. Holland Sport was believed to have been more concerned with refereeing decisions than with the behaviour of its own fans (*De Spartaan*, no. 653, March 1970: 12). The football association eventually lifted the punishment imposed on Sparta, arguing that Sparta's board and security staff 'had done everything in their powers' and that 'home supporters were not involved in the incident' (*De Spartaan*, no. 656, June, 1970: 2).

Fan protests have occasionally taken on a more organized form. In 1974 the official fan club campaigned against a fine of 7,500 guilders [approximately 3,400 euro] imposed on the club due to alleged deficiencies in the containment of away supporters (during a match at Het Kasteel an away fan threw an empty beer bottle onto the pitch, which hit the referee). Supporters protested against the decision and urged people to make a small donation. A similar campaign was initiated by local newspaper *Het Vrije Volk*. Central to the protests were the arguments that it was unfair to blame the club for the persistent misbehaviour of opposing supporters, that Sparta's financial situation was such that it could not easily afford the fine and that the club was already undertaking major improvements in security measures, such as erection of perimeter fences and the repair of fences damaged by visiting fans. The campaigns raised enough money to pay the fine (*De Spartaan*, no. 695, January 1974: 1; *De Spartaan*, no. 697, April 1974: 7).

Adding to the widespread belief among Sparta supporters that the authorities failed to effectively reduce football hooliganism was a more general concern over the declining attendances in Dutch professional football in the 1980s. Sparta supporters regarded football hooliganism as one of the main reasons for this decline. Estimates on the number of Sparta supporters who stopped attending matches due to experiences of spectator violence varied from 'a few hundred' to 'ten to fifteen per cent' of the home crowd (*De Spartaan*, no. 790, July 1984: 9l; *De Spartaan*, no. 768, November 1981). This development allegedly deepened the club's financial problems and was related to another factor: like most smaller clubs, Sparta failed to attract substantial numbers of new young supporters and therefore its fan base was ageing rapidly. This issue was also considered one of the reasons why 'our fans are quieter than the youthful thugs [at other clubs]. Good for Sparta's image, but bad news for our treasurer' (*De Spartaan*, no. 801, September 1985: 5). Supporters were convinced that it was predominantly the 'decent' part of the audience that stayed away, a development that disproportionately affected 'friendly' clubs like Sparta:

> We were thrilled not only by the victory, but also by the nice atmosphere. If one compares that with the riots provoked by Utrecht, Den Haag and Feyenoord supporters [...] we should be happy with our quiet Spangen. The decent part of the public stays away because of those riots and this mostly affects 'decent' clubs such as Haarlem and Sparta (*De Spartaan*, no. 776, September 1982: 9).

The extent and seriousness of football hooliganism and the decline in attendances were attributed not only to the behaviour of violent others or to the authorities' failure to tackle the problem, but also to the extensive media coverage of hooligan incidents. Media reports focused on the aggressive and violent behaviour of a small minority of fans and therefore underrepresented the 'decent' behaviour of Sparta supporters. Club officials and supporters have regularly protested against this perceived injustice, claiming that the Dutch media amplified football hooliganism. Sparta's security officer argued: 'Certain sets of supporters have caused mayhem here over and over again. I have often felt the urge to call television companies and say "When there is another knifing, please don't report it. Don't give them that media attention, because it's one of the things they're after"' (personal interview, July 2004). In February 1983, *De Spartaan* published 'an alternative headline which was overlooked by the newspapers', highlighting the peaceful atmosphere during a local derby at Het Kasteel (*De Spartaan*, no. 779, February 1983: 7).

The emergence and development of youth groups at Sparta

During the second half of the 1970s Sparta experienced the emergence of a group of young fans with their own practices and territory inside the stadium: the Castle Side. Contrary to the popular belief that all sides were heavily involved in football hooliganism, the Castle Side had a rather positive image within Sparta's fan community: 'perhaps not large in numbers, but of much more value to the club than any other side' (*ProSparta*, vol. 5, no. 6, 23 October 1985: 23). Predominantly consisting of young men in their late teens and early twenties, members of the Castle Side sought to create an intimate and passionate atmosphere inside the stadium. They developed a sense of friendship, community and ingroup solidarity celebrating their club's 'friendly' image.

> If someone appears to lose himself, others will intervene like 'come on, use your brains, think before you act'. That's what you hear on the terraces. That's why our group is hardly ever involved in riots, because we know each other as a group and therefore we do not respond to the provocations of rival supporters. We rather search for the safety of the police than create some sort of small war. There's no point in that, really (member of Castle Side in *ProSparta*, vol. 5, no. 6, 23 October 1985: 27).

Sparta supporters did not regularly engage in competitive violence, but a small group of young fans was occasionally involved in incidents of vandalism, missile throwing and minor inter-fan fighting. These incidents were commonly framed within the fan community as a minor and temporary excess and as a kind of 'contamination' (e.g. *De Spartaan*, no. 699, June 1974: 7). From this viewpoint, some of the more 'decent' supporters copied the behaviour of the hooligan groups at Feyenoord, Ajax, FC Utrecht and FC Den Haag. The media were seen as playing a central role in this process of imitation. Although Sparta supporters did not actively seek violent confrontation with opposing fan groups, some fans occasionally responded to provocations or attacks by rival supporters. Young fans also regularly walked towards the away section during home matches in order to taunt opposing fans. Considering the limited opportunities for physical confrontation and retaliation inside the stadium due to fencing and police presence, these taunts can be seen as a relatively safe means for subduing one's rival without resorting to violence (Marsh, 1978: 17). Furthermore, young fans were occasionally involved in the ransacking of gas stations or restaurants on their journey to away matches. Their search for excitement and fun featured centrally in this activity. As the former chairman of the official fan club commented:

> I recall two occasions in particular. A group of supporters ransacked a restaurant and a gas station. Just for fun really. They loved it, walking around with all sorts of crap. Barbie dolls, toy glasses, table cloths. In all honesty, I have done it myself once and there is no excuse, it's pretty pathetic. At present there are more stewards travelling on the coaches who keep an eye on it. They summon you to stay close to the coach during stops. (Personal interview, July 2003)

A small group of fans named the SR1888 (Sparta Rotterdam 1888) was particularly renowned for their occasional involvement in minor incidents of violence and vandalism, mainly as a form of experimentation characteristic of young males (see Chapter One). Certain individuals within this group held a reputation for their heavy drinking, an activity that features centrally in their match-day activities. For many group members, their involvement in the club and the group was a major source of excitement contrasting with the pressures of everyday life. Alcohol consumption seems to trigger their occasional boisterous and aggressive behaviour, for example in response to provocations by rival fans or to perceived injustices (i.e. refereeing decisions, the underachievement of players, aggressive police methods). According to a safety officer, the fans 'can cause considerable problems when they are drunk, but afterwards they often apologize when realizing how they have behaved' (personal interview, July 2004). For example, during an away match at Willem II on 21 September 2004 a drunken supporter assaulted a steward even though other Sparta fans tried to stop him, arguing that his behaviour was unreasonable (personal observations, September 2004). The influence of alcohol on the behaviour of some supporters is recognized by fans themselves:

> Alcohol was a major problem for me. I simply didn't care about anything, you know. I would challenge rival supporters without thinking really. Banning order, a couple of times in prison, divorce, one big mess it was. I had to stop drinking and eventually I did. It really helped me. Now I think more before I act and I haven't been in trouble since. (Personal interview, July 2003)

The development of local fan policies and mechanisms of social control

Security and safety policies at Sparta have developed in accordance with national and international regulations. In the mid-1980s the Dutch football association urged clubs to play a more substantial role in the containment of spectator violence by investing in their own security regime. Sparta was one of the first football clubs in the Netherlands to appoint a security officer and to establish a steward organization. Security officers and stewards sought to establish a fruitful relationship with supporters, emphasizing the club's hospitality towards its customers and, more generally, Sparta's 'friendly' image. Through maintaining a close relationship with fans club officials attempted to enhance informal social control among supporters. They noticed that rather than being premeditated or organized, the occasional violence caused by young Sparta fans emerged principally as a reaction to perceived injustices (i.e. the underachievement of players, refereeing decisions, sloppy club management, aggressive police methods) or provocations by rival fans. As a former security officer remembered: 'Violence occurred at specific moments, when they felt it to be a legitimate response, for example when the club was in a bad situation. But at those moments they could go absolutely mental' (personal interview, July 2004). The following police report shows that incidents of this kind may still occur:

> Sparta supporters were frustrated because they expected their team to get points against Fortuna Sittard. Their frustration was acted out against coaches and home fans, and later against the police. [...] The police charged the crowd to secure the safe retreat of 16 coaches carrying Fortuna fans. [...] Consequently, a group of Sparta fans went to the [local] police station [...] to lodge complaints against the police. At the police station officers spoke with a delegation of fans and after a few hours order was temporarily restored (Rotterdam-Rijnmond Police report, 8 April 2001).

To prevent disorder club officials seek to create a basis for mutual understanding with so-called 'risk' supporters. They argue that club representatives often have a more positive and calming influence on supporters than the (riot) police. Conversations with supporters take place on match days as well as during the week, for example by inviting fans to discuss a recent incident or development. Club officials also apply this personal approach as much as possible to the settlement of banning orders and arrests. In the case of minor offence the security officer may decide to refrain from punishment and to communicate this view to the police and the football association. Supporters may first get a warning (a so-called 'yellow card') before receiving a banning order or fine. At the same time, the club's security policy is guided by principles of consistency and deterrence. Banning orders are imposed straight after the arrest to increase the deterrent effect, that is, to show supporters that their actions have immediate consequences. The banning order prohibits individuals to attend home and away matches and occasionally includes an additional condition which prohibits their presence within a radius of two kilometres of the ground on match days. A deputy security officer summarizes this approach as follows:

> We can immediately send the banning order to the football association, but we have always had one step before that. First we use more informal measures of punishment, the more personal approach. We used to give

'yellow cards' which were remitted after a period of good behaviour. Simply to give people a second chance. But nowadays it's mainly banning orders we are dealing with. The problem is that it may take four or five months before the football association notifies you. We act in a different way. If we know what you have done, we will notify you straight away that you have been banned. I think you have to, because otherwise those people hang around for months and gradually lose the sense of direct punishment. Our approach works for most offenders I would say. (Personal interview, July 2004)

Many Sparta fans regard the banning order as a serious punishment since it obstructs them from attending home and away matches. It is extremely difficult to defy a banning order at home matches due to the compactness of the stadium, camera surveillance and steward and police observation. SR1888 members have nevertheless been creative in circumventing banning orders. For example, during the stadium's renovation in the late 1990s supporters climbed up a construction site that overlooked the stadium, enabling them to watch the game. Police and security officers appreciated the action and decided not to arrest them.

Club officials and the police seek to apply a similar approach to the containment of away fans. This approach is based on the belief that visiting fans should be treated as guests and that aggressive policing merely incites aggressive and violent behaviour. Sparta supporters have repeatedly criticized the club's 'lenient' approach because of their negative experiences at certain Dutch football grounds. They often feel unfairly treated by police officers or by clubs' security staff. Stewards and security officers who regularly accompany Sparta supporters to away matches acknowledge this complaint: 'we know our fans and they know we will defend their interests if necessary. There have been occasions when we have had to defend our fans from being assaulted by the police for no obvious reasons. We always say "let us deal with it first and if we can't handle it we will call you in for back-up"' (personal interview with security officer, July 2004). Due to the low profile of Sparta supporters, the security risks of an upcoming match are principally determined by the reputation and dispositions of opposing fans. Police chiefs and club officials devote much of their attention to the containment of visiting supporters, for instance by arranging their escort to and from the ground. They also consider the probability of 'third party' intervention. For example, when Sparta receives Ajax there is a serious chance that Feyenoord hooligans will attend the event in order to confront their rivals. In recent years club and police strategies have come to focus more sharply on the behaviour and dispositions of a small group of Sparta fans. I will examine this issue in the following section.

Overview of the reproduction of Sparta's non-hooligan traditions

Both historically and at present violence is framed within Sparta's fan community as 'not for the likes of us'. Violent conduct is principally attributed to the 'rough' and 'uncivilized' other. In other words, violence is a central theme in Sparta supporters' delimitation of the borders of the category 'we', as opposed to 'them'. The creation of collective others 'is a requirement, through the dynamics of stereotyping and identity contrast, for helping to set boundaries and mark off the dynamics of the we' (Appadurai, 2006: 50). Club officials play a significant role in this process in two ways: on the one hand, by defining incidents provoked by Sparta fans as a minor and temporary excess or as a more or less logical response to perceived injustices; and, on the other hand, by sustaining the hooligan reputations of certain sets of fans through emphasizing their persistent and 'mindless' violence.

Sparta's 'friendly' reputation produces a relatively sanguine and non-aggressive approach on the part of visitors to Het Kasteel (cf. Williams et al., 1988: 41). Hooligan groups travelling to Spangen normally do not anticipate violent confrontation because of the low-key profile of Sparta supporters: 'Sparta doesn't have any hooligans. I mean, nothing compared to what we've got. I don't dislike them or anything, I simply can't be bothered' (personal interview with Feyenoord hooligan, November 2004). Because of the negative sanctioning of hooligan behaviour at Sparta and the relatively non-aggressive approach on the part of opposing fans, young supporters interested in becoming involved in football hooliganism are likely to either follow one of the more notorious football clubs (i.e. Feyenoord) or eschew their hooligan proclivities. As a club director argued:

233

Sparta is not of interest to those who want to fight. Local boys come to watch us six times and six times nothing happens. So there is no fun for them and they will probably go elsewhere. If you are young and you want to riot, you go to Feyenoord and not to Sparta. Sparta is too boring in this sense. (Personal interview, August 2003)

Although this process of cultural reproduction is durable, in the remainder of this chapter I will show that it is not immutable, evidence of which is the recent emergence of a hooligan formation at Sparta.

Contesting traditions? The rise and development of the Sparta Youth Crew

Club and police strategies targeting spectator violence at Sparta are based on the belief that Sparta supporters do not actively seek violent confrontation with opposing fan groups. This assumption has been challenged in recent years by the emergence of a small group of fans overtly identifying with football hooliganism. The Sparta Youth Crew (SYC), founded in 1999, has come to attract a number of young males, some of whom have been supporting Sparta since their childhood. Within years the SYC transformed from a spontaneous, relatively unorganized group of like-minded friends into a more cohesive fan group that regularly engages in violent confrontation with opposing hooligan groups. Its founders were strongly influenced by the reputations and exploits of hooligan formations in the Netherlands and Britain. Their knowledge of football hooliganism was enhanced by direct interactions with hooligans, media reports and hooligan books and websites.

The core of the group consists of 15 young men in their late teens and early twenties, but for 'high-profile' matches the formation can increase to up to 50 people. SYC members are occasionally accompanied by a few supporters in their thirties, whose status among peers is based on their fighting ability and seniority. Females play a marginal role within the group. Only one girl was temporarily involved in the group as the girlfriend of a male hooligan; on one occasion, in April 2001, she was arrested and banned for insulting a police officer. Furthermore, all hooligans are white. Race categories do not play a major role in their activities, but some hooligans display a certain degree of hostility towards immigrants, especially towards those who are seen as having 'taken over' the Spangen area. Certain SYC members have used right-wing symbols and chants as a means for the provocation of outsiders:

> I once bought a shirt of the NVU [Nederlandse Volks-Unie; Dutch People's Union], and so have others. We wear those shirts not because we are loyal supporters of the NVU, but rather as a way of provocation. You know, the looks on people's faces are priceless. I love to shock them. But I would never wear the shirt to work or anything. (Personal interview with SYC member, July 2003)

On the other hand, the hooligans refuse to allow right-wing youths to join the group because 'they are a completely different type of people who have nothing to do with us. Those skinhead types wouldn't fit in very well' (personal interview with SYC member, July 2003).

Few of the group's core members live in Rotterdam and those who do are not concentrated in one area of the city. In fact, none of the group members grew up in Spangen. The vast majority of hooligans still live with their parents in towns such as Brielle, Nieuwerkerk aan den IJssel, Vlaardingen, Zevenkamp and Delft. Although the hooligans celebrate a hard masculine identity based on physical prowess, their collective identity is also constructed in relation to Feyenoord hooligans and certain other Dutch hooligan formations. Whereas the latter are portrayed as 'rough, hard-core criminals', the Sparta hooligans view themselves as a more sophisticated, fashionable 'fighting crew' and hooliganism is commonly regarded as a temporary lifestyle. As one hooligan put it:

> Feyenoord hooligans have very different backgrounds. I mean, many of them have no education, both parents on drugs, brought up in a culture of violence. Our group is completely different. We come from stable families, quite well-off, have certain values in life, an education. They will probably still be doing their business when they're 35. I certainly won't. I have others goals in life, you know. (Personal interview, July 2003)

235

At the same time, however, Sparta hooligans acknowledge the widespread reputation of the hooligan formation at Feyenoord: 'You have to respect them because of what they have done. They are one of country's leading hooligan groups.'

Many SYC members are enrolled in universities, while some have already completed their university degree. Full-time occupations vary from teaching in primary or secondary schools to health care professionals and a printing-office employee. Only one of the group's core members is a builder.[1] Sparta hooligans also claim to adhere more strictly to the hooligan ethos than many other hooligan formations. Three basic 'rules of disorder' SYC members claim to observe are: never to attack non-hooligan supporters, never to carry weapons other than leather belts, umbrellas or glass bottles, and never to inflict more injury than necessary on a defeated rival (i.e. when lying helplessly on the ground).

Several hooligans are explicitly concerned with the casual designer fashion, especially with brands such as Stone Island, Burberry and Aquascutum, and they spend a significant proportion of their earnings to keep up with the 'right gear'. SYC members also produce and sell certain types of clothing and accessories, such as T-shirts, jumpers and pins with the group logo (the pin displays a combination of the group name and the Stone Island logo). Their encounters with rival hooligan groups can in part be viewed as 'style wars' (Redhead and McLaughlin, 1985), as the following comment by an SYC member suggests: 'The police prevented the fight, but it was a good day after all. Some of the Go Ahead Eagles hooligans later said how impressive we looked, I mean, the gear we were wearing. Much better than theirs obviously. So it was a kind of victory after all, even without the violence' (personal interview, September 2005). Others, however, reject these style wars and emphasize the essence of hooliganism: 'The whole concern with designer brands is silly really. I don't give a shit about it, you know. For me it's only about fighting, friendship and excitement. That's what hooliganism is about, isn't it?' (personal interview with SYC member, October 2004).

The first incident SYC members were involved in had a profound impact on the group's subsequent development. After an away match against Willem II in Tilburg, on 18 December 1999, an SYC member was found seriously injured after being assaulted by home supporters. The incident generated deep-seated hostility between the opposing fan groups. It also increased group cohesion and the young fans' desire to enhance their status in the hierarchy of hooligan oppositions. The SYC began to travel to away matches more regularly by train, eschewing the official coach arrangements which they previously preferred. This mode of travel provided new opportunities for enacting hooligan rivalries. Police surveillance was rare on regular train services and few local hooligan groups anticipated their arrival because of the low-key profile of Sparta supporters. SYC members also began to socialize more frequently outside the football context, organizing visits to pubs and nightclubs and a Summer holiday to Salou, Spain. Seeking to avenge the 1999 incident, Sparta hooligans have repeatedly challenged their equivalents at Willem II. An intended confrontation between the two groups after a home match in 2000 was prevented by the police and stewards, but on 31 January 2001 SYC members successfully challenged their rivals before an away match in Tilburg. In the build-up to the match SYC members taunted Willem II hooligans by telephone and on the Internet. On match day a group of 40 young men, accompanied by members of SR1888, arrived early by train and gathered in pubs in the centre of Tilburg. Fighting and missile throwing erupted when the hooligans were attacked by home fans. Police officers soon arrived at the scene and kept the two sets of fans at bay. They escorted the Sparta supporters to the stadium, but they failed to prevent the rival groups from pelting each other with glasses and cans.

These early incidents enhanced the SYC's reputation within the Dutch hooligan subculture, gradually changing the expectations of rival fan groups. The SYC established violent rivalries with a number of hooligan groups and these formations increasingly confronted the Sparta hooligans. For example, prior to an away match in Doetinchem, on 24 November 2001, members of the De Graafschap's Spin Side contacted SYC hooligans to arrange a confrontation near the Doetinchem railway station. Sparta hooligans accepted the invitation and travelled to

Doetinchem in two transit vans. They were caught by surprise on arrival, being attacked by a much larger group of local hooligans. The aggressors fled before police officers arrived at the scene (*De Gelderlander*, 26 November 2001). Sparta's relegation to the First Division in 2002 had a significant impact on the development of football hooliganism, intensifying the antagonism between Sparta hooligans and a number of lower-league hooligan formations. SYC members repeatedly attempted to intimidate and humiliate hooligans of local rival Excelsior. On 3 December 2002 a group of approximately 25 Sparta hooligans arrived at Woudestein, East Rotterdam, an hour before kick-off. Their early arrival by underground took the police by surprise, enabling SYC members to attack young Excelsior supporters drinking in a bar. A similar incident occurred in the following season, on 28 November 2003. SYC members damaged a pub where Excelsior supporters were drinking and provoked several minor fights. The riot police prevented escalation by keeping the two sets of fans at bay. The Sparta hooligans were escorted back to the underground station and five arrests were made.

During the club's period in the First Division, between 2002 and 2005, the SYC established a deep-seated rivalry with hooligan formations at Go Ahead Eagles and FC Dordrecht, among others. In November 2002 a group of young Go Ahead Eagles hooligans attacked SYC members at the Deventer railway station. Sparta hooligans were on their way back from their team's away match against Heracles Almelo. When the train pulled in at Deventer station their carriage was attacked by local hooligans, who had awaited their arrival. Punches were thrown and hooligans fought each other with leather belts. The local hooligans fled when police officers arrived at the scene in order to avoid arrest. Similar incidents occurred in March 2003, when on their way to Deventer nine SYC members clashed with De Graafschap hooligans. On arrival in Deventer, Sparta hooligans were once again confronted by their counterparts at Go Ahead Eagles.

SYC members regard football hooliganism as a key source of excitement and fun in their lives as opposed to their everyday routines at school and at work, which are perceived as boring and unchallenging:

> People say, like, you've got your studies and your job so why engage in fighting. But university is just so fucking boring, you know. Most students

are absolute wankers, you know, and the classes are boring. Being with my mates and planning a fight is sort of an outlet, to get away from it all. (Personal interview, September 2004)

SYC members are fascinated with fighting in the football context and with enhancing their group's status in the hierarchy of hooligan oppositions. Their key aim is to successfully challenge rival hooligan formations, preferably on the opponent's own territory. Getting run on home territory (i.e. in your own city or at your team's ground) is regarded a major humiliation. Such events are celebrated as glorious victories and reproduced in chants directed at the opponent, such as '*Rennen in je eigen stad!*' ('Running in your own city!') and 'Who the fucking hell are you?'. The *post facto* meaning of the fight is always negotiable, both within and between hooligan formations, as is illustrated by the comments of one SYC member: 'They said it was our fault because we failed to break through the police escort after the match. That is bullshit. We ran them in their own city. Now it is their turn to restore the balance, not ours' (personal interview, September 2004).

Although violence is one of the main focal concerns of SYC members, it is not the only source of group identity. The core of the group consists of close friends who socialize regularly outside the football context. Group membership provides the young hooligans with a sense of belonging, friendship and identity. As one hooligan commented: 'For many of us friendship, belonging and adventure are just as important as fighting, if not more important. I mean, if it was only about violence you could just beat up anybody in the streets. Hooliganism is much more than that.' Furthermore, although fighting is perceived as a major source of excitement, the vast majority of SYC members reject the use of violence outside the football context. They take pride in confronting rival hooligan formations, but demonstrating their hard masculinity in other contexts does not seem to generate the same excitement and prestige. As one hooligan commented: 'Beating up someone in a nightclub or a pub simply doesn't do it for me. There's no honour in that. But if you fight rival hooligan groups, that's pure excitement. You're in the newspapers and other clubs hear, like, Sparta hooligans have done such and such' (personal interview, July 2003). In recent years, however, SYC members have occasionally been involved in fights in pubs and nightclubs, usually resulting from conflicts with other customers.

Group members' aggressive response to minor conflicts with outsiders can be viewed in terms of their strong feelings of ingroup solidarity and their defence of collective honour and reputation: 'if one of us gets in trouble, the others will back him up' (personal interview, September 2004).

For several SYC members their hooligan identity is not confined to match days only. Although fighting is central to their activities, it constitutes a negligible length of time in their lives (cf. King, 2001: 570). Discussions of fights, on the other hand, are lengthy and ubiquitous. Sparta hooligans relive and evaluate past incidents and they fantasize about upcoming events. They also keep up to date with developments in the Dutch hooligan scene on a daily basis via Internet and contacts within hooligan circles. Their collective memory and informal codes of legitimate action are shaped by intersubjective agreement, within the group as well as in interaction with opposing hooligan formations. Leading SYC members maintain temporary contacts with rival hooligans to arrange or evaluate confrontations or to discuss ongoing police investigations. These contacts are in part based on rival hooligans' mutual interest in experiencing the 'rush' of football violence, allowing rival formations to synchronize their activities in order to escape police observation. One SYC member explained this 'rush' in the following terms:

> The rush is enormous, especially when you fight a group that is larger than yours. In Dordrecht we had 30 people but many of us ran away. They always talk about how crazy they are, but in the heat of the moment they ran. Especially those who are only occasionally present, friends of friends. So we were standing there with three people facing a much larger group. That's the buzz, you know, but also the fear. And when it's all over you're still standing strong. Amazing! It's an incredible adrenalin rush. It's shit, though, that all our mates ran away. (Personal interview, July 2003)

In addition to impermanent contacts with members of several Dutch hooligan formations, SYC members have a more permanent relationship with FC Haarlem hooligans. The friendship between the two groups in part derives from the hooligans' similar social backgrounds (i.e. relatively highly educated and predominantly middle-class; cf. Korthals, 2005) and their clubs' comparable popular

240

images. Group members regularly attend each other's matches and they also meet outside the football context. At times the two groups have jointly confronted mutual opponents. On 4 November 2001, 58 supporters were arrested before a match between local rivals Telstar and Haarlem, amongst whom a number of SYC members. They were eventually cleared by the court due to lack of incriminating evidence. During a match between Telstar and Sparta, on 18 November 2002, an alliance of 50 SYC members and 30 Haarlem hooligans damaged a fence in an attempt to confront home supporters. Post-match confrontation was prevented by the police. SYC members have also been joined on occasion by (individual) hooligans of other clubs.

The hooligans' relationship with the media is complex and ambiguous. On the one hand, media coverage of Sparta fan culture tends to reproduce the club's popular image of a 'friendly' club, thwarting the SYC's attempts to secure their status as a 'respectable firm' within the hooligan subculture. At the same time, SYC members are aware of the harmful effects media reporting may have on their activities. As one hooligan argued:

> It's nice to be in the newspapers, but the reporting has to be proportional. The problem is that these stories may distort the reality of football hooliganism at Sparta. I mean, if people think we have a group of 150 lads they will show up with similar numbers or they will not show up at all if their numbers are inferior. So they will either overestimate us or there will be no one to fight at all. (Personal interview, July 2003)

This comment reveals the hooligans' self-image of a relatively small-size, close-knit group, as opposed to some of the quantitatively larger hooligan formations in Dutch football, for example the hooligan group at Feyenoord. According to one hooligan: 'The Feyenoord lads have asked us a couples of times if we want to fight them, but it's like David versus Goliath, or a war between Luxemburg and the United States. There is no point really.' Another major effect of media attention is that it may generate additional controls and impositions or create unrest within the fan community. The latter effect could be observed in the aftermath of an incident on 21 November 2003. Before a match between Sparta and Heracles Almelo, 75 away supporters were arrested for fighting, missile throwing and aggressive behaviour towards the police at the railway station Rotterdam-Alexander. Later that night the 75 Heracles fans were released, but on their way home by train they were pelted with stones and bottles. A 30-year-old Heracles supporter was seriously injured after being hit on the head by a brick. Initial media reports claimed that the incident was the result of a fight between Heracles and Sparta supporters (*NOS Journaal*, 21 November 2003). Sparta fans immediately condemned the incident, but doubted if SYC members were really the aggressors. If so, many fans argued, it would seriously damage the club's 'friendly' reputation and place Sparta 'on one level with Feyenoord'. SYC members publicly denied their involvement, accusing instead a group of FC Dordrecht hooligans. Heracles supporters endorsed these accusations. Subsequent media reports omitted any reference to Sparta supporters. An official inquiry into the incident also made no reference to the SYC, but neither to the alleged involvement of FC Dordrecht hooligans (Auditteam Voetbalvandalisme, 2004: 5-7).

The incident also highlights the sensitivity of Sparta supporters about the issue of hooliganism. Football hooliganism is generally attributed to the violent other and regarded as 'not for the likes of us'. SYC members' identification with hooliganism can therefore be viewed as contestation of the dominant fan identity at Sparta. Through their regular involvement in football hooliganism, SYC members contest the 'friendly' fan identity celebrated by Sparta supporters. At the same time, their activities contain elements of compliance with Sparta fan culture. Several hooligans are active members of the local fan community. They maintain close contacts with certain club officials, contribute to fan club magazines and independent fanzines or are involved in the 'TIFO team' (named after the *tifos* characteristic of Italian ultras) established to create a more colourful and vocal atmosphere inside the stadium. Furthermore, the hooligans construct their collective identity in terms of the perceived differences between themselves and certain larger, more notorious hooligan formations. As we have seen, SYC members define themselves as a sophisticated, fashionable 'fighting crew', as opposed to the 'less educated', 'hard-core criminals' at clubs such as Feyenoord and ADO Den Haag.

Crucially, the emergence of the SYC has not resulted in a general redefinition or rejection of the 'friendly' fan identity since the hooligan group is comparatively small and principally operates away from football grounds, escaping self-monitoring within the fan community and regularly circumventing formal social controls. Most non-hooligan supporters are simply unaware of the occurrence of hooligan confrontations and hooliganism is therefore not (yet) viewed as an immediate threat to the collective identity of Sparta fans. Club officials have also deliberately downplayed recent hooligan incidents in order to secure the club's 'friendly' reputation, seeking to avoid extensive media coverage of the subject. The 'friendly' image, it is argued, is one of Sparta's main assets and should be cherished: 'If we want to be a kind of cult club, which we could be considering our history and culture, I think it is crucial to eradicate hooliganism. At the same time, we try to keep information about incidents away from the press, because it might damage our reputation. I mean, media reports often exaggerate things' (personal interview, November 2004).

Hooligans and law enforcers: strategies and interactions

The activities and dispositions of the Sparta Youth Crew present a challenge for security policies. Whereas spectator violence at Sparta has historically been spontaneous and relatively uncommon, SYC members actively seek to confront rival hooligans and to escape police observation. Opportunities for collective violence are comparatively limited in and around football grounds due to pervasive controls and impositions. The Rotterdam-Rijnmond Police also anticipates potential trouble spots at home matches, notably the entrance to the away section of the ground. Further away from the ground, for example in the vicinity of Rotterdam's main railway station and in the city centre, controls and impositions are perceived by hooligans as being relatively weak. These locations are central to the activities of the SYC. Sparta hooligans also seek to escape police and steward observation by using regular train services or, less commonly, cars or transit vans on their journey to away matches, especially when trouble is anticipated or pre-arranged. Security and police officers regularly have difficulty gathering intelligence on the hooligans' activities and intentions since they have not established fruitful contacts with members of the group. Following a series of incidents in 2004 and 2005, the Rotterdam-Rijnmond Police started an investigation into the activities of the SYC. Although the inquiry

243

sent out a message to the hooligans that they were now monitored more closely, the investigation was closed after a few months due to lack of evidence. Security officers acknowledge that they have insufficient knowledge of the hooligan group to adequately assess the threat of football hooliganism. The club's deputy security officer argued:

> Usually we don't have any information on what their intentions are. That's a huge difference with the past, when we always found out one way or another what the expectations of supporters were. With the SYC it's far more difficult. They will never tell you what they are up to. I mean, many of them are nice guys who you can talk to and have a drink with, but they will never disclose information on their activities. So basically we don't know how and when they will travel, for example. Neither do we know their backgrounds or the offences they commit, not until they are arrested. (Personal interview, July 2004)

The vast majority of hooligan confrontations involving SYC members takes place away from football grounds, for example in city centres, at railway stations or at pubs. Police officers and club officials are unaware of some of these incidents and usually few arrests are made due to hooligans' 'hit-and-run' tactics (i.e. they tend to disperse before the police arrive at the scene). The police occasionally seems to underestimate the threat of hooliganism because of the lack of reliable pre-match intelligence. For example, Sparta's home match against FC Dordrecht on 16 May 2003 was categorized by the authorities as having a low potential for disorder (a so-called 'Category A' match). Within hooligan circles, however, rumour had it that the opposing hooligan groups would attempt to confront each other before the match. Outside the ground an alliance of Dordrecht and Feyenoord hooligans attacked a group of 30 SYC members. After prolonged and serious fighting police officers, many of whom had to be called in from adjacent police districts, dispersed the two sets of fans. One Feyenoord supporter was arrested for insulting a police officer.

Similarly, on 21 September 2004 the SYC fought Willem II hooligans before a cup match between Willem II and Sparta in Tilburg. The groups had pre-arranged a confrontation in the centre of Tilburg. A group of approximately 30 SYC members travelled to Tilburg by train, deliberately keeping a low profile in order to escape police observation. On arrival in Tilburg the hooligans realized that the police were unaware of their whereabouts or intentions. They walked to the city centre and started drinking in a pub. Having just received a phone call from one of the Willem II hooligans, a leading SYC member told the rest of the group that their opponents wished to withdraw from the confrontation since they were already on their way to the stadium. Within seconds a group of 15 Willem II hooligans gathered outside the pub intending to attack the Sparta supporters. SYC members responded through a rapid process of resource mobilization, collecting glasses, bottles, cans, umbrellas and leather belts as weapons. They ran onto the streets and attacked their opponents. After a brief fight the local hooligans retreated. A second attack was launched by the Sparta hooligans, chasing their rivals down the street. As the police arrived at the scene, three SYC members serving a ban started to make their way home in order to avoid arrest. Police officers escorted the other SYC members to the ground, but no one was arrested for their involvement in the fight. Attempts by local hooligans to confront the SYC after the match were frustrated by the police, who decided to escort the visiting supporters back to the railway station. Sparta hooligans realized that the fighting could well have ended in arrest if only the police had made more effort to investigate the matter. 'Everything was caught on camera, but you forget that in the heat of the moment. We are lucky that the police haven't used the footage to find out who were involved' (personal interview, September 2004).

Conclusion

In this chapter I have argued that the collective identity of Sparta supporters is constructed in relation to the 'rough' and 'uncivilized' other. This creation of collective others, through stereotyping and identity contrast, can be dated back to the club's early beginnings. Elite club Sparta regarded the emergence of working-class clubs such as Feyenoord with disdain because of their perceived lack of discipline. The construction of self and the other in Sparta fan culture historically contained a strong element of class consciousness. Sparta and Feyenoord represented the distinctive social realities North and South of the river Meuse and the social distance between the upper and lower classes in Rotterdam. These contrapuntal identities persist today even though the rivalry between the two clubs has somewhat declined and the areas they represent have changed dramatically over the last four decades.

The habitus of Sparta fans tends to exclude all the behaviours that would be negatively sanctioned (Bourdieu, 1990: 55-56). Violent behaviour is commonly regarded as unacceptable because it is attributed to the 'rednecks' of Feyenoord (and other notorious fan groups in Dutch football), generating a high degree of informal social control among fans. Sparta's image of a 'gentleman's' club is commonly reproduced in media reports and by club officials stressing the 'friendly' behaviour of Sparta fans, as opposed to the perceived hooligan problems at certain Dutch clubs. Occasional incidents of spectator violence are presented by fans, media and authorities as isolated incidents or are consciously ignored (Giulianotti, 1995: 214). The popular image of Sparta supporters also produces a relatively sanguine and non-aggressive approach on the part of opposing fans (Williams et al., 1988: 41). Because of the negative sanctioning of hooligan behaviour at Sparta and the relatively non-aggressive approach on the part of opposing fans, young supporters interested in becoming involved in football hooliganism are likely to either follow one of the more notorious football clubs (i.e. Feyenoord) or eschew their hooligan dispositions.

The 'friendly' identity of Sparta supporters has been challenged in recent years by a small group of young fans regularly participating in football hooliganism. The emergence of football hooliganism at Sparta in the late 1990s raises three theoretical issues. First, the creation of the hooligan formation contained a strong element of mimicry. The young fans copied the style and practices of domestic and foreign hooligan formations, which were perceived as more prestigious than their own practices. They increasingly sought to enhance their group's status in the hierarchy of hooligan oppositions by confronting rival hooligan formations. Football hooliganism at Sparta did not stem from, as Ian Taylor (1971; 1971a) has suggested, a break in the traditional relationship between the club and its fans. Rather, hooligans regard their involvement in hooligan violence as generating excitement and risk in their otherwise 'unexciting' lives. Second, Sparta hooligans are characterized by their relatively middle-class backgrounds and high levels of formal education, contradicting the emphasis in several theories on the lower-class backgrounds of football hooligans. Football hooliganism at Sparta cannot be explained in terms of hooligans' 'societal vulnerability' (Van Limbergen and Walgrave, 1988), but rather by the excitement and fun associated with the hooligan lifestyle.

Third, the emergence of football hooliganism at Sparta highlights to some degree the changeability of the fan habitus. Hooligans contest the 'friendly' identity of Sparta supporters and distinguish themselves from the perceivedly 'boring' and 'non-masculine' forms of fandom at the club. At the same time, however, their hooligan identity also contains elements of compliance with Sparta fan culture. Several hooligans are also active members of the fan community and they define themselves in opposition to the 'hard-core criminals' at certain other clubs (i.e. Feyenoord). In other words, Sparta hooligans construct a complex and subtle identity that simultaneously resists the club's non-hooligan image and complies with Sparta supporters' self-image as being 'civilized' and 'well-spoken'. Crucially, football hooliganism is not (yet) viewed as an immediate threat to the collective identity of Sparta supporters due to the group's relatively small size and the fact that they principally operate away from football grounds, escaping self-monitoring within the fan community and regularly circumventing formal social controls. Most non-hooligan supporters are simply unaware of the occurrence of hooligan confrontations and club officials have deliberately downplayed hooligan incidents in order to secure the club's 'friendly' reputation. At the same time, both club officials and supporters stress that, for the club's image of 'decency and tradition' to remain intact, football hooliganism has to be dealt with effectively.

8

Orgulloso de ser perico: Politics, Violence and the Ultras of RCD Espanyol

Introduction

The ultras of Reial Club Deportiu Espanyol are commonly perceived as one of the most violent and racist fan groups in Spanish football.[1] This persistent stigma is closely related to wider representations of the club in Catalonia. Espanyol has long been regarded by FC Barcelona supporters and Catalan nationalists as 'the enemy within', as the embodiment of the centralist state within Catalonia. Despite their geographical proximity, Espanyol and FC Barcelona have come to symbolize two diametrically opposed social, cultural and political conceptions. These contrasting conceptions are reflected in the contrapuntal identities of the clubs' supporters and, in a heightened or distorted form, in the competitive violence between the two clubs' militant fan groups. The case of Espanyol highlights the intertwinement of politics and football and the ways in which different types of supporters deal with stigmas in different ways, co-shaping the development of and responses to football hooliganism. It also shows the subtle yet vital interactions and negotiations between hooligans, non-hooligan supporters, club officials and police officers and their effects on football hooliganism.

The emergence and development of football hooliganism at Espanyol should be understood within the context of the politics of Catalan football and, more specifically, the deep-seated local rivalry between Espanyol and FC Barcelona. I therefore begin this chapter with an analysis of the image and fan culture of Espanyol and the historical antagonism between the two local rivals. Second, I examine the rise of the ultras and their involvement in football hooliganism. The final part of the chapter discusses the escalation of inter-group rivalries, the effects of official and grassroots responses and recent transformations in the ultra subculture. I seek to show that football hooliganism at Espanyol has changed considerably in recent years due to profound transformations in the local ultra subculture and increased controls and impositions.

Fan culture and the politics of Catalan football

Throughout most of the club's history Espanyol has been viewed with considerable disdain within Catalonia. Central to the club's negative image is the deep-seated local rivalry with FC Barcelona, which plays a key role in the construction of the collective identity of Espanyol supporters. Espanyol was founded in 1900 as the Sociedad Española de Foot-ball by a group of local university students led by Angel Rodriguez Ruiz, the son of the dean of the University of Barcelona. In 1903 the club changed its name to Club Español de Fútbol and in 1912 King Alfonso XIII added the title Real (Royal). The club was founded in part in reaction to FC Barcelona, which was created a year earlier and consisted principally of foreign players (see Chapter Nine). Whereas FC Barcelona provided football facilities mainly to foreigners, Espanyol aimed to make similar services available to the local people (i.e. Catalans and Spanish). A few years after its foundation Espanyol merged with FC Català, which was renowned for its locals-only policy (although the club also fielded Scotsmen) (García Castell, 1968: 23).

Despite Espanyol's historical ties with the local university and its explicit aim to provide the local population with football facilities, the club gradually obtained the image of a 'fascist' club due in part to wider socio-political developments in Catalonia. With the rise of Catalan nationalism Espanyol increasingly came to be viewed as 'the enemy within', as a representative of the centralist Spanish government within Catalonia (Duke and Crolley, 1996a: 28). The club's name – Español, written in Castilian (see note number one) – was considered as being hugely provocative (Ball, 2001: 99). Espanyol's 'very existence came increasingly to be seen as a crude insult by Catalan nationalists who supported Barcelona, making encounters between the two teams a recipe for division and violence' (Burns, 2000: 85). Catalan nationalists accused the club of receiving substantial support from the state authorities, notably during the military dictatorships of Miguel Primo de Rivera (1923-1929) and Francisco Franco (1939-1975). Franco is believed to have helped Espanyol on various occasions, for example in the club's cup victory in 1940 (e.g. Sobrequés Callicó, 1998: 272). Critics of Espanyol perceive the activities of a small group of Espanyol fans in the 1920s as symbolizing the club's 'fascist', 'anti-Catalan' nature. This fan group, the Peña Deportiva Ibérica, was founded in 1923 within Barcelona's fascist circles to promote the principles of national unity and 'Spanishness' in football and other spheres of Catalan society (Artells, 1972: 190; see Chapter One). The group consisted of a few hundred affiliates, among whom civil servants, students and army officials, who opposed the 'anti-Spanish' and 'separatist' politics of FC Barcelona. The group regularly assaulted FC Barcelona supporters during local derbies and caused serious injuries to spectators (Culla Clarà, 1977: 50).

Espanyol's 'fascist' image needs to be understood within the context of the historical rivalry with FC Barcelona. Local derbies between Espanyol and FC Barcelona have always evoked deep-seated collective emotions and the first signs of rivalry can be dated back to the early beginnings of both clubs. Early matches between the two clubs were fuelled with hostility on the part of both players and fans and regularly spilled over into violence (Sobrequés Callicó, 1998: 269-273). For example, during a cup match at Espanyol on 20 June 1909 hundreds of home fans invaded the pitch and threatened the referee with a lynching if he allowed an FC Barcelona goal to stand (Burns, 2000: 85). Three years later, on 24 and 25 March 1912, a double cup match between the two teams required police intervention after violence erupted between rival players and fans. In the 1920s the rivalry between Espanyol and FC Barcelona began to take on a more hostile dimension due to political tensions and manifest conflict between directors, players and fans of the two clubs (Sobrequés Callicó, 1998: 271). On 23 November 1924, the sending-off of FC Barcelona's star player Josep Samitier triggered a shower of coins raining down from the terraces. The game was cancelled and provoked a hostile debate between the two clubs as to who was to blame. The military authorities decided that the match should be replayed behind closed doors, a decision that infuriated the supporters. While the match was played behind closed doors, the fans massed outside the stadium and engaged in prolonged fighting (Burns, 2000: 85-86).

The rivalry between FC Barcelona and Espanyol deepened during the first decades after the Spanish Civil War (1936-1939). During this period the two clubs came to symbolize two diametrically opposed social, cultural and political

250

conceptions: Catalanism versus anti-Catalanism, anti-Spanishness versus Spanishness and integration versus non-integration (Colomé, 1999: 90). FC Barcelona became the symbol of an oppressed nation, whereas Espanyol was perceived to represent the centralist Spanish government and the right-wing military of Franco's Spain (Duke and Crolley, 1996a: 28; Kuper, 1994: 88). The late Manuel Vázquez Montalbán, a celebrated writer and staunch FC Barcelona fan, wrote:

> Barça was the symbol of the political position of the national bourgeoisie and of the small Catalan bourgeoisie until the Civil War; after, it was the only form of expression of a set of sentiments. The main evidence of this affirmation lies in the fact that the integrated immigrants are supporters of Barça, the non-integrated, of Español (1972: 7-8).

As we will see, this image of Espanyol as 'non-integrated' and overtly 'fascist' is nowadays heavily contested by Espanyol supporters.

Spain underwent a process of rapid economic modernization in the late 1950s and early 1960s. Catalonia, as the most economically advanced region, along with the Basque Country, was in the vanguard of this modernization and experienced a large influx of newcomers from other parts of Spain (Hargreaves, 2000: 29; Figueres, 2003; Molinero and Ysàs, 1999). Those arriving in Catalonia perceived FC Barcelona as an effective method for integration into Catalan society. This development contributed to a historical break in the evolution of both clubs, which saw FC Barcelona transforming into a flourishing club with over 100,000 members and with one of the world's most impressive football stadia, and Espanyol in a modest club with 20,000 members (Colomé, 1999: 90). As a result of this development the local rivalry has gradually transformed from a two-way rivalry into an unrequited rivalry. FC Barcelona supporters currently view Real Madrid as their main opponent, whereas the hatred of Espanyol towards their local rivals remains strong.

According to Espanyol fans, the discontinuity in the historical development of the two clubs was in part caused by the systematic amplification of the club's fascist image by Catalan nationalists and institutions. While not denying the historical connections between some club officials and fans and the centralist government (e.g. the Franco regime), many supporters argue that the club was founded exclusively as a sports entity and has remained so ever since. To explicitly subscribe to one specific political view would be to break with the club's original spirit, a spirit that has enabled Espanyol to maintain its position as one of Catalonia's largest football clubs for over a century (Segura Palomares, 2001: 71). The view that football and politics are two separate things that should be kept apart is reflected in the official club anthem: *El deporte es tu único objetivo* ('Sport is your only objective'). It seems that during the period of intense politicization Espanyol's ambiguous and undefined nature – in the sense that the club was administered and supported by people from a variety of social backgrounds and with a range of political beliefs – facilitated the creation of the club's negative image. Espanyol was, in the words of former manager Javier Clemente, 'neither in power nor in opposition.' As the director of a fan organization commented:

> The fact that Espanyol never explicitly backed a certain political position has been exploited by Barcelona. An image has been created of Espanyol as a pro-Franco movement. That is how it works. If one keeps repeating that the club is fascist, politically incorrect, then for many people who love football but do not support Barça following Espanyol is an unattractive alternative. Because it is an ugly, right-wing club. Based on a half truth the stereotype was created, with major future implications. (Personal interview, March 2004)

Local rivalry and the making of Espanyol fan culture

In reaction to the club's unfavourable situation Espanyol supporters have created a particular understanding of what it means to be *orgulloso de ser perico* ('proud to be an Espanyol fan').[2] This collective identity is constructed in relation to local rival FC Barcelona, which is portrayed as an 'arrogant' club that promotes a biased version of Catalan history. Espanyol fans emphasize that while their club is truly local in its origins (i.e. through its historical ties with the University of Barcelona); FC Barcelona is essentially a 'foreign' club. These foreign roots are mocked in songs such as: 'They think they are very Catalan, but were founded by a Swiss.'

Supporters contend that accusations of fascism similarly apply to FC Barcelona, evidence of which are the right-wing sympathies of former club chairmen Josep Lluís Núñez and Joan Gaspart (e.g. *El Triangle*, 21 June 2000). Espanyol fans also accuse their opponents of exploiting their favourable social, economic and political position at the expense of other Catalan football clubs. They argue that, driven by the ambition to overpower all others, FC Barcelona deliberately frustrates the progression of smaller clubs (e.g. *El Periódico*, 27 September 2003). For example, shortly after Espanyol finished second in the 1988 UEFA Cup FC Barcelona signed on two of the team's key players. Arguably, FC Barcelona's recruitment policies have not merely disadvantaged Espanyol, but also smaller clubs such as Gimnàstic Tarragona and UE Lleida and the indoor hockey team of Igualada. Several smaller Catalan football clubs have also served as meeting places for the expression of nationalist sentiments, but they have never been able to match FC Barcelona in constructing a powerful political and cultural identity (García Candau, 1996: 241-242). This power inequality is explained by one supporter as follows:

> All those things that have damaged us, that is the hatred that has grown. David versus Goliath, but with unequal means. It is more a matter of principle than a sports or political thing. Because I am Catalan too, but in a different way. I despise their arrogance and the way in which they sell their image. (Personal interview with the chairman of an Espanyol fan club, May 2004)

Fans' resentment is also directed against the institutions that are believed to promote FC Barcelona as a major symbol of Catalan identity. The daily sports papers *El Mundo Deportivo* and *Sport* devote around twenty-five pages each to FC Barcelona and only two pages to Espanyol. Other Catalan newspapers, such as *El Periódico*, come close to ignoring the club: 'no one really wants to write about Espanyol, only journalists who happen to be staunch supporters. FC Barcelona is far more exciting and challenging' (interview with a journalist of *El Periódico*, March 2004). The Catalan television channel TV3, funded by public taxes, devotes approximately twelve times more time to FC Barcelona than to Espanyol (calculations by the author, March to May 2004). According to Espanyol supporters, the overpowering

253

media attention for FC Barcelona is not merely a logical consequence of the latter's success and popularity, but it also underlines the persistence of the stereotypes surrounding Espanyol. From this viewpoint, the Catalan media deliberately stigmatize Espanyol in order to promote FC Barcelona as the club people should be supporting. As an Espanyol fan argued:

> Barça's dictatorship just doesn't end. This weekend nearly every news medium published three negative items on our club. To publish these few hours before Barcelona – Espanyol is not a way of destabilization? No, then what is it? Thank you for this majestic lesson in pseudo-journalism (*Blanc i Blau*, vol. 10, no. 697, 3 May 2004: 22).

The perceived unfair treatment of their club occasionally leads the ultras to insult local media (e.g. '*Puta TV3*') or to physically attack journalists or their equipment.

Over the last decade Espanyol has actively sought to improve its image and to strengthen its ties with the local community. An important step taken by the club was to change its name from Castilian 'Real Club Deportivo Español' to Catalan 'Reial Club Deportiu Espanyol de Barcelona'. Club officials argue that government and media representatives have begun to realize that Espanyol 'is not a refuge for the centralist military and non-integrated immigrants' (personal interview with a board member, May 2004). Despite these changes, the club's stigma still persists today. Staunch FC Barcelona fans continue to portray the club as being fascist and anti-Catalan:

> Espanyol are the traitors of Catalonia within Catalonia. They are not Catalans but Spaniards. They are proud of representing Spain. They see us as a team full of foreigners while they are supposedly an authentic Spanish club. But that's just one way of looking at things. I am proud of the fact that Catalonia is such an open society and that a Swiss founded Barça. But they are exactly the opposite: very closed and exclusively for Spaniards. They don't belong here really, do they? They shouldn't be here at all. (Personal interview with FC Barcelona supporter, April 2004)

For example, the Espanyol fan group Sarrià Nord, which explicitly identifies with Catalan separatism, is still systematically excluded by FC Barcelona fans from participating in the organized support of the Catalan 'national' team because, according to the latter, 'there is no way Espanyol fans can be genuine Catalans' (personal interviews with members of Sarrià Nord and Escamots Catalans, May and June 2004).

Espanyol fan culture revolves around the contrapuntal identities of the two largest football clubs in Catalonia. The collective identity of Espanyol supporters is constructed in opposition to FC Barcelona, which is portrayed as 'arrogant' and 'factitious'. Fan identity is based on supporters' unconditional loyalty to the club in the face of its permanent stigmatization by outsiders. This process of distinction also features centrally in the collective identity of the ultras, although, as I will show in the following section, in a heightened or distorted form. The ultras have transformed the club's 'fascist' image into a key symbol of group identity, distinguishing them from their rivals at FC Barcelona and generating recurrent inter-group violence.

Siempre contra la peste culé: the rise of the ultras

The image of Espanyol as a fascist, anti-Catalan club is reproduced not only by significant others, but also by a section of the fan community. Just as the Peña Deportiva Ibérica was historically perceived by outsiders as the maximum exponent of Espanyol's political tendencies, the ultra group Brigadas Blanquiazules (Blue and White Brigades) is nowadays viewed as a similar symbol of the club's fascist nature. The origins of the ultra group lie in the segregation of the crowd by age from the mid-1970s onwards. In the second half of the 1970s the fan club Gran Penya Espanyolista Manigua attempted to create a more vocal and colourful atmosphere inside Espanyol's Sarrià stadium through the display of flags, drums and chants.[3] The South Stand (*Gol Sur*), which was inhabited by members of Manigua and the *peña* (official fan club) Els Incansables, became the main point of reference for young supporters. The segregation of the crowd by age really began to take off in 1981 with the creation of the youth group Penya Juvenil, many of whose founding members were previously involved in Manigua. In contrast to the more traditional *peñas*, Penya Juvenil explicitly sought to unite the club's youth support by

255

reproducing the passionate atmosphere characteristic of the Italian ultra subculture. The youth group gradually came to replace Manigua's function in the stadium.

Young Espanyol fans were particularly inspired by the 1982 World Cup hosted by Spain. For many Espanyol fans this event facilitated their first direct contact with fan groups from countries such as Italy, England, Argentina and Brazil. Young supporters had the opportunity to personally observe the practices of foreign fan groups, which were commonly perceived as more prestigious than indigenous forms of football fandom. As a club historian remembered:

> Thousands of Italians, with their shouting and their flags [...] responded to the thousands of Brazilians who [...] were dancing the samba, enervating, sensual and continuous. It was a hallucinating experience. Many Espanyol members who were present cried of emotion observing their beloved Sarrià being transformed into the centre of a global fiesta broadcasted by televisions all over the world (Segura Palomares, 2000: 351).

The World Cup experience brought about an increase in the activities of young Espanyol fans, who increasingly began to use more complex choreographed displays and pyrotechnical elements, such as flares and smoke pots. Penya Juvenil received various types of support from the club, including premises for storage within the stadium, material, travel arrangements for away matches, and financial support. In order to stimulate the group's recruitment activities, the club also rewarded Penya Juvenil 500 *pesetas* (3 euros) for every new member. The non-violent character of Penya Juvenil contrasted with the emerging aggressive masculinity among members of FC Barcelona's youth group Boixos Nois (see Chapter Nine). During local derbies at Sarrià in the early 1980s members of Boixos Nois repeatedly intimidated and assaulted young Espanyol supporters. The fact that away fans were located right next to Penya Juvenil in the South Stand, without any form of segregation, made the Espanyol fans an easy target.

In the 1984/85 season a small group of affiliates of Penya Juvenil decided to stand up to the provocations and attacks by FC Barcelona fans. They criticized Penya Juvenil for being too 'soft' and lenient, arguing that the group's honour had to be defended. Their ambition to create a more aggressive alternative was in part enhanced by their interactions with Italian ultras. During their visit to a match between AC Milan and Internazionale a small group of Espanyol fans experienced the intimidating atmosphere created by AC Milan's ultra group Brigate Rossonere, which they sought to reproduce at Espanyol (*Revista Hinchas*, 2, March 1990). In the build-up to a local derby at Sarrià in 1985, rumour had it that Espanyol fans had created a hooligan group named Eagles Korps with the explicit aim of confronting their local rivals. Later that year the ultra group Brigadas Blanquiazules was founded (the group's name is a combination of the colours of the team, blue and white, and term 'brigades' copied from Italian ultra groups named *brigate*).

The emergence of Brigadas Blanquiazules indicated an important development in Spain's and in Barcelona's political far right: the eruption within right-wing circles of youth groups originating from football grounds and peripheral districts. Rather than being influenced or led by official right-wing formations, the ultra group emerged in the absence of a formally organized far right, which was fragmented and incapable of confronting the more dynamic and successful independence movement in Catalonia. The autonomous character of Brigadas was also determined by the fact that, in the 1980s and early 1990s, right-wing formations such as Juntas Españolas, Frente Nacional and the Círculo Español De Amigos De Europa (CEDADE) refused to integrate skinheads and football ultras within their ranks. The ultras were perceived to generate unrest and lack party discipline, thereby damaging the public image of the political groups (Casals, 1998: 71-72). From its early beginnings, however, informal leaders of the ultra group maintained loose relationships with traditional right-wing organizations, for instance with Juntas Españolas and its juvenile branch Juntas Jóvenes, within which they acted as an unofficial order and participated in meetings (Viñas, 2004: 161). Media reports have repeatedly stressed the connections between Brigadas Blanquiazules and the far right, at first with Juntas Españolas and later as a militant section of CEDADE, the neo-Nazi party with the largest following in Spain until its official dissolution in 1993 (e.g. *Avui*, 15 March 1987; *El Observador*, 21 February 1991; *El Periódico*, 24 February 1991; *El Periódico*, 10 January 1993; *El Triangle*, 8 December 2000).

The politicization of members and affiliates of Brigadas Blanquiazules tends to take place by osmosis and through contacts with specific environments – football matches or (skinhead) music concerts – rather than as a result of ideological training or fixed and consistent political ideologies (Adán Revilla, 1998: 123; Casals, 1998: 72; Spaaij and Viñas, 2005a: 145). Many group members do not express a profound knowledge of National Socialism or (neo-)fascism, but they nevertheless identify with the values or actions closest to it. The ultras' political militancy and aesthetics illustrate their search for social visibility and provocation and their (symbolic) resistance to the 'system'. Only a minority of group members, especially older ones, have a more profound knowledge of political theory. According to them, a distinction can be made between youths who attend football matches to express their political views (i.e. *fútbol por la política*) and those who adopt certain political beliefs to conform to group identity (i.e. *política por el fútbol*). Especially from the late 1980s onwards Brigadas Blanquiazules has come to attract growing numbers of young skinheads who principally identify with the ultra scene and attendant political symbology. Club officials subscribe to the idea that there are varying degrees of involvement in politics among the ultras:

> I don't care if they sing fascist songs outside football, but inside the stadium you can't do it for the sake of the club. More and more ultras seem to understand that, but the core doesn't. They want to express to their political views no matter what. The ideology of these people is actually quite diverse. Many ultras don't have a clue, whereas some are very educated and they know exactly what they do and why they do it. You can discuss their issues in a serious and constructive way, despite the fact that I have very different beliefs. The group leaders know very well what they say and think. But the younger skinheads often don't know at all what it's about. (Personal interview, May 2004)

Despite the fact that many group members do not have a profound knowledge of right-wing ideologies, these ideologies are central to the construction of group identity. The collective identity of members of Brigadas Blanquiazules, based on a mixture of club loyalty, neo-fascism, Spanish nationalism and hard masculinity, is diametrically opposed to Boixos Nois' identification with Catalan nationalism. These opposing group identities reflect, in a heightened and distorted form, the contrasting popular images of the two clubs they represent. The ultras' adherence to

Spanish nationalism can in some cases be explained by their family backgrounds. Some group members come from politically active, reactionary families (Viñas, 2004; Salas, 2003; *El Triangle*, 3 September 1990; *Avui*, 4 March 2001; *El Triangle*, 14 March 2001). Moreover, relatively few of the (older) ultras' parents were born and raised in Catalonia or speak Catalan at home. Many group members therefore regard Spain rather than Catalonia as their *patria*. Most ultras are not, as is often suggested, anti-Catalan but rather anti-separatist. They strongly oppose Catalan political nationalism and independence, but at the same time they appreciate Catalonia as one of the country's most prosperous and advanced regions. As one ultra argued: 'nearly all of us are Catalans and we are proud of being so, as well as Spanish [...] The only people we hate very deeply are separatists and all those who follow Pujol [former president of Catalonia]' (*Ultras Pericos*, no. 0, 1994: 1). Another ultra summarized the political beliefs of members of Brigadas Blanquiazules as follows: 'None of us are anti-Catalan. We see Catalonia as a part of Spain. We seek to defend Spain as a whole against the invasion of foreigners. From the start the group has been right-wing and nationalistic, but always in a varied way with different specific ideologies' (personal interview, May 2004).

The social composition of Brigadas Blanquiazules has changed substantially over time. All group members are white both historically and at present, reflecting the general lack of black and minority ethnic fans at the club. In the late 1980s and early 1990s the group consisted predominantly of young males in their teens and early twenties. At present, however, the group also includes a significant number of men in their thirties, most of who have been involved in the group since their late teens or early twenties. Temporal variations can also be observed in the class composition of the group. Although the class backgrounds of the ultras have always been diverse, initially the group primarily consisted of young men from (upper) middle-class backgrounds. The ultras' socio-political identity appealed to many young fans from higher up the social scale, and the club's location in the upmarket Sarrià district meant that the group drew a large part of its support from this area. Several of these 'well-off' ultras, so-called *niños pijos* ('posh kids'), held a widespread reputation for their violent and racist proclivities. Journalistic and police descriptions of football hooliganism at Espanyol have repeatedly emphasized the central involvement of *pijos* in Brigadas Blanquiazules (*El País*, 9 December

1986; *El Periódico*, 24 February 1991; *El Periódico*, 3 November 1991; Salas, 2003; De Antón and Pascual de Riquelme, 1990: 109).

Although several group members can still be categorized as 'middle class', the class composition of Brigadas Blanquiazules has become more heterogeneous over time as a result of the group's explosive growth in the second half of the 1980s. The number of group members increased rapidly during this period, from 80 in 1985 to approximately 300 two years later, and the group came to attract growing numbers of working-class youths. The group's rapid expansion resulted from a combination of five factors: the increasing popularity of the ultra and skinhead subculture among young males throughout the country; the group's growing reputation within Catalonia; the unprecedented media attention for the ultra and hooligan subculture; Espanyol's League success in the 1986/87 season (finishing third in the Premier League) and the club's successful UEFA Cup run in the 1987/88 season; and the decline, and the dissolution in 1988, of Penya Juvenil after the death of its chairman. During this period Brigadas Blanquiazules also increased its organization by introducing official group membership, ticket and travel arrangements and merchandising. One ultra described this process of growth as follows: 'In the early years our group grew rapidly. Many local boys who never went to football started to attend matches because of our reputation. They wanted to be part of the action. That was the pulling power of the ultra scene in those years' (personal interview, May 2004).

The escalation of football hooliganism

Members of Brigadas Blanquiazules have identified with the use of violence from the group's early beginnings. They tend to resolve inter-group conflict or a single provocation through the use of violence. Group members are notorious for their involvement in various types of violence within and outside the football context, including violent robberies.[4] Furthermore, the ultras hold a reputation for intimidating and assaulting ethnic minorities, homosexuals, transvestites or individuals related to opposing youth subcultures (i.e. left-wing skinheads or punks). In a 1993 television documentary on the skinhead subculture, a leading member of Brigadas Blanquiazules justified such attacks in the following way:

I am fascist and a skinhead is just that [...] because he wants to throw all the foreign rubbish out of Spain, niggers, Jews and the whole bunch. Senseless violence is not all the skinheads do. They defend what is theirs and this means to fight the reds [communists], separatists, Jews, punks and other scum of society (TVE, *Informe Semanal*, 26 October 1991).

Racial and xenophobic expressions can also be found in the group's fanzines and on its website: 'Brigadas Sieg Heil [...] I believe that such a son of a bitch [referring to Desmond Tutu] deserves to have his balls cut off by his nigger brothers and his cousins the monkeys' (*Gol Sur Ultrazine*, 19 April 1988).

In the football context, Brigadas Blanquiazules has established violent rivalries with a number of fan groups. From the start, the group's main rival has been Boixos Nois, as expressed in the battle-cry *siempre contra la peste culé* ('always opposed to the Barça plague'). The rivalry between the two groups reflects, as we have seen, the historical antagonism between Espanyol and FC Barcelona and is based in part on political opposition. Members of Brigadas Blanquiazules also consider as enemies fan groups adhering to left-wing, separatist or anti-fascist beliefs, for instance Herri Norte Taldea (Athletic Bilbao), Brigadas Amarillas (Cádiz CF), Peña Mujika (Real Sociedad) and Indar Gorri (Osasuna). At the same time, Brigadas Blanquiazules maintains a long-standing friendship with members of Ultras Sur (Real Madrid) due to their shared right-wing beliefs and hatred towards Boixos Nois. Members of the two groups regularly attend each other's matches and, at times, they have jointly confronted opposing formations. Espanyol ultras are also in contact with certain foreign (right-wing) fan groups, notably Brigate Gialloblù at Hellas Verona.

Central to the development of football hooliganism at Espanyol in the second half of the 1980s and the early 1990s was the escalation of the competitive violence between Brigadas Blanquiazules and Boixos Nois. Inclined to defend and enhance their group's status in the hierarchy of hooligan oppositions, the two groups became entangled in a spiral of escalating violence in which each incident increased the probability of future, more serious incidents. To retain or re-establish one's honour and reputation, the opposing hooligan formation has to respond effectively to

261

defeat since 'a failure to respond threatens to make retrospectively ridiculous the pretensions of all in the attacked group' (Katz, 1988: 141). The first large-scale confrontation between the two fan groups took place during and after a local derby at the Camp Nou stadium, on 12 October 1986. Espanyol ultras viewed this event as an opportunity for avenging previous attacks and intimidation by FC Barcelona hooligans and for enhancing their group's reputation for toughness. After the match a group of one hundred young Espanyol fans attacked rival supporters at a pub near the ground. During the assault the pub was seriously damaged and seven people had to be taken to hospital. The incident intensified the rivalry between the two groups and their willingness to physically dominate the other. Furthermore, the disorder set off an unprecedented wave of media attention for spectator violence at football matches in Spain. Newspapers reported that efforts to contain the misbehaviour of the ultras had proved largely ineffective (*El País*, 14 October 1986; *La Vanguardia*, 14 October 1986; *Avui*, 14 October 1986). In an interview with the daily sports newspaper *Sport*, Espanyol chairman Antoni Baró assured that:

> The measures we have adopted to avoid conflicts are effective inside our stadium, where we have separated them [Brigadas Blanquiazules] from Penya Juvenil, but outside the stadium we cannot do anything, much to our regret because their actions are damaging the image of Espanyol and our fan base as a whole. (*Sport*, 17 October 1986)

The growing official and public concern over the behaviour of the ultras was further enhanced by the emergence of the skinhead subculture on the terraces of the Sarrià stadium. The rise of a skinhead element among Brigadas Blanquiazules, at first no more than 50 young males, added to the group a common style and uniform (cropped hair, sta-prest trousers, bomber jackets with right-wing symbols, Doctor Martens boots, Lonsdale or Fred Perry tops) and an increased sense of collective identity celebrating aggressive masculinity and physical toughness. The skinheads also increased the visibility of right-wing ideologies within Brigadas Blanquiazules. In the South Stand of the Sarrià stadium group members routinely displayed banners with swastikas, white power and Celtic crosses and the group's official logo, a *Totenkopf* (skull and crossbones) derived from the German SS (e.g. *Revista Hinchas*,

2, March 1990; *Super Ultra*, 1, October 1989; *El País*, 9 December 1986). More recently, since the prohibition of Nazi symbols inside football stadia, the ultras have also come to use more covert symbols, such as the sign 88 (each 8 stands for the eighth letter in the alphabet; 88 thus stands for HH, short for Heil Hitler). As part of their neo-Nazi ethos, the skinheads celebrate the muscular, athletic body and therefore strongly oppose the consumption of drugs. For example, the consumption of marihuana is considered as *algo de rojos* ('reds', communists) or *de musulmanes* (Muslims, especially North Africans).

Espanyol's participation in the UEFA Cup in the 1987/88 season gave Brigadas Blanquiazules the opportunity to interact more directly with prestigiously perceived foreign ultra and hooligan formations. For example, the UEFA Cup Match between Espanyol and AC Milan, on 4 November 1987, was overshadowed by violent clashes between local ultras and members of AC Milan's ultra group Fossa dei Leoni. Home fans attacked one of the coaches carrying Milan ultras. The Italians, allegedly armed with pit helmets and baseball bats, responded to the attack by pelting their rivals with bricks, bottles and other objects, injuring four Espanyol fans (*El Día*, 6 November 1987). After the match young Espanyol fans attacked Italian fans and damaged cars with Italian number plates. In the aftermath of the event newspapers emphasized the international hooligan reputation of Brigadas Blanquiazules: 'Sad: the blue-and-white ultras are on a European level' (*Sport*, 6 November 1987; cf. *La Vanguardia*, 5 November 1987; *El País*, 5 November 1987).

The series of hooligan incidents in 1986 and 1987 and the visibility of right-wing symbols inside the stadium generated widespread official and media concern over the behaviour of the ultras. Following attacks by Espanyol fans on the referee, the linesmen and a visiting player during a home match against Real Zaragoza, on 31 October 1987, the football authorities decided to close Sarrià for one match. Club officials condemned the decision, arguing that the punishment was completely disproportionate. Vice chairman Fernando Martorell argued: 'I am sure that if the incidents that occurred in Sarrià had taken place in the Camp Nou or the Santiago Bernabéu [Real Madrid's stadium], nothing would have happened' (*El País*, 5 November 1987; cf. *La Vanguardia*, 5 November 1987). Espanyol also denied responsibility for the violence that marred the match against AC Milan. The club claimed that it had done everything in its power to prevent disorder and that events outside the stadium were the responsibility of the police (*Sport*, 6 November 1987). Director Pedro Tomás highlighted the good behaviour of the ultras: 'I disagree with the statement that Brigadas Blanquiazules is a nightmare to Espanyol. On the contrary, there is no reason to complain. They are young men who spend matches supporting the team without ceasing' (*La Vanguardia*, 6 November 1987). Behind the scenes, however, the club sought to increase its influence on the ultras. The new club chairman Julio Pardo called for a dialogue between the club and the ultras in an attempt to bring about the legalization of Brigadas Blanquiazules, transforming the group into an official *peña*. The group's legalization was seen as both a new impulse to the club's youth support (which had suffered from the dissolution of Penya Juvenil) and a means for reducing football hooliganism. The club considered the term *brigadas* too controversial and therefore opted for the more neutral name Juventudes Blanquiazules (Blue-and-white Youth) (*Super Ultra*, 3, February 1990). The legalization of the group was never effectuated due to the reluctance of the ultras.

Overview of the emergence and early development of football hooliganism

The emergence of football hooliganism at Espanyol contains a number of elements. The creation of a hooligan group was preceded by the segregation of the crowd by age. Groups of young fans began to congregate in the section behind one of the goals, transforming the area into their exclusive territory to the exclusion of the older football citizenry. Brigadas Blanquiazules separated from the main youth group in reaction to the intimidation and assaults by young FC Barcelona supporters. The group was heavily influenced by the Italian ultra movement and merged foreign elements of football culture (i.e. rituals, symbols, names of Italian ultra groups) with indigenous features (i.e. specific political oppositions). The ultra group explicitly identifies with the use of violence in inter-group rivalries, distinguishing itself from the more pacified youth group at Espanyol. Group members' celebration of aggressive masculinity and right-wing ideologies intensified over time, especially after the eruption of the skinhead subculture. The emergence of football hooliganism was not caused by changes in the relationship between football clubs and their audience, as Taylor (1971; 1971a) has suggested, but rather by developments in

Spanish youth subcultures and the transnational and national diffusion of subcultural practices. Central to understanding the emergence and early development of football hooliganism at Espanyol are the ongoing processes of imitation and distinction among the ultras. In the remainder of this chapter, I will describe the development of, and responses to, football hooliganism at Espanyol.

The crisis of football hooliganism: official and grassroots responses

The violent rivalry between Espanyol and FC Barcelona hooligans established in the second half of the 1980s escalated in the early 1990s. The assault on a 21-year-old Boixos Nois member, on 1 December 1990, triggered the most violent incident in the history of both groups. On 13 January 1991, five members of Boixos Nois launched a premeditated revenge attack on 19-year-old Frédéric Rouquier and 16-year-old José María Arboleas, both affiliates of Brigadas Blanquiazules, after Espanyol's home match against Sporting Gijón. Rouquier died from stabbing wounds and Arboleas was seriously injured. The young man accused of assassinating Rouquier was convicted to twenty years and ten months imprisonment, whereas two of his friends were sentenced to seventeen years in prison (*El Periódico*, 3 May 1994). The murder generated widespread official and public concern over the escalating violence in Spanish football. Media coverage of the ultra and skinhead subculture increased considerably during this period. A variety of special reports and background articles were published in newspapers and magazines as well as a number of television documentaries on the subject. Local newspapers reported how Brigadas Blanquiazules and Boixos Nois controlled different areas of the city as well as certain suburbs and villages in Catalonia (*El Periódico*, 3 November 1991).

Meanwhile, the involvement of members of Brigadas Blanquiazules in violent incidents at home and away matches continued. Violent confrontations between Espanyol and FC Barcelona hooligans also took place at other locations, for example in the local nightlife. Particular pubs, nightclubs and streets were routinely regarded as established territory for one side or another. The entry of opposing groups to these spaces was usually considered as deliberately transgressive and assumed to be intimidating (cf. Giulianotti and Armstrong, 2002: 229). Rival

265

hooligans occasionally visited each other at work and at home. Espanyol ultras also held a reputation for their recurrent involvement in violent incidents during the Día de la Hispanidad (National Day), on 12 October. For example, on 12 October 1991, a group of approximately 400 right-wing youths, most of them affiliated to Brigadas Blanquiazules, attacked several people in the centre of Barcelona (*El País*, 13 October 1991; *La Vanguardia*, 20 October 1991). During this period the ultras actively sought to confront their opponents. As one ultra commented:

> In the early 1990s there were far more violent confrontations, not only between us and Boixos Nois, but also with other fan groups and youth groups. Our mentality was also somewhat different. Back then we really went out looking for violence. We used to travel to away matches the night before and harass local ultras or punks in bars and nightclubs. So really it wasn't limited to the stadium. (Personal interview, March 2004)

A year after the death of Frédéric Rouquier, Espanyol experienced a different kind of tragedy. Only minutes before the start of a home match against Cádiz CF, on 15 March 1992, 13-year-old Guillermo Alfonso Lázaro was seriously injured by a maritime flare launched from the opposite stand. He later died in hospital. Police arrested a 39-year-old and a 57-year-old man, neither of whom were connected to Brigadas Blanquiazules. Both men confessed their crime and admitted that they had underestimated the danger of the flare (Segura Palomares, 2001: 480-485; *ABC*, 17 March 1992). Although the ultras played no part in the tragedy, the incident came to have a negative impact on their activities since it was framed by the authorities and the media as yet another sign of the escalating violence in Spanish football. A series of legal measures were introduced in a bid to prevent spectator violence and hooliganism. Flares, weapons, alcohol consumption and symbols that incite violence (i.e. right-wing symbols) were prohibited. Additionally, police presence and the segregation of opposing fans was extended at home and away matches and a special police unit was created with the task of investigating the local ultra and skinhead scene. For so-called 'high-risk' matches (*partidos de alto riesgo*), the ultras were escorted to and from the ground by the police. The club also began to co-operate more intensively with the police and created the post of security co-ordinator.

266

These changes in police and security operations brought about a gradual transformation in the ultra scene at Espanyol. Until the 1990s the activities of the ultras were largely unimpeded by official controls. Relatively few offenders were arrested and punishments were rather lenient. Most offenders were merely ejected from the ground or fined. The severe prison sentences imposed on members of Brigadas Blanquiazules and the steady increase in police presence at football matches in the early 1990s led more and more ultras to perceive the risk of apprehension and serious punishment as a deterrent. As one ultra argued:

> In the late eighties and early nineties virtually every match was accompanied by some form of violence. In the 1990s the authorities began to respond to the violence through tougher laws and controls. Especially a few years after the death of Frédéric Rouquier the sentences became far more serious. I was convicted to two years in prison for a relatively minor offence. You should keep in mind that these measures were taken during a period of social panic. But they did result in a decline in violence. When the punishment became really threatening, I mean no longer a fine but a serious prison sentence, that was when a lot of people started to refrain from fighting. Well, except for the radical core. Because some guys reacted by waving knives and guns around, also in nightclubs, as part of the rivalry with Boixos Nois. (Personal interview, March 2004)

Another important consequence of the controls and punishments was their negatively perceived effect on the match-day experience of the ultras. Their skinhead attire made them the subject of extensive searches and police observation. Several ultras adopted a more moderate appearance, for example by growing their hair, in order to reduce these negative consequences: 'On the way to the stadium the police stopped you about seven times. In and around the stadium there was police everywhere. After a while I just had enough and changed my appearance' (personal interview with an Espanyol ultra, March 2004). Many members of Brigadas Blanquiazules nevertheless continue to adhere to the skinhead style, which remains a dominant influence among the ultras today.

The increase in government responses to football hooliganism coincided with an important development within Espanyol's fan community. Following the team's relegation in the 1992/93 season, a joint effort was made by the club and the ultras to integrate the club's youth support. At that stage the different youth groups were located in different parts of the ground. The Peña Juvenil Españolista, founded in 1991, occupied the North Stand of the Sarrià stadium, whereas Brigadas Blanquiazules was still located in the South Stand. The club's motivation for engaging in a collaboration of this kind was twofold. The principal aim was to secure the team's immediate return to the Premier League. The vocal and colourful support of young fans and ultras was seen as a potential advantage to this campaign. The secondary aim of the project was the containment of football hooliganism through the integration of the different youth groups and the improvement of informal social control among young supporters.

The joint operation was put into practice in the 1993/94 season under the name Irreductibles (Unconquerables), derived from Lazio Roma's Irriducibili due to contacts between members of the two groups (in part based on their shared right-wing sympathies), the group's status within the Italian ultra scene and the fact that Irriducibili was also a combination of distinctive youth groups (personal interviews with founders of Irreductibles, February 2004; Viñas, 2005: 133). Irreductibles initially consisted of three distinctive fan groups: Brigadas Blanquiazules, Peña Juvenil Españolista and Peña Universitaria. The two main groups involved in the project, Brigadas Blanquiazules and Juvenil, were opposites regarding their attitudes towards the use of politics and violence in football. Peña Universitaria, which consisted of local university students, did not perceive itself as an ultra group and principally focused on the organization of debates at universities and colleges, seeking to improve the club's image and to attract new club members. After a short period of participation Peña Universitaria decided to abandon Irreductibles and to return to the group's core functions.

Irreductibles rapidly transformed into a prestigious fan group. The group was repeatedly voted one of the most successful ultra groups in Spain by readers of the leading national fanzine *Super Hincha*. The 2,000 young fans occupying the

South Stand of the Sarrià stadium established a widespread reputation for their ambitious choreographies. Furthermore, during this period the level of violence seemed to be declining, even though minor incidents of fighting, missile throwing and vandalism continued to occur. In addition to the aforementioned factors, one of the reasons for this decline was Irreductibles' explicit behavioural codes with regard to the use of politics and violence, creating a degree of informal social control. These behavioural codes were formalized in the group's manifesto, which contained five basic rules: 1) represent the club colours inside and outside the stadium; 2) support the team in a continuous manner; 3) no politics; 4) no violence; 5) unite as a single voice, with a sportsmanlike and Espanyol-minded spirit (Manifest Gol Sud Sarrià, 1994). The project leaders believed that inter-group differences could only be overcome and the project could only succeed by formulating explicit behavioural codes with regard to politics and violence. As a co-founder of Irreductibles argued:

> Our only condition was that there would be neither politics nor violence inside the stadium. We explicitly refused to engage in the nationalist issue. It is true that, in general, a right-wing, pro-constitutional tendency also exists among members of Juvenil, though in a more moderate form, but we argued that attending football matches should be about Espanyol, not about Spain or Catalonia. Many members of Brigadas Blanquiazules did not agree with that. We did not want Spanish flags in our area of the ground, despite the fact that many of us were as pro-Spanish as Brigadas. We knew that if we wanted to attract more people and create a positive image for the club, it would be impossible to exhibit these flags. (Personal interview, March 2004)

The relationship between leading members of Brigadas Blanquiazules and Juvenil deteriorated in 1997, resulting in verbal abuse, intimidation and physical violence. Juvenil soon decided to abandon the South Stand to avoid conflict escalation. The conflict within Espanyol's fan community reflected to some degree the club's problematic situation. Financial problems and the outdated infrastructure of the ground (i.e. poor facilities and not conforming to all-seater requirements) forced Espanyol to move to Barcelona's Olympic Stadium. The final match at the beloved

Sarrià stadium, on 21 June 1997, was characterized by a mixture of sadness and anger. After the final whistle dozens of fans invaded the pitch in order to collect a personal souvenir (e.g. a piece of the pitch or a part of the goal nets). Ultras fought with the police, damaged parts of the ground and threw seats and flag poles onto the pitch (*El País*, 22 June 1997).

The move to the Olympic Stadium had a significant impact on the activities and containment of the ultra groups. Juvenil and Brigadas Blanquiazules now occupied opposite parts of the ground, seated areas had replaced the terraces and the stadium was located in an isolated part of Barcelona. According to Brigadas Blanquiazules, the group's move to a separate section of the stadium was another attempt by the club to isolate the group from the rest of the home crowd and to frustrate the group's ability to recruit new members (*Ultras Español*, no. 159, 12 December 1999). At the same time, however, the ultras wished to continue as an autonomous, unofficial fan group acting 'alone against all others' (*Ultras Español*, no. 177, 18 March 2001). Meanwhile, Juvenil gradually recaptured its original spirit. Explicitly rejecting the use of politics and violence in football, the group organized large choreographed displays and almost 1,000 fans to its *curva*. A renewed attempt to integrate the different fan groups resulted in the eruption of inter-group and intra-group conflict causing the fragmentation and polarization of the local ultra scene. Members of Juvenil were forced to travel separately to away matches and relied heavily on the police for their safety. The conflict within the fan community led many ultras to move to different parts of the ground, either individually or in small groups.

In 2003 another attempt to unite the increasingly fragmented youth groups was initiated. The Curva Jove seeks to revive the spirit of Irreductibles and to improve the club's image within Catalonia. Brigadas Blanquiazules initially participated in the project, but after a short period of time the group decided to separate itself from the other youth groups. Although the radical core of Brigadas Blanquiazules refused to give up their political activism, several group members decided to abandon their involvement in right-wing politics and competitive violence in the football context for the club's sake, causing a major schism in the group. The Curva Jove consists of a number of fan groups and small subgroups led by Peña Juvenil Españolista and Eternos. The latter group initially had approximately 60 members, most of them males in their late twenties and early thirties who were previously core members of Brigadas Blanquiazules. Many of them were also centrally involved in football hooliganism. They argued that Brigadas Blanquiazules had failed to progress over time into a more dynamic and open ultra group, due in part to intra-group conflicts, and that the group had therefore become increasingly alienated from the rest of the fan community. Eternos opposes to the expression of right-wing politics and competitive violence at football matches. Although the individual political beliefs of Eternos members are in many cases similar to those of affiliates of Brigadas Blanquiazules, the former distinguish themselves by their refusal to allow politics to overshadow football and to transform their political beliefs into a symbol of group identity. As one ultra explained:

> Within the Curva Jove there are quite a few people who would love to display Spanish flags and right-wing symbols, but the problem is that it would offend the rest of the home crowd. So you have a choice. You either bring your flag and evoke resentment or you leave your flag at home. We choose the latter option. Our principal aim is to co-operate with other fans and not to isolate ourselves. (Personal interview, March 2004)

The non-violent, apolitical fan model advocated by the Curva Jove appeals to large numbers of young and older Espanyol fans. The Curva Jove presently has over 2,000 affiliates, among which a substantial number of women (around 20 per cent) and young boys. The group is commonly praised for its positive contribution to Espanyol fan culture and received certain kinds of support from the club (i.e. free and reduced-price tickets, storage space inside the stadium). At the same time, supporters criticize the club for its passive, lenient attitude towards the Brigadas Blanquiazules. The right-wing and violent proclivities of the Brigadas Blanquiazules are seen by both fans and club officials as damaging the club's image and threatening spectator safety. Although the expansion of the club's security regime from the 1990s onwards has effectively reduced opportunities for large-scale hooligan confrontations inside the stadium, many supporters argue that the club continues to facilitate Brigadas Blanquiazules free or reduced-price tickets and travel arrangements, despite the fact that the group does not have an official status

271

(i.e. as a *peña*). As one ultra put it: 'The club tolerates Brigadas Blanquiazules in order to avoid conflicts. The group receives certain facilities. Officially this support does not exist, but in reality this kind of facilitation has been going on for a long time' (personal interview, March 2004).

Club officials deny this informal policy of facilitation and stress that they are only in contact with certain informal leaders and intermediaries to gather intelligence on the ultras' intentions and expectations. Members of Brigadas Blanquiazules argue that although they used to receive various types of support, nowadays the club only facilitates match tickets. The club's reluctance to provide storage space is seen as being part of club directors' attempts to isolate the group from the rest of the crowd, thereby frustrating the group's recruitment of new members. The ultras also condemn the club's bid to improve its image through public support for the Curva Jove and the name change from Castilian 'Español' to Catalan 'Espanyol'. The ultras consequently refuse to integrate the latter name in their displays and fanzines. They have occasionally protested against the team's underachievement and poor club management through abusive graffiti messages, intimidation or physical violence directed against players or club officials (e.g. *El Mundo*, 16 July 1993). Certain informal leaders have also criticized the club's transfer policies. As one club director commented: 'Some of the lads call me sometimes to discuss a transfer. They say, like, "don't you dare to sign on that negro, we only want white players at our club"' (personal interview, June 2004). This attitude towards black players is reflected in one of the group's songs: 'We don't want coloured players, we prefer Tamudo because he is white and Spanish.'

Supporters have also accused certain players of failing to take a clear stance on the racism and violence provoked by Brigadas Blanquiazules. Players have occasionally given interviews to the group's fanzine editors or were photographed displaying scarves or T-shirts with the group logo. One Espanyol player was quoted as saying: 'A group like yours is always necessary, a group that, when the match is dead, does not cease to support the team, a group that adds different ideas' (*Ultras Español*, no. 177, 18 March 2001). Certain (former) players are known for their regular facilitation of tickets to members of Brigadas Blanquiazules (Chacón García, 2004). Players and club officials have also participated in the annual lottery organized by the group. A fanzine contributor commented on this issue: 'We have

272

sold lottery tickets to all staff members and players. They all bought tickets for 1000 pesetas [6 euros], with some notable exceptions. [...] Staff members all paid a minimum of 5000 [30 euros]' (*Ultras Español*, no. 52, 1 January 1994).

Recent transformations in football hooliganism

The extent and seriousness of football hooliganism at Espanyol declined considerably from the mid-1990s onwards, although members of Brigadas Blanquiazules are still regularly involved in incidents such as vandalism, missile throwing, racial abuse and (minor) fighting. The decline in football hooliganism was in part caused by changes in police and security operations, as we have seen in the previous section. Increased controls and punishments significantly reduced the opportunities for collective violence in and around football grounds. Due to the persisting influence of the skinhead style, it is relatively easy for the police to identify and control the ultras. Furthermore, although the group continues to attract a limited number of new members, its opportunities for recruitment and expansion are thwarted by constrictive controls in and around the ground and the club's attempts to isolate the group from the rest of the fan community, making it impossible for non-members to occasionally enter the section of Brigadas Blanquiazules inside the stadium. These developments contributed to the substantial decline in the size and activities of the group in recent years. According to a fanzine contributor, 'urgent measures need to be taken to avoid the more than likely dissolution of the group' (*Ultras Español*, no. 170, 4 November 2000; see also *Ultras Español*, no. 159, 12 December 1999).

Other developments that had a negative effect on the size and activities of Brigadas Blanquiazules are internal power struggles and conflicts, which led several members to abandon the group, the growing popularity of the more moderate Curva Jove and the ageing of long-standing group members, many of whom have stopped attending matches on a regular basis due to changes in their lives (i.e. family, children, job careers, alternative leisure interests). With regard to internal power struggles, one ultra argued: 'I simply don't feel at ease there anymore, because I don't like it when people tell me what to do. I go to football to relax, to get away from the daily routine. I don't need somebody to tell me that I cannot smoke a joint when I feel like it simply because he opposes drugs. That is my business and nobody else's. That is why the Curva Jove appeals to me more now' (personal interview, May 2004). Another major reason for the decline in football hooliganism over the last decade, some ultras argue, is the group's reluctance to adapt to the new circumstances, for example by transforming into a more casual-type collectivity. As one ultra indicated: 'Nowadays it is almost impossible to confront opposing groups. Many people put it down to police strategies, but that is only one side of the story. The decline in violence is also related to the way in which the ultras behave themselves. They are showily dressed, sing and yell the whole time, display flags and political symbols. It is simply too easy for the police to identify and control us, except for when they screw up' (personal interview, June 2004). Attempts by a small section of Brigadas Blanquiazules to transform the group into a casual-style hooligan formation were frustrated by informal group leaders because of their reluctance to give way to new cultural influences at the expense of the typical ultra and skinhead attire characteristic of Brigadas Blanquiazules since the group's early beginnings.

Violent confrontations between Brigadas Blanquiazules and Boixos Nois have become rare in recent years. The deep-seated inter-group rivalry has gradually transformed into a more ritualized, verbal conflict which is mainly enacted through verbal abuse, threats and occasional (usually minor) incidents. The decline in physical confrontation was closely related to increased police controls, generational changes within the two groups and the changing political identity of Boixos Nois (see Chapter Nine; cf. Viñas, 2004: 236). Occasional incidents during local derbies are predominantly spontaneous, for example in reaction to perceived injustices (i.e. a refereeing decision, brutal police methods), and may also involve members of the Curva Jove. During an ill-tempered derby on 13 December 2003, the sending-off of Espanyol player Iván de la Peña triggered a violent response on the part of the ultras. Members of the Curva Jove threw various missiles onto the pitch and tried to scale the fences. The police struggled to keep the fans at bay. At the other end of the ground, affiliates of Brigadas Blanquiazules set fire to seats and banners. In the aftermath of the event supporters and club officials accused the referee of 'causing' the disorder because of his disproportionate decisions (the referee gave fourteen yellow cards and four red cards as the match ended with just eight players on either side) (*El Mundo*, 14 December 2003; *Sport*, 14 December 2003). A similar scene took place on 16 October 2004 during a derby at the Olympic Stadium. Brigadas Blanquiazules destroyed hundreds of seats, tore down fences and ripped out paving stones. Ultras fought with the police inside and outside the stadium. Seven supporters were fined 3,000 to 6,000 euros. Three ultras were banned for five months (*El 9*, 21 October 2004; *Mundo Deportivo*, 21 October 2004; *Sport*, 19 October 2004).

Coinciding with the decline in football hooliganism at Espanyol from the mid-1990s onwards was an increase in other types of violence provoked by the ultras. There have been multiple conflicts between Brigadas Blanquiazules and other fan groups at Espanyol over the last decade. In addition to intra-group conflicts and animosity between leading members of the Brigadas Blanquiazules and Juvenil, ideological differences between Brigadas Blanquiazules and certain separatist and apolitical fan groups within Espanyol's fan community, notably the peña Sarrià Nord, have occasionally resulted in verbal abuse, intimidation and physical violence. Several Espanyol fans choose not to attend certain 'high-risk' away matches, notably at the Camp Nou, because they resent, or are afraid of, sharing the away section with the radical ultras. In recent years there has also been a conflict between the Brigadas Blanquiazules and members of the Curva Jove. Some of the Curva Jove's members, including those who were formerly part of Brigadas Blanquiazules, have been abused and threatened because of their collaboration with the club and the success of their group. Central to this conflict is the *protagonismo* of both groups, that is, their aim to be the largest and most influential ultra group at the club. Related to this issue are the financial interests involved in the ultra subculture (i.e. membership fees, match tickets, travel arrangements, merchandising), which at times have been a source of intra-group and inter-group conflict.

The relationship between Brigadas Blanquiazules and the police has somewhat deteriorated in recent years due to territorial conflicts. Members of Brigadas Blanquiazules normally tolerate the passive presence of police officers in their section of the ground, but at times they respond in an aggressive or violent manner to the 'illegitimate' invasion of their territory. Their hatred towards the police is reflected in logos and symbols such as ACAB (All Cops Are Bastards). The ultras have also occasionally attacked journalists. For example, on 6 March

275

2005, after a home match against Levante UD, a group of ultras bashed the editor and editor-in-chief of the club newsletter *Blanc i Blau* in a parking area near the stadium. The journalists received several punches and kicks. They had enraged the ultras by publishing an article condemning the racial abuse of the Brigadas Blanquiazules against Espanyol goalkeeper Carlos Kameni. Two senior group members, aged 39 and 33, were arrested because of the incident. Local and national media condemned the incident and reported that at the residence of one of the two detainees – who had an ample criminal record for violent disorder and affray – police had found an abundant supply of Nazi and skinhead material such as badges, flags, photographs, videotapes, books and offensive weapons (e.g. *Diario As*, 10 March 2005).

Conclusion

Football hooliganism at Espanyol demonstrates the temporal variability of phenomenon. Football hooliganism at Espanyol was at its peak in the late 1980s and early 1990s. During this period various serious confrontations took place between Brigadas Blanquiazules and opposing fan groups. Espanyol ultras were also regularly involved in racial abuse and violence and attacks on members of opposing subcultures (i.e. punks and anti-fascist skinheads). Central to the escalation of football hooliganism during this period was the fierce rivalry with FC Barcelona's Boixos Nois. Espanyol hooligans actively sought to enhance or secure their reputation for toughness, both individually and collectively, and were heavily influenced by prestigious foreign fan groups and youth subcultures, notably Italian ultra groups and the British skinhead subculture. The extent and seriousness of football hooliganism at Espanyol declined from the mid-1990s onwards due in part to changes in police and security operations and to the internal development of Brigadas Blanquiazules. At the same time, a gradual increase has taken place in intra-group conflict, conflicts between Espanyol fan groups and violence against the police. Members of Brigadas Blanquiazules are also regularly involved in missile throwing, vandalism, racial abuse and small-scale fighting.

The degrees of planning and co-ordination involved in football hooliganism at Espanyol are currently generally limited, contrasting with the premeditated attacks on FC Barcelona hooligans and other fan groups in the late 1980s and early 1990s. In the present-day situation Espanyol ultras do not normally go to great lengths to escape police observation. Many ultras refuse to give up their skinhead attire and political symbols and they eschew the casual style characteristic of British hooligan groups, despite the fact that their conspicuous appearance alerts police officers. The ultras continue to view the football ground as a major site for cultural and political contestation and social visibility. The public expression of their political beliefs and their hatred towards the 'separatists' of FC Barcelona are regarded by many ultras as more fundamental to the maintenance of group identity than the regular involvement in hooligan confrontations.

The case of Espanyol casts doubt on the universal applicability of sociological theories that explain football hooliganism as a predominantly lower-working-class phenomenon (e.g. Dunning et al., 1988; Taylor, 1971; Clarke, 1978). The class composition of Brigadas Blanquiazules is heterogeneous and the group historically incorporates a significant proportion of middle-class youths. Over time the group has come to attract growing numbers of working-class youths eager to 'make a name' for themselves on the terraces. The ultras view aggressive masculinity and right-wing politics as a central source of group identity, distinguishing them from both the Catalan nationalists of FC Barcelona and the 'poofs' and 'nerds' of the more moderate fan groups within Espanyol's fan community. The collective identity of the ultras mirrors, in a heightened or distorted form, the historical antagonism between Espanyol and FC Barcelona. Whereas club officials and the majority of supporters attempt to change Espanyol's persistent stigma, Brigadas Blanquiazules celebrate the club's alleged fascist tendencies. The visibility of the ultras and their political beliefs reproduces the popular image of Espanyol as a fascist club.

9

Cultural Heritage at Stake?
The Emergence and Development of Football
Hooliganism at FC Barcelona

Introduction

'Catalonia is not Spain'. This single phrase on a banner displayed during matches of the *selecció catalana* (the unofficial Catalan national football team) symbolizes the collective identity of FC Barcelona supporters. 'Barça' is one of the world's largest and most influential football clubs yet it distinguishes itself, first and foremost, by its historical social and cultural function within Catalonia. The collective identity of FC Barcelona is constructed in relation to the 'fascist', 'centralist' other, notably Real Madrid and Espanyol. This othering – a way of defining and securing one's own identity through the stigmatization of the other – is also closely reflected, in a heightened and distorted form, in the identity of the militant fan group Boixos Nois. Group members are strongly influenced by developments in British and Italian football and youth culture, but they also celebrate the core values of FC Barcelona fan culture. Over time, however, the group's identification with football hooliganism and right-wing extremism has come to challenge the club's 'friendly' image and anti-centralist, Catalan legacy. Moreover, the case of FC Barcelona illustrates the complex and shifting interactions between hooligans, law enforcers, club officials and non-hooligan supporters.

This chapter is divided into four parts. In the first section, I will examine the development of Barça fan culture and the collective identity of FC Barcelona supporters. I will then describe the emergence and early development of football hooliganism at FC Barcelona. The third part of the chapter analyzes the escalation and crisis of football hooliganism and the fragmentation of Barça's youth groups. In the final section I will discuss recent official responses to football hooliganism and the subtle yet vital interactions and negotiations between militant fans and club officials.

Més que un club: the meaning and identity of FC Barcelona

The meaning and identity of FC Barcelona have evolved considerably over time. The club's culture has been shaped by a combination of foreign and local influences. The Swiss businessman Hans Kamper (who adopted the Catalan name Joan Gamper) founded the Foot-Ball Club Barcelona in 1899 with the intention of promoting football in Barcelona. In its early years, 'Barça' mainly fielded foreigners living and working in Catalonia. These foreigners, with the exception of Gamper, were not associated with Catalan nationalism. This situation began to change as early as the 1910s when the club aligned more explicitly with Catalanism and became the largest sports entity in Catalonia. During this period the club changed its official language from Castilian to Catalan. FC Barcelona gradually evolved into an important symbol of Catalan political, social and cultural identity and came to be regarded by its supporters as *més que un club* ('more than a club'). For many fans, participating in the club had less to do with the game itself and more with the club's transformation into a potent symbol of collective identity (Burns, 1999: xi; Kuper, 1994: 92; Góngora, 1996).

Barça's identity gained force during the military dictatorships of Miguel Primo de Rivera (1923-1929) and Francisco Franco (1939-1975). During the Primo de Rivera regime Catalan nationalism was severely oppressed. All people participating in the club in any form were suspected of sympathizing with Catalan separatism. FC Barcelona supporters at times openly defied the regime, acts which infuriated the military authorities. In June 1925, when a part of the crowd booed an orchestral version of the Spanish anthem, the authorities threatened to close the Camp Nou stadium for a period of six months. The end of the Primo de Rivera regime and the instalment of the Second Spanish Republic, in 1931, intensified the identification of FC Barcelona with Catalan Republicanism but, due to the intense politicization of this era, many citizens appeared to distance themselves from football.

What became rarefied into an almost obsessive political climate coincided with a drop in membership numbers at Barça. The downward trend partly reflected the loss of earnings in a time of recession, but it also suggested that too many Catalans were simply too caught up with arguing in the streets and in parliament to take time off to watch football (Burns, 1999: 99).

One of the events that have come to symbolize the oppression suffered by the club most took place shortly after the outbreak of the Civil War (1936-1939). On 6 August 1936, FC Barcelona chairman and representative of the pro-independence political party Esquerra Republicana de Catalunya (ERC) Josep Sunyol was murdered by Falangist soldiers. The death of Sunyol – later dubbed 'the martyr of *barcelonisme*' – is seen as one of the club's truly defining moments (*El Periódico*, 22 July 1998; Ball, 2001: 116-117).

The Franco regime constitutes the most thorough attempt in the history of Spain to subordinate the country to central control (Hargreaves, 2000: 28; Shaw, 1987: 182-183). Franco tried to destroy all institutions that held traces of regionalism or separatism and languages other than Castilian were prohibited. The authorities perceived Catalonia as a serious threat to the state's well being and Barça, like Athletic Bilbao in the Basque Country, as a club with separatist tendencies which had to be controlled and eliminated (Figueres, 2003: 169-176). The Franco regime implemented a policy of cultural genocide that deeply affected the club. Any sign of independence or opposition was brutally suppressed. The Catalan language and key symbols of Catalan nationhood, such as the *senyera* (the Catalan flag), the *estelada* (the flag of Catalan independentism), the national hymn Els Segadors and the Catalan dance (the *sardana*) were proscribed (Hargreaves, 2000: 28). Barça was also forced to change its name to Castilian 'Barcelona Club de Fútbol'. The state police investigated alleged underground activities of club members. Notwithstanding these constrictive controls, during the reign of Franco supporting Barça was one of the few means available for the public expression of the Catalan sentiment, which was more effectively oppressed in other spheres of social and cultural life. The only major institution in Catalonia that was in a position to publicly defend Catalan culture and language against centralist repression was the

280

Church, most notably the Abbey of Montserrat (Hargreaves, 2000: 25). Although the military authorities were determined to strip Barça of its political, social and cultural identity, it seems that Franco did not see the nationalistic demonstrations taking place at football grounds as a potential danger to social and political order. In fact, Franco appears to have been conscious that football as a mass sport could be utilized to his favour by functioning as a kind of 'escape valve', that is, as an outlet for regional tensions (Shaw, 1987: 185; Duke and Crolley, 1996a: 37). Sport was perceived as a means for the unification and neutralization of the masses and, therefore, crowds had to be drawn to the stadium again (Burns, 1999: 130; 134-135; Ball, 2001: 101).

Towards the end of the Franco regime, in the 1960s and early 1970s, FC Barcelona underwent a process of Catalanization. This process was set off by a new generation of club officials who were strongly influenced by cultural and political developments in Catalonia, most notably the growth of the cultural and political resistance movement and the militancy of a group of Catalan intellectuals who perceived the club as one of the most powerful symbols of the Catalan identity. A number of dramatic incidents reinforced the process of Catalanization, such as the 'caso Guruceta'. During a cup match between FC Barcelona and Real Madrid at the Camp Nou stadium, on 6 June 1970, referee Emilio Guruceta awarded the visiting team a controversial penalty. Infuriated by the referee's 'favour' to the 'regime's team', a section of the home crowd invaded the pitch and fought with the police.

The meaning of FC Barcelona developed in the context of the profound demographic changes from the late 1950s onwards. In the late 1950s and early 1960s Spanish society underwent a process of rapid economic modernization. Catalonia and the Basque Country, as the state's most economically advanced areas, were in the vanguard of the modernization process. Catalonia attracted large numbers of Castilian-speaking immigrants, particularly from the South of the country where the standard of living was comparatively low (Hargreaves, 2000: 29; Molinero and Ysàs, 1999; Figueres, 2003).[1] Many of those arriving in Catalonia viewed Barça as an effective means for integration into Catalan society. Barça became a magnet for working-class immigrants whose priority it was to assimilate to the Catalan way of life (Vázquez Montalbán, 1972: 7-8; Ball, 2001: 102; Kuper,

1994: 89). The club's fan base expanded rapidly during this period. In contrast, local rival Espanyol had more and more difficulty attracting new fans (see Chapter Eight).

The construction of collective identity: Barça and the eternal rivals

The construction of FC Barcelona as a major symbol of Catalan nationalism occurred in relation to the club's two major historical rivals, Real Madrid and Espanyol. The identity of FC Barcelona supporters thus lies in the perceived differences between self and the other. The creation of collective others 'is a requirement, through the dynamics of stereotyping and identity contrast, for helping to set boundaries and mark off the dynamics of the we' (Appadurai, 2006: 50). In this context, Vázquez Montalbán (2005) has argued that 'if Real Madrid did not exist, we Catalans would have to invent them.' The same argument also applies to the local rivalry between FC Barcelona and Espanyol. The antagonism between the two clubs can be dated back to their early beginnings (see Chapter Eight for a more in-depth analysis). Local derbies were often fuelled with hostility and regularly spilled over into violence on and off the pitch (Sobrequés Callicó, 1998: 271-272; García Castell, 1968: 105). Espanyol increasingly came to be seen by Catalan nationalists as representing the centralist government, that is, as 'the enemy within'. Whereas FC Barcelona came to symbolize the oppressed people of Catalonia, Espanyol was perceived to favour the right-wing military of Franco's Spain (Duke and Crolley, 1996a: 28; Góngora, 1996: 237). Espanyol's 'very existence came increasingly to be seen as a crude insult by Catalan nationalists who supported Barcelona, making encounters between the two teams a recipe for division and violence' (Burns, 2000: 85).

The rivalry between the two clubs deepened during the first decades after the Spanish Civil War. During this period FC Barcelona and Espanyol came to symbolize two diametrically opposed social, cultural and political conceptions: Catalanism versus anti-Catalanism, anti-Spanishness versus Spanishness and integration versus non-integration (Colomé, 1999: 90). As we have seen in Chapter Eight, the rivalry between the two clubs gradually transformed from a two-way rivalry into an unrequited rivalry. FC Barcelona became the more successful of the two clubs, with over 100,000 members and with one of the world's most impressive

282

football grounds, and increasingly considered Real Madrid as its major rival. Consequently, some FC Barcelona supporters have changed their perception of their local opponents. For example, FC Barcelona's club historian wrote:

> [I]t is easy to see that, with the changing of times, the characteristics of the typical Espanyol supporter have changed sufficiently. Nowadays he is not that Castilian functionary of the post-war era, overtly centralist, or that Catalan reactionary and Spanish nationalist, or that Andalusian immigrant of the 1960s who originally supported Real Madrid and who, in Catalonia, found a white branch on the road to Sarrià [Espanyol's historical home] (Sobrequés Callicó, 1998: 277).

But despite the gradual improvements in the relationship between the two clubs, the deep-seated stigmas and stereotypes remain strong today. Many FC Barcelona fans still see Espanyol as a fascist, anti-Catalan club. Whether or not to support Espanyol is, in their view, not simply a matter of football allegiance, but rather a particular world view: 'The choice between supporting Barça or Espanyol is largely determined by what you stand for in life and which ideas are promoted in your family. Most Espanyol fans are fascists and really support Madrid' (personal interview with FC Barcelona fan, May 2005).

The hostility between the country's two most successful football clubs, FC Barcelona and Real Madrid, materialized significantly later, but has gradually come to overshadow the local rivalry between Barça and Espanyol. The strives between FC Barcelona and Real Madrid mirror in many respects the very essence of twentieth-century Spanish history (Ball, 2001: 23). The first signs of rivalry between the two clubs can be dated back to the 1910s, but only after the Civil War did it come to take on a more hostile dimension (García Candau, 1996: 8; Sobrequés Callicó, 1998: 284-287). Real Madrid, founded in 1902 by the brothers Juan and Carlos Padrós Rubió, was regarded as 'the regime's team' during the reign of Franco. In many ways Real Madrid fulfilled the role of a national team during the Franco period. The regime benefited greatly from Real Madrid's international prestige since many foreigners identified the excellence of the team with the state of the Spanish political system which it indirectly represented (Fernández Santander,

1990: 155; Shaw, 1985: 38-39). According to FC Barcelona supporters, evidence of the close relationship between Real Madrid and the Franco regime can be found in the favourable refereeing decisions the *blancos* received and which, according to many, continue today:

> The chain of refereeing errors in favour of the Madrid team does not seem to end [...] They have been given 13 points this season [...] The refereeing against Atlético was merely another chapter in a season full of "human errors" in favour of the whites (*Sport*, 19 April 2004).

There are several documented examples of spectator violence at matches between FC Barcelona and Real Madrid during Franco's reign. During a cup semi-final in Madrid, on 13 June 1943, police intimidated the Barcelona players and home fans insulted and assaulted chairman Enric Piñeyro and other board members. Piñeyro, a loyal Francoist appointed by the Spanish football federation to lead FC Barcelona, was so appalled by the hostility his team received that he resigned irrevocably. On 11 July 1968, during a League match between the two teams in Madrid, a section of the home crowd pelted Barcelona players with bottles. Two years later, on 6 June 1970, frustrated FC Barcelona fans invaded the pitch of the Camp Nou stadium. Some of the more militant fans engaged in a running battle with the police. Dozens of fans were beaten indiscriminately by the police amidst cries of '*Policía asesina*' ('police murderers') (Burns, 1999: 169). The hostility between the two sets of fans remains strong today, but the level of physical violence has declined. Emotions occasionally spill over into violence. When Luis Figo, who was transferred from Barcelona to Madrid, returned to the Camp Nou on 22 October 2000 he was continuously abused and pelted with a shower of coins, three mobile phones, several half-bricks and a bicycle chain (Ball, 2001: 19). Two years later, on 23 November 2002, Figo was once again pelted with various objects, including a suckling's head and a bottle of whisky, during the *clásico* at the Camp Nou. On that occasion, FC Barcelona chairman Joan Gaspart accused Figo of provoking the incidents. Days later Gaspart withdrew his accusations (*El Periódico*, 24 November 2002; *El Periódico*, 28 November 2002).

Franco's death in November 1975 set off important transformations in the Spanish political system. While Franco's dictatorship was seen to be loosening its grip during the 1960s and early 1970s, his death marked the official beginning of the transition to democracy. The 1978 Constitution regulated the creation of seventeen *Comunidades Autónomas* with varying degrees of autonomy in legislation and administration. Catalonia has a comparatively large degree of autonomy and the use of the Catalan language in everyday life is increasing (*La Vanguardia*, 22 April 2004; *El Periódico*, 22 April 2004). Despite the process of democratization, the experience of Franco's oppressive regime is responsible for the salience of Catalan nationalism today and for the tension that still exists between Catalonia and the Spanish state in the new democratic Spain (Hargreaves, 2000: 29). Barça continues to function as one of the main symbols of Catalan identity. A survey published in 2000 revealed that the Catalan television audience regard FC Barcelona and former president of Catalonia Jordi Pujol as the two most dominant symbols of Catalanism (*El Periódico*, 28 March 2000).

At the same time, the transition to democracy influenced the ways in which FC Barcelona manifests itself at a political, social and cultural level. Barça's is one of the four Spanish football clubs that have remained in mutual ownership. In this democratic structure, *socis* (club members; *socios* in Spanish) have considerable influence since they elect the club's chairman. Critics argued that even though the *socis* retained their right to vote in club elections, during the presidency of Josep Lluís Núñez (1978-2000) their rights were seriously reduced not only on a social level, but also concerning the club's economic activity (Carabén et al., 1999; Laporta, 2002). They stressed the lack of transparency in accounting procedures and the diminishing participation of club members' contributions to the club's global income. The contribution of revenue from season tickets to the club's whole budget declined steadily in comparison with new sources of income such as television rights, sponsoring and merchandising (Bañeres, 2000; Carabén, 1999). Núñez's reign, often referred to as *nuñisme*, was considered to undermine Barça's core principles. Many regarded his leadership style as 'aggressive' or even 'treacherous and mafia-like' (Carabén et al., 1999). Despite this overt criticism, Núñez was able to maintain his position as chairman until his resignation in 2000. He was succeeded by long-standing vice-chairman Joan Gaspart. Gaspart's resignation in February 2003 paved the way for L'Elefant Blau (the Blue Elephant), an opposition movement led by lawyers Joan Laporta and Sebastía Roca and supported by, among others, former FC Barcelona player and manager Johan Cruijff. The club elections were won by L'Elefant Blau representative Laporta, FC Barcelona's current *president*.

The contemporary situation of FC Barcelona is characterized by a combination of Catalanization and economic activity on a global scale. On the one hand, club officials stress the club's important cultural and social function within Catalonia and promote FC Barcelona as a potent symbol of the Catalan identity. On more than one occasion Laporta has stressed that his main objective is to 're-Catalanize' the club. He believes that Barça is a key instrument to promote the image of Catalonia worldwide (e.g. *El Punt*, 28 March 2004). To preserve the sanctity of their colours, Barça is still reluctant to wear shirt advertising (cf. Kuper, 1994: 87). On the other hand, FC Barcelona embraces many of the transnational developments in the football industry stimulating its economic activity. Barça's new economic model launched to overcome its financial deficit features an increasing income from television and media and marketing – a total of 95.2 million euros, 59 per cent of the club's entire income (162.7 million euros) (*Barça: Revista oficial FC Barcelona*, December 2003: 30-31; *Diario As*, 19 May 2004). The club's economic activity is part of a wider campaign to convert Barça into the world's most powerful sports institution. Central to this *Gran Repte* ('Big Challenge') is the club's desire to increase the number of fans. In Laporta's first season as chairman the total number of *socis* grew from 106,000 to over 120,000. Nearly 200 new members signed up per day (data provided by FC Barcelona, June 2004; *El 9*, 2 April 2004). Millions of people worldwide identify with Barça, many of whom have little or no affiliation with the Catalan cause. Barça currently has more than 1,000 active *penyes* (official fan clubs). Hundreds of *penyes* are located in other parts of Spain, including Madrid. Paradoxically, some of these official fan clubs have criticized what they consider the marginalization of non-Catalan fans in club politics (*El Periódico*, 14 September 2003; interviews with members of the Peña Barcelonista de Madrid, April 2004). One fan explained this paradox as follows:

Do the club directors seek to return to the origins of the club as a symbol of nationalism and resistance? Or do they want to control the market in terms of increasing their shares and fan base? If Barça really wanted to represent Catalonia, it should only field Catalan players, refuse to participate in the Spanish league, forbid its players to join the Spanish national team, only contract local sponsors, and so on. In reality the club is much more open-minded to maximize its profit and sporting potential. (Personal interview, March 2004)

Despite FC Barcelona's transformation into one of the largest and most successful football clubs worldwide, the club's cultural heritage continues to strongly influence the collective identity of its (Catalan) supporters. In the following section, I will show that the meaning and identity of FC Barcelona are also central to the identity formation of the militant youth groups at the Camp Nou and the emergence of football hooliganism.

Passió blaugrana sense límits: the emergence of football hooliganism at FC Barcelona

The Camp Nou stadium holds a reputation for its serene atmosphere. Occasional applauding is overshadowed by the silence and grumbling of the majority of home fans, especially when things do not seem to go their way (Winkels, 1998: 66; King, 2000: 126; *Super Hincha*, vol. 4, no. 29, February 1996: 37). Only on very special occasions, such as the *clásico* against Real Madrid or a high-profile European Cup match, do Barça fans transform the ground into one of the most impressive sites in world football. In the late 1970s young supporters increasingly criticized the lack of atmosphere created by the club's traditional fan clubs. Responding to a growing demand for a more active approach to football fandom, in 1981 a group of 50 young supporters around former club athlete Josep Tortosa founded the fan group Boixos Nois (Crazy Boys). The young fans transformed the lower tier of the South Stand into their exclusive territory to the exclusion of the older football citizenry. They benefited greatly from the tickets distributed by the club at various elementary and secondary schools in Barcelona in order to attract more young fans to the club (*Hinchas y Supporters*, vol. 1, no. 0, August 1995: 14). From the start Boixos Nois integrated young fans from diverse social backgrounds with the objective to provide colourful and vocal support to the team and the Catalan cause, as reflected in the group's battle-cry *passió blaugrana sense límits* (Barça passion without limits). A Boixos Nois member explained the group's philosophy as follows:

> We often criticize the people in the box seats and other stands for always complaining and booing players. I hate that. I rather support the team for the full ninety minutes. That's the main difference. They come to see the spectacle; we prefer to create the spectacle. You can compare it with my love for the opera. I rather listen to it at home than go to the Liceu [a theatre in Barcelona], because I don't like the type of people who go there. It's the same in football. It's about the way you experience the event. (Personal interview, April 2004)

The group also regularly criticized club officials, managers and players who were perceived as underperforming or damaging the club's core principles and cultural heritage (*Super Hincha*, vol. 6, no. 56, July 1998: 26).

Boixos Nois was strongly influenced by developments in foreign football cultures. The 1982 World Cup hosted by Spain was an important source of inspiration and enabled young Barcelona fans to observe and interact with foreign fan groups, notably Italian, Brazilian and English supporters. More generally, growing television broadcasting of European football matches increased the young fans' awareness of foreign spectator cultures, especially the British and Italian: 'The increasing transmission by television of big European matches enabled us to observe the extreme differences existing between the spectacular brilliance of their terraces and the silent paleness of ours' (Strubell, 1998: 48). Many rituals and symbols were directly derived from British terrace culture, for example the group's official logo, the English bulldog. These foreign elements were perceived as being more prestigious than their own style of support. The arrival of English manager Terry Venables and Scottish player Steve Archibald in the 1984/85 season stimulated the display of English and Scottish flags on the South Stand. The group also began to use songs such as 'God save the queen' and 'When the saints go marching in' (*Super Hincha*, vol. 4, no. 35, September 1996: 5). Boixos Nois members also travelled to Britain and other countries to personally experience foreign football cultures. As one Boixos Nois member remembered:

> Britain has always been our main influence. And Italy to a lesser extent. That was more something of later youth groups at Barça, with their large choreographies. In the 1980s Boixos Nois had some of those *tifos* too, with flares and banners. But mostly it's people that have been to England and, to a lesser degree, to Italy and Argentina. And those are the influences we brought back with us. (Personal interview, May 2004)

Within a few years Boixos Nois expanded to a maximum of 700 affiliates and transformed into an influential peer model for the militant fan groups emerging across Spain. The group's vocal and loyal support to the team and its allegiance to Catalanism contributed to its positive image among FC Barcelona players and supporters. During this period the group sought to advance its internal cohesion and organization through the sale of membership cards and the creation of a 'press office'. In 1986 the group's first official sections were created, in Mataró and Madrid. Group members also began to sell T-shirts, photographs and other merchandise to boost the group's financing of choreographed displays and travel to away matches. Despite this increase in the level of organization, even at this early stage Boixos Nois could not be viewed as a homogeneous group. In the mid-1980s two different tendencies co-existed within the group: on the one hand, the Super Boixos, consisting of the group's founding members, and, on the other hand, a sector that identified more explicitly with Catalan separatism. The latter section consisted of young fans closely related to political organizations such as the Front Nacional de Catalunya (FNC) (Viñas, 2005: 125).

The rapid expansion of Boixos Nois coincided with a change in the behaviour of a section of its members. In the early years the occasional incidents provoked by group members were usually limited to vandalism, but young fans now began to identify with the use of physical violence in inter-group rivalries. The first violent confrontation took place during the 1983 Spanish Cup Final against Real

Madrid in Zaragoza, when Boixos Nois members fought with members of the rival ultra group Ultras Sur. Two developments led to an increase in the extent and seriousness of football hooliganism at FC Barcelona. First, Boixos Nois established a violent rivalry with young fans of local rival Espanyol. During local derbies at Espanyol's Sarrià stadium in the early 1980s Boixos Nois intimidated and attacked members of Espanyol's youth group Peña Juvenil. In response to these aggressions a group of Espanyol fans created the more radical fan group Brigadas Blanquiazules (see Chapter Eight). This development set in motion a spiral of escalating hostility and violence that mirrors to some degree the historical antagonism between the two clubs. Second, several Boixos Nois members began to identify closely with the hooliganism that was going on in other European countries. The Heysel disaster, on 29 May 1985, and attendant media coverage stimulated their identification with, and imitation of, British hooligan groups. As one Boixos Nois member recalled:

> We thought that Heysel was a reaction of the Italians to attacks by Liverpool fans. I remember watching that game on television. Cheering on the English hooligans and waving my Union Jack. Heysel certainly increased my awareness of hooliganism. And I loved it. Politically, however, the English do not interest me very much. I've been at Celtic in Glasgow. The religious backgrounds there, that is much closer to our affairs. (Personal interview, April 2004)

The widespread official and public concern over spectator behaviour in the aftermath of the Heysel disaster caused a sea change in the authorities' perception and treatment of Boixos Nois. The club and police sought to contain what they considered the growing problem of violence, missile throwing and vandalism. Police presence and searches were extended on the South Stand, a CCTV system was installed, opposing fans were segregated and, to prevent crushes, the South Stand was divided into eight different sectors by fences. For high-profile matches security measures were further extended, for example during the European Cup quarter final between FC Barcelona and Juventus, on 5 March 1986. A total of 800 police officers were deployed to contain the 5,000 Italian fans attending the match. During the match Boixos Nois members provoked the visiting supporters by displaying a banner with the text 'Thank you Liverpool for Juve's deaths', referring to the 32 Italian fans that died at the Heysel stadium the year before. The new security measures failed to prevent violent confrontations between Boixos Nois and Brigadas Blanquiazules. In the aftermath of a violent clash between the two groups on 12 October 1986, FC Barcelona director Eduard Combas admitted that security officers experienced serious problems in containing spectator violence inside the stadium.[2] Opposing supporters were not effectively segregated and young fans carried flag poles and wore belts that were later used as weapons. No arrests were made and none of the participants were identified, despite the comparatively large number of police officers at the match, almost twice the standard amount of 100 (*El País*, 14 December 1986).

The relationship between the club and Boixos Nois has been complex and inconsistent from the start. The identification of a large proportion of Boixos Nois members with left-wing Catalan nationalism and separatism contrasted with chairman Núñez's perceived dictatorial rule and reactionary beliefs: 'We could not understand that the club was led by a person whose behaviour and ideas go against everything the club stands for' (personal interview with former member of Boixos Nois, March 2004). The group repeatedly demanded the resignation of Núñez and openly defied the chairman through chants and banners. Núñez, on the other hand, considered the group's political activism and violence a threat to his authority. The young fans felt that their activities were being closely monitored by the chairman's plain-clothes 'safety guards'. These guards, popularly known as *los morenos* ('the browns'), allegedly carried out 'dirty work' for the chairman, such as the intimidation of electoral opponents and 'overcritical' journalists and the removal of anti-Núñez banners. The relationship between the club and Boixos Nois deteriorated in the late 1980s. Following a number of incidents inside the stadium the group was exiled to the upper tier of the South Stand, but this move merely enhanced the group's internal fragmentation. Boixos Nois divided into a variety of subgroups, notably Supporters Barça, Blaugranes Sud, Gamper Nois and Cèl·lules Blaugranes. The latter subgroup, many of whose founding members were related to the left-wing separatist organization Moviment de Defensa de la Terra (MDT), refused to abandon the lower tier. Meanwhile, incidents of missile throwing, vandalism and fighting continued both inside and outside the stadium.

In the late 1980s FC Barcelona also experienced the eruption of the skinhead subculture among young supporters. The skinheads, at first no more than 50, introduced a particular dress style as well as a new ideology, namely right-wing Catalan nationalism, gradually transforming the dominant ideology among Boixos Nois members from left-wing separatism into right-wing separatism. Many left-wing Boixos Nois members abandoned the group as the right-wing element became more dominant. By the early 1990s the group consisted of three categories: left-wing separatists, right-wing separatists and apolitical hooligans. Although this diversity occasionally caused intra-group conflict, for example between left-wing and right-wing subgroups, politically opposed factions united in anticipation of violent confrontation with rival fan groups with centralist beliefs, most notably Brigadas Blanquiazules and Ultras Sur. Over time, however, intra-group conflict became increasingly persistent and undermined the internal cohesion of Boixos Nois.

The skinheads copied the dress style of their British counterparts, notably the cropped hair, sta-prest trousers, Doctor Martens boots, Lonsdale and Fred Perry tops. References to the British skinhead scene were evident, for example the group's banner with the text 'Boixos Oi!' referring to the Oi! music originating from London's East End, which was becoming increasingly popular in Catalonia (Viñas, 2001: 90-93). The skinheads' fascination with the British music and hooligan scene was regularly expressed in the group's official fanzine *Bulldog*. Their political beliefs were in most cases not the result of ideological formation, but rather of osmosis and contacts with specific environments such as football matches and (skinhead) music concerts (Adán Revilla, 1998: 123; Casals, 1998: 72; Spaaij and Viñas, 2005a: 145). Their ideology was in many cases also inconsistent. As a former Boixos Nois member commented:

> There have been some remarkable transformations. Left-wing fans who transform into right-wing skinheads over night. I have photographs of people with swastikas who were left-wing separatists before. Some have even been in prison because of their alleged involvement in Terra Lluire [a left-wing revolutionary armed organization dissolved in 1995]. Those people's beliefs are very superficial. They merely follow changes in fashion. (Personal interview, April 2004)

But although many right-wing skinheads do not express a profound knowledge of National Socialism or (neo-)fascism, they identify with the values or actions closest to it. Their emphasis on aggressive masculinity and violence as a means for acquiring prestige among peers and intimidating outsiders has contributed to the escalation of football hooliganism at FC Barcelona. Moreover, members of Boixos Nois have regularly displayed Nazi symbols at football grounds and abused and assaulted those considered 'inferior' (i.e. ethnic minorities, homosexuals, transvestites, Jews) (Spaaij and Viñas, 2005a: 147; Viñas and Spaaij, 2006: 57-58). For example, on 6 October 1991 right-wing skinheads affiliated to Boixos Nois assassinated a transvestite and assaulted beggars in a park in Barcelona (*La Vanguardia*, 8 October 1991).

Overview of the emergence and early development of football hooliganism

The emergence of football hooliganism at FC Barcelona highlights the ways in which foreign cultural influences merge with local traditions and legacies. Young FC Barcelona supporters were heavily influenced by British, and to a lesser extent Italian, fan and youth cultures, elements of which were merged with local features (i.e. Barça's cultural heritage and the deep-seated political oppositions in Spanish football). Barcelona fans' fascination with and mimicry of British and Italian fan and youth subcultures was enhanced by the interaction with foreign fan groups during the 1982 World Cup and in European club competitions, as well as through media coverage of foreign fan cultures and incidents of hooliganism.

The emergence of football hooliganism at FC Barcelona also sheds light on sociological approaches to the subject. Taylor's (1971; 1971a) explanation of football hooliganism as the democratic response by working-class fans to changes in football cannot fully account for the manifestation of football hooliganism at FC Barcelona. The rise of Boixos Nois should principally be viewed as part of the segregation of the crowd by age, that is, of the increasing social distance between young and older supporters. The young fans criticized the passive and bourgeois attitudes of older supporters and sought to introduce a more active, progressive approach to football fandom. The involvement of some young supporters in football hooliganism increased from the mid-1980s onwards, principally as a result of the growing influence of the British hooligan and skinhead subcultures. In the following section, I will examine in detail the development of the militant youth groups and football hooliganism at FC Barcelona.

Fragmentation and crisis: the development of inter-group relations

Following an agreement with the club to control the violent elements within its ranks, in the 1990/91 season Boixos Nois returned to its original territory in the lower tier of the South Stand. A sizeable subgroup chose to remain in the upper tier. Sang Culé Cor Català (Barça Blood, Catalan Heart), founded in January 1991, aimed to improve the atmosphere in the upper tier and publicly distanced itself from the growing influence of neo-fascist and neo-Nazi tendencies within Boixos Nois. Although officially the group's only conditions were loyalty to the team and the Catalan cause, most group members sympathized with left-wing Catalanism. The group reached a maximum of 600 members and also supported FC Barcelona's other sporting teams, such as basketball, handball and indoor hockey. Sang Culé is widely known for its regular involvement in political demonstrations, aid campaigns and anti-racism (Strubell, 1998: 55; Spaaij and Viñas, 2005a: 159).

Sang Culé members generally oppose the use of physical violence at football matches and in other spheres of society, although some fans argue that 'at particular moments it may seem the best solution to problems' (*Torcida Antifeixista*, no. 0, September 1994). Some of the more militant affiliates differentiate between the different contexts of violence, arguing that while football hooliganism is a senseless activity, the use of violence in political conflict is legitimate at times: 'You can hit someone or throw a bottle, but you don't want to seriously injury someone. Risking your life for football makes no sense. For me, personally, politics is worth taking a step further in terms of the use of violence. That is my priority' (personal interview, April 2004). Occasionally, however, the different contexts of violence overlapped. For example, in April 1993 the anti-fascist skinhead and member of Boixos Nois' official section in Valencia Guillem Agulló was murdered by affiliates of the ultra group Yomus (Valencia CF). A week later, on 18 April, members of Yomus displayed a banner with the text 'Guillem jódete' ('Guillem fuck you') during a home match against Albacete. Although the murder was politically motivated rather than related to the football context, the following season left-wing FC Barcelona fans mobilized hundreds of people to confront Yomus in Valencia. The group consisted of Sang Culé members, anti-fascist Boixos Nois members and anti-fascists *de la calle* (i.e. those who were not related to any of the militant fan groups in football). Only the right-wing element within Boixos Nois refused to participate in the confrontation, causing a major schism in the group.

Two years before the creation of Sang Culé, another youth group was founded at the opposite end of the stadium. The fan group Almogàvers, named after fourteenth-century Catalan mercenaries who ransacked parts of Europe, sought to improve the atmosphere inside the stadium and to promote Barça as a dominant force in European football. Several of the groups founding members had travelled to Italy, Argentina and Britain and they imported elements of these foreign fan cultures into their own activities. The group emulated the constant vocal support of English and Argentinian crowds in combination with the giant choreographed displays of Italian ultras. Whereas Boixos Nois members overtly identified with football hooliganism, Almogàvers distinguished itself by its non-violent, apolitical fan model characterized by the organization of large, spectacular choreographed displays. The group's article of association prohibits the use of physical violence among its members. Both Almogàvers and Boixos Nois benefited from FC Barcelona's on-field successes in the early 1990s. Both groups had a maximum of 900 members and, during high-profile matches, both sections of the ground contained nearly 4,000 fans. At this stage, the relationship between the two groups was relatively respectful and pacified, despite their contrasting dispositions and activities. A healthy rivalry existed in terms of who could produce the most spectacular displays and attract the most fans to their groups, although Boixos Nois members tended to view Almogàvers as 'soft' and 'too apolitical for a club as FC Barcelona' (personal interviews, June 2006).

Despite the internal fragmentation of Boixos Nois and the gradually increasing controls and impositions, in the late 1980s and early 1990s the extent and seriousness of football hooliganism increased dramatically. This increase was signalled most obviously in the numerous encounters between members of Boixos

Nois and Brigadas Blanquiazules inside and outside football stadia. The latter group had evolved into a 'worthy' opponent with a widespread reputation for toughness:

> In the early days we travelled to Sarrià and took liberties. There was no resistance really. But this changed after a few years, when the Espanyol ultras started to fight back. People also started to carry knives. There was a much bigger risk in going there. (Personal interview with member of Boixos Nois, March 2004)

The growing competitive violence between Boixos Nois and Brigadas Blanquiazules was reflected in a number of violent incidents. On 3 September 1988 the two groups fought each other near the ground after a local derby that was marred by vandalism and missile throwing. On 1 December 1990, a 21-year-old Boixos Nois member was beaten and stabbed by an affiliate of Brigadas Blanquiazules at a bus stop in Barcelona. The perpetrator was sentenced to eighteen years in prison. The spiral of escalating violence culminated in the death of an Espanyol fan, on 13 January 1991. Five members of Boixos Nois launched a premeditated attack on 19-year-old Frédéric Rouquier and 16-year-old José María Arboleas, both affiliates of Brigadas Blanquiazules, after Espanyol's home match against Sporting Gijón. Rouquier died from stabbing wounds and Arboleas was seriously injured. The young man accused of murdering Rouquier was convicted to twenty years and ten months imprisonment, whereas two of his friends were sentenced to seventeen years in prison (*El Periódico*, 3 May 1994).

The murder of Rouquier generated unprecedented official and public concern over football hooliganism and was considered a low point in the history of the Spanish ultra subculture (*El País*, 15 January 1991; *El Periódico*, 24 February 1991). In reaction to the increasing police controls and media stigmatization in the aftermath of the incident, a group of right-wing skinheads heavily involved in football hooliganism eschewed their conspicuous appearance and adopted the casual style characteristic of British hooligans (see Chapter Three). The aim of this transformation was twofold. On the one hand, the skinheads sought to lower their profile in order to escape police observation and successfully challenge their opponents (*Super Hincha*, vol. 4, no. 37, November 1996: 4). On the other hand, the casual style was viewed by the hooligan as a status symbol distinguishing them from the less sophisticated appearance of the skinheads and the ultras.

The subgroup Casuals FCB, created in 1992 and consisting of 50 young men, was in the vanguard of this development. Group members prefer leisure clothing such as Umbro, Kappa and Adidas to their previous skinhead attire: 'We identify with the English hooligan movement, leaving aside the poofy Italian ultra. [...] We adopt an unusual sports attire to distinguish ourselves from the urban tribes' (*Casuals FCB*, no. 1, 1992: 1). Casuals later distanced itself from Boixos Nois, continuing as an autonomous faction. Paradoxically, despite their interest in circumventing official controls, group members regularly display a large banner with the group's name on it. Their key aim to fight opposing hooligan groups sits somewhat uneasily with their focus on public visibility and provocation. Casuals' reputation was reinforced in recent years by media reports on the group's neo-fascist tendencies and, in particular, its alleged ties with the British right-wing organization Combat 18 (*El País*, 23 January 2003; *Sport*, 23 January 2003; *El Triangle*, 7 January 1998). In the mid-1990s some notorious Espanyol hooligans joined the group after conflicts among members of Brigadas Blanquiazules (Seara Ruiz and Sedano Jiménez, 2001: 128; *Super Hincha*, vol. 10, no. 100, March 2002: 21-24).

Another fan group at FC Barcelona, Inter City Culé (ICC), was similarly influenced by developments in British football hooliganism. Created in the 1994/95 season by former members of Cèl·lules Blaugranes, ICC derives its name from West Ham United's Inter City Firm (ICF). ICC members viewed that hooligan confrontations had to be planned more carefully due to the growing police controls in and around football grounds. ICC members eschew the skinhead attire and the forms of dress and club emblems worn by non-hooligan supporters and regularly travel to away matches by train (*Super Hincha*, vol. 4, no. 37, November 1996: 4-5). The group is relatively small and close-knit and seeks to remain so in order to avoid intra-group conflict. The core of the group consists of fifteen men who have known each other for years, but for high-profile matches the formation can call on the services of up to 50 young men. Unlike their English peers, the ICC has a clear political tendency. Group members sympathize with left-wing separatism and they strongly oppose the fascism and racial discrimination of the right-wing element within Boixos Nois: 'Those people believe that one race is inferior to another. I think that's nonsense because race is not Catalonia's defining characteristic. I mean, both Catalonia and FC Barcelona have strong immigrant traditions. That's a historical fact. I don't believe in race categories, but in the Països Catalans, the Catalan territories' (personal interview, April 2004). One of the ICC's main objectives is to fight rival fan groups, especially those identifying with right-wing extremism. Its members embrace the 'original' hooligan spirit and condemn what they consider 'senseless violence':

> We consider ourselves hooligans, which means we only fight rival hooligans, people who are willing to engage in violent confrontation. I would never attack a father attending a football match with his son even if he happens to support Real Madrid. That makes no sense and is considered inappropriate. (Personal interview, April 2004)

The ICC's involvement in football hooliganism has decreased significantly in recent years. Most group members are well in their thirties. They have families and demanding careers and therefore less time to travel to away matches on a regular basis. The group does no longer actively seek violent confrontation with rival fan groups, but it continues to passionately support the team at home matches.

Grada Joven: the road to unity?

In the early 1990s FC Barcelona's militant fan groups and the local sports newspaper *El Mundo Deportivo* initiated a campaign to integrate the different groups into a Grada Joven (Youth Terrace). Some club officials perceived the ritualized aggression and violence of the young fans as a threat to public order and were afraid that the fan groups would turn against chairman Núñez collectively. These objections thwarted the fruitful co-operation between the club and the young fans. The club eventually agreed to designate the lower tier of the North Stand, which was converted to 1,000 seats in accordance with UEFA regulations, to the club's youth groups. Leaders of the fan groups strongly disapproved with the limited space since together they had nearly 2,000 members. In their view, the club violated prior agreements to create space for 4,000 supporters. They nevertheless agreed to

298

participate in the project. The basis of the Grada Joven project was a written agreement between the different groups, which prohibited the collective expression of (left-wing and right-wing) political ideologies inside the stadium, because this was seen as undermining inter-group and intra-group relations. At the same time, Boixos Nois attempted to improve its public profile and internal social control by converting into an official *penya*, stressing that it had successfully eliminated the 'senseless violence' of some of its members (*Mundo Deportivo*, 22 August 1995: 18).

The Grada Joven integrated four autonomous fan groups with diverging dispositions: Boixos Nois, Almogàvers, Sang Culé and Unibarçataris.[3] Boixos Nois members considered their group as the only genuine militant fan group in terms of seniority, reputation and toughness. Members of the other groups generally opposed to what they considered the 'senseless' football hooliganism of Boixos Nois. As a member of Unibarçataris commented:

> We have to fight the false idea that the most loyal young supporter is the one who most violently defends the colours of his team, who is the most aggressive and provocative [...], who is the toughest and most dangerous [...] There are no reasons that justify violence against a youth merely because he supports a different team. Those who do not think like this are a cancer to football and to society (*Quicir*, no. 9, March 1995: 8).

Although group leaders explicitly sought to prevent inter-group and intra-group conflict, the relations between the different groups gradually deteriorated. *Protagonismo* (power struggle) and political antagonism resulted in intimidation and violence. In 1997 Sang Culé abandoned the Grada Joven and moved to the upper tier of the South Stand. The remaining groups separated in 1999, with Boixos Nois staying in the North Stand and Almogàvers being forced to move to the South Stand.

The conflict within Barça's fan community escalated in 1997. On 20 December 1997, before a home match against Atlético Madrid, Boixos Nois wanted to celebrate a minute of silence in memory of a 26-year-old Boixos Nois member who died only days before. The man was convicted on multiple occasions for violent assault and other crimes (*La Vanguardia*, 23 December 1997; *El Mundo*, 24

299

December 1997; *El País*, 13 January 1998; *El Triangle*, 14 January 1998). In 1991 he featured in a Spanish television documentary on skinhead gangs. When asked by the interviewer if it would be a crime to murder a transvestite, he answered 'no' (*ABC*, 30 April 1996; *El País*, 27 March 1996). Boixos Nois threatened the club officials that if they refused to co-operate, the group would abandon its designated area and possibly provoke serious disorder. Although at first the club management refused to give in to the demand, it eventually agreed in order to avoid conflict escalation (*La Vanguardia*, 23 December 1997). Before the match, Boixos Nois displayed a large banner with the text 'Sergi, we will never forget you.' To express their disapproval with the club's permissiveness, a group of fans located in the upper tier of the South Stand whistled during the minute of silence and yelled 'Nazis get out of the Camp Nou.' Around 100 Boixos Nois members immediately abandoned their area of the ground in search of members of Sang Culé, who were held responsible for the defiant actions. The police and security staff failed to prevent the group from moving through the stadium and assaulting several supporters. Two fans had to be taken to hospital; one of them suffered a skull fracture.

In the aftermath of the incident Sang Culé announced its official dissolution. The group later re-emerged and currently has approximately 100 members, of which 40 per cent is female. An important part of Sang Culé, including the group's founding members, have created a new fan group called Dracs 1991. This group sympathizes with left-wing Catalan nationalism and explicitly opposes the use of violence. Dracs 1991 currently has 200 members and operates at FC Barcelona's other sporting teams, including basketball, handball, indoor hockey and indoor football. Neither Sang Culé nor Dracs 1991 attend football matches collectively due to the intense inter-group conflicts in recent years, although some group members visit the Camp Nou on an individual basis.

The incident which occurred on 20 December 1997 generated extensive commentary on the perceived flaws in FC Barcelona's security regime. Chairman Núñez was heavily criticized for devoting more time to honouring a convicted hooligan than to the commemoration of one of the club's founding fathers, former chairman Josep Sunyol, who was murdered by Falangist soldiers in 1936 (*El Periódico*, 14 November 1999; *El Triangle*, 14 January 1998). While club officials insisted that the disorder was merely an isolated incident, supporters claimed that they were regularly abused, intimidated and physically attacked by the hooligans (*Sport*, 11 November 2004; *El Periódico*, 1 September 1999; *El Triangle*, 7 January 1998; *El País*, 28 April 1999; *El Periódico*, 27 December 2003; *Sport*, 28 December 2003; *El 9*, 23 January 2003; *Mundo Deportivo*, 23 January 2003). Several supporters do not attend away matches anymore because of the hostile and aggressive atmosphere. As a member of a militant fan group commented:

> For the last eight years we haven't been able to advertise ourselves due to the climate of intimidation and violence. We have stopped recruiting new members and organizing publicity campaigns. We simply cannot operate in such a hostile environment. We haven't been able to travel to away matches as a group because there is always some sort of trouble. A few people go on a regular basis, but the atmosphere is hostile and cold. (Personal interview, March 2004)

The group Casuals FCB has been at the centre of recent conflicts within Barça's fan community, causing several long-standing Boixos Nois affiliates as well as members of other militant fan groups to abandon their groups. The group, most of whose members are in their twenties and thirties, has also been centrally involved in recent incidents of hooliganism, missile throwing and vandalism. FC Barcelona hooligans fought with Real Zaragoza fans after an away match in Zaragoza on 16 January 2000. In September 2002, Casuals and Boixos Nois members fought with hooligans of Club Bruges before a Champions League match at the Camp Nou. The hostility between the two groups was fuelled by the fact that the Belgian fans had damaged the away section of the stadium on a previous occasion. In the build-up to the match Belgian fans threatened Boixos Nois via telephone and the Internet. When two Boixos Nois members were insulted and pelted with bottles while approaching a bar where away fans were drinking, a fight erupted between 30 Belgian fans and a dozen Boixos Nois affiliates. Other Boixos Nois and Casuals members attacked the Bruges hooligans with sticks, bottles and knives. Five home fans were arrested, four of whom were released before kick-off (*Super Hincha*, vol. 11, no. 111, February 2003: 10-11; *El Periódico*, 23 January 2003).

On 18 January 2003, during a home match against Valencia, Casuals members provoked a number of serious incidents. Boixos Nois and Casuals protested against the club's decision to install segregation fences separating the group from the rest of the home crowd. The protest ended in the vandalism of walls, glass and toilets. Hooligans also assaulted security staff and journalists. The Catalan Secretary of Sport, who watched the game from the box seats, was hit by a can. A 28-year-old Casuals member was arrested for throwing a flare onto the pitch. He was already serving a ban for damaging a television camera inside the stadium (*La Vanguardia*, 23 January 2003; *El Periódico*, 1 February 2003; *El Periódico*, 21 January 2003).

The transformation of Boixos Nois from the late 1980s onwards had a major impact on the network of inter-group allegiances and rivalries. The group's historical friendship with militant fan groups in the Basque Country, based on their shared allegiance to left-wing separatism, has gradually transformed into fierce rivalry following a number of incidents provoked by right-wing FC Barcelona hooligans. For example, two Basque anti-fascist skinheads were assaulted by Boixos Nois members near the Camp Nou stadium after a match between FC Barcelona and Athletic Bilbao, on 29 January 1995. At the same time, left-wing Barça supporters still maintain close ties with Basque fan groups such as Herri Norte Taldea (Athletic Bilbao), Peña Mujika (Real Sociedad) and Indar Gorri (Osasuna). Furthermore, Boixos Nois' traditional friendship with Frente Atlético (Atlético Madrid), based on their hatred towards Real Madrid, has also diminished over time. The two groups officially ended their allegiance in the mid-1990s following a number of violent incidents (*Super Hincha*, vol. 4, no. 37, November 1996: 5). However, a recent court case against Casuals members reported on a 'connection between organized crime in Madrid and Barcelona that emerged from violent groups operating at football grounds.' One of the accused was an alleged member of both Casuals and Frente Atlético (*Sport*, 6 May 2004).

Overview of the escalation and crisis of football hooliganism

The case of FC Barcelona challenges to some extent the definition of football hooliganism proposed in this book. On the one hand, the regular involvement of a

302

number of young fans in violent confrontations with rival hooligan groups in Spain and Europe closely reflects this definition. Barcelona hooligans established violent rivalries with the ultra groups of Barça's historical rivals Espanyol and Real Madrid. Furthermore, the group sought to enhance its status in the hierarchy of hooligan oppositions by confronting several other fan groups, some of which were previously considered 'allies' based on shared political sympathies. On the other hand, FC Barcelona hooligans have also regularly intimidated and attacked Barça supporters. Inter-group and intra-group conflict came to a height in the second half of the 1990s as a result of the increased power struggle and political antagonism between and within militant fan groups. Many of the original Boixos Nois members abandoned the group due to their disapproval of the political tendencies and 'senseless' violence of a section of the group. Ongoing internal fragmentation resulted in the decline in size and activities of the group, while at the same time new groups and subgroups emerged with their own practices and dispositions. The Grada Joven project failed to successfully integrate these different groups and seems to have merely enhanced the inter-group and intra-group conflict within Barça's fan community. In the remainder of this chapter, I will examine the responses of the authorities to the perceived threat of violence at FC Barcelona.

'Zero tolerance': the transformation of FC Barcelona's security regime

As we have seen in the previous section, journalists and supporters have repeatedly criticized FC Barcelona's lack of commitment to containing or eradicating football hooliganism. According to one journalist:

> The board, security officials and police knew perfectly well who they [the hooligans] were and where they could be found […] but no one did anything to stop the escalating violence […] There exists a relationship between those in power and the most violent faction of Boixos Nois. It's like an unwritten pact, but they mutually support each other (*Mundo Deportivo*, 23 January 2003).

In January 2003, a group of *socis* protested against the club's permissiveness towards the violent behaviour of some Barça supporters (*El Periódico*, 21 January 2003; *La Vanguardia*, 23 January 2003; *El País*, 23 January 2003). Former chairmen Josep Lluís Núñez and Joan Gaspart were believed to maintain close relations with some of Boixos Nois' and Casuals' most radical members. Gaspart has publicly expressed his sympathies for Boixos Nois on various occasions, claiming that he would join the group as soon as he resigned as chairman (*El Periódico*, 23 January 2003; *El Mundo*, 10 October 2003; *Avui*, 24 June 1987). He also possesses group membership card number one since the group's conversion into an official fan club. Boixos Nois members are therefore occasionally referred to as 'the chairman's boys' (*El Periódico*, 23 January 2003).

Although the club attempted to contain hooligan violence inside the stadium through the introduction of several security measures, in the 1990s and early 2000s the dominant informal policy was one of co-optation and facilitation. The club facilitated Boixos Nois storage space inside the stadium to store banners and flags, but the group also allegedly kept objects such as sticks and iron bars (*La Vanguardia*, 26 February 2004; *Diario As*, 22 April 2005). The club also facilitated free and reduced price tickets to members of Boixos Nois and Casuals, allowing several group members to enter the stadium without paying (*El Triangle*, 7 January 1998; *El Periódico*, 3 May 2002; *El Periódico*, 21 January 2003; *Avui*, 23 January 2003; Burns, 1999: 34-35). Group members habitually sold part of the tickets to finance the activities (personal interviews with Boixos Nois members, 2004; *El Periódico*, 26 February 2004). Notorious hooligans travelled to away matches with the team and stayed in the same hotel on more than one occasion. These travels were reportedly paid for by the club and supervised by the club's deputy security officer (*El País*, 30 August 1999; *El Periódico*, 29 January 2002; *El Periódico*, 26 February 2004; *Sport*, 26 February 2004). Club officials have also employed notorious hooligans in their private businesses, notably as security staff in private parkings. In return, Boixos Nois members publicly supported Núñez and Gaspart during club elections, occasionally intimidated electoral opponents and their supporters, and promised to refrain from violent activity inside the stadium. For example, during the elections of December 2000, Boixos Nois affiliates sought to assault electoral candidate Lluís Bassat, who was granted police protection (*Avui*, 24 July 2000; Seara Ruiz and Sedano Jiménez, 2001: 129).

In response to the growing demand for appropriate action against the violent elements within Barça's fan community, in the early 2000s FC Barcelona extended and specialized its security regime. In January 2003 the club announced the introduction of new security measures with a total cost of over two million euros (*El Periódico*, 16 January 2003). With the new measures the club intended to prevent incidents such as the missile throwing during a home match against Real Madrid on 22 November 2002. On that occasion, the Spanish football federation (RFEF) had ordered FC Barcelona to play two matches behind closed doors (a punishment that has yet to be implemented). The club installed glass walls to isolate the lower tier of the North Stand and the South Stand from the rest of the stadium, despite the government's strong opposition to the plan because of the risk of crushes.

The isolation of Boixos Nois inside the stadium did not result in a marked decline in violence. On 22 August 2003, three members of Casuals assaulted two Moroccan men inside the stadium during a friendly match against the Argentinian team Boca Juniors. Both victims needed medical treatment (*El Periódico*, 5 September 2003; *El País*, 5 September 2003). The three men arrested for the attack had an ample criminal record, including public disorder, robbery and drug trade. One of them, a 31-year-old male, was previously sentenced to 18 years in prison for his role in the assassination of Espanyol fan Frédéric Rouquier in 1991. He was released in November 2002 (*Avui*, 5 September 2003; *El País*, 5 September 2003; *El Periódico*, 6 September 2003). In October 2003, police arrested a member of Casuals suspected of being involved in a failed kidnapping attempt. The 32-year-old male was allegedly part of a criminal organization. His criminal record included drug trade, extortion, violent disorder and robbery. According to senior police officers, the man's criminal history 'reflects to perfection the profile of the majority of Casuals members' (*Avui*, 24 October 2003; personal interviews with senior police officers, 2004).

Joan Laporta's victory in the 2003 club elections marked a sea change in the club's security regime. A central issue in Laporta's electoral campaign was the urgent need to eradicate spectator violence. An estimated 90 per cent of the *socis* supported the zero tolerance policy introduced by the new club management (*Sport*, 11 September 2003). Local and national media heightened the profile of the campaign by stressing the urgency of the problem (e.g. *La Vanguardia*, 23 October 2003; *Sport*, 31 October 2003; *Sport*, 26 November 2003). FC Barcelona's zero tolerance policy consists of a number of security measures seeking to reduce the power and activities of Boixos Nois and Casuals inside the stadium. The club abolished all the privileges it traditionally facilitated, such as storage space, tickets, travel arrangements and money. The gates to the lower tier of the North Stand (gates 87, 88 and 89) are strictly controlled by police and security staff. Supporters are searched to prevent the introduction of illegal objects and need identification and a club membership card or season ticket to enter the area of the ground. These security measures contrast starkly with the club's lenient approach in previous years. As FC Barcelona's safety and security officer commented:

> For the first time the club has a very active anti-hooligan policy. Previous strategies were always temporary and never persistent. When Boixos Nois resisted, the measures were simply stalled. At present we are developing an unprecedented safety and security regime. When I started my position here there was no such thing as safety and security management. Of course there were people working on it, but no one made an effort to really reduce football hooliganism. And, as you know, all files on Boixos Nois members mysteriously disappeared. (Personal interview, May 2004)

Journalists estimated that at the first home game after the introduction of these new security measures only 20 Boixos Nois members were allowed into the stadium. Their habitual territory within the ground was therefore nearly empty (*El Periódico*, 31 October 2003; *Sport*, 31 October 2003). During the match Boixos Nois members repeatedly yelled: 'A real member stands outside.' During the rest of the season the situation remained virtually unchanged since on average only 50 Boixos Nois affiliates were given access to the territory. However, it is important to note that the group was already in decline during the period prior to the new security regime, principally due to intra-group conflicts and group members' overt identification with right-wing extremism. Furthermore, several Boixos Nois members have moved to other sections of the ground to circumvent the pervasive controls and impositions.

Conflict between the new club management and Boixos Nois surfaced from the moment Laporta was elected as chairman. On 22 August 2003, Laporta announced that Boixos Nois blackmailed the club: 'For fifteen days they have been asking us for money and tickets, but we will not give in' (*El Periódico*, 23 August 2003). When asked why the group would do such a thing, Laporta answered: 'It's because they always got what they wanted in the past' (NPS, 2005) On its official website Boixos Nois denied the allegations and called Laporta a liar. Group members have repeatedly protested against the club's new security regime. The group announced on its website that it would refrain from vocally supporting the team as long as its members were denied access to the stadium. During a home match against Valencia, on 5 October 2003, group members abandoned their territory and displayed a banner with the text 'This is the terrace you want', referring to the lack of atmosphere at the Camp Nou. The fans also continuously abused the chairman with chants such as 'Laporta, son of a bitch, you will not throw us out' and 'Laporta incompetent, Núñez president', which can be heard at virtually every home and away match of FC Barcelona. Boixos Nois and Casuals members have also threatened Laporta with intimidating graffiti messages, some of which at the chairman's family home (*El Periódico*, 14 November 2003; *El Periódico*, 9 September 2003; *El Periódico*, 6 December 2003).

In February 2004, a court case against members of a criminal organization involved in drug trade, extortion and kidnapping revealed that they had been offered money (reportedly 30,000 euros) to assault Laporta. Seven suspects were alleged members of Casuals. The money was presumably offered by the club's former deputy security officer who, during the command of Núñez and Gaspart, had the task of controlling Boixos Nois. These accusations have strengthened club officials' belief that the hooligans pose a serious threat to the club's and fans' well-being:

> Until we started our current policy Boixos Nois and Casuals had some very exclusive privileges which no other *penya* had. That has grown over the years. The radical core is no fan group, but has developed into a delinquent group involved in drug and weapon trade. We are not merely talking about

fights or flares. No, these people have accepted money for assaulting the chairman [...] The exclusive privileges are over now. That is a major loss for group members and therefore they resist and intimidate us. (Personal interview with FC Barcelona director, March 2004)

FC Barcelona's zero tolerance policy is supported by governing bodies and football representatives throughout Spain. The club attempts to spur on other clubs to adopt a similar policy. Club officials have hosted conferences and seminars to disseminate knowledge on the prevention of football hooliganism. The two league matches against Deportivo La Coruña in the 2003/04 season were used to commemorate the death of Deportivo fan Manuel Ríos Suárez (see Chapter Three). Before the match at the Camp Nou the two teams displayed a banner with the text 'No to violence'. FC Barcelona also created a 'wall against violence' near the ground. Hundreds of fans and tourists signed the wall, but so did Boixos Nois members spraying the wall with graffiti.

Despite the praise and support FC Barcelona's zero tolerance policy has received, the club's security regime has a number of important secondary effects. First, the containment and reduction of football hooliganism is limited to the stadium and to home matches only. Violent incidents continue to take place outside the stadium, albeit less frequently than in the past. Casuals and Boixos Nois members usually drink in bars near the Camp Nou and in this area they regularly challenge or attack rival supporters, despite police presence. Away matches also remain a major site for inter-group confrontation, including the intimidation and assault of other FC Barcelona supporters. Boixos Nois and Casuals members regularly abuse or threaten FC Barcelona supporters and steal their banners, flags or drums. They occasionally pelt them with bottles and other objects and physically confront them. They also seek to confront opposing fans or try to gain access to the stadium without paying, for example by intimidating or assaulting security staff (personal observations, 2004). Large-scale confrontations are nevertheless relatively uncommon due to two major reasons: increased police and security controls in and around football grounds, and the comparatively small number of group members regularly attending home and away matches compared to the 1980s and 1990s. Occasionally, however, FC Barcelona hooligans succeed in escaping police observation in order to confront opposing fans. For example, on 17 August 2006 a group of around 100 FC Barcelona hooligans launched a premeditated attack on young supporters of Espanyol near the Olympic Stadium, two hours before the kick-off of the Super Cup match between the two teams. They were armed with bricks, sticks, baseball bats and knives. Ten hooligans were arrested.

Second, although Joan Laporta initially emphasized that the club would distinguish between 'violent' and 'non-violent' fans within Boixos Nois and other militant fan groups (*La Vanguardia*, 10 September 2003), in reality the club's commitment to eradicating spectator violence affects all group members. The failure to acknowledge the group's diversity has led to further polarization between the club and Boixos Nois. Although Boixos Nois and Casuals are essentially distinctive groups with partly diverging interests, they now increasingly protest collectively against the club management. In May 2004, the club banned the chairman of Boixos Nois, who was accused of verbal abuse and attempted assault on Laporta after a handball match on 14 February 2004 (*La Vanguardia*, 14 May 2004; *El Periódico*, 14 May 2005). The man was generally considered a 'non-violent person devastated by what has happened to his fan group' (personal interview with an FC Barcelona fan, May 2004; cf. *El País*, 8 February 1998). Some long-standing supporters argued that, rather than expelling him, the club should have used him as an intermediary between the moderate and more violent elements within Boixos Nois.

Other militant fan groups, notably Almogàvers and Sang Culé, have also suffered from the zero tolerance policy. They feel that the club misjudges their passionate yet non-violent approach to football fandom and disregards their positive social function within the fan community. Furthermore, they argue that the club has done little to protect them from being subjected to intimidation and violence, especially at away matches and outside the stadium. The club has not (yet) convened a meeting with leaders of these groups to discuss these issues. As the editor of a sports newspaper argued:

> The club reacts very strongly, but on the basis of insufficient information. I don't say good or bad, but there is a clear lack of information. Perhaps a different strategy would prove more effective. To start with, they should speak to all radical, non-violent fan groups, with their historical leaders and

309

representatives. I really don't understand why the club doesn't incorporate the non-violent fan groups. They are the future of the club's youth support and the key to the promotion of a pacified fan model. (Personal interview, May 2004)

Conclusion

The escalation and persistence of football hooliganism at FC Barcelona can in part be explained by the historical lack of commitment on the part of the club to reduce spectator violence. The club's informal policy was long characterized by facilitation. Hooligans received various privileges, including tickets, storage space, travel arrangements and money. The police regularly complained about the club's reluctance to identify offenders. The relationship between club officials and hooligans also in part explains the nature of football hooliganism at FC Barcelona. Hooligan confrontations are relatively uncommon inside the stadium due to two factors. On the one hand, increased security and police controls limit the opportunities for collective violence within the ground. On the other hand, the privileges provided by the club have led to the (partial) displacement of violence. These privileges are part of an informal agreement between the club and hooligans to refrain from violence inside the ground in order not to damage the club's reputation. Club officials have repeatedly denied responsibility for incidents outside the stadium, arguing that these are beyond their control and the responsibility of the police. FC Barcelona's current security regime also has limited effect on violence outside the ground and at away matches. Increased police observation away from the stadium and at away matches has diminished but not eradicated the opportunities for violent confrontation.

The class composition of FC Barcelona's hooligan formation illustrates the temporal variability of football hooliganism. It also contradicts to some degree Dunning et al.'s (1988) explanation of football hooliganism as essentially a lower-working-class phenomenon. Boixos Nois has been characterized by its heterogeneous class composition, integrating young fans from a variety of social backgrounds, predominantly from the working class and middle class. From the late 1980s the group came to attract increasing numbers of young men from working-

310

class backgrounds. This development was principally caused by Boixos Nois' growing status in the hierarchy of hooligan oppositions. At the same time, the expansion of right-wing tendencies within the group led several left-wing fans, many of whom came from relatively middle-class backgrounds, to abandon the group. In the 1990s the group also attracted a number of young men from relatively 'troubled' backgrounds. These men grew up in a social environment in which the use of physical violence was part of everyday life. A percentage of these men were heavily involved in criminal activities outside the football context. The hooligan formation at FC Barcelona is nevertheless still characterized by its heterogeneous class composition and includes a significant proportion of relatively high educated 'middle-class' youths.

Another issue that is central to understanding football hooliganism at FC Barcelona is the role of politics in identity formation, closely reflecting the major fault line in contemporary Spanish society. Hooligans originally constructed their collective identity in relation to their club's historical rivals Real Madrid and Espanyol. In accordance with the cultural heritage of FC Barcelona, this identity was primarily constructed in terms of the contrasting political beliefs between self and the other, that is, left-wing Catalan separatism versus centralist 'fascism'. Hooligans also celebrated a hard masculine identity distinguishing them from the 'soft' and 'sissy' fan groups at the club. Over time, however, the collective identity of FC Barcelona hooligans became challenged by internal developments, most notably the rise of right-wing tendencies. Due to the growth of right-wing influences football hooliganism at FC Barcelona gradually became characterized by a high level of intra-group and inter-group conflict, resulting in internal fragmentation and the decline in group membership. What we find in this case is that when subgroup differences (in political allegiance) become more and more emphasized, ingroup identity gradually breaks down and gives way to newly emerging oppositional identities, resulting in overt hostility and confrontation and, eventually, in the collapse of the hooligan formation and the rise of new fan identities. At the same time, a small group of fans continues to identify closely with football hooliganism, occasionally provoking serious violence.

Giulianotti has argued that the 'postmodern' epoch of football hooliganism 'is signalled most obviously by changes in its political and media treatment' (1999:

311

50). There are no signs of such changes at FC Barcelona. The current official and media concern over football hooliganism resembles in many respects the moral panic over skinhead hooligan violence in the early 1990s. I would argue instead that the shift from 'modern' to 'late modern' football hooliganism is signalled by two developments. First, although FC Barcelona hooligans have long been aware of the opportunities for making profit of their group's reputation (i.e. through the sale of membership cards, T-shirts, jumpers, flags, and so on), in recent years football hooliganism has become increasingly commodified. Boixos Nois members have discovered the Internet as a means for commercial activity, selling products such as clothing, videotapes and DVDs. Second, contemporary football hooliganism at FC Barcelona is characterized by a combination of inter-group and intra-group conflict which in part contradicts the definition of football hooliganism proposed in this book. Political antagonism and power struggles lie at the heart of the conflicts within Barça's fan community. These conflicts challenge the club's cultural heritage and popular image as a major symbol of Catalanism.

10

Club Cultures and Subcultures: Why Context Matters

Introduction

What are the overlaps and dissimilarities in the extent and nature of football hooliganism in different countries and at different football clubs? How can they be explained? Cross-cultural variations in football hooliganism are often ignored or explained away in terms of comforting stereotypes. In social science research, these variations are usually addressed only in the most general of terms. No systematic and detailed comparative research into football hooliganism has been produced. This study seeks to provide a sociological understanding of the phenomenon through a comparative analysis of football hooliganism in different national and local settings. It identifies patterns of similarity and difference in the extent and nature of, and responses to, football hooliganism in London, Rotterdam and Barcelona.

Football hooliganism is both relational and nested within the ritual and collective symbolism of each fan culture. Developing a deeper understanding of football hooliganism therefore not only requires analysis of the ways in which hooligan identities are produced and reproduced, but also of how locality is produced through patterns of ritual and cultural life. In this context, Appadurai (1999: 231) has suggested that locality 'is never an inert primitive or a given, which pre-exists whatever arrives from outside itself.' Locality 'has always had to be produced, maintained and nurtured deliberately.' The local is not a fact but a project (see also Gupta and Ferguson, 1997: 6). My approach reflects to some degree the findings of Back et al.'s (2001) research into racism in football. They argue that 'the football stadium provides one context in which local identity can be ritually defined, regardless of the changes taking place in its immediate environment and patterns of migration' (2001: 43). The fan cultures of particular football clubs share common ritual elements, but at the same time each fan culture exhibits distinct forms of prescribed formal ritual behaviour and symbolism.[1] Back and his colleagues conclude that the frequency, and to some extent the form, of the racism they

313

encountered at football grounds varied greatly between clubs. These differences can to some degree be understood, they argue, by appreciating the ways in which the various fan cultures either inhibit or facilitate the expression of particular styles of racism. In the remainder of this book I will show that their argument also applies to football hooliganism.

In the final chapters of this book I will analyze the four theoretical themes outlined in Chapter Two. In Chapter Eleven I will discuss the development of anti-hooligan policies and the interactions and negotiations between hooligans and law enforcers. Chapter Twelve focuses on the construction of hooligan identities and the attractions of the hooligan subculture. In the present chapter I will examine the role of societal fault lines in fuelling and contouring football hooliganism and the degree and forms of social organization involved in football hooliganism. This chapter is divided into three parts. In the first part, I examine the emergence and diffusion of football hooliganism in different national and local settings. I will show that important commonalities can be identified in the emergence and diffusion of the phenomenon, but also some specific variations which mirror the major fault lines of the three countries under consideration. The second part demonstrates the importance of national and local contexts for understanding football hooliganism. I argue that the precise nature and development of football hooliganism can only be fully understood within the context of particular local arenas, that is, within individual 'club cultures'. In these local arenas societal fault lines and wider developments in football culture interact with more specific elements co-shaping the manifestation of football hooliganism. In the final part of the chapter, I will analyze the social organization of football hooliganism in different national and local settings, emphasizing the importance of local context.

The emergence and diffusion of hooligan subcultures

Comparative analysis of football hooliganism in the three countries and at the six clubs under consideration reveals a number of general patterns regarding the emergence and diffusion of hooligan subcultures.[2] The first major cross-national commonality is that the emergence of football hooliganism involved a process rather than a sudden break with the past. The emergence of a hooligan subculture was preceded by the segregation of football crowds by age. Certain sections of football grounds gradually became the exclusive territory of groups of young fans to the exclusion of the older football citizenry (so-called 'youth ends', 'sides', *gradas* or *curvas*). These youth groups became increasingly competitive in terms of the defence and invasion of each other's territory. Several (sections of these) groups began to identify closely with the use of violence in inter-group rivalry.

Another resemblance is the importance of certain specific events on the subsequent development of the youth groups. In England, the 1966 World Cup had the twofold effect of attracting large numbers of young fans to the game and thus stimulating the growth of the youth groups, while, at the same time acting as a catalyst for the materializing of football hooliganism as a perceived social problem. In the Netherlands, the widely reported disorder during the 1974 UEFA Cup Final between Feyenoord and Tottenham Hotspur had a similar effect: it put the issue of football 'hooliganism' on the Dutch political agenda while, at the same time, it enhanced the interest of young Dutch supporters in English terrace culture and football hooliganism. The 1982 World Cup constituted a landmark in the development of youth groups in Spanish football, enhancing young fans' awareness of and admiration for British and Italian fan models. Furthermore, the Heysel disaster and its aftermath had a major impact on the development of official policies targeting football hooliganism in each of the three countries.

In addition to these cross-national resemblances, there are also some specific dissimilarities in the emergence and diffusion of football hooliganism in England, the Netherlands and Spain. One major dissimilarity is the differential time frame of the process. Football hooliganism in its contemporary sense emerged in England in the 1960s, in the Netherlands in the 1970s, and in Spain in the 1980s. The relatively late emergence of football hooliganism in Spain seems to be principally a consequence of the specific political situation in the country until the mid-1970s. Only from the mid-1970s, with the transition to democracy, did the awareness-knowledge of Spanish youths increase rapidly and did various foreign youth subcultures become available and visible in cities such as Madrid, Barcelona, Valencia and Seville.

How do these cross-national resemblances and dissimilarities relate to the emergence and diffusion of hooligan subcultures in local settings? A first commonality is the importance of certain specific events. Apart from the aforementioned national and international events, there are also local events that need to be taken into consideration. Examples of such events are the attacks by FC Barcelona hooligans on Espanyol fans in the early 1980s, which triggered the formation of a hooligan group at the latter club, and West Ham United's on-field successes in the mid-1960s, which attracted large numbers of young fans to the club.

On the basis of the local trajectories described in Chapters Four to Nine a more detailed understanding of the issue can be generated, eliciting contextual nuances in the emergence and diffusion of football hooliganism. Central to the process of emergence are five major developments:

1. Segregation of football crowds by age. Young supporters increasingly congregated in groups and began to form an autonomous social category within the ground.

2. Emergence of youth groups with their exclusive territory and own tastes and practices. Groups of young fans began to congregate in a particular area of the ground, usually in the cheaper sections directly behind one of the goals. This area was increasingly considered their exclusive territory to the exclusion of the older football citizenry. The groups developed their own repertoires and rituals, such as in chants, symbols and insults.

3. Emergent rivalry between opposing groups of young fans. Competition between rival fan groups increased as they attempted to offer the most intensive support.

4. Specific territorial claims on ground space. Territoriality became a key component in the interaction between opposing groups of young fans. 'Taking' and defending one's territory inside the stadium became a major focus for these groups.

5. Growing commitment to securing collective and individual reputations for toughness. The focus on territoriality resulted in young fans' growing commitment to physically confronting opposing groups and gaining status among peers. Thus a 'game' on the terraces emerged, parallel to the match on the pitch. Or, as Farin and Hauswald (1998) call it, *eine dritte Halbzeit* (a third half).

One important qualification needs to be made with regard to these developments. The emergence of football hooliganism at Espanyol in the mid-1980s was characterized by a sixth development: differentiation of the youth group in terms of dispositions to competitive violence. The newly emerging ultra group Brigadas Blanquiazules not only sought to distinguish itself from the older football citizenry and from opposing hooligan groups, but also from the comparatively pacified nature of the established youth group Peña Juvenil. Although the vast majority of ultras originated from this group, they now increasingly referred to affiliates of the youth group as 'softies' lacking the *cojones* ('balls') of the 'real' ultras.

But although in the case of Espanyol this sixth development was more visible and explicit than at the other clubs, I would argue that in all cases some degree of symbolic opposition between hooligan formations and the larger youth groups from which they originated was present. In this context, it is important to reiterate that only a section of the youth groups regularly engaged in violent confrontation. Typically, during fights, non-participants caught in the midst of proceedings would back away (cf. Giulianotti and Armstrong, 2002: 222). It seems that as a result of processes of distinction, increased surveillance and segregation within the ground, the displacement of football hooliganism and the relocation of fan groups, hooligan formations have gradually become more symbolically (and often physically) separated from the general youth support, developing a kind of elite self-conception.

Channels of transnational and national diffusion

Two major channels of transnational and national diffusion can be distinguished. First, mass media channels are often a rapid and effective means to create 'awareness-knowledge', that is, to inform an audience of potential adopters about the existence of an innovation (Rogers, 1983: 17). Mass media channels are all those means of transmitting messages that involve a mass medium, such as television, newspapers, the Internet, and so on, which enable a source of one or a few individuals to reach an audience of many. Media coverage of fighting at football matches contributed to: (i) the view of football grounds as places where fighting

317

could be engaged in; (ii) increased imitation and competition between opposing youth groups; and (iii) the social construction of football hooliganism as a disturbing social problem. In Spain and in the Netherlands, early media coverage of football hooliganism principally focused on the 'English disease' and, to a lesser degree, on developments on the Continent. English media coverage, on the other hand, primarily zoomed in on domestic incidents and very occasionally on Latin American crowd disorder. This difference in early media focus can be explained by the fact that the hooligan subculture in English football emerged significantly earlier than in the other two countries.

Second, the diffusion of football hooliganism took place through interpersonal channels. These interpersonal channels involved 'face-to-face exchange in persuading an individual to adopt a new idea, especially if the interpersonal channel links two or more individuals who are near-peers' (Rogers, 1983: 18). Thus, a key aspect of the diffusion of football hooliganism is the direct observation of, and interaction with other, more prestigiously perceived fan groups. The style and practices of English hooligan formations were viewed by several Spanish and Dutch young fans as more prestigious and rewarding than native forms of football fandom. Spanish youth groups were also heavily influenced by the Italian ultra subculture, from which they copied the large choreographed displays and certain modes of organization (i.e. membership cards, the division of labour). Interaction with foreign fan groups took place in the context of friendly matches, European club competitions and international tournaments. Another important component of this early transnational interaction was the rise of the fan or hooligan tourist. Several Dutch and Spanish fans made trips to England to experience English terrace culture, elements of which were imported into their own styles of support, including names, symbols and rituals. Inter-group interaction also seems to have been a major factor in the national diffusion of football hooliganism. The growing reputation and misbehaviour of certain domestic hooligan groups triggered the rapid expansion of the hooligan subculture within each of the three countries. Fan groups with an early notoriety functioned as a yardstick by which the newly emerging hooligan groups measured their own activities.

Although these two channels of diffusion were central to the emergence and diffusion at the six clubs under consideration, there are also significant local and intra-city variations. With regard to the influence of media coverage, a distinction should be made between, on the one hand, the two London clubs and, on the other hand, the Rotterdam and Barcelona clubs. English media coverage of foreign incidents of spectator violence was relatively limited in the 1960s and does not seem to have had a significant impact on the emergence of football hooliganism at West Ham United or Fulham. At the four continental clubs, growing television and press coverage of British and European football matches increased young supporters' consciousness of foreign football cultures and attendant youth subcultures. Whereas Feyenoord and Sparta supporters principally focused their attention on English terrace culture, young FC Barcelona supporters introduced several elements of British as well as Italian fan cultures into their own forms of support. Espanyol ultras were primarily influenced by the Italian ultra movement and the English skinhead subculture.

Interestingly, the case of Sparta shows that the introduction of elements of foreign terrace culture (names, symbols, rituals) did not automatically lead to the adoption of a hooligan style. Young Sparta fans constructed their own fan practices in relation to the 'hooligan other', explicitly rejecting such type of activity. The actual attractiveness of the hooligan subculture on newly emerging youth groups, such as Sparta's Castle Side, seems to have principally depended on fans' specific perceptions of self and the other, that is, on the perceived prestige of the hooligan image and on the degree of congruence between this hooligan image and supporters' habitus and collective fan identity.

Comparable local variations can be observed in the transnational diffusion of football hooliganism through direct observation and interaction. Only at three of the six football clubs – Feyenoord, FC Barcelona and Espanyol – did interaction with foreign hooligan and fan groups play a significant role in the emergence of football hooliganism. The disorder during the 1974 UEFA Cup Final strengthened the identification of several young Feyenoord fans with the hooligan style. Young Espanyol and Barcelona fans' fascination with, and mimicry of, British and Italian fan and youth subcultures was intensified through interaction with foreign fan groups during the 1982 World Cup and in European club competitions. At the other football clubs direct interaction with opposing fan groups was largely limited to domestic leagues.

Media coverage and direct interaction were also the two main channels of national diffusion of football hooliganism, albeit to varying degrees. At West Ham United and Fulham, attempts by visiting supporters to 'take' the home end stimulated local groups of young fans to defend their territory both symbolically and physically, and to increasingly go out and try to invade the turf of opposing groups. Media portrayal of football grounds as places where fighting could be engaged in seems to have attracted increasing numbers of young fans eager to 'make a name' for themselves on the terraces. This process of self-selection was particularly evident at West Ham, while in West London most prospective practitioners did not gravitate towards Fulham, but rather towards the more notorious youth group at Chelsea.

Spanish media reporting on domestic incidents of football hooliganism was still very limited at the time when the hooligan subculture first emerged in Barcelona, in the first half of the 1980s. Although not directly influencing the emergence of football hooliganism, media coverage had a twofold effect on the early development of the phenomenon at FC Barcelona and Espanyol. On the one hand, it amplified the reputations of the two hooligan groups, thereby intensifying the inter-group rivalry and drawing more prospective practitioners to the groups. On the other hand, it contributed to the defining of football hooliganism as a growing social problem that required immediate action, urging the football and government authorities to take appropriate counter-measures. The latter development should also be viewed within the context of the aftermath of the Heysel stadium disaster. An important intra-city dissimilarity is that, unlike the situation at FC Barcelona, the materializing of football hooliganism at Espanyol was strongly influenced by young fans' direct interaction with domestic fan groups. Football hooliganism at Espanyol emerged as a more or less direct response to the intimidation and violence provoked by young FC Barcelona fans during local derbies in the early 1980s.

Striking intra-city dissimilarities in the channels of national diffusion can also be found in Rotterdam. The emergence of a hooligan subculture at Feyenoord, in the mid-1970s, was not so much precipitated by media coverage of domestic hooligan incidents. Feyenoord's hooligan group can be viewed as 'early adopters' of the hooligan style in the Netherlands. Interaction with other major 'sides', notably FC Utrecht's Bunnikzijde, had a profound impact on the early development of the youth group, increasing inter-group rivalry and territorial identifications and, gradually, dispositions to competitive violence in the football context.

The emergence of football hooliganism at Sparta followed a very different trajectory. Two separate phases need to be distinguished. The first phase relates to the early diffusion of football hooliganism in the Netherlands, in the 1970s. During this period a comparable 'side' emerged at Sparta, but no hooligan formation was created. Despite, or perhaps due to, the omnipresence of media coverage and observations of notorious Dutch hooligan groups, young Sparta fans tended to perceive the hooligan style as non-prestigious and unattractive and, above all, as a symbol of the 'uncivilized other' (i.e. Feyenoord). In sum, while at Feyenoord the process of emergence involved the five aforementioned developments, at Sparta only the first three developments materialized in the 1970s. The second phase involves the emergence of a hooligan formation at Sparta in the late 1990s. The formation of this group contained a strong element of mimicry, as a small number of young fans began to imitate the style and practices of domestic and foreign hooligan formations, which were perceived as more prestigious than their own forms of fandom. Their awareness and knowledge of hooligan violence was stimulated by the Internet and media reports as well as through regular interaction with Dutch hooligan formations during home and away matches.

Key issues in the emergence and diffusion of hooligan subcultures

In this section, I have sought to show that a number of general aspects and developments can be identified in the emergence and diffusion of football hooliganism in different national and local settings. Table 10.1 summarizes these aspects and developments. Local hooligan subcultures can be categorized in terms of the degree to which fan groups were relatively earlier in adopting the hooligan style than fan groups at other clubs. Following Rogers (1983: 247-251), five categories of adoption are distinguished: innovators, early adopters, early majority, late majority, and laggards. The comparative case study presented in this book reveals a number of important issues regarding the emergence and diffusion of football hooliganism.

Table 10.1 Summary of the commonalities and differences in the transnational and national diffusion of football hooliganism.

Country/club	Category of adoption	Channels of diffusion
England	Innovators (1960s)	Emergence of a national network of inter-group rivalries and competitive violence. National diffusion through media coverage and interpersonal comunication.
West Ham United	Early adopters within England (mid-1960s)	Interaction with, and media coverage of, domestic hooligan formations. Key event: disorder provoked by Manchester United fans in 1967.
Fulham	Early adopters within England (mid-1960s)	Interaction with, and media coverage of, domestic hooligan formations. Key event: attacks by opposing fans in second half of 1960s.
Netherlands	Early adopters (mid-1970s)	Interaction with, and media coverage of, foreign and domestic hooligan formations. Key event: disorder provoked by Tottenham Hotspur fans in 1974.
Feyenoord	Early adopters within the Netherlands (mid-1970s)	Interaction with, and media coverage of, foreign and domestic hooligan formations. Key event: disorder provoked by Tottenham Hotspur fans in 1974.
Sparta	Laggards/ late majority within the Netherlands (late 1990s)	Interaction with domestic hooligan groups. Media coverage of domestic and foreign hooligan formations.
Spain	Late majority (early 1980s)	Media coverage of, and interaction with, foreign ultra and hooligan groups. Key event: 1982 World Cup.
Espanyol	Early majority within Spain (mid-1980s)	Interaction with domestic fan groups. Media coverage of foreign fan groups. Key event: disorder provoked by FC Barcelona fans in early 1980s.
FC Barcelona	Early adopters within Spain (early 1980s)	Media coverage of, and interaction with, foreign fan groups.

First, they shed new light on the applicability of sociological theories on the subject, in particular the work of Taylor (1971; 1971a) and Clarke (1976; 1978). Taylor's explanation of football hooliganism as the democratic response by working-class fans to changes in football seems to focus disproportionately on the bourgeoisification of the game as causing the eruption of the hooligan subculture. The emergence of football hooliganism can be viewed as a consequence of the segregation of football crowds by age and the rise of youth ends with their own cultural practices and tastes. In this context, Clarke's notion of youth subcultural styles is of particular interest (see also Hughson, 1997). He argued that youth subcultures, including football hooliganism, functioned as a symbolic attempt for young working-class males to resolve 'essential problems' in their lives. Although this explanation seems plausible for the early stages of the hooligan subculture in England and, to a lesser degree, in the Netherlands, the emergence of ultra and hooligan formations in Spanish football was more closely related to the political transition of Spanish society in the late 1970s and early 1980s (see Chapter Three; cf. Acosta and Rodríguez, 1989; Viñas, 2005). The ultra subculture functioned as a site for cultural and political contestation, as a symbolic attempt by young fans to create a space and identity of their own in a changing society. Thus, although the Spanish ultra subculture was heavily influenced by Italian and English fan and youth subcultures, these foreign influences merged with indigenous developments and features, creating a youth movement that met the specific needs of local male adolescents.

Second, although English hooligan formations provided, and to some degree still provide, the benchmark against which the newly emerging hooligan groups judged their performance, the adopting groups tended to merge the English hooligan style and other elements of English terrace culture and youth subcultures (e.g. the skinheads and mods) with their own distinctive cultural forms (see Chapter One; cf. Dunning et al., 2002: 223). Football hooliganism is thus essentially a glocal phenomenon. In this context, Rogers (1983: 17) has correctly argued that 'an innovation is not necessarily invariant during the process of its diffusion and adopting an innovation is not necessarily a passive role of just implementing a standard template of the new idea.' It is important to note that football hooliganism in Spain was also heavily influenced by the Italian ultra subculture, which added aspects of organization and choreography to the fan groups.

Third, once a hooligan subculture was established in the adopting country, its national diffusion depended principally on local practices and interactions.

Nationally, the hooligan style was initially transmitted by innovators and early adopters. Trips of increasing numbers of young football fans from the North of England to their team's away matches in the South, from the mid-1960s onwards, intensified the territorial concerns and social cohesion of youth groups in the South of the country. In the Netherlands, the four major sides played a key role in the national diffusion of football hooliganism in the second half of the 1970s. Their styles of support were increasingly copied by groups of young fans at football clubs in other parts of the country. In Spain, the militant fan groups Ultras Sur and Boixos Nois functioned as a yardstick by which the newly emerging fan groups measured their own activities. At the same time, however, we should be aware that the extent and persistence of hooligan subcultures vary considerably across localities, as I have shown in an earlier section.

Fourth, the absence or restricted availability of mass media channels may prevent or slow down the diffusion of football hooliganism. The relatively restricted availability of awareness-knowledge of foreign fan and youth subcultures during the last military dictatorship in Spain seems to be one of the key reasons why football hooliganism emerged significantly later in that country. This finding corresponds with studies of football hooliganism in Eastern Europe. The emergence of a hooligan subculture in Eastern Europe seems to have been delayed by the relative isolation, restricted media coverage and rigorous repression under the communist regimes (Duke and Slepička, 2002: 60; cf. Harsányi, 2005: 3).

In addition to these four general issues, the empirical data also highlight the importance of more subtle processes of diffusion, for example the spread of specific symbols, rituals and clothing styles. The diffusion of new stylistic elements takes place through ongoing processes of distinction and imitation within and between hooligan formations. The diffusion of (elements of) the hooligan subculture should be viewed as a dynamic and relational process involving 'centrifugal as well as centripetal directions of transmissions (spreading from core to periphery and vice versa), top-down as well as bottom-up adoption processes, and creative reinvention' (Chabot and Duyvendak, 2002: 728).

One of the main conclusions that arise from comparative analysis of the emergence and diffusion of football hooliganism is that, on the Continent, football hooliganism underwent a process of cultural creolization as indigenous fan groups merged the adopted patterns with their own distinctive cultural forms. Although the hooligan and skinhead subcultures were initially typical English working-class youth subcultures, their transnational diffusion meant that they were reinterpreted to fit local needs and traditions, in some cases independent of their original class context. Striking examples of this glocalization can be found at the two Catalan clubs, where the skinhead and hooligan subcultures attracted large numbers of young middle-class fans who merged these foreign styles with political extremism. The process of glocalization is crucial to understanding national variations in the nature of football hooliganism and can to some degree be explained by the concept of fault lines. The fault lines of particular societies shape specific 'established-outsider figurations' in which intense ingroup bonds and correspondingly intense antagonisms towards outgroups are liable to develop (Dunning, 1999: 158).

The national fault lines outlined in Chapter Two co-shape local and intra-city fan and hooligan rivalries.[3] The centre-periphery cleavage in Spanish society is reflected, for example, in the contrapuntal identities of FC Barcelona and Real Madrid supporters and hooligans, and in the deep-seated local and political rivalry between FC Barcelona and Espanyol fans and hooligans. The expression of regional and (sub-)nationalist identities in Spanish society and football is also crucial to understanding the national network of inter-group alliances and rivalries in Spanish football hooliganism, which is predominantly based on political identity. Reflecting the strong sense of local and regional identity in contemporary Dutch society, the fierce hatred between Feyenoord and Ajax supporters and hooligans can in part be understood by the contrapuntal identities of the two cities these clubs represent. Furthermore, the rivalry between Feyenoord and Sparta supporters historically contains a strong element of class consciousness which continues to inform mutual perceptions and collective identities. The class cleavage in English society is reflected in the working-class nature of football hooliganism at West Ham United and, to a lesser extent, in the manifestation of football hooliganism at Fulham in the late 1960s and early 1970s (during this period most Fulham hooligans came from local working-class council estates).[4] One of the differences that these variable patterns may make, Dunning argues, is that certain fault lines as bases for football hooliganism may draw in more people from higher up the social scale. Examples of this kind can be found at FC Barcelona and Espanyol. The hooligan formations at these clubs are characterized by their heterogeneous class composition. Furthermore, the hooligan group at Sparta predominantly consists of comparatively highly educated, middle-class males.

Although the concept of fault lines constitutes a convenient point of departure for generating a deeper understanding of football hooliganism as a transnational phenomenon, it is not without its problems. One of the main dilemmas is how to account for local and temporal variations in the social backgrounds of football hooligans. A striking example of this dilemma is the difference in the social backgrounds of Feyenoord and Sparta hooligans, and to a lesser extent of Espanyol and FC Barcelona hooligans, as I will show in the following section (see also Table 10.2). A more specific analysis of the complex social, historical and cultural factors that shape local manifestations of football hooliganism is needed to fully grasp these intra-city variations.

Additionally, the concept of fault lines seems to focus almost exclusively on variations in the *nature* of football hooliganism, largely neglecting important differences in the *extent* of the phenomenon. The latter issue is important because, as we have seen, not every country or club is equally affected by football hooliganism. The comparatively lower frequency of hooligan confrontations in Spanish football can to some degree be explained by the politicized nature of the game, but in an indirect and complex way, that is, through an examination of the evolution of the ultra subculture in Spain and its emphasis on public visibility and political allegiance. Moreover, analysis of the contemporary extent of the hooligan subculture in Spanish football should take into consideration the popularity and prestige among young fans of the alternative fan model developed by the more pacified ultra groups, which challenges the hard masculine identity of the hooligans. Another difference is the deterrent effect of the longer travel distances to away matches in Spain, especially since most matches are played on Sunday afternoon or on weekdays. Apart from local and regional derbies and high-profile matches (e.g. a cup final or a

European Cup match), the number of visiting supporters and hooligans is generally comparatively small. A consequence of the comparatively small number of away fans is that the 'other' is less frequently physically present, limiting the opportunities for enacting hooligan rivalries. In the following section, I will examine in more detail local and national variations in the extent and nature of football hooliganism.

The extent and nature of football hooliganism: national and local contexts

Before analyzing the extent and nature of football hooliganism in different local settings, I will first outline the main resemblances and dissimilarities in football hooliganism at a national level. Two major patterns can be identified in the present-day extent of football hooliganism in England, the Netherlands and Spain.[5]

The first major development is that contemporary hooligan confrontations tend to be relatively small-scale in terms of the number of participants, but may still cause serious damage or injuries and, very occasionally, fatalities. In each of the three countries the number of regular participants in football hooliganism, so-called 'hard-core' hooligans, has somewhat diminished. Most long-standing hooligan groups have fewer core members than in the past, especially in England and Spain. The number and size of self-identifying hooligan groups in Spanish football – as opposed to the numerous relatively pacified ultra groups – are comparatively small. At the same time, however, each of the three countries has experienced the emergence of new generations of young male fans becoming involved in football hooliganism, sometimes as separate 'youth cores'. In the Netherlands, a gradual shift has taken place from a situation in which a small number of quantitatively large hooligan groups dominated the hooligan scene, to a more heterogeneous and fragmented pattern in which several larger and smaller groups engage in competitive violence.

The second development is that mass confrontations between rival hooligan groups inside the stadium have generally become less common, mainly as a consequence of the reduced opportunities for fighting within the ground. Nevertheless, collective violence and, in particular, relatively small-scale hooligan encounters occasionally take place within the premises of the stadium. Hooligan encounters outside the ground are relatively common in England and the

327

Netherlands, but a major difference is that, in the Netherlands, the number of quantitatively large hooligan formations is comparatively limited.[6] Hooligan confrontations in Spain, inside the stadium as well as away from the ground, are less common, especially from the mid-1990s onwards, but have by no means disappeared. Key reasons for the general decline in Spanish football hooliganism from the mid-1990s are the transformations in the ultra subculture, the increased containment and surveillance in and around football grounds, and the relatively small number of away fans at most football matches in Spain.

The comparatively low level of football hooliganism in Spain requires an additional explanation. Part of the dissimilar nature of Spanish football hooliganism lies in the availability and the prestige of the ultra subculture among young fans. Although the two fan models are closely related – the hooligan cores in Spanish football tend to be located within or on the fringes of much larger ultra groups – their basic meanings are different. As I have argued in Chapter One, ultra groups are primarily concerned with providing colourful and vocal support to the team and their dispositions to violence vary. Collective reputations are secured through public visibility and the organization of large choreographed displays. In addition, sections of several ultra groups consider physical violence against local or political rivals to be legitimate or rewarding. Only a small minority of their members can be defined as hooligans in that they actively seek violent confrontation with opposing hooligan formations. Importantly, many of the more pacified ultra groups explicitly oppose the use of violence in inter-group rivalries, thereby contesting the hooligan identity. Members of these groups are socialized into a subculture in which hard masculinity is less appreciated than constructive fanaticism (i.e. the preparation of choreographed displays, participation in the organization of the group, active fandom). These groups also tend to have a comparatively large number of female members.[7]

A third general commonality is that hooligans do not merely fight rival hooligans, but may also engage in other types of violence, ranging from damage to property to violence against police officers. Of particular interest in a comparative context is the diverging level of intra-group conflict and violence between fan groups of one football club. Both intra-group conflict and violence between fan groups of one football club are comparatively common in Spain. A major increase in these types of violence took place in the first half of the 1990s, due to the intense politicization of the Spanish ultra subculture and the rise of new fan groups challenging the hegemony of the established hooligan formations. Both types of violence are major elements of contemporary football hooliganism in Spain, even though in the past few years intra-group and inter-group conflicts have in many cases become somewhat less manifest. Some degree of intra-group conflict has also been present in English and Dutch football hooliganism, but generally to a lesser extent than in Spain. The comparatively high level of violence between fan groups of one football club in Spain can be explained by the fact that, unlike the situation in England and the Netherlands, most clubs have multiple (often politically opposed) militant fan groups on their terraces which may develop a deep-seated rivalry as part of their strive for status or to secure the privileges facilitated by their clubs (see Chapter Eleven). This type of violence is usually inflicted by hooligan formations on more pacified groups of young fans, but it may also take the form of inter-group fighting.

Related to the issue of violence against fan groups of the same club is another major cross-national dissimilarity: the politicized nature of the Spanish ultra and hooligan subculture. This key feature of Spanish football hooliganism closely reflects the dominant fault line in contemporary Spanish society. Many ultra and hooligan groups use political ideologies as key symbols of collective identity. This political element simultaneously stimulates – through the construction of exclusivist ingroup and outgroup identities based on political allegiance – and reduces inter-group violence. The explicit identification of several hooligan formations with right-wing or left-wing extremism means that they tend to focus on their public visibility rather than on developing strategies for escaping public and police observation, for example through adopting the casual style characteristic of English and Dutch hooligans. Their emphasis on public visibility and provocation provides opportunities for agents of social control to closely monitor their activities. Furthermore, some ultra groups have formed prolonged (yet fragile and negotiable) alliances based on shared political ideologies, reducing the conflict and violence between previously opposing groups.

329

In addition to resemblances and variations at a national level, important patterns of similarity and difference can be identified in the extent and nature of football hooliganism at different clubs within a single city, as is shown in Table 10.2. Football hooliganism at West Ham peaked in the 1970s and the first half of the 1980s, a period characterized by numerous violent confrontations and occasional fatalities. From the late 1980s onwards football hooliganism gradually diminished in terms of both the number of regular participants and the frequency of hooligan confrontations. Increased controls and punishments and the ageing of core group members, among other factors, seem to have played an important role in this decline. Recent incidents suggest that football hooliganism has not disappeared and that a reduced group of West Ham fans, including young recruits, continue to seek pleasurable emotional arousal through confrontations with opposing hooligan formations.

The persistent hooligan subculture at West Ham United contrasts with the relatively low level of football hooliganism at Fulham FC. Similar to its East London counterpart, in the second half of the 1960s Fulham witnessed the emergence of a group of young fans seeking violent confrontation with rival fan groups. But unlike the situation at West Ham, football hooliganism at Fulham remained a comparatively minor phenomenon in terms of the size and reputation of the hooligan group and the frequency and seriousness of hooligan confrontations. Importantly, the hooligan subculture at Fulham was also far less persistent. Football hooliganism at Fulham gradually diminished from the mid-1970s onwards, mainly due to the club's declining situation – falling attendances, mid-table position in Division Two – and the growing reputation of the hooligan group at neighbouring Chelsea FC. In recent periods there has been no comparable hooligan group actively seeking confrontation with opposing fans. Occasional incidents of inter-fan fighting have been spontaneous and usually responses to provocations or assaults by rival supporters.

Table 10.2   Summary of the similarities and differences in the extent and nature of football hooliganism.

Club	Extent*	Nature of hooligan violence	Size of hooligan group (core/periphery)**	Social composition of hooligan group (gender/age/ethnicity/class)
West Ham United	Medium in late 1960s High in 1970s and early 1980s	Relative shift from confrontations inside stadium to encounters away from ground.	150/400 until late 1980s	All male. Gradual shift in age structure, from 15-25 in late 1960s and 1970s, to 17-45 at present.
	Medium from late 1980s onwards	Gradual increase in levels of planning and co-ordination. Occasional violence against security staff, stewards or police, usually small-scale.	50/300 from 1990s	Mixed ethnic composition, but predominantly white. Predominantly working-class, though currently more heterogeneous than in the past.
Fulham	Low/medium in late 1960s and first half of 1970s	Decline in confrontations in and around the ground from mid-1970s.	50/100 until mid-1970s	All male; none at present. Age range was 15 to 25.
	Absent from 1980s onwards	No self-identifying hooligan formation at present. Occasional incidents of spectator violence are mostly spontaneous.	None from late 1970s	Predominantly white; none at present. Predominantly working-class; none at present.
Feyenoord	Medium from mid-1970s High in 1980s and 1990s	Relative shift from confrontations inside stadium to clashes away from ground, also on non-match days. Gradual increase in levels of planning and co-ordination, including pre-arranged confrontations.	150/400 until late 1990s	All male. Gradual shift in age structure, from 15-25 in 1970s and 1980s, to 15-45 at present. Mixed ethnic composition, but predominantly white. Predominantly working-class, though currently more heterogeneous than in the past.
	Medium from late 1990s onwards	Recent polarization between hooligans and the police, including intimidation and violence. Occasional violence against security staff and stewards, usually small-scale.	100/400 from late 1990s	
Sparta	Absent until late 1990s.	Emergence of hooligan group in late 1990s.	None until late 1990s	All male. Age range is 17 to 25. All white. Predominantly middle-class.
	Medium in late 1990s and early 2000s	Confrontations exclusively away from ground. Relatively high degree of planning and co-ordination, including pre-arranged confrontations.	15/50 from late 1990s	

331

Espanyol	High in second half of 1980s and early 1990s	Relative shift from confrontations inside stadium to encounters away from ground. Gradual increase in planning and co-ordination, but relatively low levels of planning and co-ordination at present.	100/300 until mid-1990s	All male. Gradual shift in age range, from 15-25 in 1980s and early 1990s, to 15-35 at present. All white.
	Medium in late 1990s	Medium intra-group and inter-group conflict within fan community from mid-1990s.	50/100 from late 1990s	Class composition was mixed but predominantly middle-class until early 1990s; currently heterogeneous.
	Low/medium in early 2000s	Recent polarization between hooligans and the police, including violent incidents. Occasional violence against security staff, stewards and journalists, usually small-scale.		
FC Barcelona	High in second half of 1980s and early 1990s	Relative shift from confrontations inside stadium to clashes away from ground. Gradual increase in planning and co-ordination, but relatively low levels of planning and co-ordination at present.	200/400 until late 1990s	All male. Gradual shift in age structure, from 15-25 in 1980s and early 1990s, to 15-35 at present.
	Medium in late 1990s and early 2000s	Serious intra-group and inter-group conflict within fan community from 1990s. Occasional violence against security staff, stewards and journalists, usually small-scale. Occasionally premeditated attacks on opposing fans.	50/100 from early 2000s	All white. Heterogeneous class composition.

Note:

*Measured in terms of the frequency and seriousness of hooligan confrontations.

** I use the categories 'core' and 'periphery' to differentiate between levels of commitment and participation. The core relates to regular participants (i.e. core group members), whereas the periphery concerns the maximum number of hooligans, for example for high-profile matches (including 'semi-retired' hooligans, followers, marginal participants).

I must stress that *it is extremely difficult to quantify hooligan membership due to the fluid boundaries of the hooligan subculture and the varying size of hooligan formations,* depending, among other factors, on hooligans' expectations and the intensity of inter-group rivalries. The numbers shown in this table should be viewed as rough estimates which serve to compare the extent and the development of the phenomenon in different local contexts. [9]

Similar intra-city variations can be found in the two Rotterdam cases. At Feyenoord, football hooliganism has been a persistent phenomenon since the mid-1970s. Although in recent years the frequency of hooligan confrontations has declined, hooligan encounters continue to occur. In contrast, the level of football hooliganism at Sparta has been comparatively low. Inter-group fighting has been relatively uncommon and when incidents occurred they usually involved spontaneous violence related to provocations by opposing fans, alcohol abuse or events on the pitch. Only as recently as the late 1990s did a self-identifying hooligan group emerge at the club, resulting in a marked increase in inter-fan fighting away from the ground. This recent development constitutes a major discontinuity in the history of spectator behaviour at the club, contradicting its popular image as a 'friendly' club. At the same time, it is important to stress that football hooliganism at Sparta has remained comparatively minor in terms of the number of regular participants (see Table 10.2).

Compared to the striking intra-city variations in the London and Rotterdam cases, football hooliganism at the two Barcelona clubs developed in a relatively uniform way. Football hooliganism at Espanyol and FC Barcelona culminated in the second half of the 1980s and the first half of the 1990s. The frequency of hooligan confrontations gradually diminished from the mid-1990s onwards due in part to internal transformations and increased controls and surveillance. During this period the manifestation of football hooliganism at the two clubs also grew increasingly dissimilar because of internal developments. Moreover, intra-group conflict and violence between fan groups of one club have been comparatively common at FC Barcelona and, to less extent, at Espanyol from the 1990s onwards, closely mirroring the general development of Spanish football hooliganism. The upsurge in this type of violence was closely related to the increased politicization of the ultra and hooligan subcultures and processes of internal fragmentation. Some degree of intra-group conflict can also be observed at West Ham United and Feyenoord, especially in the early phase of football hooliganism at these clubs. Intra-group conflict is uncommon at Sparta and Fulham.

A comparison of the number of regular participants in football hooliganism also reveals significant local and intra-city variations. An important trend is that, with the exception of the hooligan formation at Sparta, the number of regular participants has somewhat decreased over time. This decline is most evident at West

Ham United, Fulham, FC Barcelona and Espanyol (see Table 10.2). Intra-city variations in the number of core hooligans are particularly striking in Rotterdam and London. The hooligan formation at Feyenoord consists of approximately 100 core members, whereas the hooligan group at Sparta has only 15 core members. And while at Fulham no self-identifying hooligan group currently exists, the hooligan formation at West Ham United has gradually declined from 150 to around 50 core members. The hooligan formation at FC Barcelona was substantially larger historically than its equivalent at Espanyol, principally because of Barça's much larger fan base. Comparable variations can be identified in the social composition of hooligan groups.

The social composition of hooligan formations

The comparative case study presented in this book contains a wealth of empirical data on four classical sociological categories: gender, age, ethnicity and class. I will briefly indicate the main patterns of local and intra-city variation with regard to these four categories.

The *gender* of football hooligans is strikingly homogeneous, as is stressed by several scholars of football hooliganism (Dunning et al., 1988; Armstrong, 1998; Giulianotti, 1999; Alabarces, 2005). Hooligan formations consist almost exclusively of males. Although in each hooligan formation there are some female members in the periphery of the group, usually as partners of male members, their involvement in fighting is generally limited. This is also the case in Barcelona, even though the average percentage of women in the militant fan groups tends to be comparatively high (see note number four). In each of the six cases, football hooliganism is essentially a male practice and revolves around the construction of hard masculine identity. Through engaging in hooligan encounters male fans construct a notion of self based on physical prowess and hyperheterosexuality, distinguishing them from the 'non-males' and 'poofs'. Only in very exceptional cases is this hard masculinity identity 'granted' to women, although in those cases their identity is still constructed in relation to the male macho. Consider the following discussion between two Sparta hooligans:

G	We have never had any women in our group really.
B	Well, just one. Remember N?
G	True, but she was only there as the girlfriend of M, wasn't she?
B	But she was tougher than all of us. I used to see her beating up big blokes, you know. She wasn't afraid of anyone. I mean, look at all the hangers-on that run away even before the fight kicks off. She never did that.
G	You're right, but once M left the group we didn't see her anymore, did we? I mean, she was never a full member or anything.

Two major patterns can be identified in the *age structure* of hooligan formations. Football hooliganism emerged as, and continues to be, a predominantly juvenile phenomenon. The majority of core participants in football hooliganism is between 15 and 25 years old, as is shown in Table 10.2. This observation corresponds with previous findings (Marsh et al., 1978; Dunning et al., 1988; Armstrong, 1998). However, my research also indicates that the age structure of hooligan formations has broadened over the years and has come to include growing numbers of older participants. The changing age structure of hooligan groups is most evident at West Ham United and Feyenoord, where several core hooligans are in their thirties and forties. The main reason for this development is that a number of older hooligans continue to participate in football hooliganism, albeit many of them on a less frequent basis (i.e. as 'semi-retired' practitioners). A comparable development has taken place at Espanyol and FC Barcelona. While in the late 1980s and early 1990s the age of core participants in football hooliganism ranged from 15 to 25 years, the contemporary age structure is considerably wider, including a significant proportion of hooligans who are in their late twenties and early thirties.

Older hooligans have usually been involved in the group since their late teens or early twenties and are still attracted to the 'buzz' of football violence, despite important changes in other areas of their lives (i.e. marriage, children, job careers). In many cases their emotional attachment to hooligan violence was established during a period that is now perceived as the 'heydays' of football hooliganism at their clubs and in their countries. Many of the older hooligans are nostalgic about this period in which official controls and surveillance were less pervasive and large-scale hooligan confrontations were comparatively frequent. Furthermore, they tend to view today's young hooligans as increasingly alienated from the original hooligan ethos (i.e. using weapons, attacking non-hooligan supporters, less loyal to the team) (see Van der Torre and Spaaij, 2003; Spaaij, 2002). This romanticized view of their violent pasts corresponds with Foer's (2004: 89-114) description of 'the sentimental hooligan'. Importantly, an additional explanation for the involvement of older hooligans that has been neglected by scholars of football hooliganism are the financial interests and rewards attached to group membership. I will discuss this issue in Chapter Twelve.

Although the *ethnic composition* of hooligan formations varies considerably across localities, the vast majority of football hooligans at the six clubs are white. In some hooligan groups 'whiteness' is seen as a major distinguishing feature and a central source of collective identity, most notably at Espanyol and FC Barcelona. In these groups, hooliganism is closely related to the deployment of 'race' categories as part of racist repertoires, including violent attacks on immigrants (see also Spaaij and Viñas, 2005a; Viñas and Spaaij, 2006). These repertoires are not fixed or unchangeable, as the case of FC Barcelona clearly demonstrates. It was only after the eruption of the skinhead subculture, in the second half of the 1980s, that group members began to turn collectively to the use of racist language and symbology. In contrast, the hooligan formations at West Ham United and Feyenoord are characterized by their heterogeneous ethnic composition. Although the vast majority of group members are white, there is also a significant proportion of 'black' and minority ethnic participants. Importantly, several of these participants hold a reputation for physical prowess and are endowed with a hypermasculinity to be feared, for example a subgroup nicknamed 'riot negroes' at Feyenoord.

Some of the leading theoretical approaches to the subject matter explain football hooliganism in terms of *class* relations, that is, in terms of the structure and culture of the lower strata of the working class (e.g. Dunning et al., 1988). The empirical data cast doubt on the universal applicability of this explanation. Important spatial (and temporal) variations exist in the class backgrounds of football hooligans. Only in two of the six cases, Feyenoord and West Ham United, do the vast majority of football hooligans come from (lower) working-class backgrounds. Importantly, the working-class element in football hooliganism at Feyenoord contrasts with the comparatively middle-class backgrounds of Sparta hooligans. The overwhelming majority of Sparta hooligans are relatively highly educated and live in comparatively affluent towns or city districts.

The social backgrounds of Espanyol and FC Barcelona hooligans are comparatively heterogeneous and have altered over the years. In the second half of the 1980s a large proportion of football hooligans at Espanyol came from (upper) middle-class backgrounds. The rapid growth of the ultra group in the late 1980s resulted in a heterogenization of the social backgrounds of group members, including the influx of increasing proportions of working-class youths. Members of the militant fan group at FC Barcelona come from all levels of the class hierarchy, although over the years gradually many middle-class fans abandoned the group due to internal fragmentation and politicization. Looking at it from a developmental perspective, the general conclusion can be drawn that football hooliganism emerged as a specifically working-class youth subculture in the 1960s in England, but over time the phenomenon has come to attract a wider variety of male adolescents. The specific class backgrounds of football hooligans depend principally on specific social, cultural and historical circumstances at a local and national level.

Intra-city variations in the manifestation of football hooliganism also shine a new light on the thesis of 'ordered segmentation' as developed by Dunning and his colleagues (1988) (for a critique, see Giulianotti and Armstrong, 2002). This thesis asserts that hooligan groups emerge as a fluid pattern of unification of geographically discernable rival (local) gangs when challenged by a common 'enemy'. Dunning and his colleagues found that gangs that regularly fought each other during the week tended to unite on match days under the banner of the club to confront opposing fan groups. There is certainly evidence for the idea of fluid patterns of unification. For example, in the late 1960s rival gangs in East London united on match days to 'see off' the challenge by visiting fans. This pattern of unification, however, does not necessarily involve geographically distinguished groups, but may also develop in terms of political allegiance, as in the case of Spain. Moreover, most of the hooligan groups under consideration currently draw participants from diffuse locales and not merely from local estates. Although a significant proportion of West Ham and Feyenoord hooligans lives in local areas, an important part of the group members does not, or no longer. The two hooligan formations in Barcelona also draw their support from a variety of locales, both within and outside Catalonia.[8]

The national and intra-city variations described in this section illustrate the great practical heterogeneity of football hooliganism. Significant variations occur in the extent and nature of football hooliganism in different countries as well as at different clubs within a single city. Furthermore, temporal, within-case variations are in some cases even more striking than these spatial variations, as is shown in Table 10.2. In the following section, I will discuss in more detail local and temporal variations and resemblances in the social organization of football hooliganism.

The social organization of football hooliganism

One of the central themes addressed in this book is the social organization of football hooliganism. Comparative analysis of football hooliganism in different local settings reveals a number of crucial issues regarding this theme. A first important cross-local similarity is that a significant proportion of the violence provoked by members of hooligan formations is relatively spontaneous, erupting, for example, in reaction to provocations by rival fans, aggressive policing or events on the pitch. Apart from this spontaneous element, several hooligan formations have developed increasing levels of planning and co-ordination, principally as a response to growing controls and surveillance. Hooligan formations at West Ham United, Feyenoord and Sparta regularly seek to escape police observation by using alternative modes of travel and dress.[10] Confrontations involving these groups are occasionally carefully planned or pre-arranged.

Although football hooliganism at FC Barcelona and Espanyol is generally less organized, certain hooligan subgroups at these clubs have sought to escape police observation through the adoption of a casual dress style and the use of alternative modes of travel. In general, characteristic of football hooliganism at FC Barcelona and Espanyol is the continuing emphasis on public visibility (in dress, symbols, activities), which can in part be explained by the groups' intense politicization and imitation of Italian ultra groups. Moreover, the vast majority of confrontations involving these hooligan formations are currently neither carefully planned nor pre-arranged, contrasting starkly with the premeditated clashes between

Espanyol and FC Barcelona hooligans in the late 1980s and early 1990s. Occasionally, however, FC Barcelona hooligans launch premeditated attacks on opposing fans outside the stadium (see Chapter Eight).

Another major commonality is that despite the advanced level of social organization of several hooligan formations, their degree of formal organization is limited. The hooligan groups under consideration have no formal structures, hierarchies or formal leaders, other than certain informal leader figures and 'main faces' (based on their seniority, physical prowess or organizational skills). Hooligan confrontations do not result from formal hierarchies but from a combination of common interests (i.e. in fighting), opportunities for rapid resource mobilization, inter-group contacts established over the years, and familiarity with certain urban spaces (i.e. football grounds, routes to stadia, railway stations, city districts). There exists a major discrepancy between the elements of formal organization in the militant fan groups at Espanyol and FC Barcelona (i.e. their board, official membership, recruitment campaigns) and the relatively unorganized nature of violent confrontations.

Although the precise degree and forms of social organization involved in football hooliganism depend om local circumstances, the hooligan formations under consideration can all be characterized as loose associations with fluid boundaries. These associations resemble in some respects Yablonsky's (1959; 1962) concept of the 'near group'. The near group has five basic features: (i) the roles of group members are not precisely defined; (ii) the group as a whole has limited cohesion and tends to be impermanent; (iii) there is a minimum consensus among participants about the entity's norms; (iv) the members and participants are constantly shifting; and (v) leadership is often vague and confused (Yablonsky, 1962: 9). Crucial to understanding hooligan formations is that there are different levels of commitment to the group (i.e. core participants, followers, 'semi-retired' practitioners, marginal participants, 'wannabes'). Group cohesiveness decreases as one moves from the centre of the group to the periphery. The core of the formation tends to be relatively permanent and cohesive, consisting of people that have been participants for a lengthy period of time (5-10 years, or even longer), although not necessarily, or no longer, on a weekly basis (i.e. picking their clashes carefully depending on their expectations). These core members are central to the collectivity's social

339

organization and they are role models in their group. The periphery of the group is constantly shifting, depending, among other factors, on expectations of upcoming events and opportunity structures for collective violence (see Van der Torre and Spaaij, 2003).

Hooligan formations as loose associations: characteristics and dilemmas

Football hooliganism can be viewed as a trendy, fashionable youth subculture with fluid boundaries. Hooligan formations resemble in some respects the 'neo-tribes' (*tribus*) described by Maffesoli (1996) and the 'urban tribes' (*tribus urbanas*) outlined by Costa and his colleagues (1996). Focusing on the temporary and fluid nature of modern group identity, Maffesoli's concept of neo-tribes shows the shifting nature of collective associations between individuals as societies become increasingly consumer orientated. For Maffesoli, the neo-tribe is 'without the rigidity of the forms of organization with which we are familiar, it refers more to a certain ambience, a state of mind, and is preferably to be expressed through lifestyles that favour appearance and form' (1996: 98). From this point of view, the hooligan group is not a central focus for the individual but rather 'one of a series of foci or 'sites' within which the individual can live out a selected, temporal role or identity before relocating to an alternative site and assuming a different identity' (Bennett, 1999: 605; cf. Shields, 1992).

The concept of neo-tribes has much in common with other descriptions of collective associations that are consciously and freely chosen on the basis of mutual sentiment and emotional feeling (e.g. *bunds*; see Hetherington, 1994). A shared characteristic of such loose associations is that people will rapidly enter and leave. They remain members in part because of the emotional satisfaction that they derive from common goals or shared social experiences, albeit of a temporary sort (Urry, 2000: 143). Another helpful concept is the 'community lite' (*lichte gemeenschap*) described by Duyvendak and Hurenkamp (2004). They argue that people's quest for identity-related distinction has not resulted in the kind of excessive individualization emphasized by scholars such as Putnam (2000). What has changed, they argue, is the nature of collectivities: weak ties have replaced strong ties, membership is temporary and freely chosen, and people can participate at once in multiple

340

networks. Like the neo-tribe, these 'communities lite' are flexible and dynamic and they are characterized by loose affiliation. The frameworks of both neo-tribes and communities lite are closely related to the concept of 'lifestyle', since loose associations are, in essence, lifestyles and relate to styles of consumption (Bauman and May, 2001: 156). The concept of lifestyle regards individuals as 'active consumers whose choice reflects a self-constructed notion of identity' (Bennett, 1999: 607; cf. Chaney, 1996). Consumerism offers the individual new ways of negotiating class issues and individuals may select lifestyles which are in no way indicative of a specific class background.

Although the concepts of neo-tribes, communities lite and lifestyle are helpful to understanding the fluid boundaries of hooligan subcultures, there is a number of fundamental problems in applying these concepts to football hooliganism. A first, in my view minor, issue is that, confusingly, the term 'tribes' carries very strong connotations of the kind of fixity and rigidity its advocates so strongly dismiss (Hesmondhalgh, 2005: 24; Van der Loo and Van Reijen, 1997: 227). The most important common feature of the tribe, in both its traditional and its (post)modern sense, is that its members feel that they have more in common with each other than with neighbouring groups. This sense of communality both binds the members of a tribe together and distances them from non-members (Marsh, 1988: 10). In other words, both the traditional tribe and the neo-tribe set themselves apart from other groups (the outgroup) and seek to underline their separate identity (the ingroup). A key difference is that the group identity and 'membership' associated with the neo-tribe is essentially fluid, temporary and based on styles of consumption rather than on, for example, kinship.

A second problem is that the concept of neo-tribes, offering a recognition of the instable and temporary nature of group affiliation, may be too polarized a presentation of the alternatives to subcultural theory. Although British subcultural theorists (e.g. Hall and Jefferson, 1976; Clarke, 1976) might have overestimated the boundedness and permanence of group identities, to merely offer instability and temporariness as alternatives does not get us very far (cf. Hesmondhalgh, 2005: 24). The problem here is that the subculture of football hooliganism is characterized by its permanent and persistent nature. The main hooligan formations in England, the Netherlands and Spain have been active for over two or three decades. And

341

although, of course, there have been a number of generational changes, several older hooligans are still centrally involved in these groups as they have been for one or more decades. More specifically, I have argued in the previous chapter that there are different levels of commitment to the group. Group cohesiveness decreases as one moves from the centre of the group to the periphery. Thus, while the periphery of the group is constantly shifting, the core of the formation tends to be relatively permanent and cohesive, consisting of people that have been regular participants for a lengthy period of time

A third problem is the issue of access to hooligan formations. Consumer-oriented neo-tribes and communities lite are characterized by their voluntary, temporary commitment on the basis of mutual sentiment and emotional feeling. Individuals can rapidly enter and leave, quite unlike the constrictive nature of many traditional forms of community. Neo-tribes, as Bauman and May (2001: 156) have argued, do not undertake to monitor degrees of conformity at a collective level. They do not have boards or admission committees to decide who is admitted and who is excluded from membership, nor do they employ gatekeepers. They have no institution of authority which may pronounce on the correctness of members' behaviour. Individuals can therefore wander freely from one neo-tribe to another simply by changing their styles of consumption. Access to the neo-tribe is thus not regulated by the neo-tribe itself, but merely by the market.

I do not find the 'access through consumption' thesis completely convincing when applied to football hooliganism. First, in hooligan formations there *is* a kind of institution of authority which may pronounce on the correctness of members' behaviour. Although informal codes of legitimate action are regularly violated, issues such as mutual solidarity and effective response to defeat or threat are fundamental to the maintenance of hooligan identities. The *post facto* meaning of a fight is highly negotiable and contestable, yet in the course of this negotiation individuals of greater status are likely to have a greater influence (King, 2001: 580). Also, failing to 'back up' your mates during a confrontation can lead to expulsion or retaliation. There thus exist power relations within hooligan formations that co-shape the 'rules' of appropriate conduct.

Second, membership should not be viewed as a homogeneous category since there are various types of hooligan membership, ranging from 'wannabes' and followers to core group members. Access to these different types of membership not only depends on the individual's 'power to buy', but also on one's status within the group (i.e. seniority, fighting skills). Although hooligans can take upon themselves a variety of social roles, few roles can be performed without some sort of (medium-term) reputation management, that is, one has to demonstrate that one is 'capable' (i.e. as a good fighter or organizer). For example, for some young men their bodies facilitate masculine agency, enabling successful construction of self as 'more masculine' than others (Messerschmidt, 1999; see Chapter Twelve). I would argue that although the market regulates some aspects of the hooligan lifestyle (e.g. the purchase of match tickets, hooligan gear, drugs or alcohol), core membership can only be achieved within the group over time and is always negotiated. The boundaries of football hooliganism are fluid, but the core of hooligan formations – quantitatively minor, but comparatively influential in the construction and maintenance of group identity and in the social organization of hooligan confrontations – is usually less easily accessible. As one Feyenoord hooligan put it:

> Over the years we have become a more close-knit group wary of outsiders. The core of the group all know each other and it is difficult for new recruits to join. Of course there are a lot of hangers-on, but that's more the periphery of the group, you know. So although it's not very organized, you've got a small group of experienced hooligans that people look up to and that kind of set the example for the younger kids.

A fourth problem is the issue of power inequalities. The empirical data provided in this book show that the hooligan lifestyle may exist more or less independently from the individual's socio-economic position. This does not mean, however, that structural issues are unimportant in understanding young males' involvement in football hooliganism. Although access to neo-tribes is based on free choice, the genuine accessibility of lifestyles is determined by the prospective practitioners' ability to buy. Marketed lifestyles are therefore not distributed evenly or randomly. 'Beneath the claim that suggests achievement is within the reach of all lies the reality of ascription that is set according to an unequal distribution of the ability to pay' (Bauman and May, 2001: 160). There are several factors that might limit or

343

constrain accessibility to neo-tribes: marginalization, disempowerment, unequal access to education, and so on (cf. Hesmondhalgh, 2005: 25).

I would argue that access to hooligan formations is equally constrained by power inequalities. Let me give four examples. First, football hooliganism is gendered. Women have far less access to hooligan lifestyles and even when they do gain entry to hooligan formations, their opportunities for establishing a reputation for toughness and their involvement in fighting are usually very limited. Football hooliganism is essentially a male phenomenon revolving around the construction of hard masculine identity. Second, in some hooligan groups ethnicity is viewed as a distinguishing characteristic. We have seen how Espanyol and FC Barcelona hooligans construct part of their collective identities in terms of perceived differences between self and the 'inferior races'. Gaining entry to these hooligan groups is comparatively difficult for 'black' and minority ethnic youths. In fact, neither of the two hooligan formations have any 'black' or minority ethnic members.

Third, the accessibility of the hooligan lifestyle is to some degree age-group specific. The vast majority of football hooligans are young males, although, as we have seen in the previous chapter, there is a growing number of older participants. Older practitioners are sometimes looked upon with disapproval: 'Some geezer of 25 years old being a football hooligan, to my age, has got to be a total tosser to still be doing this' (former West Ham hooligan); 'I will not be doing this for the rest of my life, you know. I mean, it's great for the moment but in a few years I will probably have other things on my mind: a career, a family, and all that' (Sparta hooligan). The latter comment reveals another inequality related to age: time. Older hooligans generally have less time on their hands for sustaining a hooligan lifestyle – attending football matches, socializing with the group, engaging in violent confrontations – due to changes in other areas of their lives (family, children, career). Some older hooligans continue as semi-retired practitioners: 'I don't hang around with the boys all the time anymore because I've got kids now. But when trouble is expected, I am usually there' (Feyenoord hooligan). Entering the group at a later age (i.e. over 25 years old) is relatively difficult since the individual would also have less credibility among established group members. The overwhelming majority of older hooligans interviewed for this study first became involved in football hooliganism in their teens.

Fourth, there are geographical constraints on access to the hooligan lifestyle. People living in rural areas without a local (professional) football club, or those living close to a club without a hooligan 'firm', have to go to greater lengths to 'buy into' the hooligan subculture since they would have to travel to the nearest football club to fully 'consume' their lifestyle. Although this may seem a minor issue considering contemporary transport options and the omnipresence of football clubs in most (Western) societies, it actually relates to my central argument that the manifestation of football hooliganism should be examined within particular club cultures and is structured by the habitus of supporters. For young men supporting a football club with a deep-seated 'friendly' fan identity (i.e. Sparta or Fulham) the hooligan lifestyle is generally less easily accessible and less attractive than for male adolescents following one of the more notorious clubs (i.e. Feyenoord or West Ham United). The former would have to either change club allegiances or find like-minded individuals at his club to create a new hooligan formation, as in the case of the Sparta Youth Crew.

In conclusion, although some degree of 'free choice' is certainly available in the construction of one's identity, access to the hooligan lifestyle is constrained by the practical inequality of consumers, that is, differences in gender, age, ethnicity, and so on. Traditional sociological categories remain relevant for predicting which groupings of people can and will become centrally involved in football hooliganism. Local context and club culture play a crucial role in this process. At the same time, the concepts of neo-tribes and lifestyle point to an important transnational development: the commodification of football hooliganism. I will discuss this theme in Chapter Twelve.

Conclusion

In this chapter, I have sought to show the importance of national and local contexts for understanding football hooliganism. Important variations in the extent and nature of football hooliganism occur not only between countries, but also within countries and within individual cities. Furthermore, there are striking temporal variations in the manifestation of football hooliganism. Although national and local overlaps and dissimilarities can in part be explained in terms of transnational diffusion and

345

societal fault lines, the precise nature and development of football hooliganism can only be fully understood by taking into consideration the particular local arenas in which hooligan subcultures are embedded. In these local arenas general fault lines and wider developments in football culture interact with more specific elements co-shaping the manifestation of football hooliganism. In other words, systematic and detailed comparison of the local arenas in which hooligan subcultures are embedded enables us to develop a deeper understanding of football hooliganism as a transnational phenomenon. In the next chapter I want to extend this argument by focusing on the fourth theoretical theme outlined in Chapter Two: the interactions and negotiations between hooligans and significant others and the effects of policies targeting football hooliganism.

11

Transformations in Football Hooliganism:
Formal and Informal Policies and Their Effects

Introduction

Manifestations of football hooliganism change over time. Changes in the extent and nature of football hooliganism are often explained in terms of wider transformations in the game or in leisure culture (see Chapters One and Three). In this chapter I will show that transformations in football hooliganism cannot always be adequately explained by reference to such wider developments, since changes are also triggered by developments and interactions at a local level. To generate a deeper understanding of the development of football hooliganism over time, it is important to differentiate between national and local contexts. Football hooliganism is not only contoured and fuelled by societal fault lines and (trans)national developments, but also by more specific cleavages as well as by the specific interactions and negotiations that take place within local arenas.

I successively discuss three major issues regarding the development of football hooliganism: the development of anti-hooligan measures; the interactions and negotiations between hooligans, police officers, club officials and non-hooligan supporters; and the changing geographical meaning of the stadium. The first two issues are characterized by their great local variability, whereas the third aspect can be viewed as a comparatively universal element of the development of football hooliganism. These issues closely reflect the fourth theoretical theme outlined in Chapter Two, which focuses on the interactions and negotiations between hooligans and significant others and the effects of policies targeting football hooliganism.

347

Tackling football hooliganism: the development of anti-hooligan policies

A general transnational development is that policies targeting football hooliganism have gradually become more standardized and specialized in accordance with international and national regulations. Contrasts in anti-hooligan policies have gradually diminished (see Chapter Three). The expansion and formalization of European information exchange networks is but one example of this development. I would nevertheless argue that the precise effects of, and reactions to, these policies principally depend on how policies are implemented and received at a local level. Strategies for reducing football hooliganism should be viewed as a combination of top-down and bottom-up processes involving a great deal of adaptation and negotiation at a local level. Elsewhere I have argued that important local and intra-city variations occur in club and police strategies (Spaaij, 2005; 2005b). For example, the degree of proactivity in policing football matches in West London is remarkably higher than in East London, despite the fact that both areas fall under the same police force, the Metropolitan Police Service (see Chapters Three and Five).

Examples of local and intra-city variation can also be found at the six clubs under consideration, depending, among other factors, on local interpretations of the problem. The (perceived) persistence of football hooliganism at Feyenoord and equally persistent pressures by international and national governing bodies to tackle the problem have meant that repressive and techno-preventative policies have evolved rapidly over the years. The Feyenoord stadium was recently awarded by the UEFA as one of the safest football grounds in Europe. The high perimeter fences characteristic of the 1970s and 1980s have been removed, a tunnel entrance for visiting supporters has been constructed, and the stadium has been made all-seater. Moreover, the policing of Feyenoord hooligans is not limited to match days, but includes full-time intelligence operations. A team of intelligence officers and spotters is responsible for gathering and disseminating intelligence on the behaviour and intentions of known and suspected hooligans. The club has also introduced a special membership scheme for away matches. In contrast, the security regime at Sparta is relatively low-key and restricted to match days only, mainly due to the club's 'friendly image' and the historically low level of violent behaviour of home supporters. Only at 'high-risk' matches is the number of police officers temporarily

348

increased and are additional regulations put in use (i.e. a restrictive membership scheme).

Similar intra-city variations apply to the local priority of social preventive fan projects. Although there is a tradition of social preventive projects in football in the Netherlands, the extent and implementation of these projects varies considerably across localities. Feyenoord is the only one of the clubs under consideration that participates in a fan project specifically targeting football hooliganism. However, even at Feyenoord important within-case variations can be observed. The first fan project was created in 1988 but, by the mid-1990s, the project had lost most of its original priority and content. The long-term effect of the project has therefore been minimal. Only as recently as 2005 a new pilot project was introduced by the municipality in cooperation with the club and the local police. This project explicitly concentrates on deterring young supporters from becoming structurally involved in hooliganism. No comparable fan project exists at Sparta, mainly because of the low priority of football hooliganism at this club. Instead, the club and municipality have introduced a community scheme aimed at strengthening the ties between the club and its local environment as a means for attracting new young supporters.[1]

A comparison of security policies at West Ham United and Fulham reveals similar intra-city variations. Although security and safety issues at both clubs have become increasingly specialized from the late 1980s onwards, the policing of football hooliganism at West Ham receives a higher priority and is therefore more pervasive, including sophisticated intelligence operations. Police operations at home and away matches of Fulham are generally comparatively low-profile. Pre-match intelligence gathering principally concentrates on the 'threat' of rival supporters. For football intelligence officers in West London, the policing of Fulham supporters has a relatively low priority, for example when compared to local rivals Chelsea and Queen's Park Rangers. While extensive surveillance and intelligence structures are operating in West London, they are generally utilized in a less pervasive manner at Fulham due to the 'friendly' profile of Fulham fans and, specifically, because of the absence of a hooligan formation.

The security policies at Espanyol and at FC Barcelona have, for a long time, developed in a similar way. Comparable repressive and techno-preventative measures were taken to curb the escalation of football hooliganism in the second half of the 1980s and the first half of the 1990s. In the early 1990s the police began to invest in the collection, analysis and exchange of intelligence concerning the hooligan formations at the two clubs. Security officers were contracted and CCTV and control rooms were installed, all in accordance with national regulations. Compared to the situation at the English and Dutch clubs, the issuing of banning orders and the arrest of suspected offenders remains rather limited, due in part to the more reactive police strategy and the replacement of police officers by private security staff and stewards within the ground.

But despite the overlaps in the development of security regimes at FC Barcelona and Espanyol, in recent years the clubs' attitudes towards football hooliganism have evolved in different directions. The security regime at Espanyol has remained relatively stable over the last five years, whereas the situation at FC Barcelona featured a radical transformation in the club's commitment to tackling football hooliganism. Under the leadership of chairman Joan Laporta the club now actively attempts to stop militant fans from attending home matches through strict identification regulations, banning orders and extensive searches. As I will show in the following section, the club's current security regime contrasts starkly with previous informal club policies.

The above examples show that although policies targeting football hooliganism have become increasingly standardized and specialized, at a local level there remains room for adaptation and negotiation. In many cases implementers develop their own, informal policies which may diverge to some degree from the official policies that policy makers have set out for them (cf. Rosenthal et al., 1996: 91-92). Before examining in more detail how informal policies are produced through interactions and negotiations between hooligans and law enforcers, two major dilemmas of the realization of anti-hooligan policies should be mentioned.

A first dilemma is that, at least for a long time, football clubs have tended to avoid full responsibility for tackling football hooliganism. A common argument is that football hooliganism is essentially a societal problem rather than a football problem, and therefore the responsibility of governments. Considering the fact that nowadays hooligan confrontations tend to take place away from the ground, one could rightfully argue that such 'gang' rivalries have little connection to the game itself. In recent years there seems to have emerged an awareness of shared responsibility, in which all related organizations cooperate in order to reduce football hooliganism. Within this interorganizational network, the club – as the organizer of the event – is given a central responsibility, for example in expanding its steward organization, exchanging intelligence with other partners and contributing to or reducing the costs of policing football. In reality, there appear to be local variations in the extent to which clubs fulfil this responsibility. The efficacy of anti-hooligan policies in part depends on the participation of football clubs, some of which seem to lack a sense of urgency in the project even though they tend to agree with the substantive ends of the policy.[2] Spanish clubs in particular have been accused of ducking the issue (Spaaij and Viñas, 2005; Durán González, 1996). At clubs such as West Ham United and Feyenoord, club officials only really took to the project of reducing football hooliganism after persistent international and national pressures and sanctions, in the 1980s and 1990s respectively. I will elaborate on this first dilemma in the following section.

A second dilemma of the realization of policies targeting football hooliganism is that recipients anticipate and react to these measures. Four general strategies of resistance to these policies can be distinguished: circumvention (e.g. pre-arranged disorder away from the ground), disregard (e.g. attacking rivals regardless of surveillance and punishment), fraud (e.g. using fake identity cards or forcing access to the ground without a ticket) and appeal (e.g. formal complaints against the police or appeal against banning orders). Although it has become increasingly difficult to escape controls and punishments in the football context, several hooligan formations go to great lengths to do so in order to successfully confront their opponents and avoid arrest. West Ham, Feyenoord and Sparta hooligans regularly seek to circumvent official travel arrangements monitored by the police, opting for alternative modes of travel allowing free movement. Hooligan confrontations are occasionally pre-arranged in order to escape official controls. Some Feyenoord hooligans are well-informed about police strategies through the collection of intelligence. In general, the increased controls and punishments have produced what can be termed the 'calculating' hooligan. Experienced football hooligans tend to anticipate opportunity structures for collective violence. They are most conscious of when to refrain from violence or how to avoid arrest. It is for this reason that comparatively many young recruits and 'wannabes' eager to prove themselves to peers are arrested in and around football grounds (Spaaij, 2001; Van der Torre and Spaaij, 2003).[3]

Street-level negotiations: the importance of social interaction

The calculating behaviour of experienced football hooligans poses major challenges for law enforcement. Football hooligans not only seek to escape controls and impositions, but also tacitly negotiate formal policies. The social interaction between football hooligans and law enforcers can be viewed as a form of mutual adjustment. Street-level interactions between hooligans and police officers produce more informal and unofficial sets of rules than the formal ones known publicly (O'Neill, 2005: 189; Van der Torre, 1999). These informal rules co-exist with, and may contradict, formal policies. The nature and evolvement of local manifestations of football hooliganism should therefore be viewed not only in terms of intra-group developments and effects of official policies, but also in terms of the subtle yet vital negotiations and interactions between hooligan and law enforcers. Let me first discuss the main themes in the interaction between hooligans and police officers.

The police are one of the main agents of social control at football matches. They are an integral part of football culture. O'Neill (2005: 191-192) correctly argues that the overall boundaries between the police and supporters can be seen as interdependent. 'Police and fans need each other in order to define themselves and yet the personal crossing of identity and performance boundaries means that they can understand each other.' For the police, football provides an opportunity to present themselves to outsiders as an effective and cohesive group. Supporters in turn need the police to be there to give them an extra target for their ritual insults but also to protect them. The relationship between the police and self-identifying hooligans involves similar aspects. Crucial to understanding the development of local manifestations of football hooliganism are the subtle negotiations between hooligans and police officers during orderly and relatively uneventful moments of match days. These negotiations produce the informal rules of interaction by which the performers involved align their actions (O'Neill, 2005: 190). Let me examine this issue in more detail through a number of empirical themes.

First, power relations in the interaction between hooligans and police officers are not simply determined by the law. Hooligans and ultras have varying degrees of power and autonomy, depending on local circumstances and controls. Especially in Barcelona, hooligans' territory within the ground – and in pubs around the ground – is generally avoided by the police. Although police officers surround the section of the stadium, they avoid entering that territory as much as possible. The entrance of police usually provokes a highly combative reaction from the hooligans and ultras, the consequences of which are unpredictable (cf. De Biasi, 1998: 223). An example of this process is the recent polarization between Espanyol ultras and the police, after police officers had, according to the ultras, 'illegitimately' invaded their territory – as opposed to the usual passive police presence in their section. Similarly, FC Barcelona hooligans have protested against the current zero tolerance policy which is seen as dramatically reducing their autonomy and free movement within their section of the ground. Although at the clubs under study CCTV systems are commonly used to identify offenders, hooligans' and ultras' territory inside the stadium is, to varying degrees, a place for tolerated transgressions (i.e. the consumption of drugs, abusive songs, fireworks, aggro). Different informal rules apply in this territory than in other parts of the ground, and steward and police strategies and priorities are adjusted accordingly (e.g. a focus on conflict de-escalation rather than on strict policing).

Second, the above examples illustrate that perceived police transgressions can result in a deterioration in relations between police officers and hooligans and non-hooligan supporters. Stott and Reicher (1998: 371) have argued that 'where the (police) outgroup is seen as generically aggressive, then any outgroup intervention is liable to be perceived as signifying impending attack.' In such a context, even those who otherwise reject norms of violence may join in violence against the police as an attempt to stop aggression (see King, 1995; 1999). I would like to extend this argument to include the 'legitimate rights' claimed by football hooligans in relation to the police, for example with regard to 'minor offences' such as the consumption of drugs, verbal insults and minor damage to property (see Spaaij, 2001; 2002). Violation of informal agreements may lead to immediate escalation, as in the case of Feyenoord. Feyenoord hooligans at time retaliated against police officers because of their alleged disproportionate and aggressive methods. Hooligans and non-hooligan supporters have also filed formal complaints against riot police officers for similar reasons.

Third, differences in the mutual perceptions of hooligans and police officers may produce differences in the threat of violence against the police. At Sparta, for example, the relationship between police officers and hooligans is comparatively distant and impersonal. Police operations and intelligence gathering away from the ground are usually limited since spectator behaviour at Sparta is generally perceived as unproblematic, enabling hooligans to regularly circumvent police observation and confront their opponents. There have also been relatively few arrests away from the ground. Sparta hooligans do not perceive the police as fundamentally inhibiting opportunities for collective violence and, therefore, prefer to avoid contact with police officers rather than attempting to influence or intimidate the police.

Differences in mutual perceptions also vary according to the types of police teams involved. Riot police officers are generally viewed by hooligans as 'hooligans in uniform' seeking pleasurable emotional arousal through 'legitimately' assaulting football fans. Hooligans may also seek to identify, and retaliate against, plain-clothes officers. Variations in hooligans' perceptions of police forces and teams also depend on local circumstances. Some FC Barcelona hooligans and fans differentiate between members of the national police force (Cuerpo Nacional de la Policía) and the Catalan police force (Mossos d'Esquadra). The former is commonly perceived as anti-Catalan and neo-Francoist and is therefore treated with great suspicion and hostility. This differential perception is of particular importance since from the 2005/06 season football matches in Barcelona are policed by the Catalan police, as part of the region's expanding autonomous functions. This change in organization and attendant perceptions may also come to (negatively) affect the relationship between Espanyol ultras and the police, considering the ultras' overt opposition to (symbols of) Catalan nationalism. In a similar way, several Espanyol hooligans anticipated encounters with the Guardia Civil (the Spanish civil guard) as being particularly challenging. This police force used to police many of the away matches of Espanyol's former indoor football team. Holding a reputation for 'brutal' and provocative policing methods, the Guardia Civil was viewed by several hooligans as being 'up for it', that is, as constituting a willing opponent. Although often resulting in arrest, confrontations with the Guardia Civil were perceived as peak experiences.

354

Research into football hooliganism has largely neglected the role of football clubs. Football clubs are key partners in the implementation of formal policies targeting football hooliganism as well as in the production of informal sets of rules. The relationship between club officials and hooligans is dynamic and complex. Although a football club may seem like a homogeneous entity which directly implements formal policies and within which there is a broad consensus regarding the urgency of the issue, often this is not the case. Important local and intra-city variations occur in unofficial, informal club policies. These informal policies co-exist with, and may to some degree contradict or thwart, official policies targeting football hooliganism. In Table 11.1 six types of clubs' informal styles of dealing with the issue are distinguished. I must emphasize that these informal policies may shift over time and may occur in combination.

Let me illustrate the types listed in Table 11.1 through a comparison of the six football clubs under consideration. The management of football hooliganism at FC Barcelona and Espanyol in the first half of the 1980s can be characterized as 'facilitation'. To stimulate their youth support and the vocal and colourful support to the team, both clubs facilitated members of militant fan groups free or reduced-price tickets and storage facilities within the premises of the stadium and subsidized their travel to away matches. This policy significantly reduced the efficacy of formal security measures, enabling hooligans and ultras to establish a degree of legitimacy and autonomy as well as stimulating the groups' expansion. In the second half of the 1980s both clubs came to increasingly view football hooliganism as a disturbing problem seriously damaging their public images. But although publicly condemning football hooliganism, no real effort was made to curb the problem at grass roots level. Characteristically, the two clubs argued that they did everything in their power to tackle the problem but that they were not responsible for incidents outside the ground.

Table 11.1   Types of informal club policies in dealing with football hooliganism

Style	Underlying assumption(s)*	Strategy
Denial/downplaying	(a) Problem is exaggerated by the media (b) Need for prevention of damage to the public image of the club	Denial or downplaying of the extent and seriousness of the issue.
Exculpation	Hooliganism is a societal problem and the club is merely a victim	Emphasis on club's inability to deal with a societal problem and on the responsibility of governments.
Facilitation	(a) Recruitment of new (young) fans (b) Need for upbeat support for team (c) Hooligans as a useful force (d) Fear of retaliation	Facilitation of logistic and/or finan- cial support to hooligans or ultras.
Toleration	(a) Problem is not extremely pressing (b) Problem will disappear by itself (c) Need for upbeat support for team (d) Fear of retaliation	No active approach to tackling the issue apart from the adoption of formal measures.
Co-optation	(a) Problem is serious and persistent (b) Hooligans are also committed fans who are here to stay (c) Repression alone will not effectively reduce the problem	Dialogue with hooligans as a means for reducing violence.
Repression	(a) Problem is serious and damages the club's public image (b) Repressive measures will reduce the problem	Crackdown on offenders through banning orders and pervasive controls.

Note:

* The underlying assumption involves one or more of those proposed, depending on the individual case.

At certain points in time, however, FC Barcelona intended to curb the violent behaviour of its militant fans inside the stadium. In 1986 the militant fan group was moved to a different section of the ground to reduce missile throwing and damage to the stadium. This measure failed to have the intended effect. Attempts to let members of the militant fan group self-police their area of the ground, as a form of co-optation, also failed to reduce violence within the ground but, instead, increased the group's status and legitimacy. In the 1990s the club sought to integrate and legalize the different youth groups in order to enhance the internal and external social controls over their behaviour. The club also attempted to persuade hooligans to refrain from violence inside the stadium by facilitating them certain privileges (match tickets, travel arrangements, money). At the same time close personal contacts remained between certain club officials and informal hooligan leaders. These club officials seem to have perceived the hooligans as a useful force, for example in intimidating electoral opponents and their supporters in club elections. The hooligans, on the other hand, were reluctant to give up the privileges they had acquired over the years. The police regularly criticized FC Barcelona for not disclosing information on participants in hooligan encounters. The informal club policy transformed radically in 2003, shifting from facilitation and toleration to repression. The new chairman Joan Laporta launched a zero tolerance policy aimed at actively reducing the threat of football hooliganism in the Camp Nou (see Chapter Nine).

Different informal policies characterize the security regimes at Sparta and Feyenoord. Following the recent emergence of football hooliganism, club officials at Sparta have developed a more differentiated approach featuring a combination of co-optation and repression. On the one hand, the club implements formal security and safety procedures as laid out by the Dutch football association. The club's safety officer plays a key role in this process and is known for his 'rigid' implementation disliked by most fans. On the other hand, certain club officials prefer a more flexible approach to tackling football hooliganism. Instead of imposing prolonged banning orders on all offenders, they differentiate between perceivedly different types of offenders. While some core hooligans are perceived as being persistent offenders requiring tough punishment, others are seen as basically 'good lads' with a deep affection for the club. In order not to alienate the latter category, the club engages in dialogue and proposes informal compromises (e.g. the suspension of a banning order after a period of good behaviour). These compromises tend to contradict formal regulations, but are perceived by key club officials as being more effective in the long term.

A combination of repression and co-optation also characterizes current informal club policies at Feyenoord. Key club officials see dialogue and mutual understanding as the only viable alternative to strict repression. Co-optation is viewed as indispensable since many core hooligans are also long-standing fans who will probably stay with the club for most of their lives. By creating a mutual understanding, club officials have sought to positively influence the behaviour of the hooligans. Repression may fail to offer a long-term solution but is nevertheless viewed as a necessary strategy to deal with the most persistent offenders. It is important to note, however, that the club's style of co-optation has resembled in some ways informal policies of toleration or facilitation. For example, Feyenoord facilitated several hooligans free tickets to home and away matches, thwarting the efficacy of formal policies. This type of facilitation diminished from the late 1990s onwards as the chairman increasingly distanced himself from the hooligan group. Furthermore, the club's responses to football hooliganism were principally triggered by persistent national and international pressures in the 1990s. Before this period, the dominant informal policy was more one of exculpation and toleration. As with most football clubs, security and safety issues have long been receiving a relatively low priority on the club's agenda.

Compared to the more subtle negotiations between club officials and hooligans in Rotterdam, the interactions at West Ham United are relatively distant and formal. At various stages, however, negotiations between club officials and hooligans have been more informal and flexible. For example, the club sought to employ notorious hooligans as club stewards in order to enhance the social control among young fans. This initiative proved unsuccessful because the hooligan stewards' control over the behaviour of young supporters was actually limited. Most of them did not take their job very seriously and were principally motivated by the arrangement of free entrance to grounds and free travel to away matches. More recently, the club engaged in dialogue with some (former) hooligans regarding the imposition and lifting of banning orders.

In conclusion, two major dilemmas emerge from the discussion of informal club policies in dealing with football hooliganism. The first dilemma is that between repressive and more co-optive club strategies. Many of the club officials interviewed for this project emphasized that total repression does little to eradicate the problem.

Instead, it may lead to a deterioration in relations between the club and its fans. At the same time, club officials tend to stress that repressive and techno-preventative measures have effectively reduced the frequency and seriousness of hooligan incidents within football grounds. Their ideas about what the extent of the problem is at their club and which exact strategy should be employed varies considerably, as we have seen in this section.

The second dilemma is that some football clubs underplay, or have long underplayed, their role in the prevention of football hooliganism. Their attitudes towards the issue can to some degree be explained by the 'ambiguous' position of the football club. While usually unwelcoming hooligan support (with the exception of the 'hooligans as a useful force' category), the clubs tend to encourage what contemporary scholars call the 'carnivalesque' (Giulianotti, 1991; 1999). This paradox is highlighted by Hughson (1997: 252) in his analysis of the hooligan support at Sydney United:

> While wanting an orderly form of spectatorship, sporting administrators also seek colourful displays of banners and flags which are attractive to television audiences. In the case of Australian soccer, the dilemma of these competing demands is compounded by the perilously low attendance rates at NSL [National Soccer League] matches. Understandably, soccer officials would be reluctant to turn away any paying customers. Accordingly, BBB [Bad Blue Boys] members greet the Sydney United committee's predicament with characteristic arrogance. As one member put it, 'They need us more than we need them.'

Although facilitation is perhaps the most radical type of informal club policy in this context, this strategy can also be found at some other major European football clubs. For example, the development of a hooligan formation at Paris Saint German was encouraged by the chairman's offering of cheap tickets, subsidizing of travel to away matches and lending of premises for storage of drums and flags (Hare, 2003: 78-79; Mignon, 2001). What starts as a noble initiative to boost the club's youth support may inadvertently result in the emergence or growth of a hooligan subculture. It seems that once a certain legitimacy or privilege is granted to hooligan formations it is extremely difficult to take it away from them at a later stage, evidence of which are the current situations at FC Barcelona and Espanyol. Hooligans may seek to secure their status through intimidation or violence. This may give rise to fear of retaliation on the part of club officials, creating a kind of status quo in which the hooligan formation is officially condemned, yet unofficially tolerated.

Contestation from below: interaction between hooligans and non-hooligan supporters

In the previous sections I have examined the interactions between hooligans, police officers and club officials and their effects on local manifestations of football hooliganism. In addition to these interactions, we should also take into consideration the negotiations between hooligans and non-hooligan supporters. Although this type of interaction has been largely neglected in studies of football hooliganism, the empirical evidence provided in this book highlights the importance of the issue. I would argue that non-hooligan supporters, or former hooligans, can play an important role in the prevention of football hooliganism, although this role is complex and requires long-term effort.

Striking examples of 'contestation from below' can be found at Espanyol and FC Barcelona, where newly emerging youth groups challenged the hard masculine identity of hooligan formations. The success and persistence of these alternative fan identities have varied considerably. A first initiative by young Espanyol supporters was the Irreductibles project launched in the 1993/94 season. In this case, neutralization of the violence and right-wing politics of members of ultra group Brigadas Blanquiazules was only a secondary aim, a necessary condition for co-operation between the different youth groups involved. The major aim was to enhance the vocal and colourful support for the team through unification of the club's youth support. The current Curva Jove campaign involves more explicit contestation of violence and politics within the ground. This joint operation of the club's more pacified youth groups, including former hooligans, currently consists of over 2,000 affiliates and has contributed considerably to the construction of an alternative, non-violent fan identity at Espanyol.

Fan initiatives at FC Barcelona have been more diverse and more directly related to the issue of hooliganism. The formation of the youth group Almogàvers in 1989 can be viewed as the first collective contestation of football hooliganism at FC Barcelona, promoting a pacified, apolitical fan model. The youth project Grada Joven, in the 1990s, expanded the focus on promoting non-violence by uniting the club's main youth groups, including the hooligan formation. Overall, the alternative fan groups and identities at FC Barcelona have failed to challenge and alter the hard masculine identity of the hooligans. Intimidation and violence has forced them to significantly reduce their activities or abandon the football scene altogether. At the other four clubs under consideration no comparable contestation of the hooligan identity has occurred. Although only marginally related to the issue of hooliganism, fan organizations at West Ham United and Feyenoord have challenged racism in football.

The changing geographical meaning of the stadium

Comparative analysis of the development of football hooliganism over time highlights a fundamental transformation in the landscape of football hooliganism: the displacement of hooligan confrontations and attended changes in the geographical meaning of the stadium. Constrictive security measures have fundamentally reduced the opportunities for violent confrontation inside the stadium. In each of the three countries under consideration the occurrence of large-scale fighting between rival hooligans is nowadays comparatively uncommon within football grounds. The gradual displacement of football hooliganism entailed a shift from inter-group rivalry and confrontation inside the stadium (i.e. the ground as front stage) to a situation in which new locations became the dominant places where hooligan rivalries were enacted (i.e. the ground as back region) (Giulianotti and Armstrong, 2002: 224; see Chapter One). The process of displacement is not a singular development and should be understood as a variable product of ongoing interaction between hooligan formations and law enforcers, which continues today.

This multi-layered transformation is described in a masterly way by Giulianotti and Armstrong (2002: 221-228) with regard to English and Scottish football hooliganism and includes three key developments:

1. Segregation of home and visiting supporters within football grounds. The number of police officers inside grounds was increased and perimeter fencing within and between ground terraces was introduced in order to prevent the movement of large numbers of young fans and inter-group confrontations. The segregation of football supporters within grounds had a number of unintended consequences. First, initial segregation tended to be spatially incomplete and failed to prevent occasional confrontations between rival groups of young fans. Second, in several cases 'home' hooligans also abandoned the youth groups and moved into the stand nearest to the visitors. Third, although segregation between opposing groups became increasingly constrictive over time, opportunities remained for more material objections to impositions, for example smashing seats in the visitor's end or throwing missiles into the opposition's end (ibid.: 223).

2. Relocation of hooligan confrontations from football grounds to new locales. For committed football hooligans, the segregation of football supporters within grounds and the attendant relocation of fan groups altered the geographical meaning of the stadium. The football ground now became a back region in which interaction between the competing hooligan formations was usually denied, but where analysis and post-mortems between rivals could still be shared and disputed. The new locales for enacting rivalries became more context-bound and variable, such as train stations, pubs and city centres, and the streets en route to these sites. Rivalries were fought within the general time specifications of 'match day'; thus, the spaces in which these could be legitimately played out expanded proportionately (ibid.: 224).

3. Further relocation and growing co-ordination and planning of hooligan confrontations. In reaction to increased police surveillance and control outside grounds on match days, several hooligan formations developed more complex strategies, including new modes of transport (train services, private coaches, cars or transit vans). It is generally the objective of both sides to be spatially removed from public and police observation, quite unlike early confrontations within grounds. Hooligans may also confront

362

each other outside match days or be joined by 'third party' forces (i.e. additional opponents, such as other hooligan groups or local groups of young men) (ibid.: 225-226).

How do these developments relate to transformations in football hooliganism in a comparative context? In general, at each of the six clubs under study the segregation of home and visiting supporters and other security measures have led to a gradual decline in hooligan confrontations inside the stadium. These are now comparatively rare, but not inexistent. Other types of violence (e.g. damage to property, missile throwing) continue to occur in and around football grounds. It must be stressed that the shift from hooligan confrontations within the ground to encounters away from the ground is relative rather than absolute. Early hooligan rivalries were already, although less commonly, enacted around or en route to the ground. For example, the first major confrontation between FC Barcelona and Espanyol hooligans, in 1986, took place outside a pub near the Camp Nou stadium. Earlier incidents, notably attacks on individual group members, also took place away from the ground. At West Ham United and Feyenoord, and to a lesser degree at Fulham, early hooligan rivalries were also enacted both inside and outside the ground, including confrontations en route to the ground. At this early stage, members of hooligan groups also occasionally caused damage to trains and the property of local residents and shopkeepers (cf. Van der Brug, 1988: 278).

There are important local variations in the aforementioned developments. Perhaps the most striking dissimilarity can be found at FC Barcelona, and to a lesser extent at Espanyol, where the segregation of home and visiting supporters failed to prevent, or perhaps stimulated, the eruption of intra-group violence and violence directed at non-hooligan supporters of the same club. Only recently have non-hooligan supporters come to be more successfully protected from intimidation and assault by the more militant supporters within the fan community, for example through the erection of glass walls (FC Barcelona) and fences (Espanyol) seeking to isolate the radical fan groups from the rest of the home crowd. At away matches such 'double segregation' is unavailable since generally all visiting fans are located in a single section of the ground. Moreover, the displacement of football hooliganism at FC Barcelona was not merely the result of increased controls inside the stadium, but also of the club's attempts to persuade hooligans to refrain from violence within the ground by rewarding them with certain privileges (match tickets, travel arrangements, money) (see Chapter Nine; cf. Viñas, 2006: 268-270).

Another major variation is that the shift from the stadium as being a front stage for football hooliganism to being a back region is not equally evident at all six clubs. At Sparta the transformation in the geographical meaning of the stadium never really materialized because of the prolonged absence of a hooligan formation. By that time, opportunities for collective violence within the ground were already reduced considerably by a range of security measures introduced over the years in accordance with national and international policies. Thus, from its formation in the late 1990s, the hooligan group at Sparta has sought to confront its opponents where this was most likely to succeed: away from the ground, at railway stations, in city centres or in pubs.

Dissimilar to the changes in the geographical meaning of the stadium for football hooliganism at West Ham United and Feyenoord, the ground still plays a central role in the practices of the hooligans and ultras of Espanyol and FC Barcelona. In the previous chapter I have noted these groups' heavy emphasis on public visibility and politics, both inside and outside the stadium. Their continuing focus on public visibility can to some degree be explained as part of these groups' management of reputation in relation to other militant fan groups of the same club. Such inter-group competition may overshadow their dispositions to violent confrontation with opposing hooligan groups. Thus, whereas English and Scottish hooligan groups tend to view the public spectacle of having to stroll through a host city with police escort as a pointless exercise (Giulianotti and Armstrong, 2002: 225), some Spanish hooligan groups see this as a relatively safe and successful type of public 'protest'. However, when hooligan confrontations do occur, they tend to take place outside the ground, in the streets or in pubs. In the late 1980s and early 1990s, the deep-seated rivalry between FC Barcelona and Espanyol hooligans regularly erupted into clashes away from the ground and on non-match days.

By a way of conclusion, I would therefore argue that local variations in the geographical meaning of the ground for football hooliganism are not one of kind but of degree. Physical confrontations between rival hooligan formations nowadays tend to take place away from the ground, mainly as a reaction to constrictive security regimes in and around the stadium. This points to a major dilemma in the prevention of football hooliganism. Policies targeting football hooliganism may produce unintended consequences that significantly reduce the efficacy of the policies. A major consequence of the imposition of controls and punishments was to displace the problem into areas where the controls were, or were perceived by hooligans as being, weak or non-existent (Dunning, 1999: 153; Spaaij, 2005: 7). The process of displacement has been neither simple nor nonlinear. Rather we should speak of a cycle of displacement involving several phases and processes, culminating, in some cases, in the emergence of pre-arranged hooligan encounters outside match days and far removed from football grounds. Each phase in the process has been followed by a widening of controls, first to the immediate vicinities of grounds and then to the major points of entry into the towns and cities where matches were played (Dunning, 1999: 152). The cycle of displacement is crucial to understanding the nature and development of football hooliganism today and the (intended and unintended) effects of anti-hooligan measures. In the following section I examine this process in more detail through an analysis of the local implementation of, and reactions to, club and police policies.

Conclusion

Transformations in football hooliganism cannot be adequately explained in terms of general transnational and national developments. Rather, we should also take into consideration the subtle yet vital interactions and negotiations between hooligans, police officers, club officials and non-hooligan supporters. These negotiations create informal and unofficial sets of rules that co-exist with, and may contradict, formal policies. Although formal security policies have become increasingly standardized and national and local contrasts therein seem to have diminished, football clubs and police teams develop their own informal styles of dealing with football hooliganism, depending in part on local interpretations and priorities. In addition, hooligans develop strategies for coping with formal and informal policies, including elements of both compliance and resistance. It is a major task for academics to scrutinize the complex and dynamic interactions and negotiations involved in football hooliganism. Comparative analysis of football hooliganism should not be reduced to broad, macro-structural comparison, but should seek to integrate different levels of analysis, including the manifestation and evolvement of football hooliganism in local arenas. It is at this local level that formal and informal rules are most visibly negotiated and contested. In sum, the issues discussed in this chapter reveal that: (i) most security measures have secondary consequences reducing their intended effect and transforming the manifestation of football hooliganism; (ii) a discrepancy between formal and informal policies targeting football hooliganism tends to exist; and (iii) football fans themselves may be powerful agents in the prevention of football hooliganism and the construction of non-violent fan identities.

The issues discussed in this chapter and in Chapter Ten contribute to a deeper understanding of football hooliganism as a transnational phenomenon. However, due to the focus on detailed comparative analysis of national and local features and variations, certain crucial aspects have remained largely unexplored. How do hooligans experience their involvement in football violence? What are the meanings of football hooliganism for its participants? Why do some fans, rather than others, find this sort of activity attractive and rewarding? Why is football hooliganism such a persistent phenomenon and why has it not yielded to public efforts to eradicate or contain it? These questions, which closely reflect the second theoretical theme outlined in Chapter Two, are addressed in the final chapter of this book. I will examine in detail the construction of hooligan identities and the attractions of the hooligan subculture.

12

Constructing Hooligan Identities

Introduction

In the previous chapters I have examined the extent and nature of, and responses to, football hooliganism in different national and local contexts. The aim of this final chapter is to develop an empirically grounded, sociological understanding of football hooliganism through comparative analysis of the second theoretical theme outlined in Chapter Two: the construction of hooligan identities and the attractions of the hooligan subculture. This chapter is divided into three parts. In the first part I will show that despite the importance of local and national context and specificity, it is possible to identify a number of key aspects of football hooliganism as a transnational phenomenon. The second part focuses on the manifestation of football hooliganism in fan cultures. I argue that variations in the extent of football hooliganism can to some degree be understood by acknowledging the ways in which fan cultures either inhibit or facilitate football hooliganism. In the third part, I will demonstrate that football hooliganism remains an attractive lifestyle for several young men, closely related to the growing commodification and mediatization of the phenomenon. This issue is crucial to understanding the persistence and social diversity of hooligan subcultures.

Focal concerns of football hooliganism

In the previous chapter I have demonstrated the importance of local and national contexts for understanding and explaining football hooliganism. Despite the great practical heterogeneity of football hooliganism, a number of key aspects can be identified in the construction and maintenance of hooligan identities at the six football clubs under consideration. These aspects should be viewed as key elements of football hooliganism as a transnational phenomenon. I distinguish six focal concerns: excitement and pleasurable emotional arousal; the construction of hard

367

masculine identity; territorial identifications; the individual and collective management of reputation; solidarity and belonging; and sovereignty and autonomy. Although some of these aspects have been identified individually or in combination in previous studies of football hooliganism (Dunning et al., 1988; Marsh, 1978; Armstrong, 1998; Giulianotti, 1999; Giulianotti and Armstrong, 2002; Kerr, 1994), only in conjunction do they enable a profound understanding of football hooliganism as a transnational phenomenon. It is important to note that although the general features and social mechanisms involved have a lot in common, their specific contents and intensity vary across localities depending on local and national circumstances.

Excitement and pleasurable emotional arousal

The excitement and pleasurable emotional arousal associated with violent confrontation is one of the key components of the hooligan experience and is a recurrent theme in the narratives of football hooligans, as I have demonstrated in Chapter One.[1] Hooligans are essentially thrill seekers and fighting is one of their main acts to counter boredom and experience high emotional arousal. Many hooligans perceive conventional lifestyles and careers as boring and unchallenging:

> People say, like, you've got your studies and your job so why engage in fighting. But university is just so fucking boring, you know. Most students are absolute wankers, you know, and the classes are boring. Being with my mates and planning a fight is sort of an outlet, to get away from it all. (Sparta hooligan)

Group membership and violent confrontation provide a chance to experience immediate sensation in the form of pleasurable excitement, which is often referred to as an adrenalin rush and 'better than sex'. Compare the following statements: 'The kick of fighting your rivals is overwhelming. You cannot really understand it unless you're in it. It gives you a sense of power, a sense of control. It's an absolute high.' (Feyenoord hooligan); 'Fighting is pure excitement' (Sparta hooligan); 'The buzz is enormous; it's an incredible adrenalin rush' (Sparta hooligan). Hooligans' will to violence reveals that football hooliganism may be viewed in part as 'just for kicks', as a goal in itself, that is, autotelic violence (Schinkel, 2004: 20-21). For hooligans, the pleasurable excitement associated with violent confrontations can only be achieved by violence itself, even though certain alternatives for violence (parading, aggro, pisstaking) may generate a comparable yet less intense 'rush'.

In their seminal piece *The Roots of Football Hooliganism* Eric Dunning and his colleagues (1988: 209-210) relate the meaning of fighting directly to lower-working-class culture. They argue that for lower-working-class males:

> Fighting is an important source of meaning, status and pleasurable emotional arousal. [...] Correspondingly, there is a tendency for them to 'back down' less frequently than males from other areas and also on occasions actively to seek out fights and confrontations. Of course, males generally in our society are expected to defend themselves if attacked, but they are less likely than lower-working-class males to be the initiators in this regard.

I have sought to demonstrate in this book that hooligan confrontations are an important source of identity and pleasurable emotional arousal not merely for lower-working-class males but for a wider variety of young males. The 'buzz' of football violence should not be understood as merely an epiphenomenon of social class, but rather as a constituent element of football hooliganism worldwide. Importantly, football hooliganism emerged as a specifically working-class youth subculture in the 1960s in England, but over time the phenomenon has come to attract a wider variety of male adolescents.

Intimately related to the 'buzz' of hooligan violence is the issue of (overcoming) fear. The narratives of football hooligans reveal that fear is a recurrent theme in preparing for and participating in violent confrontation. Courage is demonstrated not by a complete absence of fear, but rather by showing sufficient discipline to perform when one is afraid (Collins, 1995: 189-190; see Chapter One). Overcoming fear is crucial, for example, in confronting a quantitatively superior group, and it is precisely the overcoming of fear that generates the greatest pleasurable emotional arousal: 'We were standing there with three people facing a much larger group. That's the buzz, you know, but also the fear' (Sparta hooligan); 'I always thought I would never be seriously injured, that hooliganism was pretty safe. Recent fights have made me realize that it is not, and that it may backfire one day as it did for some others' (Sparta hooligan); 'Without fear hooliganism wouldn't give such an adrenalin rush. It is because of this fear that you get such a thrill, because you don't know what will happen next' (Feyenoord hooligan). Football hooliganism therefore has to retain an element of physical risk in order to enable intense peak experiences. Without the element of danger, excitement would be reduced dramatically (Kerr, 2005: 111). In the management of individual reputation, however, fear is often ascribed to others, whether they are opposing or fellow hooligans:

> The issue of fear, well, I know what you mean. I understand that. I have seen a lot of that in my mates and I think it is healthy to some degree. 'Cos you keep your wits about you, you know? But for myself, I have never been afraid. Honestly, never in my life. I know I can look after myself. (West Ham hooligan)

The construction of hard masculine identity

Hooligan formations celebrate a hard masculine identity based on physical prowess. A key aim of all hooligan groups is to successfully challenge their rivals through intimidation and violence as a way of securing or enhancing their status as a good 'firm' in the hierarchy of hooligan oppositions (Armstrong, 1994: 299). Hooligans' hard, hyperheterosexist masculine identity is constructed primarily in relation to perceived differences between self and the other. The other (i.e. opposing hooligans) is systematically demasculinized through ritual denigration of their physical and heterosexual prowess (real men versus 'poofs' or 'boys'; heterosexual dominant versus gay subordinate), the object of which is to attain an unambiguous sense of one's own masculinity by questioning the masculinity of opponents (cf. Free and Hughson, 2003: 151).

Football hooligans' construction of hard masculine identity is also linked to the deployment of race categories. Several Espanyol and FC Barcelona hooligans deploy such categories in constructing their own positional superiority, denigrating 'blacks' and 'blackness' as inferior categories. In contrast, at West Ham United and Feyenoord several 'black' participants are endowed with a hypermasculinity to be feared. 'Black' hooligans are often perceived by fellow group members as superior fighters and as having great mutual solidarity, appearing as daunting oppositional threats: 'this large black guy, he was fucking mental' (Feyenoord hooligan); 'these riot negroes are crazier than the whole lot' (Sparta hooligan about 'black' Feyenoord hooligans) (cf. Armstrong, 1998: 280). In these cases, it appears that 'blackness' is:

> reproduced as a racist category equated to raw physicality, to the sheer *embodiment* of masculine labor power, hence a caricatured hypermasculinity against which the 'lads'' masculine performances could be measured and the reproduction of ambivalence toward the 'Other' of '*black*' hypermasculinity (Free and Hughson, 2003: 141). (emphasis in original)

Although an overt concern with a self-image of hypermasculinity is characteristic of all hooligan groups under study, the construction of hard masculine identity is always located in particular spaces and times. At FC Barcelona and Espanyol, for example, hooligans construct their hard masculine identity not only in terms of physical prowess and sovereignty, but also in terms of political allegiance (i.e. neo-fascism or radical Catalan nationalism). Their masculine identities can be seen to contain elements of indigenous middle-class masculinity as well as of the values celebrated in some British working-class youth subcultures (e.g. the skinheads), which the Spanish hooligans introduced into their own cultural practices. In contrast, hooligan formations at West Ham and Feyenoord celebrate the core values of their traditional local working-class communities and industries, notably a focus on physical strength and the ability to 'look after oneself.' Here we see a strong cultural connection between admired masculinity and violent response to threat. Violence is not merely glorified, it is also so closely tied to masculinity that 'aggression becomes central to the boy's notion of manhood' (Campbell, 1993: 31). From a young age, these boys cultivate 'looking hard': 'I cultivated a way of walking. I mean, I walked perfectly normal up until I was about nine [years old], but then I

371

learned to walk hard, you know. Everybody did. And you cultivated that because it looked hard' (West Ham hooligan).

The above quotation shows that hard masculine identities are not only socially constructed and context-dependent, they are also inextricably related to the body as a meaningful construction itself. Messerschmidt (1999: 200) has shown that different masculinities emerge from practices that reflect different bodily resources, arguing that 'our bodies constrain or facilitate social action and, therefore, mediate and influence social practices.' For some young men, their bodies facilitate masculine agency, enabling successful construction of self as 'superior' to other boys. Due to the capacity for power that they embody, the fighting group is an arena where these male adolescents can bodily express themselves through physical confrontation. 'Within the collective setting of "me and my boys," such practices as individual and group assaultive violence were particularly attractive, providing a public ceremony of bodily domination over and humiliation of others' (Messerschmidt, 1999: 217).

Similar constructions of the body and masculinity can be found in football hooliganism. Individual and collective reputation and status rely principally upon bodily capacity. 'Being a good fighter' and being able to 'look after oneself' are viewed as major virtues, and the tallest and physically strongest male adolescents are usually talked about admiringly by peers. The response of peers to their conduct co-shapes the masculine meaning and image constructed by these hooligans through the practice of fighting: 'People looked up to me 'cos I was big for my age and a good fighter, you know. I was always with older boys and the most notorious gangs in the area' (former West Ham hooligan).

Three issues need to be addressed with regard to the construction of the body. First, it must be emphasized that hooligans do not equally possess this bodily capacity and that the 'good fighter' role is not the only social role available to members of hooligan formations (i.e. 'organizers', 'nutters', 'jokers'). These roles are both accorded to individuals by the group, and performed by the individuals themselves, with varying degrees of seriousness (Giulianotti and Armstrong, 2002: 219). Second, fighting abilities are negotiated and contested, as I will show in the discussion of the individual and collective management of reputation. Third, the construction of the body is also context-dependent. For example, hooligan formations at Espanyol and FC Barcelona construct bodily capacity not merely in terms of fighting ability, but also in terms of physical and mental health. As part of their neo-Nazi ethos, they celebrate the muscular, athletic body and, in the case of Espanyol, abstention from drug use – for example, the consumption of marihuana is considered as *algo de rojos* ('reds', communists) or *de musulmanes* (Muslims, especially North Africans). In contrast, in Argentinian football hooliganism *ser gordo* (being fat) is considered a major virtue, since it is a sign of a bodily capacity to fight and resist. For Argentinian fans, the 'fat man' is better prepared for fights than muscular, well-trained bodies or than those of normal weight. These overweight bodies should be viewed as 'non-hegemonic' or 'oppositional': they are part of an aesthetics that is different from the dominant masculinity in Argentinian society (Alabarces, 2005: 2). Furthermore, the consumption of drugs is viewed as a symbol of hard masculine identity and distinguishes the 'real man' from the 'non-male.'

Individual and collective management of reputation

Participation in football hooliganism enables supporters to gain status and prestige among peers. Within hooligan formations, individual reputations are established principally by demonstrating courage, fighting skills and an aura of hypermasculinity. Getting run, collectively, or running away, individually, during confrontations is perceived the gravest humiliation and defeat. But although reputations for toughness are established through successfully challenging rival hooligans, it is crucial that these results are communicated effectively, both internally and externally. Reputations are won or lost merely by intersubjective agreement. Collective and individual reputations for toughness and the *post facto* meaning of confrontations are highly negotiable and open to contestation, both between rival groups and within hooligan formations (cf. Giulianotti and Armstrong, 2002: 218; Armstrong, 1994: 320). Individuals of greater status are likely to have a greater influence in the course of this negotiation (King, 2001: 580). Apportioning honour between contestants is, nevertheless, very rarely settled in full. For example, the legitimacy of a recent attack by West Ham hooligans on a pub frequented by their Tottenham Hotspur rivals was heavily contested by the latter group, claiming that the attack did not constitute a 'defeat' since there were no hooligans inside the pub at that time (see Chapter Four). Contestation also occurs within hooligan formations, as in the case of older Feyenoord hooligans' condemnation of their younger counterparts' 'queer-bashing' activities (see Chapter Six).

Hooligans continuously engage in impression and reputation management. The dramaturgic metaphor introduced by Goffman (1959) is helpful to understanding hooligans' presentation of self. Goffman argued that all social interaction is like a theatrical performance in which actors perform one of the many roles available to them, depending on the situation in which they find themselves. Extending Goffman's (1959) analysis of self-presentation, Emler and Reicher's (1995: 112-113) concept of reputation management identifies two great problems for all actors on the stage of everyday life: reputations can decay without constant attention, but they can also persist to frustrate all efforts at personal change or betterment. Reputation management therefore requires that 'one must as far as possible act in ways that are consistent with the reputation to which one lays claim. Additionally, however, one must attend to publicity; there is no guarantee one's achievements will be broadcast.' Friends and enemies must be informed.

As Goffman observed, in all performances there can be problems of 'expressive control' caused by momentary lapses, slips and accidents which would convey impressions other than those intended. Therefore, one must also be prepared for reputation repair work, that is, to go out and 'put the record straight' (Emler and Reicher, 1995: 113). To retain or re-establish its honour and reputation, the hooligan formation has to respond effectively to (the threat of) defeat. In this context, Katz (1988: 141) has argued that once an attack by another group becomes public knowledge, 'a failure to respond threatens to make retrospectively ridiculous the pretensions of all in the attacked group.' He correctly asserts that:

> At this point, the history of posturing arrogance by the attacked group suddenly becomes a heavy commitment. What had been playfully under the group's control is now out of its hands; the group may no longer determine unilaterally to back off because other elite-styled groups see a prize in its defeat. Whether it delivers or receives the first blow, it has become controlled by its own symbolism.

The collective management of reputation is thus central to the evolvement and escalation of inter-group rivalry. Past events and disagreements between opposing groups can become important reference points in sustaining great hostility and triggering violent responses. This spiral of escalating violence has been particularly evident in the rivalries between FC Barcelona and Espanyol hooligans, Feyenoord and Ajax hooligans, and West Ham and Millwall hooligans. In such deep-seated inter-group hostilities serious injuries and deaths are relatively likely to occur. On the other hand, prestigious hooligan groups tend to consider many opposing formations as not worthy of confronting due to these formations' lack of status: 'Why would we attack inferior groups? I mean, of course you have to respond to challenges and this may happen spontaneously, but we wouldn't go out and seek to confront them. They simply aren't worth it, and there is usually no particular rivalry with these groups either' (Feyenoord hooligan). The latter groups, however, are often particularly eager to inflict damage on the more prestigious groups as a way of enhancing their status in the hierarchy of hooligan oppositions. Examples of this process are the occasional attacks by less prestigious hooligan formations on alleged members of West Ham's hooligan group, even though in reality these often turn out to be non-hooligan supporters (see Chapter Four). A similar dynamic can be observed at an interpersonal level in the 'added value' of attacking informal hooligan leaders or notorious fighters: 'Everybody was talking about this Rolo, like he was a real mean bastard, you know. He was the one to take on. So on match day I told my mates, "look, I will get this Rolo and beat the shit out of him"' (former West Ham hooligan).

Territorial identifications

Territorial identifications play an important role in the construction of hooligan identities and inter-group rivalries. Hooligans identify specific spaces as their home 'turf' or territory. Space, in this sense, does not simply exist as an ontological fact; it is endowed with social meanings and regimes of signification (Lefebvre, 1991).[2] The emergence of youth ends with their exclusive territory within the ground was accompanied by a shift in territorial claims on ground space. While the ground had always been a central source of 'topophilia', groups of young fans increasingly began to regard their specific sections of the ground as home turf to be defended against outsiders, that is, opposing fan groups. Violation of this 'sacred' space was frequently the immediate cause of the severest of conflict displays (Marsh, 1978: 99). Visiting fans attempted to 'take' the home territory to demonstrate their toughness, while the home fans would try to expel them.

Territorial identifications are not limited to the football ground. The gradual decline in opportunities for fighting within football grounds had the unintended consequence of increasingly relocating hooligan encounters from football grounds to new locales, altering the geographical meaning of the ground for football hooliganism (see Chapter Eleven; cf. Giulianotti and Armstrong, 2002: 224). Contested urban spaces include the areas surrounding the ground, pubs, railway stations, city districts or entire cities. As one former West Ham hooligan put it:

> What we wanted to do as a group, we wanted to defend our territory in the East End of London, which was West Ham, but we also wanted to go out to other parts of London and up and down the country to say 'we are the hardest, we are the best and we can take on anybody if we want to'.

Importantly, home turf is defended only against opposing groups of young fans who share, fundamentally, the same values (i.e. a will to violent confrontation). There is no question of excluding everyone else except your own immediate group (Marsh, 1978: 99). Thus, as we have seen, honour is lost rather than earned when a hooligan formation allows or promotes attacks on non-hooligan supporters or bystanders. Notwithstanding this broadly shared moral convention (which is regularly violated), I have demonstrated that important local and national variations occur in hooligans' sense of how honour and reputation are won. Among certain groups of Spanish right-wing skinhead fans, individual and collective prestige can be won by assaulting or intimidating ethnic minorities, transvestites or members of rival, non-hooligan youth subcultures (i.e. punks, left-wing skinheads), all of which are perceived as 'inferior' categories. Occasionally hooligans' territorial identifications blur informal codes of legitimate action. In February 2006, a group of 70 Ajax hooligans attacked and sought to set fire to the 'supporters' home' of ADO Den Haag, a hangout for both hooligans and non-hooligan supporters. During the attack three non-hooligan fans were injured. Later that night the police prevented a group of 150 Den Haag hooligans from travelling to Amsterdam to avenge the attack on Ajax hooligans' own turf.

As we have seen in Chapter One, hooligans' territorial identifications are characterized by a degree of fluidity. Hooligans regularly form temporary alliances on a variety of shifting levels (Dunning et al., 1988: 201-202). Domestic alliances have occurred between Sparta and Haarlem hooligans and between Espanyol and Real Madrid ultras. In addition, West Ham hooligans have temporarily suspended domestic antagonisms when supporting the English national team, jointly taking on foreign opponents. Transnational alliances can also be observed, for example between Feyenoord and Antwerp hooligans, between FC Barcelona and Genoa hooligans, or between Espanyol and Hellas Verona ultras. Both domestic and transnational alliances are continuously negotiated and can be suspended or shifted.

Special reference should be made here of the expression of intra-city hooligan rivalries in cities with two or more professional football clubs (of which London, Rotterdam and Barcelona are but three examples). In these intra-city rivalries there is, at the everyday level, a stronger contextualization of time and space in distinguishing the legitimate and illegitimate pursuit of hooligan rivalries (Giulianotti and Armstrong, 2002: 229). To enable the continuation of other forms of social identity the intra-city rivals' full dispensation to initiate violence is rather inhibited. In the majority of social spaces oppositions between hooligan formations tend to be functionally suppressed and intra-city rivalries are generally regarded as sanctioned only within match-day contexts. For example, two hooligan rivals living only two streets away from each other in a central district of Barcelona seem to have achieved some form of informal agreement as to the suspension of their animosities in everyday life:

> Of course, we run into each other all the time. Usually I just nod and walk on. Honestly, there is no point in confronting him in the streets, is there? I mean, where would that end? He knows where I live and I know where he lives. It's a different story when our groups meet on match days. I mean, we have fought each other on various occasions over the years. But during the week there is this kind of mutual understanding. (Espanyol hooligan)

377

Or, as a West Ham hooligan previously working as a bouncer in a London night club commented: 'In all my years as a bouncer I have never been assaulted by rival hooligans. They knew I was working there, but there was no point in mixing up these things, you know. My work had nothing to do with football.' Interestingly, rival hooligans have also occasionally jointly organized and worked as bouncers at dance parties and sporting events.

In many cases some form of balance in the distribution of access to leisure resources is achieved. Particular pubs, nightclubs and streets are routinely regarded as established territory for one side or another. The entry of opposing groups to these spaces is therefore regarded as deliberately transgressive and assumed to be intimidating, unless other explanations exist (Giulianotti and Armstrong, 2002: 229). A striking example of this negotiation of leisure resources is the intra-city rivalry between FC Barcelona and Espanyol hooligans, especially in the early 1990s (see Chapters Eight and Nine). At other moments, however, hooligan encounters at concerts, dance parties or political manifestations have erupted into fighting. Furthermore, the personalization of animosities between individual rivals, usually founded in prior engagements, can threaten to break into a restoration of collective violence (Giulianotti and Armstrong, 2002: 229). In the Netherlands, minor conflicts between opposing hooligans during dance events have increasingly transformed such events into legitimate sites for contestation.

Finally, it should be mentioned that the intensity of intra-city hooligan animosities varies considerably across localities. Whereas the intra-city rivalries between several London-based hooligan formations and between FC Barcelona and Espanyol hooligans have been particularly fierce, the rivalry between Feyenoord and Sparta hooligans has been principally non-violent. The relationship between the two groups is vertical to some degree, in the sense that differences in size and reputation are comparatively large. Sparta hooligans are principally concerned with confronting certain lower-league rivals with whom they have established deep-seated animosities, while many Feyenoord hooligans do not consider their local rivals worthy of confronting due to their lack of status: 'Sparta doesn't have any hooligans. I mean, nothing compared to what we've got. I don't dislike them or anything, I simply can't be bothered' (Feyenoord hooligan).

Although violent confrontation is the highpoint of the hooligan's existence and crucial to the construction of collective and individual reputations, it is not the only source of meaning and identity in football hooliganism. Hooligan formations provide their members with a sense of belonging, mutual solidarity and friendship. As one Sparta hooligan put it:

> For many of us friendship, belonging and adventure are just as important as fighting, if not more important. I mean, if it was only about violence you could just beat up anybody in the streets. Hooliganism is much more than that.

Narratives of hooligans reveal how group members claim to 'look after one another' and stick together through thick and thin. Group members are often also among their closest friends and collective experiences strengthen their sense of togetherness: 'When I was in jail, my mates looked after my mum. I'll never forget that, you know. They are my true friends' (Feyenoord hooligan). It is this combination of belonging, recognition and reputation that enables the young males to achieve a sense of personal worth and identity (cf. Marsh et al., 1978). The group is commonly perceived by hard-core hooligans as a major influence in their lives, at least for some time, and some view the group as a substitute for family: 'I always felt that the West Ham lads were my family more than my home family, despite me coming from a stable family. [...] Maybe we found a family we never had at home' (West Ham hooligan).[3] Affection for the group tends to be deepest among core members and within close-knit subgroups rather than in the periphery of the group.

The group is also a source of unofficial protection and remedy for grievances. Relations with ingroup members are characteristically those of protection rather than aggression. Even when there is conflict within a group it is normally less serious or significant than conflict between groups (Patrick, 1973). Although some degree of intra-group conflict can be found in most hooligan formations (see Chapter Ten), on very few occasions this conflict does overshadow inter-group hostilities. A notable exception is the contemporary manifestation of football hooliganism at FC Barcelona, which is characterized by an exceptionally high level of intra-group anxiety and intimidation. What we find in this case is that when subgroup differences (e.g. in political allegiance) become more and more emphasized, ingroup identity gradually breaks down and gives way to newly emerging oppositional identities, resulting in overt hostility and confrontation and, eventually, in the collapse of the hooligan formation and the rise of new fan identities. This development can be viewed in terms of the microscopic processes of distinction and imitation described in this book (for example in Chapter One).

The sense of group membership is also rewarding in a different sense: it enables peak experiences. Part of the 'buzz' of football hooliganism seems to lie not in violence itself, but in a transcendent, sensual quality of 'being with the mob': 'We were mob-handed and everybody at the place [a boxing arena] was afraid of us, including the bouncers. It was an incredible feeling, a real adrenalin rush' (Feyenoord hooligan). The group is ultimately a place where many things are happening at the same time in a more or less chaotic and spontaneous manner. In this context, Katz (1988: 144) has emphasized:

> the delight in discovering the spiritual power of a collective posturing as deviant: how, once the group is constituted, a coherent line of action can spring spontaneously from chaos. The very unpredictability of actions and reactions makes 'being with the mob' predictably exciting. Otherwise unimaginable, transcendent possibilities are now sensed as real.

Besides benefits from group membership there are also duties and risks. Individual interests are linked with those of the hooligan group as a whole. There is an interdependence of individual action and group fate, which makes it quite distinct from vandalism or theft: 'Non-participation in these latter activities may violate group norms, it may show one to be cowardly or boring, but it does not actively let down other group members. So individuals may also get involved in fights to protect their fellow group members' (Emler and Reicher, 1995: 198). Individuals must protect the group's honour, even at the risk of personal injury, if they are to enjoy the benefits which come from membership of the group (King, 2001: 574). I vividly recall an example from my fieldwork among Sparta hooligans. In the aftermath of a confrontation between Sparta and FC Dordrecht hooligans, one Sparta hooligan was questioned by other group members as to his whereabouts during the fight, since they suspected he had run off during the fight. He claimed that he got hit by a riot police officer's baton and suffered a concussion. This story was confirmed by other group members who witnessed the incident. Although his story was eventually accepted, unconvinced group members paid extra close attention to his behaviour on following occasions: 'There's just too many guys who say they want to fight but shit their pants when it goes off. We can't rely on people like that' (Sparta hooligan). On the other hand, when faced by a much larger group, collective fleeing is sometimes deemed appropriate, although it does mean the group will 'lose face'. As one Feyenoord hooligan commented:

> A lot of people say, like, 'I never run away, I always stand my ground.' That's just non-sense. Listen, if I had never run away during a fight, do you think I would still be here today? I mean, if they confront you with fifty or one hundred people and you are there with ten men, you have to run, don't you? It's simply too dangerous, especially since they might be armed with knives or whatever.

The pressure to participate in violent confrontation does not merely come from the ingroup. Even if a person wishes to avoid a fight, this wish may be ignored by the opposing group. Merely as a member of a rival group this person becomes a target. In fact, individuals do not even have to be in a group in order to become the focus of aggression, they only have to be identified as members of another hooligan group. Just as ingroup pressures can commit individuals to confront members of the outgroup, so outgroup assumptions can draw people into conflict without it being individually wanted (Emler and Reicher, 1995: 198). Examples of this kind are the several attacks on individuals allegedly affiliated to the hooligan formations of FC Barcelona and Espanyol in the late 1980s and early 1990s.

381

Closely related to the collective management of reputation are the issues of sovereignty and autonomy. Football hooligans seek to present a self-image of being capable of 'looking after oneself', both collectively and individually. This presentation of self contains a number of elements. The first element relates to the presentation of self as a militant force of sovereign rule. Hooligan formations find violence 'compellingly attractive as a means of sustaining the aura of dread that is an essential element in their project of elite rule' (Katz, 1988: 137). But violence is not the only way in which sovereignty can be displayed. An important element of hooligan rivalries is the great deal of symbolic opposition and ritualized aggression involved. In its purest form, this 'aggro' is 'the art of subduing one's rival simply by conning him into thinking that his cause is lost from the outset. The aim is to achieve the end that a violent assault might but without resorting to violence' (Marsh, 1978: 17). A key component of aggro is bluff; taunts, 'eyeing each other up' from a distance and graffiti are very much part of this act. Provocation and intimidation of the opponent and, more generally, of the 'outside world' is also enacted through symbols, dress and language. For example, references to 'ultraviolence' and one of its main exponents, the character of Alex in Stanley Kubrick's controversial film of Anthony Burgess's (1962) *A Clockwork Orange*, have been widespread. FC Barcelona and Espanyol hooligans use such references in their displays and fanzines, whereas for a short period of time Fulham hooligans carried walking sticks.[4]

Aggro is closely related to another routine practice of hooligan formations: parading. Parading – within the ground, on local streets and on foreign turf – is the process of walking in apparent unison past a relatively stationary public while displaying insignia of membership in a diffusely threatening group (Katz, 1988: 142). The thrill of the parade may also be achieved by reversing the relationship between viewer and viewed, as when hooligans pace about a public location, gesturing defiance and shouting insults at will. No practice of violence is necessary. Parading plays an important part in the collective management of reputation, allowing the group to sustain its tough image. Moreover, aggro and parading are routine practices that, in addition to violence, are universally employed to raise the spirit of the group and to prevent boredom. As we have seen, hooligans seek to counter the boredom and restraints of everyday life. Consequently, as Katz (1988: 142) has correctly argued, 'perhaps the greatest danger to the survival of the fighting group as an entity that embraces the lived experience of members is not the strength of other gangs or pressure from the police, but boredom.'

I would argue that the threat of boredom is, in fact, in part related to pressure from agents of social control. Although on the one hand police surveillance and security measures in and around football grounds enable relatively non-injurious symbolic opposition, on the other hand they limit opportunities for fighting and, thus, for experiencing pleasurable emotional arousal. This may explain why hooligan encounters nowadays tend to occur away from football grounds and why several hooligan formations go to great lengths to escape police observation. When intent on confronting opponents, parading is considered undesirable since it frustrates attempts to remain unnoticed by the police. I recall an incident with the Sparta Youth Crew on an inter-city train. One hooligan provoked passengers and revealed the identity of the group by shouting abuse and chants such as 'Rotterdam Hooligans'. He was told off by the group's informal leaders for attracting the police's attention even before they had gotten off the train: 'Shut up, we don't want to be noticed by the police, remember. We don't want them to await us at the platform, do we?' On other occasions, when opportunities for fighting are seen as limited or when a group fears the opponent (e.g. on foreign turf) or is not prepared to fight, parading can become the main practice for that day. I have shown in Chapter Ten that hooligans groups at FC Barcelona and Espanyol often prefer public visibility over violent encounter due to their focus on the provocation of outsiders, notably through their skinhead attire and neo-Nazi symbology. In this case, the public spectacle of having to stroll through a host city with police escort is seen as a relatively safe and effective form of public protest.

To sum up, while they are important elements of the hooligan experience, aggro and parading alone cannot satisfy the needs of committed hooligans. There has to be at least the threat of physical violence. Aggro and parading should therefore be viewed in addition to violence rather than as replacing physical confrontation. Football hooliganism cannot simply be viewed as non-injurious symbolic opposition since (the negotiation of) violent confrontation is a key component of the hooligan identity and management of reputation. One has to show that one is 'for real', at least occasionally.

Hooligans' presentation of self as sovereign rulers is closely related to their sense of autonomy, that is, their perceived ability to make their own decisions about what to do rather than being influenced by someone else or being told what to do. Two issues are of particular interest here. First, hooligans' sense of autonomy develops in relation to the continuous social interaction between themselves and agents of social control. Throughout the text I have stressed that this type of interaction is a key component of the manifestation and development of football hooliganism. In Chapter Eleven it was demonstrated that formal policies are tacitly negotiated, producing informal sets of rules. Police officers are generally accepted as being part of the 'game', yet hooligans regularly attempt to manipulate, disrupt or circumvent security regimes.

Second, several hooligan groups have been successful in 'playing up' their media image as 'paramilitary forces' that engage in meticulously planned confrontation, demonstrating a sense of arrogance of being the toughest 'firm' in the country. Self-identifying hooligans appear on television programmes and documentaries, in press reports, in books, and so on. Experienced hooligans are particularly recognizant of the constructed nature of fan and hooligan reputations and resemble, in some respects, the 'post-fan' described by Giulianotti (1999). However, unlike Giulianotti's 'post-fan', they are, to varying degrees, still involved in violent confrontation, either as core group members or as 'semi-retired' practitioners. Hooligans can also be viewed as successful entrepreneurs. Although often publicly condemning the commodification and mediatization of football culture, experienced hooligans creatively 'cash in' on the demand for hooligan memorabilia. I will address this issue in more detail in the final section of this chapter.

Focal concerns of football hooliganism: elements of resistance and compliance

The focal concerns described in this section are key aspects of football hooliganism transnationally. I would argue that football hooliganism involves elements of both resistance and compliance. The hooligan subculture should not be viewed as a counter-culture that is alienated from the values appreciated in the dominant culture. Many of the values celebrated in the hooligan subculture reflect to some degree conventional values in (Western) society, for example norms of masculinity and the quest for excitement and 'thrills'. Rather than being alienated from adult, conventional values, football hooligans celebrate a distorted and heightened version of these conventional values through the deviant influences of peer pressure. In this context, Miller's (1958) theory of lower-class adolescent gangs underlined the similarities between gang and parent culture, arguing that the characteristics and behaviour of lower-class gangs reflect, in a distorted or heightened form, the features of the entire working-class population. Although Miller's theory applies in many respects to the hooligan formations at West Ham United and Feyenoord, I would suggest that the characteristics and behaviour of hooligan formations do not merely reflect, in a distorted or heightened form, the core features of the lower working class, but rather what Matza and Sykes (1961) have called a subterranean value system. Matza and Sykes argued that the values of delinquents are not deviant, opposed to the larger society, but reflect the subterranean values of a society:

> the delinquent may not stand as an alien in the body of society but may represent instead a disturbing reflection or a caricature. [...] The delinquent has picked up and emphasized one part of the dominant value system, namely, the subterranean values that coexist with other, publicly proclaimed values possessing a more respectable air. These subterranean values [...] bind the delinquent to the society whose laws he violates (1961: 717).

Two subterranean values are of particular interest in this context. First, the search for adventure, excitement and thrills is a subterranean value that exists side by side with the values of security and routinization (cf. Elias and Dunning, 1986). Displays of 'daring' and the search for excitement – as opposed to the routine – are acceptable and desirable in society at large, but only when confined to certain circumstances such as sport, recreation and holidays (Matza and Sykes, 1961: 716). Second, the idea of aggression as a proof of toughness and masculinity is widely accepted in Western cultures. 'The ability to take it and hand it out, to defend one's rights and one's reputation with force, to prove one's manhood by hardness and physical courage – all are widespread' (ibid.: 717). More generally, Matza and Sykes argued that the dominant society exhibits a widespread taste for violence, since fantasies of violence in books, movies and on television are everywhere at hand (see also Schinkel, 2004). I will elaborate on this theme in the final part of the chapter, when I discuss the commodification of football hooliganism. In the following section, I analyze the manifestation of football hooliganism in fan cultures.

Habitus and the manifestation of football hooliganism in fan cultures

One of the central arguments developed in this book is that manifestations of football hooliganism vary considerably across localities. I have demonstrated that football hooliganism is not an evenly distributed phenomenon and that important variations occur in its extent and nature at an intra-city level, that is, between different football clubs within a single city. The argument I would like to put forward here is that fan habitus and attendant collective fan identities strongly influence patterns of behaviour and should therefore be viewed as a partial explanation for intra-city differences in the extent and nature of football hooliganism. I agree with Robson (2000: 54) that 'it is untenable to posit the outlines of a definitive, all-encompassing habitus. Rather, it may be possible to summarize a number of key themes which [...] have structured particular sensibilities and orientations out of extraordinary processual histories.' Furthermore, it is important to emphasize that collective fan identities are not homogeneous, but instead continuously negotiated and contested. I focus here on the dominant collective identities in fan cultures, temporarily neglecting the fact that distinctive types of fan identities can be identified within, or in addition to, these dominant fan identities.[5]

The concept of habitus, as developed by Bourdieu (1984), is of particular use here because it maintains a focus on the structural-processual positionings of class-based collectivities.[6] The importance of social class as a meaningful sociological category is heavily contested in postmodernist social theory. More specifically, recent research into English football culture has emphasized the major structural changes in the class composition of football crowds as well as in the working class itself (Giulianotti, 1999: 147). These changes can be observed, to varying degrees, in each of the six case studies. Furthermore, in Chapter Ten I have demonstrated that the class backgrounds of football hooligans vary across localities. Football hooliganism emerged as a specifically working-class youth subculture in the 1960s in England, but over time the phenomenon has come to attract a wider variety of male adolescents. At the same time, however, the persistence of fan identities demonstrates how elements of cultural continuity are reproduced in ever shifting circumstances in ways that are both adaptive and cohesive (cf. Robson, 1997: 2). The habitus, then, is a system of durable and transposable collective dispositions which ensure the active presence of past experiences, an embodied history internalized as a 'second nature' (Bourdieu, 1990: 56). Painter (2000: 242) describes habitus as:

> the mediating link between objective social structures and individual action and refers to the embodiment in individual actors of systems of social norms, understandings and patterns of behaviour, which, while not wholly determining action [...] do ensure that individuals are more disposed to act in some ways than others.

Striking examples of the continuing importance of social class in the reproduction of collective fan identities can be found at Feyenoord and West Ham United. Both clubs have deep-seated working-class traditions that continue to inform their fan cultures in the sense that they shape a social consciousness which invests in masculine embodiment, physical skills and prowess, despite significant changes in the social composition of their fan bases (both clubs attract an increasing number of middle-class fans) and in the working-class districts these clubs represent. Although an emphasis on masculine norms and identities is characteristic of many supporter cultures, it is especially in modern industrial heartlands like these that 'hard' masculine norms are reproduced and appreciated (cf. Giulianotti, 1999: 155). In the cases of Feyenoord and West Ham class remains a meaningful sociological category for explaining football hooliganism, even when fans' and hooligans' material conditions and the social demography of the areas which these clubs represent change.

The concept of habitus can also be used to explain intra-city differences in the extent of football hooliganism. The relatively low level of football hooliganism at Fulham and Sparta can be understood in terms of collective fan identities at these clubs. These fan identities are continuously constructed and secured, 'not only by facing the present and future but also by reconstructing the collectivity's earlier life' (Alexander, 2004: 26). The fan identities are constructed in relation to the perceived differences between self and the other. Habitus is thus not only a sense of one's place, but it is also a sense of the other's place. The significant others are systematically portrayed as 'rough' and 'uncivilized', producing a sense of self that stresses the appropriateness of civilized, non-violent behaviour.

The habitus of Sparta and Fulham supporters 'tends to guarantee the "correctness" of practices and their constancy over time, more reliably than all formal rules and explicit norms' (Bourdieu, 1990: 54). The habitus informs fan behaviour in two ways. On the one hand, it tends to generate all the 'reasonable' behaviours which are possible within the limits of objective regularities, 'and which are likely to be positively sanctioned because they are objectively adjusted to the logic characteristic of a particular field, whose objective future they anticipate.' On the other hand, the habitus 'tends to exclude all "extravagances" ("not for the likes of us"), that is, all the behaviours that would be negatively sanctioned because they are incompatible with the objective conditions' (Bourdieu, 1990: 55-56). Importantly, the non-hooligan image of these clubs also informs opposing supporters' and hooligans' expectations of the behaviour of the home crowd and usually results in a non-aggressive approach.

The collective identities of Fulham and Sparta supporters are informed to some degree by class consciousness. This class consciousness is principally visible at Sparta, where ingroup and outgroup relations are produced not merely in terms of differences in club allegiance (Sparta versus Feyenoord), but also in terms of the perceived differences between the clubs' traditional social environments (North versus South of the river Meuse; middle-class versus working-class). Fulham fan identity is informed to some degree by middle-class and upper-working-class values, distinguishing itself from typical working-class clubs and their perceived 'rough' crowds (i.e. West Ham United, Portsmouth, Cardiff City). With regard to Chelsea, narratives of Fulham fans reveal perceived differences between the 'flash', 'hypercommodified' Chelsea area (with Chelsea Village as its major symbol) and the more authentic, traditional Fulham (with Craven Cottage as its key symbol). These findings resemble in some respects the research carried out by Williams and his colleagues (1988) at Watford FC. They argued that 'hooligan behaviour does not rest easily within the general framework of club activities or alongside the reputation established locally and outside Watford by the "friendly" club' (1988: 41). They concluded that the generally affluent and cosmopolitan audience attracted by the club is the main reason for the absence of football hooliganism at Watford: '[T]he kind of audience attracted by Watford is crucial in understanding the club's non-hooligan traditions. These traditions are, in turn, important in limiting the hooliganism of local fans and in producing a relatively sanguine and non-aggressive approach on the part of visitors to Watford' (1988: 41).

The construction of non-violent fan identities cannot, however, be fully explained in terms of class consciousness. Rather, it needs to be viewed in conjunction with more culturally and historically specific aspects, including the meaning of local football rivalry in identity formation and specific club histories. For example, any explanation of the relatively low level of football hooliganism at Fulham and its decline from the mid-1970s onwards needs to take into consideration a number of factors, such as the club's declining on-field successes and the growing reputation of Chelsea's hooligan formation, which encouraged many local prospective practitioners to join the ranks of the latter. The construction of 'friendly' fan identities should be viewed in terms of continuous processes of social distinction, of defining one's identity in opposition to a hated other (in these cases Chelsea and Feyenoord). At a time when the other came to hold a widespread reputation for football hooliganism, Fulham and Sparta fans increasingly defined themselves as non-hooligans. Association with non-violence thus became a major differential characteristic in the production and reproduction of the collective identities, an effective way of claiming moral superiority over the other. The non-hooligan identity is reproduced through informal and formal social controls, as we have seen in Chapter Eleven.

Because of the negative sanctioning of hooligan behaviour at Fulham and Sparta, young supporters interested in becoming involved in football hooliganism are likely to either follow one of the more notorious football clubs or eschew their

389

hooligan proclivities. Giulianotti (1995: 196) has referred to these processes in his analysis of Scottish fan culture:

> Those Scottish soccer casuals travelling with the national side tend to eschew the hooligan habitus for the duration of the tournament. [...] Alternatively, there are hooligan formations such as the Hibs casuals which are alienated by the Scottish support's persona. A handful have marked out their fundamental antipathy towards the reputation of Scottish fans by following English supporters to fixtures abroad, in the hope of either witnessing or getting caught up in football-related violence.

Crucial to the maintenance of 'friendly' fan identities is also that incidents of spectator violence, which may occasionally occur, 'are presented by fans, media and authorities as isolated incidents or, more commonly, consciously ignored' (Giulianotti, 1995: 214). Supporters and club directors at Sparta and Fulham have regularly publicly complained about the disproportionate punishments their clubs received for relatively minor incidents, while the 'real troublemakers' at other clubs were allegedly being dealt with insufficiently by the authorities. The 'friendly' fan identity at Fulham is also secured by fans' reconstruction of the manifestation of football hooliganism at the club in the late 1960s and early 1970s, which is generally viewed as a minor and temporary 'excess'. Hooligan incidents involving Sparta supporters have generally been downplayed by club officials in order to maintain the club's positive public image. Media representations continue to portray Sparta as one of the country's most 'friendly' football clubs.

It is important to reiterate that habitus is durable but not immutable or eternal (Bourdieu and Wacquant, 1992: 133). Bourdieu regards habitus as an open concept since actors' dispositions are constantly subjected to a range of different experiences. The dispositions that comprise habitus may be affected by new experiences in terms of being either reinforced or modified. In other words, while each habitus is set by historical and socially situated conditions, it also allows new forms and actions. Although Bourdieu anticipates that most experiences will serve to reinforce actors' habitus (as people are more likely to encounter situations and interpret them according to their pre-existing dispositions rather than to modify their feelings), he does accept that changes may occur (Hillier and Rooksby, 2002: 6; Bourdieu, 2002: 29).

The empirical data show that contestation of 'friendly' or hooligan identities may take on more successful and durable forms. On the one hand, recent developments at Espanyol reveal how hooligan identities can be successfully challenged by a more pacified fan identity. This contestation should be viewed within the context of the historical public image of Espanyol within Catalonia and the club's recurrent attempts to change this image (see Chapter Eight). On the other hand, the recent emergence of a hooligan formation at Sparta demonstrates how a small group of young fans may challenge the 'friendly' fan identity through the introduction of a hooligan style. Yet, as we have seen in Chapter Seven, the emergence of football hooliganism at Sparta has not resulted in a general redefinition or rejection of the 'friendly' fan identity, since the hooligan group is comparatively small and principally operates away from the ground, escaping self-monitoring within the fan community as well as regularly circumventing formal social controls. Hooliganism is therefore not (yet) viewed as an immediate threat to non-violent fan identity.

My argument that fan and hooligan identities are not merely a product of class-specific lifestyles can be further illustrated by the fan cultures of FC Barcelona and Espanyol. By the early 1920s, and especially after the Spanish Civil War, FC Barcelona and Espanyol came to symbolize two diametrically opposed social, cultural and political conceptions: Catalan nationalism versus anti-Catalanism, anti-Spanishness versus Spanishness, and integration versus non-integration. Whereas FC Barcelona came to symbolize the oppressed people of Catalonia, Espanyol was perceived to favour the right-wing military of Franco's Spain. Although in recent years the political aspect of the rivalry has somewhat diminished, the habitus of both sets of fans still closely reflects these deep-seated mutual perceptions, as the active presence of past experiences. Fan identity at FC Barcelona is constructed as part of the club's presentation of self as 'more than a club', that is, as a powerful symbol of Catalan nationalism. In contrast, the dominant fan identity at Espanyol is produced in opposition to the 'treacherous', 'hypercommodified' other. Most Espanyol fans seek to alter their club's persistent stigma which they claim is being reproduced time and again by the other and institutions affiliated to it (i.e. media, government). Class consciousness plays a relatively minor role in the construction of these contrapuntal identities. I have demonstrated in earlier chapters that the formation of hooligan identities at the two clubs should be understood within the context of these contrapuntal identities and that, accordingly, they are less related to class relations.

Fan and hooligan identities and the impact of serious violence

Collective fan identities and their social, cultural and historical underpinnings are not only crucial to understanding local manifestations of football hooliganism, but also to understanding the precise effects of violent incidents on fan communities. Comparable incidents of spectator violence produce variable outcomes, adding to the spatial and temporal variability of the phenomenon under consideration. In other words, the precise effects of violent incidents are also context-dependent. These effects principally depend on the *post facto* meaning of the incident as negotiated by hooligans and significant others (i.e. non-hooligan supporters, opposing hooligans, club officials, police, media).

Let me illustrate this point by briefly discussing the reversal theory explanation of football hooliganism proposed by John Kerr (2005; 1994). Kerr stresses that football hooliganism has to retain an element of physical risk and that, in this sense, 'stabbings, beatings, and occasional deaths are necessary' (2005: 111). However, Kerr argues, there must be a balance, 'with enough danger to maintain the perception of risk but not so much that the risk becomes too great, because then any protective frame will be "broken" and many of the participants will drop out.' This psychological protective frame resembles in some respects the embodied boundaries and restraints produced by the habitus. Kerr applies the idea of a protective frame to the violent confrontation between Feyenoord and Ajax hooligans on 23 March 1997. He concludes that:

> Many of the Feijenoord [*sic*] hooligans who attended the confrontation at Beverwijk *would likely have been* buoyed up by the media attention and their success against Ajax hooligans. For most, [the death and injuries] *would not have been* sufficient to break the paratelic protective frame that encompasses their hooligan activity. Quite the opposite: knowledge of the

death and injuries *would have been likely* to enhance the challenge, danger, and excitement associated with hooligan fighting. Consequently, further hooligan aggression and violence by Feijenoord [*sic*] hooligans was almost inevitable (2005: 111; emphasis added).

Kerr's analysis of the hooligan confrontation at Beverwijk is incorrect in three respects, which has important theoretical implications. These flaws seem to be principally a consequence of the speculative nature of Kerr's approach, as he relied solely upon media reports and did not actually witness the confrontation or interrogate its participants (hence the various speculations emphasized in the above quotation). First, opposite to what Kerr suggests, the confrontation was not pre-arranged and the hooligans were not 'totally successful in outwitting the police' (2005: 104). Second, in their attempt to explain the immediate causes of the confrontation, Kerr and De Kock (2002: 5) seem to place too much emphasis on the provocative insult by a Feyenoord hooligan as an affront that could not be ignored by Ajax hooligans: 'Probably feeling humiliated with the television coverage of their earlier failings, the insult produced a reactive negativistic response and at the same time acted as a challenge.' Although there is some truth in their argument, any understanding of the incident should take into consideration the deep-seated hostility between Feyenoord and Ajax hooligans and the spiral of escalating violence that preceded the incident, starting in the 1980s (see Chapter Six; Van der Torre and Spaaij, 2003; Van Gageldonk, 1996).

Third, and most important for present purposes, Kerr seems to misinterpret the immediate and medium-term consequences of the confrontation. The fighting at Beverwijk cannot simply be viewed as enhancing the challenge and excitement associated with hooligan encounters since for many Feyenoord hooligans the event did 'break' their paratelic protective frame, to use Kerr's words. Four issues are relevant here: (i) the death of an Ajax hooligan, and the confrontation as a whole, was not celebrated as a victory but rather as a defeat for both parties. Most core participants argued that things had gone too far;[7] (ii) many Feyenoord hooligans had 'a very bad feeling' beforehand, largely eroding the excitement and anticipation related to the confrontation; (iii) the confrontation had negative consequences for its participants, including constrictive security measures, prolonged banning orders,

393

prison sentences, fines and a (temporary) decrease in group cohesion; (iv) in the following seasons the police registered a marked decline in incidents of violence provoked by Feyenoord hooligans (CIV, 1998). At present, several long-standing hooligans are no longer, or less centrally, involved in the group and the frequency and seriousness of physical confrontations between Ajax and Feyenoord hooligans have diminished.[8]

The discussion of the precise effects of serious violence on hooligan identities is theoretically interesting because it shows that violence does not necessarily lead to more violence. Death and serious injury tend to have a deep impact on the development of football and hooligan rivalries, but the type of impact may vary considerably depending on the *post facto* meaning of the incident as negotiated by hooligans, non-hooligan supporters and other participants in local arenas (i.e. club, police, media). The framing of violent incidents is thus not merely a matter of negotiation within and between hooligan formations, but also takes place within wider fan communities, especially at football clubs with a deep-seated 'friendly' fan identity. I will illustrate this argument with four examples that can be distinguished along two dimensions: (i) the context of the incident (hooligan related/non-hooligan related); (ii) the effects of the negotiation (conflict escalation/de-escalation). The four examples are listed in Table 11.1. These examples highlight the more specific football-related and hooligan-related 'cleavages' that fuel and contour the development of fan cultures and hooligan subcultures.

Table 12.1   The impact of serious violence on fan and hooligan identities.

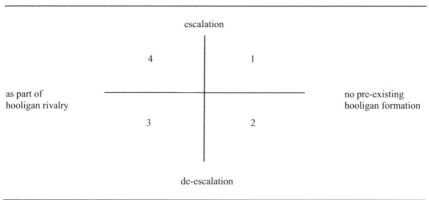

1   *Violence leads to the escalation of inter-group rivalry at a club without a*
        pre-existing hooligan formation.

The first example involves the escalation of inter-group rivalry at a football club without a pre-existing hooligan subculture. The escalation of violence can be viewed as contestation of the dominant fan discourse by a small section of fans, resulting in the emergence of a hooligan subculture. An example of this kind is the assault on a young Sparta fan in 1999. The young male was seriously injured by a group of Willem II hooligans in Tilburg. Although occasional, relatively minor incidents of spectator violence involving Sparta fans had occurred before, this particular incident was perceived by a small group of young fans, including the victim, as a major event that had to be avenged. The incident generated a deep-seated hostility between the two opposing fan groups and contributed to the group's increasing identification with football hooliganism. The group began to travel more regularly by train, eschewing the official coach arrangements they had previously preferred, to increase the opportunities for challenging their rivals. In 2001 a group of approximately 40 Sparta hooligans confronted their opponents at Willem II before a match in Tilburg. This incident led to a further escalation of the rivalry and violence between the two groups (see Chapter Seven).

2   *Violence leads to de-escalation and the revision of collective fan identity at*
        a club without a pre-existing hooligan formation.

The second example involves the revision of the dominant 'friendly' fan identity at a club without a pre-existing hooligan subculture. In contrast with the first example, violence now triggers an acute discomfort into the core of the collectivity's sense of identity. While in the first example the meaning of the incident is principally negotiated by a small group of fans in their construction of an alternative collective identity, in the second example the violent incident deeply affects the fan identity as a whole. The type of negotiation characteristic of the latter reflects in many respects the concept of cultural trauma (Alexander et al., 2004; Sztompka, 2000). A cultural trauma represents a fundamental threat to established individual and collective identity. Such trauma occurs when collective actors 'decide' to represent social pain as a fundamental threat to their sense of who they are, where they came from, and where they want to go. Insofar as collectivities' traumas are thus experienced, the collective identity will become significantly revised. This identity revision means that there will be a searching re-remembering of the collective past. Once the collective identity has been reconstructed in this way, there will, at some point in time, be a period of 'calming down'. The spiral of signification flattens out, affect and emotion become less inflamed, preoccupation with sacrality and pollution fade. Charisma becomes routinised, effervescence evaporates, liminality gives way to reaggregation (Alexander, 2004).

A striking example of collective trauma in football fan identity is the death of a Fulham fan in 1998. After an away match at Gillingham a brief fight broke out between opposing fans near the ground. A 24-year-old Fulham supporter died from head injuries after hitting his head on the side of the kerb. In the aftermath of the incident, representations of the event focused on the nature of the pain, the nature of the victim, the relation of the victim to the wider audience and attribution of responsibility. In Chapter Five I have demonstrated how these four issues were negotiated within the fan community and also between Fulham fans and supporters of other football clubs (e.g. Gillingham). The death of the Fulham supporter resulted in a revision of the 'friendly' fan identity, focusing on the representation of violence as 'not for the likes of us'. Club officials, local police officers and influential fans (e.g. fanzine editors) all played a key role in the process of identity reconstruction.

3   *Violence leads to de-escalation of inter-group violence as part of a hooligan rivalry.*

The third example is the de-escalation of hooligan violence. A violent incident can lead to a revision of the hooligan identity based on intersubjective agreement that 'things have gone too far'. Such revision may lead to a decrease in physical violence between members of opposing hooligan groups, even though this will remain highly negotiable and open to contestation. The death of an Ajax hooligan during the confrontation at Beverwijk may serve as an example here. This death shocked not only the wider fan communities of Ajax and Feyenoord, but also the hooligan formations themselves. Although there had been a series of violent confrontations between both groups in the past, this was the first murder associated with the inter-group rivalry. Fatalities were always a potential risk, especially with the carrying of weapons and home-made bombs, but death was never the major aim of either side. A major consequence of the confrontation was that it challenged informal codes of legitimate action as well as the pleasurable emotional arousal associated with hooligan encounters. The confrontation was also a major incentive for the authorities to crackdown on both hooligan formations through special police investigations, constrictive controls, tough penalties and prolonged banning orders.

At the same time, however, the short-term de-escalation of inter-group violence has not led to an overall decline in spectator violence at fixtures between the two clubs in the medium term, for example missile throwing, damage to property and violence against the police and players. Fixtures between the two teams remain loathed and always contain the possibility of spilling over into violence. Furthermore, the confrontation at Beverwijk and the celebration riot in 1999 have attracted new young recruits to the hooligan scene at Feyenoord. It is important to emphasize, therefore, that de-escalation in the short term can coexist with escalation in the medium term.

4   *Violence leads to escalation of inter-group violence as part of a hooligan rivalry.*

The fourth example involves the escalation of hooligan rivalries. This example is the 'classical' type of inter-group conflict, in which opposing hooligan formations become entangled in a spiral of escalating violence. The violent incident principally affects hooligan identities and leads to extensive negotiation between opposing groups as part of their collective management of reputation. To retain or re-establish one's honour and reputation, the opposing hooligan formation has to respond effectively to defeat since 'a failure to respond threatens to make retrospectively ridiculous the pretensions of all in the attacked group' (Katz, 1988: 141). The case studies presented in this book provide numerous examples of this type of conflict escalation. Two brief examples illustrate the nature of the escalation. First, early confrontations between Espanyol and FC Barcelona hooligans set off a spiral of inter-group violence that culminated in the murder of an Espanyol fan in 1991. Second, the death of a Millwall fan in 1978 became a focal point in the mutual perceptions and expectations of hooligan formations at West Ham United and

Millwall. Millwall hooligans sought to avenge what they perceived as intentional murder, while West Ham hooligans constructed the incident as a sign of their superiority over their South East London rivals.

After analyzing the manifestation of football hooliganism in fan cultures and the variable outcomes of violent incidents on the construction of fan and hooligan identities, in the following section I will examine in more detail the commodification of football hooliganism and its effects on the attractions and persistence of the hooligan subculture.

The commodification of football hooliganism

The main issue social scientists have sought to explain is why some young men, rather than others, might find football hooliganism an attractive and rewarding activity. From a postmodernist perspective, Armstrong (1998: 308) has argued that research is unable to find a neat equation as to what 'makes' the hooligan. He contends that the individual 'selects various groups and locations to spend time with, in effect playing with identity, selecting commodities and expressing opinions that may be contradictory and may exist independently of a person's socio-economic background.' Football hooliganism is 'the thing to do for many young men who [seek] risk and excitement.' For the participants it is a fashion that some pursue longer than others (1998: 309). Football hooliganism, as a temporary lifestyle, is available and attractive not only to young men from the lower strata of the working class, but to a wider range of male adolescents seeking excitement and reputation for toughness. The class composition of hooligan formations depends principally on national and local circumstances (i.e. social, cultural and historical specificity, national and local fault lines).

The permanence and persistence of football hooliganism at various clubs and in various countries can be viewed in terms of the continuing prestige of the hooligan lifestyle among several young men seeking excitement and adventure. I have demonstrated how participation in football hooliganism can provide pleasurable excitement and a sense of belonging, two values that are widely accepted in Western societies. The question remains why football hooliganism has not (yet), unlike so many other youth fashions and subcultures, become 'unfashionable' or passé, despite some important transformations in the phenomenon.[9] Part of the 'seductions' of football hooliganism seem to lie in the visibility of the phenomenon. What makes the hooligan lifestyle particularly attractive for prospective practitioners is that it appears so temptingly close and within reach (cf. Bauman and May, 2001: 158).

On the one hand, young supporters attending football matches can witness the daunting presence, aggro (taunts, gestures, provocations) and, occasionally, the (threat of) violence of hooligan formations. For some young men, the image of sovereignty such groups like to create can be truly tempting: 'The first time I attended a match with my friends from school I was struck by the physical appearance of the hooligans. They were not boys, but big men. Big men doing their business. I was very impressed by that. They ruled the terraces, you know' (Feyenoord hooligan). On the other hand, the prestige of football hooliganism is in part stimulated by its public staging. The mass media alter the very possibilities of interaction and dialogue, 'remaking the public sphere through highly mediated forms of quasi-interaction, producing new ways of conceiving of self and identity and generating fundamentally new performatives' (Urry, 2000: 180). Central to such a (global) public stage are various images, as well as face-to-face conversation and more straightforward informational flows. The mass media publicly stage what might otherwise remain private (ibid.: 181).

The mediatization of football hooliganism is, of course, by no means new. What is new in the contemporary period is that football hooliganism is increasingly commodified.[10] This commodification plays into the demand for hooligan memorabilia and 'substitutes' for physical violence. Police measures against football hooliganism may have reduced the opportunities for experiencing the rush of hooligan confrontations in and around football grounds, especially in Western Europe, yet this rush remains highly desirable to large numbers of prospective practitioners (Giulianotti, 1999: 53). The audience is heterogeneous, ranging from young 'wannabes' and people who wish to glance at this violent subculture to the nostalgic or entrepreneurial hooligan. The commodification of football hooliganism seems to contain a mixture of voyeurism, identification through consumption, hooligan nostalgia and financial gain.

Playing into this heterogeneous demand, a transnational market in the reproduction and simulation of football hooliganism – in print, film and video games – has emerged. The available products include an ever-expanding variety of hooligan autobiographies, real-time video clips, documentaries and fictional movies, all of which celebrate and romanticize the hooligan subculture (see Chapter Four). With regard to the various fan memoirs of British (former) hooligans, Redhead (2004: 395-396) has noted that so-called 'hit and tell' literature 'is unashamedly partisan and boastful, recounting 20 years, or more, of violent male football fandom associated with a particular British league club and its 'mob'.' Similar modes of reproduction can be found in certain football fanzines. It has been suggested that fanzines engage in continued contestation over cultural institutions (Jary et al., 1991). There are nevertheless important differences in the specific functions of football fanzines. Some fanzines actually contest the cultural properties of non-hooligan supporters, emphasizing the hard masculinity celebrated by football hooligans. Certain 'ultrazines' and 'hoolizines' explicitly promote the use of violence in inter-group rivalries (see Chapter Two).

The commodification of football hooliganism has also been visible in film and video industries. Recently two new movies were released in various European and non-European countries: *The Football Factory*, based on the book by John King (1997), and *Hooligans*, starring Elijah Wood. Certain hooligan autobiographies are currently being reworked into a movie, including *Soul Crew* (Jones and Rivers, 2002). In 2002 the controversial video game *Hooligans: Storm over Europe*, in which the player commands a group of football hooligans into battle, was released in Europe and the United States. This fictional type of hooligan entertainment is viewed by many hard-core hooligans with a kind of disdain, since 'these impure replicas of genuine violence appear over-simulated and unbelievable, in the same way that "soft-core" sex suddenly becomes staged and false when set against hard-core pornography and its immersion in the action' (Giulianotti, 1999: 54). At the same time, the process of commodification seems to confirm what some hooligans consider the hypocrisy of outsiders: 'People condemn our behaviour and call for the authorities to lock us up. But I think that, in reality, many of them would love to be like us. They just haven't got the guts for it. They condemn us while in fact they admire us for our courage and physical prowess' (Feyenoord hooligan). In this context, Matza and Sykes (1961: 717) have argued that 'delinquents simply translate into behaviour those values that the majority are usually too timid to express.'

The emergence of a transnational market in hooligan entertainment and memorabilia has had the important effect of facilitating (prospective) practitioners to 'buy into' the hooligan lifestyle. There are numerous types of casual wear that young men buy to associate themselves with football hooliganism, such as Stone Island, Aquascutum and Burberry. Moreover, brands such as Hooligan Streetwear and Pitbull seem to explicitly target (prospective) practitioners. All hooligan formations under consideration sell their own merchandising, such as T-shirts, jackets, hats and DVDs. Boixos Nois is even a registered brand name. The Internet plays a key role in group merchandising and global reputation management. Most hooligan groups have their own websites which offer a range of material on the subject of football hooliganism, such as press reports, real-time video clips and message boards where self-identifying hooligans exchange experiences and threats. There are also international websites focusing on the hooligan subculture in general. Of particular interest here is the rise of a virtual 'hooligan community'. On special websites prospective participants and self-declared hooligans alike are involved in day-to-day interaction, ranging from provocations and threats to the dissemination and exchange of hooligan material (photographs, video clips, films). However, increased opportunities for maintaining such (transnational) relations do not necessarily result in a physical expansion of hooligan formations. 'Cyber hooliganism' and attendant virtual hooligan identities may, for some young men, be a (relatively safe and anonymous) substitute for physical violence (see Van der Torre and Spaaij, 2003; 2003a).

Ongoing processes of commodification and mediatization not only make the hooligan lifestyle appear temptingly accessible, but they also create an additional motive for experienced football hooligans. Selling hooligan memorabilia, or acting as self-declared 'hooliologists' for media or movie productions, has proved a lucrative business for some hooligan entrepreneurs. Experienced hooligans may also benefit from their hooligan reputation and their contacts within hooligan circles in other areas of leisure culture, for example in organizing dance events or music festivals, or in the drug trade. This financial aspect of the hooligan subculture is commonly neglected in academic research, even though it may constitute a key motive for older hooligans to stay involved in the group. In the Spanish ultra subculture, potential sources of financial profit include the sale of group membership cards, tickets, travel to away matches, fanzines, merchandising and, occasionally, money provided by clubs. As one Espanyol ultra commented: 'What you have to understand is that some people may have different reasons for staying around. I have been in such a position myself for years. There is a lot of the money involved in the ultra scene, you know.' The same seems to be true for most of the larger Southern European ultra groups. According to a leader of an Italian ultra group:

> You are talking big money. I mean, the income of certain groups is over one million euros. The fortune of the main ultra groups is estimated at three million euros. Intelligent people take advantage of that by making a decent living out of their activities. And why shouldn't they? The whole fucking world is earning money off football fans: clubs, players, journalists, sociologists. Why can't we?

To sum up, the hooligan lifestyle appears temptingly accessible due to its public staging and commodification. This type of access is principally confined to the periphery of hooligan formations, that is, superficial or temporary participation or merely self-identification through consumption rather than active participation and group membership. Although this may be a first step towards the individual's more regular participation in football hooliganism, this is not necessarily the case; most followers and 'wannabes' never evolve into core group members. At the same time, the public staging and commodification of football hooliganism seem to have enhanced processes of imitation among young supporters, as we have seen in the discussion of the transnational and national diffusion of hooligan subcultures in Chapter Ten.

Although they have been dealt with extensively throughout this book, questions as to why within the identified collective categories some young men, and not others, find football hooliganism an attractive and rewarding activity remain particularly relevant. Why does only a relatively minor part of all young football fans engage in hooliganism, even at clubs with deep-seated hooligan traditions? Or, to return to the fan habitus described at the beginning of this chapter, how and under which circumstances may similar dispositions result in different individual actions? In this context, Armstrong and Harris (1991: 455-456) have argued that future research should attempt to discover why some young men engage in hooligan behaviour while most, from exactly the same class backgrounds, do not. They give one suggestion, namely, that in various types of society young men form relationships with one another that in certain ways supplement, or even substitute, relationships with the family. Although their argument reflects to some degree the focal concern of solidarity and belonging outlined in this chapter, I would argue that it does not get us much further, since one could simply ask: why do some young fans use hooligan groups to form such relationships, while others turn to pacified fan groups?

We have seen that although the habitus is durable, actors' dispositions are constantly subjected to a range of different experiences in a way that either reinforces or modifies them (Bourdieu and Wacquant, 1992: 133). In addition to the themes raised in this chapter, one other practical experience can be viewed as influencing dispositions to participation in football hooliganism: peer pressure. I have argued that football hooligans celebrate a distorted and heightened version of the subterranean values in society through the deviant influences of peer pressure. More specifically, the characteristics and behaviour of hooligan formations can be viewed to some degree as a radical caricature of the fan cultures in which they are embedded, displaying elements of both compliance and resistance. For example, whereas West Ham United and Feyenoord hooligans celebrate a heightened version of the core values of the working-class communities they 'represent', Espanyol hooligans tend to glorify their club's persistent neo-fascist stigma. Sparta hooligans, on the other hand, promote a self-styled, middle-class image that reflects in some respects the dominant 'friendly' fan identity at the club. These collective representations are dynamic and changeable, but they tend to be reasonably durable.

Crucial in understanding how some young fans come to celebrate such a distorted or heightened version of conventional values are the deviant influences of peer pressure. Friendship groups are one of the main sites for young males' socialization and identity formation. Young males tend to gravitate towards friends for a sense of belonging and identity, seeking prestige among peers, often by

403

adopting a tough or masculine attitude (see Chapter One). Many hooligans interviewed for this study spoke about how they first became involved in football hooliganism through their friends or school mates. Participation in football hooliganism usually evolves gradually through increasing contacts with like-minded peers and role models. Compare the following statements:

> I used to attend matches with my dad, but when I was fifteen I started going with my mates from school. And some of them knew some of the older boys who were involved in hooliganism. So we started hanging out with them and we sort of copied their behaviour to get noticed. We looked up to them, you know, they were what we called real tough guys. (Feyenoord hooligan)

> My dad and my uncle used to take me to Espanyol, but they stopped going after we got relegated. I was thirteen years old. My dad gave me money to go with my cousin. Gradually we got to know people and I became fascinated by the skinhead style. At first I stood with the young skinheads, because the older ones kept among themselves. That is how I grew into the group, step by step, meeting new people and building a reputation for toughness. (Espanyol hooligan)

In combination with the key themes addressed in this chapter, the issue of peer groups brings us yet another step closer to understanding why some young males, and not others, find football hooliganism an attractive and rewarding activity. It remains extremely difficult to account for some of the specific interpersonal variations I encountered in the course of this study. On more than one occasion, I was surprised to find (twin) brothers with diverging interests in football hooliganism. Despite their similar demographics and physical appearance, one brother might be centrally involved in football hooliganism while the other might not, even though the latter also liked to watch and play football. One indication may be that, despite overlaps in peer groups, they tended to gravitate towards different friendship groups due to their partly diverging leisure interests. In these cases, perhaps we need to look closely at (other) predisposing factors and triggering causes which lead to a stronger will to violence in some people than in others (cf. Schinkel, 2004: 26-27). However, examples of this kind are rare and do not impair the themes addressed in this chapter.

Conclusion

In this book, I have analyzed football hooliganism by systematic and detailed comparison of the manifestation of hooligan subcultures in different national and local contexts. The first step towards providing a deeper understanding of football hooliganism was to demonstrate the great practical heterogeneity of the phenomenon. Throughout the text I have stressed the importance of local context and social interaction in the manifestation of football hooliganism and the construction of hooligan identities. I have argued that to fully grasp the nature and sources of the phenomenon we should move beyond generality towards a more specific analysis of the ways in which football hooliganism is nested within particular fan communities. Detailed comparative analysis of the complex and dynamic local manifestations of football hooliganism constitutes a major counterweight to the many prevailing stereotypes and popular fallacies, such as those claiming that the issue is equally acute everywhere. Importantly, such analysis also reveals striking within-case variations, highlighting the dynamic and changeable nature of the phenomenon.

The four theoretical themes addressed in this book in combination generate a deeper understanding of football hooliganism as a transnational phenomenon. On the basis of these themes it is possible to answer the central question formulated in the Introduction: how can we explain the extent and nature of football hooliganism at different football clubs and in different countries, and variations therein over time? I have demonstrated that national and local contexts play a crucial role in shaping the extent and nature of football hooliganism. The transnational diffusion and glocalization of the hooligan subculture described in Chapter Ten and the focal concerns and commodification described in this chapter explain how football hooliganism evolved into a transnational and persistent phenomenon. At the same time, the concept of fault lines helps to explain why the (English) hooligan style did not remain invariant during the process of its diffusion and how it merged with local practices and traditions.

In addition to these cross-national commonalities and variations, I have identified striking intra-city differences which cannot be adequately explained in terms of transnational diffusion or societal fault lines. Rather, these differences should be viewed within the context of particular local arenas, that is, within individual 'club cultures'. In these local arenas societal fault lines and wider (global) developments in football culture interact with more specific elements co-shaping the manifestation of football hooliganism. The extent and nature of football hooliganism vary greatly between clubs and need to be understood by appreciating the ways in which fan cultures either inhibit or facilitate football hooliganism (i.e. through their social, cultural and historical specificity). The habitus and collective identity of supporters, and attendant processes of distinction and imitation, strongly influence patterns of behaviour and should therefore be viewed as a partial explanation for intra-city differences in the extent of football hooliganism.

Furthermore, transformations in football hooliganism over time cannot be adequately understood in terms of general (trans)national developments. Rather, they need to be viewed as variable outcomes of: (i) the interactions and negotiations within and between hooligan formations; (ii) formal and informal policies targeting football hooliganism; and (iii) the subtle yet vital interactions and negotiations between hooligans, police officers, club officials and non-hooligan supporters. The interactions and negotiations between hooligan and significant others are crucial to the construction and maintenance of hooligan identities and produce the informal rules of interaction by which the performers involved align their actions. Only by taking into account how these various factors interact in local arenas we can fully understand the precise nature and development of football hooliganism.

Although the principal aim of the study has been to generate a deeper understanding of the phenomenon rather than to provide a comprehensive list of practical recommendations, it must be said that the themes addressed in this book contain a number of (indirect) prescriptive elements with regard to formal and informal policies targeting football hooliganism. Most importantly, my research shows the continuing persistence of the phenomenon, despite all the efforts to contain or eradicate it. More specifically, I have shown that a discrepancy between

406

formal and informal policies tends to exist and that most security measures have secondary consequences significantly reducing their intended effect and transforming football hooliganism. These findings reflect my earlier argument that although international structures and concerted responses are required, prevention strategies should fundamentally be based on local practices and designed to fit local needs (Spaaij, 2005). The prevention of football hooliganism requires the continuous and long-term commitment of a variety of institutions and agents, including football clubs and local fan communities.

Apart from such practical implications, the research also has implications for sociological theory. The focus of this book on context-dependence does not impair the development of an empirically grounded, sociological understanding of the phenomenon under consideration. The specific features and social mechanisms identified in the case studies can be used to compose a more general theoretical framework for understanding and explaining football hooliganism as a transnational phenomenon. This is precisely what I have sought to do in this study. The proposed theoretical framework maintains its emphasis on local context, but at the same time it offers a more general understanding of the extent, nature and development of football hooliganism. I have also argued that a number of key common features and social mechanisms can be identified in the construction of hooligan identities: excitement and pleasurable emotional arousal; the construction of a hard masculine identity; territorial identifications; the individual and collective management of reputation; solidarity and belonging; and sovereignty and autonomy. I see these features and processes as the key focal concerns of football hooliganism as a transnational phenomenon.

Further research is needed to empirically test and refine the theoretical approach proposed in this book. I would suggest that future comparative research into football hooliganism should primarily engage in in-depth analysis of hooligan subcultures and identities and transformations therein, and the ways in which these subcultures and identities are embedded in football fan cultures. Specific themes of interest are the ever-evolving processes of distinction and imitation involved, the subtle yet vital interactions and negotiations between hooligans and law enforcers, the complex intertwinement between the local and the global, and the ongoing commodification of football hooliganism. These themes closely reflect, and may fruitfully contribute to, major issues in contemporary social theory.

Notes

Introduction

1   The term 'Panopticon' was, of course, not invented by Foucault but taken from the work of the English philosopher Jeremy Bentham, whose book *Panopticon or the Inspection House* was published in 1791. Foucault developed the concept further in his analysis of the formation of the disciplinary society.

2   All translations of interviews, fanzines, newspaper reports, literature and official documents quoted in this book are mine. This includes translations from Dutch, Spanish, Catalan as well as French, German, Italian and Portuguese.

Chapter 1

1   It must be noted, however, that every form of spectator violence, including fighting between rival fans, is observable, to varying extents, throughout the history of football (Dunning et al., 1984; Vamplew, 1983; Hutchinson, 1975; Walvin, 1994; Holt, 1981).

2   I am aware that the following overview might be flawed by the shortage of available research on football-related violence in parts of Asia (e.g. North and South Korea, Iran) and Africa (e.g. Algeria, Morocco, Egypt), and in the Americas (e.g. Mexico, Costa Rica). A second major problem is that the overview is based on secondary sources, that is, on interpretations of primary sources. For example, Hua's (2004) research into football 'hooliganism' in China groups together several types of violence, including missile throwing directed at referees and players, vandalism and fighting. This broad definition of 'hooliganism' makes it difficult to assess the precise nature of inter-fan violence at football matches in China.

3   Some early commentators saw the emergence of English football hooliganism as cross-cultural 'contamination' in which English fans allegedly copied the violent behaviour of Argentinian fans (cf. Taylor, 1969: 204).

4   Similar observations have been made with regard to football in Sierra Leone (Richards, 1997).

5   The 'societal vulnerability' thesis of Belgian scholars Van Limbergen and Walgrave (1988) may be considered a notable exception. This approach will not be discussed here separately since it has much in common with the 'Leicester School' approach.

6   Concept coined by Stanley Cohen in his analysis of the stigmatization of British youth subcultures in the 1950s and 1960s (Cohen, 1972).

7   The globalization of fan cultures should thus not be viewed as merely involving local adaptation of a global product or practice, as the localization of the global. I would argue that in many fan cultures, especially at 'smaller' clubs, local traditions and practices continue to exert a strong influence over patterns of behaviour. Globalization should therefore not be viewed as one larger region (the global economy and culture) simply replacing the smaller regions (individual societies, regions, localities) (see Urry, 2000: 33; Albrow, 1996: 211; Ritzer, 2004: 163).

8   The terms 'front region' and 'back region' are derived from Goffman (1959). According to Goffman, all social interaction is like a theatrical performance in which actors perform one of the many roles available to them, depending on the situation (front stage) in which they find themselves. They must also provide the audience for another actor and determine whether the performance is believable. When away from the particular situation in the 'back region' or 'backstage' area, the role can be dropped because the previous audience will not usually be present, and the actor can relax into another role. Goffman defines this 'backstage' as a place, relative to a given performance, where the impression fostered by the performance is knowingly contradicted as a matter of course' (1959: 112).

9   There are important resemblances between the hooligans' notion of honour and that which is found in various cultural and historical contexts (see for example Peristiany, 1966; Riches, 1986).

10 Data gathered during my position as Visiting Lecturer and Research Fellow at the University of Seville in 2005 and 2006.

11 Juvenile delinquency therefore seems to be only marginally related to social circumstances. However, the types, seriousness and frequency of offending may be influenced by social conditions, such as material circumstances and the appreciation of aggressive masculine behaviour in certain (sections of) societies (cf. Van den Brink, 2000: 42).

12 Moffitt's use of the term 'antisocial' is problematic since football hooliganism, and much juvenile delinquency in general (cf. Emler and Reicher, 1995: 120), is *social* in two senses. It is a socially visible activity and it is also frequently a group activity.

Chapter Two

1 These statistics say little about the real scope of the 'hooligan' problem at the mentioned clubs. They cover only one season, may reflect policing strategies rather than the level of spectator violence, and most of the arrests were made at one or few specific incidents (NCIS, private correspondence, December 2004; Spaaij, 2005).

2 These statistics have largely similar limitations to those identified in the previous footnote. Additionally, they do not distinguish between the various types of offence at the mentioned clubs.

3 An additional flaw of these statistics is that they do not provide any details on the number of arrests for 'violent disorder' per club. The arrest rates presented in Table 2.4 include all types of offences, ranging from the vandalism of property and the possession of an offensive weapon to violent disorder. On average, approximately 35% of all arrests concern violent or public disorder (CIV, 2003: 23-24). In England, this percentage is 48% (Home Office, 2004).

4 Smaller clubs with similar arrest records are excluded for the sake of brevity, for example FC Eindhoven.

5 This stigma was reinforced at an international level in the aftermath of the racial abuse during Spain's friendly match against England on November 17, 2004, which was fiercely condemned in the British and international press (Spaaij and Viñas, 2005a; Viñas and Spaaij, 2006).

6   A case study can be defined as 'an empirical inquiry that investigates a contemporary phenomenon within its real-life context, especially when the boundaries between phenomenon and context are not clearly evident; and [...] [that] relies on multiple sources of evidence' (Yin, 1994: 13).

7   Flyvbjerg (2001: 66-87) argues that one of the major misunderstandings about the nature of the case study as a research method is that one cannot generalize on the basis of an individual case and that, therefore, the case study cannot contribute to scientific development. He claims that 'the strategic choice of case may greatly add to the generalizability of a case study' (2001: 75). A good example in football research are the findings of Marsh and his colleagues (1978). Their theory of 'the rules of disorder' was based on a single case (Oxford United in the 1970s), but has been widely accepted as characteristic of fan behaviour in other times and places (e.g. Dal Lago, 1990).

8   Passive observation means that the ethnographer is present at the scene of action but does not participate or interact with other people to any great extent. Moderate observation occurs 'when the ethnographer seeks to maintain a balance between being an insider and an outsider, between participation and observation' (Spradley, 1980: 60). It is important to note that I have deliberately sought to avoid 'active' or full participation in the sense of trying to learn and master the behaviour of hooligans and to participate in it to the fullest possible extent.

Chapter Three

1   The Chester Report (1968) found a substantial increase in the number of cases of 'disorderly behaviour by spectators'. From 1946 to 1960 an average of 13 cases was brought to the attention of the Football Association. The number nearly doubled, to an average of 25 per season, between 1960 and 1965. It is difficult to assess to what extent this increase reflects a real upsurge in spectator violence rather than changes in official and public perceptions or modes of registration.

2   Most Premier League clubs currently attract a more heterogeneous audience in terms of class composition. Despite the continuing dominance of white male

support, a slight increase in female attendance across the leagues has been observed, although some sociologists have criticized this observation (Sir Norman Chester Centre, 2002: 5-6; 2002a; 5; 2001: 5; cf. I. Waddington et al., 1996; J. Williams, 1996). In terms of attracting minority ethnic support, the situation at most League clubs remains quite bleak. Arsenal and Queen's Park Rangers are, arguably, the only English professional football clubs that attract an ethnically-mixed crowd to any real degree (Sir Norman Chester Centre, 2002: 6; 2002a: 5-6).

3   The author has personally experienced this issue on a number of occasions while casually observing fights at Euston and King's Cross railway stations in Central London. At times I only later found out, through contacts within police and hooligan circles, which groups had been involved.

4   It must be stressed, however, that the conversion to seats is less appreciated by fans emotionally attached to the experience of watching the match from the terraces (e.g. Bormans, 2002). In the Netherlands and in other parts of Europe there is extensive debate on whether standing areas should be re-introduced in certain parts of certain grounds. In the 2003/2004 season a pilot was conducted with 'safe standing' at FC Groningen, SC Heerenveen and Go Ahead Eagles (Van der Torre, 2004).

Chapter Four

1   The word 'Cockney' is often used to refer to white working-class inhabitants of East London, or those originating from the East End.

2   East London has a long history of immigration. Through the port of East London wave after wave of newcomers arrived. In an attempt to evade religious persecution in their native France, the Protestant Huguenots fled to Britain in the fifteenth century. Many were attracted by the prosperity of the capital and were drawn to Spitalfields, which under their influence became a centre of the country's textile and clothing industry. In the late nineteenth and early twentieth century, for example, Jewish immigrants from Russia and Eastern Europe arrived by the same route, fleeing from religious persecution and settling around

413

Whitechapel and Spitalfields (Young and Willmott, 1992: xvi; White, 2002: 138).

3   Also located in East London is the more modest club Leyton Orient FC. Leyton Orient was founded in 1881 as the football team of the Glyn Cricket Club. In 1888, the club took the name of Orient, after the Orient Steam Navigation Company based in East London. After the Second World War, with the club having moved to its current home in Leyton, the name was eventually changed into Leyton Orient.

4   The rivalry between East London and South East London males began before either club was formed, in the days when Thames Ironworks and Millwall Ironworks shipbuilding companies were rivals for the same contracts. Employees of the rival companies occasionally engaged in violent confrontations (Belton, 2003: 51-52). The feeling of conflict between the dockers was transferred back into the club rivalry.

5   My reconstruction of this incident, and of other recent incidents, is principally based on reports provided by the Metropolitan Police and the British Transport Police, unless stated otherwise.

6   The data were compiled by film producer Ian Stuttard for the *Hooligan* documentary (*The Times*, 13 January 1986).

Chapter Five

1   Whitting (1970: 216) on the other hand, has suggested that the idea of a football team came from the young men themselves rather than from their patrons at St Andrews Church.

2   Fulham's cup performance peaked in 1975, when the club reached the FA Cup Final. The final was lost 2-0 to West Ham United, but it was nevertheless perceived a 'high-water mark' of the club's '30-year golden age that followed World War Two' (Turner, 2004: 128).

3   At the same time, the area began to attract growing numbers of manual and unskilled workers from the West Indies, the Caribbean and Africa. These developments have produced a situation of contrasts. On the one hand, the gentrifiers added new prosperity to the area. Many of the traditional

manufacturing activities disappeared, with a consequent loss of manual jobs. Instead a 'service class' emerged – a group of people, generally between the ages of 25 and 35, with a high disposable income and service-oriented labour. On the other hand, although the borough of Hammersmith and Fulham (as it is named since 1965) is among the leaders in average house prices within London, it also suffers serious deprivations. Large, older council estates in the area suffer from poor environments which exacerbate the social and economic problems of those who live there (Hammersmith and Fulham Council, 2002).

4   Detailed accounts of the development of the ground issue in the 1980s and early 1990s can be found in Turner (1994: 180-185) and *TOOFIF* (no. 10, March 1990).

5   During the spell of Japanese player Junichi Inamoto at the club, from 2002 to 2004, some 300 Japanese fans regularly attended home matches, of which 80 were season ticket holders and dozens travelled to away matches as well (data provided by Fulham FC, December 2003). Most of them stopped visiting Craven Cottage when Inamoto's spell at Fulham ended.

6   One of these songs went as follows: 'The famous Danny Eccles [a notorious Chelsea hooligan], said there was one man he afeared, it was not Arsenal's Johnny Hoy, but Fulham's Mickey Beard.' Beard was one of the recognized 'leaders' of Fulham's hooligan formation in the late 1960s and early 1970s.

7   Despite Chelsea's problematic situation in parts of the 1970s and 1980s; Chelsea played in Division Two in the 1975/76 and 1976/77 seasons, from 1979/80 to 1983/84, and in the 1988/89 season.

8   Posted on http://vote.sparklit.com.

9   One Internet website claimed that a small group of Fulham supporters fought a larger group of Croatian hooligans after the UEFA Cup match between Hajduk Split and Fulham, on 19 September 2002. The two groups reportedly threw bottles and glasses at each other. Police separated the two factions but home fans succeeded in stealing a few flags from the Fulham fans (posted on www.ultrasworld.com/news20.htm). Moreover, before the FA Cup match between Fulham and Burnley, on 16 February 2003, a Fulham supporter tried to confront a group of visiting supporters (police report, February 2003). This minor incident was not listed in the NCIS or BTP logs.

Chapter Six

1 For an analysis of intelligence-led policing at Feyenoord, see also Spaaij, 2002.

2 In the Netherlands the Mayor is responsible for public order. The country is divided into 25 police regions. Each region has its own police force under the administrative management of the mayor of the largest or most central town in the region. In the case of the Rotterdam-Rijnmond Police force the Mayor of Rotterdam is the *korpsbeheerder* (administrator).

Chapter Seven

1 These data were gathered in 2003 and 2004 and may therefore be somewhat dated.

Chapter Eight

1 The club's name has changed several times throughout its history. For the sake of consistency, I use the Catalan spelling (used since 1994). It must be noted that the Spanish spelling (Real Club Deportivo Español) prior to 1994 has been important in shaping the club's image in Catalonia as a 'non-Catalan' club.

2 *Perico* literally means parakeet. *Perico* (or *periquito*) was the club's early nickname and since 1975 it is the club's official symbol. As Segura Palomares (2001: 105-110) has pointed out, the nickname *perico* was originally derived from a cartoon cat (*el gato Periquito*) rather than from a parakeet.

3 The Sarrià stadium no longer exists. The club moved to the Olympic Stadium in in Barcelona in 1997.

4 Senior police officers have suggested that most of these robberies are not committed for financial gain, since the perpetrators often belong to 'well-to-do' families, but merely serve as a justification for starting a fight (e.g. *El Periódico*, 19 December 1993).

Chapter Nine

1 In the Catalan context, the term 'immigrant' has two distinctive meanings. First, it refers to people who migrated to Catalonia from other parts of Spain. Second, it refers to people who have arrived from outside Spain (Gore, 2002: 92).

2 For a description of the incident, see Chapter Eight.

3 The latter group consisted of approximately 200 university students and graduates.

Chapter Ten

1 Songs, for example, are largely drawn from a relatively limited repertoire of (international hit) melodies (cf. Bromberger, 1993: 96).

2 Diffusion is defined by Rogers (1983: 5) as 'the process by which an innovation is communicated through certain channels over time along members of a social system. It is a special type of communication, in that the messages are concerned with new ideas.' Rogers argues that the type of communication involved is a two-way process of convergence, rather than a one-way, linear act in which one individual seeks to transfer a message to another.

3 On city-based fan identities and rivalries in France and Italy, see Bromberger et al. (1987; 1993) and Hare (2003).

4 I am aware that my choice to study two clubs from London may have led to an under-representation of the centre-periphery cleavage in English society.

5 Quantitatively, one potential indicator is the statistics on football-related arrests listed in Chapter Three. In the 2003/04 season 3,010 arrests were made at English league matches, 1,837 at Dutch football matches and only 53 in Spain. Regretfully, these figures are not compatible to any real degree due to the different match categories included (league matches only for England, and league, cup and European Cup matches only for Spain) and the fact that the figures are unweighted (e.g. not related to the total number of matches or spectators). Moreover, as we have seen, these statistics say little about the specific phenomenon under consideration.

6   A major reason for this dissimilarity seems to be that, in the Netherlands, there are comparatively few football clubs which attract similarly large crowds (e.g. average home attendances of over 20,000). I must stress, however, that the size of hooligan groups may vary considerably over time, depending on local circumstances. For example, at ADO Den Haag the number of regular participants in football hooliganism has gradually diminished as a result of the club's prolonged stay in the First Division (between 1992 and 2003) and the ageing of long-standing hooligans. Many regular participants stopped being regularly involved in football hooliganism, while the number of young recruits remained quantitatively limited. This example illustrates the importance of within-case comparison.

7   On average, the percentage of women within ultra groups is 10 to 20 per cent, although in a few cases this percentage is much higher (up to 50 per cent). Several ultra groups include official 'female sections', subgroups that consist exclusively of women.

8   Both groups have official sections and affiliates throughout the country and beyond (e.g. in France and Italy) (see Chapters Eight and Nine).

9   In the case of Espanyol and FC Barcelona it is relatively difficult to determine the maximum number of hooligans (i.e. core plus periphery) because of the larger militant fan groups in which they are embedded. Several affiliates of these groups do not normally identify with football hooliganism, although for high-profile matches or during confrontations some might occasionally join the ranks of the hooligans. While the militant groups as a whole have been larger, only a section of their members can be categorized as 'hooligans', 'followers' or 'marginal participants' in football hooliganism.

10 The casual dress style is particularly popular among these hooligan formations (see Chapter Three). Ironically, this common fashion tends to make hooligan formations identifiable to the police as well as to non-hooligan supporters. As one Feyenoord hooligan commented: 'Nowadays, if you really wanted to escape police observation in and around football grounds you would have to return to the ordinary dress pattern. You know, wearing scarves and hats. That is the only way not to stick out from the main football crowd.'

Chapter Eleven

1   This scheme is comparable to the community schemes at Fulham and West Ham United, neither of which explicitly target football hooliganism. In contrast, in Barcelona there are no social preventive or community schemes of this kind. This dissimilarity can to some degree be explained by the general lack of commitment to social prevention programmes at a national level as well as by the institutionalized nature of fan clubs at Espanyol and FC Barcelona. Most fan clubs are official, autonomous *peñas* which exert some degree of social control over their members and organize social activities. The fan clubs are also organized in so-called 'federations' that function as platforms for dialogue with the club. These features limit the need for more centralized fan projects, even though their effects on football hooliganism seem to have been minimal due to hooligan groups' withdrawal from institutional arrangements in favour of their own subcultural practices. In the 1990s the regional government of Catalonia attempted to improve the dialogue between clubs and young supporters, but this dialogue has been *ad hoc* and thwarted by what we may call the 'distorted' relationship between hooligans and the clubs.

2   Dependence on others who lack a sense of urgency in the project is one of the key reasons why a project or policy may fail to facilitate the means for effectuating it, as is described in a masterly way in Pressman and Wildavsky's (1973) classic study of implementation.

3   This does not mean, of course, that experienced hooligans are never arrested (e.g. in the heat of the moment), but rather that they are most conscious of police and camera surveillance. 'Nutters' in particular are renowned within hooligan circles for their 'irrational' behaviour (cf. Marsh et al., 1978). In each hooligan formation one or more nutters with ample arrest records can be found.

Chapter Twelve

1   The intense emotional states associated with violent conduct are, of course, not limited to football hooliganism. Comparable accounts are provided by many juvenile delinquents in general. For example, from a psychoanalytic perspective,

Coleman (1980: 5) argues that the need for intense emotional states, 'including delinquent activities, drug and mystical experiences,' is a key feature of adolescence.

2   We have seen in Chapters Four to Nine that spatial affinity is by no means limited to football hooligans. Crucially, place attachment is a key feature of football culture in general (e.g. Bale, 1993; Giulianotti and Armstrong, 2002).

3   My argument here contradicts to some degree Sánchez Jankowski's study of youth gangs in America. He argued that intra-group solidarity should not be overestimated: 'Regardless of what they say, over time it becomes apparent that members of gangs really do not think of their fellow members as brothers. Gang members are fundamentally loners who have chosen to participate not because the gang represents a family (with brothers) that they have been deprived of, but because they perceive it to be, at least in the short run, in their best interest' (1991: 148).

4   An ultra group at Juventus is explicitly named *Drughi*, after Alex's friends in violence. Moreover, Armstrong (1998: 236-237) has noted that in the early 1970s some young Sheffield United fans wore boiler suits, boiler hats or pit helmets, and a few fans carried walking sticks or wore face make-up. Watt (1993: 121-122) has described the use of walking sticks on Arsenal's North Bank and at other London youth ends.

5   For example, in Chapter Five, I have shown how some long-standing Fulham fans distinguish themselves to some degree from the new fans the club has been attracting in recent years. In this context, Giulianotti (2002) provides an interesting taxonomy of supporter identities in football, advancing four ideal types of spectator identity: supporters, followers, fans and *flâneurs*.

6   The term 'habitus', basically meaning 'second nature' or 'embodied social learning', was also regularly used by Elias (2000 [1939]). Bourdieu traces the term back to, among others, Hegel, Husserl, Weber and Durkheim (cf. Paulle, 2005: 74).

7   Despite some opposite claims posted on the Internet and provocations by Feyenoord hooligans during the first match between the two teams since the confrontation at Beverwijk, waving large inflatable hammers referring to the murder weapon, accompanied by verbal insults directed at the Ajax hooligans.

8   This does not mean, of course, that there have not been any encounters between the two groups over the last five years. However, recent incidents included damage to property, missile throwing and attacks by Ajax hooligans on players of the Feyenoord reserves team rather than inter-group fighting.

9   Some academics have argued that football hooliganism has indeed 'disappeared' (see the discussion in Dunning, 1999: 132-139). My research shows that this is not the case, despite important transformations in the phenomenon.

10   This commodification is, of course, not limited to football hooliganism, but rather it is a key feature of post-industrial societies, which influences the project of the self and the establishing of lifestyles (Giddens, 1991: 197). In his analysis of the commodification of British football, Giulianotti (2002: 26-27) takes commodification not as a single process but as an ongoing process, often involving the gradual entry of market logic to the various elements that constitute the object or social practice under consideration. He argues that the marked intensification of this process in recent years is of a different order to that which was experienced up until the late 1980s, and which might now be described as a period of hypercommodification, driven by extraordinary and different volumes of capital that have entered football from new sources. On the commodification of English football, see also Dunning (1999: 121-129).

Bibliography

Abbink, J. (2000) 'Preface: Violation and violence as cultural phenomena', in G. Aijmer and J. Abbink (eds), *Meanings of violence: A cross cultural perspective*, Oxford and New York: Berg, pp. xi-xvii.

Abbink, J. (1999) 'Violence, ritual, and reproduction: Culture and context in Surma dueling', *Ethnology*, vol. 38, no. 3, pp. 227-242.

Abma, R. (1990) *Jeugdcultuur en tegencultuur: Een theoretische verkenning*, Nijmegen: SUN.

Acosta Naranjo, R., and F. Rodriguez Fernandez (1989), *Los jóvenes "ultras" en el fútbol sevillano*, Sevilla: Ayuntamiento de Sevilla.

Adán Revilla, T. (2004) 'Ultras: Culturas del fútbol', *Revista de Estudios de Juventud*, vol. 64, no. 4, pp. 87-100.

Adán Revilla, T. (1998) 'Ultras e hinchas: Política y violencia en el fútbol en España (1982-1997), in Consejo Superior de Deportes, *Política y violencia en el fútbol*, Madrid: Ministerio de Educación y Cultura, pp. 107-129.

Adán Revilla, T. (1996) *Ultras y skinheads: La juventud visible*, Oviedo: Ediciones Nobel.

Adán Revilla, T. (1993) 'Nuevos escenarios, viejos rituales: Los "ultras" del fútbol', *Revista de Antropología Social*, no. 2, pp. 149-166.

Adang, O.M.J. (2002) 'Collectief geweld tussen voetbal-"supporters": Organisatie, groepsprocessen en sociale identiteit', *Tijdschrift voor Criminologie*, vol. 44, no. 2, pp. 172-181.

Adang, O.M.J. (2000) 'Jonge mannen in groepen: Een geweldige combinatie?' *Justitiële verkenningen*, vol. 26, no. 1, pp. 72-80.

Adang, O.M.J. (1998) *Hooligans, autonomen, agenten: Geweld en politie-optreden in relsituaties*, Alphen aan den Rijn: Samsom.

Adang, O.M.J. (1997) 'Van voetbalvandalisme naar voetbalcriminaliteit?', *Tijdschrift voor de Politie*, vol. 60, no. 11, pp. 26-30.

Adang, O.M.J. (1988) 'Voetbalvandalisme geobserveerd', *Tijdschrift voor Criminologie*, no. 4, pp. 302-312.

Adang, O.M.J., and C. Cuvelier (2001) *Policing Euro 2000: International*

police co-operation, information management and police deployment,
Ubbergen: Tandem Felix.

Aijmer, G., and J. Abbink (eds) (2000) *Meanings of violence: A cross cultural perspective*, Oxford and New York: Berg.

Alabarces, P. (2005) 'Fútbol, violencia y política en la Argentina: Ética, estética y retórica del aguante', in J. Aquesolo Vegas (ed.), Actas del X Congreso Internacional de Historia del Deporte, Sevilla: CESH.

Alabarces, P. (ed.) (2003) *Futbologías: Fútbol, identidad y violencia en América Latina*, Buenos Aires: CLACSO.

Alabarces, P. (2002) ''Aguante' and repression: Football, politics and violence in Argentina', in E. Dunning, P. Murphy, I. Waddington and A.E. Astrinakis (eds), *Fighting fans: Football hooliganism as a world phenomenon*, Dublin: University College Dublin Press, pp. 23-36.

Alabarces, P., M. Conde and C. Dorado (eds) (2005) *Hinchadas*, Buenos Aires: Prometeo.

Alabarces, P., R. Coelho and J. Garriga Zucal (2000) '"Aguante" y represión: Fútbol, violencia y política en el fútbol en la Argentina', in P. Alabarces (ed.), *Peligro de gol: Estudios sobre deporte y sociedad en América Latina*, Buenos Aires: CLACSO, pp. 211-229.

Albrow, M. (1996) *The global age*, Cambridge: Polity.

Alegi, P. (2004) ''Like cows driven to a dip': The 2001 Ellis Park stadium disaster in South Africa', *Soccer and Society*, vol. 5, no. 2, pp. 233-247.

Alexander, J. (2004) 'Toward a theory of cultural trauma', in J. Alexander, R. Eyerman, B. Giesen, N.J. Smelser and P. Sztompka (eds), *Cultural trauma and collective identity*, Berkeley: University of California Press, pp. 1-28.

Alexander, J., R. Eyerman, B. Giesen, N.J. Smelser and P. Sztompka (eds) (2004) *Cultural trauma and collective identity*, Berkeley: University of California Press.

Allan, J. (1989) *Bloody casuals: Diary of a football hooligan*, Glasgow: Famedram.

Anderson, B. (1983) *Imagined communities: Reflections on the origin and spread of nationalism*, London and New York: Verso.

Andersson, T. (2001) 'Swedish football hooliganism, 1900-1939', *Soccer and*

423

Society, vol. 2, no. 1, pp. 1-18.

Andersson, T., and A. Radmann (1998) 'Fans in Scandinavia', in A. Brown (ed.), Fanatics! Power, identity and fandom in football, London and New York: Routledge, pp. 141-157.

Appadurai, A. (2006) *Fear of small numbers: An essay on the geography of anger*, Durham and London: Duke University Press.

Appadurai, A. (1999) 'Globalization and the research imagination', *International Social Science Journal*, vol. 51, no. 160, pp. 229-238.

Archetti, E.P. (1999) *Masculinities: Football, polo and the tango in Argentina*, Oxford and New York: Berg.

Archetti, E.P. (1996) 'In search of national identity: Argentinian football and Europe', in J.A. Mangan (ed.), *Tribal identities: Nationalism, Europe, sport*, London: Frank Cass, pp. 201-219.

Archetti, E.P. (1992) 'Argentinian football: A ritual of violence?', *International Journal of the History of Sport*, vol. 9, no. 2, pp. 209-235.

Archetti, E.P., and A.G. Romero (1994) 'Death and violence in Argentinian football', in R. Giulianotti, N. Bonney and M. Hepworth (eds), *Football, violence and social identity*, London: Routledge, pp. 37-72.

Armstrong, G. (2002) 'Talking up the game: Football and the reconstruction of Liberia, West Africa', Identities: Global Studies in Culture and Power, vol. 9, pp. 471-494.

Armstrong, G. (1998) *Football hooligans: Knowing the score*, Oxford and New York: Berg.

Armstrong, G. (1994) 'False Leeds: The construction of hooligan confrontations', in R. Giulianotti and J. Williams (eds), *Game without frontiers*, Aldershot: Arena, pp. 299-326.

Armstrong, G., and R. Giulianotti (eds) (2001) *Fear and loathing in world football*, Oxford and New York: Berg.

Armstrong, G., and R. Giulianotti (eds) (1999) *Football cultures and identities*, London: Macmillan Press.

Armstrong, G., and R. Giulianotti (1999a) 'From another angle: Police surveillance and football supporters', in C. Norris, J. Morgan and G. Armstrong (eds), *Surveillance, closed circuit television and social control*,

Aldershot: Ashgate, pp. 113-135.

Armstrong, G. and M. Young (1997) 'Legislators and interpreters: The law
and "football hooligans"', in G. Armstrong and R. Giulianotti (eds),
Entering the field: New perspectives on world football, Oxford and New
York: Berg.

Armstrong, G., and D. Hobbs (1994) 'Tackled from behind', in R. Giulianotti,
N. Bonney and M. Hepworth (eds), *Football, violence and social identity*,
London: Routledge, pp. 196-228.

Armstrong, G., and R. Harris (1991) 'Football hooligans: Theory and
evidence', *Sociological Review*, vol. 39, no. 3, pp. 427-458.

Artells, J.J. (1972) *Barça, Barça, Barça*, Barcelona: Laia.

Astrinakis, A.E. (2002) 'Subcultures of hard-core fans in West Attica: An
analysis of some central research findings', in E. Dunning, P. Murphy, I.
Waddington and A.E. Astrinakis (eds), *Fighting fans: Football
hooliganism as a world phenomenon*, Dublin: University College Dublin
Press, pp. 88-105.

Atyeo, D. (1979) *Blood and guts: Violence in sports*, New York: Paddington.

Auditteam Voetbalvandalisme (2004) *Vier incidenten rond uitwedstrijden en
vrij reizende supporters*, Den Haag: Ministerie van Binnenlandse Zaken.

Back, L., T. Crabbe and J. Solomos (2001) *The changing face of football:
Racism, identity and multiculture in the English game*, Oxford and New
York: Berg.

Back, L., T. Crabbe and J. Solomos (1999) 'Beyond the racist/hooligan
couplet: Race, social theory and football', *British Journal of Sociology*,
vol. 50, no. 3, pp. 419-442.

Bailey, K.D. (1994) *Methods of social research*, 4th ed., New York: The Free
Press.

Bairner, A. (2002) 'The dog that didn't bark? Football hooliganism in Ireland',
in E. Dunning, P. Murphy, I. Waddington and A.E. Astrinakis (eds),
Fighting fans: Football hooliganism as a world phenomenon, Dublin:
University College Dublin Press, pp. 118-130.

Balcells, A. (2004) *Breve historia del nacionalismo catalán*, Madrid: Alianza
Editorial.

Balcells, A. (1996) *Catalan nationalism: Past and present*, London: Macmillan.

Bale, J. (2000) 'The changing face of football: Stadiums and communities', *Soccer and Society*, vol. 1, no. 1, pp. 91-101.

Bale, J. (1993) *Sport, space and the city*, London and New York: Routledge.

Ball, P. (2001) *Morbo: The story of Spanish football*, London: WSC Books.

Bandyopadhyay, K. (2005) 'In search of a football ground in twentieth century urban Bengal', *Soccer and Society*, vol. 6, no. 1, pp. 69-78.

Bañeres, E. (2004) *Estimada Basilea*, Barcelona: Mundo Deportivo.

Bañeres, E. (1988) 'Les forces vives amenacen l'intrús', *Diari de Barcelona*, 31 January.

Barruti, M. (1990) *El món dels joves a Barcelona: Imatges i estils juvenils*, Barcelona: Ayuntamiento de Barcelona.

Bauman, Z., and T. May (2001) [1990] *Thinking Sociologically*, 2nd ed., Oxford: Blackwell.

Becker, H.S. (1963) *Outsiders: Studies in the sociology of deviance*, New York: The Free Press.

Beiu, A. (2005) 'Football related violence in Romania', in J. Aquesolo Vegas (ed.), *Actas del X Congreso Internacional de Historia del Deporte*, Sevilla: CESH.

Belton, B. (2003) *Founded on iron: Thames Ironworks and the origins of West Ham United*, Stroud: Tempus.

Belton, B. (1999) *Days of iron: The story of West Ham United in the Fifties*, Derby: Breedon Books.

Belton, B. (1997) *Bubbles, hammers and dreams*, Derby: Breedon Books.

Ben-Porat, A. (2001) '"Biladi, Biladi": Ethnic and nationalistic conflict in the soccer stadium in Israel', *Soccer and Society*, vol. 2, no. 1, pp. 19-38.

Benke, M., and R. Utz (1989) 'Hools, Kutten, Novizen und Veteranen: Zur Soziologie gewalttätiger Ausschreitungen von Fußballfans', *Kriminologisches Journal*, vol. 21, no. 2, pp. 85-100.

Bennett, A. (1999) 'Subcultures or neo-tribes? Rethinking the relationship between youth, style and musical taste', *Sociology*, vol. 33, no. 3, pp. 599-617.

Bieleman, B., A. de Jong, H. Naayer and J. Nijboer (2004) *Evaluatie supporters-project Groningen*, Groningen: Intraval.

Blok, A. (2000) 'The enigma of senseless violence', in G. Aijmer and J. Abbink (eds), *Meanings of violence: A cross cultural perspective*, Oxford and New York: Berg, pp. 23-38.

Blok, A. (1997) 'Het narcisme van kleine verschillen', *Amsterdams Sociologisch Tijdschrift*, vol. 24, no. 2, pp. 159-187.

Blok, A. (1991) 'Zinloos en zinvol geweld', *Amsterdams Sociologisch Tijdschrift*, vol. 18, no. 3, pp. 189-207.

Blokdijk, P., and B. Warbroek (2004) *Leven met Feyenoord: Getuigenissen van clubliefde*, De Fontein.

Bodin, D., L. Robène and S. Héas (2005) *Sport and violence in Europe*, Strasbourg: Council of Europe Publishing.

Bol, M.W. (1998) 'Gedragsbeïnvloeding van voetbalvandalen', *Proces*, vol. 77, no. 1, pp. 17-21.

Bol, M.W., and C.J. van Netburg (1997) *Voetbalvandalen/voetbalcriminelen*, Den Haag: WODC.

Booth, C. (1902) *Life and Labour of the People in London*, 17 vols., London: Macmillan.

Bormans, R. (2002) *'Feyenoord bedankt!' De supporters en hun club*, Nijmegen: SUN.

Bormans, R. (1996) *'Vandaag houden we ons gedeisd?!' Een cross-nationale studie naar voetbalvandalisme en beleid*, Unpublished dissertation, Rotterdam: Erasmus Universiteit Rotterdam.

Bot, W. (1994) *Leve Feyenoord één*, Amsterdam: De Arbeiderspers.

Bottenburg, M. van (1994) *Verborgen competitie: Over de uiteenlopende populariteit van sporten*, Amsterdam: Bert Bakker.

Bouman, P.J., and W.H. Bouman (1952) *De groei van de grote werkstad: Een studie over de bevolking van Rotterdam*, Assen: Van Gorcum.

Bourdieu, P. (2002) 'Habitus', in J. Hillier and E. Rooksby (eds), *Habitus: A sense of place*, Aldershot: Ashgate, pp. 27-34.

Bourdieu, P. (1998) *La domination masculine*, Paris: Éditions du Seuil.

Bourdieu, P. (1990) *The logic of practice*, Stanford: Stanford University Press.

427

Bourdieu, P. (1984) *Distinction: A social critique of the judgement of taste*, London: Routledge.

Bourdieu, P. (1977) *Outline of a theory of practice*, Cambridge: Cambridge University Press.

Bourdieu, P., and L. Wacquant (1992) *An invitation to reflexive sociology*, Chicago: University of Chicago Press.

Brimson, D. (2003) *Eurotrashed: The rise and rise of Europe's football hooligans*, London: Headline.

Brimson, D., and E. Brimson (1998) *Derby days: The games we love to hate*, London: Headline.

Brimson, D., and E. Brimson (1997) *Capital punishment: London's violent football following*, London: Headline.

Brimson, D., and E. Brimson (1996) *Everywhere we go: Behind the matchday madness*, London: Headline.

Brimson, E. (1999) *Tear gas and ticket touts: With the England fans at the World Cup*, London: Headline.

Brink, G. van den (2000) 'Agressieve jongeren: Een cultuurhistorische bespiegeling', *Justitiële Verkenningen*, vol. 26, no. 1, pp. 35-47.

British Transport Police (2004) *Force Football Unit Annual Report 2003-2004*, London: BTP.

British Transport Police (2003) *Annual Report 2002-2003*, London: BTP.

Bromberger, C. (1997) 'Formes et sens de la passion partisane chez les *ultras* du football', in M. Comeron (ed.), *Quels supporters pour l'an 2000?*, Bruxelles: Éditions Labor, pp. 17-31.

Bromberger, C. (1993) 'Fireworks and the ass', in S. Redhead (ed.), *The passion and the fashion: Football fandom in the New Europe*, Aldershot: Avebury, pp. 89-102.

Bromberger, C., A. Hayot and J.-M. Mariottini (1993) ''Allez l'O.M., Forza Juve': The passion for football in Marseille and Turin, in S. Redhead (ed.), *The passion and the fashion: Football fandom in the New Europe*, Aldershot: Avebury, pp. 103-151.

Bromberger, C., A. Hayot and J.-M. Mariottini (1987) 'Allez l'O.M.! Forza Juve!', *Terrain*, 8, pp. 8-41.

Brown, A. (ed.) (1998) *Fanatics! Power, identity and fandom in football*, London and New York: Routledge.

Brown, A. (1998a) 'United we stand: Some problems with fan democracy', in A. Brown (ed.), *Fanatics! Power, identity and fandom in football*, London and New York: Routledge, pp. 50-67.

Brown, A., and A. Walsh (2000) 'Football supporters' relations with their clubs: A European perspective', *Soccer and Society*, vol. 1, no. 3, pp. 88-101.

Brug, H.H. van der (1994) 'Football hooliganism in the Netherlands', in R. Giulianotti, N. Bonney and M. Hepworth (eds), *Football, violence and social identity*, London: Routledge, pp. 174-195.

Brug, H.H. van der (1986) *Voetbalvandalisme: Een speurtocht naar verklarende factoren*, Haarlem: De Vrieseborch.

Brug, H.H. van der, and M. Marseille (1987) *Voetbalvandalisme en beleid*, Haarlem: De Vrieseborch.

Brug, H.H. van der, and M. Marseille (1983) *Achtergronden van vandalisme bij voetbalwedstrijden*, Haarlem: De Vrieseborch.

Brug, H.H. van der, and J. Meijs (1989) 'Waarom de Nederlandse supporters niet vochten bij de EK in Duitsland', *Tijdschrift voor Criminologie*, no. 3, pp. 169-194.

Brug, H.H. van der, and J. Meijs (1988) 'Voetbalvandalisme en de media', *Tijdschrift voor Criminologie*, no. 4, pp. 336-347.

Budge, I. (1996) 'Great Britain and Ireland: Variations on dominant party government', in J. Colomer (ed.), *Political institutions in Europe*, London and New York: Routledge, pp. 18-61.

Buford, B. (1991) *Among the thugs*, London: Arrow.

Burgers, J. (2001) 'Rotterdam, kleine sociaal-economische geschiedenis van een havenstad', in G. Engbersen and J. Burgers (eds), *De verborgen stad: De zeven gezichten van Rotterdam*, Amsterdam: Amsterdam University Press, pp.13-28.

Burgers, J., and G. Engbersen (2001) 'De wrok van Spangen: Opkomst en neergang van een arbeidersbuurt', in G. Engbersen and J. Burgers (eds), *De verborgen stad: De zeven gezichten van Rotterdam*, Amsterdam: Amsterdam University Press, pp. 251-261.

Burgess, A. (2000) [1962] *A clockwork orange*, London: Penguin.

Burnett, C. (2002) 'The 'black cat' of South African soccer and the Chiefs-Pirates conflict', in E. Dunning, P. Murphy, I. Waddington and A.E. Astrinakis (eds), *Fighting fans: Football hooliganism as a world phenomenon*, Dublin: University College Dublin Press, pp. 174-189.

Burnett, C. (2002a) 'The killing fields of soccer: Violence, villains and victims', *African Journal for Physical, Health Education, Recreation and Dance*, vol. 8, no. 1, pp. 149-160.

Burns, J. (2000) *Barça: A People's Passion*, London: Bloomsbury.

Butler, T., and M. Rustin (eds) (1996) *Rising in the East? The regeneration of East London*, London: Lawrence & Wishart.

Cachet, L., and E.R. Muller (1991) *Beslissen over voetbalvandalisme: Een permanent probleem,* Arnhem: Gouda Quint.

Campbell, A. (1993) *Men, women, and aggression*, New York: Basic Books.

Campbell, B., and A.L. Dawson (2001) 'Indecent exposures, Men, masculinity and violence', in M. Perryman (ed.), *Hooligan wars: Causes and effects of football violence*, Edinburgh and London: Mainstream, pp. 62-76.

Canter, D., M. Comber and D.L. Uzzell (1989) *Football in its place: An environmental psychology of football grounds*, London: Routledge.

Carabén, A. (1999) 'Nuñolàndia 1999', *El País*, 3 September.

Carabén, A., A. Godall, J. Laporta and J. Moix (1999) 'The struggle for democracy at Barcelona FC', in S. Hamil, J. Michie and C. Oughton (eds), *A game of two halves? The business of football*, Mainstream: Edinburgh.

Carrabine, E., P. Cox, M. Lee and N. South (2002) *Crime in modern Britain*, Oxford: Oxford University Press.

Carrol, R. (1980) 'Football hooliganism in England', *International Review of Sports Sociology*, vol. 15, no. 2, pp. 77-92.

Casals, X. (1998) *El fascismo: Entre el legado de Franco y la modernidad de Le Pen (1975-1997)*, Barcelona: Destino.

Casals, X. (1997) '"Boixos" i "Brigadistas": Una lectura ideológica', *L'Avenç*, no. 211, pp. 52-55.

Casals, X. (1995) *Neonazis en España: De las audiciones wagnerianas a los skinheads (1966-1995)*, Barcelona: Grijalbo.

Castro Moral, L. (1986) *Violencia el el deporte de competición*, Unpublished dissertation, Madrid: Instituto de Ciencias de la Educación Física y del Deporte.

Chabot, S., and J.W. Duyvendak (2002) 'Globalization and transnational diffusion between social movements: Reconceptualizing the dissemination of the Gandhian repertoire and the "coming out" routine', *Theory and Society*, vol. 31, no. 6, pp. 697-740.

Chacón García, A. (2004) *Violencia blanquiazul*, Unpublished dissertation, Barcelona: Johan Cruyff Academy.

Chaney, D. (1996) *Lifestyles*, London: Routledge.

Chester, N. (1968) *Report of the Committee on Football*, London: HMSO.

Chisari, F. (2004) '"The cursed cup": Italian responses to the 1985 Heysel disaster', *Soccer and Society*, vol. 5, no. 2, pp. 201-218.

CIV (2004) *Jaarverslag seizoen 2003-2004*, Utrecht: CIV.

CIV (2003) *Jaarverslag seizoen 2002-2003*, Utrecht: CIV.

CIV (2002) *Jaarverslag seizoen 2001-2002*, Utrecht: CIV.

CIV (2001) *Jaarverslag seizoen 2000-2001*, Utrecht: CIV.

CIV (1998) *Jaarverslag seizoen 1997-1998*, Utrecht: CIV.

CIV (1993) *Jaarverslag seizoen 1992-1993*, Utrecht: CIV.

CIV (1991) *Jaarverslag seizoen 1990-1991*, Utrecht: CIV.

Clarke, J. (1978) 'Football and working class fans: Tradition and change', in R. Ingham (ed.), *Football hooliganism: The wider context*, London: Interaction, pp. 37-60.

Clarke, J. (1976) 'The skinheads and the magical recovery of community', in S. Hall and T. Jefferson (eds), *Resistance through rituals: Youth subcultures in post-war Britain*, London: Hutchinson, pp. 99-102.

Clarke, J. (1973) *Football hooliganism and the skinheads*, Stencilled Occasional Paper, Birmingham: Centre for Contemporary Cultural Studies.

Clarke, J., S. Hall, T. Jefferson and B. Roberts (1976) 'Subcultures, cultures and class: A theoretical overview', in S. Hall and T. Jefferson (eds), *Resistance through rituals: Youth subcultures in post-war Britain*, London: Hutchinson, pp. 9-74.

Cloward, R.A., and L.E. Ohlin (1960) *Delinquency and opportunity*, New York: The Free Press.

Coakley, J.J. (1978) *Sport in society: Issues and controversies*, St. Louis: The C.V.

Mosby Company.

Coalter, F. (1985) 'Crowd behaviour at football matches: A study in Scotland', *Leisure Studies*, vol. 4, pp. 111-117.

Cocheret, Ch. A. (1963) *'Sparta!' Een Rotterdamse Voetbalclub 1888 – 1963*, Rotterdam: Nijgh & Van Ditmar.

Cohen, A.K. (1955) *Delinquent Boys*, New York: The Free Press.

Cohen, A.P. (1993) Self consciousness: An alternative anthropology of identity, London: Routledge.

Cohen, P. (1972) 'Sub-cultural conflict and working-class community', Working Papers in Cultural Studies no. 2, Birmingham: Centre for Contemporary Cultural Studies.

Cohen, S. (1972) *Folk devils and moral panics*, London: Paladin.

Colaers, C., and K. van Limbergen (1987) 'Voetbalvandalisme: Maatschappelijke en socio-psychologische achtergronden', *Streven*, vol. 54, pp. 1001-1010.

Coleman, J.C. (1980) *The nature of adolescence*, London: Methuen.

Coleman, S. (1990) *Hillsborough and after: The Liverpool experience: First report*, Ormskirk: Centre for Studies in Crime and Social Justice.

Collins, R. (1995) 'Gewelddadig conflict en sociale organisatie: Enkele theoretische implicaties van de sociologie van de oorlog', in J. Goudsblom, B. van Heerikhuizen and J. Heilbron (eds), *Hoofdstukken uit de sociologie*, Amsterdam: Amsterdam University Press, pp. 185-202.

Colomé, G (1999) 'Conflictos e identidades en Cataluna', in S. Segurola (ed.), *Fútbol y pasiones políticas*, Madrid: Temas de Debate, pp. 169-174.

Colomé, G. (1997) 'Futbol i identitat nacional a Catalunya: FC Barcelona i RCD Espanyol', *L'Avenç*, no. 211, pp. 32-35.

Colomé, G. (1997a) 'La péninsule ibérique dans la tourmente des *ultras*: Le cas de la Catalogne', in M. Comeron (ed.), *Quels supporters pour l'an 2000?*, Bruxelles: Éditions Labor, pp. 82-90.

Colomé, G. (1995) *Le RCD Español de Barcelona: Du lieu commun au stade*, Unpublished paper, Barcelona: Universitat Autónoma de Barcelona.

Colomer, J. (1996) 'Introduction', in J. Colomer (ed.), *Political institutions in Europe*, London and New York: Routledge, pp. 1-17.

Colovic, I. (2002) *The politics of symbol in Serbia*, London: Hurst & Co.

Colovic, I. (1999) 'Nacionalismos en los estadios de Yugoslavia', in S. Segurola (ed.), *Fútbol y pasiones políticas*, Madrid: Temas de Debate, pp. 139-146.

Comeron, M. (2002) *The prevention of violence in sport*, Strasbourg: Council of Europe Publishing.

Comisión Nacional contra la Violencia en Espectáculos Deportivos (2004) *Actividades de la Comisión Nacional contra la Violencia en Espectáculos Deportivos en 2004*, Madrid: Consejo Superior de Deportes.

Comisión Nacional contra la Violencia en Espectáculos Deportivos (2003) *Actividades de la Comisión Nacional contra la Violencia en Espectáculos Deportivos en 2003*, Madrid: Consejo Superior de Deportes.

Connell, R.W. (2000) *The men and the boys*, Cambridge: Polity.

Consejo Superior de Deportes (1998) *Política y violencia en el fútbol*, Madrid: Ministerio de Educación y Cultura.

Conversi, D. (1996) *The Basques, the Catalans and Spain: Alternative routes to nationalist mobilisation*, London: Hurst.

Corrigan, P. (1979) *Schooling the smash street kids*, London: Macmillan.

COS (2004) *Demografische gegevens 2003*, Rotterdam: Centrum voor Onderzoek en Statistiek.

COS (2003) *Demografische gegevens Rotterdam*, Rotterdam: Centrum voor Onderzoek en Statistiek.

Costa, P-O, J.M. Pérez Tornero and F. Tropea (1996) *Tribus urbanas*, Barcelona: Paidós.

COT (2002) *Openbare orde: Ernstige verstoringen, ontwikkelingen, beleid*, Alphen aan den Rijn: Kluwer.

COT (2000) *Een drugsscene op Zuid (de Millinxbuurt): Een model voor de strategische analyse van drugsscenes*, Alphen aan den Rijn: Samsom.

COT (1999) *Voetbal en geweld: onderzoek naar aanleiding van rellen en plunderingen bij een huldiging in Rotterdam (25 april 1999)*, Alphen aan den Rijn: Samsom.

COT (1998) *De Amsterdam Arena: Evaluatie van de veiligheidsorganisatie*, Amsterdam: Politie Amsterdam-Amstelland.

Cotass (1995) *Persconferentie Stichting Cotass*, Hilversum, 30 August.

Council of Europe (1998) *Report on Spanish fulfilment of the European Convention*

433

on *Spectator Violence 1987-1997*, Strasbourg: COE.

Council of Europe (1985) *European Convention on Spectator Violence and Misbehaviour at Sports Events*, Strasbourg: COE.

Council of the European Union (2003) *Situation report on football hooliganism in the Member States of the European Union*, Brussels: COE.

Council of the European Union (2002) *Report on football hooliganism in the Member States of the European Union*, Brussels: COE.

Courakis, N. (1998) 'Football violence: Not only a British problem', *European Journal on Criminal Policy and Research*, vol. 6, no. 2, pp. 293-302.

Crain, M. (1997) 'The remaking of an Andalusian pilgrimage tradition: Debates regarding visual (re)presentation and the meanings of "locality" in a global era', in A. Gupta and J. Ferguson (eds), *Cultural, power, place: Explorations in critical anthropology*, Durham and London: Duke University Press, pp. 291-311.

Crolley, L., and D. Hand (2002) *Football, Europe and the press*, London: Frank Cass.

Cross, R.J. (1998) 'The Teddy Boy as Scapegoat', *Doshisha Studies in Language and Culture*, vol. 1, no. 2, pp. 263-291.

Csikszentmihalyi, M. (1975) *Beyond boredom and anxiety*, San Francisco: Jossey-Bass.

Culla Clarà, J.B. (1977) 'L'extrema dreta a Catalunya durant la República', *L'Avenç*, no. 6, pp. 48-54.

Custers, T., and S. Hamersma (2005) 'De genese van het fenomeen hooliganisme in Nederland', in R.F.J. Spaaij (ed.), *Supportersgedrag en hooliganisme in het Nederlandse voetbal*, Amsterdam: Universiteit van Amsterdam, pp. 5-49.

Dal Lago, A. (1990) *Descrizione di una battaglia: I rituali del calcio*, Bologna: Il Mulino.

Dal Lago, A., and R. De Biasi (1994) 'Italian football fans: Culture and organization', in R. Giulianotti, N. Bonney and M. Hepworth (eds), *Football, violence and social identity*, London: Routledge, pp. 73-89.

De Antón, J., and A.P. Del Riquelme (1990) *Factores que promueven la violencia en el deporte con especial referencia al fútbol*, Madrid: Consejo Superior de Deportes.

De Biasi, R. (1998) 'The policing of hooliganism in Italy', in D. Della Porta and H. Reiter (eds), *Policing protest: The control of mass demonstrations in Western democracies*, Minneapolis and London: University of Minnesota Press, pp. 213-227.

Delgado, M. (2002) 'Estética e infamia: De la distinción al estigma en los marcajes culturales de los jóvenes urbanos', in C. Feixa, C. Costa and J. Pallarés (eds), *Movimientos juveniles en la Península Ibérica*, Barcelona: Ariel, pp. 115-143.

Della Porta, D., and H. Reiter (eds) (1998) *Policing protest: The control of mass demonstrations in Western democracies*, Minneapolis and London: University of Minnesota Press.

Dijk, A.G. van, H.H. van der Brug and R.P. van Uffelen (1992) 'Preventie voetbalvandalisme', in C. Sas and M. Herweijer (eds), *Uitvoering van beleid: Blinde vlek bij bestuurders of hobby van onderzoekers?*, Den Haag: Platform Beleidsanalyse, pp. 155-166.

Dijk, A.G. van, N.C. Hilhorst and R.P. van Uffelen (1991) *Eindrapportage experimenten voetbalvandalisme en jeugdwelzijn*, Rijswijk: Ministerie van WVC.

Dijk, B. van (2002) *Samenvatting evaluatie sociaal preventief supportersbeleid 1998-2002*, Amsterdam: DSP.

Dijk, B. van, E. van Dijk, M. Koekkoek and B. Perrels (2000) *Eerste meting evaluatie sociaal-preventief supportersbeleid*, Amsterdam: DSP.

Dimeo, P. (2001) '"Team loyalty splits the city in two": Football, ethnicity and rivalry in Calcutta', in G. Armstrong and R. Giulianotti (eds), *Fear and loathing in world football*, Oxford and New York: Berg, pp. 105-118.

Downes, D. (1982) 'The language of violence', in P. Marsh and A. Campbell (eds), *Aggression and violence*, Oxford: Blackwell.

Drew, B. (1999) 'Policing Euro '96', in S. Frosdick and L. Walley (eds), *Sport and safety management*, Oxford: Butterworth-Heinemann, pp. 239-251.

Duke, V. (1991) 'The sociology of football: A research agenda for the 1990s', *Sociological Review*, vol. 39, no. 3, pp. 627-645.

Duke, V., and P. Slepička (2002) 'Bohemian rhapsody: Football supporters in the Czech Republic', in E. Dunning, P. Murphy, I. Waddington and A.E. Astrinakis (eds), *Fighting fans: Football hooliganism as a world phenomenon*, Dublin:

University College Dublin Press, pp. 49-61.

Duke, V., and L. Crolley (2001) '*Fútbol*, politicians and the people: Populism and politics in Argentina', *International Journal of the History of Sport*, vol. 18, no. 3, pp. 93-116.

Duke, V., and L. Crolley (1996) 'Football spectator behaviour in Argentina: A case of separate evolution', *Sociological Review*, vol. 44, pp. 272-293.

Duke, V., and L. Crolley (1996a) *Football, nationality and the state*, Harlow: Longman.

Dunning, E. (2000) 'Towards a sociological understanding of football hooliganism as a world phenomenon', *European Journal on Criminal Policy and Research*, vol. 8, no. 2, pp. 141-162.

Dunning, E. (1999) *Sport matters: Sociological studies of sport, violence and civilization*, London and New York: Routledge.

Dunning, E. (1994) 'The social roots of football hooliganism: A reply to the critics of the "Leicester school"', in R. Giulianotti, N. Bonney and M. Hepworth (eds), *Football, violence and social identity*, London: Routledge, pp. 128-157.

Dunning, E., P. Murphy, I. Waddington and A.E. Astrinakis (eds) (2002) *Fighting fans: Football hooliganism as a world phenomenon*, Dublin: University College Dublin Press.

Dunning, E., P. Murphy and I. Waddington (2002a) 'Towards a global programme of research into fighting and disorder', in E. Dunning, P. Murphy, I. Waddington and A.E. Astrinakis (eds), *Fighting fans: Football hooliganism as a world phenomenon*, Dublin: University College Dublin Press, pp. 218-224.

Dunning, E., P. Murphy and I. Waddington (1991) 'Anthropological versus sociological approaches to the study of soccer hooliganism: Some critical notes', *Sociological Review*, vol. 39, no. 3, pp. 459-478.

Dunning, E., P. Murphy and J. Williams (1988) *The roots of football hooliganism: An historical and sociological study*, London: Routledge and Kegan Paul.

Dunning, E., P. Murphy and J. Williams (1986) 'Spectator violence at football matches: Towards a sociological explanation', *British Journal of Sociology*, vol. 37, no. 2, pp. 221-244.

Dunning, E., P. Murphy and J. Williams (1986a) '"Casuals", "terrace crews" and "fighting firms": Towards a sociological explanation of football hooligan

436

behaviour', in D. Riches (ed.), *The anthropology of violence*, Oxford: Blackwell, pp. 164-183.

Dunning. E., P. Murphy, J. Williams and J. Maguire (1984) 'Football hooliganism in Britain before the First World War', *International Review for the Sociology of Sport*, vol. 19, no. 3, pp. 215-240.

Dunning, E., J. Maguire, P. Murphy and J. Williams (1982) 'The social roots of football hooligan violence', *Leisure Studies*, vol. 1, no. 2, pp. 139-156.

Dunning, E., J. Maguire, P. Murphy and J. Williams (1981) 'If you think you're hard enough', *New Society*, vol. 57, no. 980, pp. 342-344.

Durán González, J. (1996) *El vandalismo en el fútbol: Una reflexión sobre la violencia en la sociedad moderna*, Madrid: Gymnos.

Durán González, J. (1996a) 'Hinchadas radicales en el fútbol', *Temas para el debate*, vol. 14, no. 1, pp. 37-40.

Durán González, J. (1995) *El fenómeno de las jovenes hinchadas radicales en el fútbol: Un análisis sociológico figuracional sobre una forma de conflicto social: Su situación en España*, Unpublished Ph.D. thesis, Madrid: Universidad Complutense de Madrid.

Durán González, J. (1992) 'El vandalismo en el fútbol en España: Un problema social y político a la espera de un tratamiento científico', *Sistema*, no. 110-111, pp. 155-174.

Durán González, J. (1991) 'El vandalismo en el fútbol: Análisis sociológico de un proceso. Su incidencia en la prensa española: El caso de El País', *Revista de Investigación y Documentación sobre las Ciencias de la Educación Física y del Deporte*, vol. 7, no. 19, pp. 25-47.

Duteweerd, I.B. (1997) *De rush van het rellen: Een onderzoek naar de achtergronden van supportersgeweld bij voetbalwedstrijden in het algemeen en FC Twente in het bijzonder,* Unpublished dissertation, Enschede: Universiteit Twente.

Duyvendak, J.W., and M. Hurenkamp (2004) *Kiezen voor de kudde: Lichte gemeenschappen en de nieuwe meerderheid*, Amsterdam: Van Gennep.

Dwertmann, H., and B. Rigauer (2002) 'Football hooliganism in Germany: A developmental sociological study', in E. Dunning, P. Murphy, I. Waddington and A.E. Astrinakis (eds), *Fighting fans: Football hooliganism as a world phenomenon*, Dublin: University College Dublin Press, pp. 75-87.

Eckstein, H. (1975) 'Case study and theory in political science', in F. Greenstein and N. Polsby (eds), *Handbook of political science*, Reading: Addison-Wesley, pp. 79-138.

Edensor, T., and F. Augustin (2001) 'Football, ethnicity and identity in Mauritius: Soccer in a rainbow nation', in G. Armstrong and R. Giulianotti (eds), *Fear and loathing in world football*, Oxford and New York: Berg, pp. 91-103.

Ek, R. (1996) *Hooligans: Fakten, Hintergründe, Analysen*, Worms: Cicero Verlag.

Elias, N. (2000) [1939] *The civilizing process: Sociogenetic and psychogenetic investigations*, London: Blackwell.

Elias, N. (1971) 'The genesis of sport as a sociological problem', in E. Dunning (ed.), *The sociology of sport: A selection of readings*, London: Frank Cass, pp. 88-115.

Elias, N., and E. Dunning (1986) *Quest for excitement: Sport and leisure in the civilizing process*, Oxford: Blackwell.

Elias, N., and J.L. Scotson (1965) *The established and the outsiders*, London: Frank Cass.

Elliot, D., and D. Smith (1999) 'Waiting for the next one: Management attitudes to safety in the UK football industry', in S. Frosdick and L. Walley (eds), *Sport and safety management*, Oxford: Butterworth-Heinemann, pp. 86-107.

Elliot, D., and D. Smith (1993) 'Football stadia disasters in the United Kingdom: Learning from tragedy', *Industrial & Environmental Crisis Quarterly*, vol. 7, no. 3, pp. 205-229.

Emler, N., and S. Reicher (1995) *Adolescence and delinquency: The collective management of reputation*, Oxford: Blackwell.

Emmenes, A. van (1972) *Oorsprong en ontwikkeling van de voetbalsport in Nederland*, Den Haag: KNVB.

Engbersen, G., and J. Burgers (eds) (2001) *De verborgen stad: De zeven gezichten van Rotterdam*, Amsterdam: Amsterdam University Press.

Engbersen, G., C.J.M. Schuyt, J. Timmer and F. van Waarden (1993) *Cultures of unemployment: A comparative look at long-term unemployment and urban poverty*, Boulder and Oxford: Westview Press.

Erikson, E.H. (1968) *Identity: Youth and crisis*, New York: W.W. Norton.

438

Erpecum, I. van (2003) 'Hooligans in de EU', *SEC*, vol. 17, no. 4, pp. 5-7.

Evans, R., and M. Rowe (2002) 'For club and country: Taking football disorder abroad', *Soccer and Society*, vol. 3, no. 1, pp. 37-53.

Farin, L., and H. Hauswald (1998) *Die dritte Halbzeit: Hooligans in Berlin-Ost*, Berlin: Tilsner.

Featherstone, M. (1990) 'Global culture: An introduction', in M. Featherstone (ed.), *Global culture: Nationalism, globalization and modernity*, London: Sage, pp. 1-14.

Feixa, C. (2003) 'Un antropólogo en el fútbol', in F.X. Medina and R. Sánchez (eds), *Culturas en juego: Ensayos de antropología del deporte en España*, Barcelona: Icaria, pp. 73-102.

Feixa, C., and J.S. Juris (2000) 'Football cultures', *Social Anthropology*, vol. 8, no. 2, pp. 203-208.

Feixa, C., C. Costa and J. Pallarés (eds) (2002) *Movimientos juveniles en la Península Ibérica*, Barcelona: Ariel.

Ferguson, A. (2003) *Pandora's Fulhamish box*, Whitton: Ashwater.

Fernández Santander, C. (1997) *A bote pronto: El fútbol y sus historias*, Madrid: Temas de Hoy.

Fernández Santander, C. (1990) *El fútbol durante la guerra civil y el franquismo*, Madrid: San Martín.

Fernández Villanueva, C. (1998) *Jóvenes violentos*, Barcelona: Icaria.

Ferwerda, H. (2000) 'Jeugdcriminaliteit en de rol van de groep: de groep als negatieve voedingsbodem', *Tijdschrift over Jongeren*, no. 1, pp. 34-44.

Ferwerda, H. (1999) *Werken in de luwte: Over supporterscoördinatoren en de sociaal-preventieve aanpak van voetbalvandalisme*, Arnhem: LOS.

Ferwerda, H., and O. Adang (2005) *Hooligans in Beeld: Van informatie naar aanpak*, Zeist: Kerkebosch.

Ferwerda, H., and L. Gelissen (2001) 'Voetbalcriminaliteit. Veroveren hooligans het publieke domein?', *Justitiële Verkenningen*, vol. 27, no. 1, pp. 84-94.

Ferwerda, H., J. Jakobs and B. Beke (1996) *Signalen voor toekomstig crimineel gedrag*, Den Haag: Ministerie van Justitie.

Figueres i Artigues, J.M. (2003) *Història contemporània de Catalunya*, Barcelona: UOC.

Finn, G.P.T. (1994) 'Football violence: A societal psychological perspective', in R. Giulianotti, N. Bonney and M. Hepworth (eds), *Football, violence and social identity*, London: Routledge, pp. 90-127.

Finn, G.P.T., and R. Giulianotti (eds) (2000) *Football culture: Local contests, global visions*, London: Frank Cass.

Flyvbjerg, B. (2001) *Making social science matter: Why social inquiry fails and how it can succeed again*, Cambridge and New York: Cambridge University Press.

Foer, F. (2004) *How soccer explains the world*, New York: Harper Collins.

Football Trust (1991) *Digest of football statistics: 1990-1*, London: Football Trust.

Foucault, M. (1977) *Discipline and punish: The birth of the prison*, New York: Pantheon.

Francia, F. (1994) 'I sostenitori del Pisa', *Rassegna Italiana di Criminologia*, vol. 5, no. 3.

Francis, M., and P. Walsh (1997) *Guvnors*, Bury: Milo Books.

Free, M., and J. Hughson (2003) 'Settling accounts with hooligans: Gender blindness in football supporter subculture research', *Men and Masculinities*, vol. 6, no. 2, pp. 136-155.

Freud, S. (1961) [1930] *Civilization and its discontents*, New York: W.W. Norton.

Freud, S. (1947) [1917] 'Das Tabu der Virginität', in *Sigmund Freud: Gesammelte Werke*, vol. 12, Frankurt am Main: Fischer, pp. 161-180.

Frith, S. (1987) *Jeugdsociologie*, Groningen: Wolters-Noordhoff.

Frosdick, S., and P. Marsh (2005) *Football hooliganism*, Cullompton: Willan.

Frosdick, S., and J. Sidney (1999) 'The evolution of safety management and stewarding at football grounds', in S. Frosdick and L. Walley (eds), *Sport and safety management*, Oxford: Butterworth-Heinemann, pp. 209-220.

Frosdick, S., and L. Walley (eds) (1999) *Sport and safety management*, Oxford: Butterworth-Heinemann.

Frosdick, S., M. Holford and J. Sidney (1999) 'Playing away in Europe', in S. Frosdick and L. Walley (eds), *Sport and safety management*, Oxford: Butterworth-Heinemann, pp. 221-238.

Frosh, S. (1994) *Sexual difference: Masculinity and psychoanalysis*, London: Routledge.

Gageldonk, P. van (2000) *Eurohooligans*, Amsterdam: Nijgh & van Ditmar.

Gageldonk, P. van (1999) *Geen woorden maar daden: Het drama van Beverwijk en hoe het verder ging met de hooligans van Feyenoord*, Amsterdam: Nijgh & van Ditmar.

Gageldonk, P. van (1996) *Hand in hand: Op stap met de hooligans van Feyenoord*, Amsterdam: Nijgh & van Ditmar.

Galeano, E. (1997) *Football in sun and shadow*, London: Fourth Estate.

Gallagher, M., M. Laver and P. Mair (1995) *Representative government in modern Europe*, 2nd ed., New York: McGraw-Hill.

Galvani, M., and J. Palma (2005) 'La hinchada de uniforme', in P. Alabarces (ed.), *Hinchadas*, Buenos Aires: Prometeo, pp. 161-182.

García Candau, J. (1996) *Madrid-Barça: Historia de un desamor*, Madrid: El Pais Aguilar.

García Candau, J. (1980) *El futbol sin ley*, Madrid: Penthalón.

García Castell, J. (1968) *Història del futbol català*, Barcelona: Aymà.

García Ferrando, M. (1990) *Aspectos sociales del deporte: Una reflexión sociológica*, Madrid: Alianza.

Garland, J., and M. Rowe (2001) *Racism and anti-racism in football*, Basingstoke and New York: Palgrave.

Garland, J., and M. Rowe (2000) 'The hooligan's fear of the penalty', *Soccer and Society*, vol. 1, no. 1, pp. 144-157.

Garland, J., and M. Rowe (1999) 'The 'English disease': Cured or in remission? An analysis of police responses to football hooliganism in the 1990s', *Crime Prevention and Community Safety: An International Journal*, vol. 1, no. 4, pp. 35-47.

Garriga Zucal, J. (2005) '"Soy macho porque me la aguanto": Etnografía de las prácticas violentas y la conformación de identidades de género masculino', in P. Alabarces, M. Conde and C. Dorado (eds), *Hinchadas*, Buenos Aires: Prometeo, pp. 39-58.

Garriga Zucal, J. (2005a) 'Pibitos chorros, fumancheros y con aguante : El delito, las drogas y la violencia como mechanismos constructores de identidad en una hinchada del fútbol', in P. Alabarces, M. Conde and C. Dorado (eds), *Hinchadas*, Buenos Aires: Prometeo, pp. 59-72.

Gemeente Rotterdam (2003) *Rotterdam zet door: Op weg naar een stad in balans*,

Rotterdam: Gemeente Rotterdam.

Gennep, A. van (1960) [1908] *The rites of passage*, Chicago: The University of Chicago Press.

George, A.L., and A. Bennett (2005) *Case studies and theory development in the social sciences*, Cambridge: MIT Press.

Giddens, A. (1997) *Sociology*, 3rd ed., Cambridge: Polity.

Giddens, A. (1991) *Modernity and self-identity: Self and society in the late modern age*, Cambridge: Polity.

Gilman, M. (1994) 'Football and drugs: Two cultures clash', *International Journal of Drug Policy*, vol. 5, no. 1, pp. 40-51.

Giltay Veth, N. (1982) 'Wangedrag van supporters: Enige juridische aspecten', in R. Siekmann (ed.), *Voetbalvandalisme*, Haarlem: De Vrieseborch, pp. 105-115.

Giner, S. (2000) *Los españoles*, Barcelona: Plaza & Janés.

Giner, S. (ed.) (1998) *La societat catalana*, Barcelona: Institut d'Estadística de Catalunya.

Giner, S. (1984) *The social structure of Catalonia*, Sheffield: The Anglo-Catalan Society.

Giulianotti, R. (2002) 'Supporters, followers, fans and *flâneurs*: A taxonomy of spectator identities in football', *Journal of Sport and Social Issues*, vol. 26, no. 1, pp. 25-46.

Giulianotti, R. (2001) 'A different kind of carnival', in M. Perryman (ed.), *Hooligan wars: Causes and effects of football violence*, Edinburgh and London: Mainstream, pp. 141-154.

Giulianotti, R. (1999) *Football: A sociology of the global game*, Cambridge: Polity.

Giulianotti, R. (1999a) 'Hooligans and carnival fans: Scottish football supporter cultures', in G.

Armstrong and R. Giulianotti (eds), *Football cultures and identities*, London: Macmillan Press, pp. 29-40.

Giulianotti, R. (1995) 'Football and the politics of carnival: An ethnographic study of Scottish fans in Sweden', *International Review for the Sociology of Sport*, vol. 30, no. 2, pp. 191-223.

Giulianotti, R. (1995a) 'Participant observation and research into football hooliganism: Reflections on the problems of entrée and everyday risks',

Sociology of Sport Journal, vol. 12, no. 1, pp. 1-20.

Giulianotti, R. (1994) 'Scoring away from home: A statistical study of Scotland football fans at international matches in Romania and Sweden', *International Review for the Sociology of Sport*, vol. 29, no. 2, pp. 171-200.

Giulianotti, R. (1994a) 'Social identity and public order: Political and academic discourses on football violence', in R. Giulianotti, N. Bonney and M. Hepworth (eds), *Football, violence and social identity*, London: Routledge, pp. 9-36.

Giulianotti, R. (1993) 'Soccer casuals as cultural intermediaries', in S. Redhead (ed.), *The passion and the fashion: Football fandom in the new Europe*, Aldershot: Avebury, pp. 153-205.

Giulianotti, R. (1991) 'Scotland's tartan army in Italy: The case for the carnivalesque', *Sociological Review*, vol. 39, no. 3, pp. 503-527.

Giulianotti, R., and G. Armstrong (2002) 'Avenues of contestation: Football hooligans running and ruling urban spaces', *Social Anthropology*, vol. 10, no. 2, pp. 211-238.

Giulianotti, R., and G.P.T. Finn (2000) 'Old visions, old issues: New horizons, new openings? Change, continuity and other contradictions in world football', in G.P.T. Finn and R. Giulianotti (eds), *Football culture: Local contests, global visions*, London: Frank Cass, pp. 256-282.

Giulianotti, R., and J. Williams (eds) (1994) *Game without frontiers: Football, identity and modernity*, Aldershot: Arena.

Giulianotti, R., N. Bonney and M. Hepworth (eds) (1994) *Football, violence and social identity*, London: Routledge.

Glass, R. (1963) *London: Aspects of change*, London: Centre for Urban Studies.

Goffman, E. (1973) [1959] *The presentation of self in everyday life*, New York: The Overlook Press.

Goldstein, J.H. (ed.) (1983) *Sports violence*, New York: Springer-Verlag.

Góngora Martin, A. (1996) 'Deporte y sociedad: Estudio de un caso: El F.C. Barcelona como un fenómeno constructor de identidad colectiva', in M. García Ferrando, J.R. Martinez Morales (eds), *Ocio y deporte en España*, Valencia: Tirant lo Blanch, pp. 215-248.

Goodhead, G. (2003) *Us v them: Journeys to the world's greatest football derbies*, London: Viking.

Gooptu, S. (2005) 'Celluloid soccer: The peculiarities of soccer in Bengali cinema', *International Journal of the History of Sport*, vol. 22, no. 4, pp. 689-698.

Gore, S. (2002) 'The Catalan language and immigrants from outside the European Union', *International Journal of Iberian Studies*, vol. 15, no. 2, pp. 91-102.

Guibernau, M. (2000) 'Nationalism and intellectuals in nations without states: The Catalan case', *Political Studies*, vol. 48, pp. 989-1005.

Gupta, A., and J. Ferguson (1997) 'Culture, power, place: Ethnography at the end of an era', in A. Gupta and J. Ferguson (eds) *Culture, power, place: Explorations in critical anthropology*, Durham and London: Duke University Press, pp. 1-31.

Guttmann, A. (1986) *Sports spectators*, New York: Columbia University Press.

Haan, W. de, E. de Bie, C. Baerveldt and C. Bouw (1999) *Jeugd en geweld: Een interdisciplinair perspectief*, Assen: Van Gorcum.

Hakkert, A., A. van Wijk, H. Ferwerda and T. Eijken (1998) *Groepscriminaliteit*, Den Haag: Ministerie van Justitie.

Hall, S. (1978) 'The treatment of "football hooliganism" in the press', in R. Ingham (ed.), *Footballhooliganism: The wider context*, London: Interaction, pp. 15-36.

Hall, S., and T. Jefferson (eds) (1976) *Resistance through rituals: Youth subcultures in post-war Britain*, London: Hutchinson.

Hammersmith and Fulham Council (2002) *Borough profile 2002: A borough profile of Hammersmith and Fulham*, London.

Hannerz, U. (1996) *Transnational connections: Culture, people, places*, London and New York: Routledge.

Hannerz, U. (1992) *Cultural complexity: Studies in the social organization of meaning*, New York: Columbia University Press.

Hannerz, U. (1987) 'The world in creolisation', *Africa*, vol. 57, no. 4, pp. 546-559.

Hans, D., and J. Wolff (1928) *Sparta, 1888-1928*, Rotterdam: E. de Bont & Zoon.

Hare, G. (2003) *Football in France: A cultural history*, Oxford and New York: Berg.

Hargreaves, J. (2000) *Freedom for Catalonia? Catalan nationalism, Spanish identity and the Barcelona Olympic Games*, Cambridge: Cambridge University Press.

Harper, C. (1990) *A study of football crowd behaviour*, Lothian and Borders Police, mimeo.

Harris, M. (1984) 'The Doc Martens angels', *New Society*, vol. 68, no. 1122, pp.

307-309.

Harrison, P. (1974) 'Soccer's tribal wars', *New Society*, vol. 29, no. 622, pp. 602-604.

Harsányi, L. (2005) *Report on hooliganism, racism, anti-Semitism and intolerance in Slovak football*, Bratislava: Ludia proti rasizmu.

Hart, P. 't, and B. Pijnenburg (1988) *Het Heizeldrama: Rampzalig organiseren en kritieke beslissingen*, Alphen aan den Rijn: Samsom.

Hartsuiker, J.F. (1977) *Rapport van de projectgroep vandalisme door voetbalsupporters*, Den Haag: Ministerie van Justitie.

Hay, R. (2001) '"Those bloody Croatians": Croatian soccer teams, ethnicity and violence in Australia, 1950-99', in G. Armstrong & R. Giulianotti (eds), *Fear and loathing in world football*, Oxford and New York: Berg, pp. 77-90.

Hay, R. (1998) 'A new look at soccer violence', in D. Hemphill (ed.), *All part of the game: Violence and Australian sport*, Petersham: Walla Walla, pp. 41-62.

Haynes, R. (1995) *The football imagination: The rise of football fanzine culture*, Aldershot: Arena.

Haynes, R. (1993) 'Marching on together', in S. Redhead (ed.), *The passion and the fashion: Football fandom in the new Europe*, Aldershot: Avebury, pp. 13-31.

Hebdige, D. (1979) *Subculture: The meaning of style*, London and New York: Routledge.

Hebdige, D. (1976) 'The meaning of mod', in S. Hall and T. Jefferson (eds), *Resistance through rituals: Youth subcultures in post-war Britain*, London: Hutchinson, pp. 87-98.

Heijs, L., and A. Mengerink (1993) *Stewarding in Nederland*, Apeldoorn: VUGA.

Hesmondhalgh, D. (2005) 'Subcultures, scenes or tribes? None of the above', *Journal of Youth Studies*, vol. 8, no. 1, pp. 21-40.

Hetherington, K. (1994) 'The contemporary significance of Schmalenbach's concept of the bund', *Sociological Review*, vol. 42, no. 1, pp. 1-25.

Hill, S. (1976) *The dockers*, London: Heinemann.

Hillier, J., and E. Rooksby (2002) 'Introduction', in J. Hillier and E. Rooksby (eds), *Habitus: A sense of place*, Aldershot: Ashgate, pp. 3-25.

Hirschi, T. (2002) [1969] *Causes of Delinquency*, Berkeley: University of California Press.

Hobbs, D. (1988) *Doing the business: Entrepreneurship, the working class, and detectives in the East End of London*, Oxford: Clarendon Press.

Hobbs, D., and D. Robins (1991) 'The boy done good: Football violence, changes and continuities', *Sociological Review*, vol. 39, no. 3, pp. 551-579.

Hobsbawm, E. (1983) 'Introduction: Inventing traditions', in E. Hobsbawm and T. Ranger (eds), *The invention of tradition*, Cambridge and New York: Cambridge University Press, pp. 1-14.

Holdaway, S. (1977) 'Changes in urban policing', *British Journal of Sociology*, vol. 28, no. 2, pp. 119-137.

Holland, B. (1997) 'Surviving leisure time racism: The burden of racial harassment on Britain's black footballers', *Leisure Studies*, 16, pp. 261-277.

Holt, R. (1990) *Sport and the British: A modern history*, Oxford and New York: Oxford University Press.

Holt, R. (1981) *Sport and society in modern France*, Basingstoke and London: Macmillan Press.

Homann, B., M. Löffelholz and R. Schwart (1991) 'Fanprojekte bundesweit: Gesichtspunkte der Evaluationsforschung', *Schriftenreihe der Polizei-Führungsakademie*, no. 3, pp. 131-142.

Home Office (2004) *Statistics on football-related arrests & banning orders: Season 2003-2004*, London: Home Office.

Home Office (2003) *Statistics on football-related arrests & banning orders: Season 2002-2003*, London: Home Office.

Home Office (2002) *Statistics on football-related arrests & banning orders: Season 2001-2002*, London: Home Office.

Hoogerwerf, A. (1996) *Geweld in Nederland*, Assen: Van Gorcum.

Hopcraft, A. (1988) [1971] *The football man: People and passions in soccer*, London: Simon & Schuster.

Horak, R. (1991) 'Things change: Trends in Austrian football hooliganism from 1977-1990', *Sociological Review*, vol. 39, no. 3, pp. 531-548.

Horak, R., and W. Maderthaner (1997) *Mehr als ein Spiel: Fußball und populare Kulturen im Wien der Moderne*, Wien: Löcker Verlag.

Horak, R., W. Reiter and K. Stocker (1987) 'Football violence in Austria: A report on a study of fan subculture and soccer hooliganism', in T. O'Brien (ed.),

European conference on football violence, Preston: Lancashire Polytechnic, pp. 59-65.

Houlihan, B. (1991) *The government and politics of sport*, London and New York: Routledge.

Hout, B. in 't (1969) *Rotterdam voetbalstad no. 1*, Rotterdam: Wijt.

Hua, T. (2004) 'Football "hooligans" and football supporters' culture in China', in W. Manzenreiter and J. Horne (eds), *Football goes east: Business, culture and the people's game in China, Japan and South Korea*, London: Routledge, pp. 87-101.

Hughson, J. (2002) 'Australian soccer's "ethnic" tribes: A new case for the carnivalesque', in E. Dunning, P. Murphy, I. Waddington and A.E. Astrinakis (eds), *Fighting fans: Football hooliganism as a world phenomenon*, Dublin: University College Dublin Press, pp. 37-48.

Hughson, J. (1997) 'The Bad Blue Boys and the "magical recovery" of John Clarke', in G. Armstrong and R. Giulianotti (eds), *Entering the field: New perspectives on world football*, Oxford and New York: Berg, pp. 239-259.

Huijzer, D. (1998) *Dat zijn nou typisch Feyenoorders*, Leiden: Uitgeverij Krikke.

Hulsteijn, G. (2005) 'Voetballen op het internet: De rol van fansites binnen de subcultuur van het hooliganisme', in R.F.J. Spaaij (ed.), *Supportersgedrag en hooliganisme in het Nederlandse voetbal*, Amsterdam: Universiteit van Amsterdam, 2005, pp. 167-198.

Hutchinson, J. (1975) 'Some aspects of football crowds before 1914', in Society for the Study of Labour History, *Conference proceedings: The working class and leisure*, Paper no. 13, University of Sussex, mimeo.

Ibarra, E. (2003) *Los crímenes del odio: Violencia skin y neonazi en España*, Madrid: Temas de Hoy.

Ignatieff, M. (1998) The warrior's honor: Ethnic war and the modern conscience, New York: Henry Holt.

Ingham, R. (ed.) (1978) *Football hooliganism: The wider context*, London: Interaction.

Inglis, S. (2001) 'All gone quiet over here', in M. Perryman (ed.), *Hooligan wars: Causes and effects of football violence*, Edinburgh and London: Mainstream, pp. 87-94.

Jaime-Jiménez, O., and F. Reinares (1998) 'The policing of mass demonstrations in Spain: From dictatorship to democracy', in D. Della Porta and H. Reiter (eds), *Policing protest*, Minneapolis: University of Minnesota Press, pp. 166-187.

Janssen, J. (1989) 'Delinquentie als "crime de passage"', *Jeugd en Samenleving*, vol. 19, no. 2, pp. 114-129.

Jareño Ruíz, E. (1998) 'La comunicación al servicio de la prevención social de los grupos de seguidores ultras', Paper presented at the Seminario Internacional sobre la gestión del hooliganismo y las estrategias de prevención en Europa, Lieja.

Jary, D., J. Horne and T. Bucke (1991) 'Football "fanzines" and football culture: A case of successful "cultural contestation"', *Sociological Review*, vol. 39, no. 3, pp. 581-597.

Johnes, M. (2004) '"Heads in the sand": Football, politics and crowd disasters in twentieth-century Britain', *Soccer and Society*, vol. 5, no. 2, pp. 134-151.

Jones, D., and T. Rivers (2002) *Soul Crew: The inside story of Britain's most notorious hooligan gang*, Bury: Milo Books.

Joustra, W., and Y. Kuiper (2001) *SC Heerenveen: Spelen met traditie*, Amsterdam: Thomas Rap.

Junger-Tas, J. (1996) 'Youth and violence in Europe', *Studies on Crime and Crime Prevention*, vol. 5, no. 1, pp. 31-58.

Junger-Tas, J. (1994) 'Nature and evolution of the criminality of young adults', in European Committee on Crime Problems, *Young adult offenders and crime policy*, Strasbourg: Council of Europe Press, pp. 14-58.

Katz, J. (1988) *Seductions of crime*, New York: Basic Books.

Keman, H. (1996) 'The Low Countries: Confrontation and coalition in segmented societies', in J. Colomer (ed.), *Political institutions in Europe*, London and New York: Routledge, pp. 211-253.

Kerr, J.H. (2005) *Rethinking aggression and violence in sport*, London and New York: Routledge.

Kerr, J.H. (1994) *Understanding soccer hooliganism*, Buckingham and Philadelphia: Open University Press.

Kerr, J.H., and H. De Kock (2002) 'Aggression, violence and the death of a Dutch soccer hooligan: A reversal theory explanation', *Aggressive Behavior*, vol. 28, no. 1, pp. 1-10.

King, A. (2002) *The end of the terraces: The transformation of English football in the 1990s*, rev.ed., London and New York: Leicester University Press.

King, A. (2001) 'Violent pasts: Collective memory and football hooliganism', *Sociological Review*, vol. 49, no. 4, pp. 568-585.

King, A. (2000) 'Football fandom and post-national identity in the New Europe', *British Journal of Sociology*, vol. 51, no. 3, pp. 419-442.

King, A. (1999) 'Football hooliganism and the practical paradigm', *Sociology of Sport Journal*, vol. 16, no. 3, pp. 269-273.

King, A. (1997) 'The postmodernity of football hooliganism', *British Journal of Sociology*, vol. 48, no. 4, pp. 576-593.

King, A. (1995) 'Outline of a practical theory of football violence', *Sociology*, vol. 29, no. 4, pp. 635-641.

King, J. (2000) *FC Barcelona: Tales from the Nou Camp*, London: Macmillan.

King, J. (1997) *The football factory*, London: Vintage.

King, M., and M. Knight (1999) *The naughty nineties*, Edinburgh and London: Mainstream.

King, M., and M. Knight (1999a) *Hoolifan: 30 years of hurt*, Edinburgh and London: Mainstream.

KNVB (2003), *Handboek veiligheid: Voorwaarden, voorschriften en aanbevelingen ter bevordering van de orde en veiligheid in de Nederlandse voetbalstadions*, Zeist: KNVB.

Köster, M. (2005) 'Weer trekken wij ten strijde: Onderzoek naar de opkomst, ontwikkeling en huidige situatie van NEC's harde kern', in R.F.J. Spaaij (ed.), *Supportersgedrag en hooliganisme in het Nederlandse voetbal*, Amsterdam: Universiteit van Amsterdam, pp. 50-89.

Korr, C.P. (1986) *West Ham United: The making of a football club*, London: Duckworth.

Korr, C.P. (1978) 'West Ham United Football Club and the beginnings of professional football in East London, 1895-1914', *Journal of Contemporary History*, vol. 13, no. 2, pp. 211-232.

Korthals, J. (2005) 'Fanatieke supporters: Een onderzoek naar uitingsvormen en drijfveren', in R.F.J. Spaaij (ed.), *Supportersgedrag en hooliganisme in het*

Nederlandse Voetbal, Amsterdam: Universiteit van Amsterdam, pp. 136-166.

Kozanoglu, C. (1999) 'Beyond Edirne: Football and the national identity crisis in Turkey', in G. Armstrong and R. Giulianotti (eds), *Football cultures and identities*, London: Macmillan Press, pp. 117-125.

Kuper, S. (2000) *Ajax, de joden, Nederland*, book ed. Hard Gras no. 22, Amsterdam: L.J. Veen.

Kuper, S. (1994) *Football against the enemy*, London: Orion.

Laar, P. van de (2000) *Stad van formaat: Geschiedenis van Rotterdam in de negentiende en twintigste eeuw*, Zwolle: Waanders.

Landelijk Overleg Voetbalvandalisme (1987) *Bestrijding voetbalvandalisme: Een zaak van teamwork*, Den Haag: VNG.

Lanfranchi, P. (1997) 'La gènesi del futbol a les regions de la conca mediterrània occidental', *L'Avenç*, no. 211, pp. 12-17.

Laporta, J. (2002) 'El Barça sí que és més que un club', *El Periódico*, 14 October 2002, p. 4.

Lefebvre, H. (1991) *The production of space*, Oxford: Blackwell.

Lewis, J.M. (1982) 'Crowd control at English football matches', *Sociological Focus*, vol. 15, no. 4, pp. 417-423.

Lewis, R.W. (1996) 'Football hooliganism in England before 1914: A critique of the Dunning thesis', *International Journal of the History of Sport*, vol. 13, no. 3, pp. 310-339.

Lijphart, A. (1971) 'Comparative politics and the comparative method', *American Political Science Review*, vol. 65, no. 3, pp. 682-693.

Limbergen, K. van (1991) 'Sport als bijzondere methodiek ter preventie van delinquentie: Het fan coachingproject te Antwerpen als voorbeeld', *Revue van de Rijkswacht*, no. 120, pp. 24-31.

Limbergen, K. van, and L. Walgrave (1991) *De justitiële afhandeling van voetbalmisdrijven*, Leuven: Katholieke Universiteit Leuven.

Limbergen, K. van, and L. Walgrave (1988) *Sides, fans en hooligans: Voetbalvandalisme: feiten, achtergronden en aanpak*, Leuven en Amersfoort: Acco.

Limbergen, K. van, and L. Walgrave (1988a) 'Enkele beschouwingen bij de relatie tussen het voetbalgeweld en de mediaberichtgeving erover', *Tijdschrift voor*

Criminologie, no. 4, pp. 321-335.

Lindner, R. (ed.) (1980) *Der Fußballfan: Ansichten vom Zuschauer*, Frankfurt am Main: Syndikat.

Lipset, S.M., and S. Rokkan (1967) 'Cleavage structures, party systems and voter alignments: An introduction', in S.M. Lipset and S. Rokkan (eds), *Part systems and voter alignments*, New York: The Free Press, pp. 1-64.

Lipsky, M. (1980) *Streetlevel bureaucracy: Dilemmas of the individual in public services*, New York: Russell Sage.

Loo, H. van der, and W. van Reijen (1997) *Paradoxen van modernisering*, Bussum: Coutinho.

Mac an Ghaill, M. (1996) '"What about the boys?" Schooling, class and crisis masculinity', *Sociological Review*, vol. 44, no. 3, pp. 381-397.

Madrid, D. (2005) *Insider: Un policía infiltrado en las gradas ultras*, Madrid: Temas de Hoy.

Madzimbamuto, F.D. (2003) 'A hospital reponse to a soccer stadium stampede in Zimbabwe', *Emergency Medicine Journal*, vol. 20, no. 6, pp. 556-559.

Maffesoli, M. (1996) *The time of the tribes: The decline of individualism in mass society*, London: Sage.

Maguire, J. (1999) *Global sport: Identities, societies, civilizations*, Cambridge: Polity.

Maguire, J. (1986) 'The emergence of football spectating as a social problem 1880-1985: A figurational and developmental perspective', *Sociology of Sport Journal*, vol. 3, pp. 217-244.

Majumdar, B., and K. Bandyopadhyay (2005) '"*Ghati-Bangal* on the *Maidan*": Subregionalism, club rivalry and fan culture in Indian football', *Soccer and Society*, vol. 6, no. 2, pp. 210-226.

Malcolm, D., I. Jones and I. Waddington (2000) 'The people's game? Football spectatorship and demographic change', *Soccer and Society*, vol. 1, no. 1, pp. 129-143.

Maluquer, A. (1949) *Historia del Club de Fútbol Barcelona*, Barcelona: M. Arimany.

Marivoet, S. (2002) 'Violent disturbances in Portuguese football', in E. Dunning, P. Murphy, I. Waddington and A.E. Astrinakis (eds), *Fighting fans: Football hooliganism as a world phenomenon*, Dublin: University College Dublin Press, pp. 158-173.

Marivoet, S. (1989) *Evolução da violência associada ao desporto (1978-1987)*, Lisboa: Ministério da Educação.

Marques, M. (1987) 'Youth commitment in football fan associations: The Juve Leo case', in T. O'Brien (ed.), *European conference on football violence*, Preston: Lancashire Polytechnic, pp. 11-20.

Marsh, P. (1988) *Tribes*, London: Pyramid.

Marsh, P. (1978) *Aggro: The illusion of violence*, London: Dent.

Marsh, P. (1978a) 'Life and careers on the soccer terraces', in R. Ingham (ed.), *Football hooliganism: The wider context*, London: Interaction, pp. 61-81.

Marsh, P. (1976) 'Careers for boys, nutters, hooligans and hardcases', *New Society*, vol. 36, no. 710, pp. 346-348.

Marsh, P. (1975) 'Understanding aggro', *New Society*, vol. 32, no. 652, pp. 7-9.

Marsh, P., and A. Campbell (eds) (1982) *Aggression and violence*, Oxford: Blackwell.

Marsh, P., K. Fox, G. Carnibella, J. McCann and J. Marsh (1996) *Football violence in Europe*, Oxford: Social Issues Research Centre.

Marsh, P., E. Rosser and R. Harré (1978) *The rules of disorder*, London: Routledge & Kegan Paul.

Martialay, F., and B. De Salazar (1997) *Las grandes mentiras del fútbol español*, Madrid: Fuerza Nueva Editorial.

Martinez Calatrava, V. (2002) *Historia y estadística del fútbol español: Segunda parte*, Barcelona: Servicepoint.

Martinez Calatrava, V. (2001) *Historia y estadística del fútbol español: Primera parte*, Barcelona: Digital Center.

Mascall, P. (2002) *Celebrating Craven Cottage*, London: Fulham Football Club.

Mascall, P. (2001) 'Feeling Fulhamish', Internet Article posted on 18 July, www.fulhamfc.com.

Mason, T. (1980) *Association Football and English society 1863-1915*, Brighton: Harvester.

Matza, D. (1964) *Delinquency and drift*, New York: Wiley.

Matza, D., and G.M. Sykes (1961) 'Juvenile delinquency and subterranean values',

American Sociological Review, vol. 26, pp. 712-719.

Melnick, M.J. (1986) 'The mythology of football hooliganism: A closer look at the British experience', *International Review for the Sociology of Sport*, vol. 21, no. 1, pp. 1-21.

Merkel, U. (1999) 'Football identity and youth culture in Germany', in G. Armstrong and R. Giulianotti (eds), *Football cultures and identities*, London: Macmillan Press, pp. 52-63.

Merkel, U., and W. Tokarski (eds) (1996) *Racism and xenophobia in European football*, Aachen: Meyer & Meyer.

Messerschmidt, J.W. (1999) 'Making bodies matter: Adolescent masculinities, the body, and varieties of violence', *Theoretical Criminology*, vol. 3, no. 2, pp. 197-220.

Metropolitan Police (2003) *End of season 2002-2003 report*, London: Football Intelligence Unit.

Miermans, C. (1955) *Voetbal in Nederland: Maatschappelijke en sportieve aspecten*, Assen: Van Gorcum.

Mignon, P. (2002) 'Another side to French exceptionalism: Football without hooligans?', in E. Dunning, P. Murphy, I. Waddington and A.E. Astrinakis (eds), *Fighting fans: Football hooliganism as a world phenomenon*, Dublin: University College Dublin Press, pp. 62-74.

Mignon, P. (2001) 'Le Francais feel-good factor', in M. Perryman (ed.), *Hooligan wars: Causes and effects of football violence*, Edinburgh and London: Mainstream, pp. 165-178.

Mignon, P. (1996) 'La lutte contre le hooliganisme: Comparaisons européennes', in M. Leclerc (ed.), *Football, ombres au spectacle*, Paris: IHESI, pp. 92-107.

Mignon, P. (1994) 'New supporter cultures and identity in France: The case of Paris Saint-Germain', in R. Giulianotti and J. Williams (eds), *Game without frontiers: Football, identity and modernity*, Aldershot: Arena, pp. 273-297.

Miller, W.B. (1958) 'Lower class culture as a generating milieu of gang delinquency', *Journal of Social Issues*, vol. 14, no. 1, pp. 5-19.

Moffitt, T. (1993) 'Adolescence-limited and life-course-persistent antisocial behavior: A developmental taxonomy', *Psychological Review*, vol. 100, no. 4, pp. 674-701.

Molinero, C., and P. Ysàs (1999) *Catalunya durant el franquisme*, Barcelona: Empúries.

Moorhouse, H.F. (2000) 'Book review of "Football hooligans: Knowing the score"', *Urban Studies*, vol. 37, no. 8, pp. 1463-1464.

Moorhouse, H.F. (1991) 'Football hooligans: Old bottle, new whines?', *Sociological Review*, vol. 39, no. 3, pp. 489-502.

Moorhouse H.F. (1989) '"We're off to Wembley!" The history of a Scottish event and the sociology of football hooliganism', in D. McCrone and S. Kendrick (eds), *The making of Scotland: Nation, culture, change*, Edinburgh: Edinburgh University Press, pp. 207-227.

Moorhouse, H.F. (1984) 'Professional football and working class culture: English theories and Scottish evidence', *Sociological Review*, vol. 32, no. 2, pp. 285-315.

Morris, D. (1981) *The soccer tribe*, London: Jonathan Cape.

Mosely, P. (1997) 'Soccer', in P. Mosely, R. Cashman, J. O'Hara and H. Weatherburn (eds), *Sporting immigrants: Sport and ethnicity in Australia*, Crow's Nest: Walla Walla Press, pp. 155-173.

Mosely, P. (1995) *Ethnic involvement in Australian soccer: A history 1950-1990*, Canberra: Australian Sports Commission.

Mumford, K., and A. Power (2003) *East Enders: Family and community in East London*, Bristol: The Policy Press.

Mungham, G., and G. Pearson (eds) (1976) *Working class youth culture*, London: Routledge & Kegan Paul.

Murphy, P. (2000) 'Hooligans abroad: Football crowd disorder in Cyprus', *Singer & Friedlander's Review*, pp. 39-42.

Murphy, P., E. Dunning and J. Maguire (1998) 'Football spectator violence and disorder before the First World War: A reply to R.W. Lewis', *International Journal of the History of Sport*, vol. 15, no. 1, pp. 141-162.

Murphy, P., J. Williams and E. Dunning (1990) *Football on trial: Spectator violence and development in the football world*, London: Routledge.

Murphy, P., E. Dunning and J. Williams (1988) 'Soccer crowd disorder and the press: Processes of amplification and de-amplification in historical perspective', *Theory, Culture & Society*, vol. 5, no. 4, pp. 645-673.

Murray, B. (2000) [1984] *The Old Firm: Sectarianism, sport and society in Scotland*, Edinburgh: John Donald.

Murray, B. (1977) 'The soccer hooligans' honour system', *New Society*, vol. 42, no. 783, pp. 9-11.

NCIS (2000) *Football disorder: Season 1999-2000*, London: NCIS.

Nederveen Pieterse, J. (1995) 'Globalization as hybridization', in M. Featherstone, S. Lash and R. Robertson (eds), *Global modernities*, London: Sage, pp. 45-68.

Nicholson, M. (ed.) (2005) *Fanfare: Spectator culture and Australian Rules football*, Melbourne: Australian Society for Sports History.

Northcutt, J., and R. Shoesmith (1997) *West Ham United: An illustrated history*, Derby: Breedon Books.

NPS (2005) *Een jaar om FC Barcelona te redden*, Documentary first broadcasted on 15 June.

O'Brien, T. (ed.) (1987) *European conference on football violence*, Preston: Lancashire Polytechnic.

O'Neill, M. (2005) *Policing football: Social interaction and negotiated disorder*, Basingstoke and New York: Palgrave.

O'Neill, M. (2004) 'Policing football in Scotland', *International Review for the Sociology of Sport*, vol. 39, no. 1, pp. 95-104.

O'Neill, G. (2000) *My East End: Memories of life in cockney London*, London: Penguin.

Ornstein, L. (1982) 'De F.C. Bunnikzijde', *Vrij Nederland*, 9 January, pp. 2-22.

Orwell, G. (1989) *Homage to Catalonia*, London: Penguin.

Oudenaarden, J. (1994) *Feyenoord: Een beeld van een club*, Rotterdam: Phoenix & den Oudsten.

Painter, J. (2000) 'Pierre Bourdieu', in M. Crang and N. Thrift (eds), *Thinking space*, London: Routledge, pp. 239-259.

Pallarés, J., C. Costa and C. Feixa (2002) 'Okupas, makineros, skinheads: Ciudadania y microculturas juveniles en Cataluña', in C. Feixa, C. Costa and J. Pallarés (eds), *Movimientos juveniles en la Península Ibérica*, Barcelona: Ariel, pp. 89-114.

Palmer, A. (2000) *The East End: Four centuries of London life*, London: John Murray.

Panfichi, A., and J. Thieroldt (2002) 'Barras bravas: Representation and crowd violence in Peruvian football', in E. Dunning, P. Murphy, I. Waddington and A.E. Astrinakis (eds), *Fighting fans: Football hooliganism as a world phenomenon*, Dublin: University College Dublin Press, pp. 143-157.

Patrick, J. (1973) *A Glasgow gang observed*, London: Eyre Methuen.

Paulle, B. (2005) *Anxiety and intimidation in the Bronx and the Bijlmer. An ethnographic comparison of two schools*, Amsterdam: Dutch University Press.

Pearson, G. (1998) 'The English disease? Socio-legal constructions of football hooliganism', *Youth and Policy*, vol. 60, no. 1, pp. 1-15.

Pearson, G. (1983) *Hooligan: A history of respectable fears*, London: Macmillan.

Pearson, J. (1995) [1972] *The profession of violence: The rise and fall of the Kray twins*, 4th ed., London: Harper Collins.

Peffer, R. (1984) 'Catalonia: Spain's country within a country', *National Geographic*, vol. 165, no. 1, pp. 95-127.

Peiser, B., and J. Minten (2003) 'Soccer violence', in T. Reilly and A.M. Williams (eds), *Science and Soccer*, 2nd ed., London and New York: Routledge, pp. 230-241.

Peitersen, B. (1990) 'Roligan: Un modo d'essere dei tifosi danesi', in A. Roversi (ed.), *Calcio e violenza in Europa*, Bologna: Il Mulino, pp. 169-186.

Pennant, C. (2005) *Top boys*, London: John Blake.

Pennant, C. (2002) *Congratulations: You have just met the I.C.F.*, London: John Blake.

Pennant, C. (2000) *Cass*, London: John Blake.

Pennant, C., and M. King (2003) *Terrace legends*, London: John Blake.

Pennant, C., and M. Smith (2002) *Want some aggro?* London: John Blake.

Peristiany, J. (ed.) (1966) *Honour and shame: The values of Mediterranean society*, Chicago: University of Chicago Press.

Perryman, M. (ed.) (2001) *Hooligan wars: Causes and effects of football violence*, Edinburgh and London: Mainstream.

Phillips, D. (1987) 'Football fans and the police', in T. O'Brien (ed.), *European conference on football violence*, Preston: Lancashire Polytechnic, pp. 31-38.

Pieloor, R.A., B. van de Meer and M. Bakker (2002) *F-Side is niet makkelijk!* Utrecht: Het Spectrum.

Pilz, G.A. (1996) 'Social factors influencing sport and violence: On the "problem" of football hooliganism in Germany', *International Review for the Sociology of Sport*, vol. 31, no. 1, pp. 49-66.

Pilz, G.A. (1991) 'Eskalation von Gewalt in Zusammenhang mit dem Fussbalgeschehen', *Schriftenreihe der Polizei-Führungsakademie*, no. 3, pp. 114-129.

Pimenta, C.A.M. (2003) 'Torcidas organizadas de futebol: Identidade e identificações, dimensões cotidianas', in P. Alabarces (ed.), *Futbologías: Fútbol, identidad y violencia en América Latina*, Buenos Aires: CLACSO, pp. 39-55.

Pimenta, C.A.M. (2000) 'Violência entre torcidas organizadas de futebol', *São Paulo em Perspectiva*, vol. 14, no. 2, pp. 122-128.

Pintér, O., and J. van Gestel (2002) 'Football's fighting fans: The Hungarian case', in E. Dunning, P. Murphy, I. Waddington and A.E. Astrinakis (eds), *Fighting fans: Football hooliganism as a world phenomenon*, Dublin: University College Dublin Press, pp. 106-117.

Piotrowski, P. (2004) 'Soccer hooliganism in Poland: Its extent, dynamism and psycho-social conditions', in R. Jackson (ed.), *(Re)constructing cultures of violence and peace*, Amsterdam and New York: Rodopi.

Podaliri, C., and C. Balestri (1998) 'The *Ultràs*, racism and football culture in Italy', in A. Brown (ed.), *Fanatics! Power, identity and fandom in football*, London and New York: Routledge, pp. 88-100.

Politie Rotterdam-Rijnmond (1999) *Vuurwerk na de huldiging: Evaluatie van het optreden rond de huldiging van Feyenoord op 25 april 1999*, Rotterdam.

Porta, M. (1995) *Del franquisme als Jocs Olímpics (1975-1992)*, Barcelona: Barcanova.

Portelli, A. (1993) 'The rich and the poor in the culture of football', in S. Redhead (ed.), *The passion and the fashion: Football fandom in the new Europe*, Aldershot: Avebury, pp. 77-87.

Powley, A. (1999) 'Fighting talk', *When Saturday Comes*, no. 149, pp. 34-36.

Pratt, J., and M. Salter (1984) 'A fresh look at football hooliganism', *Leisure Studies*, vol. 3, no. 2, pp. 201-230.

Pressman, J.L., and A. Wildavsky (1973) *Implementation*, Berkeley and Los

Angeles: University of California Press.

Pujol, J., J. Tussel, G. López Casasnovas, J. Arango and J. Triadú (2002) *Cataluña hoy*, Barcelona: Generalitat de Catalunya.

Punch, M. (1982) 'Voetbal en geweld', in R. Siekmann (ed.), *Voetbalvandalisme*, Haarlem: De Vrieseborch, pp. 117-125.

Putnam, R.D. (2000) *Bowling alone: The collapse and revival of American community*, New York: Touchstone.

Redhead, S. (2004) 'Hit and tell: A review essay on the soccer hooligan memoir', *Soccer and Society*, vol. 5, no. 3, pp. 392-403.

Redhead, S. (1997) *Post-fandom and the millennial blues: The transformation of soccer culture*, London and New York: Routledge.

Redhead, S. (ed.) (1993) *The passion and the fashion: Football fandom in the new Europe*, Aldershot: Avebury.

Redhead, S. (1991) 'Some reflections on discourses on football hooliganism', *Sociological Review*, vol. 39, no. 3, pp. 479-486.

Redhead, S., and E. McLaughlin (1985) 'Soccer's style wars', *New Society*, vol. 73, no. 1181, pp. 225-228.

Reis, H.H.B. dos (2003) 'Os espectadores de futebol e a problemática da violência relacionada à organização do espetáculo futebolístico', *Revista Paulista de Educação Física* , vol. 17, no. 2, pp. 85-92.

Reville, N.J. (1988) 'A sporting theory of justice', *The Law Society's Gazette*, vol. 85, no. 24, pp. 12-14

Richards, P. (1997) 'Soccer and violence in war-torn Africa: Soccer and social rehabilitation in Sierra Leone', in G. Armstrong and R. Giulianotti (eds), *Entering the field: New perspectives on world football*, Oxford and New York: Berg, pp. 141-157.

Richardson, W. (1993) 'Identifying the cultural causes of disasters: An analysis of the Hillsborough football stadium disaster', *Journal of Contingencies and Crisis Management*, vol. 1, no. 1, pp. 27-35.

Riches, D. (ed.) (1986a) *The anthropology of violence*, Oxford: Blackwell.

Riches, D. (1986) 'The phenomenon of violence', in D. Riches (ed.), *The anthropology of violence*, Oxford: Blackwell, pp. 1-27.

Ritzer, G. (2004) [1993] *The McDonaldization of society*, Thousand Oaks: Pine

Forge Press.

Roadburg, A. (1980) 'Factors precipitating fan violence: A comparison of professional soccer in Britain and North America', *British Journal of Sociology*, vol. 31, no. 2, pp. 265-276.

Roberts, J.V., and C.J. Benjamin (2000) 'Spectator violence in sports: A North American perspective', *European Journal on Criminal Policy and Research*, no. 8, pp. 163-181.

Robertson, R. (1992) *Globalization*, London: Sage.

Robertson, R. (1995) 'Glocalization: Time-space and homogeneity-heterogeneity', in M. Featherstone, S. Lash and R. Robertson (eds), *Global modernities*, London: Sage, pp. 25-44.

Robson, G. (2000) *No one likes us, we don't care: The myth and reality of Millwall fandom*, Oxford and New York: Berg.

Robson, G. (1997) *Class, criminality and embodied consciousness: Charlie Richardson and a South East London habitus*, Occasional Paper, London: Goldsmiths College.

Rodríguez, J. (1995) 'El derby de los ultras', *Cambio 16*, no. 1254, pp. 48-52.

Rodríguez, J. (1993) 'Historia de un vándalo', *El País Semanal*, vol. 18, no. 148, pp. 20-32.

Rodríguez Díaz, A. (2003) 'Los jóvenes ultras del fútbol andaluz', *Anduli: revista andaluza de ciencias sociales*, no. 2, pp. 107-124.

Rodríguez Díaz, A. (1994) *Las hinchadas juveniles en el fútbol andaluz*, Sevilla: Junta de Andalucía.

Rogers, E.M. (1983) [1962] *Diffusion of innovations*, New York: The Free Press.

Romero, A.G. (1986) *Muerte en la cancha (1958-1985)*, Buenos Aires: Nueva América.

Rood-Pijpers, E. (1995) 'Een sociografische schets van de wijken Afrikaanderwijk, Bloemhof en Hillesluis', in E. Rood-Pijpers, B. Rovers, F. van Gemert and C. Fijnaut (eds), *Preventie van jeugdcriminaliteit in een grote stad*, Arnhem: Gouda Quint, pp. 191-214.

Rosenthal, U., A. Ringeling, M. Bovens, P. 't Hart and M. van Twist (1996) *Openbaar bestuur: Beleid, organisatie en politiek*, Alphen aan den Rijn: Samsom.

Rovers, B. (1995) 'De criminaliteit in de drie wijken', in E. Rood-Pijpers, B. Rovers, F. van Gemert and C. Fijnaut (eds), *Preventie van jeugdcriminaliteit in een grote stad*, Arnhem: Gouda Quint, pp. 215-263.

Roversi, A. (1996) 'El sociólogo y el ultra: Los estudios sobre el gamberrismo en el fútbol', in Consejo Superior de Deportes, *Valores sociales y deporte: Fair play versus violencia*, Madrid: Ministerio de Educación y Cultura, pp. 69-93.

Roversi, A. (1992) *Calcio, tifo e violenza: Il teppismo calcistico in Italia*, Bologna: Il Mulino.

Roversi, A. (1991) 'Football violence in Italy', *International Review for the Sociology of Sport*, vol. 26, no. 4., pp. 311-330.

Roversi, A., and C. Balestri (2002) 'Italian ultras today: Change or decline?', in E. Dunning, P. Murphy, I. Waddington and A.E. Astrinakis (eds), *Fighting fans: Football hooliganism as a world phenomenon*, Dublin: University College Dublin Press, pp. 131-142.

Salas, A. (2003) *Diario de un skin: Un topo en el movimiento neonazi español*, Madrid: Temas de Hoy.

Salvini, A. (1988) *Il rito aggressivo: Dall' aggressività simbolica al comportamento violento: il caso dei tifosi ultras*, Firenze: Giunti.

Sánchez Jankowski, M. (1991) *Islands in the streets: Gangs and American urban society*, Berkeley: University of California Press.

Sandvoss, C. (2003) *A game of two halves: Football, television and globalization*, London and New York: Routledge.

Savornin Lohman, P.M. de, and F.H. ter Bruggen (1987) *Voetbalvandalisme buitenspel: Onderzoek naar de mogelijkheden van een jeugdwelzijnsbenadering van voetbalvandalisme*, Rijswijk: Ministerie van WVC.

Schadee, N. (2002) *Een rijk geheugen: Geschiedenis van Rotterdam 1270-2001*, Rotterdam: Historisch Museum Rotterdam.

Schinkel, W. (2004) 'The will to violence', *Theoretical Criminology*, vol. 8, no. 1, pp. 5-31.

Schneider, T. (1991) 'Fan-Projekte: Erfahrungen, Anforderungen', *Schriftenreihe der Polizei-Führungsakademie*, no. 3, pp. 104-113.

Schuyt, C.J.M. (1993) 'Jeugdcriminaliteit in groepsverband', *Delikt en Delinkwent*, vol. 23, no. 6, pp. 499-510.

Scraton, P. (2004) 'Death on the terraces: The contexts and injustices of the 1989 Hillsborough disaster', *Soccer and Society*, vol. 5, no. 2, pp. 183-200.

Scraton, P. (1999) *Hillsborough: The truth*, Edinburgh: Mainstream.

Seara Ruiz, J.M., and D. Sedano Jiménez (2001) *Radiografía de los grupos ultras en acontecimientos deportivos*, Madrid: Dykinson.

Segura Palomares, J. (2001) *Cent anys d'història del RCD Espanyol de Barcelona*, Barcelona: Fundació Privada RCD Espanyol de Barcelona.

Segura Palomares, J. (1974) *Historia del RCD Español*, Bilbao: Gran Encliclopedia Vasca.

Segurola, S. (ed.) (1999) *Fútbol y pasiones políticas*, Barcelona: Temas de debate.

Senado (1990) *Dictamen de la comisión especial de investigación de la violencia en los espectaculos deportivos, con especial referencia al futbol*, Madrid: Senado.

Shaw, D. (1987) *Fútbol y franquismo*, Madrid: Alianza Editorial.

Shaw, D. (1985) 'The politics of "fútbol": Spanish football under Franco', *History Today*, 35, pp. 38-42.

Shields, R. (1992) 'Spaces for the subject of consumption', in R. Shields (ed.), *Lifestyle shopping: The subject of consumption*, London: Routledge, pp. 1-20.

Shimizu, S. (2001) 'The study of supporter cultures', *Japan Journal of Sport Sociology*, 9, pp. 24-35.

Shoemaker, D.J. (2000) *Theories of delinquency*, New York and Oxford: Oxford University Press.

Short, J.F, and F.L. Strodtbeck (1965) *Group process and gang delinquency*, Chicago: University of Chicago Press.

Siekmann R. (ed.) (1982) *Voetbalvandalisme*, Haarlem: De Vrieseborch.

Signy, D. (1968) *A pictorial history of soccer*, London: Hamlyn.

Sir Norman Chester Centre for Football Research (2002) *The FA Premier League national fan survey 2001: Summary Report*, Leicester: University of Leicester.

Sir Norman Chester Centre for Football Research (2002a) *Football League supporter surveys 2001*, Leicester: University of Leicester.

Sir Norman Chester Centre for Football Research (2001) *Football League supporter surveys 2000*, Leicester: University of Leicester.

Sir Norman Chester Centre for Football Research (2000) *FA Premier League survey 1999*, Leicester: University of Leicester.

Smith, M.D. (1983) *Violence and sport*, Toronto: Butterworths.

Smith, M. (2004) *For the claret and blue*, London: John Blake.

Sobrequés Callicó, J. (1998) *FC Barcelona: Cent anys d'historia*, Barcelona: Edi-Liber.

Sobrequés Callicó, J. (1995) *FC Barcelona: Su historia y su presente*, Barcelona: Edi-Liber.

Sonneveld, H. (1986) *Vijftig Kasteeljaren*, Haarlem: De Vrieseborch.

Spaaij, R.F.J. (2005) 'The prevention of football hooliganism: A transnational perspective', in J. Aquesolo Vegas (ed.), *Actas del X Congreso Internacional de Historia del Deporte*, Sevilla: CESH, pp. 1-10.

Spaaij, R.F.J. (ed.) (2005a) *Supportersgedrag en hooliganisme in het Nederlandse voetbal*, Amsterdam: Universiteit van Amsterdam.

Spaaij, R.F.J. (2005b) 'Het succes van de Britse voetbalwet: Kanttekeningen en best practices', *Tijdschrift voor de Politie*, vol. 67, no. 1/2, pp. 4-8.

Spaaij, R.F.J. (2002) 'Het informatieproces rond voetbalwedstrijden: Structuur, knelpunten, kansen', *Tijdschrift voor de Politie*, vol. 64, no. 11, pp. 26-31.

Spaaij, R.F.J. (2001) *Hooligans, politie en informatie: een vloeiende combinatie?*, Unpublished dissertation, Leiden: Universiteit Leiden.

Spaaij, R.F.J., and C. Viñas (2005) 'Passion, politics and violence: A socio-historical analysis of Spanish ultras', *Soccer and Society*, vol. 6, no. 1, pp. 79-96.

Spaaij, R.F.J., and C. Viñas (2005a) '"A por ellos": Racism and anti-racism in Spanish football', *International Journal of Iberian Studies*, vol. 18, no. 3, pp. 141-164.

Spradley, J.P. (1980) *Participant observation*, Forth Worth: Harcourt Brace Jovanovich College Publishers.

Stevenson, T.B., and A.K. Alaug (2001) 'Competition and cooperation: Football rivalries in Yemen', in G. Armstrong and R. Giulianotti (eds), *Fear and loathing in world football*, Oxford and New York: Berg, pp. 173-186.

Stokkom, B. van (2000) 'Het mannelijke ego: Over onzekerheid, hoge eigendunk en agressie', *Justitiële Verkenningen*, vol. 26, no. 1, pp. 48-59.

Stokvis, R. (2003) *Sport, publiek en de media*, Amsterdam: Aksant.

Stokvis, R. (1991) 'Voetbalvandalisme in Nederland', *Amsterdams Sociologisch*

Tijdschrift, vol. 18, no. 3, pp. 165-188.

Stokvis, R. (1989) *De sportwereld: Een sociologische inleiding*, Alphen aan den Rijn: Samsom.

Stott, C., and S. Reicher (1998) 'How conflict escalates: The inter-group dynamics of collective football crowd "violence"', *Sociology*, vol. 32, no. 2, pp. 353-377.

Stott, C., and S. Reicher (1998a) 'Crowd action as intergroup process: Introducing the police perspective', *European Journal of Social Psychology*, vol. 28, pp. 509-529.

Stott, C., P. Hutchison and J. Drury (2001) 'Hooligans abroad? Inter-group dynamics, social identity and participation in collective "disorder" at the 1998 World Cup Finals', *British Journal of Social Psychology*, vol. 40, no. 3, pp. 359-384.

Strubell, T. (1998) *Les penyes barcelonistes*, Barcelona: Editorial Barcanova.

Sugden, J., and A. Bairner (1986) 'Observe the sons of Ulster: Football and politics in Northern Ireland', in A. Tomlinson and G. Whannel (eds), *Off the ball*, London: Pluto, pp. 146-157.

Suttles, G. (1968) *The social order of the slum*, Chicago: University of Chicago Press.

Sztompka, P. (2000) 'Cultural trauma: The other face of social change', *European Journal of Social Theory*, vol. 3, no. 4, pp. 449-466.

Takahashi, Y. (2002) 'Soccer spectators and fans in Japan', in E. Dunning, P. Murphy, I. Waddington and A.E. Astrinakis (eds), *Fighting fans: Football hooliganism as a world phenomenon*, Dublin: University College Dublin Press, pp. 190-200.

Taylor, I. (1991) 'English football in the 1990s: Taking Hillsborough seriously?', in J. Williams and S. Wagg (eds), *British football and social change: Getting into Europe*, Leicester and London: Leicester University Press, pp. 3-24.

Taylor, I. (1989) 'Hillsborough, 15 April 1989: Some personal contemplations', *New Left Review*, 177, pp. 89-110.

Taylor, I. (1987) 'Putting the boot into working class sport: British soccer after Bradford and Brussels', *Sociology of Sport Journal*, vol. 4, no. 2, pp. 171-191.

Taylor, I. (1982) 'On the sports violence question: Soccer hooliganism revisited', in J. Hargreaves (ed.), *Sport, culture and ideology*, London: Routledge and Kegan

Paul, pp. 152-196.

Taylor, I. (1971) 'Football mad: A speculative sociology of football hooliganism', in E. Dunning (ed.), *The sociology of sport: A selection of readings*, London: Frank Cass, pp. 352-377.

Taylor, I. (1971a) 'Soccer consciousness and soccer hooliganism', in S. Cohen (ed.), *Images of deviance*, Harmondsworth: Penguin.

Taylor, I. (1969) 'Hooligans: Soccer's resistance movement', *New Society*, vol. 14, no. 358, pp. 204-206.

Taylor, R. (1991) 'Walking alone together: Football supporters and their relationship with the game', in J. Williams and S. Wagg (eds), *British football and social change: Getting into Europe*, Leicester and London: Leicester University Press, pp. 111-129.

Thornton, P. (2003) *Casuals: Football, fighting and fashion: The story of a terrace cult*, Lytham: Milo Books.

Thornton, S. (1997) 'General introduction', in K. Gelder and S. Thornton (eds) *The subcultures reader*, London and New York: Routledge, pp. 1-7.

Toledo, L.H. de (1994) 'Transgressão e violência entre torcedores de futebol', *Revista USP*, vol. 22, pp. 92-101.

Torre, E.J. van der (2004) *Staanplaatsen in voetbalstadions: Een onderzoek naar veiligheid*, Alphen aan den Rijn: Kluwer.

Torre, E.J. van der (1999) *Politiewerk: Politiestijlen, community policing, professionalisme*, Alphen aan den Rijn: Samsom.

Torre, E.J. van der (1996) *Drugstoeristen en kooplieden*, Arnhem: Gouda Quint.

Torre, E.J. van der, and R.F.J. Spaaij (2003) *'Rotterdamse' hooligans: aanwas, gelegenheidsstructuren, preventie*, Alphen aan den Rijn: Kluwer.

Torre, E.J. van der, and R.F.J. Spaaij (2003a) 'Harde-kern hooligans: Verder dan geweld', *Tijdschrift voor de Politie*, vol. 65, no. 7/8, pp. 28-33.

Trivizas, E. (1980) 'Offences and offenders in football crowd disorders', *British Journal of Criminology*, vol. 20, no. 3, pp. 276-288.

Tummers, T. (1993) *Architectuur aan de zijlijn: Stadions en tribunes in Nederland*, Amsterdam: D'ARTS.

Turner, D. (2004) *Fulham Football Club: The official 125 year illustrated history*, Derby: Breedon Books.

Turner, D. (1994) *Cottage chronicles: An anecdotical history of Fulham Football Club 1879-1993*, Bordon: Northdown Publishing.

Unzueta, P. (1999) 'Fútbol y nacionalismo vasco', in S. Segurola (ed.) (1999) *Fútbol y pasiones políticas*, Barcelona: Temas de debate, pp. 147-167.

Urry, J. (2000) *Sociology beyond societies: Mobilities for the twenty-first century*, London and New York: Routledge.

Vamplew, W. (1994) 'Violence in Australian soccer: The ethnic contribution', in J. O'Hara (ed.), *Ethnicity and soccer in Australia*, Campbelltown: Australian Society for Sports History, pp. 1-15.

Vamplew, W. (1994a) ''Wogball': Ethnicity and violence in Australian soccer', in R. Giulianotti and J. Williams (eds), *Game without frontiers: Football, identity and modernity*, Aldershot: Arena, pp. 207-223.

Vamplew, W. (1992) 'Sports crowd disorder: An Australian survey', in J. O'Hara (ed.), *Crowd violence at Australian Sport*, Campbelltown: Australian Society for Sports History, pp. 79-111.

Vamplew, W. (1983) 'Unsporting Behavior: The control of football and horse-racing crowds in England, 1875-1914', in J.H. Goldstein (ed.), *Sports violence*, New York: Springer-Verlag, pp. 21-31.

Vázquez Montalbán, M. (2005) *El fútbol: Una religión en busca de un Dios*, Madrid: Debate.

Vázquez Montalbán, M. (1972) 'Arquelogia i subcultura', in J.J. Artells, *Barça, Barça, Barça: FC Barcelona, esport i ciutadania*, Barcelona: Laia, pp. 7-8.

Vázquez Montalbán, M. (1969) 'Barça! Barça! Barça!', *Triunfo*, 25 October.

Verkamman, M. (2002) 'Rood Wit gaat nooit verloren: S.P.A.R.T.A.', *Trouw*, 25 May, p. 19.

Verleyen, K., and S. De Smet (1997) *Hooligans*, Leuven: Davidsfonds.

Vermeer, E., and R. van Vrijaldenhoven (1994) *De klassieker*, Amsterdam: Windroos.

Veugelers, W., and J. Hazekamp (1984) *Inside Z-side: 'Voetbalvandalen' in woord en beeld*, Groningen: Xeno.

Viñas, C. (2006) *Tolerància zero: La violència en el futbol*, Barcelona: Angle.

Viñas, C. (2005) *El mundo ultra: Los radicales del fútbol español*, Madrid: Temas de Hoy.

465

Viñas, C. (2004) *Skinheads a Catalunya*, Barcelona: Columna.

Viñas, C. (2001) *Música i skinheads a Catalunya: El so de la política*, Barcelona: Diputació de Barcelona.

Viñas, C., and R.F.J. Spaaij (2006) 'Medidas y políticas de intervención acerca del racismo y la xenofobia en el fútbol español', *Sistema*, no. 192, pp. 51-76.

Vrcan, S., and D. Lalic (1999) 'From ends to trenches, and back: Football in the former Yugoslavia', in G. Armstrong and R. Giulianotti (eds), *Football cultures and identities*, London: Macmillan Press, pp. 176-185.

Vreese, S. de (2000) 'Hooliganism under the statistical magnifying glass: A Belgian case study', *European Journal on Criminal Policy and Research*, vol. 8, no. 2, pp. 201-223.

Vrijaldenhoven, R. van (1996) *Feyenoord tegen de rest van de wereld: Vijfendertig jaar Europa Cup en Wereld Cup voetbal*, Amsterdam: Luitingh.

Waddington, D. (1992) *Contemporary issues in public disorder: A comparative and historical approach*, London: Routledge.

Waddington, I., D. Malcolm and R. Horak (1998) 'The social composition of football crowds in Western Europe', *International Review for the Sociology of Sport*, vol. 33, no. 2, pp. 155-169.

Waddington, I., E. Dunning and P. Murphy (1996) 'Research note: Surveying the social composition of football crowds', *Leisure Studies*, vol. 15, pp. 209-214.

Wagg, S. (1984) *The football world: A contemporary social history*, Brighton: Harvester.

Walgrave, L. (ed.) (1996) *Confronterende jongeren*, Leuven: Leuven University Press.

Walton, J.K. (2001) 'Basque football rivalries in the twentieth century', in G. Armstrong and R. Giulianotti (eds), *Fear and loathing in world football*, Oxford and New York: Berg, pp. 119-133.

Walton, J.K. (2001a) 'Football and identities: England and Spain', in F.J. Caspistegui and J.K. Walton (eds), *Guerras danzadas: Fútbol e identidades locales y regionales en Europa*, Navarra: UENSA, pp. 19-29.

Walvin, J. (1994) [1975] *The people's game. A social history of British football*, London: Allen Lane.

Walvin, J. (1986) *Football and the decline of Britain*, London: Macmillan.

Wann, D.L., M.J. Melnick, G.W. Russell and D.G. Pease (2001) *Sport fans: The psychology and social impact of spectators*, New York and London: Routledge.

Ward, C. (1989) *Steaming in: Journal of a football fan*, London: Simon and Schuster.

Ward, C., and S. Hickmott (2000) *Armed for the match: The troubles and trial of the Chelsea Headhunters*, London: Headline.

Warren, I. (1993) 'Violence in sport: some theoretical and practical issues in the Australian context', Paper presented at the Second National Conference on Violence, Australian Institute of Criminology, Canberra, 15-18 June.

Warren, I. (1995) 'Soccer subcultures in Australia', in C. Guerra and R. White (eds), *Ethnic minority youth in Australia: Challenges and myths*, Hobart: NCYS, pp. 121-131.

Warren, I. (2003) *Football, crowds and cultures: Comparing English and Australian law and enforcement trends*, Campbelltown: Australian Society for Sports History.

Warren, I., and R. Hay (1998) 'Order and disorder at sporting venues', in D. Hemphill (ed.), *All part of the game: Violence and Australian sport*, Petersham: Walla Walla Press, pp. 63-85.

Watt, T. (1993) *The end: 80 years of life on the terraces*, Edinburgh and London: Mainstream.

Weber, M. (1968) *Economy and Society* (trans. G. Roth and G. Wittich), Berkeley and Los Angeles: University of California Press.

Whannel, G. (1979) 'Football crowd behaviour and the press', *Media, Culture and Society*, vol. 1, pp. 327-342.

White, J. (2002) *London in the twentieth century*, London: Penguin.

White, R., and J. Wyn (2004) *Youth and society: Exploring the social dynamics of youth experience*, Oxford and New York: Oxford University Press.

Whitting, P.D. (1970) *A history of Fulham*, London: Fulham History Society.

Wijnen, H. van (1989) *De Kuip: De geschiedenis van het stadion Feyenoord*, Utrecht: Veen.

Williams, J. (2001) 'Who you calling a hooligan?', in M. Perryman (ed.), *Hooligan wars: Causes and effects of football violence*, Edinburgh and London: Mainstream, pp. 37-53.

Williams, J. (2001a) 'The costs of safety in risk societies', *The Journal of Forensic Psychiatry*, vol. 12, no. 1, pp. 1-7.

Williams, J. (1996) 'Surveying the social composition of football crowds: A reply to Waddington, Dunning and Murphy', *Leisure Studies*, vol. 15, pp. 215-219.

Williams, J. (1991) 'Having an away day: English football spectators and the hooligan debate', in J. Williams and S. Wagg (eds), *British football and social change: Getting into Europe*, Leicester and London: Leicester University Press, pp. 160-184.

Williams, J., E. Dunning and P. Murphy (1989) *Hooligans abroad: The behaviour and control of English fans in continental Europe*, 2nd ed., London: Routledge & Kegan Paul.

Williams, J., E. Dunning and P. Murphy (1989a) *The Luton Town members scheme: Final report*, Leicester: University of Leicester.

Williams, J., E. Dunning and P. Murphy (1988) *Football and spectator behaviour at Watford: 'The friendly club'*, Leicester: University of Leicester.

Williams, J., E. Dunning and P. Murphy (1986) 'The rise of the English soccer hooligan', *Youth and Society*, vol. 17, no. 4, pp. 362-380.

Williams, J., E. Dunning and P. Murphy (1984a) 'Come on, you whites', *New Society*, vol. 68, no. 1122, pp. 310-311.

Williams, R. (2001) 'From Rochdale to Rio via Rome: Hooliganism is alive and kicking', *The Guardian*, 2 February.

Winkels, E. (1998) *De eenzame kampioen*, book ed. Hard Gras no. 15, Amsterdam: L.J. Veen.

Wolff, P. (1971) *Geen woorden maar daden: De roemruchte historie van topclub Feyenoord*, Baarn: De Boekerij.

Yablonsky, L. (1962) *The violent gang*, New York: Penguin.

Yablonsky, L. (1959) 'The delinquent gang as a near-group', *Social Problems*, vol. 7, pp. 108-117.

Yin, R.K. (1994) *Case study research: Design and methods*, 2nd ed., Beverly Hills: Sage.

Young, K. (2002) 'A walk on the wild side: Exposing North American sports crowd disorder', in E. Dunning, P. Murphy, I. Waddington and A.E. Astrinakis (eds), *Fighting fans: Football hooliganism as a world phenomenon*, Dublin:

University College Dublin Press, pp. 201-217.

Young, K. (2000) 'Sport and violence', in J. Coakley and E. Dunning (eds), *Handbook of sports studies*, London: Sage, pp. 382-407.

Young, K. (1986) '"The killing field": Themes in mass media responses to the Heysel stadium riot', *International Review for the Sociology of Sport*, vol. 21, no. 2/3, pp. 253-265.

Young, M., and P. Willmott (1992) [1957] *Family and kinship in East London*, Berkeley and Los Angeles: University of California Press.

Zaragoza, A. (1994) 'Notes per a una lectura sociològica del Nuñisme i del Fútbol Club Barcelona', in N. Puig and A. Zaragoza (eds), *Lectures en sociologia de l'oci i de l'esport*, Barcelona: University of Barcelona, pp. 66-72.

Zevenbergen, C. (1986) *Rotterdamse voetbalglorie 1886-1986*, Rotterdam: Sijthoff.

Samenvatting (Dutch summary)

Deze studie bespreekt de omvang en aard van supportersgeweld rond voetbalwedstrijden vanuit een internationaal-vergelijkend perspectief. Het hooliganisme werd lange tijd beschouwd als hoofdzakelijk een 'Engelse ziekte', die langzaam maar zeker ook het Europese vasteland heeft 'geïnfecteerd'. Dit beeld is niet langer dominant. Enerzijds zijn sommige Britse wetenschappers ervan overtuigd geraakt dat juist in het Verenigd Koninkrijk het hooliganisme gedurende de jaren negentig in intensiteit is afgenomen. Anderzijds wijzen recente studies op vergelijkbare gewelddadige competitie tussen groepen voetbalsupporters in diverse Europese en Latijns-Amerikaanse landen. Het hooliganisme is in de loop der jaren verworden tot een persistente, transnationale subcultuur.

De persistentie van het hooliganisme noopt tot nader onderzoek, in de eerste plaats omdat een viertal centrale theoretische thema's onvoldoende bestudeerd is. Deze thema's vormen tezamen de basis voor een beter begrip van het hooliganisme als transnationaal fenomeen. Het eerste thema is de wijze waarop de aard van het supportersgeweld mede wordt gevormd door de scheidslijnen (*fault lines*) van individuele landen. Een tweede onderwerp dat centraal staat, is de sociale constructie van hooliganidentiteiten en de aantrekkingskracht van de hooligansubcultuur op jonge mannen. Het derde thema is de sociale organisatie van supportersgeweld. Het vierde en laatste thema is de interactie tussen hooligans en 'significante anderen' (politiefunctionarissen, clubbestuurders, supporters, rivaliserende hooligangroepen) en de ontwikkeling en effecten van beleidsmaatregelen.

Deze vier thema's worden in dit boek bestudeerd door middel van een vergelijkende analyse van het hooliganisme in verschillende landen en bij verschillende voetbalclubs. De analyse richt zich tevens op ontwikkelingen en variaties in de tijd. De centrale vraagstelling van het onderzoek luidt: hoe kunnen we de omvang en aard van het hooliganisme bij verschillende clubs en in verschillende landen, en variaties daarin door de tijd, verklaren? Het empirisch onderzoek spitst zich toe op drie West-Europese landen – Engeland, Nederland en Spanje – en zes

470

West-Europese voetbalclubs, namelijk: West Ham United FC en Fulham FC (beide uit Londen); Feyenoord en Sparta Rotterdam (beide uit Rotterdam); en RCD Espanyol en FC Barcelona (beide uit Barcelona). De belangrijkste databronnen zijn (semi-gestructureerde) interviews, participerende observatie, beleidsdocumenten, fanzines, mediaberichtgeving, videobeelden en (hooligan)websites.

Het boek bestaat uit drie delen. Het eerste deel (Hoofdstuk Een en Twee) bespreekt de wetenschappelijke literatuur over supportersgeweld en benoemt de centrale aspecten van het hooliganisme. Hooliganisme wordt gedefinieerd als gewelddadige competitie tussen rivaliserende supportersgroepen. Tegelijkertijd wordt aangegeven dat deze specifieke vorm van geweld onlosmakelijk verbonden is met andere soorten van geweld, bijvoorbeeld vandalisme of geweld tegen de politie. Hoofdstuk Een analyseert het debat in de sociale wetenschappen over de oorzaken, aard en gevolgen van hooliganisme. Geconcludeerd wordt dat het ontbreekt aan systematisch en gedetailleerd vergelijkend onderzoek naar supportersgeweld. In Hoofdstuk Twee werk ik dit argument uit aan de hand van de vier bovengenoemde thema's. Hoofdstuk Twee bespreekt tevens de methodologie van het onderzoek.

Het empirisch onderzoek dat ten grondslag ligt aan deze studie wordt uiteengezet in het tweede deel van het boek. Hoofdstuk Drie geeft een algemene schets van de genese en ontwikkeling van de hooligansubculturen in Engeland, Nederland en Spanje. Ook wordt ingegaan op de ontwikkeling van het voetbalvandalismebeleid. Geconstateerd wordt dat het beleid in de drie landen in toenemende mate gelijkvormig is geworden door onderlinge afstemming en internationale regelgeving, maar dat er desondanks belangrijke variaties blijven voortbestaan in zowel de problematiek als het beleid. In de hoofdstukken Vier tot en met Negen verschuift het perspectief naar een gedetailleerde beschrijving van het hooliganisme en beleid bij de zes voetbalclubs. Aan de hand van de vier centrale thema's worden per club de genese en ontwikkeling van het fenomeen in kaart gebracht. Daarnaast worden de genomen beleidsmaatregelen en de effecten hiervan op lokaal niveau tegen het licht gehouden.

Hoofdstuk Vier analyseert de ontwikkeling en aard van het hooliganisme bij West Ham United. De hooligangroep die zich rond deze club heeft gevormd vanaf het midden van de jaren zestig van de vorige eeuw heeft een internationale reputatie verworven. Deze reputatie is met name gebaseerd op de vele grootschalige

471

geweldsincidenten in de jaren zeventig en tachtig en weerspiegelt de geweldsreputatie van Oost-Londen in het algemeen. Vanwege de toenemende veiligheidsmaatregelen binnen en buiten de stadions, heeft het geweld zich geleidelijk verplaatst naar andere locaties (bijvoorbeeld treinstations, pubs, routes naar het stadion) en tijdstippen. Ook is de planning en coördinatie van confrontaties toegenomen. Vanaf het einde van de jaren tachtig is de kern van de groep in omvang afgenomen en is ook de frequentie van gewelddadige confrontaties gedaald, grotendeels als gevolg van politiecontroles en andere veiligheidsmaatregelen. Het hooliganisme bij West Ham United is echter geenszins verdwenen, zoals blijkt uit recente incidenten en de nieuwe aanwas van jonge hooligans.

Hoofdstuk Vijf behandelt de ontwikkeling van het hooliganisme bij Fulham FC. Het hooliganisme bij Fulham beperkt zich tot de jaren zestig en zeventig van de vorige eeuw. Echter, ook gedurende deze periode was het hooliganisme zowel kwantitatief als kwalitatief beperkt in vergelijking met de relatief ernstige incidenten bij diverse Engelse voetbalclubs. Deze bevinding wordt verklaard uit de specifieke collectieve identiteit van Fulhamsupporters, die zich afzet tegen het gepercipieerde 'onbeschaafde' gedrag van supporters van sommige andere clubs, met name lokale rivaal Chelsea. Deze notie van 'zelf' en de 'ander' werd mede versterkt door de dood van een Fulhamsupporter in 1998. Dit incident veroorzaakte een 'cultureel trauma' dat het voortbestaan van de collectieve identiteit van Fulhamsupporters ter discussie stelde en dat uiteindelijk leidde tot de herbevestiging van deze identiteit.

Hoofdstuk Zes bespreekt de genese en de ontwikkeling van het hooliganisme bij Feyenoord. Geconstateerd wordt dat de collectieve identiteit van de hooligans belangrijke overeenkomsten vertoont met de dominante identiteit van Feyenoordsupporters. Deze identiteit is grotendeels gebaseerd op de historische en culturele kenmerken van de club. In de jaren zeventig van de vorige eeuw was het supportersgeweld relatief ongeorganiseerd. Met het ontstaan van gewelddadige rivaliteiten tussen verschillende supportersgroepen is de bereidheid om geweld te gebruiken toegenomen. Hooligans zien zich ook in toenemende mate genoodzaakt om de confrontatie op te zoeken op andere locaties en tijdstippen, als reactie op veiligheidsmaatregelen binnen en buiten de stadions. Hoewel vanaf het einde van de jaren negentig, in de periode na de rellen bij Beverwijk (1997), een groot aantal leden van de oude harde kern minder actief is geworden of is weggevallen, is tevens

472

een nieuwe generatie jonge hooligans opgestaan die actief de confrontatie zoekt met rivaliserende groepen. De hooligans slagen er geregeld in veiligheidsmaatregelen te omzeilen of te manipuleren.

Hoofdstuk Zeven zoomt in op de ontwikkeling en de aard van het hooliganisme bij Sparta Rotterdam. De beperkte omvang van het hooliganisme weerspiegelt het positieve, 'vriendelijke' imago van de club. Dit imago is historisch geconstrueerd ten opzichte van de 'onbeschaafde', 'gewelddadige' ander, met name lokale rivaal Feyenoord. Tot voor kort kenmerkte Sparta zich door ontbreken van een hooligantraditie. Pas aan het einde van de jaren negentig van de vorige eeuw ontstond een kleine groep jonge mannen die zich identificeert met de subcultuur van het hooliganisme. Gewelddadige confrontaties doen zich vrijwel uitsluitend voor buiten de stadions en worden gekenmerkt door een relatief hoge graad van planning en coördinatie. De autoriteiten zijn tot op heden niet in staat geweest om deze ontwikkeling een halt toe te roepen, mede door de gebrekkige informatiepositie van de politie.

Hoofdstuk Acht bespreekt de ontwikkeling van de hooligansubcultuur bij Espanyol en de historische rivaliteit tussen Espanyol- en Barcelonasupporters. Het hooliganisme bij Espanyol wordt gekenmerkt door zijn politieke lading, met name de extreemrechtse sympathieën van hooligans. De politieke identiteit van Espanyolhooligans moeten worden gezien als een radicale versie van het historisch imago van Espanyol in Catalonië als een 'fascistische', 'anti-Catalaanse' club. De collectieve identiteit van supporters en hooligans wordt geconstrueerd ten opzichte van de Catalaans-nationalistische identiteit van FC Barcelona. De rivaliteit tussen Espanyol- en Barcelonahooligans bereikte haar hoogtepunt aan het einde van de jaren tachtig en aan het begin van de jaren negentig. Gedurende deze periode vonden frequent gewelddadige confrontaties plaats tussen beide groepen, zowel op wedstrijddagen als in het dagelijks leven. Vanaf het midden van de jaren negentig is de intensiteit van de rivaliteit afgenomen als gevolg van strictere veiligheids-maatregelen en interne ontwikkelingen binnen beide groepen.

Hoofdstuk Negen analyseert de oorsprong en de ontwikkeling van het supportersgeweld bij FC Barcelona. De hooligangroep, die ontstond aan het begin van de jaren tachtig, identificeerde zich aanvankelijk met (links) Catalaans nationalisme en separatisme. Met de opkomst van de skinheadsubcultuur transformeerden zowel de politieke sympathieën van veel hooligans (toenemende populariteit van extreemrechtse ideologieën) als de intensiteit van het supportersgeweld. De escalatie van het hooliganisme leidde niet alleen tot diverse grootschalige confrontaties met rivaliserende groepen, maar ook tot persistente interne conflicten. De oorspronkelijke groep viel uiteen en er ontstonden nieuwe subgroepen die tevens de confrontatie zoeken met supporters van hun eigen club. Het clubbestuur heeft lange tijd onvoldoende grip gehad op deze ontwikkelingen en zelfs gedurende sommige perioden actief bijgedragen aan de escalatie van het supportersgeweld door bepaalde gunsten te verlenen aan hooligans (gratis toegangskaarten, gratis vervoer naar uitwedstrijden, opslagruimte in het stadion, geld). De recente omslag in het beleid, van gedogen naar repressie, heeft geleid tot een slepend conflict tussen hooligans en clubbestuurders, hetgeen gepaard gaat het bedreigingen en geweld.

In het derde en laatste deel van het boek worden de individuele *case studies* met elkaar vergeleken. Hoofdstuk Tien analyseert twee centrale theoretische thema's: de wijze waarop de scheidslijnen van individuele samenlevingen vorm geven aan nationale en lokale vormen van hooliganisme, en de sociale organisatie van het hooliganisme. Het eerste thema wordt bezien vanuit een ontwikkelingsperspectief, waarin het proces van transnationale diffusie centraal staat. Het hooliganisme ontstond in Engeland in de jaren zestig van vorige eeuw als een jeugdsubcultuur onder jonge mannen uit de arbeidersklasse. De diffusie van de hooligansubcultuur naar het continent ging gepaard met een proces van glokalisering. Buitenlandse invloeden vermengden zich met nationale en lokale culturele tradities, waardoor het hooliganisme in verschillende landen en steden een eigen karakter kreeg. Nationale variaties in de aard van het hooliganisme kunnen tot op zekere hoogte worden verklaard uit verschillen in de scheidslijnen van individuele landen. Deze scheidslijnen zijn sociale klasse en regionale ongelijkheden (Engeland); de expressie van regionale en lokale culturele identiteiten (Nederland); en de centrum-periferie-scheidslijn (Spanje). Deze scheidslijnen genereren specifieke wij/zij-figuraties; intense wij-gevoelens gaan gepaard met vijandige gevoelens ten opzichte van buitenstaanders. Zij beïnvloeden de rivaliteit tussen supportersgroepen en de collectieve identiteit van hooligangroepen. Hoewel het scheidslijnconcept een belangrijk beginpunt is voor het verklaren van nationale en lokale variaties in het hooliganisme, moeten ook de meer specifieke sociale, historische en culturele factoren die ten grondslag liggen aan lokale vormen van hooliganisme in de analyse worden betrokken.

Het tweede thema dat centraal staat in Hoofdstuk Tien is de sociale organisatie van hooliganisme. Verscheidene hooligangroepen plannen en coördineren in toenemende mate gewelddadige confrontaties met rivaliserende groepen, hoofdzakelijk als reactie op stricte beleidsmaatregelen en politiecontroles. Het tijdstip en de plaats van confrontaties worden soms van tevoren afgesproken met vertegenwoordigers van rivaliserende groepen. Bij Espanyol en FC Barcelona is momenteel echter nauwelijks sprake van dergelijke strategieën. Ook bij Fulham doet de bovengenoemde trend zich niet voor, vanwege de afwezigheid van een hooligangroep. Ondanks de toegenomen sociale organisatie van diverse hooligangroepen, is hun formele organisatie zeer beperkt. De bestudeerde groepen hebben geen formele structuren, hiërarchieën of formele leiders, maar slechts informele leiderfiguren (gebaseerd op hun senioriteit, vechtreputatie of organisatiekwaliteiten). Gewelddadige confrontaties tussen hooligangroepen zijn niet het gevolg van formele hiërarchieën, maar van een combinatie van gedeelde interesses en belangen, mogelijkheden voor snelle *resource mobilization*, contacten tussen rivaliserende groepen en bekendheid met bepaalde publieke ruimten (bijvoorbeeld voetbalstadions, wegen, treinstations, stadscentra).

Hoewel de precieze organisatiegraad en strategieën variëren naar tijd en plaats, kunnen de bestudeerde hooligangroepen alle worden gekarakteriseerd als losse verbanden met fluïde grenzen. Een centraal kenmerk is dat er verschillende niveaus van groepslidmaatschap bestaan, variërend van harde-kernleden tot meelopers, halve uittreders en *wannabes*. De groepscohesie is relatief sterk in de kern van de groep, maar zwak in de periferie. De kern van de hooligangroep is meestal relatief duurzaam en samenhangend en bestaat uit personen die gedurende langere tijd deel uitmaken van de groep (vijf tot tien jaar, of zelfs veel langer), zij het niet noodzakelijkerwijs (of niet meer) op een wekelijkse basis. De kernleden vormen de spil van de groep's sociale organisatie en fungeren als rolmodel. De periferie van de groep verandert voortdurend en is mede afhankelijk van de specifieke verwachtingspatronen van hooligans rond voetbalwedstrijden.

Hoofdstuk Elf bespreekt de interactie tussen hooligans en 'significante anderen' en de effecten van beleid. Geconstateerd wordt dat veranderingen in de omvang en aard van hooliganisme niet voldoende kunnen worden verklaard uit nationale scheidslijnen en transnationale ontwikkelingen. Het is van cruciaal belang ook de specifieke scheidslijnen en interacties binnen lokale contexten te analyseren. Centraal staan de sociale interacties tussen hooligans, politiefunctionarissen, veiligheidspersoneel, clubbestuurders en supporters. Deze interacties creëren informele gedragsregels die kunnen botsen met het formele beleid. Ondanks het feit dat beleidsmaatregelen in toenemende mate zijn gestandaardiseerd en nationale en lokale contrasten zijn afgenomen, ontwikkelen voetbalclubs en politieteams een eigen informele stijl van aanpak, die mede afhankelijk is van lokale interpretaties en prioriteiten. Daarnaast ontwikkelen hooligans strategieën om ongewenste beleidsmaatregelen te omzeilen of te verzachten. Een bekend voorbeeld hiervan is de geleidelijke verplaatsing van hooliganconfrontaties van binnen naar buiten de stadions, naar locaties en tijdstippen waarop de ordehandhaving minder effectief wordt geacht. Het hoofdstuk sluit af met een drietal algemene conclusies: (i) de meeste veiligheidsmaatregelen hebben onbedoelde effecten die de effectiviteit van het beleid reduceren en die kunnen leiden tot een transformatie van de aard van het hooliganisme; (ii) er bestaat in veel gevallen een significante discrepantie tussen formeel en informeel beleid; (iii) voetbalsupporters kunnen een belangrijke rol spelen in de preventie van supportersgeweld en in de constructie van niet-gewelddadige supportersidentiteiten.

Hoofdstuk Twaalf analyseert de sociale constructie van hooliganidentiteiten en de aantrekkingskracht van de hooligansubcultuur op jonge mannen. In het eerste deel van het hoofdstuk wordt betoogd dat, ondanks het heterogene karakter van het hooliganisme, een zestal aspecten ten grondslag ligt aan hooliganidentiteiten. Deze zes aspecten zijn: aangename emotionele opwinding (de kick van geweld); de constructie van agressieve masculiniteit; territoriale identificaties; individueel en collectief reputatiemanagement; solidariteit en vriendschap; en soevereiniteit en autonomie. Deze aspecten moeten worden beschouwd als de centrale elementen van de hooligansubcultuur. Hoewel de betreffende sociale mechanismen overeenkomstig zijn, variëren de specifieke inhoud en intensiteit ervan, afhankelijk van lokale en nationale omstandigheden.

Het tweede deel van het hoofdstuk biedt een verklaring voor lokale variaties in de omvang en intensiteit van supportersgeweld door middel van een vergelijkende analyse van de habitus en collectieve identiteit van supporters van de zes onderzochte voetbalclubs. De persistentie van het hooliganisme bij Feyenoord en West Ham United kan deels worden verklaard uit de diepgewortelde arbeiderstradities van beide clubs. De supportersculturen van deze clubs benadrukken met name specifieke normen van 'harde' masculiniteit en fysieke kracht, ondanks het feit dat de sociale samenstelling van de supportersscharen in de loop der jaren belangrijke veranderingen heeft ondergaan. Deze normen worden gereproduceerd, in een verhoogde en meer dwingende vorm, in de collectieve identiteit van hooligans. Eenzelfde proces zien we, weliswaar in een andere vorm, terug bij de hooligangroepen bij Espanyol en FC Barcelona. De gewelddadige competitie tussen beide groepen moet worden bezien in de context van de historische politieke rivaliteit tussen beide clubs. Deze politieke context vormt de basis voor zowel de dominante supportersidentiteit als voor de collectieve identiteit van hooligans. Klassentegenstellingen en –bewustzijn spelen hierbij een veel minder prominente rol, hetgeen zijn weerslag vindt in de heterogene sociale compositie van beide hooligangroepen.

De relatief beperkte omvang van het hooliganisme bij Fulham en Sparta kan deels worden begrepen uit de collectieve supportersidentiteiten bij deze clubs. Deze identiteiten worden geconstrueerd op basis van de gepercipieerde verschillen tussen het 'zelf' en de 'ander'. De ander – in de eerste plaats respectievelijk Chelsea en Feyenoord – wordt bestempeld als 'onbeschaafd' en 'gewelddadig', terwijl in de constructie van het zelf de wenselijkheid van 'beschaafd' en niet-gewelddadig gedrag wordt benadrukt. Het 'vriendelijke' imago van deze clubs wordt veelal gereproduceerd door significante anderen (media, supporters, autoriteiten), bijvoorbeeld doordat wangedrag van supporters wordt getypeerd als een eenmalig incident of simpelweg wordt ontkend.

Hoewel de collectieve identiteiten van supporters en hooligans vaak duurzaam zijn, treedt soms ook min of meer succesvol verzet op. Recente ontwikkelingen bij Espanyol tonen aan dat de hooliganidentiteit op den duur kan worden overschaduwd door een alternatieve, niet-gewelddadige supportersidentiteit, hetgeen kan leiden tot een significante afname van het hooliganisme. Aan de andere kant wijst de recente opkomst van een hooligangroep bij Sparta erop, dat supporters zich ook met succes tegen een diepgewortelde 'vriendelijke' supportersidentiteit kunnen verzetten. In dit laatste geval valt op dat deze ontwikkeling niet heeft geleid tot een algehele herdefiniëring of verwerping van de dominante identiteit, maar dat het hooliganisme zich veeleer in de marge van de supportersgemeenschap afspeelt, namelijk buiten de formele en informele sociale controle om. Juist hierdoor heeft de hooligangroep zich gedurende de afgelopen jaren kunnen profileren binnen de Nederlandse hooligansubcultuur.

In het derde deel van Hoofdstuk Twaalf ga ik in op de commodificatie van het hooliganisme. De persistentie van het hooliganisme kan worden gezien als een gevolg van de prestige van de hooliganlevensstijl onder jonge mannen die op zoek zijn naar uitdaging en avontuur. Mediatisering en commodificatie spelen een belangrijke rol in de promotie van de hooliganlevensstijl onder jongeren. Het ontstaan van een transnationale markt op het gebied van hooliganentertainment en daaraan gerelateerde producten (onder andere boeken, films en kleding) draagt bij aan de toegankelijkheid en zichtbaarheid van de subcultuur. Deze ontwikkeling creëert daarnaast nieuwe motieven voor ervaren hooligans, die hun ondernemingsgeest aanwenden voor financieel gewin.

Het boek sluit af met een aantal conclusies. De centrale bevinding van de studie is dat context van grote invloed is op de precieze omvang en aard van het hooliganisme. Er bestaan niet alleen belangrijke verschillen tussen landen, maar ook binnen landen en binnen steden. Daarnaast doen zich belangrijke variaties voor in de tijd, hetgeen het belang van een historisch-vergelijkend perspectief onderstreept. Hoewel overeenkomsten en verschillen in het hooliganisme deels kunnen worden verklaard uit transnationale diffusiepatronen en nationale scheidslijnen, kan men de precieze aard en ontwikkeling van het hooliganisme alleen begrijpen wanneer men oog heeft voor de specifieke contexten waarin hooligansubculturen zijn ingebed. Systematische en gedetailleerde vergelijking van deze contexten stelt ons in staat om de oorzaken en transnationale dimensies van het hooliganisme beter te begrijpen.

Index

Printed in Great Britain
by Amazon.co.uk, Ltd.,
Marston Gate.